HEALTHY EMERGENCY SUBSTITUTIONS

IF YOU DON'T HAVE THIS . . .	USE THIS . . .	ADJUSTMENTS
Alcohol (rum, sherry or brandy), 1 teaspoon	1 teaspoon vanilla extract	Vanilla is strongly flavored, so if more than 1 teaspoon is needed, make up the difference with fruit juice.
Baking powder	$\frac{1}{4}$ teaspoon baking soda + $\frac{5}{8}$ teaspoon cream of tartar	No change.
Bread crumbs, 1 cup	$\frac{3}{4}$ cup crushed crackers	Adjust seasonings to compensate for salt (if any) in the crackers.
Broth (beef or chicken), 1 cup	1 bouillon cube in 1 cup water	Bouillon is saltier than broth, so you may want to dilute 1 cube in 2 cups water.
Butter, 1 cup	$\frac{7}{8}$ cup vegetable oil	Oil causes a looser crumb in baked products, so work gently to prevent crumbling.
Buttermilk, 1 cup	1 cup low-fat or nonfat plain yogurt	For baking, no change needed. In casseroles, you may want to use $\frac{3}{4}$ cup, because the yogurt is denser.
Cornstarch, 1 tablespoon	2 tablespoons all-purpose flour	The flour will cause a somewhat duller appearance, so it's best used for gravies, stews or other mixed combos.
Herbs, fresh, 1 tablespoon	1 teaspoon dried	Dried herbs are stronger, so add them earlier in the recipe.
Lemon juice	Half as much vinegar	This is not recommended for baked goods.
Milk, skim, 1 cup	$\frac{1}{3}$ cup nonfat dry milk mixed with $\frac{3}{4}$ cup water	No change for baking.
Mustard, prepared, 1 teaspoon	1 teaspoon powdered mustard	Powdered mustard is concentrated, so use it sparingly.
Olive oil	Equal amount of any vegetable oil	The consistency will be the same, but the flavor will change.
Roasted red peppers	Equal amount of pimentos	No change.
Tomato juice, 1 cup	$\frac{1}{2}$ cup tomato sauce + $\frac{1}{2}$ cup water	Tomato sauce has more added salt, so adjust your seasonings accordingly.
Sour cream, 1 cup	1 cup evaporated skim milk + 1 tablespoon lemon juice	To speed curdling, microwave on high power for 30 seconds.
Tomato sauce, 1 cup	$\frac{3}{8}$ cup tomato paste + $\frac{1}{2}$ cup water	No change.
Vinegar, 1 teaspoon	2 teaspoons lemon juice	Adjust seasonings for changed flavor.

PREVENTION'S

The
Healthy
Cook

PREVENTION'S

The Healthy Cook

The Ultimate Illustrated Kitchen Guide to Great Low-Fat Food

Featuring 450 Homestyle Recipes and Hundreds of Time-Saving Tips

By the Food Editors of **PREVENTION** Magazine Health Books

Edited by Matthew Hoffman and David Joachim

Rodale Press, Inc., Emmaus, Pennsylvania

Copyright © 1997 by Rodale Press, Inc.

Illustrations copyright © 1997 by Judy Newhouse
Cover illustration copyright © 1997 by Pamela Rossi

All rights reserved. No part of this publication may be reproduced or
transmitted in any form or by any means, electronic or mechanical,
including photocopying, recording or any other information storage
and retrieval system, without the written permission of the publisher.

Special thanks to Fante's Gourmet Kitchenware Shops, Philadelphia,
for providing technical assistance to the illustrator.

Prevention is a registered trademark of Rodale Press, Inc.

Printed in the United States of America on acid-free ∞,
recycled paper ♻

Library of Congress Cataloging-in-Publication Data

Prevention's the healthy cook : the ultimate illustrated kitchen guide
   to great low-fat food / by the food editors of Prevention Magazine
   Health Books ; edited by Matthew Hoffman and David Joachim.
     p. cm.
   Includes index.
   ISBN 0–87596–310–2 hardcover
   1. Low-fat diet—Recipes. I. Hoffman, Matthew. II. Joachim, David
date. III. Prevention Magazine Health Books. IV. Title:
Healthy Cook
RM237.7.P744 1997
641.5'638—dc20   96–27695

**Distributed in the book trade by
St. Martin's Press**

 4 6 8 10 9 7 5   hardcover

PREVENTION'S THE HEALTHY COOK EDITORIAL STAFF

EDITOR: Matthew Hoffman

RECIPE EDITOR: David Joachim

MANAGING EDITOR: Jean Rogers

CONTRIBUTING EDITOR: Sharon Sanders

CONTRIBUTING WRITERS: Rob Eshman; John D. Forester, Jr.; Linda Gassenheimer; Mary Goodbody; Susie Heller; Jenna Holst; Donna C. Liotto; Holly McCord, R.D.; Tom Ney; Jill O'Connor; Mara Reid Rogers; Jay J. Solomon

ASSISTANT RESEARCH MANAGER: Carol Svec

BOOK PROJECT RESEARCHER: Sandra Salera-Lloyd

RESEARCHERS AND FACT CHECKERS: Elizabeth A. Brown, R.D.; Christine Dreisbach; Bernadette Sukley

RODALE TEST KITCHEN DIRECTOR: Tom Ney

RODALE TEST KITCHEN MANAGER: JoAnn Brader

RECIPE DEVELOPMENT: JoAnn Brader; Madelaine D. Bullwinkel; Anita Hirsch, R.D.; Jenna Holst; David Joachim; Tom Ney; Beatrice Ojakangas; Linda M. Rosensweig; Lorna J. Sass; Sue Spitler; Phyllis Stein-Novack

RODALE TEST KITCHEN STAFF: Cindy Litzenberger, Debbie Schuberth, Lee Speed, Robin Wieder, Nancy Zelko

NUTRITION CONSULTANTS: Anita Hirsch, R.D.; Holly McCord, R.D.; Linda R. Yoakam, R.D.

EDITORIAL CONSULTANTS: Nancy Baggett, Ruth Glick

COPY EDITOR: Kathy D. Everleth

ASSOCIATE ART DIRECTOR: Faith Hague

BOOK DESIGNER: Elizabeth Otwell

COVER AND LAYOUT DESIGNER: Darlene Schneck

ILLUSTRATOR: Judy Newhouse

COVER ILLUSTRATOR: Pamela Rossi

STUDIO MANAGER: Stefano Carbini

TECHNICAL ARTISTS: J. Andrew Brubaker, Karen Lomax

MANUFACTURING COORDINATOR: Patrick T. Smith

OFFICE STAFF: Roberta Mulliner, Julie Kehs, Bernadette Sauerwine, Mary Lou Stephen

RODALE HEALTH AND FITNESS BOOKS

VICE-PRESIDENT AND EDITORIAL DIRECTOR: Debora T. Yost

DESIGN AND PRODUCTION DIRECTOR: Michael Ward

RESEARCH MANAGER: Ann Gossy Yermish

COPY MANAGER: Lisa D. Andruscavage

BOOK MANUFACTURING DIRECTOR: Helen Clogston

In all Rodale Press cookbooks, our mission is to provide delicious and nutritious low-fat recipes. Our recipes also meet the standards of the Rodale Test Kitchen for dependability, ease, practicality and, most of all, great taste. To give us your comments, call 1-800-848-4735.

Contents

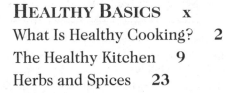

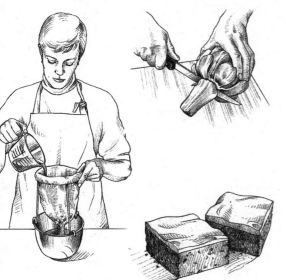

Introduction

Break out the confetti and balloons! At last—after years of testing what works (and what doesn't)—we at *Prevention* magazine are ready to bring you a master plan for healthy cooking that you can stick with forever.

Prevention's The Healthy Cook is America's newest, most authoritative kitchen companion. More than two years in the making, it distills the wisdom and expertise of dozens of the nation's top chefs, nutritionists and other culinary professionals. The Rodale Press Test Kitchen worked overtime testing hundreds of recipes to ensure that each and every one is both delicious and easy to make. We can confidently guarantee that this is *the* cookbook that you'll reach for when you need to know the basics for preparing delicious food that's also very good for you.

What makes *Prevention's The Healthy Cook* so special?

☞ It's easy to love. The days are gone when "healthy" food was brown, heavy and tasteless. The recipes in *Prevention's The Healthy Cook* are truly delicious. Say good-bye to fat, salt and sugar by the cupful. You won't miss them.

☞ It's complete. Cooks of all skill levels will turn to *Prevention's The Healthy Cook* for indispensable advice for virtually every kitchen technique, from sharpening knives to making soups, stews and low-fat pie crusts.

☞ It's recipe-packed. *Prevention's The Healthy Cook* contains hundreds of recipes and simple variations. No matter what's on your menu—muffins, a light salad for lunch, steamed tuna, healthy meat loaf, a complete holiday spread—you'll find it here.

☞ It's illustrated. *Prevention's The Healthy Cook* contains more than 400 illustrations that are clear, clean and beautiful. Whether you're boning a chicken, kneading bread, peeling a tomato or turning fish on the grill, *Prevention's The Healthy Cook* will show exactly what you need to do.

☞ It's packed with advice from expert cooks. To make this book as exciting and informative as possible, we've filled it with special features to help you get the most from your kitchen. "Helpful Hints" are quick tips providing shortcuts, instructions and behind-the-scenes savvy. "Is It Good for You?" boxes give the nutritional lowdown on some of your favorite foods. "Be My Guest" boxes offer exciting low-fat recipes from some of America's top chefs, including Jacques Pépin and Charlie Trotter. The "Quick!" symbol assures you that the recipe can be completed, beginning to end, in 30 minutes or less.

Prevention's The Healthy Cook is more than just another cookbook. It's really the summing up—the essence, if you will—of the health-giving strategies that we at *Prevention* have been developing, testing and perfecting for nearly 50 years. *Prevention's The Healthy Cook* brings the gift of better health to you and your family.

Enjoy.

Mark Bricklin

Mark Bricklin
Editor, *Prevention* Magazine

Healthy
Basics

WHAT IS HEALTHY COOKING, PAGE 2

THE HEALTHY KITCHEN, PAGE 9

HERBS AND SPICES, PAGE 23

What Is Healthy Cooking?

Happily, good nutrition and healthy cooking are coming into their own after years of growing pains. But for healthy cooks of yesteryear, the outlook wasn't so rosy. Back then, it took a lot of imagination just to create meals that weren't bad for you, let alone that tasted good. Not surprisingly, many cooks didn't bother—or gave up after a few halfhearted and often unsuccessful efforts.

There simply wasn't a lot of support for healthy diets. Many so-called healthy cookbooks featured vegetables drenched in eggs, cheese, butter and salt. Many of the early cookbooks that did cut back on fat and salt left a lot to be desired—namely, taste.

The supermarket was a high-fat danger zone. Low-fat versions of fatty foods such as salad dressings, sour cream and mayonnaise didn't exist. Frozen vegetables came locked in high-fat sauces. The few reduced-sodium foods were pathetically bland. Cuts of beef were much higher in fat. Even finding nonfat yogurt was iffy.

Before 1994, manufacturers weren't required to provide complete nutritional labels on their products. Remember those days? You had to guess how much fat, cholesterol, sodium or calories they contained—or own a shelf of reference books that would tell you what was lurking within.

Today, of course, a lot has changed. By law, almost all supermarket foods have labels that tell us what's inside. Supermarket shelves are packed with low-fat and nonfat alternatives to high-fat foods. And with years of experience behind them, chefs nationwide have perfected a new American cuisine featuring dishes with fabulous flavors and textures that don't depend on fat and salt.

THE HEALING POWER OF FOOD

A vast amount of scientific research has shown that what you eat plays a tremendous role in what happens to your health. For example:

☞ A major 1989 U.S. government report concluded that eating a better diet reduces the risk of cancer, heart disease, high blood pressure, stroke and diabetes.

☞ It has been estimated that up to 70 percent of all the cancer cases in the United States are probably related to diets that are too high in fat and calories and too low in vegetables and fruit.

It's really not surprising that food has such a huge impact on our lives. Assuming that you have three meals a day (and most of us have more, counting snacks), you eat nearly 1,100 times a year. That's 1,100 chances to have a positive—or negative—influence on your health. And that's just in one year.

Are there some doubts out there? Right up front, let's confront a few of the barriers that may keep you from eating healthier food. According to surveys, most people say that healthy food takes too much time to fix, it doesn't taste good enough and nutrition guide-

READING LABELS

For years, food companies could pretty much decide on their own what nutrition information to put on a package. It wasn't always easy to tell what you were getting or how much. Today, federal regulations require most foods to carry labels with a detailed accounting of what's inside. Here's what to look for.

☞ **Serving size.** This tells what the nutrition information on the label is based on. For example, your favorite frozen yogurt might contain 4 grams of fat. That looks good—until you realize that the serving size is half a cup. If you're in the mood for a bigger snack, you might be getting more fat than you planned on.

☞ **Calories.** If the calories are high, pass it by.

☞ **Grams of total fat.** If you're not sure what your personal fat budget is, see page 7. Ask yourself if this food fits reasonably into your daily goals, or if you'll blow your whole fat budget in one sitting.

☞ **Saturated fat and cholesterol.** If you eat mainly vegetables, fruits, grains and beans and if you also keep total fat intake low, you really don't have to check these numbers, since they will stay low automatically. Just keep in mind that you should have no more than 300 milligrams of cholesterol a day. For women, 45 to 50 grams of fat a day is about the maximum; men should limit themselves to 55 to 60 grams of fat a day.

☞ **Sodium.** Remember that 2,400 milligrams should be your upper limit for one day.

☞ **Daily nutrients.** Look at the "percent DV" for dietary fiber and certain nutrients (vitamins A and C, calcium and iron) at the bottom of the label. The designation stands for percent of Daily Value, the amount recommended in one day. The higher the numbers, the better.

With breakfast cereals, always look for dietary fiber to be 20 percent DV or higher. For dairy products, always check calcium and choose products with the highest percent DV of calcium. A serving of milk, the gold standard, has 30 percent DV.

lines are too darned confusing to follow.

First things first. Healthy cooking can be very easy. Once you know a few basics, preparing healthy food is as automatic and essential to your well-being as wearing seat belts. It doesn't take any longer to prepare than food that's bad for you.

Second, taste can certainly be an issue. It's true that once you remove large amounts of fat and sugar from food, the amount of taste may go down. But there are many easy strategies to get low fat and high flavor all in the same meal.

Finally, there's simply no reason for nutritional advice to be confusing. Put your calculator away. Ultimately, it all comes down to a simple principle: Using less fat and sugar and using more unprocessed fruits, vegetables and whole grains will lower your health risks and still give you plenty of natural flavor. Sounds easy, doesn't it? It is.

KEEP IT SIMPLE

To a large extent, healthy cooking means designing meals that focus on the "fabulous four"—vegetables, fruits, whole grains and beans. Here's why. Study after study reveals major health benefits linked to diets rich in these foods.

☞ People who eat five or more servings of vegetables and fruits every day have half the cancer risk of people who eat one serving or less.

☞ Men who eat more vegetables and fruits lower their chances of having a stroke.

☞ Diets high in wheat bran reduce the risk of colon and breast cancer.

☞ Adding beans or oat bran to your diet cuts high cholesterol levels.

The great thing about healthy cooking is that the essential foods are ones that you're already using every day. All you have to do is use more of them—more often. Here are some ideas.

Score with extra vegetables. When planning your vegetable menu, experts suggest aiming for three or more servings a day, with a serving being ½ cup, or about the size of a tennis ball. The only major exception is raw, leafy greens; try to get two servings.

Most Americans eat only two servings of vegetables a day, or less. So until three servings a day becomes automatic for you, make it a habit to count up your servings. It's that important.

Get plenty of fruit. Aim for two servings a day, at least. Most Americans average one serving of fruit or less. So count your fruit during the day, too, until two servings becomes automatic.

Here's a helpful tip: Breakfast is an easy meal to work fruit into. Have citrus juice or slice fruit onto a bowl of cereal. Always keep fruit on hand for grab-and-go snacks, too.

Enjoy convenience fare. While many people prefer fresh fruits and vegetables, frozen and canned varieties aren't so bad either. In fact, research shows that they hold their own with fresh produce when it comes to good nutrition.

☞ One study compared fresh, frozen and canned vegetables and fruits. After cooking, the levels of vitamins A and C were about the same for all forms.

COUNTING FIBER

You can't taste dietary fiber or season it or dress it up with sauce. Yet it's a key ingredient in the healthy cook's kitchen. Getting enough fiber in your diet can help lower cholesterol, prevent constipation and help control weight problems, among many other things.

Experts advise getting 25 grams or more of fiber every day. Here's an easy way to estimate your intake without getting bogged down in fiber charts.

☞ For every serving of whole-grain foods, count 2 grams of fiber.

☞ For every serving of refined-grain products, count 1 gram of fiber.

☞ For every serving of fruits or vegetables, count 2 grams of fiber.

☞ For every serving of beans, count 5 grams of fiber.

If, by the end of the day, you've had three servings of vegetables, two of fruit, three of whole-grain foods, three of refined-grain foods and one of beans, you're up to 24 grams of fiber. Add a high-fiber breakfast cereal, and you have it made.

☞ Precut fresh vegetables sealed in special packaging may retain more beta-carotene than fresh vegetables sold loose at the produce counter.

In addition, don't assume that all canned vegetables are high in salt. Some are, but more and more products are made with no salt added. So check the labels; you may be pleasantly surprised.

The bottom line? Eat whatever form of fruits and vegetables fits your lifestyle. You get lots of

Salt

Is It GOOD for You?

You can't live without sodium. It plays a crucial role in muscle contraction, nervous system function and maintenance of your body's fluid balance. A little salt is certainly good for you.

But what about salt added to foods? This is where things get more complicated. Experts agree that salt isn't the evil spice that people once thought it was. Yes, it occasionally may play a role in raising blood pressure. But for most people, adding moderate amounts of salt to food doesn't seem to cause problems. It appears that some people are sensitive to salt's effects while others aren't.

Incidentally, it's not necessarily the saltshaker that causes problems. Canned and processed foods tend to contain more sodium than fresh foods. For instance, ½ cup home-cooked red kidney beans without salt has less than 2 milligrams of sodium; ½ cup canned red kidney beans has 436 milligrams.

This is not to say that you should resume loading up your food with salt. Quite the opposite. Most people soon get used to the taste of less salt after about three months and start to find foods seasoned the old way too salty.

vitamins and fiber no matter which form you choose. The only bad choice is eating no fruits and vegetables.

Bring on the grains. Experts recommend that we eat six or more servings of grain foods every day. That sounds like a lot, but in most cases, it's easily done. A slice of bread, for example, counts as one serving. So does ½ cup cooked rice. Or half a bagel. Or ½ cup cooked pasta.

There is one caveat, however. When counting grain servings, it's critical that at least three out of six are whole-grain foods. Sadly, most grains are refined before they reach us. That means that two nutrient-rich parts of the grain are removed: the bran and the germ. Even though manufacturers add back iron and some B vitamins, we lose hard-to-get zinc, magnesium, copper and vitamin E. Lots of fiber is lost, too. That's why when you go with the grain, you should go with the whole grain.

Check the label. The only way to be sure that you're getting quality is to look at the list of ingredients on the label; otherwise, you may get fooled. The first ingredient should say "whole wheat" or "whole-wheat flour." If it says "wheat flour" or "enriched wheat flour," it's not whole grain.

Don't be taken in by slick advertising. For example, "Country Wheat Bread" sure sounds whole grain, but it probably isn't. Don't trust the color, either. It's easy to make a wholesome-looking brown loaf that contains only processed—and minimally healthful—ingredients. Reading the label is the one way to be sure that you're getting high-quality, nutritious food.

Put beans on the table. Dried beans, lentils and peas are the best sources of total fiber and soluble fiber (the cholesterol-shrinking kind). They're also a rich source of folate, which helps prevent birth defects and heart disease. Best of all, they're inexpensive. This makes it easy to get at least one serving of beans a day.

THE CASE AGAINST FAT

It wasn't so many years ago that "healthy" cooks conscientiously filled their kitchens with vegetables, fruits and whole grains and then slathered every recipe with butter, cheese, sour cream, mayonnaise and other high-fat foods.

People didn't know it then, but fat is *the* saboteur in any healthy diet. Why is fat such a problem? Consider:

☞ High levels of blood cholesterol invite heart disease, the number one cause of death for Americans. Reducing your cholesterol level by as little as 5 percent may help cut your risk of heart attack by 10 percent.

☞ A very low fat diet with plenty of fruits and vegetables has been shown to actually reverse the buildup of deposits in blood vessels that make heart attacks more likely.

☞ Low-fat diets have been linked to lower rates of colon cancer and prostate cancer.

☞ One study found that women with diets low in fat have a 34 percent lower risk of endometrial cancer compared with women on high-fat diets.

☞ Because low-fat diets make weight loss easier, they help prevent obesity, another foe of good health. Weighing too much makes us prone to high blood pressure, diabetes and heart disease. Obesity raises the risk of strokes in men and breast cancer in women.

☞ Another study found that women who followed a low-fat diet for a year reported feeling more energy and less depression. They also lost nine pounds each.

☞ A study of people over age 45 found that those who ate the most saturated fat had an 80 percent greater chance of developing early retina degeneration than those who ate the least. Early retina degeneration is the leading cause of legal blindness among people over 65.

COOKING LEAN

There are many ways for healthy cooks to reduce fat in their diets. The trick is to maintain flavor in the process. Here are some strategies for you to try.

Always check the label. Most of us fill the grocery cart without ever taking a close look at food labels. But when you're trying to cut fat from your diet, food labels are like road maps showing you when you're on course—and when you're about to stray.

For example, if you look at the label on a jar of mayonnaise, you'll find that 1 tablespoon has 11 grams of fat. If your total fat budget for the day is 44 grams, 2 tablespoons of mayo on your sandwich uses up half your day's allowance—not such a good deal. A better bet might be to use low-fat or nonfat mayo. Or pick another sandwich helper, such as mustard, which has only 1 gram of fat per tablespoon.

Choose the right oil. You doubtless already know that not all fats are created equal. Saturated fats, the kind found in red meats, cause the most damage; monounsaturated fats, like olive oil, in small amounts may actually be beneficial, by reducing the amount of bad LDL cholesterol in your body and possibly increasing the good HDL cholesterol. A study in Greece found that women using the most olive oil had the lowest rates of breast cancer. But moderation is key; too much of any fat, even a "good" fat, can cause problems.

Beware of butter and margarine. While each contains a different kind of fat—butter has saturated fat, while margarine contains trans-fatty acids—neither is especially good for your diet. Use them in small amounts. (For a closer look at the butter-versus-margarine debate, see page 475.)

Add seafood to your diet. Most seafood is extremely low in saturated fat. It's true that some types, like shrimp and lobster, contribute more than a little cholesterol to the diet, but their rock-bottom fat content and saturated fat profile make them heart-healthy.

Salmon, a super source of omega-3 fatty acids, is a particularly good choice. One study found that eating an average of 3 ounces of salmon once a week seemed to cut the risk of certain fatal heart attacks in half.

FIGURING YOUR FAT BUDGET

Given the dangers of a diet that's too high in fat, it's important to know your fat budget—the number of grams of fat that you can have each day and still be within healthy limits. Many doctors recommend a diet in which no more than 25 percent of your total calories come from fat.

To know how much fat you can have, you first need to know the number of calories required to maintain your body at a healthy weight, even if that's not what you weigh right now. (Your healthy weight is, quite simply, one that you can maintain by eating a nutritious, low-fat diet and exercising daily.)

Start by taking your healthy weight and multiplying it by 12 if you're fairly inactive. If you're moderately active (for example, you do aerobic exercise for 30 minutes three times a week), multiply the weight by 15. If you're very active (exercising for at least 60 minutes four or more times a week), multiply by 18. The result tells you how many calories you need. Once you've figured out your calories, it's easy to find your fat budget using the chart below.

HEALTHY CALORIE INTAKE	FAT BUDGET (G.)
1,200	33
1,400	38
1,600	44
1,800	50
2,000	55
2,200	61
2,500	69
2,800	77

Look for lite. Take advantage of new low-fat or nonfat versions of mayonnaise, margarine, butter, sour cream, cream cheese and other traditionally fatty foods. The fat and calorie savings can often be enormous. For example, a tablespoon of regular margarine contains 100 calories, while an equal amount of fat-free margarine contains only 5 calories.

Keep in mind, however, that fat-free doesn't mean calorie-free. If you eat a whole package of fat-free cookies, for example, you may not get much fat, but you will get nearly a whole day's worth of calories—and practically no fiber, vitamins or minerals. Check those labels!

Cut back on meats. The old days of throwing a humongous steak on the grill every night are gone. Here's why: Meat is a major source of fat, especially saturated fat—the very type that's most harmful to good health if you eat too much of it. A study in the Netherlands found that women who eat meat more than five times a week have more than twice the breast cancer risk of women who eat meat two times a week or less. Diets high in meat have also been linked to colon cancer and prostate cancer.

More and more Americans report that they're becoming "sometime vegetarians"—that is, they're eating several meatless meals each week. But can't healthy cooks have meat? If they want it, you bet! To enjoy satisfying, stick-to-your ribs dishes without ruining your healthy diet, follow these guidelines.

☞ Serve no more than one 3-ounce portion of meat, fish or poultry—the size of a cassette tape—in one day.

☞ Use meat as a flavoring ingredient in casseroles, salads and stews, instead of using it as the main feature on your plate. (Limiting meat or even going meatless won't jeopardize your protein intake, since protein is also found in grains, beans, dairy foods and vegetables.)

☞ Use cuts of beef with the least fat. A 3-ounce portion of London broil (flank steak) has 9 grams of total fat and 4 grams of saturated fat. By comparison, 3 ounces of beef tenderloin has 15 grams of total fat and 6 grams of saturated fat.

Low Fat, High Flavor

Fat is bad for your heart, bad for your arteries and bad for your waistline. So why do you love it so? Because fat, for all its negatives, carries a lot of flavor to food. That's why when you cut back on fat, you have to boost the flavor of your food.

Homemade horseradish is great way to fire up almost any meal. Best of all, it's easy to prepare. Here's how.

Remove the leaves from a horseradish root and use a vegetable peeler to shave off the top layer of skin.

Chop the root into pieces, then grind it in a food processor or blender with enough vinegar to moisten. Don't puree the root; you want it to have texture.

Store the horseradish in a glass container with a tight-fitting lid; it will keep, refrigerated, for up to three months.

Pork tenderloin is another low-fat meat.

☞ Remove skin from poultry. A 3-ounce piece of chicken breast with skin has 7 grams of fat. Without the skin? Only 3 grams.

The Pleasures of Dairy

It's hard to imagine cooking without the creaminess and flavor that dairy products contribute to food. Dairy foods aren't used just for their taste and texture, of course. They also provide abundant calcium—the mineral we need to help prevent fragile bones. The Daily Value of calcium for men and women under age 50 is 1,000 milligrams. From 50 on, women who are not on estrogen should try for 1,500 milligrams.

That sounds like a lot. And in fact, most women get only half the calcium that they need. But by focusing on the right foods, you can get enough calcium almost automatically. Look for foods that have about 300 milligrams of calcium per serving. (On food labels, 30 percent DV for calcium signifies 300 milligrams.) Which foods fit the bill?

☞ An 8-ounce serving of nonfat or 1% low-fat milk

☞ An 8-ounce serving of some nonfat and low-fat yogurts (check the labels to make sure)

☞ 1 ounce of many low-fat and nonfat cheeses (again, check the labels)

☞ An 8-ounce serving of some calcium-fortified nonfat and low-fat soy milks

If you can't work three to four servings of these high-calcium foods a day into your regular diet, make up any difference with a calcium supplement.

We've been focusing on the benefits of dairy, but there's also a downside. Dairy is naturally high in fat—unless you're careful to buy low-fat or nonfat versions of all your favorites.

The Healthy Kitchen

You've promoted grains and vegetables from supporting roles and made them star players. You're cutting back on red meat and other forms of dietary fat. You're eating smarter than ever before. But are you really well-equipped for healthy eating?

Having the right cookware, appliances and utensils can make an enormous difference in how you cook. Obviously, people with only a deep-fat fryer at their disposal have limited options. Outfitting your kitchen with the proper tools, on the other hand, will enable you to prepare the types of meals that enhance health: those that are low in fat, high in fiber and livened with a delicious abundance of fruits, vegetables and grains.

Besides, as any chef can tell you, having good equipment makes cooking easier and more fun, so you'll do it more often.

What you don't need is a kitchen full of specialized gear just to put healthy food on the table. What you do need is quality gear. A knife that quickly loses its edge—or that never had much of an edge to begin with—is hardly a bargain. The same goes for pots and pans that are extremely cheap. They may look great and the price may be right, but will they hold up? Don't count on it.

Take a cue from experts: Buy only equipment that works as hard as you do. Think of it as a long-term investment, and you won't be tempted to settle for second best.

MATERIAL NEEDS

You use your pots and pans every day, so buy equipment that will hold up. The best cookware is made from heavy-duty material—heavy enough to heat evenly without developing hot spots, yet light enough so that you can handle them without fatigue. Pots and pans should sit solidly on the burner, so you don't have to chase them around the stove top during cooking, yet they should also be light enough so that you can handle them without fatigue.

Handles should be strong, attached securely and free of any wobble. Lids should fit tightly and have solidly attached knobs. Remember that some types of handles and lid knobs get hot. Know ahead of time which type you're getting and whether or not you'll need pot holders handy.

When choosing cookware, it's also important to consider factors such as appearance and ease of cleaning. Copper cookware, for example, takes on a lovely burnish, but it also requires frequent polishing. Stainless steel, on the other hand, not only looks good but also is virtually maintenance-free.

Here's a rundown of some of the more popular cooking materials.

☞ **No-stick surface.** For the healthy cook, pots and pans lined with no-stick materials are ideal. They have slick, nearly impermeable surfaces, which means that you can cook food with

LOW-FAT COOKWARE

No-stick cookware is called for throughout the recipes in this book. It's the healthiest choice for cooking without added fat. If you don't have no-stick cookware, regular cookware can easily be substituted. Just use a little extra no-stick spray so that the food doesn't stick.

For baking, line baking sheets, jelly-roll pans, cake pans and loaf pans with parchment paper, which is a ready-made, disposable no-stick surface. It's available near the wax paper in most supermarkets and kitchen stores. Simply cut a piece to fit your bakeware and bake as directed.

little or no added fat. Plus, cleanup is a breeze. In most cases, a quick rub with a little soapy water is all that's needed.

One drawback to some no-stick surfaces is that they scratch easily—and once the coating is gone, so is the stick-free advantage. To prevent this, reach for plastic or wooden utensils instead of metal. This will also help keep little bits of the surface from flaking into food. (If flaking should occur, be aware that the material is nontoxic.)

Scratching isn't a problem with the newer generation of no-stick ware, whose special finish is guaranteed not to scrape off, burn off or scrub off for at least 20 years. These pans can withstand high temperatures and the use of metal utensils. Don't let price deter you from buying a quality product that will last for many years to come.

☞ **Stainless steel.** For durability, light weight and rugged good looks, stainless steel cookware is the first choice of many home cooks. The wonderfully shiny surface is attractive and easy to clean. And since stainless is a nonreactive metal, it will not impart any

aftertaste or discoloration to food.

Unfortunately, stainless steel is a notoriously poor conductor of heat. To provide for faster heating times, manufacturers have no choice but to make the metal very thin. While this speeds the cooking time, it also has the tendency to allow hot spots to form, which can cause food to stick and burn.

It's generally best to avoid pure stainless cookware. A better choice is to buy products that incorporate an aluminum core or copper bottom with the stainless steel. This combines the durability, sharp appearance and easy cleaning of stainless steel with the improved conductivity and even heating of the other materials.

☞ **Cast iron.** For even heating, durability, excellent heat retention and low cost, this traditional favorite is hard to beat. Its main drawback is that larger pans are very heavy. Also, cast iron will rust if not properly seasoned and then dried thoroughly after each use.

The surface of cast iron is riddled with thousands of small pits, which is why new cast-iron pans require seasoning to prevent food from sticking. Here's how to season cast iron.

1. Warm a new pan over low heat and peel off the label.

2. Remove from the heat and wash the pan with warm, soapy water, rubbing thoroughly with a bristle brush or plastic bun. Then rinse and dry the pan completely.

3. Pour in ¼ cup vegetable oil (use more if the pan is large) and coat the entire inside surface by rubbing it with a paper towel. Then pour out the excess oil, leaving a thin film on the bottom and sides. If you have other pans to season, you can reuse the same oil.

4. Bake the pan in a 300° oven for 1 hour. Turn off the oven and allow the pan to remain in it until cool, at least 2 to 3 hours.

5. Remove the cold pan from the oven. Place it on the stove over medium-high heat and let it stand for 5 minutes. Remove the pan from the heat (the handle will be hot) and cool completely. The pan is ready to use.

Pans are typically seasoned when new, although you may want to repeat the process if food begins sticking.

After using cast iron, wash it by hand with hot water and liquid dish soap. Do not scour the pan. To keep the pan from rusting, dry it very thoroughly, preferably by wiping it first with a towel to remove most of the water, then placing it over low heat for a few minutes until completely dry.

If food has stuck to the surface, let the pan cool after cooking. Sprinkle coarse salt into the pan and rub it well with a paper towel to remove the particles. Then wash the pan lightly and dry as above.

Cast iron is an excellent choice for high-heat cooking, such as sautéing, as well as for slow-cooking foods like stews. Be aware that tomatoes and tomato sauce may discolor when cooked in cast iron. It's not recommended that you either store or marinate food in cast iron.

Some cast iron is lined with enamel. While this lends durability and promotes even heating, it typically requires the addition of more oil during cooking to prevent food from sticking.

☞ **Aluminum.** For quick and even heating, choose this highly conductive metal. Quality aluminum cookware rarely develops hot spots, and it's light enough to handle easily.

Aluminum is soft, however, and it generally begins to pit with long-term use. Food shouldn't be stored in aluminum, as the metal can impart a bitter taste to the food. In addition, acidic foods like tomatoes can cause discoloration. For the benefits of aluminum without the drawbacks, you may want to buy aluminum lined with stainless steel. Heavy-gauge anodized aluminum, which has a dark gray finish, can work well, too.

If your aluminum does discolor, clean it with a mixture of two teaspoons cream of tartar and one quart water. Boil the mixture in the pan for 10 minutes, then rinse the pan out.

There has been concern over whether or not there is a link between aluminum and Alzheimer's disease, but there is no conclusive

Helpful Hint

Simmering tomato sauce or other acidic foods for an extended time in cast-iron cookware can increase your intake of dietary iron. It has been shown, for instance, that spaghetti sauce simmered for a few hours in a cast-iron pot has an increase in iron from 3 milligrams to 50 milligrams.

evidence that use of aluminum cookware or foil poses any health risk.

☞ **Copper.** For cooks who want what is generally considered the best cooking material available, durable, long-lasting copper is the answer. Chefs swear by its performance, while bemoaning its admittedly astronomical price and its tendency to need frequent polishing to maintain its beauty.

If you decide to take the plunge and invest in high-quality copper cookware, make sure that it's lined with tin, silver, stainless steel or some other nonreactive material. Copper itself is highly reactive. When it comes in contact with acidic foods, harmful by-products can be produced that could get into your system. Over time, they could accumulate and possibly cause physical damage.

It is safe, however, to beat raw egg whites in unlined copper bowls. Unlike acidic foods, egg whites don't react harmfully with the metal. And chefs have long recognized that egg whites beaten in copper bowls achieve greater volume than those beaten in other types of bowls.

Copper pots have traditionally been lined with tin, which provides fast, even heating. Tin is fairly soft, however, so pans that are heavily used may eventually require retinning. Silver is also a soft metal. Stainless steel linings, while poorer conductors than tin, have the advantage of being virtually indestructible.

In some countries, copper pans are often sold unlined. While these are perfectly adequate for storing dry goods or for hanging on a wall, they aren't meant for cooking.

CHOICE POTS AND PANS

Skillets, saucepans and sauté pans are the backbone of the healthy kitchen. Unlike those bright orange fondue pots or fancy custard molds that you got for wedding gifts, which probably haven't been off your shelf in years, your pots and pans see heavy service almost every day. It's essential that they be both rugged and easy to use.

The least expensive way to buy pots and pans is in a set. But you should ask yourself if pieces included in the set are actually things that you need and will use often. In the long run, it may be better to pay a little more for just the pots that you'll use every day than to get a "bargain" set where half the pieces rarely get used.

In the interest of saving space and money, it's always worth looking for cookware that does double duty: a saucepan that comes with a double-boiler insert, for example, or lids that fit more than one piece.

Whether you're a new cook just getting started or you're looking to acquire some extra inventory, here are some basic pots and pans that no healthy kitchen should be without.

☞ **Heavy-gauge skillets.** These are for sautéing, stir-frying and all-purpose use. Common sizes are 8″ (small), 10″ (medium) and 12″ (large). The larger sizes are more versatile, although you may have trouble hefting the extra weight. If you want only one skillet, the 10″ size is a good choice.

☞ **Wok.** This is the perfect choice if you make stir-fried meals a lot, although a skillet is sufficient if you only stir-fry occasionally. The high heat and large surface area provided by a wok make it ideal for cooking with little added fat. Some woks are made with a no-stick surface. Round-bottom woks are often recommended for gas stoves, while flat-bottom ones are sold for electric ranges. Some chefs recommend flat-bottom woks for both types of stoves, since they're more stable and allow more contact with the heat. Electric models are also available. No matter what type you choose, make sure that it has a lid.

Woks can be used for more than just stir-fries. By putting an inch or two of water in the bottom and inserting a steamer basket, you can easily convert your wok to a steamer. It's excellent for steaming fish, poultry and vegetables.

☞ **Pressure cooker.** This cooks with moist heat at high temperatures, which means that you can prepare food with no added fat—and in a fraction of the time needed for regular stove-top cooking. This is particularly important for healthy cooking, since many delicious and nutritious foods, such as beans and legumes, are extremely slow-cooking otherwise.

Modern models are safe and foolproof to use. Just be sure to follow the manufacturer's directions. A 6-quart capacity is good for most recipes. A model with two handles makes handling it easier.

☞ **Stove-top grill.** This combines the low-fat benefits of grilling with the convenience of cooking indoors. Often made from cast iron, a stove-top grill fits directly over the existing burners; no modifications are necessary.

☞ **Heavy-gauge saucepans.** These are the

workhorses of the kitchen. Chances are, you'll use these every day for making sauces, hot cereals, rice, soups and more. They're also ideal for steaming vegetables. Chefs recommend having a 1½-quart (small) saucepan for all-purpose use and a 2- to 3- quart (medium) saucepan for steaming and boiling.

☞ **Heavy-gauge Dutch oven.** This comes in handy for large batches of soups, stews and chili. It's also good for boiling pasta, making stock and cooking pot roast. Get one that's at least 6 quarts.

No matter how small your kitchen or how simply you're trying to outfit it, you'll want one or more of the following. They're bigger-ticket items than small gadgets, but they earn their place by saving time or letting you cook without fat.

☞ **Microwave.** Although the microwave will never replace a regular stove or oven, it's indispensable for quickly preparing foods like

THE LOW-FAT ARSENAL

Forget the deep fryer and the butter curler. One of the first steps in creating a healthy kitchen is to get the right tools. Here are a few specialized items that we use at the Rodale Test Kitchen.

Ribbed frying pans allow fat to drain away from food during cooking.

A fat separator has a bottom spout that lets you pour out the fat-free juices at the bottom—a must for defatting stock and making healthy gravy.

A slotted broiler allows meat fat to drip into the pan beneath.

A soapstone griddle has a natural no-stick surface, so you don't need oil.

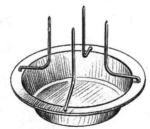

A chicken roaster collects rendered fat in the pan below.

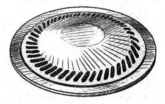

Stove-top grill toppers allow you to grill meat, fish and vegetables without using oil.

vegetables, chicken cutlets and fish fillets without fat. (For more on microwaves, see page 54.)

☞ **Food processor or blender.** These appliances aren't entirely interchangeable, but you can get by with one or the other if you don't want to spring for both. Blenders are especially good at pureeing thin liquids like soups and drinks. Food processors quickly chop vegetables and cubed meat, shred foods with ease and thoroughly blend thick mixtures. A mini-processor comes in handy for chopping herbs, garlic and other foods in small quantities.

Another option is the immersion blender, also called a handheld blender. It's good for pureeing soups and sauces right in the saucepan or whipping up low-fat shakes right in the glass.

A low-tech pureeing device is the old-fashioned food mill. It makes smooth applesauce, lump-free mashed potatoes and creamy soups with just a little energy expenditure on your part.

☞ **Electric mixer.** Either a portable mixer or a standing model is probably in order. If you bake a lot of bread, you may want a standing mixer with a dough hook. On the other hand, if you rarely bake cakes or cookies and prefer to mash things like potatoes by hand, you can get by with simple tools such as a wire whisk, some wooden spoons and a potato masher. Your equipment should reflect your needs.

Knives: A Cook's Best Friend

Whether you're peeling an onion, chopping broccoli or trimming fat from a roast, a sharp knife makes the work go faster.

"Safety is the biggest reason for keeping your knives sharp," says Tom Ney, director of the Rodale Test Kitchen in Emmaus, Pennsylvania. "A knife that's dull enough to slip off a tomato is still sharp enough to cut your fingers."

A top-quality knife can be made of carbon steel, stainless steel or high-carbon stainless. Most people prefer knives made from high-carbon stainless, which holds its edge and shiny

appearance for a long time and is still relatively easy to sharpen.

A good knife is solid and well-balanced; it should feel comfortable in your hand. Some knives have wooden handles that are securely riveted in place. Others have plastic handles that are molded around the metal. Both kinds hold up well, and you should pick the one that feels better to you.

You don't need a huge selection of knives, but having a few sizes and styles to choose from will make your kitchen tasks go much easier. Here's a list of the basics.

☞ **3″ or 4″ paring knife.** This is essential for paring, peeling, mincing and slicing small items, such as garlic or scallions.

☞ **6″ boning knife.** The strong, flexible blade is indispensable for trimming fat and for removing bones from chicken, meat and fish.

☞ **8″ or 10″ chef's knife.** This is an all-purpose knife with a slightly curved edge. The shape allows for a rocking motion that makes it ideal for chopping, dicing, mincing and julienning. It also does a great job slicing meat, fish and poultry.

☞ **6″ or 8″ serrated knife.** This is perfect for slicing tomatoes and bread. Serrated blades have the added advantage of never needing sharpening.

☞ **8″ or 10″ carving knife.** The long, slender blade is extremely flexible—perfect for cutting thin slices from a turkey, roast or other meats.

Protecting Cutlery

Knives that are well-constructed and made from superior material are always expensive; don't expect to buy a quality knife for $3.99. On the other hand, good knives last a lifetime if they are cared for properly. For speed, efficiency and a satisfying feel, good knives are worth the investment.

They're also worth taking care of. To keep your blades in good shape and cutting-sharp, chefs recommend these tips.

HOW TO SHARPEN YOUR KNIVES

Do you have a drawerful of kitchen knives that don't cut? It's not hard to sharpen a knife on a whetstone. Even if you don't do it right the first time, you won't ruin the knife. Just try again.

Here's a lesson from Tom Ney, director of the Rodale Test Kitchen in Emmaus, Pennsylvania, for keeping all your knives tomato-cutting sharp.

Place the sharpening stone on a slightly moist kitchen towel or paper towel to prevent slipping. Position the stone near the counter's edge. Dot mineral oil along the stone and smear it into a light, even coating.

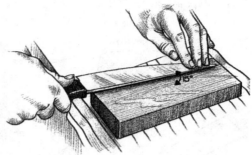

Position the edge of the knife against the upper left-hand corner of the stone. Tilt the blade toward the stone at an angle of about 15 degrees.

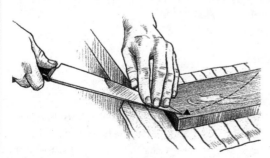

Move the blade in an arc, so that the knife point slips off the lower right-hand corner of the stone. Steady the back of the blade with your fingertips as you move the knife. Repeat 10 to 20 times.

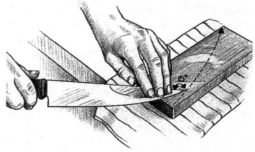

Turn the knife over, position it against the lower right-hand corner of the stone and slide the knife back in an arc in the other direction. Repeat 10 to 20 times.

KINDS OF CUTS

The food processor has eliminated some of the tedium from large-scale chopping, slicing and dicing. But for most smaller jobs, cutting by hand is faster—and more precise.

The type of cut that you need depends on the dish being prepared. Dicing, for example, is usually recommended for sautés, because you want items to cook quickly and release all their flavor to the oil. Chopping, however, is better for retaining texture and crunch.

Take a look at the "chop shop" below to see what cuts you need.

Mincing. This means cutting food into small pieces, usually less than ⅛″. Mincing is the smallest cut and is often used for garlic, shallots and fresh herbs. It vastly increases the cooking area, helping foods release all their flavors.

Chopping. This involves cutting food into irregular ¼″ to ½″ pieces. The small pieces provide a large surface area for quick cooking, yet they are large enough to hold their basic shape and texture. Onions are often chopped, as are carrots, celery and tomatoes.

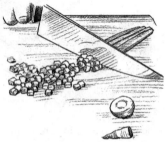

Dicing. Unlike the chop cut, this involves cutting food into *uniform* ¼″ cubes. Dicing is often used when appearance is important, as with a cold salad.

Keep them in a rack. Nothing dulls a knife faster than throwing it in a kitchen drawer, where its delicate edge will be banged, abraded and chipped by every other piece of metal that's banging around in there with it.

To protect the edges, store good knives in a free-standing rack or attach them to a magnetic strip. You'll always know where they are, and they'll stay sharp.

Wash them by hand. Dishwashers and soaking are out for knives. Too much water and harsh detergents dull and distort both handles and blades. (And leaving a sharp knife submerged in soapy water invites cuts.) Instead, wipe and dry each knife immediately after using it. Then return it to the rack, where it will be ready for next time.

Keep the edge. While any good knife needs occasional grinding—either on a whetstone at home or at your local knife shop—regularly using a sharpening steel is the best way to preserve the edge. Unlike grinding, which

Cubing. A larger cut than a dice, cubing means cutting food into uniform cubes or squares that can range from about ½″ to 2″. Often used for salads and stir-fries, cubed vegetables retain their shape and texture while still cooking quickly.

Julienning. With this cut, food is sliced into thin strips or sticks, usually about ⅛″ thick. Julienning exposes a large surface area for quick cooking— as, for example, when using carrots in a stir-fry—yet it provides an even, elegant shape.

Shredding. Done on a grater, shredding cuts food into long, uneven strips. It's usually used for raw dishes that don't require distinctive shapes, like coleslaw. Shredding is much coarser than grating, which is often used for hard cheeses like Parmesan and for vegetables that need to be nearly minced.

Slicing. Sliced food is cut into pieces of uniform thickness. Like a julienne, the slice provides a lot of surface area for cooking, yet it is large enough to retain crunch.

abrades metal from the edge, "steeling" it every few times you use it straightens the edge, keeping it sharp all the time.

Use them on wood. Plastic cutting boards are extremely hard on knives. Wood cutting boards have more give than plastic and are more forgiving on a knife's delicate edge.

Before you start cutting, lay a slightly damp dish towel underneath your cutting board. This will keep the board steady and prevent it from skating. At the same time, it will catch run-off—

the juice from a roast, for example—before it hits the counter.

HEALTHY BAKING

Whether you're making muffins or meat loaf, good-quality bakeware is essential. No-stick surfaces usually require no greasing; some may require just a light coating of no-stick spray. Ovenproof glass bakeware also resists sticking and is a good choice. When using glass, however,

Using a Steel

The edge of a knife is lined with many thin, sharp pieces, like the teeth on a saw. Under the force of repeated use, the teeth gradually bend to either side. This is what causes sharp knives to get dull.

The easiest way to keep the edge straight and keen between regular sharpenings is to employ a steel every time you use the knife. Here's how.

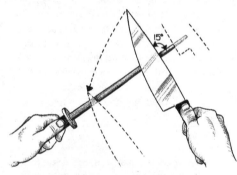

Hold the lower edge of the blade against the tip of the steel at an angle of about 15 degrees. Pull the blade across the steel, sliding the knife down as you go.

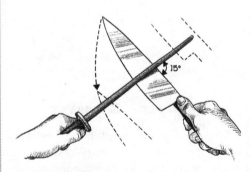

Reverse the knife and hold the other side of the edge against the tip of the steel and curve it down. Do about five sweeps of each side.

be sure to reduce the oven temperature by 25°, because glass conducts and retains heat better than metal.

Unless you do a lot of baking, you don't need a large selection of extravagant equipment. Stocking up on the following essentials will cover most situations that you're likely to encounter.

☞ Broiler pan (Made with a grooved surface and slots leading to a drip pan underneath, a broiler pan is ideal for cooking meats at high temperatures. Fat is liquefied and drains away.)

☞ Metal roasting pan with rack (This allows heat to circulate evenly around the food, while at the same time letting fat drain off. To keep cleanup time to a minimum, it's a good idea to choose a no-stick rack. The most versatile size for a roasting pan is about 11″ × 17″.)

☞ Mixing bowls

☞ Heavy-duty no-stick baking sheets

☞ Heavy-duty no-stick jelly-roll pan (a baking sheet with a rim)

☞ Glass baking dishes (8″ × 8″, 8″ × 12″ or 9″ × 13″)

☞ Glass or metal pie plates (9″ and 10″)

☞ Loose-bottom tart pans, (8″ or 9″)

☞ No-stick cake pans (8″ and 9″)

☞ No-stick bundt pan

☞ No-stick loaf pans

☞ No-stick muffin pans (Using paper or foil liners with regular muffin pans will serve the same purpose: helping speed cleanup while enabling you to cut back on oil.)

☞ Oven-to-table casserole or baking dishes, in assorted shapes and sizes

☞ Ramekins or custard cups (6 ounces)

☞ Springform pan, (8″ or 9″)

Filling Your Drawers

Walk into any kitchen supply store, and you'll see hundreds of wonderful gadgets, ranging from traditional potato peelers to high-tech battery-powered pepper mills.

The allure of gadgets is their promise of making life easier, faster and more efficient—

with a little fun thrown into the bargain. While many kitchen gadgets really are worth their weight in gold, many others are destined to spend their entire lives buried in the back of a junk drawer.

To prevent your kitchen drawers from turning into artifact museums, make it a point to stock up only on items that you're pretty sure you'll use—as opposed to those that just seem "neat." While you're at it, keep a sharp eye out for gadgets (for example, fat strainers) that can help cut fat from your daily meals; there are many to choose from. (See "The Low-Fat Arsenal" on page 13.)

Here are a few things that are especially useful. This list is divided into two parts: basics and extras. Which gadgets you'll want depends on what type of cooking you do and which foods you generally prepare. Someone who never uses wine probably won't need a corkscrew, for instance.

Basics

- ☞ Can opener
- ☞ Collapsible metal steamer basket
- ☞ Fat separator
- ☞ Flat skimmer, mesh or plastic, for removing fat from soups and stews
- ☞ Four-sided stainless steel box grater
- ☞ Funnel
- ☞ Glass measuring cups for liquids
- ☞ Graduated measuring spoons
- ☞ Graduated metal or plastic measuring cups for dry ingredients
- ☞ Instant-read thermometer

- ☞ Ladle
- ☞ Metal spatula
- ☞ Pepper mill
- ☞ Plastic spatula for no-stick pans
- ☞ Potato masher
- ☞ Rolling pin
- ☞ Rubber spatula or scraper
- ☞ Slotted spoon
- ☞ Strainer or colander
- ☞ Timer
- ☞ Tongs
- ☞ Vegetable peeler
- ☞ Wire whisk, 8″ to 10″, preferably stainless steel
- ☞ Wooden or plastic spoons

MEASURING UP

For most recipes—especially those for baked goods—accurate measuring is essential for success. You'll need two different types of cups, which are not interchangeable.

Glass measuring cups are used for liquid ingredients, including thick liquids like honey and molasses. The most common sizes are 1 cup, 2 cups and 4 cups. To use, place the cup on a flat surface and bend over so that you're at eye level with it. Pour in the liquid until it rises to the appropriate mark.

Dry measuring cups come in sets that generally include ¼-, ⅓-, ½- and 1-cup sizes. (Sometimes ⅛-cup and 2-cup sizes are also available.) They're most often made of metal or plastic. To use, spoon dry ingredients, such as flour, sugar or cornmeal, into the cup until it's overflowing; level off the ingredient with the flat side of a knife. (You can level off ingredients like rice, dried fruit and chopped nuts with your fingers.)

Helpful Hint

When you need just a touch of a hard cheese like Parmesan or Cheddar to liven up a dish, try shaving some off with a citrus zester instead of a grater. This will give you exactly the amount that you need, and you won't have to clean a large grater.

Extras

- ☞ Bamboo or metal skewers
- ☞ Blender
- ☞ Cake saver
- ☞ Cheesecloth
- ☞ Citrus zester
- ☞ Cooling racks
- ☞ Corkscrew
- ☞ Egg beater
- ☞ Egg separator
- ☞ Egg slicer (useful for slicing any soft food like mushrooms)
- ☞ Food processor
- ☞ Food scale
- ☞ Freezer/refrigerator thermometer
- ☞ Garlic press
- ☞ Ginger grater
- ☞ Hand juice reamer
- ☞ Icing spatula
- ☞ Kitchen scissors or shears
- ☞ Kitchen twine
- ☞ Meat pounder
- ☞ Meat thermometer
- ☞ Melon baller
- ☞ Metal pastry scraper
- ☞ Oven thermometer
- ☞ Parmesan cheese grater
- ☞ Pastry bags and tips
- ☞ Pastry brush
- ☞ Pie server
- ☞ Pizza cutter
- ☞ Pizza stone
- ☞ Plastic spray bottle, for misting olive oil or vegetable oil on pans or over salads (When buying a spray bottle, make sure that it's equipped with an adjustable nozzle. Oil will clog the spray mechanism of ordinary nozzles.)
- ☞ Swivel peeler
- ☞ Yogurt funnel

ADDED PLEASURES

As is evident from the sheer number of kitchen supply stores, cook's catalogs and other merchandising outlets that have sprung up to satisfy cooks' needs, there's really no limit to the kinds of kitchen equipment that you can buy.

Once you're well-supplied with the basics, it's time to ask yourself what, if any, additional equipment you need. It really depends on how much cooking you do and what style or styles you lean toward. If you do a lot of baking, for example, you may find yourself looking at specialty items like heavy-duty mixers or porcelain-lined double boilers that another cook would rarely or never use.

One advanced item that every cook can benefit from is a large stockpot. While it's possible to get along without it, having an 8- to 10-quart pot will make your life much easier when it's time to make stock for freezing or when you're preparing soup or stew to feed a large group.

If you enjoy fresh juices, you'll almost certainly want to consider an electric juicer. A good one is fairly expensive, but the massive engine and heavy-duty construction mean that you'll be using it for many years to come.

Many cooks also find themselves eyeing small electric spice mills. Although the traditional mortar and pestle will certainly help you extract the freshest flavors from dried spices, they aren't nearly as fast—or as much fun.

A hot-air corn popper will appeal to someone who eats a lot of popcorn and doesn't want the fat that comes from the old-fashioned oil-based method. The hot-air popper also produces a cheaper, lower-fat, lower-calorie, lower-sodium snack than you get from commercial microwave packages.

SAFETY IN THE KITCHEN

Cooking for friends is a cozy notion, but if bacteria crash the party, the experience may set

TAKING TEMPERATURES

Whether you're proofing yeast or roasting a turkey, hitting exactly the right temperature can make the masterpiece—or spell disaster. Here are several ways to check the heat.

Meat thermometer. This typically has settings for different meats right on the dial. You insert the thermometer into raw meat and leave it in place during cooking. Position the thermometer in the center (away from the bone) of the meat.

Freezer/refrigerator thermometer. Foods spoil if the temperature is not sufficiently low. Leave the thermometer in place, without opening the door, for at least six hours. Make sure the freezer reads 0°F or less; the refrigerator temperature should be no higher than 40°F.

Instant-read thermometer. While somewhat more expensive than other thermometers, it's generally more accurate. You get a reading within 30 seconds and can use the thermometer to gauge everything from the doneness of roasts to the temperature of water used to proof yeast.

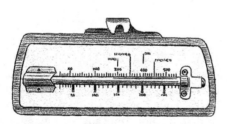

Oven thermometer. Actual oven temperatures don't always match the setting on the dial, so it's important to check the heat with an oven thermometer. Place the thermometer in a cold oven. Heat the oven at 325° for 30 minutes. If the readings don't match, you'll need to make adjustments, up or down, in your cooking times.

Candy thermometer. When making candy, a few degrees one way or the other can spell the difference between success and failure. Some candy thermometers are made of glass and should be prewarmed in a glass of hot tap water before being placed in boiling liquid.

your stomach in motion. Food poisoning can occur any time you swallow bacteria, which tend to accumulate on food that's been improperly stored for long periods at room temperature. In most cases, however, illness is easily prevented. To keep your kitchen a safe haven, here's what you need to do.

Keep foods chilled. Bacteria, like people, are most comfortable where it's warm. Leaving food that should be refrigerated out on the counter for long periods is, for bacteria, like putting out the welcome mat.

It's best to leave foods in the refrigerator until you're ready to use them. If you're prepping ingredients—especially meats or seafood—ahead of time, put them back in the refrigerator as soon as you're done. Then bring them out again just before you're ready to start cooking.

Defrost meats slowly. It's best to defrost meats overnight by moving them from the freezer into the refrigerator. If you need them faster, thaw them in the sink under cold running water or follow the directions that came with your microwave. If you use the microwave, be careful, or portions of the food might end up cooked before the rest is thawed. With either quick method, use the meat immediately.

Don't thaw meat by leaving it on the counter, however. By the time it's thawed, bacteria may have found a home—and will soon be moving on to you.

Wash it well. After cutting chicken, meat or fish, always wash the knife and cutting board in hot, soapy water before using them to prepare other ingredients. This will prevent bacteria from winding up on the next ingredient—like lettuce for the salad—that you're working with.

When you're done cooking, scouring the cutting board with a mild bleach solution will kill bacteria that may be hiding inside cuts or scratches in the wood or plastic. Use ⅓ cup bleach to 1 quart water. Then wash it in hot, soapy water.

Keep meats separated. If you've ever presided over a barbecue, chances are that you've put raw meat on a platter, transferred it to the grill, then returned the cooked meat to the same platter. While bacteria in meat are usually killed during cooking, those still on the platter are alive and can reinfect the cooked meat.

Always use a separate plate for the cooked meats. Washing the extra dishes is less inconvenient than spending time sick in bed.

Be careful with marinades. Marinate meat, poultry and seafood in the refrigerator if the time involved is more than about 30 minutes. Take special care with the leftover marinade. To use it as a sauce or in a sauce, place it in a saucepan and bring it to a full boil. To use the raw marinade as a basting medium, especially when broiling or grilling, stop basting about 5 minutes before the food is ready. Discard any leftover raw marinade.

Rinse chicken well. Since bacteria that sometimes live on poultry aren't always killed during cooking, it's important to rinse chicken well under cold running water before cooking. If you're roasting a whole bird, be sure to rinse out the cavity, too. Then wash the sink well with hot, soapy water.

Chill it fast. Though there are myths to the contrary, you needn't let hot foods cool before putting them in the refrigerator. That idea is probably left over from the days of old-fashioned ice boxes, when hot food would melt the ice. The fact is that the more time any food spends in the warm air, the greater the risk of contamination. To store food, package it in small portions so that it can chill all the way through quickly.

Herbs and Spices

The days of bland, spiceless foods are becoming a distant memory as today's cooks broaden their seasoning repertoires and expand their spice racks. Formerly exotic spices like cumin, coriander and cloves are now being used in kitchens every day. Some cooks, bypassing most offerings in the dried-spice aisle, have taken to growing their own herbs for the freshest tastes imaginable.

Herbs and spices enhance and invigorate any meal while adding virtually no calories, sodium or fat. Furthermore, their vibrant and uplifting presence reduces the need for adding large amounts of salt, cream or butter to a dish. In short, there has never been a better time to learn about the world of herbs and spices. In the following pages, you'll discover many healthy and inventive ways to perk up your meals with a little bit of this and a touch of that.

WHAT'S THE DIFFERENCE?

Is it an herb or is it a spice? Good question, and there's no easy answer. In the broadest sense, you can use this gauge: If you can grow it at home, it's an herb. If it grows in the tropics, it's a spice. So basil would be an herb and cinnamon, a spice.

Some sources define herbs as the leaves of certain annual or perennial plants that do not have woody stems. Again, basil would be an herb, but bay leaves, which grow on a laurel tree, wouldn't.

Other sources insist that leaves are generally called herbs, while seeds, roots, fruits, flowers and bark are spices. So the fresh leaves of coriander, fennel and dill would be herbs, while the dried seeds of the same plants would be classified as spices.

Some say that herbs are green and have a more subtle taste, and that spices are shades of brown, black or red with more dramatic, pungent flavors. To further muddy the waters, a common dictionary definition of *herb* is "a plant valued for its medicinal, savory or aromatic qualities." In that regard, those seasonings that we would otherwise classify as spices—such as nutmeg, black pepper and allspice—qualify as herbs.

In the end, it doesn't really matter what you decide to call them. Let the botanists debate the issue. Your mission is to stock a variety of herbs and spices, use them with abandon and enjoy them.

THE WORLD OF HERBS

Whether you grow them on the patio or buy them at the grocery store, herbs are a most valuable asset in the healthy kitchen. They enhance and amplify almost any part of a meal, from savory soups, tossed salads and sautéed chicken to broiled fish, marinated meats, breads and dessert.

You can buy herbs fresh or dried; most cooks use both forms, depending on the dish being prepared and what's currently available at the supermarket.

(continued on page 28)

KITCHEN MATCH-UPS

Rosemary goes on chicken, but what complements squash? You like dill on fish, but will it work with dips? There are dozens of common herbs and spices to choose from. The list below will help you make good flavor matches.

HERB/SPICE	CHARACTERISTICS	COMMON USES
Allspice	Dark brown or reddish tropical round berries with hints of cinnamon, cloves and nutmeg	Caribbean soups, marinades, savory sauces, chutneys, curries, spice cakes, sweet breads, puddings and fruit desserts
Anise seeds	Tiny seeds with a licorice flavor	Seafood, chowders, sweet breads, cakes and cookies
Basil	Sharp, refreshing green leaf with hints of mint, anise and pepper (varieties include sweet basil, cinnamon basil, lemon basil, ruffled basil, opal or purple basil and Thai basil)	Pesto, red sauces, tomato salads, green salads, Italian soups, vinaigrettes and pasta dishes
Bay leaf	Pale green leaf with a subtle woodsy flavor and brittle texture	Bouquet garni, poaching liquids, soup, stews and marinades; always remove the bay leaf before serving
Caraway seeds	Small seeds with a licorice scent	Rye bread and biscuits, roasted poultry, eastern European dishes, root vegetables and cabbage dishes (coleslaw)
Cardamom seeds	Hints of citrus and ginger	Curry dishes, rice puddings, pickles, chutneys, flat breads and sweet breads; can be bought ground or in the pod; to use, break the pods to free the seeds, then crush the seeds
Celery seeds	Subtle celery flavor	Coleslaw, salad dressings, pickles, poultry stuffings and potato salad
Chervil	Delicate green leaf with hints of parsley, anise and celery; has the appearance of very fine Italian parsley leaves	Sauces for chicken and fish, egg dishes and salads; used in fines herbes
Chives	Tender green shoots with faint onion and scallion flavor	Creamy soups, chowders, dips, egg dishes, vinaigrettes and salads; used in fines herbes; chive blossoms make colorful garnishes
Cilantro	Pungent flavor; appearance is similar to Italian parsley	Asian, Mexican and Indian dishes; salsa, rice, beans, curries, peanut sauces and chicken and fish dishes
Cinnamon	Sweet and fragrant	Poultry rub, pilafs, curries, cakes, muffins, rice puddings, pumpkin soups and pies and winter squash dishes and mulled drinks

Herb/Spice	Characteristics	Common Uses
Cloves	Intense, burnt-orange scent and fragrant, pungent flavor	Indian curries and chutneys, rice dishes, sweet breads, muffins, spice cakes, winter squash soups and purees, mulled drinks
Coriander seeds	Lemony, musky flavor	Prevalent in Thai and Indian curries, Middle Eastern legume dishes, Mexican dishes, black bean soup, Asian peanut sauces and pickles
Cumin seeds	Earthy, rustic flavor	Salsa, Indian curries, Mexican rice and grain dishes, black bean soup, hummus, Tex-Mex chili, chicken, fish, guacamole and chutney
Dill	Refined feathery green strands with distinctive lemony caraway flavor	Vichyssoise, sauces for fish and chicken, seafood chowders, cucumber salads and chilled bisques and yogurt dips
Dill seeds	Similar in flavor to caraway seeds but milder	Gravlax, potato salads, mashed root vegetables, pickles
Fennel	Feathery fronds similar to fresh dill, with a slight licorice taste	Italian tomato sauces, sausage, fish dishes, pickles and European desserts
Fennel seeds	Slightly sweet with a licorice-anise taste	Breads, Mediterranean fish stews, borscht, cabbage dishes
Garlic	Pungent, strongly scented member of the onion family	Virtually all savory dishes, including soups, salads, pesto, garlic bread and stir-fries; prevalent in Italian, Mexican, Indian, French and Middle Eastern dishes; roasting makes garlic's flavor milder
Ginger	Slightly sweet, pungent flavor with spicy aroma	Chinese dishes, curries, carrot and sweet potato dishes, chicken, fish, meats, gingerbread, cakes, pumpkin pie, fruit salads; available fresh, ground and candied; the forms are not interchangeable
Horseradish	Very hot and pungent	Sauces for roast beef, chicken, fish and eggs; salad dressings, cocktail sauce, sandwiches, borscht; available as a whole root or grated
Lemon balm	Green leaf with citruslike taste and grassy perfume	Fruit jams, jellies, light soups, fruit salads, sorbets and teas; seasonal herb often found in farmer's markets
Lemon grass	Sturdy, pale green-to-white tightly furled stalk with mild lemony flavor	Stir-fries, Asian soups, peanut sauces, soy-based sauces and marinades and chicken and fish dishes; sold primarily in Asian markets; available fresh and dried

(continued)

KITCHEN MATCH-UPS—CONTINUED

HERB/SPICE	CHARACTERISTICS	COMMON USES
Lovage	Strong celery taste	As a substitute for celery in potato salads, stuffings and stews; stalks can be braised as a vegetable
Mace	Very similar to nutmeg but more pungent and intense	Sauces for vegetables, puddings, cakes, muffins, sweet breads and fruity desserts; mace is the outer covering of the nutmeg seed
Marjoram	Small green petals with oregano-like resinous flavor	Tomato sauce, fish, red meat, poultry, grains, marinades, sauces for pasta, soups, dressings and dips; can be used in place of oregano; prevalent in Italian and Greek cuisine
Mint	Forest-green to dark green leaves with refreshing, palate-cleansing taste and clean nuance	Fruity salads, condiments for lamb and game, light soups, tabbouleh, yogurt sauces, desserts, jelly and teas; comes in many varieties such as peppermint, spearmint, lemon mint, pineapple mint, apple mint and orange mint
Mustard seeds	Powerfully pungent	Forms the basis of many condiments, such as pickles and chutney
Nutmeg	Sweet, fragrant flavor with hints of allspice, cinnamon and mace	Cakes, sweet breads, rice dishes, fruit salads, muffins, pancakes, vegetable and broccoli soups and poultry marinades and sauces
Oregano	Dark green petals have resinous pine-needle flavor similar to marjoram	Italian and Mexican soups, chili, salads, pasta sauces, Greek salad dressing, marinades, grilled vegetables, sauces for chicken and meat, pilafs and pasta dishes; prevalent in Italian, Mexican and Greek cooking
Paprika	A dark red powder made from certain dried peppers, it varies from mildly sweet to hot	Spanish and Hungarian stews, chowders, chicken, broiled fish, roasted or mashed potatoes and Tex-Mex chili
Parsley	Has a refreshing flavor with grassy undertones; Italian flat-leaf parsley has a slightly stronger flavor than curly parsley	Soups, dressings, sauces, dips, marinades and meats; fish, vegetable or chicken dishes; anything with potatoes, grains or pasta
Peppercorns, black	Black, roundish dried berries with a spicy floral taste	Soups, stews, salads, meat, poultry, fish, vegetables, dressings and egg dishes
Peppercorns, white	Grayish-white berries with a smooth peppery flavor	Creamy, light-colored soups, sauces and dressings; interchangeable with black pepper
Poppy seeds	Tiny blue-gray seeds with a slightly sweet, nutlike flavor	Noodle dishes, salad dressings, coleslaw, breads, rolls, cakes, quick breads, pastries

Herb/Spice	Characteristics	Common Uses
Rosemary	Narrow needlelike leaves with a fragrant evergreen scent	Lamb, pork, poultry, potato chowders, summer squash, roasted root vegetables, grilling marinades and focaccia; sturdy rosemary sprigs can be used as skewers for grilled vegetables
Saffron	Mild aromatic scent with rich yellow-orange hue	Spanish paella, curries, sweet breads, Spanish and Middle Eastern rice and grain dishes and Milanese risotto
Sage	Pale green to silvery leaves with earthy, musky flavor	Poultry stuffing, stewed white beans and soup, vegetable and legume dishes, pasta sauce and Italian soups; dried sage has a stronger presence than its fresh counterpart
Savory	Summer savory is mild and grassy; winter savory is spicier	Legume dishes (especially lima beans and lentils), poultry and vegetable entrées
Sesame seeds	Mild, sweet, nutty flavor	Breads, Middle Eastern spreads like hummus, casseroles, salads, cakes; toasting the seeds releases their rich nutlike flavor
Star anise	Star-shaped brown pod containing eight shiny seeds; similar in flavor to anise seeds but more bitter	Chinese dishes, teas, baked goods; an ingredient in Chinese five-spice powder (along with cinnamon, cloves, fennel seeds and Szechuan pepper)
Szechuan pepper	Similar in size to black peppercorns with a mildly hot, pungent flavor	Chinese dishes
Tarragon	Long feathery green leaves with a subtle anise flavor	Sautéed chicken, pasta salad, potato salad, seafood entrées, egg dishes, mustard sauces and vinaigrettes; used in herbes de Provence and fines herbes
Thyme	Tiny greenish-gray petals with a pungent earthy flavor and strong scent	Potato and fish chowders, squash bisque, vinaigrettes, marinades, roasted vegetables, mushrooms, potatoes, bean dishes, poultry and wild rice; appears in bouquet garni; varieties include common thyme, French thyme, English thyme and lemon thyme
Turmeric	Mildly pungent flavor with yellowish-orange hue; often substituted for the more expensive saffron for its color	Gives mustard pastes, curries and rice dishes a brilliant yellow glow
Vanilla bean	Sweet, mellow, aromatic flavor	Cakes, cookies, sweet breads, muffins, fruit desserts, poached pears and rice pudding

☞ The advantage of fresh herbs is their vibrant taste. The drawback is they must be stored in the refrigerator, and even so, they're highly perishable.

☞ Dried herbs have a slightly duller taste than fresh. They have a much longer shelf life, however, and will stay fresh at least six months when stored in a dark, cool, dry place.

☞ You can substitute three parts fresh herbs for one part dried.

Using Fresh Herbs

Until a few years ago, the only way to have fresh herbs was to grow your own. These days, just about every supermarket and specialty store stocks a variety of different kinds. To get the best tastes, here's what chefs advise.

Keep them cold. Fresh herbs are extremely perishable and should be kept in the refrigerator at all times.

☞ Wet leaves spoil quickly. This is especially true of delicate herbs like cilantro and basil. Before storing them, pick over the herbs, discard any bad leaves and dry the remaining ones well with a paper towel.

☞ The best way to store herb sprigs is by standing the bunch in a glass filled halfway with water. Then place a plastic bag loosely around the top.

☞ If your refrigerator is short on shelf space, wrap the herbs in a paper towel, place them in a resealable plastic bag and store them in the produce drawer.

Clean them well. Before using fresh herbs, check them for grit or other dirt. If needed, rinse them well under cold running water, then pat dry. Discard woody or thick stems as well as any discolored or torn leaves. Then chop into pieces and add to whatever you're preparing.

The finer you chop herbs, the more flavor they release. Sometimes, however, you may want a coarser chop—for a yogurt dip, for example—to add additional texture to the dish.

Add them late. When preparing hot dishes

CHOPPING HERBS

Fresh herbs should be chopped finely to release all their tantalizing flavors. Here are three ways to prepare them fast.

Holding a scissors in one hand and a bunch of herbs in the other, snip small pieces from the end.

The two-handled razor-sharp mezzaluna provides a rocking action that's ideal for mincing herbs.

A large chef's knife also provides a rocking action that minces herbs finely. Using the point as a pivot, rock the knife over the herbs until all the pieces are about the same size.

like minestrone or rice pilaf, add the herbs toward the end of the cooking time to prevent the delicate flavors from dissipating.

Or season early. For cold dishes like herb-marinated carrots or potato salad, adding the herbs before refrigerating the dish will allow the flavors to meld and mingle together.

Using Dried Herbs

Convenient to use and store, dried herbs make it easy to have a variety of different flavors on hand. Dried herbs come in three forms: whole, crumbled and ground.

The relatively large size of whole and crumbled herbs allows them to retain their freshness

---

DRYING GARDEN HERBS

To combine the fresh taste of garden herbs with the longevity of dried, many chefs grow and dry their own. Here's how.

Rinse the leafy herbs briefly under cold running water. Shake off excess moisture and pat dry with a paper towel.

Long-stemmed herbs, like thyme and rosemary, can be tied together in a bouquet, then hung upside down in a dry, well-ventilated area for three to six days, or until crumbly.

Herbs with large leaves, such as basil and Italian flat parsley, can be spread on a mesh screen and left for several days in a dry, well-ventilated area.

Herbs are suitably dried when they crumble easily when rubbed between your fingers. Carefully strip the leaves (leaving them whole, if possible) from the stems and store in a dark, airtight container in a cool, dry, dark place. Dried herbs retain their flavor for up to one year, but since you'll have new ones available come warm weather, there's no point in hoarding your harvest.

much longer than the ground kind. To extract the most flavor from whole herbs, crush them well before using, either between your fingers or using a mortar and pestle. Even crumbled herbs benefit from being rubbed between your fingers to release their essential oils.

Ground herbs are very convenient to use, but they have a short shelf life. Also, they tend to be somewhat less flavorful than whole or crumbled herbs.

Check for freshness. Before using dried herbs, grab a pinch from the bottle and take a sniff: It should have a strong, distinctive aroma. If the smell is barely there or if the color appears weak and strawlike, the herb has probably given up its flavors and should be replaced.

Add them early. Whereas fresh herbs should be added late in the cooking process, dried herbs should be added early; the prolonged contact with heat and moisture causes them to release their flavors.

Store them carefully. Dried herbs that haven't been ground have an excellent shelf life and generally retain their flavors for six months or longer when stored in tightly covered containers in a cool, dark place. Left uncovered, however, they can give up their flavors in as little as a few days.

THE WORLD OF SPICES

Unlike herbs, which are used both fresh and in dried forms, spices, such as cinnamon, pepper and cardamom are always used dry. Spices, which include seeds, bark, roots or berries, add fragrance and depth to dishes.

Spices generally come to market in one of two forms: whole (like cinnamon sticks, allspice berries, peppercorns, whole cloves, caraway seeds and cumin seeds) and ground. Despite their robust appearance, spices do not last indefinitely. Ground spices lose potency after about six months; whole spices last one to two years.

The advantage of ground spices is that they're easy to use. You just spoon them out of the container. As with ground herbs, however, they lose flavor on the shelf fairly quickly. Many cooks prefer buying whole spices, then grinding them as needed. There is, after all, no comparison between freshly ground black pepper and the preground stuff, for instance.

Using Spices

It's hard to imagine, in our world of international commerce and high-speed transportation, that everyday spices such as pepper were once exceedingly valuable commodities. For cooks today, however, spices are both plentiful and inexpensive. To get the best flavors every time, here's what chefs advise.

Store them carefully. Although whole spices retain their flavors much longer than ground, both types should be stored in airtight containers in a cool, dark place.

Cook them long. Unlike fresh herbs, which give up their flavors almost instantly, whole

Helpful Hint

Contrary to logic and convenience, the worst place to store seasonings is above the stove. Heat from cooking severely shortens their shelf life. In addition, never shake herbs or spices right from the jar into a simmering pot. Rising steam will get into the bottle, remain trapped there and turn the seasonings moldy. Instead, either use a measuring spoon or shake the flavoring into your hand. And always recap the container tightly after use.

spices are slow to reveal themselves. They are best used in long-simmering soups, stews, stocks or poaching liquids or in fermented items such as pickles.

☞ To extract flavor from whole spices without actually leaving them in the food or digging them out one at a time, you can wrap them in cheesecloth, tie the bundle with string and drop it into the pot. Then remove it when you're finished cooking. A metal tea ball also works well. Either method is best with liquid dishes like brothy soups and poaching liquids for foods such as fish, chicken and fruit.

☞ To add a robust edge to any whole spice, you can toast it briefly, either in a dry no-stick skillet or in the oven on a baking sheet. Spices should be toasted until they're just slightly brown and aromatic.

A *Pepper Primer*

Black pepper is by far the world's most popular spice. Made by picking and then drying immature green peppercorns, black pepper adds an aromatic sharp pungency to dishes. Believe it or not, pepper even shows up in some sweet foods like certain cakes and even French toast.

While black pepper graces almost every table, there are a number of other pepper varieties as well.

☞ **Green peppercorns.** Used more as a colorful garnish than a flavoring agent, green peppercorns do lend a slightly pungent flavor to food. Unlike black pepper, however, they generate little "heat." They're available freeze-dried and packed in brine or water. After opening a container of the brine- or waterpacked peppercorns, store leftovers in the refrigerator. They'll keep for a week or two.

☞ **Pink pepper.** These come from an entirely different plant than white and black pepper. Pink pepper has a mild, almost sweet, flavor. As with green pepper, however, it's used more for its attractive appearance than for unique qualities in the taste. Like green peppercorns, they come in freeze-dried and brine- or waterpacked varieties.

☞ **Szechuan pepper.** Like pink pepper, Szechuan pepper comes from a plant not related to the peppercorn family. It has a distinctive mildly hot flavor and fragrance. Szechuan pepper is used mostly in Chinese cooking and is a prime ingredient in Chinese five-spice powder.

☞ **White pepper.** This comes from the same plant as the black variety and is also sold in the dry, loose form. With white pepper, however, the peppercorn is allowed to ripen before being picked. At that time, the outer portion is stripped away, leaving behind the white interior. White peppercorns have a smoother, slightly milder taste than the black variety. They're often used in white sauces and other light-colored dishes where black specks might detract from the aesthetics of the food.

Of course, the pepper that we use most often is black pepper. Not surprisingly, it also comes in a number of exciting varieties. To get the best pepper tastes, here's what experts advise.

Keep it whole. Although ground black pepper is convenient to use, it can lose its aromatic subtle flavors in as little as two months. To get the best flavors, buy pepper whole, then grind it just before using it.

Explore the flavors. Specialty stores stock a variety of black peppers. Each has its own flavor and heat. Some varieties you may want to try include:

☞ **Tellicherry.** Considered the most elegant pepper, Tellicherry pepper from India has a rich, bold flavor—aromatic without being overly spicy.

☞ **Brazilian.** Perhaps the most common variety in the United States, Brazilian pepper is quite sharp—hot and spicy rather than aromatic.

☞ **Malabar.** From India, Malabar pepper has a rich, well-balanced flavor.

S*haking Salt*

Perhaps no other ingredient is used as often or in so many foods as salt. Food manufacturers

(continued on page 34)

HERB BLENDS

The right combination of herbs and spices can magically transform the simplest foods into culinary treats to remember. Whether you're spicing a salad or preparing beef, poultry or lamb, an herb blend adds exciting layers of flavor. And since you can prepare dried herb blends ahead of time, you don't have to fumble with half a dozen (or more) bottles at the last minute.

Whether you're mixing a small amount to use right away or an entire bottle for future meals, here are a few blends that you may want to try. Store leftovers in dark, airtight containers in a cool, dry, dark place. Heat, light and exposure to air destroy the flavor of dried herbs and spices.

Italian Herb Seasoning

This all-purpose blend perks up the flavor of soups, stews, gravy, tomato sauce, meat loaf, lasagna, chicken cacciatore and pot roasts. Or sprinkle it on baked potatoes and pizza.

- 1 tablespoon dried oregano
- 1 tablespoon dried basil
- 1 teaspoon dried thyme

Makes about 2 tablespoons

VARIATION
• For a more zesty blend, add ½ teaspoon onion powder, ¼ teaspoon garlic powder and ¼ teaspoon crushed red pepper flakes.

Poultry Seasoning

This savory herb blend brings out the best flavors of chicken and turkey without added salt. Use it to season soups, stews, casseroles, stuffings and dumplings, too.

- 2 teaspoons dried marjoram
- 2 teaspoons onion powder
- 1 teaspoon dried thyme
- 1 teaspoon dried sage
- 1 teaspoon dried savory
- ½ teaspoon ground black pepper

Makes about 2 tablespoons

Beef Seasoning

Beef has strong flavors of its own. So we created a simple blend to enhance those natural flavors without overpowering them. Add this seasoning to almost any beef dish during cooking.

- 2 teaspoons dried parsley
- 2 teaspoons garlic powder
- 2 teaspoons onion powder
- 2 teaspoons ground black pepper

Makes about 2½ tablespoons

Vegetable Seasoning

A few shakes of this salt-free herb blend will keep your cooked vegetables from tasting bland and boring. You can use it in soups and casseroles, too.

- 1 teaspoon dried basil
- 1 teaspoon dried chervil
- 1 teaspoon dried chives
- 1 teaspoon dried marjoram
- 1 teaspoon dried parsley
- ¼ teaspoon dried savory
- ¼ teaspoon dried thyme

Makes about 2½ tablespoons

Lamb Seasoning

For great-tasting lamb, rub this herb blend into the meat before cooking.

- 2 teaspoons dried parsley
- 2 teaspoons dried rosemary
- 2 teaspoons dried thyme

Makes 2 tablespoons

Cajun Spice

Lend a bit of zip to any Creole or Cajun dish with this Louisiana seasoning. Or rub it into catfish or red snapper fillets as a "blackening" seasoning before cooking.

- 2 teaspoons paprika
- 2 teaspoons ground black pepper
- 1½ teaspoons garlic powder
- 1 teaspoon crushed red-pepper flakes
- 1 teaspoon dried thyme
- 1 teaspoon dried oregano
- 1 teaspoon onion powder
- ¼ teaspoon dry mustard

Makes about 3 tablespoons

Pumpkin Pie Spice

This delicious blend isn't just for pumpkin pie. Try it in spice cakes, cookies and sweet breads.

- 2 teaspoons ground cinnamon
- 2 teaspoons ground nutmeg
- 1 teaspoon ground ginger
- ½ teaspoon ground cloves
- ½ teaspoon ground mace

Makes about 1½ tablespoons

Chili Powder

Commercial chili powders often contain added salt. Here's a spicy salt-free recipe that's great in chili, sloppy joes, bean dishes, soups, stews and savory sauces. For a milder mix, cut back on the ground red pepper.

- 1 tablespoon ground cumin
- 1 teaspoon dried oregano
- 1 teaspoon garlic powder
- 1 teaspoon onion powder
- ½ teaspoon ground red pepper
- ½ teaspoon paprika
- ¼ teaspoon ground allspice

Makes about 2½ tablespoons

Curry Powder

Similar to the curry powders sold in stores, this recipe lends a delicious, exotic flavor to vegetable, bean and rice dishes. For the most flavor, sauté the curry powder in a little oil before adding the other ingredients. Because you're using whole seeds, you'll want to grind the mixture to a fine powder with a mortar and pestle or with a spice mill or a coffee mill reserved just for spices. Alternatively, use already ground forms of the same herbs and spices.

- 3½ teaspoons coriander seeds
- 2½ teaspoons turmeric
- 1 teaspoon cumin seeds
- 1 teaspoon fenugreek seeds
- ½ teaspoon black peppercorns
- ½ teaspoon dry mustard
- ½ teaspoon allspice berries
- ¼ teaspoon crushed red-pepper flakes
- ¼ teaspoon powdered ginger

Makes about 3 tablespoons

use it both as a preservative and a flavoring agent. At home, we add it to everything from soup and vegetables to bread and even desserts.

However, it can overwhelm the palate and crowd out other, more subtle flavors. To reduce the amount of salt in your diet and further enjoy the wide range of enticing seasonings already in your kitchen, here are a few things that you can do.

Add it early. Putting salt in food early in the cooking process allows it to thoroughly meld with the other ingredients; you get more flavor while still using less.

Don't add salt to meat, chicken or fish until the cooking is complete. Otherwise, the salt will draw out essential juices needed to keep these foods tender.

Check your spice labels. Many common seasonings include large amounts of sodium. Celery salt and garlic salt are obvious examples. But even many spice blends, including chili powder, contain salt. To cut back on salt without cutting back on flavors, avoid spices or spice blends that include salt as a key ingredient. If you need to use them, omit any further salt from your recipe.

EXTRA-SPECIAL SEASONINGS

Most people just couldn't cook without the flavor boost provided by such aromatics as fresh and dried chili peppers, fresh and dried ginger, garlic and the colorful rinds of various citrus fruits. Here are tips for getting the best from these kitchen superstars.

Chili Peppers

These fiery pods come in many varieties and cover a wide spectrum of heat, ranging from slightly sweet to explosively hot. Whether you buy them whole or powdered, chili peppers are a real boon for the healthy cook. Their heat and full flavors virtually eliminate the need for added salt or butter.

Ease the heat. Many dried peppers are uncomfortably hot; removing the inner

IS IT CHILI OR CHILE?

Which spelling of these fiery peppers you use depends more on where you live and what you're used to than anything else. Many people contend that the correct spelling of the peppers themselves is *chile*, and that *chili* should be reserved for the traditional meat-and-bean dish made with peppers and chili powder.

membranes, where the heat-activating ingredient is stored, will help keep the heat to more comfortable levels. Although the seeds themselves aren't inherently hot, they can take on heat from their proximity to the membranes. In addition, roasting chili peppers sometimes helps tame their fire, too.

Put on protection. The hot oils in chili peppers can irritate your skin as well as your taste buds. To protect your hands, wear plastic or rubber gloves while handling chili peppers. If you forget to wear gloves, be very careful not to touch your face, especially your eyes or lips, until you've thoroughly cleansed your hands.

Cut them fine. To extract the most flavor, most chili peppers should be minced before being added to soups, stews or other dishes.

To add just a hint of heat, some cooks put a single whole chili (minus the seeds and stem) into the pot for long cooking.

Put out the flames. If your mouth is hurting after taking a chili bite, experts recommend eating yogurt or cheese or taking a swig of milk. Dairy products contain a protein called casein, which washes away capsaicin, the compound in chili peppers that makes them hot.

Garlic

The slightest smell of garlic instantly triggers a fervent anticipation for the meal to come.

Whether chopped, crushed or minced—or even, for the bold of heart, eaten whole—garlic lends a distinctive touch to soups, stews, stir-fries, sautés, roasts, marinades, relishes, chutneys, sauces and pilafs. The world's menu is scented with garlic.

Keep it at room temperature. Putting garlic in the refrigerator causes it to soften and sprout, giving it a bitter taste. It's best to store garlic in a cool, dry place with adequate air circulation.

Break the skin. Perhaps the hardest part about eating garlic is getting it out of the skin. An easy way to peel garlic is to set it on the counter or cutting board and give it a sharp whack with the side of a chef's knife. The impact splits and loosens the skin, making it easy to peel off.

Try it roasted. Roasting garlic in the oven tames the sharp, pungent flavor, making it almost sweet. To roast garlic, wrap the entire head, unpeeled, in aluminum foil. Place the package in a preheated 350° oven and bake for 40 to 45 minutes, or until the garlic is very tender to the touch. Remove from the oven and let cool slightly before unwrapping.

☞ To remove garlic from a roasted clove, give it a squeeze after it cools; the garlic will squiggle from the opposite end like toothpaste from a tube.

Helpful Hint

Don't throw out garlic that has begun to sprout. Separate the cloves and plant them in your garden; the resulting garlic "chives" are great for salads, dips and dressings.

If the only garlic that you have is sprouting and you need to use it, cut each clove in half lengthwise and pull out the green sprout.

Garlic
Is It Good for You?

Garlic's role in battling heart disease has been debated ever since scientists first noticed that populations eating lots of the herb had a lower incidence of heart disease. But there is increasing evidence that the "stinking rose" provides a host of other valuable health benefits.

One study found that people with mild cases of high blood pressure who took 600 milligrams a day of a special garlic powder (a unique standardized formula) for 12 weeks showed an average drop in diastolic blood pressure of around 11 percent. They also showed a 14 percent average drop in total cholesterol and an 18 percent drop in triglycerides.

In the real world, garlic's benefits have been no less impressive. In regions where garlic (and onion, a near relative) consumption is high, the rate of gastric and colonic cancer is much lower than in areas where consumption of these foods is low. In addition, garlic has been shown to help keep blood from clotting and to have powerful antioxidant effects—that is, it helps neutralize harmful oxygen molecules in the body that can lead to heart disease.

☞ You can eat roasted garlic plain or add it to soups, potatoes, salads, dressings or sauces.

Enjoy the greens. During late spring and early summer, you will find garlic greens offered at farmers markets. Similar in appearance to thin, sturdy scallions, they have a slightly subdued garlic flavor. The greens can be chopped and added to soups, pesto, salads and tomato sauce.

Ginger

This gnarly, knobby, tropical root with the ugly outside has a wonderfully clean, citruslike taste with just a hint of bite. A popular ingredient in stir-fries, curries, peanut sauces and dishes with soy sauce, ginger is treasured in Caribbean, Indian, African and Asian cuisines.

Keep it cool. Whole ginger root can be stored in the produce drawer in your refrigerator for about two weeks. For long-term storage, it can be placed in a jar and covered with vinegar or sherry.

Peel the skin. Before using ginger, you have to peel away the tough, brown skin. The best way to do this is with a vegetable peeler or sharp paring knife.

Mince it fine. To extract the most flavor, ginger should be minced fine before using. The finer you chop it, the more flavor will be released.

Use dried for baking. Ginger that is dried and powdered is considerably sweeter and more aromatic than the fresh root. Dried ginger is most suitable for baking cakes, cookies, pumpkin pies or various sweet breads.

Citrus Rind

Although we normally eat the insides of citrus fruits and throw away the rind, this outer peel (also known as the zest) can be used to add a dash of sparkling flavor to almost any dish.

Grate it lightly. Using the fine side of a grater, gently rub the fruit back and forth. Don't press so hard that you grate the underlying white part, which can be unpleasantly bitter.

Try a zester. Perhaps the easiest way to remove rind is by using an inexpensive gadget called a zester. This quickly carves thin strips

Ginger
Is It GOOD for You?

With its strange appearance and sharp, pungent aroma, ginger looks more like something that you'd find in a medieval apothecary than in a modern kitchen.

Looks aren't always deceiving. Research has shown that ginger has powerful healing powers for a variety of conditions, ranging from upset stomach to arthritis pain.

In one study, for instance, students with motion sickness who were given ginger had less nausea and dizziness than those given the leading over-the-counter drug (Dramamine). Studies have also shown that ginger may help prevent migraines, relieve arthritis pain and lower cholesterol.

Here's the kicker. It doesn't take huge amounts of ginger to get the healing benefits. According to Charles Lo, M.D., a physician in private practice in Chicago, adding small amounts of ginger to a stir-fry will give you the healing benefits—and the great taste.

from the peel, which can then be chopped fine and added to the dish.

Use a peeler. Another way to remove rind is with a vegetable peeler. You have to be careful, however, not to peel so deeply that you get the bitter white along with the rind.

Chris Schlessinger

Big, bold flavors are what you'll find at Chris Schlessinger's three Boston restaurants: East Coast Grill, Jake and Earl's and The Blue Room. His casual cuisine is influenced by the vibrant, heavily seasoned foods of Thailand, Brazil, Singapore, Morocco and Mexico.

"Subtlety in food does not impress me. I like big, loud flavors—sweet, sour, hot, salty, aromatic, pungent, tingling— preferably all in the same bite," Schlessinger says. "Grilling is a great way to use spice mixes. Rub the spices on the outside of the food before grilling. It helps encourage a thick crust that has a lot of flavor and helps keep the inside juicy."

The following mix can be used on lamb, beef, chicken (without the skin) and game meats—and not just for grilling but for broiling and sautéing as well. How much you use is entirely up to you. If you like a strong flavor, rub it on thickly. For a milder taste, a light dusting is all you need.

East Coast Grill Spice Mix

- 2 tablespoons ground cumin
- 2 tablespoons paprika
- 1 tablespoon crushed coriander seeds
- 1 tablespoon ground ginger
- 1 tablespoon ground cinnamon
- 1 teaspoon turmeric
- 1 teaspoon ground red pepper
- 1 teaspoon dry mustard

In a large skillet, mix the cumin, paprika, coriander, ginger, cinnamon, turmeric, pepper and mustard. Place over medium heat. Stir constantly for 2 to 3 minutes, or until the first whiff of smoke appears. Remove from the heat immediately. Remove from the pan and cool completely. Store in a sealed container in a cool, dry, dark place.

Makes about ½ cup

NOTES

• For a delicious appetizer or snack, toss 1 teaspoon of the spice mix with 2 cups cooked or canned chick-peas (drained and rinsed, if canned) and 1 teaspoon olive oil or canola oil in a medium bowl. Place the seasoned chick-peas in a single layer on a no-stick baking sheet. Bake in a 400° oven, shaking the baking sheet occasionally, for 30 to 40 minutes, or until the chick-peas are crisp and golden on the outside. (Do not overcook, or the chick-peas will become tough.)

• To make healthy french fries with a unique flavor, toss 1 teaspoon of the spice mix with 1 tablespoon oil in a large bowl. Cut 3 baking potatoes lengthwise to make ¼"- to ½"-thick wedges. Add to the bowl and toss to mix. Place the seasoned potato wedges in a single layer on a no-stick baking sheet. Bake in a 475° oven, turning the potatoes occasionally, for 20 to 30 minutes, or until the potatoes are lightly browned and tender.

Mastering
Essential
Techniques

Stir-Frying, Sautéing and Poaching

The healthy cook strives to prepare food quickly and efficiently, to lock in moisture and fresh tastes and to make delicious foods without unhealthy additions of butter, oil and other unnecessary fats.

Three of the most common cooking techniques—stir-frying, sautéing and poaching—fulfill these goals admirably. What's more, you don't need new (or expensive) cookware in order to begin. All you really need is a deep skillet and a reliable source of heat.

STIR-FRYING

Wok cookery was first developed in China as a practical solution to the scarcity of cooking fuels. The quicker that food cooked, the less fuel was needed—and woks cook very quickly indeed. For today's busy cook, speed is its own reward. Few meals are quicker on the stove than stir-fries. And because high heat sears in flavors and locks in moisture, few meals are more nutritious, as long as you use only the barest amount of oil.

☞ Once you've sliced, diced or marinated the various ingredients, the actual stir-fry cooking time is typically five minutes or less.

☞ The high heat sears food almost instantly. This means that it's less likely to stick, even when you cook with little or even no added oil.

☞ Although meats are by no means excluded from stir-fries, it's usually vegetables—everything from onions and celery to broccoli, snap peas and bean sprouts—that take center stage.

☞ Stir-fries often require only one pan—a large skillet or a wok—so cleanup is a snap. Even if you make rice on the side, you can feed your entire family and do the dishes in less time than it takes to order and pick up a carry-out meal.

Basic Gear

Stir-frying is among the simplest of kitchen techniques, so you don't need a lot of fancy utensils. Here's what chefs recommend you start with.

Begin with a wok. Small stir-fries can be prepared in a skillet, but if you're feeding more than one person, a wok gives you more maneuvering room. The high sides hold a lot of food. Plus, they help keep the various ingredients in the wok—and off the counter or floor. And because a wok has a very large surface area, it's easy to move food from one hot area to the next for quicker cooking.

☞ Woks are usually made of carbon steel or aluminum because of their excellent heat conductivity. If a wok seems lightweight and flimsy, pass it by. A high-quality wok, well-cared for, will last for life.

☞ Flat-bottomed woks sit solidly on both electric and gas heating elements. The flat bottom gets sufficiently hot to cook foods quickly.

☞ Round-bottomed woks have a curved bottom and are often recommended for gas

CHOPSTICK SAVVY

To add a little excitement (and manual dexterity) to a savory stir-fry, put your fork aside and go to work with chopsticks. They're easy to clean and a snap to use—once you know how.

Balance one chopstick in the crook of your thumb, with the narrow end resting on your ring finger.

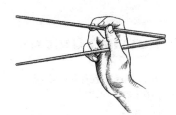

Put the second chopstick between your index and middle fingers, holding it in place with the tip of your thumb.

Holding the first chopstick steady, move the second one up and down to grab your food. For extra insurance, lean forward over your plate until you're sure that you won't slip!

stoves. They come with a metal ring that gives them stability.

☞ Some woks are equipped with one long handle, like a skillet. Others have two small handles positioned at opposite sides. The two-handled kind is attractive and easier to carry; it's often preferred for tabletop serving. The one-handled wok, although it rarely leaves the stove, is somewhat easier to handle during cooking.

☞ Because electric woks aren't confined to the kitchen, they're often used right on the table for cooking while entertaining guests. They don't get quite as hot as stove-top models, however. Cooking time is somewhat longer, and meat and vegetables may not get as tender. Electric woks often have a no-stick surface.

Season it well. If you've just bought a new steel wok, it's important to season the surface before you start cooking. Seasoning creates a protective layer inside the wok, making the pan slicker. This means that you need less fat. It makes the wok easier to clean as well. (If you have a no-stick wok, treat it as you do no-stick pans.)

☞ To season a new wok, wash it well with hot, soapy water and dry it thoroughly.

☞ Rub the inside surface with about 1 tablespoon of vegetable oil, then place the wok over medium-high heat for 15 minutes, swirling the oil to coat the sides.

☞ Remove from the heat and wipe well with a paper towel. The wok is now seasoned and ready to use.

☞ To keep the pan well-protected in the future, wash it gently with hot water and mild detergent after each use. Don't scour it, however, as this will remove the protective coating.

☞ Always dry the wok thoroughly to prevent rust. The best way is to immediately put it over heat for a few minutes after washing and towel drying. Before storing your wok, you might want to rub a couple of drops of oil over the surface with a paper towel.

Get the edge. Since stir-fries can include everything from the most tender vegetables to the toughest meats, you'll need a large, sharp knife that can handle a variety of tasks.

Many chefs prefer the Chinese cleaver, a round-handled knife with a large rectangular blade. The cleaver is tough enough to chop hard vegetables or even crack poultry bones. At the same time, it's sufficiently sharp to make quick work of tomatoes or other tender vegetables.

The wide blade makes a perfect "tray" for transferring chopped vegetables from the cutting board to the wok.

If you don't have a Chinese cleaver, try a large chef's knife, which has a long, wide blade that's ideal for chopping.

CUTTING ONIONS

Perhaps no other ingredient is used as often in stir-fries and sautés as the onion. Here's an easy way to dice this pungent bulb.

With a sharp knife, cut through the stem end, stopping just before you cut through the last layers of papery skin. Use the knife to peel back the skin.

Place the onion on end and cut it down the middle.

Set one onion half, cut side down, on a cutting board. Make several parallel horizontal cuts almost to the root end. Don't cut all the way through, or the pieces will fall apart and scatter.

Make several parallel vertical cuts, going all the way through the onion layers but, again, not cutting through the root end.

Finally, cut across the grain to make pieces of the desired size.

Stir things up. As the name suggests, stir-frying requires food to be constantly moved around the pan from one hot area to the next. It's helpful to have a variety of tools for stirring.

☞ The cooking spatula is a long-handled (usually metal) tool with curved sides; it resembles a small shovel. It makes it possible to both stir the food and lift it from one part of the pan to another. When cooking in a no-stick wok, however, care must be taken to prevent the metal spatula from scratching the surface.

☞ Long-handled wooden spoons are lightweight and inexpensive. It's good to have several on hand—not just for stirring food in the wok, but for mixing sauces as well.

☞ Metal spoons are acceptable for all-steel or aluminum woks. For woks with no-stick surfaces, however, use wood or plastic spoons.

Stir-Fry Savvy

Woks can get extremely hot, which is why the actual cooking time is often less than five minutes. Since things happen so quickly, it's important to have all your ingredients chopped, sliced, marinated or otherwise prepared before you even turn on the heat.

Give the eyes a treat. When planning a stir-fry, think not only about the taste of the ingredients but also about their appearance, alone and in combination with each other.

☞ Complement the colors. To prevent completed stir-fries from looking "flat," combine ingredients with the maximum visual effect in mind. Julienned strips of red pepper help set off a bed of caramelized onions, for example. A handful of bright green beans accents a plateful of stir-fried pork.

ORDER OF COOKING

Perhaps the most challenging part of preparing a stir-fry is ensuring that the ingredients are all done at the same time. It helps to add slow-cooking vegetables at the beginning and their quicker-cooking kin later on. (Thinly sliced meat, which cooks very quickly, is typically browned in the wok, set aside and then returned to the wok when the vegetables are almost done.) To help you time your dinner, here's a list of both slow-cooking and fast-cooking vegetables commonly used in stir-fries.

SLOW-COOKING VEGETABLES	FAST-COOKING VEGETABLES
Broccoli	Baby corn
Carrots	Bean sprouts
Cauliflower	Endive
Celery	Mushrooms
Kale	Peppers
Fennel	Snap peas
Onions	Snow peas
Parsnips	Spinach
Potatoes	Summer squash
Winter squash	Zucchini

COOKING OILS

Some oils, like those made with sesame seeds or almonds, are used mainly for flavor. Cooking oils, on the other hand, are needed to help food brown evenly and prevent it from sticking. Health experts advise using oils with a high percentage of heart-healthy monounsaturated fats. Here are some commonly available oils, along with percentages of fats—labeled monos, polys and saturated—that they contain. (You'll notice that the percents don't add up to 100. That's because there is a small amount of other fats in all oils.)

OIL	MONOS (%)	POLYS (%)	SATURATED (%)	COOKING CHARACTERISTICS
Canola	60	30	7	Light-colored, flavorless oil with a high smoking point. Good choice for cooking.
Coconut	6	2	89	A heavy oil used primarily in blended oils and shortenings. Its high saturated-fat content makes it undesirable from a health standpoint.
Corn	25	59	13	A mild-flavored, light-yellow oil with a high smoking point. It's often used for cooking as well as in salad dressings.
Olive	76	9	14	A flavorful oil ranging from pale yellow to deep green. It can be used for cooking and salad dressings, and it can be drizzled on food as a condiment. Widely considered the most healthful of the commonly used oils.
Peanut	47	32	17	A neutral flavor makes peanut oil a good choice for cooking as well as dressings. Has a fairly high smoking point and is used often for stir-frying and sautéing.
Safflower	13	76	9	Almost flavorless, it has a high smoking point, making it ideal for stir-frying and sautéing.
Sesame (oriental)	40	42	14	Its strong, nutty flavor makes it a natural for stir-fries, noodle dishes and other recipes. It breaks down at high heat, however, and should be added after cooking is done.
Soybean	24	59	15	A neutral flavor; can withstand high temperatures. Not a great salad oil but good for cooking.
Sunflower	20	67	11	A light oil commonly used for cooking and for salad dressings.

☞ Vary the shapes. Another way to make stir-fries attractive is to combine shapes. You can use thinly sliced vegetables to provide a counterpoint to thicker pieces of meat. Or combine a long, lean vegetable, like a snap pea, with squares of bell peppers.

☞ Vary the textures. Strike a balance between hard, long-cooking vegetables like broccoli or carrots and softer vegetables like bean sprouts or bok choy. Combining crunchy with soft creates anticipation and adds excitement to the meal. Of course, the more vegetables you use, the greater the variety of vitamins and minerals you'll get as well.

Go against the grain. Cutting meat crosswise into thin strips helps it marinate more thoroughly. Plus, it cooks more quickly and gets more tender than when it's cut in the same direction as the grain.

☞ Marinating strips of meat for at least 15 minutes before cooking makes them fork-tender and adds a delicate nuance to each bite.

☞ For a simple marinade, combine ¼ cup soy sauce, 2 tablespoons vinegar (such as rice or red wine), 1 tablespoon honey and 1 clove garlic, chopped.

Toss in some tofu. Also known as bean curd, tofu has a soft, slightly spongy texture that firms up when cooked, making it an ideal filler. It's also a great source of protein that takes on the flavors of whatever foods it is cooked with.

☞ Tofu comes in a variety of textures, from soft (also called silken) to firm. Firm tofu holds its shape better and is recommended for use in stir-fries.

☞ Tofu should be rinsed in cold water before using. (If you're not planning to use it immediately after bringing it home, rinse it daily and keep it submerged in fresh water.)

☞ After rinsing, press out excess water. Place the tofu between several layers of paper towels. Press with your palm. Repeat, moving to dry sections of paper, until little water is exuded. Cut it into cubes before using.

Helpful Hint

Even with sharp knives, slicing meat thinly for stir-fries can be difficult. Putting meat in the freezer for half an hour before cutting makes it firmer and easier to slice.

☞ Adding tofu to the wok during the last few minutes of cooking will heat it all the way through, while at the same time allowing it to hold its shape. Adding it too early, on the other hand, will cause it to fall apart.

☞ If you're looking to substitute tofu for ground meat, especially in a saucy stir-fry, freeze the firm variety. Thaw it, then crumble it into the sauce.

Go easy on the oil. Since woks cook so quickly and at such high heats, it takes very little oil—in some cases, as little as a teaspoon— to prevent food from sticking.

It's best to add oil when the wok is already hot. Adding oil too early causes it to break down, reducing its lubricating qualities.

Try new flavor combinations. The medley of ingredients that go into stir-fries calls out for a variety of spices and flavored liquids. The best choices for this purpose are aromatics, like ginger, garlic, slivered lemon or orange rind, chopped scallions, crushed red pepper, soy sauce or a bit of rice wine.

You can add spices directly to the stir-fry. Or combine them with soy sauce or rice wine and use as a flavorful marinade.

Add flavored liquids. To further boost the flavors of stir-fries, pour a little fat-free broth— vegetable, chicken or beef—into the wok. Or add a little white grape juice or unsweetened pineapple juice for a tangy touch.

Try new filler foods. Stir-fries are often served on a bed of rice, but there is a world of

STIR-FRYING VEGETABLES

Although this recipe features vegetables, stir-frying is an incredibly versatile technique that works equally well with chicken, seafood and red meats. Cooking occurs rapidly, locking in flavor and moisture. It's important, however, to have all the ingredients prepared—vegetables trimmed, meat sliced and sauces mixed—before you turn on the heat. Many stir-fries are served over cooked rice, as is this one. That, too, should be just about ready before you start the stir-fry.

Chinese Vegetable Stir-Fry *QUICK!*

- 1 tablespoon canola or Chinese stir-fry oil
- 1½ cups broccoli florets
- 1 tablespoon water
- ¾ cup julienned carrots
- 1½ cups snow peas, ends trimmed
- 6 fresh shiitake mushrooms, slivered
- ½ cup drained water chestnuts
- 1 clove garlic, minced
- ½ teaspoon minced fresh ginger
- 3 tablespoons reduced-sodium soy sauce
- 3 tablespoons defatted chicken broth
- 1 teaspoon cornstarch
- 2 cups hot cooked rice

Add the carrots, snow peas, mushrooms, water chestnuts, garlic and ginger. Stir-fry for 1 to 2 minutes, or until the vegetables are crisp-tender.

Heat a wok over medium heat and add the oil. Increase the heat to medium-high. Add the broccoli and water. Stir-fry for 1 minute, or until the broccoli is bright green.

In a small bowl, combine the soy sauce, broth and cornstarch; mix well to dissolve. Add to the wok and stir-fry for about 1 minute. Serve over the rice.

Makes 4 servings. Per serving: 212 calories, 4 g. fat (17% of calories), 6.9 g. protein, 38.3 g. carbohydrates, 4.2 g. dietary fiber, 0 mg. cholesterol, 432 mg. sodium

NOTE

• If fresh mushrooms are unavailable, use dried. Place 8 dried mushrooms in a small bowl. Cover with boiling water; set aside for 20 minutes. Remove and discard the stems. Use as directed.

other grains, like barley and quinoa, that also make great accompaniments. Or you can supplement the meal with noodles, like soba (buckwheat) or cellophane.

SAUTÉING

Although we often think of *sautéed* as meaning "with butter," in fact, it's a surprisingly healthful technique that requires little added fat.

In professional kitchens, sautéed foods are cooked "à la minute," meaning they're prepared to order instead of ahead of time. The reason for this is that sautéing is very fast. Food is cooked at high temperatures, although not quite so hot as those used in stir-fries.

Ingredients are often sautéed as part of a recipe. For example, onions, garlic and mushrooms are typically sautéed, then added to other ingredients that will undergo further cooking. Boneless chicken breasts and pork tenderloin, on the other hand, may be sautéed for the end result—a simple, easy-to-prepare meal that's browned and cooked all the way through.

Sauté Necessities

Since so many recipes require that ingredients be sautéed, it's not uncommon for cooks to own two or more sauté pans. A busy restaurant may have dozens. A small sauté pan, 7″ to 8″ in diameter, holds about 5 cups. A medium pan, 9″ to 10″ in diameter, holds about 8 cups. A large sauté pan, 12″ to 14″ in diameter, holds about 15 cups.

Using a pan with a no-stick surface will reduce to a minimum the amount of oil needed to sauté. The drawback is that these surfaces, while more durable today than those of the past, still tend to scratch. Using wood or plastic utensils will help keep them in good shape for years to come.

☞ Cast-iron skillets hold and conduct heat very well, making them an excellent (and inexpensive) choice in a sauté pan. And because cast iron becomes seasoned with proper use, it's possible to cook with very little added fat. The main drawback to cast iron is its weight.

OLIVE OIL— A TASTER'S GUIDE

You already know the benefits of using moderate amounts of olive oil, which is high in heart-healthy monounsaturated fats. Which type of olive oil you choose, however, depends on personal taste. Some have a strong full-bodied flavor, while others are so light that they're barely there. Here's a guide to the standard grades.

☞ **Extra-virgin.** Made from the first pressing (with acid levels under 1 percent), this is the best oil and also the most expensive. It's often used as a condiment for drizzling over fish, pasta or fresh vegetables.

☞ **Virgin.** Made from the second pressing, the acidity is a little higher than extra-virgin. It's not as delicate as extra-virgin, but it's still a good oil for sautéing or drizzling.

☞ **Pure.** This is oil that's been refined and filtered. It's not as full-flavored as the better oils, but it's a good choice for sautéing or stir-frying.

☞ **Extra-light.** This is an oil that's been heavily processed. It has a very light olive flavor and a light color. It's generally used by people who want the health benefits of olive oil, but who don't care for the taste. It can be used as a more healthy substitute for mild oils such as safflower.

☞ Tin-lined copper skillets are perhaps the best sauté pans that money can buy. (Some copper pans are lined with silver.) The high cost of copperware, however, makes them impractical for many home chefs. Further, it's often necessary to have copper relined as the inner surface wears off.

SAUTÉING CHICKEN AND VEGETABLES

The keys to a good sauté, whether you're preparing chicken, fish, meat or vegetables, are medium heat, a modest amount of oil or a liquid (such as stock, water or wine) and occasional stirring. (Although true sautéing involves some type of fat, steam-sautéing with liquid reduces the amount of fat in a recipe and still produces similar results.) It also helps to use ingredients that have been cut small or pounded thin, which allows them to cook more rapidly.

Chicken Sauté with Vegetables and Herbs   *QUICK!*

4 boneless, skinless chicken breast halves	1 large tomato, chopped
1 egg white	2 teaspoons reduced-sodium soy sauce
1 tablespoon cornstarch	1 teaspoon chopped fresh basil
2 tablespoons defatted chicken broth	1 teaspoon chopped fresh oregano
½ cup sliced mushrooms	1 teaspoon chopped fresh thyme
2 small zucchini, cut into 1" pieces	
6 scallions, chopped	

Flatten each piece of chicken by placing it between 2 sheets of wax paper and pounding it with a mallet or the flat side of a cleaver until about ¼" thick. Then cut into bite-size pieces.

In a medium bowl, combine the egg white and cornstarch until smooth. Add the chicken and stir until coated. Let the chicken stand for about 10 minutes.

☞ When "trying on" sauté pans in the store, look for one that feels balanced and comfortable in your hand and that is heavy enough to sit solidly and flat on the burner. Avoid lightweight pans, which tend to develop hot spots that cause food to burn.

☞ Many pans have handles that do not become hot during cooking. However, many others do not. To protect your hands from hot handles, try slipping a "pan handler" over the handle.

Made from heat-resistant material, these are folded and sewn pot holders that allow you to grip the handle firmly without getting burned.

Healthy Sautéing

Since sautéing, like stir-frying, uses high heats, it's important that all ingredients be prepared and ready to go before you start cooking. Herbs or seasonings should be already measured. Meat and poultry should be lightly

In a large no-stick skillet over medium heat, warm the broth. Remove the chicken from the cornstarch mixture and add to the skillet. Sauté, stirring occasionally, for 3 minutes, or just until the chicken is opaque throughout. Using a slotted spoon, remove the chicken from the skillet and set aside.

Stir in the chicken and sauté for 1 minute, or until heated through.

Add the mushrooms to the pan and stir over medium heat until the mushrooms begin to release their liquid. Add the zucchini, scallions, tomatoes, soy sauce, basil, oregano and thyme. Cook, stirring frequently, for 5 minutes, or until the vegetables are crisp-tender.

Makes 4 servings. Per serving: 169 calories, 3.2 g. fat (17% of calories), 27.8 g. protein, 6.3 g. carbohydrates, 1.3 g. dietary fiber, 69 mg. cholesterol, 177 mg. sodium

NOTES

• The chicken, vegetables and pan juices taste wonderful served over thin spaghetti or rice.

• For a more exotic flavor, replace the mushrooms with ½ cup sliced wild mushrooms such as shiitakes.

dredged in flour (when the recipe requires it) a few minutes ahead of time.

Prepare the pan. To reduce fat in recipes, many chefs season their pans. Cast iron requires the more elaborate seasoning used for woks (see page 41). Other pans, like no-stick and stainless steel, can use this quick method: First, "scour" the pan with salt. Remove the salt, apply a light film of oil, then wipe the pan well with a paper towel. The light sheen of oil will help food cook evenly while keeping the amount of fat to almost nothing.

Go easy on the oil. When using a good sauté pan, you don't need a lot of oil, either for even cooking or to prevent food from sticking. In most cases, you can put in just enough oil to moisten the bottom of the pan.

Rather than pouring oil directly into the pan, transfer some to a spray bottle. This way you can lightly mist the pan before you start cooking.

Cut back on butter. When you want the taste of butter but not much saturated fat, try brushing a little canola oil in the pan, then adding just a dot of butter for flavor. The addition of the oil has the extra benefit of helping prevent the butter from burning, which it might do if used for sautéing by itself.

Provide plenty of room. For food to cook quickly and evenly, it's important that there be plenty of room inside the pan. Place pieces of poultry or meat in a single layer with lots of space between. Don't crowd them.

If your sauté pan is too small to cook without crowding, use a second pan or prepare the food in several batches.

Do not disturb. The point of sautéing is to let food cook to a perfect golden brown. Let the food cook, undisturbed, for a few minutes in one place. Then turn or move it to another part of the pan for further cooking. It's less likely to stick if you use this method.

POACHING

The most gentle of cooking methods, poaching occurs when food is submerged in 160° to 180° liquid and carefully "simmered" until it's done. (True simmering occurs at 180° to 200°, whereas boiling occurs at 212°.) Poaching is often used as a prelude to further preparation: Chicken breasts may be poached before being sliced and added to cold chicken salad, for instance. Poaching can also be the main cooking method, as when serving hot poached salmon steaks, for example, or stuffed, rolled fish fillets.

Poaching is ideal for tenderizing poultry or for allowing fragile foods like fish to retain their natural shape, texture and delicate flavors during cooking. Poaching nearly guarantees that food will be moist and tender, and it requires no added fat.

Keep it simple. Chefs who poach frequently may require specialized gear, but most cooks can get by with a large skillet. Just make sure that

it's large enough to hold the food—a whole fish, for example—in a single layer with enough liquid to cover.

Don't poach in a cast-iron skillet, as the metal imparts a slightly off taste that becomes especially noticeable when cooking mild foods.

Choose the right liquid. Poached food is naturally mild, so it's important that the poaching liquid be rich and flavorful.

☞ You can make a simple poaching liquid by combining reduced-sodium chicken or fish broth with seasonings like finely chopped onions, garlic or carrots and peppercorns or other herbs and spices.

☞ When poaching fish, try combining clam juice, herbs (like tarragon) and flavored liquids (like lemon juice or herbal vinegar) with enough water to cover.

☞ When poaching chicken, a cooking liquid might include chicken broth flavored with rosemary and lemon juice.

Keep the action gentle. The water should be just slightly simmering, not boiling. The rigorous action of boiling could cause tender foods to fall apart or toughen.

Skin the fat. Removing skin from chicken and trimming off visible fat before poaching will keep fat in recipes to a minimum.

Lower away. Using a skimmer, a metal spatula or a strip of cheesecloth, lower food all the way into the cooking liquid; it should be completely submerged.

POACHING FISH

An extremely gentle cooking method, poaching does double duty: It cooks the food while at the same time adding flavor from the liquids used. Since fish has very tender flesh that can easily be rendered tough and dry, poaching is often the preferred cooking method. Regardless of what your catch of the day is, here's how to poach it right.

This recipe uses fish fillets, but the same technique works beautifully for fish steaks, whole fish, shellfish of all sorts and chicken pieces (especially boneless breasts). The key is to gently simmer the food until cooked through.

Poached Flounder Italian-Style *QUICK!*

1	cup defatted chicken broth
1	medium tomato, chopped
1	small green pepper, cut into strips
1	small onion, thinly sliced
1	cup thinly sliced mushrooms
1	clove garlic, minced
2	teaspoons dried Italian herb seasoning
⅛	teaspoon ground black pepper
4	skinless flounder fillets (about 4 ounces each and ¼"–½" thick)
2	tablespoons grated Parmesan cheese

In a large skillet, combine the broth, tomatoes, green peppers, onions, mushrooms, garlic, Italian herb seasoning and black pepper. Cover and bring to a boil.

Carefully add the flounder to the pan. Reduce the heat, cover and gently simmer for 3 to 6 minutes, or until the fish looks opaque all the way through when tested with a fork; do not overcook.

Using a slotted spatula or spoon, carefully transfer the flounder to a serving platter. Spoon the vegetable mixture over the flounder and sprinkle with the Parmesan.

Makes 4 servings. Per serving: 150 calories, 2.6 g. fat (16% of calories), 25 g. protein, 6.3 g. carbohydrates, 1.3 g. dietary fiber, 62 mg. cholesterol, 239 mg. sodium

POACHING TIMES

Since poached food is cooked in liquid, it can be difficult to tell exactly when it's done. Here are some guidelines.

CHICKEN

PART	AMOUNT	COOKING TIME (MIN.)
Split breasts	1½ pounds	20–25
Boneless breasts	1 pound	12–15
Boneless thighs	1½ pounds	18–22

FISH

CUT	AMOUNT	COOKING TIME (MIN.)
Chunks	1 pound	6–8
Whole fish	1 pound	6–8
Steaks	8–10 ounces	5–10
Fillet (delicate)	4–6 ounces	5–7
Fillet (rolled and stuffed)	6–8 ounces	8–10
Fillet (firm)	6–8 ounces	10–12

☞ Whole fish can be wrapped in a double thickness of cheesecloth to help hold it together. Placing it on a metal rack, especially one with handles that stick out of the liquid, can help remove the fish without breaking it.

☞ Whole fish should be started in cold liquid. Placing it in already hot liquid can cause the skin to split and may allow the exterior flesh to overcook before the interior is done.

☞ Tender foods like shellfish, boneless fish fillets and boneless chicken breasts can be added to water that is already simmering.

Check for doneness. Fish is done when it is opaque in the center. With chicken, the juices should run clear after the meat is pierced with a fork.

When poaching foods that will be served cold, stop the cooking just before cooking is completed. Then allow the food to cool in the cooking liquid.

Helpful Hint

One danger of poaching is that delicate foods sometimes fall apart in the cooking water. Adding lemon juice to the poaching liquid helps firm up delicate foods like fish, so that they hold together during cooking.

Jacques Pépin

Author, food columnist and master chef Jacques Pépin has had a major influence on American chefs since he arrived from France in 1959. Central to his philosophy is the importance of lowering fat in food without sacrificing flavor.

Poaching, he explains, is an excellent way to achieve this goal. "Poaching means immersing, or nearly immersing, food in liquid and cooking it at or just under the boiling point. The versatility of the cook is reflected in the choice of a poaching liquid. Depending on what is to be poached, you can use water, stock, fruit juice, wine, a light syrup or a mixture of these."

This salmon dish is one of Jacques' favorite recipes—high in flavor and respectably low in fat.

Salmon in Vegetable Broth with Potato Slices

- 4 medium boiling potatoes, peeled and sliced ½" thick
- 1 small leek, thinly sliced
- 1 medium carrot, thinly sliced
- 1 small zucchini, diced
- 4 large mushrooms, diced
- 2 shallots, thinly sliced
- 1 cup dry fruity white wine or nonalcoholic white wine
- 1 cup water
- 1 teaspoon salt
- ¼ teaspoon ground black pepper
- 4 salmon steaks (1¼" thick), skin removed
- 2 tablespoons butter
- 1 tablespoon olive oil

Place the potatoes in a medium saucepan. Add cold water to cover. Bring to a boil over high heat. Cover, reduce the heat to low and cook gently for 10 minutes, or until the slices are just tender when pierced with a fork. Drain, cover and keep warm while you poach the salmon.

While the potatoes are cooking, prepare the poaching liquid. In a large skillet, combine the leeks, carrots, zucchini, mushrooms, shallots, wine, water, salt and pepper. Bring to a boil over high heat. Cover, reduce the heat to low and cook gently for 10 minutes. Add the salmon to the skillet in a single layer, making sure that it's immersed in the liquid. Return the liquid to a boil, cover the pan, reduce the heat to low and simmer gently for 2½ to 3 minutes, or until the salmon is cooked through and flakes easily when tested with a fork.

Divide the potatoes among soup plates. Use a slotted spoon to remove the salmon from the liquid. Place it on top of the potatoes.

Add the butter and oil to the poaching liquid and vegetables in the skillet. Bring the mixture to a strong boil to emulsify it and create a sauce. Spoon the vegetables and sauce over and around the salmon. Serve immediately.

Makes 4 servings. Per serving: 439 calories, 14.6 g. fat (30% of calories), 31.3 g. protein, 36.3 g. carbohydrates, 3.5 g. dietary fiber, 88 mg. cholesterol, 650 mg. sodium

Microwaving, Steaming and More

Cooking with moist heat is one of the oldest and easiest cooking methods. Whether you're microwaving broccoli, steaming fish, pressure-cooking beans or slow-cooking chicken, it's also one of the healthiest.

Moist heat cooks food gently while sealing in flavor—with no added fat. In addition, it allows foods to retain much of their original character. Vegetables like corn on the cob, broccoli and snap peas taste fresh-picked and keep their shape, texture and brilliant colors. Fish and seafood maintain their delicate flavors. And poultry, even when you strip away the fatty skin, cooks up plump, juicy and moist.

Since most home cooks use the microwave more than any other moist-heat cooking method, we'll start by taking a look at the appliance that has helped put healthy cooking on the fast track.

MICROWAVING

The microwave has been in home kitchens for a long time now, and most folks are just getting around to realizing what a boon it is—not just for cooking fast but for cooking healthy as well.

Microwave ovens bombard water, fat and sugar molecules in food with high-energy waves. This causes the molecules to vibrate and build up friction, which in turn creates heat that causes cooking. Microwaving cooks faster than other methods, because the food is heated directly, rather than through a pan on the stove top or by the hot air in a conventional oven. The quick cooking means little added liquid is necessary, allowing food to retain more of its flavor and nutrients. To take advantage of the microwave and still practice kitchen safety:

☞ Never heat unopened jars of food, including baby food. Pressure from trapped steam could cause the jar to explode.

☞ Never heat foods in metal cans. Metal deflects microwaves, keeping them from heating food. It's sometimes possible to use shallow metal containers; read the directions that came with your microwave.

☞ Avoid dishes and other containers that have metal trim. Aluminum foil should be used sparingly. Arcing (or sparking) may occur, which can damage your microwave.

☞ Don't use paper towels, paper bags or other paper products made from recycled fibers. There may be small amounts of metal present that can get hot enough to ignite the paper.

☞ Never microwave eggs in the shell, as the internal rise in pressure may cause a dangerous explosion.

☞ When cooking whole eggs out of the shell, prick the yolk sac with a toothpick to prevent the yolk from bursting.

☞ Other whole foods with skins, like tomatoes, eggplant and unpeeled potatoes, need to be pricked all over with a fork to prevent bursting.

☞ When cooking food covered with plastic wrap, vent the wrap by turning back a corner to allow steam to escape.

☞ Never operate your microwave if the door is dented, warped or otherwise damaged.

☞ Never deep-fry foods in a microwave. Aside from the obvious health concerns of deep-frying, this method is especially unwise in a microwave. A fair amount of oil is needed, and it reaches a high temperature; splashing and spillage could easily occur as you remove the container from the microwave.

Microwave Cookware

While a number of manufacturers have produced lines of microwave cookware, you don't really need special equipment or dishes. Almost any cookware that you already own—with the exception of metal pots or dishes with metal rims—works well in the microwave.

☞ Round pans and rectangular pans with rounded corners are best, because they help prevent overheating at the edges.

☞ Food can be heated on white paper towels, paper plates, wax paper, freezer bags or nearly anything else that doesn't contain metal.

☞ Foods to be lightly steamed or reheated can be covered with a layer of wax paper or a dampened paper towel.

STEAM SAFETY

When uncovering a microwave dish, always begin by lifting the lid or plastic wrap on the side away from you to prevent steam burns.

Helpful Hint

To test whether or not a dish or other container is safe for microwaving, set it in the microwave next to a one-cup glass measure containing eight ounces of cool water. Microwave on high power for one minute. If the dish remains cool, it's safe to use.

☞ Plastic storage containers are generally safe for reheating food. When used for cooking, however, they may get too hot and melt. In either case, it's wise to check the bottom of the container for confirmation that it's microwave-safe.

☞ The same foods that you would cover on the stove top—like fish, vegetables or poultry—should also be covered in the microwave.

Microwaving Cereals, Grains and Vegetables

Health experts recommend eating 6 to 11 servings of grains—like rice, barley and oats—every day. Cooking grains in the microwave gives good results. It produces grains that are perfectly textured, light and fluffy without a hint of sogginess. Plus, you can cook and serve in the same dish, for easier cleanup.

Breakfast cereals like oatmeal and farina are easy to prepare one bowl at a time. Follow directions on the package for near-instant morning meals.

When it comes to longer-cooking items like regular white rice, brown rice, barley, millet and other grains, be aware that the microwave won't yield you a time advantage. Because of the large amounts of liquid involved, grains cooked in the microwave take about as long as those prepared on the stove.

Managing Microwaves

Microwave ovens are fast, efficient and easy to use. Just like conventional ovens, however, microwaves have hot zones where foods cook a little bit faster. The location of these zones varies from oven to oven. Using a carousel or turntable is one way to help foods cook evenly. Here are some other strategies to guarantee perfect microwaving.

Potatoes

Position a single potato in the center of the microwave.

Arrange two potatoes side by side.

When cooking four potatoes, use a circular pattern.

Vegetables

Vegetables like zucchini should be cut into same-size pieces.

Arrange stalk vegetables like cauliflower, broccoli and asparagus with the tender heads facing inward for slower cooking.

When cooking several halves of vegetables, like stuffed potatoes, tomatoes or squash, arrange them in a ring, leaving the center open.

Chicken

Chicken breasts containing bone should always be positioned so that the thick edges face outward, leaving the thin edges facing inward and the center of the dish empty.

Helpful Hint

When cooking grains in the microwave, boost the flavor by cooking them in low-fat broth instead of water. Use a reduced-sodium brand to maximize natural flavors and keep sodium to a minimum.

For cooking vegetables, the microwave offers tremendous advantages. It cooks the toughest vegetables crisp-tender in just a few minutes. Plus, you need very little water, which means more nutrients are retained.

☞ Use a shallow cooking container with enough room to spread cut vegetables in a single layer for even cooking. Glass bakeware is a good choice.

☞ In most microwaves, foods in the center of the plate or carousel cook more slowly than foods further out. So put quick-cooking foods in the middle and items that require more energy farther out.

☞ With a fork or knife, prick the skin of whole vegetables like potatoes or squash to let steam escape. A single potato cooked in the microwave is ready to eat in as little as three to five minutes.

☞ When cooking small, loose vegetables like peas, stir halfway through the cooking time to help them cook more evenly.

Microwaving Fish

Fresh fish and seafood are nutritious, low in fat and wonderfully easy to make in the microwave. To make the most of your catch:

☞ Use a glass baking dish or pie plate for cooking fish, shrimp or scallops. For shellfish in the shell, like clams or mussels, use a deep casserole with a cover.

☞ Shelling shrimp before cooking will help prevent the shell from sticking to the flesh.

GREAT TATER TOPPINGS

Potatoes are filling, nutritious and, when "baked" in the microwave, done in a flash—making them the perfect high-speed food. Here are some fast toppings to make them even better. The quantities given are for one serving.

☞ 1/4 cup nonfat yogurt cheese mixed with 2 tablespoons each chopped scallions, carrots and celery

☞ 1/4 cup low-fat pizza sauce topped with 2 tablespoons shredded reduced-fat mozzarella cheese

☞ 1/2 cup steamed broccoli florets topped with 2 tablespoons shredded reduced-fat Cheddar cheese

☞ 1 small tomato (seeded and diced) mixed with 1 teaspoon extra-virgin olive oil and 1 tablespoon chopped fresh basil; top with 2 tablespoons reduced-fat ricotta cheese

☞ 1/3 cup sliced mushrooms sautéed with 1 small shallot, minced; mix with 1 tablespoon whole-grain mustard

☞ 1/2 cup shredded cooked chicken breast mixed with 1/4 cup barbecue sauce

☞ Covering fish with wax paper traps heat, allowing it to cook more quickly and without drying out.

☞ Arrange fish fillets in a single layer with the thin ends tucked under to prevent overcooking. An alternate method is to arrange fish so that the narrow (faster-cooking) ends face toward the middle.

☞ To add flavor, place fish fillets or fish steaks *en papillote*—in packets of parchment paper—with herbs or thinly cut aromatic vegetables, like onions or celery.

☞ Fish is almost done when it flakes at the edges and toward the center. Remove from the microwave and let stand a few minutes to complete cooking.

☞ If fish does not flake at its recommended cooking time, increase cooking time by one-minute increments. Be careful not to overcook the fish.

Microwaving Poultry

Chicken and turkey are versatile, low in fat and inexpensive—and a snap in the microwave.

☞ Arrange boneless, skinless chicken or turkey cutlets in a single layer with the thinner (faster-cooking) portions toward the center of the dish.

FOIL FOR SLOWER COOKING

To help food in the microwave cook more evenly, apply a 1"- to 2"-wide strip of foil to parts that might otherwise cook too fast, like the center bone area of a whole turkey or chicken breast. The foil should be smoothed evenly around the food, and it shouldn't touch the oven walls, floor or door.

Helpful Hint

To make sure that your steamer doesn't run dry without your knowing it, place a few marbles in the water. If the water evaporates, the marbles will rattle, letting you know that it's time for a refill.

☞ Cook a whole or half bone-in turkey breast on a microwave roasting rack in a baking dish. Raising the meat off the oven floor will help it cook more evenly.

STEAMING

The advantage to steaming food is that the food cooks fast, at temperatures above 212° (the boiling point of water). This helps tenderize food while sealing in moisture and nutrients, and it requires no added fat. And because cooking takes place *over* water rather than in it, vitamins are retained that otherwise might boil away.

There are many types of food steamers, ranging from the Chinese bamboo steamer to the *couscoussière* of France. But the principle on which they operate is similar: Water is brought to a boil in the lower portion, while a perforated rack above holds the food. Steamers are particularly good for cooking fish, because there is less chance that the fish will dry out.

For perfect results, follow these guidelines.

☞ Add enough water so that the steamer doesn't run dry, but not so much that the water comes in contact with the food.

☞ Add herbs or spices to the water before cooking to subtly flavor steamed foods.

☞ Another way to flavor foods like chicken is to place them directly on a bed of herbs in

(continued on page 62)

STEMERS

F‌ood steamers have been used in home kitchens for hundreds of years. All of them work in roughly the same way—that is, by trapping steam to cook the food—but there are a number of different styles to choose from. All types are good for steaming vegetables, fish (whether whole, fillets or steaks), other seafood, boneless poultry cuts and traditional Chinese steamed buns and dumplings (dim sum).

Bamboo steamers have several levels, so you can cook a variety of foods—often a whole meal—at the same time. They're generally used over a wok.

Collapsible metal steamer baskets are inexpensive and versatile. They convert any pot with a tight-fitting lid into a steamer.

Electric food steamers offer the versatility of a stove-top steamer with the convenience of temperature control. They're often sold as rice cookers, but they're good for other foods also.

Pasta-draining inserts fit into a large pot and have holes all over the sides and bottom. They're most often used when cooking pasta to make draining easy, but they make serviceable steamers and are also good for steamed puddings and for large amounts of seafood in the shell.

You can improvise a steamer. Place a cooling or roasting rack in a roasting pan. Cover the pan with a tight-fitting lid or aluminum foil.

Steaming is the perfect technique for making tender, flavorful food without added fat. Vegetables and fish are popular choices for the steamer basket, but you can steam anything from bread to rice to poultry. To vary the flavors of the food, simply add broth, fruit juice or herbs to the steaming liquid. The key is to keep a tight lid on the pot during cooking.

Chicken Rolls Florentine

8	ounces fresh spinach
1½	teaspoons olive oil
1	clove garlic, minced
1	shallot, minced
1	tablespoon minced fresh rosemary
¼	cup dry bread crumbs
¼	cup crumbled feta cheese
¼	cup fat-free egg substitute
4	boneless, skinless chicken breast halves

Rinse out the saucepan and place it over medium-low heat. Add the oil, garlic and shallots; sauté for 4 minutes, or until the shallots are soft. (Do not let the garlic brown.) Add the spinach and sauté for 2 minutes.

Wash the spinach in cold water and transfer the wet leaves to a large saucepan. Cover and cook over medium heat until the spinach is just wilted. Transfer the spinach to a colander to drain and cool. When cool enough to handle, finely chop and set aside.

Transfer the mixture to a large bowl. Add the rosemary, bread crumbs, feta and egg substitute; mix well. (If the mixture does not hold together, add more bread crumbs.)

Place each piece of chicken between two sheets of wax paper. Pound with a mallet or heavy cleaver until the meat is about ¼" thick. Be careful not to tear the flesh. Set aside.

In a large saucepan, bring 1" of water to a boil. Set each chicken roll on a small piece of parchment paper or foil, then transfer to a steaming rack. Set the rack in a saucepan. Cover and steam for 15 to 18 minutes, or until the chicken is no longer pink when tested with a sharp knife.

Makes 4 servings. Per serving: 218 calories, 6.7 g. fat (27% of calories), 30.2 g. protein, 8.3 g. carbohydrates, 1.3 g. dietary fiber, 75 mg. cholesterol, 263 mg. sodium

NOTE
• If you like mushrooms, add ¼ cup finely chopped mushrooms along with the garlic and shallots. Sauté until most of the liquid evaporates.

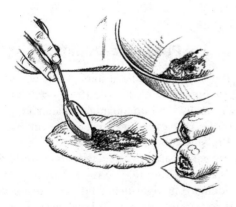

Spread equal amounts of filling on each of the four breasts. Carefully roll up each breast to enclose the filling. Secure with toothpicks, if necessary.

SETTING UP A BAMBOO STEAMER

A triple-tiered bamboo steamer is a simple, inexpensive utensil that lets you cook all the foods on your menu—from the toughest vegetables to the most delicate fish—at the same time. It's generally used with a wok. Although you can set the steamer directly in a wok, it's helpful to add a small wire rack to give it stability.

Place a wire rack in a wok. Add water, making sure that it doesn't come above the rack. Bring to a boil over high heat.

Place the basket that contains the slowest-cooking food, like chopped vegetables, nearest the water, where it's hottest.

Baskets with quicker-cooking foods, like fish, go higher up, where the temperatures are lower.

the steamer basket. The herbs will impart a delicate taste. Whatever flavorings you use should be aromatic enough to enhance the natural flavor of the food but not so strong as to overpower it.

☞ Once food is added to the steamer, the temperature of the water drops, and it will need a minute or so to return to a boil. Start your timing from the moment the water comes back to a boil.

☞ Accurate timing is important to prevent foods from being underdone or overcooked. Frequent peeking, however, lengthens the cooking time, because valuable steam escapes—so add one minute to the cooking time.

☞ Keep a large plate on the kitchen counter or on the stove near the steamer so that you'll have a place to set the insert when you remove it from over the water.

☞ Always open the steamer cover away from you to prevent burns.

PRESSURE-COOKING

Pressure cookers have come a long way since they were introduced in the 1940s—when they occasionally built up too much steam and deposited the evening's meal on the ceiling.

Pressure cookers today are constructed of heavy-gauge stainless steel with improved lid seals and pressure-release valves that prevent accidents. The tight-fitting lid traps steam, along with important vitamins and nutrients. The real advantage of pressure cookers, however, is speed: Food cooks as much as 70 percent faster than in a regular pot.

That's a real boon for the healthy cook, because some of the foods that are best for us, like beans and legumes, are notoriously slow to cook. In the pressure cooker, however, they can be ready in well under half an hour.

☞ Before using any pressure cooker, be sure to read the manufacturer's directions. In partic-

PRESSURE-COOKING BEANS

On the stove top, dry beans are terribly slow to cook. A faster way is to use a pressure cooker. Following the directions that came with your pressure cooker, cover presoaked beans with cold water, turn on the heat and adjust the pressure. The steam does the rest.

The times given here are for presoaked beans (black-eyed peas, lentils and split peas do not need presoaking) and assume that you will use the quick-release method of opening the pressure cooker. If you use the natural-release method, which allows the pressure to come down at a slow speed, actual cooking times will be even less.

BEAN	COOKING TIME (MIN.)
Adzuki	5–9
Black	9–11
Black–eyed peas (unsoaked)	9–11
Cannellini	9–12
Chick-peas	21–25
Christmas lima	8–10
Cranberry	9–12
Fava	8–12
Great Northern	8–12
Lentils (brown or French), unsoaked	7–10
Lentils (red), unsoaked	4–6
Lima (baby)	4–6
Lima (large)	5–7
Navy	6–8
Pigeon peas	6–9
Pinto	4–6
Red kidney	10–12
Split peas (unsoaked)	8–10

ular, be familiar with the locking and steam-release mechanisms.

☞ For most home kitchens, a 6-quart pressure cooker is about right, although other sizes are available.

☞ Check the pressure. Most cookers are automatically set at 15 pounds (about 250°), although some allow you to set the pressure between 5 and 10 pounds for slower cooking.

☞ Since there's so little evaporation, less liquid is needed than with standard methods.

☞ In general, don't fill a pressure cooker more than two-thirds. If you're preparing beans or grains, fill the cooker no more than halfway.

☞ Pressure cookers continue cooking even after the heat is turned off, so factor this into your calculations—especially if you opt for the natural pressure-release method, which lets the pressure fall slowly over a period of about ten minutes.

☞ Many manufacturers advise against using pressure cookers for cranberries, because the berries pop during cooking, possibly clogging the pressure-release vent. Rhubarb, which in the cooked state is stringy, may also cause the vents to clog.

☞ Other foods that some experts suggest avoiding in the pressure cooker are pasta, rice, applesauce, oatmeal, split peas and pearl barley. All are likely to foam during cooking and might clog the vent.

☞ Don't add salt or acidic liquids like tomato sauce or tomato juice when cooking beans, because this can cause the beans to toughen.

☞ If you live in a high-altitude area, a pressure cooker will let you cook foods at a much higher temperature than usual—and will therefore cook them faster.

SLOW-COOKING

Although at the other end of the speed spectrum from pressure cookers, slow cookers also make a lot of sense in today's busy world. They provide a steady, wraparound heat that cooks food slowly and evenly. This means no hot spots, virtually no supervision and, unless the cooker

MOIST HEAT COOKING TIMES

Although microwaves, steamers and pressure cookers all use moist heat, the actual cooking times vary widely. For general guidelines, use the chart below. The amounts included here are mainly for the microwave; microwave timing is very much dependent on the quantity of food being cooked.

VEGETABLE	AMOUNT	MICROWAVE SET ON HIGH (MIN.)	STEAMER (MIN.)	PRESSURE COOKER (MIN.)
Artichokes	4 medium	20–25	30–35	9–11
Asparagus	1 pound, trimmed	5–6	6–7	1½–2
Beets	1 pound	12–15	30–35	20–22
Broccoli	1 pound, cut into florets	8–12	5–7	2–3
Brussels sprouts	1 pound, with an X cut in the bottom of each	7–11	11–12	4–5
Cabbage	1 medium, cut into wedges	9–13	12–15	3–4
Carrots	1 pound, sliced	8–10	7–10	4–5
Cauliflower	1 pound, cut into florets	4–7	8–10	2–3
Corn on the cob	4 ears	10–14	10–12	3–4
Eggplant	1 medium, cut into cubes	7–10	5–7	3–4
Green beans	1 pound	10–12	7–9	2–3
Onions, small whole	1 pound	6–8	15–20	4–5
Mushrooms	1 pound, sliced	6–8	3–4	1–2
Peas, green	1 pound, shelled	5–7	8–10	Not recommended
Peas, snap	1 pound	6–10	8–10	Not recommended
Potatoes	1 whole, small new red	9–11	25–30	7–8
Spinach	1 pound	5–7	3–4	2–3
Squash, acorn or butternut	1 medium, cut and seeded	8–10	25–30	6–7
Squash, spaghetti	3 pounds, halved and seeded	7–9	25–35	14–17
Turnips	1 pound, peeled and cut	7–9	10–12	3–4
Zucchini, sliced	1 pound	4–6	8–10	2–3

runs completely dry, little risk of burning. Like other moist-heat cookers, the slow cooker makes food that's deliciously tender with little or no added fat.

Perhaps the most common slow cooker is the Crock-Pot type, which typically has only two settings: high and low. A second, more expensive variety of slow cooker has a temperature control, which allows you to set the heat—usually from about 150° to 350°. To make sure that food reaches a temperature of at least 165°, which is needed to kill bacteria, check it with a thermometer.

Most slow cookers have a removable insert. This allows you to wash the inside of the pot without lugging the whole thing—electrical wires and all—to the sink. Plus, you can fill the insert, store it in the refrigerator overnight and then place it in the cooker portion the following morning. When using a slow cooker:

☞ Trim away visible fat from meat before cooking.

☞ Layer slow-cooking root vegetables (such as carrots, parsnips and potatoes) in the bottom where it's hottest. Put the more tender items higher up.

☞ It's best to use small whole potatoes, unpeeled. They retain their shape and won't fall apart during cooking.

☞ Cut chicken into chunks and freeze it before placing it in the pot. That will slow the cooking time and prevent overcooking delicate meat.

☞ Either use a little less liquid to begin with or thicken it by sprinkling 1 teaspoon quick-cooking tapioca over the vegetables before adding meat, since stews prepared in slow cookers retain more liquid than those cooked on the stove top.

☞ Don't let curiosity slow you down. Each time you open the lid, built-up steam escapes, which can cost about 20 minutes in cooking time.

Clay Cookers

These unglazed terra-cotta pots have been around since ancient times and are enjoying a new popularity as we look for ways to eat healthier while preparing food with ease. They cook food slowly in an oven and do, indeed, take advantage of moist heat like the other techniques in this chapter.

The cooker, usually oval in shape, is made up of two deep casseroles. The top is inverted over the bottom to form a mini clay oven. Before using, immerse both the top and the bottom of the cooker in cool or tepid water for 15 minutes. Porous by nature, the clay retains moisture. Essentially, it acts like a natural steaming chamber to seal in juices in meat without basting.

Whole chickens cooked this way are amazingly tender. Clay-pot cooking also works well for vegetables, pilafs and casseroles. Plus, it cooks faster than regular oven cooking and doesn't require tending.

☞ When cooking meat, trim off as much visible fat as possible before cooking. Check for doneness with a meat thermometer.

☞ Cooking a whole chicken with the skin on will help keep the bird moist. Remove the skin before eating.

☞ Always start by placing the cooker in the center of a cold oven. Then turn on the heat to 450° to 480°.

☞ When cooking meat or poultry, remove the cover about 10 minutes before the end of cooking time and baste, using juices collected from the bottom. Cooking for an additional 10 to 15 minutes, uncovered, will help the meat brown nicely.

☞ After use, clean a clay cooker using only water and a stiff scrubbing brush; soap can impair the porous quality of the clay.

☞ Never use a clay cooker on the stove top. It's likely to crack if exposed to direct heat.

Michael Lomonaco

At Lomonaco's restaurant in New York City, Michael Lomonaco is a master at combining classic favorites with today's healthier cooking styles.

"I particularly like this steamed snapper recipe, as it allows the different ingredients to shine without being covered up with lots of fat and without the intrusiveness that sautéing or grilling can inflict on delicate foods," Lomonaco says.

Steamed Red Snapper with Coconut Broth

Coconut Broth
- 1½ cups defatted vegetable, fish or chicken broth
- ¾ cup dry sherry (optional)
- 8 basil leaves or 1 tablespoon dried basil
- 3–4 whole dried chili peppers
- 3 tablespoons unsweetened coconut milk

Fish and Vegetables
- 12–16 bok choy leaves
- 4 red snapper fillets (6 ounces each), with skin
- 2 tablespoons chopped scallions
- 2 teaspoons minced fresh ginger
- 1 teaspoon minced garlic
- Pinch of salt
- Pinch of ground black pepper
- 4 ounces leeks (white part only), chopped
- 4 ounces carrots, shredded
- 1 small turnip, thinly sliced
- 2 small stalks celery, cut on the diagonal ¼" thick
- 1 cup broccoli florets
- 8 shiitake mushroom caps

To make the coconut broth: In a large saucepan or wok, place the broth, sherry (if using), basil, peppers and milk. Bring to a boil over medium heat. Reduce the heat to low and simmer for 10 minutes.

To make the fish and vegetables: Blanch the bok choy in boiling water for 30 seconds, or until just wilted. Remove with a slotted spoon and plunge into a bowl of ice water to stop the cooking process.

Lay 3 to 4 of the leaves side by side with the edges overlapping. Place 1 snapper fillet in the center, skin side up. Repeat with the remaining leaves and fillets. Sprinkle the scallions, ginger, garlic, salt and pepper evenly over the fillets. Pull the bok choy over the fillets to enclose them in packets.

Place the leeks, carrots, turnips, celery, broccoli and mushrooms in a large steamer basket. Lay the fish packets on top of the vegetables and place the basket in the saucepan or wok.

Cover and steam for 15 to 20 minutes, or until the fish flakes easily when tested with a fork.

Discard the chili peppers and divide the fish and vegetables among 4 plates. Serve with the broth spooned over top.

Makes 4 servings. Per serving: 343 calories, 5.4 g. fat (14% of calories), 38.7 g. protein, 23.6 g. carbohydrates, 4 g. dietary fiber, 62 mg. cholesterol, 168 mg. sodium

Grilling

Can you imagine a camping trip without grilling? Or going an entire summer without hearing the sizzle of burgers or enjoying the heady aroma of slow-smoking chicken?

Like baseball and homemade ice cream, grilling is a veritable symbol of summer. At the same time, however, its influence has spread beyond the backyard and into fine restaurants nationwide. Grilling has become as sophisticated —and in some cases, nearly as pricey—as great French cooking. Nor are the entrées limited to burgers and steaks. Chicken, turkey and fish are great on the grill. So are seafood, garden vegetables and even pizza.

Grilling is more than just tasty. Because it utilizes high heats, it quickly sears foods and locks in flavors with little or no added fat. At the same time, it lends a smoky nuance and rich layering of flavors to food. You simply don't need fatty, heavily marbled meats or such fat-laden extras as butter to achieve fantastic flavors.

STOCKING UP

Buying a new grill is like getting a new car: You don't have to spend a fortune to get where you're going, although it's certainly easy to do so. If you do a lot of grilling—some chefs use their outdoor grills as much as, or even more than, their kitchen stoves—you're probably going to want a top-of-the-line model. That could amount to a sturdy, heat-controlled, multi-grilled wonder that will cook a delicate fish fillet, two whole chickens and a seven-pound buffalo brisket—possibly all at the same time.

For most cooks, however, the great thing about grilling is its essential simplicity. For basic great tastes, you don't need anything more complicated than a small grill, utensils, a reliable source of heat and a few chips of aromatic hardwood for flavor.

Grills

If you're just starting out, it's important to buy a grill that most closely suits your style of cooking. Some grills are open, while others have lids. Some chefs favor charcoal-fired grills, while others insist on propane. Here are a few points to consider.

☞ How often do you grill? If the answer is "not often," then a simple, inexpensive grill is all you need. If you grill frequently, however, you're going to want a grill that's rugged enough to stand up to hard use. You'll probably also want some special features, like movable grates, adjustable air vents and so forth. Better grills cost more, but they're wonderfully easy to use and, with proper care, will last a lifetime.

☞ Where do you grill? A large, stationary grill is ideal for backyard or patio grilling. For camping, you're going to want something lightweight and portable, like a hibachi.

☞ How much room is there? If you have a large yard and can place the grill at least several

PROFESSIONAL GRILL MARKS

To please the eye as well as the palate, serve grilled meats and vegetables with perfect crosshatch markings. Here's how to do it right.

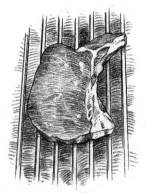

Place food on the hot grill and leave it on long enough for deep lines to appear.

Rotate the food 90° and let it cook until the crosshatch lines have formed.

Turn the food over and finish cooking on the opposite side. The side facing downward on the plate won't need fancy markings.

feet from the house, garage or other flammable objects, then a wood- or charcoal-burning grill is perfectly safe. If you'll be grilling on a wood deck or apartment terrace, however, a gas grill may be a better choice.

☞ How many appetites are you feeding? A standard-size grill is perfect for two to six people. If you like cooking for crowds, you're going to want a larger grill with wide (or even multiple) grilling areas.

Don't buy more grill than you need, however. Large grills consume more fuel, so you'll end up paying twice: once for the more-expensive grill and again for the extra fuel.

☞ How do you grill? If you think that you'll be grilling or smoking large items, like whole chickens or hams, you're going to need a grill with a lid. You'll also want adjustable heat controls for the long cooking times that large items require.

By contrast, if the only grilling that you plan to do is for hamburgers, hot dogs and small amounts of vegetables, then an open grill is all you'll need. This type of grill works perfectly well and with light use will last for years.

Helpful Hint

Metal transmits heat, which is why metal skewers cause food to cook faster. They're recommended for grilling meats and dense vegetables. For more delicate foods like fish, wooden skewers are a better choice, because they won't overcook the fish, as metal might.

GREAT GRATES

Although most grills do a satisfactory job with basic tasks, it's best to buy equipment that matches your own style of cooking. If your favorite food is burgers, for example, why bother with a top-of-the-line smoker?

Here are some of the basic grill styles and the jobs they do best.

Indoor countertop grills. Fired by electricity, these generate high heat but very little smoke. Although they won't produce the rich, smoky taste of food cooked on outdoor grills, they do create a satisfying crust—with the convenience of cooking indoors.

Braziers. The most inexpensive of all the grills, a brazier is really nothing more than a shallow pan on legs. (The hibachi is a miniversion of the brazier.) Fired by charcoal, braziers provide little control but are a good choice for cooks who grill infrequently and want something simple.

Kettles and covered cookers. Often kettle-shaped and covered with a large, domed lid, these have adjustable air vents to control the heat of the fire. Usually fired by charcoal, a kettle can be used both as a brazier-type grill or, with the lid in place, as a slow smoker.

Smokers. These tall, cylindrical cookers have tight-fitting lids and, in some cases, a number of cooking compartments inside. Fired by electricity, gas or charcoal, they cook food slowly, surrounding it in a dense cloud of smoke and steam.

Utensils

Having the right tools makes grilling easier as well as safer. Don't try to save money by buying cheap utensils, however; you'll wind up spending more as they rust, bend, splinter or break and have to be replaced. Good tools last indefinitely, so the higher initial cost pays off.

Here are a few basics that you'll want to have on hand.

☞ Aluminum drip pan
☞ Grilling basket for fish and small items like vegetables
☞ Heat-resistant gloves
☞ Heavy-duty fork with long handle
☞ Long- and short-handled metal spatulas with heat-resistant wood handles
☞ Long-handled basting brush with natural bristles
☞ Long-handled tongs for reaching over hot grills
☞ Meat thermometer
☞ Metal skewers for making kebabs
☞ Poker for moving hot coals

FISH IN A BASKET

The easiest way to keep fish in one piece is to use a grill basket.

Made of two metal grids that enclose the fish, a grill basket holds food together and helps prevent it from slipping into the fire. To keep fish from sticking, lightly oil the screens or spritz them with no-stick spray.

☞ Short-handled tongs for control when working up close

☞ Wire brush with scraper on one side, for cleaning the grill

SAFETY FIRST

Since grilling utilizes very high heats and is usually done outdoors, it doesn't take much—a sudden wind, uneven bricks or simply an out-of-bounds volleyball—to create chaos in an instant. To prevent problems, here's what grill chefs recommend.

Allow plenty of room. A blowing spark can torch fires in an instant, so set up your grill in an open area away from buildings, dry leaves or brush. If there is a breeze, position the grill so that your back will be to the wind.

Get it level. Placing the grill on rickety ground or uneven bricks could cause it to tip over and spew fire-hot coals—or, in the case of gas grills, dangerous clouds of propane. Always put the grill on a level surface, then gently rock it to make sure that the legs are secure and stable before lighting it.

Be prepared. Experienced grill chefs always keep a fire extinguisher handy in case an accident occurs. It's important, however, to read the directions ahead of time so that you know how the thing works before you need it.

Dress for safety. Hanging apron strings, billowy sleeves and flapping shirttails have a way of drifting into the fire. When working at the grill, always wear clothes that won't get in the way. It's also a good idea to keep a pair of flame-retardant mitts nearby. These make it easy to adjust the fire or grate without getting burned.

Only work outdoors. Grilling with charcoal or hardwood releases carbon monoxide, which in close quarters can be deadly. Unless you have a grill that's designed for indoor use, do your grilling outside.

Beware of old coals. Charcoal and hardwood ashes can retain their heat for hours, even when the fire is out. When cleaning the grill, wrap ashes in foil and put them in a metal container. If the coals are still hot, wrap them in foil and thoroughly douse the package with water.

LIGHTING THE COALS

Less expensive than hardwood and more aromatic than propane, charcoal briquettes are the fuel of choice for many home grillers. When it comes to lighting them, however, there are many options to choose from.

☞ **Charcoal chimneys**. With charcoal placed in an upper section and crumpled newspaper beneath, charcoal chimneys take advantage of a simple rule of nature: Heat rises. Charcoal chimneys eliminate the need for starter fluids and, if you take care of them, provide years of service.

☞ **Electric starters**. As long as your grill is near an electrical outlet, these may be your best choice. They fire up charcoal in just a few minutes, create no aftertaste and last virtually forever.

☞ **Presoaked briquettes**. These start easily, usually with a single match. Unfortunately, the fumes from the chemical starter tend to persist through the cooking process, giving an unpleasant, chemical-like taste to the food.

☞ **Quick-start fluid**. It starts easily and burns with little aftertaste. By the time the charcoal is covered with white ash, most of the chemical residue is gone. This is probably the most popular form of starter. *Never* squirt more lighter fluid onto the coals once the fire has started.

☞ **Solid starters**. Made with wood chips and paraffin, these are lightweight and easy to use. They're an excellent choice for packing in the car. The drawback is that they're more expensive than lighter fluid.

HEALTHY GRILLING

It wasn't so many years ago that a backyard barbecue meant 16-ounce steaks sizzling on the grill or a slab of baby-back ribs in the smoker. These days, however, healthy cooks have begun exploring new possibilities—not only lean meats and poultry but also grilled vegetables, seafood and even tropical fruits.

FUELS FOR THE FIRE

It used to be that grilling was synonymous with charcoal. The traditional briquettes remain an excellent choice. In addition, there are other fuels that you may want to try. Here's a rundown of the options.

☞ **Charcoal.** This is the carbon that's left behind when wood is burned very slowly in the absence of oxygen. Charcoal burns cleaner, hotter and longer than wood. Plus, it creates very little smoke or flames. The briquettes that you most often find in supermarkets are a blend of charcoal, anthracite and sawdust pressed together. Some types have other additives that help them light more easily without the addition of lighter fluid. Read the label to determine what you're getting.

☞ **Gas.** Propane is clean, efficient and very easy to control. In most cases, however, the "lava rocks" that are part of a gas grill and used to distribute heat don't get as hot as charcoal.

☞ **Hardwood.** Many grill chefs prefer the rich, smoky taste that comes from cooking with hardwoods, such as hickory, oak, grapevine, applewood and mesquite. The drawback to this method is that hardwoods require constant attention to maintain a steady heat.

☞ **Hardwood charcoal.** Made with pressed woods, this combines the convenience of charcoal with the good taste of hardwood.

To enjoy the great taste of grilling without boosting your cholesterol level or widening your waistline, here's what chefs advise.

Keep it lean. Grilling fatty meats is like throwing fat on the fire—literally and figuratively. There are many ways to enjoy grilled chicken and meats while reducing the amount of unhealthy saturated fats.

☞ Instead of buying heavily marbled beef, like sirloin, shop for leaner cuts, like flank steak and bottom round.

☞ Trim away visible fat before putting meat on the grill.

☞ Rather than grilling an entire slab of meat, look for ways to stretch it. One possibility is to cube it, soak it in marinade and put it on skewers for a full-flavored yet healthy shish kebab. Or you can simply slice it thin—for fajitas, for example, or to make a lean steak sandwich.

Explore the garden. You don't use the kitchen stove for cooking only meat, so why

MAKING KEBABS

Used as appetizers or main events, kebabs lend excitement to a meal. They're easy to make. Many cooks load the skewers before guests arrive, then put them on the grill for quick cooking. To prevent food from twisting as you turn the kebabs, use flat metal skewers or position 2 skewers parallel to each other and thread food onto both at the same time.

If you're using wooden skewers, presoak the skewers in water for 30 minutes before threading food onto them so that they don't catch fire. Since it's counterproductive to have the wood dry out before the skewers hit the grill, cook the food immediately.

Cut all ingredients to roughly the same size. For instance, slice zucchini about ½″ thick, cut peppers into uniform cubes, divide onions into wedges, keep small mushrooms whole and cut meat or poultry into 1″ to 1½″ cubes.

Slide the ingredients onto the points of 2 side-by-side skewers. Quick-cooking items, like vegetables, poultry and seafood, can be mixed on skewers. Put longer-cooking meats on separate skewers. With meat, especially, leave about ¼″ between pieces to ensure thorough cooking.

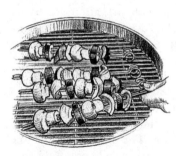

Place the skewers on the grill rack. Turn them often to prevent the food from burning.

Grilling

Is It GOOD for You?

Today's healthy grilling styles are a big improvement over the high-fat carnivorous feeds of yesteryear. But researchers say that there are still some risks linked to the grill.

When fat from meats drips on hot coals, it releases molecules called polyaromatic hydrocarbons, which may increase the risk for cancer. The risk probably isn't very large, experts agree, but there are ways to trim it still more.

COOK BEFORE GRILLING. Microwaving meat before putting it on the grill reduces the grilling time and, with it, the release of potentially harmful compounds.

GRILL LIGHTLY. Raising the meat away from the heat gives the flavor of grilling while reducing the risks.

STICK WITH LEAN MEATS. The less fat there is to drip into the fire, the fewer smoky hydrocarbons will be produced.

TILT THE RACK. Reduce the likelihood of flare-ups by making sure that fat doesn't drip directly onto the hot coals.

USE A DRIP PAN. An alternative to tilting the rack is to position a foil pan or other pan directly under the food (among the coals).

limit your choices on the grill? Grilling vegetables causes their natural sugars to caramelize, creating a smoky, slightly sweet flavor that's hard to beat.

☞ Cutting vegetables into thin slices helps them grill evenly and quickly.

☞ When grilling thick, dense vegetables like turnips and potatoes, blanch or microwave them first. When they're almost tender, move them to the grill for final cooking.

"Grease" the grill. To prevent food from sticking, lightly spray the cold grill rack with no-stick spray. Or pour a little cooking oil onto a paper towel and rub it on before heating the grill.

FOODS FOR THE GRILL

One of the great things about grilling is that even inexperienced chefs can wield a backyard spatula with almost certain success. Grilling poultry, vegetables and seafood is somewhat more complicated than flipping burgers, but not by much. With a little practice, you can turn out fine low-fat meals every time.

Helpful Hint

When grilling, here's how to test the temperature of the coals. Place your hand 4" above the center coals. Count the number of seconds that the palm of your hand can withstand the heat before you have to remove your hand. For a hot temperature, that should be 2 seconds. For a medium-hot temperature, it should be 3 seconds. Medium heat would be 4 seconds, and low would be 5 seconds.

Bastes and Marinades

The high, dry heat used in grilling means that most meats and vegetables benefit from basting or marinating.

Basting means brushing liquid or sauce on food while it grills to keep it moist. Marinating involves soaking food in a paste or liquid before grilling. The soaking time can be as little as 15 minutes or as long as 48 hours. Delicate foods like fish generally require a brief marinating time, whereas red meats may need more.

☞ When using bastes that include honey or sugar, put them on toward the end of grilling to prevent the sugars from burning.

☞ Don't add salt to bastes or marinades, as it draws moisture out of the food and makes it dry and tough.

☞ Meat and poultry can safely marinate at room temperature for up to 30 minutes. In the refrigerator, they can marinate for up to 48 hours.

☞ Meat can be marinated in a large deep-sided pan. Or you can put it in a large leak-proof bag. In either case, turn it (the food or the bag) several times to distribute the marinade.

Grilling Poultry

Whether you're preparing a boneless breast or roasting a whole bird, poultry's mild flavor and tender texture make it a natural for the grill. Chicken and turkey readily absorb the grill's smoky flavors. They're also quite forgiving: Small errors in seasonings or cooking time (as long as the meat is not undercooked) probably won't be noticed.

Helpful Hint

When making low-fat marinades, replace the oil with fat-free broth or vegetable juice. Add citrus juice or grated lemon peel for zip.

Warm it up. Before cooking chicken or turkey on the grill, let it stand at room temperature for 15 minutes. This removes the chill and helps it cook quickly and evenly.

Cook before grilling. Unless you're grilling thin strips of poultry, it's helpful to precook it—by poaching, baking or microwaving—before moving it to the grill. This helps ensure that the inside will be done as soon as the outside is properly seared.

Grill with the skin on. Leaving the skin on during grilling essentially makes each piece self-basting. Although the skin is the fattiest part of the bird, little fat is absorbed during cooking. When grilling is done, remove and discard the skin before serving.

Use cooler coals. When chicken is cooked on an open grill, drips from the skin often cause flare-ups that can burn the meat and cause a slightly greasy off flavor. To reduce flaming, put chicken on the grate after the coals have cooled somewhat. In addition, it's helpful to cook chicken as far above the coals as your grill will allow.

Cover it up. Another way to prevent drips from flaming is to cook poultry on a covered grill. The enclosed space reduces the air supply, which in turn helps prevent the fat from flaring.

Check for doneness. When cooking bone-in chicken pieces, place them on the grill, skin side down, for about 15 minutes. Then turn it and grill for another 15 to 20 minutes. When you think that the pieces are done, insert a sharp knife into the thickest piece next to the bone. The meat is done when the juices run clear.

☞ When cooking whole birds, put a drip pan underneath to collect drippings. (The charcoal is arranged around the outside of the drip pan. This indirect heat method allows large pieces of food to cook slowly.) Grill the bird, covered and with the breast down, for about 20 minutes, basting several times. Then turn the breast up and finish cooking—usually for about 15 minutes per pound. The bird is done when a

Helpful Hint

When grilling thick meats, like bone-in chicken or London broil, precook them in the microwave to ensure that they cook all the way through, while still absorbing the grill's smoky flavor. For food safety reasons, take the food directly from the microwave to the grill; don't let partially cooked meats stand.

meat thermometer inserted in the thigh but not touching bone reads 185°. Breast meat (away from the bone) should read 175°.

Grilling Fish

Firm-fleshed fish are quick to cook and among the most delicious of grill foods. It isn't difficult to grill fish, but you do have to stay alert; a minute or two (whether over or under) can make a huge difference in how it turns out.

Prepare the grill. To prevent fish from sticking, it's important to start with an impeccably clean grill. Lightly oil the grate before turning on the heat.

Get it hot. Putting fish on a cold grill will cause it to stick. Always bring the grill to cooking heat before putting on the fish.

Handle it lightly. The same flaky texture that makes fish so delicious can also spell disaster should it flake into pieces and fall into the fire. You want to handle fish as little as possible during grilling. Let it cook until one side is done, then turn and cook the other side. Turning fish more than once is tempting fate.

Test for doneness. When you think the fish is done, poke through the layers to inspect the inside. Properly cooked fish should be opaque. If it's slightly translucent, let it cook for a minute or two more, then check it again. Fish continues cooking even after it's removed from the heat, so don't leave it on the grill too long.

Grilling Seafood

It's not only fish that goes great on the grill. Lobster, shrimp and scallops make elegant treats that cook quickly and easily, taking on a smoky nuance that enhances their naturally fresh flavors.

Make it fresh. When grilling whole lobster, fresh is superior to frozen. Split it lengthwise and remove the innards. With the split side down, grill for about 6 minutes over a medium-hot fire. Then turn and cook for 4 to 8 minutes more, depending on size.

After the lobster is done, remove it from the heat. Separate the claws and return them to the grill. They require an extra 3 to 5 minutes to be properly cooked.

Avoid shrimpy shrimp. To enjoy the best flavor and texture from grilled shrimp, buy the large kind—31 to 40 shrimp per pound.

☞ A grill basket sandwiches shrimp (or other small grill foods) between screens, making it easy to turn them and preventing them from falling into the fire.

☞ When peeling shrimp before cooking, leave the tail shell intact. That makes it easier to grab the shrimp when it's time to eat.

(continued on page 78)

Helpful Hint

To prevent shrimp or small vegetables from falling through the bars, line the grill with foil, then poke holes in the foil at about half-inch intervals. An alternative is to go to a kitchen supply store and buy a piece of food-safe metal mesh or a grill basket for cooking small items.

GRILLING CHICKEN AND FISH

For combining great taste with minimal fat, you can't beat grilled foods. The following recipes illustrate basic grilling methods for two popular grilled foods: chicken and fish. For each dish, prepare the grill by coating the unheated grill rack with no-stick spray. Then light the grill according to the manufacturer's directions. Place the rack on the grill to preheat it.

When outdoor grilling isn't an option, each recipe can also be prepared under a preheated broiler instead of on the grill.

Zesty Barbecued Chicken Breasts QUICK!

- ¼ cup chili sauce
- 2 tablespoons reduced-sodium ketchup
- 1 tablespoon honey
- 1 tablespoon red-wine vinegar
- 1 teaspoon ground ginger
- 1 teaspoon Dijon mustard
- ¾ teaspoon ground black pepper
- ¼ teaspoon garlic powder
- ¼ teaspoon ground red pepper
- 4 boneless, skinless chicken breast halves (1 pound)

Grill the chicken about 4″ from the heat for 5 minutes. Turn, brush with the sauce and grill for 5 to 10 minutes, or until the chicken is no longer pink inside (test with a sharp knife). Brush the other side with the remaining sauce before serving.

In a small saucepan, combine the chili sauce, ketchup, honey, vinegar, ginger, mustard, black pepper, garlic powder and red pepper. Bring to a boil over medium heat. Remove from the heat and set aside.

Makes 4 servings. Per serving: 180 calories, 3.1 g. fat (16% of calories), 25.9 g. protein, 11.3 g. carbohydrates, 0.3 g. dietary fiber, 69 mg. cholesterol, 280 mg. sodium.

NOTE

• Because the sauce is brushed onto *cooked* chicken only, not raw chicken, it can be served at the table without bringing it to a boil again. If the sauce had been used on raw meat, you would either discard any that was left or bring it to a full boil before using, to kill any bacteria that might have been picked up from the uncooked poultry.

Grilled Tuna Steaks
with Chive and Dill Sauce *QUICK!*

⅔ cup defatted chicken broth

1 tablespoon finely minced fresh chives

1 tablespoon finely minced fresh dill or 1 teaspoon dried

1 teaspoon coarse-grain mustard

1 tablespoon olive oil

4 tuna steaks (about 5 ounces each)

In a large no-stick skillet, combine the broth, chives, dill and mustard. Bring to a boil over high heat, whisking frequently. Continue to boil and whisk for about 3 minutes, or until the sauce has been reduced to half its volume. Transfer the skillet to the side of the grill rack to keep the sauce warm.

Rub the oil over the surface of each steak. Then grill about 5½" from the heat for 4 to 5 minutes per side, or until the fish is opaque throughout (test with a sharp knife).

Remove from the grill, then drizzle the sauce equally over the tuna. Serve warm.

Makes 4 servings. Per serving: 184 calories, 4.8 g. fat (24% of calories), 33.1 g. protein, 0.3 g. carbohydrates, 0 g. dietary fiber, 62 mg. cholesterol, 124 mg. sodium

NOTES

• Using a large skillet to boil down the sauce gives lots of surface area, which cuts the time needed to evaporate excess liquid.

• This recipe works well with most any fish steak, such as swordfish or salmon.

☞ Shrimp cook very quickly; put them over medium heat for only 3 to 5 minutes.

Learn the shell game. When grilling clams, mussels or oysters, place them directly on the grill. If you look carefully, you'll notice that most shells have one half that's deeper than the other. Position the deeper half on the bottom; it will serve as a reservoir for juices. Cover and cook until the shells start opening, usually about 6 to 10 minutes.

Grilling Fruits and Vegetables

In many parts of the country, fruits and vegetables are increasingly appearing on the grill, not only at upscale restaurants but at backyard barbecues as well.

Cook them quickly. Don't overly char fruits and vegetables; this gives them an off flavor. Instead, grill them quickly, usually for about 2 to 5 minutes per side, or until grill marks first appear.

Cook them warm. For quick, even cooking, don't bring vegetables or fruit straight from the refrigerator to the grill. Let them warm to room temperature first.

Turn down the heat. Fruits and vegetables hold heat well and continue to cook after being removed from the grill. To prevent them from being overdone, remove them from the heat when they're just slightly undercooked. If you're not serving them immediately, spread them in a single layer on a tray for rapid cooling.

Add some smoke. Hardwood chips, dried herbs or citrus rinds added to the coals or lava rocks give a delicate smoky flavor that complements most fruits and vegetables.

If you're using smoke chips, be sure to close the lid in order to get the most intense flavoring.

GRILLING CORN

You don't need meat as an excuse to fire up the grill. Reach for corn on the cob instead. It's fast and easy to make and has a deliciously smoky flavor all its own. Plus, it comes ready-packed in its own wrapping.

Pull the husks halfway down and remove the silk. Pull the husks back up over the cob.

Tie the ends shut with twine or long, thin pieces of husk. Soak the ears in cold water for at least 30 minutes.

Grill for about 20 minutes, turning often.

Christopher Gross

At his four restaurants in Phoenix—Christopher's, Christopher's Bistro, Christopher's Cellar, and Arizona Cafe and Grill—chef and owner Christopher Gross has elevated grilling to an art form. And not only for fish, poultry and meat dishes but for many vegetable recipes as well.

The following recipe is simple and full of flavor. You can make the herb marinade and the roasted tomatoes the day before (roast the tomatoes in your oven overnight; warm them in a pan over your grill or in the oven before serving).

Grill the steaks over a hot fire to sear the outside and keep the inside medium-rare. Cooking time will depend on the thickness of your steaks. Allow the meat to rest for a few minutes before slicing to redistribute the juices.

Gross serves this dish with grilled corn or grilled peppers and squash.

Sirloin Steaks with Fresh Herb Marinade

Roasted Tomatoes
- 8 plum tomatoes, halved lengthwise
  Salt and ground black pepper

Herb-Marinated Steaks
- 4 cloves garlic, minced
- 5 basil leaves, finely chopped
- 2 tablespoons chopped fresh rosemary
- 2 teaspoons chopped fresh thyme
  Pinch of salt
  Pinch of ground black pepper
- 4 sirloin steaks (6 ounces each)
- 2 teaspoons olive oil

Garnish
- ½ cup chopped shallots
- 2 teaspoons olive oil

To make the roasted tomatoes: Preheat the oven to 225°.

Sprinkle the tomatoes very lightly with the salt and pepper. Place, cut side down, on a no-stick baking sheet. Place in the oven and allow to roast for 6 to 7 hours. Remove from the oven and set aside.

To make the herb-marinated steaks: In a small bowl, combine the garlic, basil, rosemary, thyme, salt and pepper.

Brush both sides of each steak with the oil. Sprinkle the herb mixture on both sides of each steak. Place the steaks on a platter, cover with plastic wrap and refrigerate for at least 2 hours.

Cook the steaks on a hot grill for 3 to 4 minutes on each side (for medium-rare), or until the desired degree of doneness is reached.

To make the garnish: In a medium no-stick skillet over medium heat, sauté the shallots in the oil for 2 to 3 minutes, or until lightly browned.

If needed, rewarm the tomatoes. Top each steak with equal amounts of the shallots and tomatoes.

Makes 4 servings. Per serving: 323 calories, 12.9 g. fat (36% of calories), 36.1 g. protein, 16.3 g. carbohydrates, 3.3 g. dietary fiber, 97 mg. cholesterol, 98 mg. sodium

Fresh
Beginnings

Salads

A bowl of leafy greens and crisp raw vegetables is one of life's finest and simplest pleasures. A well-tossed salad coated with a tangy dressing stimulates and cleanses the palate and nourishes the appetite. A garden salad is also a powerhouse of nutrients, teeming with vitamins, minerals and fiber. For your taste buds and your health, a salad day is a happy day.

Today's salads are much more vibrant and lively than yesteryear's bland and dowdy offerings of iceberg lettuce and gooey dressings. There is a wide and growing selection of leafy salad greens, including red- and green-leaf lettuce, Romaine, curly endive, exotic mizuma, tender oak leaf, radicchio, spinach and a bounty of others. Crisp leaves with colors ranging from ruby red and purple to every shade of green are appearing in supermarkets, farmers markets and gardens across the country.

Salad garnishes and dressings have also moved in a healthier, tastier direction. Tossed salads are no longer embellished with a meager slice of cucumber and a cherry tomato. An abundance of bright, nutrient-rich raw vegetables are filling up salad bowls. Easy-to-prepare light vinaigrettes are enhancing salads with enticing flavors; traditional high-sugar, high-fat, turbo-caloried salad dressings are relics of the past.

BUYING AND PREPARING GREENS

Since leafy greens and lettuces form the foundation of the garden salad, it's critical that they be crisp, clean and at the peak of freshness.

☞ Look for leafy greens that are crisp and bright-looking. Avoid those with torn or discolored leaves or those that are limp and wilted.

☞ Before storing, remove and discard discolored or damaged leaves. Remove the core with a twist of your hand or slice it with a knife. Trim off any fibrous stems.

☞ Excess water can hasten decay, so dry greens well if they're wet.

☞ Wrapping greens in a paper towel and storing them in a perforated plastic bag will help lock natural moisture in and keep greens fresh for several days in the refrigerator. For best results, remove excess air from the bag before sealing.

☞ Greens have numerous nooks and crevices that are natural traps for grit. Before using, place greens in a colander and rinse under cold running water, turning the leaves often.

☞ For greens that are exceptionally sandy, fill the sink partway with cold water. Add the greens and gently swish them around, allowing the grit to fall to the bottom of the sink. Gently

Helpful Hint

To remove the core of head lettuces such as iceberg, slam the "knob" on a cutting board or counter. This will knock it loose so that it pops right out.

LEAFY GREENS

Rich in beta-carotene and other healthful compounds, leafy greens can help protect against cancer, circulatory diseases and many problems linked to aging. As to which greens are the best, a simple, if imperfect, rule is this: The harder they are to pronounce and the more they cost, the better they taste.

GREEN	APPEARANCE	TASTE
Arugula (roquette)	Long, medium-green, sometimes scalloped leaves	Aggressive peppery taste
Beet	Reddish stems with tender leaves	Mild cabbage flavor
Belgian endive	Tight, elongated head with blanched white to pale yellow-green leaves	Slightly bitter flavor
Chard	Narrow, fan-shaped loose green leaf, with white or red veins and stems	Tastes slightly of mustard
Chicory	Bushy, frizzy head made of thick, crisp, narrow leaves with curly, frilly edges	Ranges from slightly bitter when young to extremely bitter when old
Collard greens	Large, smooth, silvery green leaves	Tastes like a cross between spinach and watercress
Dandelion	Jagged, medium-green leaves	Young leaves have a pleasant, slightly bitter flavor; older leaves are more pungent
Escarole	Broad, curly-edged, dark green leaves with pale, yellowish heart	Bitter flavor
Kale	Very curly, dark green, coarse leaves with frilly edges	Fresh, grassy flavor
Lettuce, butterhead	Small, round, loosely formed head of soft leaves	Buttery, slightly sweet flavor
Lettuce, loose leaf	Curly, loose, coarse leaves	Mild flavor
Lettuce, oak leaf	Narrow leaves with rounded edges in an oak-leaf pattern; in red and green	Extremely mild flavor with just a hint of sweetness
Lettuce, red leaf	Red tinged, large, loose leaves	Delicate flavor
Lettuce, romaine	Elongated head with large, medium to dark green leaves that branch out from a white base	Mild, sweet, nutty flavor
Mizuma (mizuna)	Light green, lacy leaves	Mildly bitter, with a slight mustard taste
Radicchio	Red, cabbagelike leaves	Sweetly bitter flavor
Sorrel	Bright green, tongue-shaped leaves	Sour flavor
Spinach	Dark green, tender leaves	Mild but musky flavor
Watercress	Dark green, dime-size glossy leaves	Spicy, peppery flavor

DRY THEM FAST

Thoroughly drying salad greens before you add dressing will help the dressing cling better, so that it doesn't slide off and slip to the bottom of the bowl. Salad spinners use centrifugal force to remove moisture.

After rinsing the leaves under running water, transfer them to the spinner basket. A few turns of the handle (or, in some models, pulls of the string) will spin the basket, shaking off the moisture.

shake off the leaves as you scoop them from the water.

☞ After washing, pat the leaves dry with paper towels or spin them dry in a salad spinner.

BEYOND LETTUCE

Today's healthy cooks want new and vibrant salads that use not only a variety of greens but also ingredients like pasta, fish, chicken and legumes. These salads can stand alone as hearty entrées.

The next time you have a taste for something fresh, bold and only partly green, here are some wonderfully simple—and wonderfully delicious—recipes to try. (See page 88 for a vinaigrette recipe that you can use as a basis for other vinaigrettes.)

☞ **Santa Fe salad.** Garnish greens of your choice with black beans, corn kernels, avocado slices, jícama slices and salsa. Dress with a cilantro-lime vinaigrette and serve with a flour tortilla. Add a bit of grilled chicken and call it a fajita salad.

☞ **Salad Caribe.** Toss greens with kidney beans and chopped cucumbers; garnish with slices of mango, kiwifruit and starfruit. Dress with a papaya vinaigrette.

☞ **Mediterranean salad.** Toss greens with endive and arugula; garnish with black olives, chick-peas and cherry tomatoes. Dress with a garlic-herb vinaigrette.

☞ **Farmers-market bowl.** Toss red oak leaf, radicchio, frisée and butterhead lettuce with

MIX AND MATCH

With so many wonderful greens to choose from, why limit your salads to just one? By combining a variety of greens, you can enjoy harmonious salads with diverse tastes and textures. Great combinations include:

☞ Romaine lettuce, curly endive and oak-leaf lettuce

☞ Spinach, green-leaf lettuce, arugula and radicchio

☞ Red-leaf lettuce, frisée, mizuma and watercress

☞ Endive, butterhead lettuce and arugula

☞ Chard, watercress, butterhead lettuce and green-leaf lettuce

☞ Romaine lettuce, spinach and red chard

shredded beets, shredded carrots, sliced yellow tomatoes and peas. Dress with a garlic vinaigrette.

☞ **Fire and spice.** Mix arugula, watercress, endive and red-leaf lettuce. Toss in slices of grilled eggplant, peppers and zucchini. Garnish with guacamole. Dress with a chili-infused vinaigrette.

☞ **Warm wilted salad.** Heat the dressing of your choice and drizzle it over greens just seconds before serving. Sturdy, assertive greens—such as curly endive, escarole, spinach and young chard—make the best wilted salads.

BEAN SALADS

Although legumes are perhaps best known for the hearty soups and stews that they inspire, their culinary potential also extends to the salad bowl. They can be used solo or combined with vegetables, pasta or salad greens.

☞ Always rinse and drain canned beans before using. When possible, use products that are low in sodium and don't have added sugar.

☞ For a light bean salad, combine two or more kinds of beans (cooked or canned) with a mixture of raw vegetables, like cucumbers, tomatoes, peppers and scallions. Dress with a vinaigrette or citrus dressing, let marinate for 30 minutes and serve.

☞ To make a spicy three-bean salad, combine black beans, kidney beans and chickpeas with minced garlic, chili peppers, lime juice, a little canola oil and seasoning to taste.

☞ Another way to give the traditional three-bean salad a makeover is to use a mixture of exotic beans, like anasazi, adzuki or green lentils.

☞ You can make a nourishing legume-and-grain salad by combining beans or lentils with a grain, like cooked rice, barley, couscous or quinoa. Add garden vegetables and toss with a vinaigrette dressing. You can also add strips of poached chicken breast or shrimp for extra protein.

☞ Remember that legumes come in fresh varieties as well as dried. Fresh snow peas and

PREPARING PEAS

Although some tasty peas come off the vine ready to eat, most have a tough, fibrous string that should be removed before cooking.

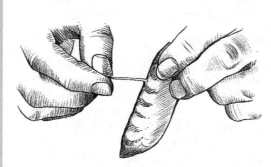

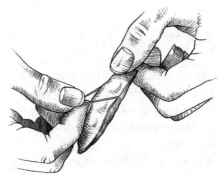

When preparing snow peas, break off the stem and slowly "zip" the string down the thicker side.

Snap peas have fibrous strings on both sides and need double stringing. Break the stem end, then pull it down the length of the pod to remove both strings at once.

snap peas are excellent legume-family additions to salads. Use them raw, lightly blanched or cooked.

GREAT GARNISHES

Like an artist's canvas, a bowl of greens is ready for the cook's embellishments, adornments and signature touches. From the basic accompaniment of tomatoes, cucumbers and other garden-variety vegetables to more exotic offerings, there is an enormous selection of appealing garnishes to choose from. Let your imagination—and taste buds—be your guide.

Vegetable Basics

If lettuce and other greens are a salad's blank canvas, then garden vegetables are the primary colors. When planning your salad, here are some points to consider.

☞ Choose tomatoes with a rich red color. Remove the cores and slice the flesh into wedges. Cut large cherry tomatoes in half.

☞ Carrots provide in beta-carotene, fiber and crunch as well as extra-vivid color. Carrots for salads can be grated or cut into thin strips or slices.

☞ Cucumbers that are waxed must be peeled before using.

Helpful Hint

To tenderize and brighten salad vegetables, plunge them into boiling water for a minute or two, then quickly chill them under running water. This process, called blanching, works especially well for green vegetables, such as broccoli, asparagus and snap peas.

☞ Thinly sliced red onion adds a sharp tang to salads. If onions are cut too thick, however, your palate may be overpowered.

☞ Sliced fresh mushrooms have an earthy, woodsy flavor. Choose mushrooms with dry flesh.

☞ All bell peppers are a good and colorful choice, but the red ones are especially high in beta-carotene. Be sure to remove the white membrane inside, which can impart a bitter taste.

Fruitful Favorites

Today's healthful salad isn't limited to the vegetable bin. Fresh fruits are often added to leafy greens—and not just as attractive garnishes.

☞ Apples, pears, nectarines and peaches can be sliced or diced and added to salads at the last minute (they'll discolor if they're added too far ahead).

☞ If cut apples or pears are not going to be used immediately, store them in cold water that's been acidulated with a little lemon or lime juice to retard browning.

☞ Raspberries, blueberries and strawberries are often added to salads for a refreshing taste of summer.

☞ Tropical fruits, such as kiwifruit, mango, papaya, starfruit and pineapple, add a wonderful tang to salads. Arranging them around the perimeter of the salad is an easy way to create an attractive centerpiece for the table.

Pantry Pleasers

When it comes to salads, fresh is best—most of the time. Particularly in mid-winter, when the selection at the greengrocer's is somewhat limited, the pantry offers a collection of staples that can add substance and variety to salads.

☞ Raisins or chopped dates, apricots, figs and other dried fruit give an interesting twist to both salads and dressings.

☞ Nuts add pleasant crunchiness to the salad bowl. Sesame seeds, poppy seeds, pumpkin seeds and sunflower seeds are also

SPRUCE UP YOUR SALAD

A vegetable garnish adds an exciting splash of color and style to a salad. Here are two whimsical shapes that are easy to make.

OLIVE RABBITS

Cut a slice lengthwise from a large unpitted green or black olive.

Carve a small triangle from the slice and discard it. The remaining piece is the "ears."

Position the olive, cut side down, and make an incision across the olive near one end. Twist the blade to open the cut, then insert the ears.

CARROT FLOWERS

Using a thick, peeled carrot, cut petals in the sides all around (there is usually room for about four).

Rock the tip back and forth to separate it from the remaining carrot.

Insert a caper or a piece of olive in the middle to give the "flower" a colorful center.

good choices. (You might want to go a little easy, though, since nuts and seeds do contain quite a bit of fat.)

☞ Tofu, which is high in protein, is a nutritious addition to salads. It can be used raw or lightly brushed with oil or marinade and roasted on the grill.

Artful Accessories

It's easy to turn a basic salad arrangement into an artistic and healthful fashion plate. The range of ingredients is limited only by your imagination—and, of course, the time of the year.

☞ Asparagus needn't be cooked to be included in a salad. You can blanch the spears by boiling them for a minute or two and refreshing them in a colander under cold running water.

☞ Fresh uncooked beets have a crisp texture and delicate flavor, making an impressive salad garnish. Simply scrub, peel and shred them.

☞ Adding thin strips or rings of bell pepper is an easy way to add color to salads. Red, yellow and orange peppers are slightly sweeter than green ones. Roasting peppers ahead of time brings out a smoky nuance and a sweeter flavor.

☞ Broccoli and cauliflower can be cut into florets and added raw. You can also blanch or steam them to temper their texture and flavor.

☞ Corn kernels add a splash of yellow. Blanch or steam them before adding. You can use fresh or frozen corn.

☞ Green peas lend a colorful touch. Blanch or steam them before adding. Use fresh or frozen peas; avoid canned peas, which are really too soft for salads and usually have more added sodium than frozen peas.

☞ Jícama has a crisp, cream-colored flesh that tastes like water chestnuts, only sweeter.

☞ Sprouts add valuable nutrients and fresh, grassy flavors to salads. Look for dry, light sprouts with a springy texture. You can use sprouted beans as well as seeds like alfalfa, radish and wheat.

☞ Radishes add a sharp, peppery taste and crisp texture to salads. Slice thinly or shred before using. Don't stop with the familiar little red ones, either; try icicle, daikon and black radishes.

THE PERFECT VINAIGRETTE

Selecting the proper dressing is the final stage in the quest for the perfect salad. All too often, however, it's also the time when even the healthiest intentions go awry.

Be choosy when selecting store-bought dressings; even a "healthy" product labeled "fat-free" could be loaded with sugar and salt. Besides, it's so easy to make your own vinaigrette, a pleasant union of oil and vinegar. The tartness of the vinegar balances the smooth nature of the oil, and a mellow mustard acts as an emulsifier to bind it all together.

It's best to use oils like canola, olive, safflower or sunflower, which are high in polyunsaturated and monounsaturated fats and low in saturated fats. You'll also need garlic, mustard and herbs like oregano, thyme and parsley. You may also want to add a touch of honey or sugar for a hint of sweetness.

☞ In a screw-top jar or a cruet, mix two parts oil to one part vinegar. This ratio isn't a magic number; all chefs have their own favorites. Don't be afraid to alter the amounts of vinegar and oil until you find the taste that's right for you.

☞ Add garlic, mustard and the herbs and spices of your choice and adjust the seasoning to your taste. Shake vigorously for a few seconds just before using.

Vinaigrettes store well when refrigerated and kept in sealed containers. In fact, they pick up a deeper character as the flavors are allowed to meld together. Vinaigrettes will keep for several weeks in the refrigerator. Be sure to whisk or shake well before serving.

Olive Oil

Is It Good for You?

Not since Popeye have people paid so much attention to olive oil. Many experts believe that this aromatic oil is a key factor in the low heart disease rate in the Mediterranean, and studies suggest that it may have a favorable impact on breast cancer rates as well.

Yet olive oil—which admittedly adds great flavor to any cuisine—is still 100 percent fat. One tablespoon contains 119 calories—about as much as in a slice of pound cake. And when you consider that some recipes use ¼ cup or more of the stuff, you can see how, in one form or another, the oil tends to stick around.

Experts agree that olive oil is a great substitute for butter, margarine or other products high in saturated fats. However, it should be used in moderation—instead of other fats and not in addition to them.

LOW-FAT DRESSINGS

More and more healthy cooks, in trying to cut the amount of fat that they use in the kitchen, have set their sights on salads. Why use mega-oil dressings, they argue, when there are so many healthier, good-tasting alternatives? Even if you do use a traditional dressing, there are ways to keep the fat content low.

Call on citrus. Whether added to vinaigrettes or squeezed directly on salad, juice from lemons, limes or oranges adds a delightful tang without adding fat.

Turn on the juicer. You can make a wonderfully fresh, low-fat dressing by combining freshly pressed juice, like apple juice, with vinegar or lemon juice, a hint of oil and chopped fresh herbs.

Bring out the buttermilk. Despite its name, buttermilk is low in fat and makes a healthful alternative to milk, cream and mayonnaise in creamy dressings. When buying buttermilk, double-check the label; some brands are lower in fat than others.

Try cottage cheese. When pureed and combined with herbs and spices, it makes a smooth and creamy low-fat dressing.

Add some culture. Yogurt, either low-fat or nonfat, can be used as a healthful replacement for regular mayonnaise or sour cream. It offers a luscious mouthfeel, and its innate mellow tanginess is easily flavored with herbs, spices and other aromatics.

Put it on the side. Rather than putting dressing directly on your salad, put it on the side of the plate. Then dip your fork into the dressing before picking up a biteful of salad. Moistening the fork gives the greens enough flavor without overpowering your taste buds or your waistline.

SALAD HERBS

A few sprigs of fresh herbs spruce up a salad with refreshing, vibrant flavors. Plus, using fresh herbs means that you can use less salt or other fatty add-ons, like cheese or bacon bits.

You can use fresh herbs whole or coarsely chopped and add them to your dressing. One classic blend is fines herbes—a mixture of tarragon, chervil and parsley. Other favored salad herbs include the following.

VINEGAR VARIETIES

A prized commodity in the healthy kitchen, vinegars bring sharp, clean flavors to the salad bowl while contributing zero fat. There are many vinegars to choose from, ranging from inexpensive jug-wine vinegars to extremely expensive imports. Which ones you choose depends entirely on your own preferences. Here are some selections.

☞ **Balsamic.** An aged, low-acid vinegar, its deep color and rich flavor lend a sophisticated touch to salads.

☞ **Cider.** This is a fruity, tart vinegar with a strong apple presence.

☞ **Champagne.** This smooth, mildly flavored vinegar has a hint of champagne.

☞ **Flavored.** Steeped with ingredients ranging from raspberries and other berries to various herbs, such as tarragon or dill, to hot chili peppers, this is often used in conjunction with "neutral" vinegars to add just a hint of extra taste.

☞ **Red wine.** This vinegar has a mellow tartness and medium body that work well with vinaigrettes. It can be combined with balsamic vinegar for a flavorful nuance.

☞ **Rice.** This has a mild, almost sweet flavor and is often used in Asian salads.

☞ **Sherry.** A mild vinegar, it has an undertone of dry sherry.

☞ **White wine.** This mildly flavored vinegar has a hint of white wine.

☞ **Basil.** A potent, summery leaf with a hint of anise and mint. Coarsely chop and add to dressings. Or add a few sprigs' worth of whole leaves to the salad itself.

☞ **Chervil.** A mildly flavored, anise-scented herb with a hint of parsley. Coarsely chop or use whole leaves.

☞ **Chives.** Delicate, thin herbal strands with a hint of scallion and onion. Chive blossoms make a brilliant salad garnish and have a strong onion flavor.

☞ **Dill.** A feathery herb with a distinctive flavor. It's best chopped and added to dressing.

☞ **Marjoram.** A fragrant herb similar to oregano, with a slight resin flavor.

☞ Mint. Ideal for light, fruity dressings and salads.

☞ **Oregano.** A mild resin flavor similar to marjoram. For a well-balanced and fragrant herb blend, combine oregano with basil, parsley and thyme.

☞ **Parsley.** An all-purpose herb with a rewarding springtime flavor. Italian, or flat-leaf, parsley is slightly sweeter than the more common curly variety.

☞ **Sorrel.** Lemon-scented leaves that can be tossed whole into a salad. Like arugula, they add a pleasantly bitter taste.

☞ **Tarragon.** A European herb with a distinctive aniselike flavor.

☞ **Thyme.** A pungent, earthy flavor that gets stronger over time. Add to dressings ahead of time and allow to marinate.

MAKING CROUTONS

Homemade croutons are easy and economical to make and are vastly superior to the rock-hard, stucco-textured versions sold in stores. Croutons add substance and crunchiness and can be made ahead of time. Here's how.

☞**Get the right bread.** Forget about using puffy white bread; it absorbs too much oil. Choose a firm-textured whole-grain bread. Day-old bread actually works better than fresh, as it's slightly hard and holds its shape during cooking.

☞ **Cut it into cubes**. After trimming the crusty edges, cut the bread into $\frac{1}{2}''$ cubes.

☞ **Prepare the oil**. Heat a large no-stick skillet and coat it with a small amount of olive oil. Add a few slivered garlic cloves and cook for a few minutes over medium heat until the cloves are lightly browned.

☞ **Start cooking**. Add the bread cubes to the skillet in a single layer (don't overfill it) and sauté them until the cubes turn light brown. Stir the bread cubes and shake the pan frequently during cooking. Remove the garlic if it begins to burn.

☞ **Set the bread aside**. After the croutons are done, transfer them to a platter lined with a paper towel. Pat dry. Let the croutons cool to room temperature before tossing into a salad.

Creative Croutons

Croutons traditionally are plain, but you can also spruce them up so that they add a little bite to your salads. Here are some possibilities.

Open the oven. Instead of sautéing bread cubes for croutons in a skillet, broil or bake them in the oven and flavor them with herbs. Lightly mist the cubes with no-stick spray and toss with a mixture of dried herbs or spices, like oregano, basil and parsley. Arrange on a no-stick baking sheet and bake or broil until lightly toasted.

Add some spice. When sautéing bread cubes, add a jalapeño or serrano pepper, halved and seeded, to the pan along with the garlic. Sprinkle a little hot-pepper sauce or ground red pepper over the croutons as they cook. Remember to use plastic gloves when handling hot peppers.

Try a taste of Asia. Adding slivers of fresh ginger along with the garlic creates croutons with an intriguing sweet-spicy taste. For more Asian flavor, add some chopped fresh cilantro.

Create a corn flavor. Rather than using wheat bread, make croutons with day-old cornbread.

Make it hearty. Firm, dark breads like rye and pumpernickel make the perfect croutons for heartier salads.

MAIN-DISH SALADS

While most of us grew up with salads on the sidelines, more and more healthy cooks are turning salads into nutritious main dishes. The next time you have a taste for something fresh and hearty, dress a platter of tossed greens with a light vinaigrette. Garnish with plenty of seasonal vegetables and voilà! An inviting dinner is born.

Really, the main thing that distinguishes a main-dish salad from a supporting player is the topping (and, of course, the size of the serving). Adding nutritious, filling ingredients guarantees that no one will leave the table hungry. Here are some suggestions.

☞ Strips of grilled or broiled boneless, skinless chicken breast add important protein to your salad without adding too much fat.

☞ Poached or grilled shellfish, such as shrimp and scallops, served hot or cold, transform the simplest serving of greens into a seafood delight.

☞ Strips of fresh, firm-textured grilled fish, such as swordfish, marlin or tuna, deliver refreshing flavor along with heart-healthy levels of omega-3 fatty acids.

☞ Thai-grilled beef (soy-marinated strips of lean meat) adds a slightly exotic, deliciously smoky taste.

☞ Extra-lean ground beef browned with taco seasoning turns an ordinary salad into a Mexican fiesta.

☞ Add cooked or canned beans like chick-peas or black beans for a richer-tasting salad that's full of fiber—not fat.

Frank Stitt

Mediterranean influences and southern grace form a winning combination at Frank Stitt's innovative Bottega in Birmingham, Alabama.

Along with pasta, pizza, risotto, seafood and game, Stitt specializes in creating truly innovative salads.

"Ingredients don't have to be expensive to be extraordinary," he says. "This recipe uses common field peas, which we get in their fresh form. We make a star out of something that usually plays a supporting role." Stitt usually recommends using fresh pinkeyes, crowders or tiny

leaf beans. In a pinch, however, frozen peas will work fine, he adds.

Stitt sometimes garnishes this special salad with okra, blanched green beans or thinly sliced country ham. And he often serves it with grilled cornbread or country sourdough bread.

Warm Field-Pea Salad

Salad

- 2 cups shelled field peas
- 1 Vidalia onion, finely chopped
- 1 carrot, finely chopped
- 1 stalk celery, finely chopped
- 1 clove garlic, crushed
  Sprig of fresh thyme
- 1 bay leaf
  Pinch of salt
- 1 dried red chili pepper
- 1 teaspoon extra-virgin olive oil

Tomato Vinaigrette

- 1 pound tomatoes, halved and seeded
- 2 teaspoons minced shallots
- 1½ teaspoons cider vinegar
- 1½ teaspoons balsamic vinegar
  Pinch of salt
  Pinch of ground black pepper
- 2 tablespoons extra-virgin olive oil
- 8 fresh basil leaves, shredded

To make the salad: Rinse the peas and discard any debris. Place in a medium saucepan. Add the onions, carrots, celery, garlic, thyme, bay leaf, salt and chili pepper. Cover by 2″ with cold water and bring to a boil over high heat. Reduce the heat to low and simmer for 20 to 25 minutes, or until the peas are tender. Skim any foam as it appears.

Drain the peas; discard the garlic, thyme, bay leaf and chili pepper. Toss the peas with the oil and set aside.

To make the tomato vinaigrette: Grill or broil the tomatoes, cut side up, until charred. Transfer to a food processor or blender. Add the shallots, cider vinegar, balsamic vinegar, salt and pepper. Process with on/off turns. With the machine running, slowly add the oil in a thin stream and blend until emulsified.

Mound the pea salad on salad plates. Drizzle with the vinaigrette and sprinkle with the basil.

Makes 4 servings. Per serving: 195 calories, 8.6 g. fat (38% of calories), 6.2 g. protein, 25.6 g. carbohydrates, 8.5 g. dietary fiber, 0 mg. cholesterol, 44 mg. sodium

Greek Salad

2 tomatoes, quartered
1 large cucumber, halved crosswise and sliced
2 sweet red peppers, diced
4 pickled peperoncini peppers, sliced into rings
2 tablespoons crumbled feta cheese
1 small sweet onion, sliced and separated into rings
1 tablespoon olive oil
⅓ cup lemon juice
1 tablespoon minced fresh oregano
1 clove garlic, crushed
4 slices Italian bread, toasted

In a medium bowl, gently toss together the tomatoes, cucumbers, red peppers, peperoncini peppers, feta and onions.

In a small bowl, whisk together the oil, lemon juice, oregano and garlic. Pour the dressing over the salad and toss gently. Serve with the bread.

Makes 4 servings. Per serving: 209 calories, 6.9 g. fat (28% of calories), 6.9 g. protein, 33.4 g. carbohydrates, 3.5 g. dietary fiber, 7 mg. cholesterol, 496 mg. sodium

NOTE

• For a richer flavor, add 12 whole or pitted kalamata olives to the salad. To pit kalamata olives, place the flat side of a sharp knife on an olive and press gently. This loosens the pit so that it can be removed easily.

Salade Niçoise

Salad
6 leaves Boston lettuce, torn
12 ounces green beans, steamed
4 small potatoes, cooked and sliced
2 plum tomatoes, sliced
2 hard-cooked egg whites, chopped
2 cans (6½ ounces each) water-packed tuna
4 scallions, thinly sliced
1 tablespoon capers

Basil Vinaigrette
1 tablespoon chopped fresh basil
1 tablespoon lemon juice
1 tablespoon red-wine vinegar
2 tablespoons Dijon mustard
2 tablespoons water
2½ teaspoons olive oil
½ teaspoon ground black pepper

To make the salad: In a large salad bowl, gently toss the lettuce, beans, potatoes, tomatoes, egg whites, tuna, scallions and capers. Cover and refrigerate for 20 minutes.

To make the basil vinaigrette: In a small bowl, whisk together the basil, lemon juice, vinegar, mustard, water, oil and pepper. Drizzle the dressing over the salad just before serving.

Makes 4 servings. Per serving: 282 calories, 4.6 g. fat (15% of calories), 29.8 g. protein, 31.5 g. carbohydrates, 1.3 g. dietary fiber, 27 mg. cholesterol, 532 mg. sodium

NOTES

• For extra flavor, rub a cut clove of garlic around the inside of the salad bowl before tossing the salad.

• Add ½ cup pitted and sliced black olives to the salad.

Caesar Salad

QUICK!

Caesar salad is notoriously high in fat. We reduced the fat and calories by using a light mayonnaise dressing and reducing the amount of olive oil used to sauté the bread. We also removed the standard raw egg because of concerns about salmonella.

1 tablespoon olive oil
1 small baguette, cut into ½" slices
½ teaspoon crushed dried rosemary
½ teaspoon onion powder
2 cloves garlic
2 anchovy fillets
¼ cup reduced-fat mayonnaise
¼ cup nonfat plain yogurt
2 tablespoons lemon juice
2 tablespoons Parmesan cheese
¼ teaspoon dry mustard
¼ teaspoon ground black pepper
6 cups torn romaine lettuce

Using a pastry brush, brush the oil onto the bread. Warm a large no-stick skillet over medium heat. Add the bread and sprinkle with the rosemary and onion powder. Sauté for 2 to 3 minutes on each side, or until golden. Transfer the bread to a wire rack and set aside.

In a food processor or blender, process the garlic and anchovies until smooth.

Add the mayonnaise, yogurt, lemon juice, Parmesan, mustard and pepper to the garlic-anchovy mixture, and process until combined. Refrigerate the dressing until ready to use.

Place the lettuce in a large bowl and toss it gently with the dressing. Serve with the baguette slices.

Makes 4 servings. Per serving: 142 calories, 9.2 g. fat (57% of calories), 5.1 g. protein, 10.5 g. carbohydrates, 1.6 g. dietary fiber, 9 mg. cholesterol, 223 mg. sodium

Roasted Vegetable Salad

1½ pounds small red potatoes, quartered
12 ounces green beans, cut into 1" pieces
2 sweet red peppers, thinly sliced
1 red onion, thinly sliced crosswise and separated into rings
½ cup defatted chicken broth
2 cloves garlic
2 tablespoons red-wine vinegar
1½ tablespoons olive oil
1 teaspoon crushed dried rosemary
¼ teaspoon ground black pepper
8 kalamata olives, pitted and sliced
1–2 tablespoons lemon juice

Preheat the oven to 425°.

Coat a 9" × 13" baking dish with no-stick spray. Add the potatoes, beans, red peppers, onions, broth and garlic. Mix well. Roast, stirring every 10 minutes, for 20 to 30 minutes, or until the vegetables are tender. Set aside.

Transfer the garlic to a small bowl and mash. Whisk in the vinegar, oil, rosemary and black pepper.

Place the vegetables in a large bowl. Add the dressing and olives. Toss to mix well. Sprinkle with the lemon juice just before serving. Serve warm or chilled.

Makes 4 servings. Per serving: 274 calories, 6.9 g. fat (21% of calories), 7.2 g. protein, 51 g. carbohydrates, 3.1 g. dietary fiber, 0 mg. cholesterol, 215 mg. sodium

Cobb Salad with Grilled Chicken

Tomato Dressing

6	tablespoons tomato juice
1½	tablespoons red-wine vinegar
2	teaspoons olive oil
½	teaspoon minced garlic
½	teaspoon Worcestershire sauce

Salad

4	boneless, skinless chicken breast halves
4	cups torn mixed lettuce
1	cucumber, thinly sliced
⅓	cup diced turkey bacon, cooked until crisp
2	tomatoes, cut into wedges
1½	tablespoons crumbled blue cheese (optional)

To make the tomato dressing: In a small bowl, whisk together the tomato juice, vinegar, oil, garlic and Worcestershire sauce.

To make the salad: Place the chicken in a glass baking dish and pour half of the dressing over the chicken, reserving the remaining dressing. Cover the dish and marinate the chicken in the refrigerator for 30 minutes.

Remove the chicken from the marinade; discard any marinade remaining in the dish.

Coat an unheated grill rack with no-stick spray. Light the grill according to the manufacturer's directions. Place the rack on the grill. Grill or broil the chicken for 5 to 8 minutes on each side, or until cooked through (test with a sharp knife). Slice into strips and set aside.

Toss the lettuce and cucumbers with the remaining dressing and place on a platter. Sprinkle with the turkey bacon, arrange the tomatoes around the edge and garnish with the blue cheese (if using). Place the chicken in the center of the salad.

Makes 4 servings. Per serving: 194 calories, 8 g. fat (36% of calories), 24 g. protein, 8.3 g. carbohydrates, 1.7 g. dietary fiber, 61 mg. cholesterol, 359 mg. sodium

VARIATION

Cobb Salad with Grilled Turkey: Replace the chicken with turkey breast tenders or cutlets.

Tricolor Pasta and Spinach Salad

QUICK!

4	cups cooked tricolor rotini
2	cups torn spinach
½	cup chopped scallions
2	tablespoons lemon juice
1	tablespoon red-wine vinegar
1	teaspoon olive oil
1	teaspoon Dijon mustard
1	clove garlic, minced
1	tablespoon chopped fresh basil

In a large bowl, combine the pasta, spinach and scallions.

In a small bowl, whisk together the lemon juice, vinegar, oil, mustard, garlic and basil. Pour the dressing over the salad and toss well.

Makes 4 servings. Per serving: 195 calories, 1.5 g. fat (7% of calories), 7.2 g. protein, 38.4 g. carbohydrates, 6.7 g. dietary fiber, 0 mg. cholesterol, 47 mg. sodium

NOTES

• To prevent pasta destined for salads from getting soggy, don't overcook it (it should still be slighty chewy in the center). Drain and run it under cold water to stop the cooking process. Toss with dressing to prevent the pasta from sticking together.

• If you prefer spinach on the softer side, blanch it in boiling water for 30 seconds, plunge it into ice water to stop the cooking process and coarsely chop before using.

• In a pinch, replace the lemon juice, vinegar and olive oil with ¼ cup fat-free Italian dressing.

Waldorf Salad

QUICK!

We lowered the fat in this classic salad by replacing the traditional mayonnaise dressing with a flavorful apple vinaigrette.

1	cup thinly sliced apples
¼	cup thinly sliced celery
½	cup seedless green grapes
1½	tablespoons apple juice
1	tablespoon lemon juice
1	teaspoon extra-virgin olive oil
½	teaspoon Dijon mustard
3	cups torn romaine lettuce
1	head Belgian endive, leaves separated
1	tablespoon coarsely chopped toasted walnuts (see note)

In a medium bowl, combine the apples, celery and grapes.

In a small bowl, combine the apple juice, lemon juice, oil and mustard; mix well. Toss the apple mixture with 1½ tablespoons of the dressing.

Place the romaine on a serving platter and arrange the endive leaves in a wheel on top of the romaine. Drizzle the greens with the remaining dressing. Place the apple mixture in the center of the platter and top with the walnuts.

Makes 4 servings. Per serving: 71 calories, 2.7 g. fat (31% of calories), 1.9 g. protein, 11.6 g. carbohydrates, 2.7 g. dietary fiber, 0 mg. cholesterol, 27 mg. sodium

NOTES

• To toast nuts, place them in a dry skillet over medium heat. Toast the nuts, shaking the pan often, for 3 to 5 minutes, or until fragrant and golden.

• For a more fruity salad, add ½ cup blueberries.

• Sprinkle the top of the salad with 1½ tablespoons crumbled blue cheese.

Rich and Creamy Coleslaw

You won't find any mayonnaise in this low-fat coleslaw. We took out the fat but left the rich and creamy texture in by using a mixture of nonfat plain yogurt and nonfat sour cream.

12	ounces green cabbage, finely shredded
12	ounces red cabbage, finely shredded
2	medium carrots, coarsely shredded
½	cup chopped scallions
½	cup nonfat plain yogurt
¼	cup nonfat sour cream
2	tablespoons chopped fresh chives
1	tablespoon cider vinegar
2	teaspoons pickle relish
1	teaspoon honey
¼	teaspoon Dijon mustard
¼	teaspoon dill, celery or caraway seeds
¼	teaspoon ground black pepper
	Pinch of paprika

In a large bowl, combine the green cabbage, red cabbage, carrots and scallions.

In a small bowl, whisk together the yogurt, sour cream, chives, vinegar, relish, honey, mustard, dill or celery or caraway seeds and pepper. Add to the cabbage mixture and toss until well-combined. Cover and refrigerate for at least 1 hour before serving. Just before serving, sprinkle with the paprika.

Makes 4 servings. Per serving: 95 calories, 0.9 g. fat (5% of calories), 5.4 g. protein, 20.3 g. carbohydrates, 4.3 g. dietary fiber, 0.5 mg. cholesterol, 100 mg. sodium

NOTE

• For extra sweetness and crunch, add ½ cup chopped sweet red peppers. Or give the salad a more tangy flavor with ½ cup thinly sliced radishes.

Macaroni Salad

2 cups cooked elbow macaroni or other tube pasta
1½ tablespoons lemon juice
1 teaspoon canola oil
¾ cup minced celery
½ cup minced fresh parsley
½ cup peeled and shredded carrots
½ cup chopped pimento-stuffed green olives
⅓ cup nonfat sour cream or nonfat plain yogurt
⅓ cup reduced-fat mayonnaise
⅛ teaspoon ground black pepper
⅛ teaspoon paprika

In a medium bowl, combine the macaroni, lemon juice, oil, celery, parsley, carrots, olives, sour cream or yogurt, mayonnaise and pepper. Cover and refrigerate for 1 hour to allow flavors to blend. Sprinkle with the paprika before serving.

Makes 4 servings. Per serving: 147 calories, 3.9 g. fat (24% of calories), 4.6 g. protein, 24.3 g. carbohydrates, 2.5 g. dietary fiber, 0 mg. cholesterol, 736 mg. sodium

NOTES

• For a bit more crunch, add ½ cup minced green peppers.
• Add 2 teaspoons minced onions or 1 tablespoon chopped fresh chives.

QUICK!
Chicken Salad

2 cups cubed cooked chicken breast
¼ cup pecans, toasted and coarsely chopped (see note on page 96)
1 small red onion, chopped
1 stalk celery, chopped
½ cup nonfat mayonnaise
1 tablespoon lemon juice
⅛ teaspoon ground black pepper
½ teaspoon dried thyme
½ teaspoon dried basil
4 leaves Romaine lettuce
4 leaves red-leaf lettuce
½ teaspoon paprika
¼ cup chopped fresh parsley

In a medium bowl, combine the chicken, pecans, onions and celery.

In a small bowl, whisk the mayonnaise, lemon juice, pepper, thyme and basil. Add the dressing to the chicken mixture and mix well.

Line 4 plates with equal amounts of the Romaine lettuce and red-leaf lettuce. Serve the salad on the lettuce and sprinkle with the paprika and parsley.

Makes 4 servings. Per serving: 168 calories, 6.4 g. fat (34% of calories), 17.5 g. protein, 10.3 g. carbohydrates, 0.9 g. dietary fiber, 44 mg. cholesterol, 427 mg. sodium

NOTES

• In a pinch, replace half of the mayonnaise with nonfat plain yogurt. You can also replace the red onions with chopped scallions.

• For an extra boost of energy-giving complex carbohydrates, add 1 cup cooked white or brown rice to the salad.

VARIATIONS

Curried Chicken Salad: Add 1 teaspoon curry powder to the dressing.
Fruited Chicken Salad: Add ¼ cup halved seedless grapes to the salad.

S pinach and Mandarin Orange Salad

QUICK!

Salad

8 cups torn spinach leaves
1 red onion, thinly sliced and separated into rings
½ cup canned mandarin orange segments, drained
2 tablespoons toasted sliced almonds (see note on page 96)

Honey-Mustard Dressing

2 tablespoons Dijon mustard
1 tablespoon honey
1 tablespoon lemon juice
1 tablespoon orange juice

To make the salad: In a large bowl, combine the spinach, onions, oranges and almonds.

To make the honey-mustard dressing: In a small bowl, whisk together the mustard, honey, lemon juice and orange juice. Pour the dressing over the salad and toss gently to combine.

Makes 4 servings. Per serving: 98 calories, 2.8 g. fat (23% of calories), 5.1 g. protein, 16.5 g. carbohydrates, 4.1 g. dietary fiber, 0 mg. cholesterol, 192 mg. sodium

NOTE

• In a pinch, use fat-free honey-mustard dressing.

T omato-and-Cucumber Salad

QUICK!

2 tablespoons red-wine vinegar or sherry-wine vinegar
1 tablespoon mustard
1 tablespoon chopped fresh cilantro or parsley
1 teaspoon olive oil
½ teaspoon ground black pepper
2 plum tomatoes, sliced
2 cucumbers, sliced
1 red onion, thinly sliced and separated into rings
1 hard-cooked egg white, diced
4 leaves red-leaf lettuce

In a large bowl, whisk the vinegar, mustard, cilantro or parsley, oil and pepper. Add the tomatoes, cucumbers, onions and egg white. Toss gently to coat.

Arrange the lettuce leaves on a platter. Top with the salad and drizzle with any remaining dressing. Serve immediately.

Makes 4 servings. Per serving: 69 calories, 1.8 g. fat (21% of calories), 3.3 g. protein, 11.8 g. carbohydrates, 1.8 g. dietary fiber, 0 mg. cholesterol, 74 mg. sodium

T una Salad

3 cans (6 ounces each) drained and flaked water-packed tuna
1 small onion, minced
½ stalk celery, minced
½ teaspoon lemon juice
1½ tablespoons chopped fresh parsley
⅓ cup nonfat plain yogurt
⅓ cup reduced-calorie mayonnaise

In a medium bowl, combine the tuna, onions, celery, lemon juice, parsley, yogurt and mayonnaise. Cover and refrigerate for 1 hour to allow the flavors to blend.

Makes 4 servings. Per serving: 139 calories, 5.9 g. fat (39% of calories), 15.8 g. protein, 4.8 g. carbohydrates, 0.4 g. dietary fiber, 24 mg. cholesterol, 232 mg. sodium

VARIATIONS

Seafood Salad: Replace the tuna with other seafood such as shrimp, crabmeat or salmon.
Tangy Tuna Salad: Replace half of the parsley with chopped fresh chives.

Couscous-and-Vegetable Salad

1½ cups water
¼ teaspoon salt
1 teaspoon + 1 tablespoon olive oil
1 cup couscous
¾ cup canned chick-peas, drained and rinsed (reserve the liquid)
½ cup frozen peas, thawed
1 medium carrot, coarsely shredded
1 small tomato, chopped
1 small sweet red or yellow pepper, chopped
2½ tablespoons currants
2½ tablespoons finely chopped fresh chives
1½ tablespoons pistachio or pine nuts
1½ tablespoons lemon juice
¼ teaspoon dried thyme
¼ teaspoon dried marjoram
Dash of angostura bitters (optional)

In a medium saucepan over high heat, bring the water, salt and 1 teaspoon of the oil to a boil. Stir in the couscous. Remove from the heat, cover and let stand for 5 minutes, or until the liquid is absorbed. Fluff with a fork.

Transfer the couscous to a large bowl. Add the chick-peas (without the liquid), peas, carrots, tomatoes, peppers, currants, chives and nuts. Toss gently until mixed.

In a small bowl, whisk together the lemon juice, thyme, marjoram, bitters (if using) and the remaining 1 tablespoon oil. Add 3 tablespoons of the reserved chick-pea liquid; discard the remaining chick-pea liquid. Mix and pour over the salad. Toss to mix well.

Cover and let stand at room temperature for 30 minutes to blend the flavors.

Makes 4 servings. Per serving: 325 calories, 7.4 g. fat (20% of calories), 10 g. protein, 55 g. carbohydrates, 12.4 g. dietary fiber, 0 mg. cholesterol, 334 mg. sodium

Tabbouleh Salad

Serve this traditional Middle Eastern grain salad on a bed of lettuce or as a sandwich in pita pockets.

¾ cup bulgur
2 cups boiling water
⅓ cup chopped scallions or onions
2 medium tomatoes, chopped
½ cucumber, sliced and quartered
⅓ cup chopped fresh parsley
⅓ cup chopped fresh mint
¼ cup lemon juice
2 tablespoons olive oil
⅛ teaspoon salt
⅛ teaspoon ground black pepper

Place the bulgur in a large bowl. Pour the water over the bulgur, cover and let stand for 20 minutes, or until the bulgur is light and fluffy. Drain excess water.

Add the scallions or onions, tomatoes, cucumbers, parsley, mint, lemon juice, oil, salt and pepper; mix gently. Cover and refrigerate for at least 1 hour.

Makes 4 servings. Per serving: 177 calories, 7.4 g. fat (35% of calories), 4.4 g. protein, 26.1 g. carbohydrates, 7 g. dietary fiber, 0 mg. cholesterol, 81 mg. sodium

NOTES

• For added crunch, mix in 3 tablespoons pistachio nuts just before serving.

• For extra flavor, soak the bulgur in a mixture of 1 cup boiling water and 1 cup hot vegetable broth.

Wild Rice Salad

1 cup wild rice, rinsed
2 tablespoons pine nuts, toasted, or sliced toasted almonds (see note on page 96)
2 green, red or yellow peppers (or a combination), cut into short strips
2 scallions, minced
1 clove garlic, minced
1 tablespoon chopped fresh basil
1½ teaspoons chopped fresh thyme
2 tablespoons red-wine vinegar
1 tablespoon lemon juice
2 teaspoons olive oil
¼ teaspoon dry mustard
1 head Boston lettuce
1 tablespoon crumbled feta cheese

In a medium saucepan, bring 4 cups water to a boil. Add the rice and boil, uncovered, for 35 minutes, or until the rice is tender but still chewy. Drain well and set aside.

In a large bowl, combine the rice, nuts, peppers, scallions, garlic, basil and thyme.

In a cup, whisk together the vinegar, lemon juice, oil and mustard. Pour over the rice mixture and toss well.

Serve on a bed of lettuce. Sprinkle with the feta.

Makes 4 servings. Per serving: 219 calories, 6.3 g. fat (24% of calories), 8.7 g. protein, 35.4 g. carbohydrates, 1.7 g. dietary fiber, 3 mg. cholesterol, 50 mg. sodium

VARIATION

Wild Rice Spinach Salad: Blanch 1½ cups chopped fresh spinach in boiling water for 30 seconds. Remove the spinach with a slotted spoon and place into a bowl of ice water to stop the cooking process; drain well. Add to the rice mixture. Add ¼ teaspoon ground nutmeg to the dressing.

Potato Salad

QUICK!

1 pound boiling potatoes
¾ cup thinly sliced celery
1 scallion, minced
3 tablespoons thinly sliced red onions
1 hard-cooked egg white, chopped
1 small plum tomato, diced
1½ tablespoons minced fresh dill
⅓ cup nonfat mayonnaise
2 teaspoons coarse mustard
2 teaspoons lemon juice
2 teaspoons olive oil
2 teaspoons apple cider vinegar
½ teaspoon reduced-sodium soy sauce
1 teaspoon honey
1 teaspoon minced fresh parsley
¼ teaspoon ground black pepper
⅛ teaspoon celery seeds

Scrub the potatoes and cut into 1″ cubes. Steam for about 15 minutes, or until tender. Place in a large bowl.

Add the celery, scallions, onions, egg whites, tomatoes and dill. Toss well.

In a small bowl, whisk together the mayonnaise, mustard, lemon juice, oil, vinegar, soy sauce, honey, parsley, pepper and celery seeds.

Pour over the potato mixture and combine well. Serve warm or chilled.

Makes 4 servings. Per serving: 152 calories, 2.7 g. fat (15% of calories), 3.4 g. protein, 29.8 g. carbohydrates, 1 g. dietary fiber, 0 mg. cholesterol, 351 mg. sodium

NOTE

• Boiling potatoes are the best choice for salads. They have waxy flesh that contains less starch than baking potatoes, so they're less likely to fall apart when cooked.

Three-Bean Picnic Salad

1¼ cups halved green beans
⅔ cup cooked or canned chick-peas, rinsed and drained
⅔ cup cooked or canned kidney beans, rinsed and drained
1 medium tomato, seeded and diced
1 tablespoon olive oil
1½ tablespoons Dijon mustard
1½ tablespoons water
1 tablespoon chopped fresh basil
1 teaspoon honey
⅛ teaspoon ground black pepper
2 tablespoons snipped fresh chives

Steam the green beans for about 5 minutes, or until crisp-tender. Place in a large bowl. Add the chick-peas, kidney beans and tomatoes. Mix well.

In a food processor or blender, combine the oil, mustard, water, basil, honey and pepper. Process until smooth. Pour over the salad. Sprinkle with the chives. Toss well. Let stand for 20 minutes before serving.

Makes 4 servings. Per serving: 158 calories, 4.9 g. fat (27% of calories), 7.4 g. protein, 23.3 g. carbohydrates, 2.6 g. dietary fiber, 0 mg. cholesterol, 84 mg. sodium

NOTES
• Use almost any combination of beans. Try fresh limas or wax beans in place of the green beans. Replace the chick-peas or kidney beans with fava, pinto, black, cranberry or anasazi beans.
• Serve in colorful lettuce cups such as radicchio or Boston lettuce and garnish with chopped fresh basil.
• For a creamier dressing, replace the water with nonfat plain yogurt.

Raspberry Dressing

QUICK!

1 cup fresh or thawed and drained frozen raspberries
¼ cup balsamic vinegar
4 teaspoons olive oil
Pinch of ground black pepper

Press the raspberries through a fine sieve into a small bowl to remove the seeds. To the resulting puree, add the vinegar, oil and pepper. Mix to combine.

Makes 1 cup. Per 2 tablespoons: 35 calories, 2.3 g. fat (59% of calories), 0.1 g. protein, 3.5 g. carbohydrates, 0.7 g. dietary fiber, 0 mg. cholesterol, 1 mg. sodium

Russian Dressing

QUICK!

Creamy and delicious, this dressing has less than half the calories of high-fat Russian dressings. Try it on green salads or as a sandwich spread or use it as a dip.

½ cup reduced-calorie mayonnaise
2 tablespoons ketchup
2 tablespoons snipped fresh chives
1 teaspoon prepared horseradish
1 tablespoon minced pickles
1 teaspoon lemon juice
1 teaspoon paprika

In a small bowl, combine the mayonnaise, ketchup, chives, horseradish, pickles, lemon juice and paprika. Mix well. Store, covered, in the refrigerator, for up to 1 week.

Makes ¾ cup. Per 2 tablespoons: 64 calories, 5.4 g. fat (74% of calories), 0.2 g. protein, 4.1 g. carbohydrates, 0.1 g. dietary fiber, 7 mg. cholesterol, 119 mg. sodium

B lue Cheese Dressing

A rich, low-fat alternative to traditional blue cheese dressing. Try it on salads or sandwiches.

- 1 cup low-fat cottage cheese
- 2 tablespoons skim milk
- 1 clove garlic, pressed or minced
- 2 tablespoons crumbled blue cheese

In a food processor or blender, combine the cottage cheese, milk and garlic. Blend until smooth. Add the blue cheese and blend just until the cheese is mixed in but still chunky. Store, covered, in the refrigerator, for up to 1 week.

Makes 1 cup. Per 2 tablespoons: 29 calories, 0.8 g. fat (26% of calories), 4 g. protein, 1.1 g. carbohydrates, 0 g. dietary fiber, 3 mg. cholesterol, 142 mg. sodium

T omato-Basil Vinaigrette

QUICK!

Garden salads and fish go especially well with this savory no-oil vinaigrette. Try it in pasta salad, too.

- 1½ cups peeled and chopped tomatoes
- 6 tablespoons white-wine vinegar
- 1 tablespoon chopped fresh basil
- 1 tablespoon chopped fresh thyme
- 1½ teaspoons Dijon mustard

In a food processor or blender, combine the tomatoes, vinegar, basil, thyme and mustard. Blend until smooth. Store, covered, in the refrigerator, for up to 2 days. Shake well before using.

Makes 1 cup. Per 2 tablespoons: 11 calories, 0.2 g. fat, (14% of calories), 0.4 g. protein, 2.6 g. carbohydrates, 0.5 g. dietary fiber, 0 mg. cholesterol, 16 mg. sodium

C reamy Parmesan-Pepper Dressing

QUICK!

- ⅔ cup dry-curd cottage cheese
- ⅓ cup buttermilk
- 1 tablespoon white-wine vinegar
- 2 tablespoons grated Parmesan cheese
- 1 teaspoon ground black pepper

Place the cottage cheese in a food processor or blender. Process for 3 minutes, or until very smooth. With the machine running, pour in the buttermilk and vinegar. Process until smooth. Add the Parmesan and pepper. Blend just until combined.

Makes 1 cup. Per 2 tablespoons: 26 calories, 0.8 g. fat (27% of calories), 3.3 g. protein, 1.3 g. carbohydrates, 0.1 g. dietary fiber, 2 mg. cholesterol, 116 mg. sodium

B alsamic Vinaigrette

QUICK!

- ½ cup defatted chicken broth
- ¼ cup balsamic vinegar
- 2 tablespoons reduced-sodium ketchup
- 2 tablespoons prepared mustard
- ½ teaspoon dried savory
- ½ teaspoon dried thyme
- ⅛ teaspoon ground red pepper

In a small jar with a tight-fitting lid, combine the broth, vinegar, ketchup, mustard, savory, thyme and red pepper. Shake well. Store, covered, in the refrigerator, for up to 1 week.

Makes 1 cup. Per 2 tablespoons: 17 calories, 0.3 g. fat (14% of calories), 0.6 g. protein, 3.3 g. carbohydrates, 0.1 g. dietary fiber, 0 mg. cholesterol, 73 mg. sodium

Creamy Italian Dressing

½ cup nonfat plain yogurt or nonfat sour cream
½ cup nonfat mayonnaise
½ cup skim milk
1 teaspoon dried Italian seasoning
½ teaspoon garlic powder
⅛ teaspoon ground black pepper

In a small bowl, whisk together the yogurt or sour cream, mayonnaise, milk, Italian seasoning, garlic powder and pepper. Store, covered, in the refrigerator, for up to 1 week.

Makes 1 cup. Per 2 tablespoons: 26 calories, 0.1 g. fat (2% of calories), 1.4 g. protein, 5 g. carbohydrates, 0 g. dietary fiber, 0.5 mg. cholesterol, 209 mg. sodium

5 EASY LOW-FAT SALAD DRESSINGS

The trick to a trim salad is watching what goes on top of it. Here are five easy ways to dress up a salad without adding a lot of fat.

☞ **Citrus juice dressing.** A little squeeze of lemon perks up mixed greens or a seafood salad. Top with ground black pepper.

For a dressing with more tropical flavor, combine lemon, orange and pineapple juices.

☞ **Flavored vinegar dressing.** Sprinkle garden salads with flavored vinegars that range from raspberry to rosemary. You can find a variety of these vinegars at your supermarket, deli or gourmet cooking shop. To make your own herb-flavored vinegars, add sprigs of fresh, well-washed herbs, such as tarragon, rosemary and thyme, to red- or white-wine vinegar. Cover tightly and let mellow for 1 week before using.

☞ **Herbed yogurt dressing.** For a creamy herbed dressing, add fresh or dried herbs—such as dill, basil, thyme, rosemary or oregano, alone or in combination—and cracked fresh pepper to nonfat plain yogurt. Thin to pouring consistency with skim milk or buttermilk. For curried yogurt dressing, use curry powder in place of fresh herbs.

☞ **Sour cream and dill dressing.** To make a quick dressing for seafood or potato salads, combine fresh or dried dill with nonfat sour cream and season to taste with salt and pepper. Thin to the desired consistency with skim milk or buttermilk.

☞ **Sour cream and salsa dressing.** To top fajitas or taco salads, combine fresh salsa and nonfat sour cream. Thin to the desired consistency with skim milk.

Soups

A steaming bowl of soup beckons with warmth and goodness. Whether as a prelude to dinner or as a light meal with crusty bread, wholesome soup leaves a lasting and memorable impression.

For centuries, a plethora of savory soups has graced the world's tables. From minestrone and pot-au-feu to the old-fashioned but venerable chicken noodle, soups have been enjoyed in every culture, region and season. Humble cauldrons and sophisticated tureens alike are a source of delightful satisfaction.

A WORLD OF FLAVORS

For every season and mood, there are many soups to choose from.

☞ **Bisque**. A pureed soup with a thin, loose consistency. Bisque was once synonymous with cream soup. Many of today's healthier recipes replace the cream with pureed potatoes, mushrooms or other vegetables mixed into a dairy-free broth.

☞ **Borscht**. A smooth beet bisque that's served hot or cold, depending on the season. Borscht is rooted in eastern European cuisine, and it is often served with a dollop of sour cream or yogurt.

☞ **Bouillabaisse**. A traditional soup from the coast of southern France prepared with fish and seafood in a well-spiced broth.

☞ **Broth**. An aromatic liquid, generally made from chicken, beef, veal, fish or vegetables.

☞ **Chowder**. A chunky potato soup often fortified with corn, carrots, celery, leeks and peppers. Chowder also may contain a variety of fish or shellfish, such as clams, oysters, scallops, lobster or haddock.

☞ **Cioppino**. A well-seasoned mixed-fish stew containing tomatoes, vegetables, red wine and herbs. Cioppino was developed in San Francisco by Italian immigrants.

☞ **Consommé**. A clear, clarified aromatic beef broth. Its crystal-clear appearance is achieved by stirring beaten egg whites into defatted broth and allowing them to coagulate with floating particles that otherwise would muddy the broth. The broth is then carefully strained.

☞ **Gazpacho**. Chilled tomato-and-vegetable soup that's a summertime favorite in Spanish and Mexican kitchens. Gazpacho can include cucumbers, hot and sweet peppers, avocados, garlic, basil, parsley or mint; the texture can be chunky or smooth.

☞ **Gumbo**. A piquant soup originating in Louisianan—as well as African and Caribbean—cooking. Gumbo can be made with almost any combination of shellfish, meat, poultry and sausage. The soup is thickened with either okra, filé (ground sassafras leaves) or a flour roux (a cooked combination of fat and flour used as a thickening agent) and spiced with hot red pepper. It's generally served over rice.

☞ **Legume soups**. Hearty, robust soups containing a multitude of beans, split peas or lentils—together or separately. Legumes are high in fiber, protein and complex carbohydrates and low in fat and sodium. Most dried legumes require soaking before cooking.

☞ **Matzo ball soup.** A traditional Jewish soup typically made with chicken broth and matzo balls (dumplings made with unleavened matzo meal). Vegetarian broths can also be used.

☞ **Minestrone.** A classic Italian soup containing beans, small pastas, tomatoes, potatoes and other seasonal vegetables.

☞ **Miso.** A Japanese broth soup flavored with miso paste (a fermented mash of soybeans and grains). Miso is rich in protein and nutrients and low in fat.

☞ **Mulligatawny.** A brothy, sweet-and-spicy Indian curry soup containing chicken, carrots, apples, raisins, rice, potatoes and tomatoes.

☞ **Pot-au-feu.** Literally meaning "pot of fire," a rustic French dish containing meat, chicken, vegetables and herbs.

☞ **Soupe au pistou.** A Provençal soup made with vegetables, herbs, potatoes and pasta, topped with a swirl of pistou—a pestolike sauce of crushed basil, garlic, olive oil and cheese.

☞ **Vichyssoise.** The classic soup made of pureed potatoes, leeks and herbs (often chives and parsley). Traditionally served cold.

SOUP IS GREAT FOOD

Soup can deliver a meal's worth of nutrients without adding unwanted fat, salt or energy-depleting sugars. Many soups abound with heart-healthy vegetables, grains, pastas and beans. What's more, as healthy cooks discover the joy of soups infused with fresh garlic, ginger, chili peppers and other lively seasonings, the saltshaker is becoming a distant memory.

Soup-making is a most forgiving kitchen endeavor. If you can chop, stir and taste, you are well-qualified. All you need is a selection of first-rate ingredients, a sturdy pot and a stirring spoon—plus time to let the process unfold. The ability to follow a recipe helps, but it is not the

prerequisite that it is with other types of dishes. Most soup recipes are intended to be general blueprints, not exact instructions.

Making soup also has the advantage of being a flextime vocation; you can prepare it hours or days ahead of time, then reheat it at your convenience. Soup actually improves with time as the flavors are allowed to blend and mingle together. In addition, most dairy-free soups freeze well for up to six months. (Dairy products such as milk and yogurt tend to separate when thawed and reheated. They should be added after the reheating phase.)

BROTH TIPS

Traditional soups derive much of their flavor from a well-cooked liquid called broth, or stock. Broth is formed by gently simmering meat, poultry or fish bones and trimmings with vegetables in a pot of water. The resulting liquid, once strained, forms the foundation for classic soups such as French onion, consommé and countless varieties of chicken soups.

It is possible to create high-flavor, low-sodium, nutritious soups even without preparing a broth from scratch. Water or reduced-sodium canned chicken broth can replace homemade broth in many cases. A well-stocked spice cabinet, a fresh supply of vegetables and a selection of fresh and dried herbs can turn these liquids into a rich-tasting base for soup. Making a healthful soup does not require blocking out an entire weekend.

Some recipes for broths and soups call for the addition of a product called soup base. Soup bases offer concentrated flavor, typically in the form of a ground paste, that enhances the broth. Many bases, however, contain significant amounts of salt, monosodium glutamate, chicken or beef fat and other unwelcome additives. You're better off devoting your resources to expanding your usage of herbs and spices.

To make great broth, here's what chefs recommend.

Despite its traditional image as a wholesome food, milk has come under increasing fire. While milk is still the drink of choice among the younger set, many adults worry that the large amounts of fat—an 8-ounce glass of whole milk contains nearly 9 grams of fat—may offset the benefits.

There's no question that milk—along with cheese, yogurt and other dairy foods—is a stellar source of dietary calcium. Calcium is an essential mineral for preventing osteoporosis, the bone-thinning disease that affects some 20 million American women. While you can get calcium in beans, some leafy vegetables and other foods, you have to eat a lot of them. Milk, by contrast, is a concentrated source; having two or three servings a day of milk or other dairy products will readily fulfill the Daily Value of 1,000 milligrams of calcium.

To get the benefits of milk without the fat, experts say, all you have to do is switch to skim or low-fat milk. If you have three servings of milk a day, for example, changing from whole to 2 percent will save 11 grams of fat. Switching to skim will save 24 grams.

Smaller is better. Cutting the bones, vegetables and other broth ingredients into small pieces increases the amount of flavor derived from them and slightly reduces the cooking time.

Keep it strong. After adding ingredients to the broth, add just enough water to cover them. Too much water results in a diluted, less-enriched broth.

Cook it slowly. You want the broth liquid to gently simmer over low heat. Avoid bringing the broth to a rolling boil. Boiling churns fat and scum back into the soup and produces a greasier broth.

Skim the surface. The advantage to gently simmering broth is that this process allows fat particles to float to the top, where they can be easily removed. Make a point of occasionally skimming both visible fat and any scum from the top of the liquid. (A shallow ladle will do the job.)

Strain the liquid. When the broth is ready—usually in about 1 to 2 hours—you'll need to strain it.

☞ Place a wide sieve or colander over a pan or bowl.

☞ Line the sieve or colander with a damp cloth or a double thickness of cheesecloth.

☞ Gradually ladle the broth into the strainer. Discard the solid remnants and return the strained liquid to a clean pot or storage container.

☞ Taste the liquid. If it's weak, boil it down until the flavor is concentrated.

Chill it fast. To prevent bacteria from growing in the hot liquid, it's important to chill broth as quickly as possible. After cooking, place the pot in a sink full of cold water and ice. Stir until cooled. Then cover and place in the refrigerator.

Properly chilled, broth will keep in the refrigerator for five to seven days. Frozen, it will keep almost indefinitely.

☞ As the broth chills, fat remaining in it will solidify on the surface. Remove with a spoon.

☞ To freeze broth, ladle the cold liquid into pint or quart containers, leaving about ½″ of headroom for the broth to expand as it freezes. To have small amounts on hand, pour some broth into ice-cube trays; when frozen, transfer the cubes to a freezer bag.

☞ When reheating broth, bring it to a boil to kill bacteria that may have accumulated.

COMMON BROTHS

While most broths are made by simmering rich, flavorful ingredients for varying lengths of time in water, there are a number of variations on this basic theme.

SKIMMING FAT

Cream isn't the only thing that rises to the top. When making stock, you'll often see fat globules rising to the surface. Here's an easy way to remove the fat without turning off the heat or chilling the stock.

Fold a sheet of paper towel in half and pull it across the top of the soup to absorb the fat. (When using a two-ply towel, peel it apart to get a single sheet.) Repeat until no more fat is visible, using new towels as needed.

Brown Broth

Also referred to as meat stock, this is the broth extracted from meat trimmings, like pot roasts, ribs, shanks, shoulders and beef and veal bones. Many brown broths also include the addition of herbs and hardy vegetables, like turnips, onions, leeks, carrots and parsnips.

Begin by browning. When making a brown broth, roast or brown ingredients in the oven first. This intensifies flavors and caramelizes sugars in the vegetables, resulting in a rich, deeply flavored broth.

☞ Combine the bones and meat trimmings in a large roasting pan.

☞ Roast at 425° for about 1 hour, or until the ingredients take on a dark color. Turn the pieces occasionally.

☞ Add vegetables to the pan after about 30 minutes.

☞ Transfer the browned meat, bones and vegetables to a large stockpot.

Salvage the drippings. To extract even more flavor for the broth, you'll want to deglaze the roasting pan. To do this, add water to the hot pan and scrape the stuck-on parts from the bottom. Add this mixture to the stockpot along with the other ingredients.

Poultry Broth

This is one of the easiest and most versatile broths to make. Simply combine an assortment of cooked or raw poultry bones—wings, backs, necks and so on—in a large stockpot. Cover with

Helpful Hint

To create a fat-free—and nearly instant—broth, pour boiling water over dried mushrooms. Soak for 15 minutes, then strain the broth.

cold water and bring to a simmer. Cook for 3 to 4 hours, skimming occasionally.

☞ Adding coarsely chopped carrots, onions, celery, garlic and a variety of herbs will impart extra flavor to the broth.

☞ Avoid adding the chicken liver, which has a dominant flavor and can also muddy the broth.

☞ To make a browned poultry broth, brown the poultry bones in the oven beforehand. Deglaze the pan and add the bones to the stockpot. The extra step yields a dark, intense broth.

☞ Leaving the brown, papery skins on onions also gives the broth some color.

Vegetable Broth

As more and more people try to reduce the amount of meat in their diets and seek ways to prepare flavorful meatless meals, all-vegetable broths become an appealing and satisfying option. Vegetable broths are economical, nutritious and low in fat.

☞ Combine a variety of vegetables and trimmings in a stockpot, cover with water and simmer for 45 to 60 minutes. The broth can include carrot peelings, bell pepper cores and ribs, onion and garlic skins, celery leaves, mushroom stems, parsley stems and so on. (You can freeze the trimmings until you have enough to make a suitable broth.)

☞ If desired, roast the vegetables in a 375° oven for 30 minutes, or until lightly browned, before cooking them in water. Deglaze the baking dish with water and add to the stockpot.

Helpful Hint

Beets impart a deep magenta hue to broth. They work best for tomato-based soups, where they will complement, and not dominate, the color scheme.

☞ Be careful about using vegetables with very assertive flavors—like broccoli—unless you want the broth to taste of them.

☞ Keep the vegetables barely covered with water. If the broth evaporates too quickly, add more water.

☞ When ready, strain the cooking liquid and discard the vegetables.

☞ For a particularly flavorful broth, add the liquid left over from steaming or blanching vegetables.

Herb Broth

Grassy, aromatic herb broths are a favorite of many restaurant chefs. The exotic flavors and fresh tastes are an especially welcome addition to the spring and summer table.

Different herbs yield different results. Rosemary, for example, adds a pine-needle nuance, while tarragon gives a sophisticated sweetness. Herb broths can also be made with dill, oregano, thyme, parsley and other favorites.

☞ Collect handfuls of a variety of fresh herbs. Combine with water in a pot and simmer for 30 to 60 minutes.

☞ When the broth is done, puree it and strain it. You can then use it as a stand-alone liquid or as a means to reinvigorate and flavor other broths that you have on hand.

Fish Broth

Fish and seafood broths take less than an hour to make. You can use shrimp, lobster or crab shells, fish carcasses and heads as well as other discarded parts.

☞ It is best to use bones from lean whitefish and avoid strong-tasting, potentially overpowering oily fish such as mackerel, tuna, smelt and herring.

☞ Using a variety of seafood will yield a fully rounded broth. You can ask your fishmonger for fish trimmings and shells. Naturally, the fresher the fish, the better the broth.

☞ Adding onions, leeks, carrots, bay leaves, thyme and parsley to the mix will complement most fish broths.

The Well-Stocked Kitchen

Just as a carpenter needs the proper hammers, saws and chisels, the soup chef must have the proper pots and pans. Fortunately, you don't have to spend a fortune to get good equipment. Basically, here's what you need.

☞ One or two large soup pots made of stainless steel (a 4- to 6-quart capacity is ideal). To prevent scorched-bottom syndrome, buy a soup pot that feels heavy for its size and that has a thick bottom. Stainless steel and enameled cast iron fare better than thin aluminum.

☞ Large stirring spoon, preferably wooden

☞ Food processor, blender or food mill for pureeing

☞ Cutting board

☞ Vegetable peeler

☞ Knives

☞ Soup ladle

☞ Strainer or colander with cheesecloth or fine mesh cloth to line it

Most well-made soups begin with sautéed vegetables. In Italian, this mix is called sofrito. The French call it mirepoix. Other chefs refer to it simply as their little secret. Regardless of the name, however, it's the key to creating a truly good soup.

Start with a sauté. To create an aromatic foundation for your soup, briefly cook a mixture of vegetables over high heat in a small amount of oil or wine. Sautéing the vegetables first—as opposed to stewing them in the broth—releases deep, long-lasting flavors and subtly sweetens the pot.

☞ Many soups begin by combining chopped onions, celery and garlic. Depending on the soup, you can also add mushrooms, zucchini, eggplant, peppers, carrots or other vegetables.

☞ In Creole and Cajun kitchens, the trio of onions, bell peppers and celery is used so often and with such great success that it's popularly known as the holy trinity.

☞ For a hot-and-spicy nuance, try adding jalapeño or serrano peppers to the sauté. For hot-and-smoky, a chipotle (smoked jalapeño) pepper works well. Asian-style soups rely on chopped fresh ginger, lemongrass and garlic.

Hold off on adding tomato. While most vegetables can be added to the pan and sautéed together, tomatoes should be added near the end. Otherwise, the juices released from the tomatoes create a stewlike mixture and keep the other vegetables from browning nicely.

Add the cooking liquid. After the vegetables are sautéed, transfer them to the soup pot, add the cooking liquid (whether water or broth), the dried seasonings, the bouquet garni (if used) and the bulk of the ingredients, such as potatoes, winter squash, carrots and root vegetables.

Hold the salt. When spicing the pot, start out with considerably less salt than you think is necessary. The soup's flavors will magnify and swell over time, and you may not need as much salt by the time the soup is finished.

Simmer slowly. Soups benefit from long spells of simmering and occasional stirring but do not require a lot of fussing or attention. During this time, a kind of culinary alchemy takes place: Potatoes, squash and other vegetables become tender, liquids thicken and garlic and herbs spread their aromatic presence. Flavors are coaxed and awakened. The soup begins to look and smell inviting.

Helpful Hint

If you accidentally put too much salt into soup, you can correct the flavor by putting in several large chunks of raw potato, which will help absorb it. Discard them after about 15 minutes. A preventive measure, of course, is not to salt the soup until it's finished cooking—and to use a light hand with the seasoning.

MAKING A BOUQUET GARNI

To provide just a hint of herbal depth and fragrance to soups and stocks, chefs use a bouquet garni (boo-KAY garn-E). Steeped in the simmering broth and removed at the finish, a bouquet garni leaves behind an aromatic presence in the liquid.

Almost any herb can be included in a bouquet garni, but parsley, thyme and bay leaves are the classic combination. If used in moderation, tarragon, basil, oregano, rosemary and marjoram can also be delicious.

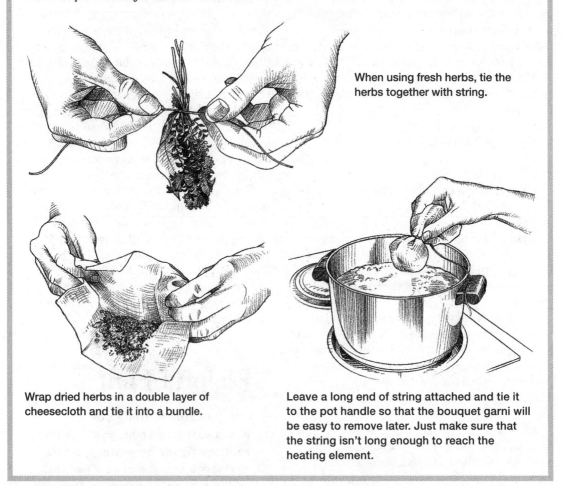

When using fresh herbs, tie the herbs together with string.

Wrap dried herbs in a double layer of cheesecloth and tie it into a bundle.

Leave a long end of string attached and tie it to the pot handle so that the bouquet garni will be easy to remove later. Just make sure that the string isn't long enough to reach the heating element.

Add the finishing touches. When the soup is nearly finished, it is time for last-minute touches. In the past, that often meant swirling in quantities of cream, butter or egg yolks, but in today's healthy kitchen, there are more inventive and nutritious ways to perk up the soup.

☞ Stir in chopped fresh parsley, basil, chives or scallions when the soup is almost done. Fresh herbs lose their potency over a long cooking time, but bring a refreshing taste when added near the finish. A twist of freshly ground pepper adds uplifting flavor, as well.

☞ Add chopped leafy soup greens—like kale, Swiss chard, escarole or spinach—to the pot about 5 to 10 minutes before the finish. They give interesting texture and color as well as valued nutrients to the soup.

☞ Collard greens take slightly longer to cook. They should enter the soup about 30 minutes before the finish.

☞ Shellfish like shrimp, scallops, oysters and clams cook in 10 minutes or less, so add them at the very end of the cooking process. Precooked fish, meat and chicken need only to be reheated to the simmering point.

☞ A dash of dry wine or lemon juice adds depth and dimension to low-sodium soup. You don't need much—only a few tablespoons. For tomato- and meat-based soups, use red wine; for chicken, fish or vegetable soups, use white wine or lemon juice.

THE THICK AND THIN OF IT

The body and texture of the soup matters almost as much as its taste. Some soups are meant to be quite thin, while others aspire to be smooth, velvety and thick. To thicken soups, chefs have traditionally relied on heavy cream, egg yolks or buttery roux. In the process, the soup's fat and cholesterol contents ballooned.

SOUPING UP THE TABLE

Soup often dazzles the taste buds while leaving the eyes unsatisfied. With a little culinary creativity, however, soup can be visually exciting. Here are some easy ways.

Serve soup inside a hollowed-out acorn squash, sugar pie pumpkin or hubbard squash. The "bowl" may be cooked or raw; if it's cooked, you can eat it when you've finished the soup.

Top soup with strips of grilled chicken breast, zucchini, bell peppers or shrimp.

Swirl pureed vegetables into soup. Choose a contrasting color for the most impact. If desired, sprinkle with chopped fresh herbs.

Homemade low-fat croutons add elegance to soups as well as substance and crunch.

With a little ingenuity and a light-handed touch, however, it is possible to thicken, not fatten, your soup. And if it's thin soup that you're after, we've included a few easy ways for making it sparkle. Here's what chefs advise.

Fire up the blender. Ladle a small amount of soup into a blender or food processor and puree until smooth. Stir the pureed mixture back into the soup and return it to a simmer. If the soup isn't thick enough, repeat until you get the desired consistency.

Be a masher. If your soup contains potatoes, dried beans, squash or tomatoes, use a potato masher to crush them. Alternately, mash them against the side of the pan with the back of a large spoon.

Add complex carbs. Throw some uncooked rice, small pasta or couscous into the pot. Cook for 15 to 20 minutes, or until the grains or pasta are tender.

Look for leftovers. Get instant last-minute thickening power from leftover mashed potatoes or pureed cooked rice or vegetables.

Reach for the can opener. To thicken a tomato-based soup, the easiest strategy is to stir in a few tablespoons of canned tomato puree.

Add some starch. Thicken Asian-style soups with equal parts of cornstarch and water; whisk the mixture into simmering soup. For other types of soup, a sprinkling of instant potato flakes works well.

Break some bread. Tossing cubed pieces of toast or stale bread into the pot is a delicious way to add both thickness and nutrients. In Italy, minestrone thickened with bread is called ribollita.

Increase the cooking time. Many soups reduce naturally, given a little extra time on the stove. Bring to a simmer and stir frequently.

While many soups are best enjoyed thick, others, like egg drop soup, are designed to be thin and loose. In most cases, it's easy to make a thick soup thinner, as long as you adjust the seasonings to compensate for the added liquid volume.

Stir in more liquids. If your soup is thick-ening up more than you like, gradually stir in hot vegetable broth or low-fat chicken broth until you reach the desired consistency.

Reach for the juice. To thin a tomato-based soup, try adding a small amount of canned or fresh tomato juice.

SOUP STAPLES

Healthy soups rely on a variety of hearty vegetables, grains, beans and pastas for substance, texture and nutrients. Here are some excellent choices.

☞ **Barley.** A pale, mildly flavored grain, barley has a chewy texture and the ability to expand to three or four times its size. It gives soup a stick-to-your-ribs quality.

☞ **Beans.** Almost any kind of bean can be used in soup, including kidney beans, black beans, chick-peas and white beans, among others. Many recipes call for soaking and precooking dried beans before adding them to the soup pot. (The beans' cooking liquid makes a flavorful broth.) Canned beans can be added near the end of the cooking process.

☞ **Butternut squash.** This tan winter squash melds wonderfully into soup and is a natural thickener. To prepare, scoop out and discard the seeds from the bulbous end of the squash, then peel the squash and dice the flesh like a potato.

☞ **Leafy green vegetables.** Kale, chard, mustard greens, dandelion, collards, escarole, spinach and other "soup greens" lend texture, color and flavor.

☞ **Leeks.** Resembling an overgrown scallion, the leek's mild onion flavor makes it a European favorite.

☞ **Lentils.** These oval-shaped legumes add substance and earthy flavors to long-cooking soups.

☞ **Parsnips.** A mildly sweet root vegetable, the parsnip can be used in place of (or with) potatoes. It's peeled and diced just like a carrot.

☞ **Pasta.** Most pastas are natural fodder for soup. Pasta is best added near the end of the cooking time (10 to 15 minutes before serving), since overcooked pasta tends to expand and absorb more broth than you thought imaginable. Small, thin pastas are ideal, such as tubetti, ditalini, small shells, orzo and angel hair. Asian noodles made from buckwheat, rice or beans are also soup-friendly.

☞ **Potatoes.** Red, blue or waxy potatoes make the best soups. (Baking potatoes tend to mush up the broth.) Leave the skin on for additional nutrients and texture.

☞ **Rice.** Long-grain white rice should be added to soup at least 15 to 20 minutes before serving; brown rice takes about 45 minutes to cook. Short-grain rices (such as Arborio) are ideal for thick, creamy soups; parboiled (converted) and long-grain rice hold their shape longer. Tender basmati breaks apart and melds into the liquid. Like pasta, rice continues to expand over time, so don't add it to the soup too early.

☞ **Rutabagas**. This large, softball-size, mild-flavored root vegetable is a candidate for long-cooking soups. Peel off the waxy protective coating before using.

☞ **Sweet potatoes.** These can be used interchangeably with white potatoes in many recipes. The orange hue and subtle sweetness add an appealing nuance as well as valuable beta-carotene.

☞ **Turnips.** These squatty, off-white root vegetables are distinguished by their radishlike flavor. They add a pleasant texture and body to soup. Their strong flavor, however, means that they're best used in moderation.

HOT-AND-SPICY SOUPS

In recent years, more and more Americans have begun discovering the joys of fiery ethnic soups, many of which derive their peppery personalities from hot chili peppers. The pungent pods offer varying degrees of heat to soups from around the world, including Mexican black bean soup, Indian and Thai curry soups, Southwestern corn chowder, Cajun gumbo and Caribbean squash bisques.

Chili peppers are high in vitamins A and C and low in fat and sodium. Plus, with chilies lighting up the pot, there is little need for salt or butter. Here are a few tips when handling and preparing fresh chili peppers.

Take precautions. It's a good idea to wear plastic or rubber gloves when handling chili pods.

Remove the seeds. The heat-activating ingredient in chili peppers—capsaicin—is concentrated where the seeds are connected to the inside walls. Remove them and the attached membranes so that you don't transform a mildly piquant sensation into one that blisters your tongue.

Know when. Add chili peppers, minced or chopped, when you are sautéing vegetables for the aromatic base.

Moderation is key. If you are new to hot cuisine, don't turn up the heat-producing fires all at once. Use chili peppers sparingly and start out with mild varieties.

HOT CUISINE

The addition of fresh chili peppers infuses soup with culinary fire. Here's an approximate heat scale, from mild to wild. (Remember to use plastic gloves when handling hot peppers.)

1. Bell pepper
2. Pimento
3. Hungarian cherry
4. Anaheim
5. Poblano/ancho
6. New Mexico
7. Peperoncini
8. Jalapeño/chipotle
9. Fresno
10. Serrano
11. Thai
12. Cayenne
13. Tabasco
14. Scotch bonnet
15. Habanero—watch out!

Jean-Louis Palladin

As a two-star Michelin chef in France, Jean-Louis Palladin understands that the secret to great soup is always to use the freshest ingredients available.

"My mother was a great cook, and I believe I have soup running through my veins," he jokes. "I put soup on every lunch and dinner menu at my restaurant."

The recipe below calls for fava beans, which you can often buy at large supermarkets. To get 1 pound shelled, buy 1½ pounds in the shell. If favas are not available, use blanched fresh peas. For a smooth soup, strain the soup after cooking.

Cold Fava Bean Soup

- 1 pound shelled fava beans
- 1 tablespoon olive oil
- 1 onion, chopped
- 3 shallots, chopped
- 1 clove garlic, chopped
- 3 sprigs fresh thyme
- 1 bay leaf
- 4 cups defatted chicken broth
  Pinch of salt
  Pinch of ground black pepper

Cook the beans in a large pot of boiling water for 7 minutes, or until the beans are tender. Drain and transfer to a bowl of ice water to stop the cooking process and set the color. Remove and discard the outer layer (the skin) from each bean. Set aside.

Warm the oil in a large skillet over medium heat. Add the onions, shallots and garlic. Cook over medium heat for 6 to 8 minutes, or until the vegetables are tender but not brown.

Add the beans, thyme and bay leaf. Cook for 5 minutes. Add the broth and simmer for 10 minutes, or until the vegetables are soft and the broth has reduced slightly.

Remove and discard the thyme and bay leaf. Puree the soup in a blender or food processor, working in batches if needed. Add the salt and pepper. Cover and refrigerate for at least 1 hour.

Makes 4 servings. Per serving: 411 calories, 4.7 g. fat (10% of calories), 27.5 g. protein, 67.6 g. carbohydrates, 17 g. dietary fiber, 0 mg. cholesterol, 345 mg. sodium

French Onion Soup

2 large onions, thinly sliced and separated into rings
5 cups defatted reduced-sodium chicken broth
3 cups defatted reduced-sodium beef broth
2 teaspoons reduced-sodium soy sauce
1 clove garlic, minced
1 bay leaf
4 slices French bread or whole-wheat bread, toasted
4 slices reduced-fat mozzarella cheese

Coat a large saucepan with no-stick spray. Warm the saucepan over medium heat. Add the onions and reduce the heat to low. Sauté for 10 minutes, or until the onions are tender.

Add the chicken broth, beef broth, soy sauce, garlic and bay leaf. Cover and bring to a boil, then reduce the heat to medium-low. Simmer for 40 minutes. Remove and discard the bay leaf.

Meanwhile, preheat the broiler. Place the bread on a rack in a broiler pan. Top each slice with a piece of mozzarella. Broil 4″ from the heat for 1 minute, or until the cheese is melted.

To serve, ladle the soup into bowls. Top with the bread.

Makes 4 servings. Per serving: 206 calories, 4.9 g. fat (22% of calories), 15.8 g. protein, 23.1 g. carbohydrates, 1.4 g. dietary fiber, 11 mg. cholesterol, 527 mg. sodium

Tomato Soup

1 tablespoon olive oil
⅓ cup finely diced onions
¼ cup finely diced celery
¼ cup finely diced carrots
1 clove garlic, minced
3 large tomatoes, peeled, seeded and diced (see note)
1 bay leaf
2 tablespoons minced fresh parsley
2 teaspoons minced fresh basil
1 teaspoon minced fresh thyme or ½ teaspoon dried
1 teaspoon minced fresh marjoram or ½ teaspoon dried
3 cups defatted chicken broth or reduced-sodium tomato juice
¼ teaspoon ground black pepper

In a large saucepan over medium heat, warm the oil. Add the onions, celery, carrots and garlic. Sauté for 5 minutes, or until the onions are soft. Add the tomatoes, bay leaf, parsley, basil, thyme and marjoram. Cover and cook over low heat for 10 to 15 minutes, or until the mixture is soft.

Gradually stir in the broth or tomato juice and bring to a boil. Reduce the heat to low, cover and simmer gently for 15 to 20 minutes, or until the vegetables are soft. Stir in the pepper. Remove and discard the bay leaf.

Makes 4 servings. Per serving: 79 calories, 3.8 g. fat (40% of calories), 4.7 g. protein, 7.9 g. carbohydrates, 1.8 g. dietary fiber, 0 mg. cholesterol, 271 mg. sodium

NOTES
• To peel tomatoes easily, dip them in boiling water for 30 seconds, or until the skins begin to crack. Remove with a slotted spoon and transfer to a bowl of ice water to stop the cooking process. When cool enough to handle, slip off and discard the skins.

(continued)

• In a pinch, replace the tomatoes with 1 can (28 ounces) Italian plum tomatoes, drained and chopped. Replace some of the chicken broth with the canned tomato juice.

VARIATIONS

Cream of Tomato Soup: Reduce the broth to 1 cup and stir into the vegetables. After cooking, puree the soup. Return to the heat and stir in 1½ cups 1% low-fat milk and ½ cup nonfat sour cream. Warm through over low heat but do not boil.

Spicy Tomato Soup: Increase the amount of onions to 1 cup. Replace the celery and carrots with 1 small chili pepper, seeded and chopped, or a pinch of ground red pepper. After sautéing the onions and peppers, add 1 teaspoon ground cumin, ½ teaspoon turmeric and ¼ teaspoon ground cardamom. Omit the parsley, basil, thyme and marjoram.

Tomato-Rice Soup: Add 1 cup cooked rice to the soup 5 minutes before the end of cooking time.

Tomato Soup with Pasta: Add 1 cup cooked orzo or small shell pasta to the soup just before serving.

until the onions are soft. Add the broth, celery, carrots, thyme, dill and pepper. Bring to a boil over medium heat.

Add the chicken and noodles. Cook for 8 to 10 minutes, or until both the chicken and noodles are tender. Stir in the parsley. Serve hot.

Makes 4 servings. Per serving: 218 calories, 2.9 g. fat (12% of calories), 28.1 g. protein, 19.3 g. carbohydrates, 1.8 g. dietary fiber, 52 mg. cholesterol, 508 mg. sodium

NOTE

• If you prefer the noodles done separately, cook them for 8 to 10 minutes in a large pot of boiling water. Drain. To serve, place the noodles in individual soup bowls and top with the hot soup.

VARIATION

Chunky Chicken-Vegetable Soup: Replace 1 cup of the broth with 1 cup canned tomatoes. Chop the tomatoes and add to the soup along with ¼ cup diced green or sweet red peppers, ½ cup fresh or frozen corn and ½ cup quartered and sliced zucchini.

Classic Chicken Noodle Soup

QUICK!

1	large onion, finely chopped
3	cloves garlic, minced
5¼	cups defatted chicken broth
½	cup sliced celery
⅓	cup sliced carrots
½	teaspoon dried thyme
½	teaspoon dried dill
⅛	teaspoon ground black pepper
4	boneless, skinless chicken breast halves (1 pound) cut into ½" pieces
3	ounces ribbon egg (no-yolk) noodles
1	tablespoon chopped fresh parsley

Coat a large saucepan with no-stick spray. Warm the saucepan over medium heat. Add the onions and garlic. Sauté for 3 minutes, or

Easy Vegetable Soup

QUICK!

1½	cups cubed potatoes
1	tablespoon olive oil
1	onion, chopped
1	stalk celery, chopped
2	cloves garlic, minced
2¾	cups vegetable or defatted chicken broth
1	cup fresh or frozen corn
½	cup fresh or frozen cut green beans
1	large tomato, chopped
½	teaspoon dried thyme
½	teaspoon dried basil
¾	cup 1% low-fat milk
	Dash of angostura bitters (optional)
¼	teaspoon salt (optional)
¼	teaspoon ground black pepper

Place the potatoes and ¾ cup water in a small microwave-safe bowl. Cover and microwave on high power for a total of 6 minutes; stir after 3 minutes. Let stand, covered, until needed.

In a large saucepan over medium heat, warm the oil. Add the onions and celery. Sauté for 5 minutes, or until the onions are soft.

Drain the potatoes and add to the saucepan. Stir in the garlic, broth, corn, green beans, tomatoes, thyme and basil. Bring to a boil. Reduce the heat to medium-low, cover and simmer for 10 minutes.

Stir in the milk, bitters (if using), salt (if using) and pepper. Warm through, stirring occasionally, for 5 minutes, but do not boil.

Makes 4 servings. Per serving: 183 calories, 4.2 g. fat (19% of calories), 5.5 g. protein, 33.6 g. carbohydrates, 2.4 g. dietary fiber, 2 mg. cholesterol, 98 mg. sodium

NOTES

• For a creamier soup, puree some of the vegetable mixture in a food processor or blender before adding the milk. Return to the saucepan, add the milk and remaining ingredients and warm through.

• The green beans can be replaced with lima beans.

QUICK!
Cream of Mushroom Soup

We cut the fat in this classic cream soup by replacing the heavy cream with a creamy mixture of evaporated skim milk and cornstarch. Thyme, parsley and a bit of nutmeg add to its great flavor.

- 1   tablespoon olive oil
- 1   tablespoon dry white wine or nonalcoholic white wine
- 12 ounces mushrooms, sliced
- ¼   cup finely chopped onions
- 1   clove garlic, minced
- 1   tablespoon chopped fresh thyme
- 2   teaspoons chopped fresh parsley
- 2   cups defatted chicken broth
- 1   cup evaporated skim milk
- 2   tablespoons cornstarch
- ¼   teaspoon ground black pepper
- ⅛   teaspoon ground nutmeg

In a medium saucepan over medium heat, warm the oil and wine. Add the mushrooms, onions, garlic, thyme and parsley. Sauté for 5 minutes, or until the mushrooms release their liquid and the vegetables are soft.

Add the broth; cover and simmer for 5 minutes over low heat. Puree the mixture in a food processor or blender. Return to the saucepan.

Meanwhile, in a small bowl, whisk together ¼ cup of the milk and the cornstarch until smooth. Slowly add to the mushroom mixture, stirring constantly, over medium heat. Stir in the pepper, nutmeg and the remaining ¾ cup milk. Cook and stir until thickened and bubbly. Cook and stir for 2 minutes more.

Makes 4 servings. Per serving: 137 calories, 3.9 g. fat (25% of calories), 9.1 g. protein, 16.9 g. carbohydrates, 1.4 g. dietary fiber, 2 mg. cholesterol, 247 mg. sodium

NOTES

• Garnish with extra chopped fresh parsley and a sprinkling of nutmeg or paprika.

• The onions can be replaced with ¼ cup chopped shallots.

• The thyme can be replaced with marjoram.

VARIATION

Creamy Mushroom-and-Barley Soup: Add 1 cup cooked barley along with the last addition of milk.

Cream of Broccoli Soup

    1   small head broccoli (about 1 pound)
    1   tablespoon canola oil
    1   cup sliced leeks (white part only)
    ½   cup sliced celery
    4   cups defatted chicken broth
    2   cups evaporated skim milk
    ¼   cup cornstarch
    1   teaspoon chopped fresh thyme
    ⅛   teaspoon ground black pepper

Cut the broccoli into florets and set aside. Trim and discard the tough fibrous skin from the stems. Coarsely chop the stems and set aside.

In a medium saucepan over medium-low heat, warm the oil. Add the leeks and celery and sauté for 8 minutes, or until the leeks are soft. Add the broccoli stems and broth. Bring to a boil, then reduce the heat to low, cover and simmer for 15 minutes. Add the broccoli florets and simmer for 10 minutes more.

Puree the mixture in a food processor or blender. Return to the saucepan.

Meanwhile, in a small bowl, whisk together ¼ cup of the milk and the cornstarch until smooth. Slowly add to the broccoli mixture, stirring constantly, over medium heat. Stir in the remaining 1¾ cups milk, thyme and pepper. Cook and stir until thickened and bubbly. Cook and stir for 2 minutes more.

Makes 4 servings. Per serving: 233 calories, 4.1 g. fat (15% of calories), 17.8 g. protein, 32.9 g. carbohydrates, 0.9 g. dietary fiber, 4 mg. cholesterol, 528 mg. sodium

NOTE

• For a decorative look, remove several small cooked broccoli florets before pureeing the soup. Add a few florets to each bowl before serving.

Creamy Cauliflower Soup

    2   cups cauliflower florets
    ½   cup chopped potatoes
    4   cups defatted chicken broth
    ½   cup sliced leeks (white part only)
    1   bay leaf
    ¼   teaspoon ground caraway seeds
    ⅛   teaspoon ground black pepper
    2   tablespoons chopped fresh chives

In a large saucepan, bring 1″ of water to a boil. Place the cauliflower and potatoes in a steamer basket and set the basket in the pan. Reduce the heat to medium-low, cover and steam for 15 to 20 minutes, or until the vegetables are tender when pierced with a fork.

Transfer to another large saucepan and add the broth, leeks, bay leaf and caraway seeds. Simmer for 20 minutes over medium-low heat. Remove and discard the bay leaf.

Puree the mixture in a food processor or blender. Return to the saucepan, add the pepper and heat through. Ladle into serving bowls and garnish with the chives.

Makes 4 servings. Per serving: 72 calories, 0.2 g. fat (3% of calories), 6.4 g. protein, 12.1 g. carbohydrates, 0.7 g. dietary fiber, 0 mg. cholesterol, 355 mg. sodium

VARIATION

Cauliflower-Cheese Soup: Stir in ½ cup shredded reduced-fat Cheddar cheese after returning the pureed mixture to the saucepan.

Carrot Soup

1½ cups defatted chicken broth
4 medium carrots, chopped
1 potato, peeled and cubed
⅓ cup orange juice
¼ cup chopped onions
2 teaspoons minced fresh ginger
1 teaspoon grated orange rind
¾ cup buttermilk
¾ cup nonfat plain yogurt
1½ tablespoons honey
¼ teaspoon reduced-sodium soy sauce
¼ teaspoon ground nutmeg or cardamom
Pinch of ground red pepper

In a medium saucepan, combine the broth, carrots, potatoes, orange juice, onions, ginger and orange rind. Cover and cook over medium heat for 25 minutes, or until the carrots and potatoes are tender. Let cool for 5 minutes.

Puree the mixture in a food processor or blender. Add the buttermilk and yogurt and blend until smooth. Return to the saucepan and add the honey, soy sauce, nutmeg or cardamom and pepper.

Makes 4 servings. Per serving: 157 calories, 0.8 g. fat (4% of calories), 7.4 g. protein, 31.1 g. carbohydrates, 0.8 g. dietary fiber, 2 mg. cholesterol, 275 mg. sodium

NOTE
• To save time, place the broth, vegetables, orange juice, ginger and orange rind in a microwave-safe 3-quart no-stick baking dish. Microwave, uncovered, on high power for 10 minutes, or until the vegetables are tender.

VARIATIONS
Dairy-Free Carrot Soup: Replace the buttermilk and yogurt with an additional 1½ cups broth.
Squash Soup: Replace the carrots with chunks of pumpkin or winter squash.

QUICK!
Italian Minestrone

1 tablespoon olive oil
⅓ cup diced onions
⅓ cup diced celery
⅓ cup diced carrots
1 clove garlic, minced
4 cups defatted reduced-sodium chicken broth
1 can (14 ounces) chopped tomatoes (with juice)
1 can (16 ounces) canned chick-peas or red kidney beans, rinsed and drained
¾ cup packed chopped escarole or spinach
¼ cup orzo pasta
1 cup sliced (½" pieces) green beans
½ cup diced zucchini
2 tablespoons chopped fresh basil

In a medium saucepan over medium heat, warm the oil. Add the onions, celery and carrots. Sauté for 5 minutes, or just until the vegetables are softened. Add the garlic and sauté for 1 minute.

Add the broth, tomatoes (with juice), chick-peas or kidney beans, escarole or spinach and orzo. Bring to a boil over high heat. Reduce the heat to medium and simmer for 10 minutes.

Add the green beans and zucchini. Cover and simmer for 5 minutes, or until the beans are tender. Stir in the basil and cook for 1 minute more.

Makes 4 servings. Per serving: 252 calories, 7.8 g. fat (27% of calories), 12.9 g. protein, 34.9 g. carbohydrates, 7.9 g. dietary fiber, 2 mg. cholesterol, 629 mg. sodium

NOTE
• Orzo is a type of small pasta that resembles grains of rice. It may be replaced with ¾ cup small shell pasta.

P QUICK! umpkin Soup

½ teaspoon canola oil
3 tablespoons minced shallots
½ teaspoon minced fresh ginger
2 cups canned pumpkin
2 cups defatted chicken broth
½ teaspoon pumpkin pie spice
½ cup evaporated skim milk
3 tablespoons nonfat sour cream

Coat a large saucepan with no-stick spray. Add the oil, shallots and ginger. Cook over medium heat for 2 minutes. Add the pumpkin, broth and pumpkin pie spice. Bring to a boil. Reduce the heat to medium-low and cook for 10 minutes.

Whisk in the milk and sour cream. Warm through but do not boil.

Makes 4 servings. Per serving: 96 calories, 1 g. fat (9% of calories), 7 g. protein, 16.6 g. carbohydrates, 3.6 g. dietary fiber, 1 mg. cholesterol, 219 mg. sodium

NOTES
• To make your own pumpkin pie spice for this recipe, combine ¼ teaspoon ground cinnamon, ¼ teaspoon ground nutmeg, a pinch of ground ginger, a pinch of ground cloves and a pinch of ground mace.
• The canned pumpkin can be replaced with 2 cups cooked and pureed pumpkin.

VARIATIONS
Apple Cider Pumpkin Soup: Reduce the broth to ½ cup and mix with 1½ cups apple cider.
Sweet Potato Soup: Replace the pumpkin with 4 cups peeled and cubed sweet potatoes. Partially cover the saucepan and increase the cooking time to 15 minutes, or until the sweet potatoes are tender. Puree the mixture in a food processor or blender. Return to the saucepan and whisk in the milk and sour cream.

B orscht

This traditional Russian soup is delicious hot or cold. Either way, its flavor improves if you let it stand overnight.

3 medium beets, peeled and shredded
4 cups vegetable broth
1½ tablespoons honey
¼ cup vinegar
1 teaspoon reduced-sodium soy sauce
2 cups shredded cabbage
½ cup tomato puree or tomato juice

In a large saucepan, combine the beets and broth. Cover and cook over medium heat for 20 to 25 minutes, or until the beets are tender.

Stir in the honey, vinegar and soy sauce. Add the cabbage, cover and cook for about 6 minutes, or until the cabbage begins to soften. Stir in the tomato puree or tomato juice and cook for an additional 10 minutes.

Makes 4 servings. Per serving: 114 calories, 0.2 g. fat (1% of calories), 3 g. protein, 26.8 g. carbohydrates, 3.5 g. dietary fiber, 0 mg. cholesterol, 305 mg. sodium

VARIATION
Chilled Orange Borscht: Omit the vinegar and soy sauce. Replace 1 cup of the broth with 1 cup orange juice. Add the orange juice to the saucepan along with 1 cup halved cherry tomatoes, 1 seeded and sliced sweet red or yellow pepper and 2 tablespoons chopped fresh ginger. Omit the cabbage. Puree the soup along with 1 small orange, peeled and sectioned, and ¼ cup chopped fresh mint. Cover and refrigerate for at least 2 hours. Swirl a dollop of nonfat plain yogurt or sour cream into each serving.

Salmon Bisque

2 teaspoons olive oil
1 medium onion, diced
1½ tablespoons all-purpose flour
2 cups defatted chicken broth
1 cup tomato puree
1 teaspoon lemon juice
1 salmon fillet (12 ounces), cut into ½″ chunks
1 tablespoon minced fresh parsley
2 teaspoons minced fresh dill
1½ cups evaporated skim milk

In a medium saucepan over medium heat, warm the oil. Add the onions and sauté for 5 minutes, or until soft. Add the flour and cook for about 3 minutes, or until light brown.

Add the broth, tomato puree, lemon juice, salmon, parsley and dill. Simmer for 10 minutes. Add the milk and heat through.

Makes 4 servings. Per serving: 251 calories, 5.4 g. fat (20% of calories), 27.8 g. protein, 22.7 g. carbohydrates, 2 g. dietary fiber, 46 mg. cholesterol, 585 mg. sodium

NOTES

• Garnish each soup bowl with a swirl of nonfat sour cream and a sprinkling of chopped fresh dill.
• In a pinch, use canned salmon instead of the fresh fillet and reduce the cooking time to 5 minutes.

Corn Chowder

1½ cups defatted chicken broth
1½ cups water
1 baking potato, peeled and diced
1 onion, diced
1 small clove garlic, minced
½ teaspoon dried thyme
¼ teaspoon ground black pepper
⅛ teaspoon dried basil
1½ cups fresh or frozen corn
½ cup diced sweet red pepper
1 small zucchini, diced
½ cup evaporated skim milk

In a large saucepan over medium-high heat, bring the broth, water, potatoes, onions, garlic, thyme, pepper and basil to a boil. Cook for 10 minutes, or until the potatoes are tender.

Let cool for a few minutes, than ladle half of the vegetables and about 1 cup of the liquid into a food processor or blender. Add ½ cup of the corn. Blend until coarsely pureed. Return to the saucepan.

Stir in the red peppers, zucchini and remaining 1 cup corn. Cook over medium heat for 8 minutes, or until the zucchini is tender. Stir in the milk and warm through.

Makes 4 servings. Per serving: 144 calories, 0.4 g. fat (2% of calories), 7.9 g. protein, 30.5 g. carbohydrates, 3.3 g. dietary fiber, 1 mg. cholesterol, 170 mg. sodium

New England Clam Chowder

We set out to make a slimmed-down version of this classic American soup. Replacing the bacon and heavy cream with lean ham and low-fat milk did the trick.

- 1⅓ cups water
- 2 dozen littleneck clams, scrubbed
- 2 medium potatoes, peeled and diced
- 1 large onion, chopped
- 2 large stalks celery, chopped
- 2 carrots, halved lengthwise and thinly sliced
- 3 tablespoons minced fully cooked lean ham
- 1 small clove garlic, minced
- 1½ teaspoons canola oil
- 1½ cups bottled clam juice
- ½ teaspoon dried thyme
- 1⅓ cups 1% low-fat milk
- ½ teaspoon ground red pepper
- ¼ cup chopped fresh parsley
- 1 small scallion, thinly sliced

In a Dutch oven or large saucepan over high heat, bring the water to a boil. Add the clams. Reduce the heat to medium-low. Cover and simmer for 5 minutes, or until the clams open. Use a slotted spoon to remove the clams; discard any that did not open. Strain the liquid through a fine-mesh strainer and set aside. Remove the clams from their shells, mince and set aside.

In the same saucepan, combine the potatoes, onions, celery, carrots, ham, garlic and oil. Cook and stir over medium heat for 5 minutes.

Stir in the reserved clam liquid, clam juice and thyme. Bring to a boil. Reduce the heat to low, cover and gently simmer for 10 minutes, or until the potatoes are tender.

Puree the mixture in a food processor or blender. Return to the pan. Stir in the milk. Bring to a simmer but do not boil. Stir in the pepper and the reserved clams.

Sprinkle with the parsley and scallions.

Makes 4 servings. Per serving: 204 calories, 4.4 g. fat (19% of calories), 14.3 g. protein, 27.4 g. carbohydrates, 2.8 g. dietary fiber, 26 mg. cholesterol, 294 mg. sodium

NOTE

• The fresh clams can be replaced with 2 cans (6½ ounces each) chopped clams. Drain the clam juice from the clams and set the clams and juice aside. Reduce the amount of bottled clam juice to 1 cup. Add the reserved clam juice and bottled clam juice to the saucepan with the thyme. After pureeing the mixture, stir in the reserved clams and heat through.

Manhattan Clam Chowder

- 2 teaspoons olive oil
- 1 onion, finely chopped
- 2 stalks celery (with leaves), chopped
- 1 small clove garlic, minced
- ¾ cup bottled clam juice
- 2 cans (6½ ounces each) chopped clams (with juice)
- 1 large potato, peeled and diced
- 1 small green pepper, seeded and chopped
- 2½ cups reduced-sodium stewed tomatoes (with juice)
- 1 cup frozen corn
- ½ teaspoon dried thyme
- ½ teaspoon dried basil
- ¼ teaspoon chili powder
- ⅛ teaspoon salt (optional)
- ⅛ teaspoon ground black pepper
- 2–3 drops hot-pepper sauce
- 1 bay leaf

In a Dutch oven or large saucepan over medium heat, warm the oil. Add the onions, celery, garlic and 2 tablespoons of the bottled clam juice. Cook, stirring, for 5 minutes, or until the onions are tender. (If necessary, add more juice during cooking.)

Drain the juice from the clams into a small bowl. Set the clams aside and add the juice to the onion mixture. Then stir in the potatoes, green peppers and the remaining bottled clam juice. Bring to a boil. Reduce the heat to medium-low, cover and simmer, stirring occasionally, for 10 to 12 minutes, or until the potatoes are tender.

Add the tomatoes (with juice), corn, thyme, basil, chili powder, salt (if using), black pepper, hot-pepper sauce, bay leaf and the reserved clams. Bring to a boil. Cover and simmer for 8 minutes, or until the flavors are well-blended. Remove and discard the bay leaf.

Makes 4 servings. Per serving: 143 calories, 2.9 g. fat (17% of calories), 4.9 g. protein, 27.8 g. carbohydrates, 3.8 g. dietary fiber, 0 mg. cholesterol, 298 mg. sodium

Chicken Gumbo

We gave this traditional Southern stew its characteristic flavor without all the fat. The key was using a well-trimmed smoked ham bone instead of fatty smoked bacon.

- 3 cups water
- 2 cups defatted chicken broth
- 1 small smoked ham bone or 2 medium smoked pork hocks, trimmed of all visible fat (about 1 pound total)
- 2 small boneless, skinless chicken breast halves (about 5½ ounces total)
- 2 cups frozen black-eyed peas
- ½ cup coarsely chopped sweet red or green peppers
- ¼ cup chopped fresh parsley
- ¼ cup long-grain white rice
- 3 large scallions, sliced
- 1 onion, chopped
- 1 stalk celery, sliced
- 2 cloves garlic, minced
- ¼ teaspoon dried thyme
- 1½ cups reduced-sodium stewed tomatoes (with juice)
- ¾ cup sliced fresh or frozen okra
- ⅛ teaspoon ground black pepper
- ⅛ teaspoon ground red pepper (optional)

In a Dutch oven or large saucepan, combine the water, broth, ham bone or pork hocks, chicken, black-eyed peas, sweet peppers, parsley, rice, scallions, onions, celery, garlic and thyme. Bring to a boil over medium-high heat. Reduce the heat, cover and simmer, stirring occasionally, for 20 minutes.

Using tongs, remove the chicken and transfer it to a plate to cool. Simmer the gumbo for 10 minutes more.

Stir in the tomatoes (with juice), okra, black pepper and red pepper (if using). Cover and simmer, stirring occasionally, for 10 minutes.

Meanwhile, cut the chicken into bite-size pieces. Add the chicken to the pan. Remove and discard the ham bone or pork hocks. Skim off and discard any visible fat from the surface of the mixture. Simmer for 5 minutes, or just until the chicken is heated through.

Makes 4 servings. Per serving: 295 calories, 4 g. fat (12% of calories), 23.2 g. protein, 43.3 g. carbohydrates, 7.5 g. dietary fiber, 34 mg. cholesterol, 324 mg. sodium

Split Pea Soup

1 cup dried green split peas, sorted and rinsed
4 cups defatted chicken broth
1 small onion, diced
1 stalk celery, chopped
1 small carrot, diced
¼ teaspoon dried thyme
1 bay leaf
2 teaspoons reduced-sodium soy sauce
2 teaspoons minced fresh dill

In a large saucepan over high heat, bring the split peas and broth to a boil. Reduce the heat to medium-low, cover and simmer for 45 minutes, stirring occasionally.

Add the onions, celery, carrots, thyme, bay leaf and soy sauce. Return to a boil over medium-high heat, then reduce the heat to medium-low. Cover and simmer for 45 minutes, stirring occasionally. Add the dill and cook for another 5 minutes. Remove and discard the bay leaf before serving.

Makes 4 servings. Per serving: 210 calories, 0.7 g. fat (3% of calories), 17.5 g. protein, 35.2 g. carbohydrates, 3 g. dietary fiber, 0 mg. cholesterol, 447 mg. sodium

NOTE
• Garnish with a swirl of nonfat plain yogurt and a sprinkling of chopped fresh dill.

VARIATION
Split Pea Soup with Ham: Add ⅓ cup fully cooked chopped lean ham along with the vegetables. Or use the same amount of turkey ham and add 2 drops liquid smoke (available in the condiment section of most supermarkets). Omit the minced fresh dill.

Lentil-and-Pasta Soup

1 tablespoon olive oil
2 stalks celery, diced
1 carrot, diced
1 sweet green pepper, diced
½ cup chopped scallions
2 cloves garlic, minced
7 cups defatted reduced-sodium chicken broth
2 cups reduced-sodium canned tomatoes (with juice)
1 cup brown lentils, sorted and rinsed
4 ounces small shell pasta
1 box (10 ounces) frozen chopped spinach, thawed and squeezed dry
2 tablespoons grated Parmesan cheese

In a large saucepan over medium heat, warm the oil. Add the celery, carrots, peppers, scallions and garlic. Cook, stirring frequently, for 5 minutes, or until the vegetables are tender. Add the broth and tomatoes (with juice); bring to a boil.

Reduce the heat to medium-low and stir in the lentils. Simmer, partially covered, for 30 minutes.

Add the pasta and spinach. Simmer for 10 to 12 minutes, or until the pasta is tender. Sprinkle with the Parmesan.

Makes 4 servings. Per serving: 426 calories, 9 g. fat (19% of calories), 27.6 g. protein, 61.4 g. carbohydrates, 2.2 g. dietary fiber, 7 mg. cholesterol, 143 mg. sodium

VARIATION
Red Lentil and Pasta Soup: Replace the brown lentils with red lentils and reduce the cooking time to 20 minutes.

Black Bean Soup

Makes 4 servings. Per serving: 183 calories, 5.6 g. fat (28% of calories), 12.7 g. protein, 29.5 g. carbohydrates, 7.6 g. dietary fiber, 0 mg. cholesterol, 510 mg. sodium

1 can (16 ounces) black beans, rinsed and drained
4 cups defatted reduced-sodium chicken broth
1 bay leaf
¼ teaspoon chili powder
1 teaspoon cumin seeds
1 teaspoon coriander seeds
2 teaspoons dried oregano
1 teaspoon dried sage
3 cloves garlic, minced
1 tablespoon olive oil
1 onion, chopped
¼ cup chopped celery leaves
¼ cup chopped fresh cilantro or parsley
1 lime, halved
2 tablespoons Worcestershire sauce

In a large saucepan, combine the beans, broth and bay leaf. Bring to a boil. Reduce the heat to medium-low and simmer for 10 minutes.

Meanwhile, in a spice grinder or with a mortar and pestle, grind the chili powder, cumin seeds, coriander seeds, oregano, sage and garlic into a paste.

In a medium no-stick skillet over medium heat, warm the oil. Add the spice paste, onions, celery and cilantro or parsley. Using a fork, squeeze the juice and pulp from the lime into the mixture. Sauté for 5 minutes, or until very fragrant. Add to the beans along with the Worcestershire sauce. Simmer, uncovered, for 30 minutes.

Allow the beans to cool slightly; remove and discard the bay leaf. Puree 1½ cups of the bean mixture in a food processor or blender.

Stir the puree back into the soup. Warm through and serve.

Beef-and-Barley Soup

8 ounces lean beef eye round, cut into ½" cubes
¼ cup all-purpose or whole-wheat flour
1½ tablespoons canola oil
2 cups diced onions
½ cup chopped celery
½ cup chopped carrots
1 bay leaf
1½ teaspoons chopped fresh thyme or ½ teaspoon dried
3 tablespoons barley
1 tablespoon reduced-sodium soy sauce
4 cups water or defatted beef broth
Juice from ½ lemon

Dredge the beef in the flour to coat.

In a large saucepan over medium heat, warm the oil. Add the beef and cook until brown on all sides. Add the onions and cook for 5 minutes, or until the onions are soft.

Add the celery, carrots, bay leaf, thyme, barley, soy sauce, water or broth and lemon juice. Reduce the heat to low, cover and simmer for 1½ hours, or until the beef is tender and the barley is cooked. Skim off and discard any visible fat from the surface of the soup. Remove and discard the bay leaf before serving.

Makes 4 servings. Per serving: 272 calories, 8.4 g. fat (28% of calories), 20.7 g. protein, 28.2 g. carbohydrates, 3.7 g. dietary fiber, 39 mg. cholesterol, 189 mg. sodium

VARIATION

Lamb-and-Barley Soup: Replace the beef with boneless lamb loin trimmed of all visible fat and cut into ½" cubes.

Black-Eyed Pea and Vegetable Stew

- 1 tablespoon canola oil
- 1 cup chopped onions
- ½ cup sliced celery
- 4 cloves garlic, minced
- 1 potato, peeled and cubed
- 1 cup chopped turnips
- 1 cup sliced carrots
- 1 can (28 ounces) reduced-sodium crushed tomatoes
- 3 cups cooked or canned black-eyed peas
- 1½ cups fresh or frozen corn
- 2 tablespoons steak sauce
- 2 tablespoons chili sauce
- 1 tablespoon molasses
- 1 tablespoon cider vinegar
- 1 tablespoon cornstarch
- 4 drops hot-pepper sauce

In a large saucepan over medium heat, warm the oil. Add the onions, celery and garlic; sauté for 2 minutes. Stir in the potatoes, turnips and carrots; cook for 2 minutes. Stir in the tomatoes and bring to a boil over medium heat. Reduce the heat to low and simmer for 10 minutes.

Stir in the black-eyed peas, corn, steak sauce, chili sauce, molasses, vinegar, cornstarch and hot-pepper sauce. Cover and simmer for 45 minutes, or until the stew is thick and the vegetables are tender.

Makes 4 servings. Per serving: 358 calories, 5.2 g. fat (12% of calories), 16.1 g. protein, 68.1 g. carbohydrates, 17.6 g. dietary fiber, 0 mg. cholesterol, 318 mg. sodium

Beef Stew

- 12 ounces boneless beef chuck arm steak, trimmed of all visible fat and cut into 1" cubes
- 1 onion, chopped
- 2 cloves garlic, minced
- 1 cup water
- 4 cups defatted reduced-sodium beef broth
- 1 bay leaf
- 2 cups sliced carrots
- 1 cup sliced celery
- 1½ cups peeled and cubed turnips
- 1½ cups peeled and cubed potatoes
- ½ teaspoon ground black pepper
- ¼ cup all-purpose flour
- 2 teaspoons dried marjoram

Coat a large saucepan with no-stick spray. Warm the saucepan over medium heat. Add the beef and cook until browned on all sides. Add the onions and garlic. Sauté for 4 minutes, or until the onions are soft.

Add the water, broth and bay leaf. Cover and bring to a boil. Reduce the heat to low and simmer for 1¼ hours.

Add the carrots, celery, turnips, potatoes and pepper. Cover and return to a boil. Reduce the heat to low and simmer for 30 minutes, or until the vegetables are tender. Skim off any visible fat from the surface of the stew. Remove and discard the bay leaf.

Remove about 1 cup of the liquid. In a small bowl, whisk together the liquid and the flour until the mixture is smooth and free of lumps. Stir into the stew. Add the marjoram. Cook and stir over medium heat until the stew thickens and begins to gently boil. Cook and stir for 1 minute more.

Makes 4 servings. Per serving: 334 calories, 8 g. fat (21% of calories), 28.9 g. protein, 37.4 g. carbohydrates, 5.5 g. dietary fiber, 56 mg. cholesterol, 196 mg. sodium

NOTES

• For a full meal, serve with whole-grain soda bread or over wide noodles.

• As with most stews, the flavor of this dish improves overnight. For the best-tasting stew, make it the night before and reheat over low heat.

• You can replace ½ cup of the carrots with ½ cup fresh or frozen peas.

VARIATION

Lamb Stew: Replace the beef with lamb loin, trimmed of all visible fat and cut into 1″ cubes.

Turkey Stew with Herb Dumplings

Turkey

1	boneless, skinless turkey breast half (1¼ pounds)
1	tablespoon nondiet tub-style margarine or butter
1	small onion, chopped
1	medium stalk celery, chopped
2½	tablespoons all-purpose flour
3½	cups defatted chicken broth
⅛	teaspoon dried thyme
⅛	teaspoon ground black pepper
1	package (10 ounces) frozen mixed peas and carrots

Dumplings

1	cup all-purpose flour
1½	teaspoons sugar
¾	teaspoon baking powder
¼	teaspoon salt
1	tablespoon canola oil
1	tablespoon cold nondiet tub-style margarine or butter, cut into small pieces
¾	cup low-fat buttermilk
2	teaspoons finely chopped fresh chives

To make the turkey: Cut the turkey crosswise into 3 or 4 large pieces.

In a Dutch oven or large saucepan over medium heat, melt the margarine or butter. Add the onions and celery. Sauté for 3 minutes, or until the onions are tender. Stir in the flour; sauté for 2 minutes more.

Add ½ cup of the broth and stir until smooth. Gradually stir in the remaining 3 cups broth. Add the turkey, thyme and pepper. Bring to a boil. Reduce the heat to low, cover and simmer for 20 minutes.

Remove the turkey (it won't quite be cooked through) and cut it into 1″ pieces.

Skim off and discard any visible fat from the surface of the stew. Return the turkey to the pan. Stir in the peas and carrots. Remove the pan from the heat.

To make the dumplings: In a medium bowl, stir together the flour, sugar, baking powder and salt. Drizzle the oil over the flour mixture. Using a pastry blender, cut the oil and margarine or butter into the flour mixture until coarse crumbs form.

Add the buttermilk and chives. Using a fork, stir until just moistened.

Drop tablespoonfuls of the dough on top of the turkey mixture, leaving a small space between the dumplings.

Return the pan to the heat. Bring the mixture to a simmer over medium heat. Reduce the heat to low. Cover and simmer for 12 to 15 minutes, or until a toothpick inserted in the center of a dumpling comes out clean.

Makes 4 servings. Per serving: 482 calories, 10.9 g. fat (21% of calories), 52.8 g. protein, 42.1 g. carbohydrates, 1.5 g. dietary fiber, 114 mg. cholesterol, 742 mg. sodium

Simply
Delicious Grains and Beans

Pasta

When you were growing up, you called it spaghetti, and it usually came with meatballs. Today, it's called pasta, and it's nearly a national obsession.

While most supermarkets stock 20 to 30 pasta shapes, there are more than 600 varieties worldwide. More and more restaurants are featuring new, ever-expanding lists of trendy pasta dishes. In some cities, there are even fast-food restaurants that serve pasta and pasta alone.

What's behind this popularity of pasta? For starters, pasta is among the healthiest foods that you can eat. A 1-cup cooked serving of noodles has about 160 calories, less than 2 percent of which come from fat. Pasta is also a good source of B vitamins. As long as you serve it with a low-fat sauce, you're dishing out a healthy meal.

In addition, most pasta dishes are fast and easy to make—no small favor after a hectic day. At its simplest, pasta is a nutritious, filling base for whatever you want to put on top of it. One suggestion: Simply sauté some vegetables, add a few chopped tomatoes or tomato sauce and some fresh herbs and serve on any type of pasta. With tortellini or ravioli, all you really need is a little olive oil and grated cheese. Never has healthy cooking been so simple—or so delicious.

A Food for the Ages

Even though the word *pasta* has only recently entered our daily lexicon, food historians believe that the food itself originated many centuries before the birth of Christ. The Roman philosopher and statesman Cicero, for example, apparently enjoyed a flat dough cut into strips, which eventually evolved into the modern-day lasagna. And Etruscan artworks from the fourth century B.C. show all of the utensils necessary for pasta making.

Perhaps it's not surprising that one of the earliest cookbooks was written by a Roman, Marcus Gabius Apicius. He talked about pasta cooked in oil and dressed with pepper and garum, a sort of all-purpose sauce that the Romans used on everything.

Although we think of pasta as being as Italian as garlic and olive oil, noodles in one form or another are nearly universal. They form an integral part of the daily diet in countries as varied as China, Japan, Greece and Egypt, as well as here in the United States.

Long-Lasting Convenience

One of the most wonderful things about pasta is that it stores extremely well. Whether you buy the dry form and store it on a pantry shelf or stock up on frozen, it's always there when you need it.

Dried Pasta

As a convenience food, dried pasta—which is really nothing more than flour and water—can't be beat. It's inexpensive, cooks quickly and can be stored almost indefinitely. And unlike fresh pasta, it's available in a remarkable variety of shapes, from macaroni and penne to shells.

Quality dried pasta is made from hard durum wheat, which is very high in gluten. This is what gives pasta its stretch and elasticity, allowing it to cook up firm and hold its shape without turning soggy.

Dried pasta also provides good value for the money, often selling for a third (or even less) the price of fresh pasta.

☞ When buying pasta, check the label to see that it contains semolina flour or durum wheat. It should have a clear yellow color.

☞ To keep pasta fresh, store it in a cool, dark place, preferably in an airtight container.

☞ Each pasta strand or piece should be well-separated when cooked. If your pasta consistently sticks together in clumps, you may want to try another brand.

☞ Dry pasta has little flavor of its own and is recommended for use with a robust sauce.

Fresh Pasta

Until recently, the only place to get fresh pasta was in expensive restaurants or specialty stores. Now it's available, either refrigerated or frozen, in supermarkets everywhere.

Unlike dried pasta, which is made with hard flour, fresh pasta is made with eggs and a softer, all-purpose flour. This not only gives it a richer flavor but also causes it to absorb sauces more readily. It also freezes well, so you can store it for several weeks or longer before using.

With its more delicate texture and flavor, fresh pasta is generally preferred with mild sauces that won't overwhelm the flavor of the noodles.

Colored and Flavored Pastas

If you've eaten in trendy restaurants lately, you've probably already discovered that pasta can be a many-splendored thing. Dozens of ingredients—from spinach and tomatoes to saffron, garlic and basil—have lent their hues and flavors to this basic food. Here are a few popular types and a description of what gives them their color or flavor.

Egg Noodles

Is It GOOD for You?

After hearing all the bad news about cholesterol, you can't help but wonder if egg noodles are really a healthy choice. After all, one egg contains about 212 milligrams of cholesterol—more than two-thirds of the Daily Value. Wouldn't we be better off putting egg pasta (along with the venerable omelet), on the *verboten* list?

While people on strict low-cholesterol diets may want to reduce their noodle noshing, one serving of egg noodles contains only 50 milligrams of cholesterol—less than the amount in one serving of extra-lean ground beef. For most people, the healthful levels of protein and complex carbohydrates in egg noodles more than offset the slight boost in cholesterol.

☞ **Beet pasta.** This is easily made at home by adding cooked and finely chopped beets to the mixture. The deep red color fades to pink during cooking. Beet pasta is excellent served with a white sauce or a cheese sauce. It can also be combined with spinach pasta for a pleasing contrast.

☞ **Black pasta.** Made by adding squid ink to the mixture, black pasta lends a dramatic note to a meal. It's best served with a light sauce that won't mask the squid flavor.

(continued on page 136)

While store-bought pasta is very good indeed, purists insist that it can never rival the delicate taste and texture of homemade. To prepare dough manually, all you really need are eggs, flour and your own two hands.

Basic Pasta Dough

- 1½ cups all-purpose flour
- 2 eggs
- 1½ teaspoons olive oil (optional)

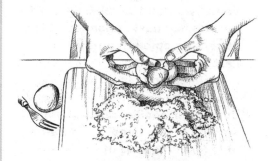

On a flat work surface, spoon 1¼ cups of the flour into a mound. Make a well in the center and break the eggs into it. Add the oil (if using) and beat together with the eggs using a fork.

As the mixture starts to thicken, set the fork aside and work with your hands, adding flour if needed, until the mixture forms a crumbly dough. At this point, it should be about the same texture as pie-crust dough.

Lightly flour the work surface and knead the dough, using the heel of your hand, until the dough becomes smooth and elastic. (Don't knead with an open hand, as your palms are too warm for the dough.)

Slowly bring the flour into the egg mixture, beating the flour and eggs with the fork.

Wrap the dough in plastic wrap or cover it with an inverted bowl and leave for about 30 minutes to rest.

Makes 8 ounces dough (enough for 4 servings). Per serving: 208 calories, 2.9 g. fat (13% of calories), 7.9 g. protein, 36.1 g. carbohydrates, 1.3 g. dietary fiber, 107 mg. cholesterol, 32 mg. sodium

NOTES

- Serve with your favorite sauce.
- To make 1 pound of dough (8 servings), use 2¼ cups flour, 3 large eggs and 1 tablespoon olive oil.
- To reduce the amount of fat and cholesterol, you can substitute 2 egg whites for one of the yolks.
- To speed preparation, place 1¼ cups of the flour in a food processor. Add the eggs and oil. Using on/off turns, process until the ingredients are mixed. Then process with on/off turns until the dough forms a ball around the blade. Add more flour if the dough is too sticky. Turn the dough onto a lightly floured surface and follow the directions for kneading.
- Pasta dough can be frozen for up to 3 months.

VARIATIONS

Beet Pasta Dough. Add 2 teaspoons pureed cooked beets to the eggs.

Herbed Pasta Dough. Add 1 teaspoon finely chopped fresh herbs, such as basil, dill, parsley or cilantro, to the eggs.

Lemon-Pepper Pasta Dough. Add 1 teaspoon grated lemon rind and ½ teaspoon ground black pepper to the eggs.

Spinach Pasta Dough. Add 2 teaspoons pureed cooked spinach to the eggs before mixing them with the flour. Or, for flecks of spinach in the dough, add 1 tablespoon thawed and squeezed-dry frozen chopped spinach.

Tomato Pasta Dough. Add 2 teaspoons tomato paste to the eggs.

Whole-Wheat Pasta Dough. Replace ¾ cup of the all-purpose flour with ¾ cup whole-wheat flour.

HAND-ROLLING DOUGH

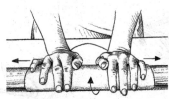

Place the dough on a lightly floured surface and roll it away from you. (But don't roll all the way to the edge.) Give the dough a quarter-turn and roll again. Continue turning the dough in the same direction to make a circle.

When the dough is about 8″ in diameter and ⅛″ thick, curl the far edge of the dough around the rolling pin. Keeping it taut, roll up the dough toward you. As you do this, slide your hands along the dough toward the ends of the pin, dragging them lightly against the surface of the pasta.

When the dough is completely rolled around the pin, unroll it and give it a quarter-turn. Wind it back onto the pin and roll it again. Continue until the dough is less than 1/16″ thick.

(continued)

MAKING YOUR OWN—CONTINUED

CUTTING PASTA

Lasagna. Cut the unrolled dough into 4″ × 6″ rectangles.

Pappardelle. Loosely fold the dough over into a long, flat roll about 3″ wide. With a sharp knife, cut the rolled sheet crosswise, making the strips about ¾″ wide.

Tagliatelle. Prepare the same way as pappardelle, but cut the strips at ½″ intervals.

Fettuccine. Cut the same way as pappardelle, but make the strips ¼″ wide.

MACHINE ROLLING AND CUTTING

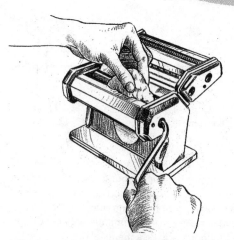

Adjust the rollers of a hand-cranked machine to the widest setting. Lightly dust about ⅛ of the dough and run it through the rollers. Reset the rollers to the next narrower setting and roll the dough through again. Continue until the dough is about 1/16″ thick.

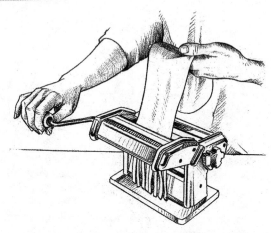

After attaching the desired cutting attachment, cut the dough to an easily managed length and run in through the machine.

Cheese Ravioli

- 8 ounces part-skim ricotta cheese
- ¼ cup grated Parmesan cheese
- 2 tablespoons fat-free egg substitute
- 2 tablespoons chopped fresh basil
- 2 teaspoons reduced-sodium tomato sauce
- ¼ teaspoon ground black pepper
- 8 ounces Basic Pasta Dough (page 132)

In a large bowl, combine the ricotta, Parmesan, egg substitute, basil, tomato sauce and pepper. Mix until just blended.

Cut the rolled-out pasta dough into sheets that are about 3″ wide and 16″ long. (To roll pasta, see the instructions on page 133.) Drop 1 tablespoon of the filling at 1″ intervals halfway down the length of each sheet.

Fold each sheet in half so that the long and short edges meet. With your fingertips, gently seal the edges and press down around each dab of filling to enclose it.

Using a pasta cutter or serrated knife, trim the edges of the dough and cut apart the ravioli. Gently crimp the edges of the ravioli with the tines of a fork to seal them closed.

Add the ravioli to a large pot of boiling water. Cook for 2 to 5 minutes, or until tender. Remove with a slotted spoon.

Makes 4 servings (about 24 ravioli). Per serving: 306 calories, 8.1 g. fat (24% of calories), 17.2 g. protein, 39.8 g. carbohydrates, 1.5 g. dietary fiber, 124 mg. cholesterol, 208 mg. sodium

NOTE

• To freeze the ravioli, sprinkle a no-stick jelly-roll pan with cornmeal. Place the ravioli in a single layer in the pan. (If a second layer is necessary, place wax paper between the layers but do not allow the ravioli to touch.) Freeze for at least 2 hours, or until solid. Transfer to freezer bags. Keeps frozen for up to 3 months.

VARIATION

Walnut Ravioli. Add 1 tablespoon finely chopped toasted walnuts to the filling.

☞ **Spinach pasta.** Made by adding cooked and finely chopped spinach to the flour, this is a good choice for a tomato or cream sauce.

☞ **Tomato pasta.** The addition of concentrated tomato paste creates a vivid orange-red color. Tomato pasta can be served with virtually any sauce, although it creates a particularly striking contrast when served with pesto.

Perhaps the greatest blessing of pasta is that you can plan, execute and serve a deliciously healthful meal in under 20 minutes. All you need is boiling water and a little bit of patience. For best results:

Start with a large pot. Pasta should be cooked in a large pot, preferably one that is taller

PASTA MADE PERFECT

While the basic ingredients used in making pasta have barely changed over hundreds of years, the noodles themselves have assumed an extraordinary variety of sizes and shapes. Each pasta shape is best suited for a particular sauce or style of cooking. In the chart below are some of the most common styles along with their recommended uses and cooking times. (When using store-bought frozen or refrigerated pastas, follow the directions on the package.)

COMMON PASTAS	WHAT IT MEANS	COOKING TIME (MIN.) DRIED	FRESH	SERVING SUGGESTIONS
Cannelloni 	Large reeds	8	½–2	The noodles' thick, sturdy sides are ideal for casseroles.
Capellini 	Fine hairs	5	2	This is best combined with a light sauce that won't overwhelm the delicate noodles.
Conchiglie 	Conch shells	10	3	The shells are often used with meat or vegetable sauces, because the folds trap the pieces. They are also used with hearty soups like minestrone, since the shells can compete equally with beans and potatoes.
Farfalle 	Butterflies	7–10	2–3	The bow-tie shape collects dressings and seasonings.
Fettuccine 	Small ribbons	8–9	1½–3	These firm ribbon shapes are often used with delicate cream sauces.

than it is wide. Plan on using at least 4 quarts of water for every pound of pasta. Cooking pasta in a pot that's too small may cause it to stick together.

Work with small batches. For pasta to cook evenly, it has to roll freely in the boiling water. Unless you have a truly gargantuan pot, don't try to cook more than 2 pounds at a time.

Wait for the boil. Putting pasta in water that's not at full boil means that it spends more time in the water than it otherwise would. This can cause the noodles to absorb too much liquid, which will make them soft and mushy.

Hold the oil. While cooks have traditionally poured a small quantity of oil into the water to prevent pasta from sticking, this really isn't nec-

COMMON PASTAS	WHAT IT MEANS	COOKING TIME (MIN.) DRIED	FRESH	SERVING SUGGESTIONS
Lasagna	Little pots	10	2–4	This thick, wide pasta holds up well during baking.
Linguine	Small tongues	5–7	1½–2	The flat, slippery shape is often used with tomato or seafood sauce.
Maccheroni	Macaroni	9–10	—	The sturdy curved elbows hold their shape and trap meat and vegetable pieces when used with robust sauces or in soups and stews. It's often used in salads, because the shape collects dressings and seasonings.
Ravioli	Little turnips	—	7–9	These are usually stuffed with meat or other fillings.
Spaghetti	Length of cord	7–9	2–3	The delicate shape goes well with light and spicy sauces.
Tortellini	Small twists	9–11	7–9	Often filled with a meat or cheese stuffing, these are usually served with a light cream sauce.
Ziti	Bridegrooms	10	—	The grooved shape clings to meat and vegetable pieces, making it ideal for chunky sauces. Also used in casseroles and salads.

MEASURING PASTA

A single serving size of dried pasta looks deceptively skimpy, which is why many cooks, nervous about running short, always take the precaution of making extra—only to discover they have enough left over to feed the neighbors.

Pasta expands considerably during cooking. A rule of thumb is to allow 2 ounces of dry pasta per serving.

Use the chart below to gauge the amount needed of different shapes.

Pasta	Dry Measure (4 servings)
Long, skinny pastas, like spaghetti	1½"-diameter bunch
Broad noodles	4 cups
Fine or medium noodles	4½ cups
Macaroni	2 cups
Rigatoni	4 cups
Ziti, rotini or fusilli	3 cups
Bow ties	4 cups
Orzo, ditalini, stelline or acini di pepe	1⅓ cups

essary. As long as you're using high-quality pasta and giving it room to roll in boiling water, it won't stick. If you are having trouble with clumping, don't add oil; change pasta brands instead.

Add it all at once. To keep control of the cooking time, it's best to put all of the pasta in the pot at one time, rather than dropping it in a little at a time.

If the pasta is too long to lie flat, just stand it on edge. As it softens and bends, immerse the remaining ends. Stir it regularly to move pasta from the bottom to the top.

Maintain the heat. It's normal for water to lose its boil once you add the pasta. To bring it back to a boil quickly, put the lid on for just a minute. As soon as the boil resumes, remove the lid and cook until the pasta is done.

Plan ahead. Since pasta continues cooking even after you remove it from the water, it's important to drain it *before* it's completely cooked. Chefs generally recommend removing pasta from the water about 1 minute before you expect it to be done.

The Done Test

Get together with three friends over a plate of spaghetti, and you'll probably hear three different methods for knowing when to remove pasta from the water.

Frustrated cooks have devised dozens of strategies for guesstimating when their dinners are done. These range from the practical (like using a timer) to the exotic (throwing a strand at the wall to see if it sticks).

It really isn't all that complicated. For perfect pasta every time, here's what chefs advise.

Take a bite. The easiest way to tell when pasta is done is to fish a piece out of the pot, douse it with cold water and then take a bite. It should be al dente, which literally means "to the tooth." In other words, it should be firm, but not soft or mushy.

Check it often. Different shapes and sizes of pasta cook at different speeds. Even different

Helpful Hint

Adding salt to boiling water along with the pasta briefly raises the temperature, preventing the boil from being interrupted. A healthier alternative is simply to add the pasta more slowly.

batches of the same pasta type may vary by a minute or two either way. So don't put your faith in the package directions; check the pasta—using the bite test—a minute or two before you think it's done. If necessary, let it cook a minute more, then test it again.

Make it fresh. Fresh pasta cooks much faster than dried. Depending on the shape, it may be ready in 1 or 2 minutes. Dried pasta, on the other hand, may take 10 or more minutes.

Draining, Serving and Storing Pasta

To prevent pasta from overcooking, it must be drained as soon as it's ready. Here's how.

☞ Using mitts or a kitchen towel to protect your hands, drain the pasta in a large, stable colander set in the sink. The steam will be extremely hot, so don't put your face over the colander, and be careful of the placement of your hands.

☞ With oven mitts on, take the handles of the colander and shake it from side to side to release excess water.

☞ When making a pasta salad, or when cooking pasta for later use, rinse it well with cold water after draining. This will stop residual heat from cooking it further. Then toss the pasta with a little oil to prevent sticking and store it in the refrigerator in a covered bowl.

☞ It's best to use dried pasta when you need to cook some ahead of time; fresh pasta is more delicate and tends to get mushy when reheated.

☞ To reheat pasta in the microwave, use high power and heat for about 1 minute. If it is not warm, continue heating, checking at 15-second intervals.

☞ The microwave works best for reheating small amounts of pasta. If you're reheating more than one serving, it may be just as fast to heat it on the stove top using boiling water.

TWICE-COOKED PASTAS

Lasagna, macaroni and cheese, baked ziti—these are among the oldest dishes in Italy. Known as *pasticci*, or twice-cooked pasta, these are casseroles in which the ingredients are prepared separately, then mixed together and baked in the oven.

Pasticci are substantial, nourishing and great to serve at buffets. They're also easy to make.

☞ Since the pasta will be cooked twice—once in boiling water and again in the oven—it's important to slightly undercook it when boiling. This will prevent it from being overdone later on.

☞ Dried pasta should be removed from the boiling water about 5 minutes before the recommended cooking time.

☞ Fresh pasta should be removed from the pot about 20 seconds after the water returns to a boil.

☞ Watery lasagna is the bane of home cooks. It's best to rinse and drain the cooked noodles while the other ingredients are being prepared. The extra draining time will help keep the finished product firm and intact.

☞ To cut lasagna into neat squares, let it stand for at least 10 minutes after baking. This gives the cheese time to solidify and allows the noodles to absorb surplus liquids.

PASTA FROM AROUND THE WORLD

Pasta is truly a universal food. In many Asian countries, noodles play a major role. They can be used as a base for sauces or to give body to soup. They can be steamed, stir-fried or coiled into thick pancakes. Noodle dumplings like wontons are always popular, and steamed rice noodles are often used for stuffing spring rolls.

While pasta in this country is most often made from wheat, in Asian countries it's more likely made from rice flour or vegetable starches like yam, soybean and potato.

Rice Noodles

Also called rice stick or rice vermicelli, these translucent noodles are usually sold dried and gathered into large skeins.

☞ To soften rice noodles, soak them in water for about 20 minutes before cooking.

☞ Rice noodles absorb flavors well, so they're often used in soups or as a base for stews or sauces.

Bean-Starch Noodles

Also called bean-thread noodles, these are made from dried mung beans and are often added to soups and braised dishes. Bean-thread noodles are often found in spring rolls too. The noodles give substance to any dish, along with a slightly chewy texture.

The noodles are difficult to cut when dry, so soak them first in warm water until they soften.

Wonton Wrappers

These versatile noodles are available fresh or frozen in many supermarkets. They can be added to soups for substance and texture. In some cases, they're used to replace the noodles used in lasagna.

Wonton wrappers can also be used to make egg rolls or filled like ravioli. To make quick wonton ravioli, use the cheese ravioli filling from the recipe on page 135. Replace the Basic Pasta Dough with 24 wonton wrappers. Place the wontons on a lightly floured work surface. Place 1 tablespoon of filling in the center of each wonton. Moisten the edges with your fingers or a pastry brush dipped in water. Fold one corner diagonally over the filling to make a triangle. With the tines of a fork, gently crimp the edges of each ravioli. Cover with a damp towel until all are done. Cook the ravioli in a large pot of boiling water for 4 to 6 minutes, or until tender. Remove with a slotted spoon.

Soba

These are square, medium-thick buckwheat noodles that are often served in soup. They can also be served cold and topped with a wide variety of condiments, like chopped scallions or horseradish.

☞ Soba is extremely long-lasting and will keep for several months when stored in an airtight container.

☞ Cook in simmering water until almost tender, then rinse under cool running water.

☞ Noodles can be cooked ahead of time, then reheated by immersing in boiling water and serving in soup.

Ramen

This is the Japanese name for Chinese-style egg noodles. They are usually sold in cellophane packages, complete with a concentrated powder for making a tasty, nutritious (but high-sodium) broth.

Lidia Bastianich

When Lidia Bastianich arrived in New York City in 1958, she brought with her an authentically Italian style of cooking that has earned her the title "First Lady" of Italian restaurants. Today, her restaurants, Felidia and Becco, serve some of the best pasta on the East Coast.

"Bread may be the 'staff of life,' but in Italy and many other parts of the world, its primacy is increasingly challenged by pasta," she says. "Pasta has become a universally favorite food."

For the recipe below, Bastianich generally uses borlotti beans, which are available in many Italian markets. If you can't find them, you can substitute cranberry beans, kidney beans or cannellini beans.

Shells and Beans with Basil

- 8 ounces dry borlotti, cranberry, kidney or cannellini beans, sorted and soaked overnight
- 2 bay leaves
- ¼ cup shredded carrots
- 2 tablespoons olive oil
- 2 cloves garlic, minced
- 1 small onion, diced
- 1 can (16 ounces) peeled plum tomatoes
  Pinch of salt
  Pinch of red-pepper flakes
- ¼ cup chopped fresh Italian parsley
- ¼ cup shredded fresh basil
- 1 pound small pasta shells

Drain and rinse the beans. Transfer to a large saucepan; add enough water to cover. Add the bay leaves, carrots and 1 tablespoon of the oil. Bring to a boil over high heat. Reduce the heat to medium and cook for 30 minutes, or until the beans are almost tender. Remove from the heat and set aside.

Meanwhile, place the remaining 1 tablespoon oil in a Dutch oven or large saucepan and warm over medium heat. Add the garlic and onions. Sauté for 5 minutes, or until the onions are golden.

Drain the tomatoes and pass through a food mill. Add to the onions along with the salt and red-pepper flakes. Cook for 10 minutes.

Drain the beans, reserving ½ cup of the cooking liquid. Add the beans and the reserved liquid to the tomato mixture. Simmer for 15 minutes, or until the beans are tender. Add the parsley and basil.

Meanwhile, cook the shells in a large pot of boiling water until just tender. Drain, add to the tomato mixture and cook over low heat for 3 to 4 minutes to blend the flavors.

Makes 6 servings. Per serving: 482 calories, 6.6 g. fat (12% of calories), 19.6 g. protein, 86.6 g. carbohydrates, 0.9 g. dietary fiber, 0 mg. cholesterol, 127 mg. sodium

QUICK!
Cheese Filling for Pasta

- 1 container (16 ounces) reduced-fat ricotta cheese (about 2 cups)
- ½ cup reduced-fat spaghetti sauce
- 3 large egg whites, lightly beaten
- ¼ cup shredded reduced-fat mozzarella cheese
- 2 tablespoons skim milk
- 2 tablespoons grated Parmesan cheese
- ½ teaspoon dried basil
- ¼ teaspoon dried oregano
- ¼ teaspoon garlic powder
- ¼ teaspoon ground black pepper

In a medium bowl, combine the ricotta, spaghetti sauce, egg whites, mozzarella, milk, Parmesan, basil, oregano, garlic powder and pepper. Mix until completely blended.

Makes 3 cups. Per ¼ cup: 55 calories, 1.7 g. fat (28% of calories), 5.7 g. protein, 4.1 g. carbohydrates, 0 g. dietary fiber, 7 mg. cholesterol, 108 mg. sodium

NOTES
• This filling will stuff 8 ounces of jumbo pasta shells (22 to 24 shells) or fill 2 dozen ravioli. It can also be used in baked ziti and lasagna.
• To make *Cheese-Stuffed Zucchini*, cut 6 medium zucchini in half lengthwise and hollow out the halves to make boats. Spoon the filling into the zucchini. Sprinkle with shredded reduced-fat mozzarella cheese and bread crumbs. Coat a no-stick baking sheet with no-stick spray. Place the zucchini on the baking sheet, cover and bake at 375° for 20 minutes. Uncover and bake for 10 minutes, or until the cheese is browned and bubbly and the filling is heated through.
• To make *Triple-Cheese Eggplant Parmigiana*, cut 1 large eggplant into ½"-thick slices. Coat a no-stick baking sheet with no-stick spray. Arrange the slices in a single layer on the baking sheet and spread the filling on each slice. Top with shredded reduced-fat mozzarella cheese and bread crumbs. Cover and bake at 375° for 20 minutes. Uncover and bake for 10 minutes, or until the cheese is browned and bubbly and the eggplant is heated through.

VARIATIONS
Cheese-and-Meat Filling for Pasta: Stir in 8 ounces cooked extra-lean ground beef, ground turkey or crumbled low-fat turkey sausage.
Cheese-and-Vegetable Filling for Pasta: Stir in 1 cup thawed frozen chopped broccoli or thawed frozen spinach, squeezed dry. Or sauté 1 cup sliced vegetables (such as zucchini or mushrooms) in 1 teaspoon olive oil, then stir into the cheese mixture.

Stuffed Shells Florentine

- 2 cups reduced-sodium spaghetti sauce
- 16 jumbo pasta shells (about 5–6 ounces)
- 1½ cups reduced-fat ricotta cheese
- 1 package (10 ounces) frozen chopped spinach, thawed and squeezed dry
- ½ cup coarsely chopped reduced-sodium stewed tomatoes
- ¼ cup grated reduced-fat Parmesan cheese
- 1 tablespoon skim milk
- 1 teaspoon dried basil
- ⅛ teaspoon ground nutmeg
- ⅓ cup shredded fat-free mozzarella cheese

Preheat the oven to 350°. Spread 1 cup of the spaghetti sauce in the bottom of a 9" × 13" no-stick baking dish and set aside.

In a large pot of boiling water, cook the shells according to the package directions.

Meanwhile, in a large bowl, combine the ricotta, spinach, tomatoes, Parmesan, milk, basil, nutmeg and half of the mozzarella.

Drain the shells. Spoon equal amounts of the filling into the shells and place them, filling side up, in the prepared baking dish. Spoon the remaining 1 cup spaghetti sauce over them.

Cover with foil and bake for 40 minutes. Uncover and sprinkle with the remaining mozzarella. Bake for 5 to 10 minutes, or until the cheese melts.

Makes 4 servings. Per serving: 358 calories, 5.8 g. fat (15% of calories), 21.8 g. protein, 55.1 g. carbohydrates, 0.4 g. dietary fiber, 12 mg. cholesterol, 643 mg. sodium

NOTES
• This filling may also be used to stuff cannelloni or manicotti.
• For a richer flavor, add ½ cup chopped roasted red peppers to the filling.

Classic Lasagna

12 lasagna noodles
½ cup fat-free egg substitute
2 cups fat-free ricotta cheese
2 cups part-skim ricotta cheese
¼ cup chopped fresh parsley
4 cups tomato sauce
2 cups shredded part-skim mozzarella cheese

Preheat the oven to 375°.

In a large pot of boiling water, cook the noodles according to the package directions. Drain.

Meanwhile, in a large bowl, combine the egg substitute, fat-free ricotta, part-skim ricotta and parsley; set aside.

Spread 1 cup of the tomato sauce in the bottom of a 9″ × 13″ no-stick baking dish. Place a layer of 4 noodles in the dish. Sprinkle with half of the mozzarella. Spread a layer of

the filling over the mozzarella. Spoon on a layer of sauce. Add a layer of 4 noodles, then top with all but ¼ cup of the remaining mozzarella. Spread on the remaining filling. Finish with the remaining 4 noodles and the remaining sauce. Sprinkle with the reserved mozzarella.

Cover loosely with foil. Bake for 30 to 35 minutes, or until the cheese is browned and bubbly and the lasagna is heated through. Let stand for 10 minutes before cutting.

Makes 10 servings. Per serving: 267 calories, 8.7 g. fat (29% of calories), 22.6 g. protein, 26.2 g. carbohydrates, 2.9 g. dietary fiber, 28 mg. cholesterol, 667 mg. sodium

NOTES
• Take care not to overcook the lasagna noodles; slightly underdone noodles are easier to handle and less likely to tear. To prevent sticking, place just-cooked, hot noodles immediately into cold water. Remove the noodles one at a time for layering. Work quickly so that the noodles remain tender yet firm.
• If your pasta pot starts to boil over, stick a wooden spoon into the water. The foam will immediately subside.

VARIATIONS
Lasagna with Meat Sauce: Brown 8 ounces extra-lean ground beef in a no-stick skillet coated with no-stick spray. Drain well and discard any excess fat. Stir the meat into the tomato sauce.
Spinach Lasagna: Rinse and remove the stems from 12 ounces of fresh spinach. Steam the spinach until wilted. Drain well and squeeze out the liquid. Chop the spinach and stir into the filling.
Zucchini Lasagna: Add 1½ cups shredded zucchini to the filling.
Mushroom Lasagna: Add 1½ cups sautéed button and/or cremini mushrooms to the filling.

Shortcut Microwave Lasagna

8   ounces extra-lean ground beef
1   small onion, chopped
1   large clove garlic, minced
4   cups reduced-fat tomato sauce
1   teaspoon dried oregano
2   containers (16 ounces each) fat-free ricotta cheese (about 4 cups)
½   cup grated reduced-fat Parmesan cheese
¼   teaspoon salt
2   cups shredded part-skim mozzarella cheese
16   no-boil lasagna noodles (8 ounces)

Coat two 8″ × 8″ microwave-safe no-stick baking dishes with no-stick spray.

In a large microwave-safe bowl, stir together the beef, onions and garlic. Cover loosely with wax paper. Microwave on high power for a total of 4 minutes; stop and stir well after 2 minutes to break up the beef.

Stir in the tomato sauce and oregano. Cover and microwave for a total of 5 minutes; stop and stir well after 2 minutes.

In a large bowl, stir together the ricotta, Parmesan, salt and half of the mozzarella.

Spread a thin layer of the meat sauce in the bottom of each baking dish. Add a layer of noodles, then a layer of the filling. Repeat the layering, using more sauce, more noodles and the remainder of the filling. Finish each lasagna with a layer of sauce, a layer of the remaining noodles and a final layer of sauce.

Place one of the baking dishes on a microwave-safe rack or an inverted microwave-safe saucer. Cover with wax paper. Microwave on high power for a total of 9 minutes; rotate the dish a quarter-turn after 5 minutes. Sprinkle with half of the remaining mozzarella. Loosely cover the dish with wax paper and let stand for 10 minutes before cutting.

Repeat the microwaving procedure with the second baking dish.

Makes 12 servings. Per serving: 211 calories, 5.5 g. fat (23% of calories), 23.3 g. protein, 19.5 g. carbohydrates, 2.2 g. dietary fiber, 23 mg. cholesterol, 635 mg. sodium

NOTE

• If you need only 6 servings, you can refrigerate one of the lasagnas for up to 2 days. For refrigerated lasagna, increase the final microwaving time to about 12 minutes.

Baked Ziti

8   ounces ziti
8   ounces low-fat Italian turkey sausage, casings removed
1   jar (27½ ounces) reduced-sodium tomato sauce
1½   cups shredded fat-free mozzarella cheese
1   tablespoon grated Parmesan cheese
2   tablespoons chopped fresh parsley

Preheat the oven to 350°. Coat a shallow 3-quart no-stick baking dish with no-stick spray and set aside.

In a large pot of boiling water, cook the ziti according to the package directions.

Meanwhile, in a large no-stick skillet coated with no-stick spray, cook and stir the sausage for 5 to 7 minutes, or until broken into small pieces and no longer pink.

Drain the ziti and place in a large bowl. Add the sausage, tomato sauce and 1 cup of the mozzarella and mix well. Spoon into the prepared baking dish.

Cover with foil and bake for 30 minutes. Uncover and sprinkle with the Parmesan and the remaining ½ cup mozzarella. Bake for 6 to 8 minutes, or until the cheese melts. Sprinkle with the parsley before serving.

Makes 4 servings. Per serving: 457 calories, 5.5 g. fat (11% of calories), 36.5 g. protein, 63 g. carbohydrates, 2.9 g. dietary fiber, 37 mg. cholesterol, 864 mg. sodium

NOTES
• This dish can be assembled a day ahead and refrigerated, then baked when needed. Increase the initial baking time 35 minutes.
• You may replace the ziti with other short tube pasta such as penne or rigatoni.

VARIATIONS
Baked Ziti with Beef: Replace the sausage with extra-lean ground beef.
Baked Ziti with Peas: Add 1 box (10 ounces) frozen peas to the mixture. They don't need to be thawed because they will cook in the oven.
Triple-Cheese Baked Ziti: When mixing the sausage and ziti, add ½ recipe (1½ cups) Cheese Filling for Pasta (page 142).

Light Manicotti

14	manicotti shells (8 ounces)
4	ounces mushrooms, sliced
4	mild chili peppers, seeded and sliced
1	jar (27½ ounces) reduced-sodium tomato-and-herb spaghetti sauce
½	teaspoon dried basil
1½	cups low-fat cottage cheese or fat-free ricotta cheese
1	cup shredded fat-free mozzarella cheese
1	tablespoon grated Parmesan cheese
1	package (10 ounces) frozen chopped spinach, thawed and squeezed dry
2	egg whites
⅛	teaspoon ground black pepper
¼	cup chopped fresh parsley

In a large pot of boiling water, cook the manicotti shells according to the package directions. Drain.

Meanwhile, coat a large no-stick skillet with olive oil no-stick spray and warm over medium heat. Add the mushrooms and chili peppers. Sauté for 2 minutes, or until the mushrooms begin to release their liquid. Remove from the heat and stir in the spaghetti sauce and basil. Spread ¼ of the sauce in the bottom of a 9″ × 13″ no-stick baking dish and set aside.

In a large bowl, mix the cottage cheese or ricotta, mozzarella, Parmesan, spinach, egg whites and black pepper. Spoon the filling carefully into the shells.

Preheat the oven to 350°.

Place the manicotti in a single layer in the prepared baking dish and pour the remaining sauce over the top. Cover with foil and bake for 25 to 30 minutes, or until hot and bubbly. Garnish with the parsley.

Makes 6 servings. Per serving: 370 calories, 8.6 g. fat (21% of calories), 24 g. protein, 47.5 g. carbohydrates, 4.3 g. dietary fiber, 3 mg. cholesterol, 460 mg. sodium

NOTE
• Be careful not to overcook the manicotti shells; slightly underdone shells are easier to handle and less likely to tear. To prevent sticking, place just-cooked, hot shells immediately into cold water. Remove the shells one at a time for stuffing. When stuffing them, use a teaspoon or a pastry bag fitted with a large tip and work quickly so that the shells remain tender yet firm.

Meat Ravioli

A mixture of seasoned ground turkey and veal replaces the usual fatty beef. Serve the ravioli plain or with your favorite sauce.

 1 teaspoon olive oil
 1 stalk celery, diced
 1 carrot, diced
 1 clove garlic, minced
 6 ounces lean ground turkey
 4 ounces lean ground veal
 ¼ cup defatted reduced-sodium chicken broth
 1 large egg white, lightly beaten
 1 tablespoon grated Parmesan cheese
 ¼ teaspoon finely crushed fennel seeds
 1 recipe (8 ounces) Basic Pasta Dough (page 132)

In a large no-stick skillet over medium heat, warm the oil. Add the celery, carrots and garlic and sauté for 3 to 5 minutes, or until the vegetables are tender. Stir in the turkey and veal. Cook and stir for 4 to 6 minutes, or until the meat is broken into pieces and is no longer pink. Stir in the broth. Reduce the heat to low, cover and cook for 1 to 2 minutes, or until the liquid evaporates.

Transfer the meat mixture to a food processor and process with on/off turns until finely chopped. Transfer to a medium bowl. Stir in the egg white, Parmesan and fennel seeds and mix well.

Roll out and fill the dough as directed for Cheese Ravioli (page 135).

In a large pot of boiling water, cook the ravioli for 3 to 4 minutes, or until they float to the surface of the pot. Remove with a slotted spoon.

Makes 4 servings (about 24 ravioli). Per serving: 350 calories, 10 g. fat (26% of calories), 24.2 g. protein, 38.8 g. carbohydrates, 1.9 g. dietary fiber, 153 mg. cholesterol, 149 mg. sodium

NOTES

• The ravioli can be assembled ahead of time and refrigerated up to 8 hours before cooking.

• Be sure to use a slotted spoon when removing ravioli from water, because fresh ravioli tend to be more delicate than store-bought.

• To make a light cream sauce for the ravioli, melt 4 teaspoons nondiet tub-style margarine in a no-stick skillet over medium-low heat. Stir in 2 tablespoons flour to make a roux (a cooked combination of flour and fat used as a thickening agent). Whisk in 2 cups evaporated or regular skim milk. Cook and stir until thick. Stir in 2 tablespoons grated Parmesan cheese. Season with salt and pepper and serve over the ravioli.

Spaghetti and Meatballs

We gave meatballs a low-fat profile and great flavor by using a combination of ground turkey breast and low-fat turkey sausage in place of regular ground beef.

 8   ounces spaghetti
 1½ slices whole-wheat bread, torn into small pieces
 4   ounces ground turkey breast
 4   ounces low-fat turkey sausage, casings removed
 2   tablespoons minced onions
 2   teaspoons minced garlic
 ½   teaspoon dried basil
 ½   teaspoon dried oregano
     Pinch of ground red pepper
 1   egg white, lightly beaten
 ½   cup defatted chicken broth

1 small onion, finely chopped
2 sweet red peppers, finely chopped
4 large tomatoes, seeded and diced
¼ cup tomato sauce

In a large pot of boiling water, cook the spaghetti according to the package directions.

Meanwhile, place the bread in a food processor or blender and process with on/off turns to make fine crumbs. Crumble the turkey breast and turkey sausage into the food processor. Add the minced onions, garlic, basil, oregano and ground red pepper and process briefly. Add the egg white and process with on/off turns until well-mixed. Shape the mixture into 1″ balls.

Coat a Dutch oven or large no-stick skillet with no-stick spray. Place over medium heat, add the meatballs and brown on all sides. Remove to a platter and set aside.

Add the broth to the pan and scrape up the cooked-on bits of meat with a wooden spoon. Add the chopped onions and sweet red peppers. Sauté, stirring frequently, for 5 minutes, or until tender. Add the tomatoes and tomato sauce. Cover and cook for 10 minutes, stirring frequently to prevent scorching. Add the meatballs and cook for 10 minutes more. Drain the pasta and serve with the meatballs and sauce.

Makes 4 servings. Per serving: 460 calories, 7.6 g. fat (15% of calories), 25.7 g. protein, 74.2 g. carbohydrates, 4.4 g. dietary fiber, 42 mg. cholesterol, 402 mg. sodium

NOTE
• To buy the leanest ground turkey available, look for products made with only turkey breast meat. Many ground turkey products also contain the dark meat and fatty skin.

Meatballs Florentine

The addition of spinach and cheese makes these delicious meatballs "florentine." Add them to soups, serve them with pasta and tomato sauce or roll them in fresh bread crumbs and bake them for meatball sandwiches.

8 cloves garlic, unpeeled
1 teaspoon olive oil
4 shallots, peeled
1 cup fresh spinach leaves
½ cup fat-free ricotta cheese
1 egg white
2 teaspoons dried oregano
½ teaspoon dried dill
½ teaspoon ground black pepper
¼ teaspoon ground nutmeg
12 ounces extra-lean ground beef
⅓ cup fresh whole-wheat or oatmeal bread crumbs

Preheat the oven to 400°.

Place the garlic on a piece of foil, drizzle with the oil and bake for 15 minutes. Trim the root end from each clove and remove the peel. Transfer to a food processor or blender. Add the shallots, spinach, ricotta, egg white, oregano, dill, pepper and nutmeg and puree.

In a large bowl, combine the beef and bread crumbs. Add the spinach mixture and mix well. Shape into meatballs using ¼ cup of meat for each.

Line a no-stick jelly-roll pan with foil. Coat a wire rack with no-stick spray and place it in the pan. Place the meatballs on the rack and bake at 400° for 20 to 25 mintues, or until brown.

Makes 4 servings. Per serving: 228 calories, 11.8 g. fat (47% of calories), 22.4 g. protein, 8.7 g. carbohydrates, 1 g. dietary fiber, 53 mg. cholesterol, 110 mg. sodium

Macaroni and Cheese

We lightened up this classic comfort food by replacing the high-fat cheese, butter and whole milk with a lean and tasty blend of cheeses and skim milk.

6	ounces elbow macaroni (about 1½ cups)
⅔	cup shredded reduced-fat Cheddar cheese
½	cup dry-curd cottage cheese
½	cup skim milk
½	cup fat-free egg substitute
¼	teaspoon hot-pepper sauce
1	teaspoon Dijon mustard
¼	cup seasoned dry bread crumbs
¼	teaspoon paprika
1	tablespoon grated Parmesan cheese

In a large pot of boiling water, cook the macaroni according to the package directions. Drain.

Preheat the oven to 375°.

Coat a 1-quart no-stick baking dish with no-stick spray. Add the macaroni and Cheddar. Toss to combine.

In a food processor or blender, puree the cottage cheese, milk, egg substitute, hot-pepper sauce and ½ teaspoon of the mustard. Pour over the macaroni and stir to combine.

In a small bowl, mix the bread crumbs with the paprika, Parmesan and the remaining ½ teaspoon mustard. Sprinkle over the macaroni. Bake for 25 minutes.

Makes 4 servings. Per serving: 321 calories, 7.1 g. fat (20% of calories), 22.1 g. protein, 40.3 g. carbohydrates, 0 g. dietary fiber, 23 mg. cholesterol, 944 mg. sodium

VARIATION

Tomato Macaroni and Cheese: Gently stir 10 halved cherry tomatoes into the macaroni mixture before adding the cheese sauce.

Pasta with Creamy Parmesan Sauce

QUICK!

8	ounces fusilli
3	tablespoons dry sherry or nonalcoholic white wine
1	tablespoon water
1	tablespoon nondiet tub-style margarine or butter
1	large onion, finely chopped
1	small clove garlic, minced
2	tablespoons all-purpose flour
½	teaspoon dry mustard
⅛	teaspoon ground black pepper
1¾	cups 1% low-fat milk
½	cup grated reduced-fat Parmesan cheese
⅓	cup nonfat sour cream
1	tablespoon chopped fresh parsley

In a large pot of boiling water, cook the fusilli according to the package directions.

Meanwhile, in a large no-stick skillet over medium heat, warm the sherry or wine, water and margarine or butter. Add the onions and garlic. Cook and stir for 7 to 8 minutes, or until the onions are tender. If the liquid begins to evaporate, add a bit more water.

Whisk in the flour, mustard and pepper. Gradually whisk in the milk. Cook and stir for 4 to 5 minutes, or until the sauce begins to thicken. Reduce the heat to medium-low to prevent the sauce from boiling. Add the Parmesan and stir until melted. Stir in the sour cream and cook over low heat for 1 to 2 minutes.

Drain the fusilli and transfer to a large bowl. Toss with the sauce. Garnish with the parsley.

Makes 4 servings. Per serving: 403 calories, 8.9 g. fat (20% of calories), 18.4 g. protein, 59 g. carbohydrates, 0.9 dietary fiber, 14 mg. cholesterol, 340 mg. sodium

L inguine with White Clam Sauce

8 ounces linguine
4 dozen littleneck clams, scrubbed
4 teaspoons all-purpose flour
2 teaspoons olive oil
3 cloves garlic, minced
3 bay leaves
2 cups defatted chicken broth
½ cup evaporated skim milk
2 teaspoons Dijon mustard
¼ teaspoon dried thyme

In a large pot of boiling water, cook the linguine according to the package directions.

Meanwhile, in a large saucepan over high heat, bring 2 cups of water to a boil. Add the clams. Reduce the heat to medium, cover and simmer for 5 minutes, or until the clams open. With a slotted spoon, remove the clams and discard any that did not open. Let the clams cool, then remove them from their shells. Mince and transfer to a large bowl. Add the flour and toss to coat; set aside.

In a large no-stick skillet over medium heat, warm the oil. Add the garlic and bay leaves and sauté for 4 minutes, or until the garlic begins to brown. Add the broth, milk, mustard and thyme. Cook and stir until the sauce is reduced by about half. Add the reserved clams. Cook and stir for 2 minutes, or until the sauce thickens.

Remove the bay leaves from the sauce and discard. Drain the pasta and toss with the sauce.

Makes 4 servings. Per serving: 247 calories, 3.8 g. fat (14% of calories), 17 g. protein, 36.4 g. carbohydrates, 0.1 g. dietary fiber, 19 mg. cholesterol, 241 mg. sodium

NOTE
• You can replace the fresh clams with 4 cans (6½ ounces each) chopped clams, drained.

S paghetti with Red Clam Sauce

8 ounces spaghetti
2 dozen cherrystone clams, scrubbed
1 tablespoon olive oil
2 cloves garlic, minced
1 small onion, chopped
3 cups canned peeled plum tomatoes, drained and chopped
2 tablespoons minced fresh parsley
½ teaspoon dried oregano
⅛ teaspoon ground black pepper
¼ cup tomato paste

In a large pot of boiling water, cook the spaghetti according to the package directions.

Meanwhile, in a Dutch oven or large saucepan over high heat, bring 2 cups of water to a boil. Add the clams. Reduce the heat to medium, cover and simmer for 5 minutes, or until the clams open. With a slotted spoon, remove the clams and discard any that did not open. Strain ½ cup of the liquid through a fine-mesh strainer into a small bowl and set aside. Let the clams cool, then remove them from their shells. Mince and set aside.

In a large no-stick skillet over medium heat, warm the oil. Add the garlic and onions and sauté for 5 minutes, or until the onions are soft. Add the tomatoes, reserved clam liquid, parsley, oregano and pepper. Simmer for 5 minutes. Stir in the tomato paste and simmer for 5 minutes.

Add the reserved clams to the sauce and simmer for 5 minutes, or until heated through. Transfer the pasta to a serving bowl and toss with the sauce.

Makes 4 servings. Per serving: 299 calories, 6.6 g. fat (20% of calories), 17 g. protein, 46.5 g. carbohydrates, 2.4 dietary fiber, 18 mg. cholesterol, 549 mg. sodium

Penne with Broccoli and Peppers

- 8 ounces penne
- 2 cups broccoli florets
- 1 tablespoon olive oil
- 1 sweet red or yellow pepper, cut into thin strips
- 3 large cloves garlic, slivered
- ½ cup vegetable or defatted chicken broth
- 1¼ teaspoons Dijon mustard
- ½ teaspoon salt (optional)
- ⅛ teaspoon ground black pepper
- 2 teaspoons balsamic vinegar
- 2 tablespoons grated Parmesan cheese (optional)

In a large pot of boiling water, cook the penne according to the package directions. Drain. Transfer to a serving bowl and keep warm.

Meanwhile, in a medium saucepan, cook the broccoli in a small amount of boiling water for 3 to 5 minutes, or until bright green and just tender. Drain.

In a large no-stick skillet over medium heat, warm the oil. Add the red or yellow peppers and sauté for 2 minutes. Add the garlic and sauté for 2 minutes.

Stir in the broth and broccoli and cook for 3 minutes. Stir in the mustard, salt (if using) and black pepper.

Toss the penne with the vegetables. Drizzle with the vinegar and toss again. Sprinkle with the Parmesan (if using).

Makes 4 servings. Per serving: 291 calories, 4.9 g. fat (15% of calories), 9.9 g. protein, 53 g. carbohydrates, 2.6 g. dietary fiber, 0 mg. cholesterol, 45 mg. sodium

NOTE

• To save time and reduce kitchen cleanup, cook the broccoli in the same pot as the penne; add it for the last 5 minutes of cooking time.

VARIATION

Penne with Broccoli Rabe: Replace the broccoli with 12 ounces broccoli rabe, cut into bite-size pieces. Reduce the blanching time to 3 minutes. If desired, add ¼ teaspoon crushed red pepper to the sautéed vegetables along with the garlic. If desired, replace the balsamic vinegar with lemon juice.

Mediterranean Pasta with Shrimp

- 8 ounces fusilli
- 1 clove garlic, minced
- 1 large onion, chopped
- 2 tablespoons dry sherry or nonalcoholic white wine
- 2 tablespoons 1 ⅓ cup defatted chicken broth
- 1 can (16 ounces) reduced-sodium stewed tomatoes (with juice)
- 1 jar (15 ounces) water-packed artichoke hearts, drained
- 5 large pimento-stuffed green olives, sliced
- 2 teaspoons dried Italian seasoning
- ¼ teaspoon ground black pepper
- 1 pound medium shrimp (40 to 50 shrimp per pound), shelled and deveined

In a large pot of boiling water, cook the fusilli according to the package directions.

Meanwhile, coat a large no-stick skillet with no-stick spray. Add the garlic, onions, sherry or wine and 2 tablespoons of the broth. Cook, stirring, over medium heat for 5 mintues, or until the onions are tender.

Add the tomatoes (with juice), artichokes, olives, Italian seasoning, pepper and the remaining ⅓ cup broth. Add the shrimp and simmer, uncovered, for 3 minutes, or until the shrimp turn pink.

Drain the fusilli. Serve topped with the shrimp mixture.

Makes 4 servings. Per serving: 490 calories, 3.5 g. fat (6% of calories), 34.6 g. protein, 80 g. carbohydrates, 6.8 g. dietary fiber, 175 mg. cholesterol, 460 mg. sodium

VARIATION

Mediterranean Pasta with Scallops: Replace the shrimp with 1 pound bay or sea scallops. The slightly smaller bay scallops have a superior flavor. If using bay scallops, reduce the cooking time to 2 to 3 minutes. If using sea scallops, cook for 3 to 6 minutes. Cook the scallops just until done; the interior should still be tender.

C avatelli with Broccoli

QUICK!

12	ounces cavatelli
2	cups broccoli florets
1	tablespoon olive oil
½	cup diced red onions
2	cloves garlic, minced
½	cup defatted reduced-sodium chicken broth
2	teaspoons balsamic vinegar
½	cup diced roasted red peppers
2	tablespoons grated Parmesan cheese
¼	teaspoon ground black pepper
2	tablespoons chopped fresh basil (optional)

In a large pot of boiling water, cook the cavatelli according to the package directions. Add the broccoli and cook for 3 to 4 minutes, or until the pasta is tender and the broccoli is bright green.

Meanwhile, in a large no-stick skillet over medium heat, warm the oil. Add the onions and garlic. Sauté for 2 to 3 minutes, or until the onions are tender. Stir in the broth and vinegar and bring to a boil. Reduce the heat to low and stir in the red peppers, Parmesan and black pepper. Cook for 1 to 2 minutes, or until heated through.

Drain the pasta and broccoli and place in a large serving bowl. Add the onion mixture and toss to mix well. Sprinkle with the basil (if using).

Makes 4 servings. Per serving: 413 calories, 5.7 g. fat (12% of calories), 16.1 g. protein, 75.8 g. carbohydrates, 3.9 g. dietary fiber, 0 mg. cholesterol, 114 mg sodium

NOTES

• For extra garlic flavor, rub the cut side of a garlic clove around the serving bowl before tossing the pasta and sauce.

• You can replace the cavatelli with bow-tie noodles or medium shells.

VARIATION

Penne with Asparagus: Replace the cavatelli with penne and replace the broccoli with 2 cups of 1" asparagus pieces.

P asta Puttanesca

QUICK!

This quick, zesty pasta dish originated among Italian women who had little time to cook and threw together what they had on the pantry shelves.

12	ounces linguine or spaghetti
1	tablespoon olive oil
1	small onion, chopped
2	cloves garlic, minced
1	can (28 ounces) stewed tomatoes (with juice)
10	kalamata olives, pitted and chopped
1	anchovy fillet, finely chopped
2	teaspoons rinsed and drained capers
½	teaspoon dried oregano
⅛	teaspoon red-pepper flakes
2	tablespoons grated Parmesan cheese (optional)

In a large pot of boiling water, cook the linguine or spaghetti according to the package directions.

Meanwhile, in a large no-stick skillet over medium heat, warm the oil. Add the onions and garlic. Sauté for 2 to 3 minutes, or until the onions are tender. Stir in the tomatoes (with juice), olives, anchovies and capers and bring to a boil. Reduce the heat to low and simmer for 10 to 15 minutes, or until the sauce thickens slightly. Stir in the oregano and red-pepper flakes and cook for 1 minute.

Drain the pasta and place in a large serving bowl. Add the sauce and toss to mix well. Sprinkle with the Parmesan (if using).

Makes 4 servings. Per serving: 433 calories, 7 g. fat (15% of calories), 13.8 g. protein, 81.2 g. carbohydrates, 2.2 g. dietary fiber, 1 mg. cholesterol, 644 mg. sodium

NOTES
• If using fresh pasta, reduce the cooking time to 3 to 5 minutes.
• You can use canned pitted black olives if kalamata olives are difficult to find.

Pasta Primavera

A tasty mixture of low-fat sour cream, low-fat yogurt and Parmesan cheese replaces the high-fat cream in this version of an Italian classic.

- 12 ounces penne
- 2 teaspoons olive oil
- 1 small onion, thinly sliced and separated into rings
- 2 cloves garlic, minced
- 2 cups thinly sliced carrots
- 2 cups thinly sliced zucchini
- 2 cups snow peas
- 1 medium tomato, chopped
- 1 cup frozen peas, thawed
- ½ cup low-fat plain yogurt
- ½ cup low-fat sour cream
- 2 tablespoons grated Parmesan cheese
- ½ teaspoon dried basil
- ¼ teaspoon ground black pepper

In a large pot of boiling water, cook the penne according to the package directions.

Meanwhile, in a large no-stick skillet over medium heat, warm the oil. Add the onions and garlic. Cook and stir for 2 minutes. Add the carrots and cook, stirring frequently, for 3 minutes. Add the zucchini, snow peas, tomatoes and peas and cook, stirring frequently, for 4 to 6 minutes, or until the vegetables are tender.

Reduce the heat to low. Remove the skillet from the heat and stir in the yogurt, sour cream, Parmesan, basil and pepper. Return the skillet to the heat and cook over very low heat for 1 to 2 minutes, or until warmed through. Do not boil.

Drain the pasta and place in a large serving bowl. Add the sauce and toss to mix well.

Makes 4 servings. Per serving: 556 calories, 11.5 g. fat (19% of calories), 20.6 g. protein, 92.4 g. carbohydrates, 6.7 g. dietary fiber, 11 mg. cholesterol, 149 mg. sodium

NOTES
• You can use almost any combination of vegetables in this dish. Sun-dried tomatoes make a nice addition.
• For variety, use other pastas, such as cut fusilli, rotini or spaghetti. Flavored pastas such as spinach or tomato pasta make a great presentation.

VARIATION
Double-Cheese Pasta Primavera: Just before serving, toss the pasta with shredded fat-free mozzarella cheese.

Bow Ties with Greens and Beans

QUICK!

Here's a quick and delicious way to get your beans, grains and vegetables, all in one dish.

- 12 ounces bow-tie noodles
- 1 teaspoon olive oil
- 2 cups broccoli florets
- 1 red onion, thinly sliced and separated into rings
- 2 cloves garlic, minced
- 1 tablespoon all-purpose flour
- 2 cups defatted reduced-sodium chicken broth or vegetable broth
- 1 bunch (about 1 pound) escarole, chopped into 1" pieces
- 1 can (16 ounces) chick-peas, rinsed and drained
- 2 tablespoons grated Parmesan cheese
- 2 teaspoons lemon juice

In a large pot of boiling water, cook the bow ties according to the package directions.

Meanwhile, in a large no-stick skillet over medium heat, warm the oil. Add the broccoli, onions and garlic. Cover and cook, stirring frequently, for 4 minutes, or until the broccoli is bright green and crisp-tender. Transfer the broccoli mixture to a small bowl. Sprinkle the flour into the skillet. Cook and stir for 1 minute. Gradually whisk in the broth until blended and smooth.

Add the broccoli mixture, escarole, chick-peas, Parmesan and lemon juice and bring to a boil. Reduce the heat to low, cover and simmer for 5 to 7 minutes, or until the vegetables are tender and the sauce thickens slightly.

Drain the pasta and place in a large serving bowl. Add the sauce and toss to mix well.

Makes 4 servings. Per serving: 536 calories, 5.6 g. fat (9% of calories), 24.4 g. protein, 99.2 g. carbohydrates, 12.1 g. dietary fiber, 0 mg. cholesterol, 581 mg. sodium

Linguine with Mushrooms and Peppers

QUICK!

- 8 ounces linguine or spaghetti
- 2 teaspoons olive oil
- 1 sweet onion, sliced and separated into rings
- 1 bay leaf
- 1 cup sliced fresh button mushrooms
- 1 cup sliced fresh cremini or shiitake mushrooms
- 2 sweet red, yellow or green peppers, cut into thin strips
- 2 cloves garlic, minced
- ½ teaspoon thyme
- ½ teaspoon oregano
- 1 tablespoon chopped fresh basil or 1 teaspoon dried
- 3 tablespoons chopped fresh parsley
- ⅔ cup vegetable broth or defatted chicken broth
- 2 tablespoons grated Parmesan cheese (optional)

In a large no-stick skillet over medium-low heat, warm the oil. Add the onions and bay leaf and sauté for about 5 minutes.

Add the button mushrooms, cremini or shiitake mushrooms, peppers and garlic and sauté for 4 minutes, or until the mushrooms begin to release their liquid. Add the thyme, oregano, basil, parsley and broth. Simmer for 5 to 7 minutes, or until the peppers are soft and the broth has reduced slightly.

Meanwhile, in a large pot of boiling water, cook the linguine or spaghetti according to the package directions. Drain. Place in a serving bowl and toss with the mushroom mixture.

Remove and discard the bay leaf. Sprinkle the pasta with the Parmesan (if using).

Makes 4 servings. Per serving: 327 calories 3.9 g. fat (11% of calories), 10.9 g. protein, 64.5 g. carbohydrates, 3.8 dietary fiber, 0 mg. cholesterol, 20 mg. sodium

Rice and Other Grains

Nutritionists have long recommended that we give rice and other grains star billings in our daily diets. Grains are high in fiber, complex carbohydrates and a variety of essential vitamins and minerals. Plus, they have zero cholesterol and practically no fat.

It's not just health experts who tout the benefits of rice, corn, wheat, quinoa and other grains. For chefs, these dietary staples provide nutritious and delicious ways to round out a menu. Used both as side dishes and main courses, grains can be teamed with meats, poultry, fish and vegetables to make filling and healthful meals.

There are literally thousands of grains, ranging from exotics like quinoa and triticale to the very familiar—and nutritious—white rice. All have one thing in common: They're remarkably easy to cook. Essentially, all grains require nothing more than water, a stint on the stove and a little bit of patience until they're done.

RICE

If there were only one item in every cook's pantry, that item would probably be rice. Nutritious, inexpensive, long-lasting and easy to use, rice is an indispensable ingredient in the healthy cook's kitchen. What's more, it goes with just about everything, from fish and stir-fries to hearty chicken stew.

Rice plays a key role in cuisines worldwide, and food experts estimate that there are as many as 40,000 varieties. Here in the United States, we can readily explore rices with a range of tastes and textures, including basmati rice from India and Pakistan, Arborio rice from Italy, Valencia rice from Spain and "sticky" rice from Japan.

The rice that you're probably most familiar with is the long-grain white variety. This is simply rice from which the brownish outer hull has been stripped. Removing the hull takes away fiber and some vitamins. However, white rice is enriched to replace some of those vitamins, so you can still enjoy the pristine fluffiness of white rice. Replace the lost fiber by combining the rice with lots of vegetables.

Storing Rice

Uncooked rice has a very long shelf life. White varieties stay fresh for up to a year when kept in a cool, dry cupboard.

Keeping rice in an airtight container prolongs its shelf life and helps prevent bugs from getting in.

Unlike white rice, brown rice has an oily outer layer that can turn rancid at room temperature. It should either be refrigerated or used within a few weeks after you bring it home from the store.

Cooked rice should be eaten fairly soon after cooking. It doesn't benefit from standing at room temperature for long periods. Store leftovers, covered, in the refrigerator for up to a week. You can even freeze cooked rice for near-instant fu-

RICE RICHES

Today's supermarkets stock dozens of different rices, each with its own taste and texture. Rice can be defined by color, the length of the grain, processing method, variety and other characteristics. Here are some terms associated with rice as well as some common varieties.

☞ **Long-grain.** Available in white and brown varieties, the grains are four to five times longer than they are wide. They cook up fluffy and well-separated. This is the most common rice used in America. Carolina, basmati and jasmine are long-grain rices.

☞ **Medium-grain.** Consisting of shorter, plumper grains that cling together, medium-grain rice is used for rice pudding, croquettes and molded dishes. Arborio, Valencia and "sushi" rice are medium-grain varieties.

☞ **Short-grain.** Soft and sticky when cooked, it's often used in Asian dishes, because it's easy to eat with chopsticks. Sticky, or sweet, rice is a short-grain type.

☞ **Parboiled.** Soaked, steamed and dried before milling, parboiled rice retains many of the nutrients that otherwise are lost during processing. Also called converted rice, it's available in white and brown.

☞ **Instant.** This is rice that has been previously cooked and dried. At home, it requires rehydrating rather than cooking, so it can be made quickly. It's available in white and brown.

☞ **Brown.** Higher in fiber and vitamin E than white rice, brown rice requires longer cooking, because the outer shell (the bran) is left intact.

☞ **Arborio.** A medium-grain rice, Arborio is prized for making risotto and other dishes requiring a firm-textured yet creamy grain.

☞ **Aromatic.** This is an umbrella term for a variety of rices that give off a nutty aroma when being cooked. Basmati, jasmine, pecan and popcorn rice are among the most popular.

☞ **Basmati.** An aromatic, long-grain rice much prized in India and Pakistan, it has a nutty taste and rich, aromatic smell. It's available in white and brown.

☞ **Jasmine.** This long-grain rice has a slight floral bouquet and is particularly good for making fried rice.

☞ **Sweet.** Also called sticky rice, this is a short, stubby grain that sticks together when cooked. It is almost completely composed of amylopectin, a type of rice starch that creates a creamy texture. Sweet rice is often used for desserts.

ture meals (microwave the rice to thaw and reheat it).

Preparing Rice

Although it's a point of pride for many cooks that they can make perfect rice, the process isn't all that difficult. If you can accurately measure

rice and water and keep an eye on the time, you'll have great rice every time.

Know when to rinse. While domestic rice can—and should—be cooked without rinsing, imported varieties may contain impurities and should be rinsed thoroughly before using. Place the rice in a sieve and rinse under cold running

White Rice

Is It GOOD for You?

Thanks to its natural bran overcoat, brown rice contains substantial amounts of vitamins, minerals and fiber. But what about white rice, which has had its bran layer removed?

As it turns out, white rice is also good food. In this country, at least, most white rice has been enriched with niacin, thiamine and iron during processing. So even though it falls somewhat short in the fiber department, it still provides an abundance of essential nutrients. Rice has no gluten and is easily digested, so people with allergies or digestive problems can indulge. In addition, white rice is rich in insoluble fiber, which may have a protective effect against bowel cancer.

water until the water runs clear. Or soak the rice in a bowl with plenty of water to cover, stirring the rice and changing the water until it's clear. Soaked rice can absorb water as it stands, so you may be able to shorten the cooking time by a few minutes.

Choose your liquid. While rice is customarily cooked in plain water, many chefs prefer to use flavored liquids, which add depth and complexity to the finished dish. Chicken and beef broths are ideal cooking liquids. Or you can add a squeeze of lemon, a splash of flavored vinegar or a sprinkling of herbs to the water.

Leave it alone. It's almost impossible for cooks not to poke, stir, investigate or otherwise tamper with works in progress, including rice. The problem is, frequently stirring rice before it's done damages the grains and can make the finished product soft and gummy. Arborio rice, which is meant to be stirred frequently during cooking, is an exception.

Watch for separation. To prevent rice from overcooking, it's a good idea to check it just before you think it should be done. If the rice still looks a little wet, it needs an extra minute or two (or more) to absorb excess water. When it's done, the grains of long-grain varieties will separate easily, without being either dry or wet and sticky. Short- and medium-grain rice will tend to clump together.

Cooking Methods

While rice is typically prepared by simmering on the stove top in a covered saucepan, it can also be boiled in an open pot, baked and microwaved with good results.

☞ **Covered saucepan.** This is one of the easiest methods for cooking rice—and certainly the most common. Follow package directions for the ratio of rice to water. (A rule of thumb is to use one part rice to two parts water, but that can vary depending on the type of rice being cooked.) Bring the water to a boil over high heat (use a large saucepan to help prevent the boil-overs that rice is prone to). Add the rice, stir once and cover with a tight-fitting lid. Reduce the heat to low and simmer until the rice is tender and the liquid is absorbed—usually 15 to 20 minutes for white rice.

Simmered long-grain rice is light and fluffy, with well-separated grains that are ideal for stir-fries, salads and side dishes.

☞ **Uncovered pot.** This is a boiling method. Instead of using just the amount of water needed, bring a large pot of water to a boil. Stir in the rice, sprinkling it gently over the surface of the water so that the water maintains its boil. Reduce the heat to medium and cook until tender. Then drain the rice and serve. The main advantage of this method is that you can monitor the progress of the rice as it cooks. The main disadvantage is the loss of some water-soluble vitamins, which get poured out with the excess water.

☞ **Baking.** The advantage of preparing rice in the oven instead of on the stove top is that there is virtually no risk of scorching or boil-overs. Also, baking rice creates a creamier grain that is often preferred as an accompaniment to roasted meat or chicken.

To bake rice, preheat the oven to 400°. Put the rice and liquid in an ovenproof saucepan or a flameproof casserole. On the stove top, bring the water to a boil. Stir, cover and transfer to the oven. Bake until the rice is tender and the liquid is absorbed. Long-grain white rice takes about 20 minutes.

For adding extra flavor to baked rice, sauté onions and garlic in the pan first. Add the rice and stir to coat. Cook for 2 to 3 minutes. Then add the liquid, bring to a boil and transfer to the oven, as described above.

☞ **Microwaving.** As with baking, you can use the microwave to prepare rice with virtually no risk of burning. And as long as you use a large enough container, the rice won't boil over. Combine the rice and water in a microwave-safe dish. Cover and microwave on high power for about 5 minutes, or until boiling. Stir the rice, cover and

microwave on medium power until the rice is tender and the liquid is absorbed.

If your microwave doesn't have a turntable, give the dish a quarter-turn two or three times during cooking.

While microwaving is an almost foolproof way to cook rice, there's no real speed advantage. It takes 15 to 20 minutes—about the same as cooking on the stove top.

Although not "authentic," microwaving is a labor-saving way to prepare risotto. You combine the rice with the full amount of liquid and cook until most of it is absorbed. Stop and stir the mixture two or three times during the cooking period—much easier than the almost-constant stirring required for stove-top risotto.

☞ **Rice cooker.** You can buy special electric appliances that automatically turn off when the rice is perfectly cooked and keep it warm until serving time. Follow the manufacturer's directions regarding the amounts of water and rice to use.

WILD RICE

Despite the name, wild rice is not a rice at all, but the seed of an aquatic grass. It's cured and toasted, which gives wild rice its characteristic nutty taste. And wild rice isn't particularly wild these days; in this country, at least, most of it is cultivated in manmade rice paddies.

Although wild rice is expensive, it has a deliciously pungent flavor that goes a long way. It's very nutritious as well.

☞ When using wild rice for a side dish (when appearance is important), look for brands with intact, well-shaped grains.

☞ When making soups or stuffings, you can save money by seeking out brands with broken, damaged grains, which are considerably less expensive than their more pristine counterparts.

☞ Before cooking wild rice, rinse it well to remove impurities or pieces of hull.

☞ To make wild rice, bring 3 cups water or broth to a boil over high heat. Stir in 1 cup wild rice. Return to a boil, stir, cover and reduce the heat to low. Cook for about 40 minutes, or until most of the grains have cracked open. The grains should have a slight crunch without being hard.

☞ Wild rice doesn't absorb liquid as readily as white varieties, so you may have to drain excess liquid before serving. Or set the pot aside, covered, for about 10 minutes, which will cause much of the liquid to be absorbed.

☞ To subdue the strong flavor of wild rice, many cooks mix it half-and-half with white rice. The two types of rice cook at different speeds, however, so it's best to mix them after cooking.

AMARANTH

A tiny grain packed with protein and calcium, amaranth has only recently found its way into American kitchens. It is commonly added to breads or other grain dishes to boost their nutritional value. Plus, its creamy-crunchy texture makes it an interesting alternative to white rice.

☞ Amaranth is a long-lasting grain that's all but impervious to pests, so it stores extremely well.

☞ Unlike rice, amaranth can absorb a relatively small amount of cooking liquid, so it's often served as a porridge, much like grits.

☞ Amaranth has a distinctive flavor—sort of like toasted sesame seeds—and is often seasoned with garlic, ginger, onions or other assertive ingredients.

☞ To make amaranth "popcorn," toast the seeds in an ungreased pan over high heat. A tablespoon of seeds produces 3 to 4 tablespoons popped seeds, which make a deliciously crunchy addition to salads, stews and soups.

BARLEY

This hearty, robust grain has always been more popular in Europe than in the United States, in large part because American tastes run to wheat. But with its slightly chewy texture and more than slightly pungent taste, barley is often used with big-flavored dishes such as lamb stew and mushroom soup.

☞ Barley can be chewy, so it's typically included in soups and stews, rather than used as a stand-alone ingredient in side dishes.

☞ A little barley goes a long way; 1 cup dried expands to about four times that size during cooking.

☞ Most barley found in supermarkets is called pearl barley—that is, it has been refined, leaving behind only the "pearl" from the center of the grain. In health food stores, however, you can buy whole, hulled barley. This contains higher levels of fiber and other nutrients.

☞ Whole barley is jaw-achingly tough, so it should be soaked overnight before cooking.

☞ While overnight soaking isn't really necessary for preparing pearl barley, some

Helpful Hint

To speed the cooking time of hard grains like wheat, rye, barley and triticale, cover them with boiling water. Let them soak at least until the water cools, then cook as directed on the package.

GREAT GRAINS

Grains are not only nutritious and delicious, they're wonderfully easy to prepare. Here are cooking instructions for some of the most common grains—and a few that aren't so common, as well.

GRAIN	COOKING TIPS	USE
Amaranth	Simmer 1 part amaranth in 3 parts water for 20 to 25 minutes	Cereal
Barley, pearl	Simmer 1 part barley in 4 parts water for 30 to 40 minutes	Side dishes, pilafs
Buckwheat groats (kasha)	Simmer 1 part groats in 2 parts water for 15 minutes	Pilafs
Bulgur	Pour 1½ cups boiling water over 1 cup bulgur and let stand for 30 minutes	Side dishes, cold salads
Cornmeal	Simmer 1 part cornmeal in 4 parts water for 30 minutes	Cereal, polenta
Couscous	Pour 1½ cups boiling water over 1⅓ cups couscous and let stand for 5 minutes	Side dishes
Hominy	Soak overnight, then simmer 1 part hominy in 3 parts water for 2½ to 3 hours	Cereal, side dishes
Millet	Simmer 1 part millet in 2 parts water for 25 to 30 minutes	Soups, stews, side dishes
Oats, old-fashioned rolled	Simmer 1 part oats in 2 parts water for 10 minutes and let stand for 2 minutes	Cereal, baking
Oats, steel-cut	Simmer 1 part oats in 4 parts water for 30 to 40 minutes	Cereal
Quinoa	Rinse before using. Simmer 1 part quinoa in 2 parts water for 15 to 20 minutes	Side dishes
Rice, brown	Simmer 1 part rice in 2 parts water for 30 to 40 minutes	Side dishes, casseroles, pilafs, soups
Rice, white	Simmer 1 part rice in 2 parts water for 15 to 20 minutes	Side dishes, casseroles, pilafs, soups
Rye berries	Soak overnight, then simmer 1 part rye berries in 4 parts water for 1 hour	Side dishes, casseroles, stews
Triticale	Simmer 1 part triticale in 4 parts water for 1 hour	Cereal, casseroles, pilaf
Wheat berries	Soak overnight, then simmer 1 part wheat berries in 3 parts water for 2 hours	Stuffings, casseroles, side dishes, cereals
Wheat, cracked	Simmer 1 part cracked wheat in 2 parts water for 25 minutes	Cereal, side dishes, salads, casseroles
Wild rice	Simmer 1 part rice in 3 parts water for 45 to 60 minute	Stuffings, casseroles, side dishes

cooks do it anyway to make the kernels fluffier.

☞ The quick-cooking form of barley is both tender and quick to prepare. It's ready in about 10 minutes and is perfectly suitable for pilafs and other side dishes.

BUCKWHEAT

Like wild rice, buckwheat is a grass and not a true grain. It has a nutty taste, which lends a distinctive accent to stuffings and side dishes. And it's a good source of B complex and E vitamins as well as iron and calcium. The roasted form of buckwheat groats is called kasha.

☞ Buckwheat is often lightly toasted and sold either whole or in coarse, medium or fine grinds. While groats take longer to cook than more finely milled varieties, they retain more of buckwheat's pleasant chewiness.

☞ When preparing kasha, many chefs stir in a beaten egg, which helps the grains cook up separately while maintaining a slight crunch. Combine the groats and a lightly beaten egg in a saucepan and stir over medium heat until the groats are dry. Add water and cook as usual.

☞ Untoasted buckwheat has a delicate flavor and can be used as an alternative to white rice.

☞ Buckwheat flour can be added to breads for a robust flavor and slightly darker color.

BULGUR

This staple of the Middle East—which is made from uncooked wheat that has been steamed, dried and crushed—resembles coarse, brown-hued grits. Commonly used in casseroles and in grain salads, bulgur is best known for its use in tabbouleh, a Middle Eastern salad that also includes chopped tomatoes, onions, parsley and mint flavored with olive oil and lemon juice.

☞ Bulgur comes in three varieties: coarse, which is used for pilafs and stuffings; medium, often used for cold salads like tabbouleh; and

fine, which is typically used for making bread and some desserts.

☞ The outer layer of bulgur contains natural oils, so the grain should be refrigerated or stored in an airtight container to prevent it from turning rancid or from attracting bugs.

☞ Bulgur can be boiled like rice by adding 1 cup bulgur to several quarts boiling water. Return the water to a boil, lower the heat and simmer for about 20 minutes. Then strain and serve.

☞ For a fluffier grain with a slight crunch, many chefs recommend soaking bulgur before cooking in cold water for 2 to 3 hours. Or pour boiling water over the bulgur and let soak for about 30 minutes.

☞ Do not confuse bulgur with cracked wheat, which takes much longer to cook and is not interchangeable with bulgur in recipes.

CORN

Used extensively throughout the United States, corn is the only grain native to the Americas. Traditionally known as maize, it can be used in many forms: fresh from the cob, for example, or dried and used as cereal, cornmeal, grits or flour.

Corn cereals are categorized by the grind. Cracked corn, for example, can be boiled or simmered to make porridge. Coarsely ground corn is used to make grits or hominy. Or it can be ground still more to make cornmeal, polenta or flour.

☞ The best cornmeal is stone-ground, as this traditional process preserves the most flavor and nutrients.

☞ As with all grains, most of corn's flavor and nutrients are found in the outer layer known as the germ. So look for whole-grain meal, which is made using the entire kernel.

☞ Whole-grain corn contains more oil than corn that has been highly processed. To prevent it from turning rancid, it's best to keep it refrigerated in an airtight container.

☞ Corn readily absorbs flavors from the liquid that it's cooked in, so you can try different tastes by cooking it in broth, milk or other flavored liquids.

☞ While traditional polenta takes about 40 minutes to cook, instant varieties are ready in about 5 minutes.

☞ Hominy is dried white or yellow corn kernels that have had their hull and germ removed. It is available dried or cooked and canned. Hominy grits are made by grinding the dried kernels and come coarse, medium and fine.

Couscous

Commonly used in North African cooking, couscous isn't a grain. Rather, it's a pastalike product made from the inner portion of durum wheat (semolina). However, couscous is cooked and used like a grain. It has a mild taste that blends well with fresh herbs and other seasonings. It's also easy to cook.

☞ Most couscous found in supermarkets is the instant variety, which is ready in about 5 minutes.

☞ For regular couscous from a Middle Eastern store, steam it for about 1 hour: Line a colander with dampened cheesecloth and pour in 1 cup couscous. Place the colander over a pot of simmering water and steam until tender.

☞ For added flavor, many chefs steam regular couscous for 30 to 40 minutes over water,

Helpful Hint

To give grains a deliciously aromatic flavor, toast them in a dry, heavy no-stick skillet. Stir frequently until the grains are golden. Then add water and cook as directed on the package, slightly reducing the cooking time.

then move the colander over a fragrant pot of stew, such as lamb, for the remaining time.

Millet

Although millet is commonly enjoyed by people in Asia and Africa, in this country, it's mainly enjoyed by birds in birdseed. For the healthy cook, however, millet is a grainy gold mine, containing a good amount of protein. In addition, it makes a pleasantly crunchy addition to other grain dishes.

☞ Millet will keep for at least a year if properly stored in a cool, dry place and kept in an airtight container.

☞ For a nutty flavor and to speed cooking time, millet can be lightly toasted in a heavy skillet before its final cooking.

Oats

A highly nutritious grain that has received accolades for its role in lowering cholesterol, the oat has gone from being fodder for horses to being a daily staple on millions of American tables. Oats are typically served in one of three forms.

☞ **Old-fashioned rolled oats.** Made from thinly sliced raw oats that have been flattened into flakes and then dried, these are the oats that we eat for breakfast or mix into dough for oatmeal cookies.

When making oatmeal for breakfast, combine 1 cup rolled oats with 2 cups water in a medium saucepan. Simmer for 10 minutes, uncovered, stirring occasionally. Remove from the heat, cover and let stand for about 2 minutes.

For a lightly nutty flavor, you can toast oats prior to cooking. Spread the oats on a no-stick baking sheet and put them in a 350° oven. Stir frequently and bake until golden brown, which should take about 10 minutes.

Toasted oats can be substituted for nuts in cookie recipes. Oats can also be used to stretch bread crumbs and add extra fiber when making stuffing or meat loaf.

☞ **Quick oats.** These are similar to rolled oats, only they are more thinly sliced and cook more quickly. Even quicker are instant varieties, which are precooked and dried; they're ready to eat after adding boiling water. As with many grains, the more processing oats receive, the more susceptible they are to nutrient loss.

☞ **Steel-cut oats.** These are rough-cut and dried, with virtually no heat used during processing. As a result, steel-cut oats retain many of their natural nutrients and can be cooked into a rich, creamy cereal with a firm texture. They can be hard to find, however, and generally must be purchased from specialty shops or well-supplied health food stores. Other names for them are Scotch oats and Irish oatmeal.

Steel-cut oats take longer to cook than rolled oats. Quick-cooking varieties are available.

QUINOA

Farmed for centuries high in the Andes Mountains of Peru, quinoa (KEEN-wa) has only recently been introduced to North America. This high-protein grain can be used as a substitute for rice in pilafs and side dishes and as a base for stews.

Rinse quinoa with cold water before using to remove the natural, bitter-tasting coating. Prepare in the same way as you would rice, mixing 1 cup quinoa with 2 cups water.

Alternatively, toast quinoa briefly in a large, dry no-stick skillet before adding water.

RYE

Rye is a hearty grain that thrives in cold climates. Look for rye berries and rye flakes—a common ingredient in granola—in health food stores. The most familiar form is rye flour, which is used to make dark breads, like black bread and pumpernickel.

To use rye berries as a side dish, soak them overnight, then simmer one part berries in four parts water until tender. Serve alone or mixed with other grains and vegetables.

WHEAT

This grain is the basis for nearly all our breads and numerous other foods that we eat every day, like cereals, crackers and pasta. In fact, wheat accounts for three-quarters of our total grain consumption.

☞ Wheat kernels, also known as wheat berries, are commonly available in health food stores. As with any whole grain, wheat contains oils that will quickly turn rancid if left out at room temperature. Stored in the refrigerator in an airtight container, however, it will keep indefinitely.

☞ When preparing wheat berries, soak them in water overnight, then cover with fresh water and simmer until tender. Use one part berries to three parts water. If not presoaked, wheat berries can take as long as 2 hours to become tender.

☞ Cooked wheat berries can be enjoyed as cereal or added to cold salads or to bread for texture and crunch.

☞ Cracked wheat is made by breaking wheat berries into coarse, medium or fine pieces. It resembles bulgur, but since it hasn't been precooked, it takes longer to prepare.

OTHER GRAINS

Among the more unusual grains available are kamut, spelt and triticale. You're most likely to find these items in health food stores. Like most other grains, these can be milled into flour. But they're available in whole form, so you can cook them as you would rice or wheat berries.

☞ Kamut is an ancient variety of high-protein wheat. It has large kernels that can be cooked into pilafs or made into salads.

☞ Spelt is another ancient variety of wheat that has large, brown kernels. You can buy it whole or rolled into flakes. It's good in granola mixtures as well as pilafs.

☞ Triticale is a nutty-sweet hybrid of wheat and rye. Look for whole berries as well as flakes. Use it as cereal or in casseroles and pilafs.

Thomas Keller

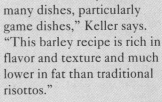

Thomas Keller calls himself a modern classicist—a traditionally trained chef who has nonetheless found himself at the forefront of many culinary trends.

Keller's restaurant in Yountville, California, The French Laundry, provides an idyllic setting to experiment with a variety of ingredients and flavor combinations.

"I like to use rice and other grains because of the richness that they add to many dishes, particularly game dishes," Keller says. "This barley recipe is rich in flavor and texture and much lower in fat than traditional risottos."

Barley Risotto

  3 tomatoes, peeled and halved crosswise
     Pinch of salt
     Pinch of ground black pepper
4–5 cups defatted reduced-sodium chicken broth
  2 cups water
  2 teaspoons olive oil
  ¼ cup chopped shallots
  2 cups barley
  ¼ cup chopped Niçoise olives
  ½ cup grated Parmesan cheese
  1 teaspoon chopped fresh marjoram

Preheat the oven to 225°.

Sprinkle the tomatoes with the salt and pepper. Coat a no-stick baking sheet with no-stick spray. Place the tomatoes, cut side down, on the baking sheet. Place in the oven and roast for 6 to 7 hours. Remove from the oven, chop and set aside.

In a medium saucepan, combine the broth and water. Bring to a boil; reduce the heat to low. Maintain the broth at a simmer.

In another medium saucepan over medium heat, warm the oil. Add the shallots and sauté for 2 minutes. Add the barley and sauté for 1 minute. Add ½ cup of the broth mixture. Bring to a simmer. Cook, stirring occasionally, until the liquid has been absorbed.

Continue to add the broth mixture in ½-cup increments. Stirring occasionally, cook until each addition of liquid has been absorbed. Continue until the barley is soft. (This should take approximately 30 to 40 minutes. You may not need all of the broth mixture.) Remove from the heat.

Set aside one-quarter of the tomatoes and one-quarter of the olives.

Stir the Parmesan, marjoram, the remaining tomatoes and the remaining olives into the barley mixture. Divide among serving bowls and sprinkle with the reserved tomatoes and olives.

Makes 4 servings. Per serving: 463 calories, 10.4 g. fat (20% of calories), 20.2 g. protein, 75.6 g. carbohydrates, 15.1 g. dietary fiber, 10 mg. cholesterol, 538 mg. sodium

S affron Rice

QUICK!

2 teaspoons olive oil
1 small onion, diced
1 small sweet red pepper, diced
2 cups defatted reduced-sodium chicken broth
½ teaspoon saffron threads
1 cup long-grain white rice

In a medium saucepan over medium heat, warm the oil. Add the onions and peppers and sauté for 2 minutes.

Add the broth and bring to a boil over high heat. Stir in the saffron and rice. Cover, reduce the heat to low and simmer for 20 minutes, or until the rice is tender and the liquid is absorbed.

Remove from the heat and fluff the rice with a fork before serving.

Makes 4 servings. Per serving: 227 calories, 3.2 g. fat (13% of calories), 5.6 g. protein, 44 g. carbohydrates, 1.8 g. dietary fiber, 0 mg. cholesterol, 35 mg. sodium

NOTE
• This rice dish tastes great with peas. Add 1 cup frozen peas along with the saffron.

I talian Wild Rice Pilaf

2 teaspoons olive oil
½ cup wild rice, rinsed and drained
½ cup long-grain white rice
2 cups defatted reduced-sodium chicken broth or water
2 tablespoons pine nuts
2 tablespoons minced fresh basil

In a medium saucepan over medium heat, warm the oil. Add the wild rice and white rice and sauté for 30 seconds. Add the broth or water and bring to a boil. Cover, reduce the heat to low and simmer for 20 minutes, or until most of the liquid is absorbed.

Meanwhile, preheat the oven to 400°. Coat a 2-quart no-stick baking dish with no-stick spray. Spoon the rice mixture into the prepared baking dish. Add the pine nuts and basil and stir well.

Bake for 10 to 15 minutes, or until the rice is tender and the liquid is absorbed.

Makes 4 servings. Per serving: 213 calories, 5.5 g. fat (23% of calories), 7 g. protein, 35 g. carbohydrates, 0.5 g. dietary fiber, 0 mg. cholesterol, 35 mg. sodium

P ork Fried Rice

QUICK!

1 tablespoon peanut oil
4 scallions, thinly sliced
⅓ cup finely chopped celery
⅓ cup finely chopped sweet red peppers
1 large clove garlic, minced
1 teaspoon minced fresh ginger
1 cup frozen peas
4 cups cooked long-grain white rice
1 cup cubed fully cooked smoked ham
3 tablespoons reduced-sodium soy sauce
⅛ teaspoon ground black pepper
½ cup fat-free egg substitute

Warm a wok or large no-stick skillet over medium-high heat. Add the oil and heat for 30 seconds, or until hot. Add the scallions, celery and red peppers. Cook and stir for 4 minutes, or until the vegetables are tender.

Stir in the garlic, ginger, peas, rice, ham, soy sauce and black pepper. Cook and stir for 5 minutes, or until heated through.

Pull the mixture to the sides of the wok and pour the egg substitute into the center. Cook, without stirring, for 2 to 3 minutes, or until set. Scrape the egg from the bottom of the wok and break it up. Stir it into the rice mixture until evenly combined.

Makes 4 servings. Per serving: 328 calories, 4.9 g. fat (13% of calories), 16.5 g. protein, 54.9 g. carbohydrates, 2.2 g. dietary fiber, 16 mg. cholesterol, 792 mg. sodium

NOTES
• For a more earthy flavor, add 1 cup quartered mushrooms along with the scallions.
• For a spicy dish, add 1 teaspoon chopped chili peppers along with the garlic.

Spanish Rice

1	tablespoon olive oil
⅛	teaspoon red-pepper flakes
¼	teaspoon ground cumin
1	cup chopped sweet red or green peppers
1	cup sliced scallions
1	large clove garlic, minced
1	cup long-grain white rice
¼	teaspoon dried oregano
2	cups defatted reduced-sodium chicken broth or vegetable broth, heated
2	cups Mexican-style stewed tomatoes (with juice)
1	tablespoon chopped fresh cilantro (optional)

In a large saucepan over medium heat, warm the oil. Add the red-pepper flakes and cumin and sauté for 2 minutes. Add the peppers, scallions and garlic and sauté for 3 minutes, or just until the vegetables are tender.

Stir in the rice, oregano and broth. Reduce the heat to low, cover and simmer for 10 minutes, or until the broth is partially absorbed.

Add the tomatoes (with juice). Cover and simmer, stirring occasionally, for 15 minutes, or until the rice is tender and the liquid is absorbed. Garnish with the cilantro (if using).

Makes 4 servings. Per serving: 276 calories, 4.3 g. fat (14% of calories), 6.7 g. protein, 52.7 g. carbohydrates, 3 g. dietary fiber, 0 mg. cholesterol, 256 mg. sodium

Basmati Rice with Tomatoes

1	tomato, coarsely chopped
2	teaspoons canola oil
¼	cup chopped onions
1	clove garlic, minced
1	teaspoon coriander seeds
⅔	cup basmati or other long-grain aromatic white rice
½	teaspoon powdered ginger
	Pinch of red-pepper flakes

In a food processor or blender, puree the tomatoes. Pour into a 2-cup glass measuring cup. Add enough water to bring the level up to 1¼ cups; set aside.

In a medium saucepan over medium heat, warm the oil. Add the onions, garlic and coriander seeds and sauté for 2 to 3 minutes, or until the onions are tender. Stir in the rice and cook for 1 minute.

Add the tomatoes and water, ginger and red-pepper flakes and bring to a boil. Reduce the heat to low, cover and simmer for 25 to 30 minutes, or until the rice is tender and the liquid is absorbed.

Remove from the heat and let stand, covered, for 10 minutes. Fluff with a fork before serving.

Makes 4 servings. Per serving: 133 calories, 3.1 g. fat (21% of calories), 3.2 g. protein, 24.3 g. carbohydrates, 0.6 g. dietary fiber, 0 mg. cholesterol, 23 mg. sodium

Dirty Rice

This Cajun specialty often features high-fat ground pork, chicken livers and giblets. We reduced the fat by using beef broth and ground round to give the rice its characteristic color.

8 ounces extra-lean ground beef round
1 large onion, finely chopped
¾ cup finely chopped celery
1 clove garlic, minced
¾ cup chopped green peppers
¾ cup defatted beef broth
2 teaspoons Worcestershire sauce
1½ teaspoons dried thyme
¾ teaspoon dried basil
¾ teaspoon dried marjoram
¼ teaspoon salt (optional)
⅛ teaspoon ground black pepper
4–5 drops hot-pepper sauce
⅓ cup chopped scallions
¾ cup long-grain white rice

In a Dutch oven or large saucepan, combine the beef, onions, celery and garlic. Cook over medium heat, breaking up the meat with a spoon, until the beef is browned. Drain the beef mixture in a strainer or colander, then transfer it to a large plate lined with paper towels. Blot the top with additional paper towels. Return the mixture to the pan.

Add the green peppers, broth, Worcestershire sauce, thyme, basil, marjoram, salt (if using), black pepper and hot-pepper sauce. Stir until well-combined. Bring to a boil, then reduce the heat to low, cover and simmer for 30 minutes. Add the scallions and simmer for 5 minutes.

Meanwhile, cook the rice according to the package directions. Fluff with a fork. Stir into the beef mixture and mix well.

Makes 4 servings. Per serving: 228 calories, 2.3 g. fat (9% of calories), 15 g. protein, 36.4 g. carbohydrates, 2.9 g. dietary fiber, 27 mg. cholesterol, 84 mg. sodium

Curried Brown Rice with Mushrooms and Peas

2 teaspoons peanut oil
½ cup chopped leeks (white part only)
1½ teaspoons curry powder
½ cup sliced mushrooms
1½ cups brown rice
4 cups reduced-sodium vegetable broth
1 cup frozen peas
½ cup chopped fresh cilantro
1½ tablespoons reduced-sodium soy sauce
¼ teaspoon hot-pepper sauce

Preheat the oven to 350°.

In a large ovenproof saucepan over medium heat, warm the oil. Add the leeks and curry powder and sauté for 1 minute. Add the mushrooms and sauté for 3 minutes, or just until the leeks are soft and the mushrooms begin to release their liquid. Stir in the rice and cook for 1 minute.

Stir in the broth, peas, cilantro, soy sauce and hot-pepper sauce and bring to a boil.

Cover the pan and bake for 40 to 50 minutes, or until the rice is tender and the liquid is absorbed. Let stand for 10 minutes. Fluff with a fork before serving.

Makes 4 servings. Per serving: 362 calories, 4.6 g. fat (11% of calories), 9.7 g. protein, 70.6 g. carbohydrates, 6.2 g. dietary fiber, 0 mg. cholesterol, 327 mg. sodium

Indian Rice with Almonds

QUICK!

1 teaspoon olive oil
1 tablespoon chopped toasted almonds (see note)
1 clove garlic, minced
¼ teaspoon red-pepper flakes
⅛ teaspoon fennel seeds, crushed
⅛ teaspoon ground cardamom
1¼ cups defatted chicken broth
1 cup quick-cooking rice
½ carrot, diced
½ sweet red pepper, diced
1 bay leaf

In a medium saucepan over medium heat, warm the oil. Add the almonds, garlic, red pepper flakes and fennel seeds and sauté for 3 minutes.

Add the cardamom, broth, rice, carrots, red peppers and bay leaf. Bring to a boil. Reduce the heat to medium-low, cover and simmer for 10 minutes, or until the rice is tender and the liquid is absorbed. Fluff with a fork. Remove and discard the bay leaf before serving.

Makes 4 servings. Per serving: 135 calories, 2.4 g. fat (16% of calories), 4.3 g. protein, 24.2 g. carbohydrates, 1.3 g. dietary fiber, 0 mg. cholesterol, 110 mg. sodium

NOTES
• To vary the flavor, replace the fennel seeds with ¼ teaspoon ground cumin. Add 4 whole cloves along with the broth.
• To toast the almonds, place them in a dry nostick skillet over medium heat. Toast the almonds, shaking the skillet often, for 3 to 5 minutes, or until fragrant and golden.

Vegetable-Rice Pilaf

QUICK!

1 teaspoon olive oil
1 medium onion, finely chopped
1 small clove garlic, minced
2 cups defatted chicken broth or vegetable broth
1 cup long-grain white rice
½ teaspoon dried thyme
½ teaspoon dried basil
⅛ teaspoon ground black pepper
1 bay leaf
¾ cup finely chopped carrots
¾ cup frozen peas

In a large saucepan over medium heat, warm the oil. Add the onions, garlic and 2 tablespoons of the broth. Cook and stir for 5 minutes, or until the onions are tender.

Add the rice, thyme, basil, pepper, bay leaf and the remaining broth. Bring to a boil, then reduce the heat to low. Cover and simmer for 10 minutes.

Arrange the carrots and peas evenly over the rice. Cover and simmer for 10 minutes, or until the rice is tender and the liquid is absorbed. Remove and discard the bay leaf. Fluff with a fork to stir in the carrots and peas.

Makes 4 servings. Per serving: 237 calories, 1.6 g. fat (6% of calories), 7.8 g. protein, 47.2 g. carbohydrates, 2.8 dietary fiber, 0 mg. cholesterol, 204 mg. sodium

Mixed-Grain Pilaf

1¼ cups reduced-sodium vegetable broth
¼ cup basmati or other long-grain aromatic white rice
¼ cup medium pearled barley
¼ cup wild rice, rinsed and drained
1½ teaspoons margarine or butter
1 sweet red or green pepper, chopped
½ cup chopped leeks (white part only)
1 teaspoon reduced-sodium soy sauce
2 drops hot-pepper sauce

In a medium saucepan over medium heat, bring the broth to a boil. Stir in the white rice, barley and wild rice. Reduce the heat to medium-low, cover and simmer for 30 to 35 minutes, or until the grains are tender and the liquid is partially absorbed. Drain thoroughly through a sieve. Spread the grains on a large no-stick baking sheet and let cool for 15 minutes.

In a large no-stick skillet over medium heat, melt the margarine or butter. Add the peppers and leeks and sauté for 4 minutes, or until tender. Stir in the grains and cook, stirring, over high heat for 2 minutes, or until heated through.

Stir in the soy sauce and hot-pepper sauce and cook for 1 minute.

Makes 4 servings. Per serving: 170 calories, 2.1 g. fat (11% of calories), 5.2 g. protein, 34.3 g. carbohydrates, 3.4 g. dietary fiber, 0 mg. cholesterol, 99 mg. sodium

NOTE
• For a delicious nutty flavor, try adding amaranth to this pilaf. (Amaranth is available in large supermarkets and health food stores.) Replace 1 tablespoon of the barley and 1 tablespoon of the wild rice with a total of 2 tablespoons amaranth.

Rice Pilaf with Spinach and Pine Nuts

1½ teaspoons reduced-calorie margarine or butter
¼ cup chopped scallions
1 tablespoon pine nuts
½ cup long-grain white rice
1¼ cups defatted reduced-sodium chicken broth
½ cup chopped fresh spinach
1 tablespoon grated Parmesan cheese
2 teaspoons grated lemon rind
Pinch of ground nutmeg
Pinch of ground black pepper

In a small saucepan over medium heat, melt the margarine or butter. Add the scallions and pine nuts. Cook and stir over medium heat for 4 minutes, or until the scallions are tender. Stir in the rice and cook for 2 minutes.

Stir in the broth, spinach, Parmesan, lemon rind, nutmeg and pepper and bring to a boil. Reduce the heat, cover and simmer for 20 to 25 minutes, or until the rice is tender and the liquid is absorbed.

Remove from the heat and let stand, covered, for 5 minutes. Fluff with a fork before serving.

Makes 4 servings. Per serving: 121 calories, 2.9 g. fat (22% of calories), 3.9 g. protein, 20.1 g. carbohydrates, 0.5 g. dietary fiber, 1 mg. cholesterol, 72 mg. sodium

Rice-and-Lentil Pilaf

       2 teaspoons olive oil
       1 cup diced carrots
       1 cup diced sweet red peppers
      ¼ cup finely chopped onions
      ¾ cup long-grain white rice
      ¼ cup brown lentils, sorted and rinsed
       2 cups defatted chicken broth
      ½ teaspoon dried thyme
      ½ teaspoon ground cumin
       1 bay leaf
       1 cup frozen peas

In a medium saucepan over medium-high heat, warm the oil. Add the carrots, peppers and onions and sauté for 2 minutes. Add the rice and lentils and sauté for 2 minutes.

Add the broth, thyme, cumin and bay leaf and bring to a boil. Reduce the heat to low, cover and simmer for 12 minutes.

Add the peas. Cover and cook for 5 to 7 minutes, or until the rice is tender and the liquid is absorbed. Discard the bay leaf before serving.

Makes 4 servings. Per serving: 262 calories, 3 g. fat (10% of calories), 11 g. protein, 48.7 g. carbohydrates, 4 g. dietary fiber, 0 mg. cholesterol, 215 mg. sodium

NOTE
• Refrigerate any leftover pilaf and serve it as a chilled salad with a low-fat vinaigrette.

VARIATION
Mexican Rice and Beans: Replace the lentils with ½ cup cooked or canned kidney beans. Add ⅛ teaspoon dried oregano along with the cumin. Replace the peas with frozen corn.

Wild Rice and Mushroom Pilaf

      1½ cups water
      ¾ cup wild rice, rinsed and drained
      1⅔ cups defatted chicken broth
      1½ teaspoons olive oil
       2 small leeks (white part only), chopped
      ¾ cup sliced mushrooms
       1 teaspoon chopped fresh thyme
      ⅛ teaspoon ground black pepper

In a large saucepan over high heat, combine the water and rice. Bring to a boil. Cover, remove from the heat and let stand for 20 minutes. Drain well and return to the pan.

Add 1½ cups of the broth and bring to a boil over medium-high heat. Reduce the heat to low, cover and simmer for 25 minutes, or until the rice is tender and the liquid is absorbed.

Meanwhile, in a large no-stick skillet over medium heat, warm the oil. Add the leeks and sauté for 3 minutes. Add the mushrooms and thyme and sauté for 3 minutes. Add the pepper and the remaining broth. Cover and simmer for 5 minutes; set aside until the rice is ready.

Add the rice to the pan and mix well.

Makes 4 servings. Per serving: 154 calories, 2.2 g. fat (13% of calories), 7.1 g. protein, 28.1 g. carbohydrates, 1.2 g. dietary fiber, 0 mg. cholesterol, 149 mg. sodium

Quinoa Pilaf with Pistachios

¾ teaspoon peanut oil
2 tablespoons shelled unsalted pistachios
½ cup chopped scallions
⅓ cup chopped dried apricots
2 teaspoons minced fresh ginger
1 clove garlic, minced
1 cup defatted reduced-sodium chicken broth or vegetable broth
2 drops hot-pepper sauce
½ cup quinoa, rinsed and drained
2 tablespoons chopped fresh cilantro

In a medium saucepan over medium heat, warm the oil. Add the pistachios and cook, stirring frequently, for 2 to 3 minutes, or until the nuts are fragrant and golden. With a slotted spoon, remove the nuts to a small bowl.

Add the scallions, apricots, ginger and garlic to the pan and cook, stirring constantly, for 2 minutes. Stir in the broth and hot-pepper sauce and bring to a boil.

Stir in the quinoa and cilantro. Reduce the heat to low, cover and simmer for 20 to 25 minutes, or until the liquid is absorbed. Remove from the heat and let stand for 5 minutes. Fluff with a fork and stir in the pistachios.

Makes 4 servings. Per serving: 145 calories, 4.3 g. fat (25% of calories), 4.8 g. protein, 23.4 g. carbohydrates, 2.5 g. dietary fiber, 0 mg. cholesterol, 23 mg. sodium

Barley-Chestnut Pilaf

QUICK!

2 cups defatted reduced-sodium chicken broth
1 cup quick-cooking barley
1 bay leaf
1 teaspoon olive oil
1 cup diced carrots
¾ cup chopped chestnuts (see note)
1 onion, diced
¼ cup sliced scallions
1 clove garlic, minced

In a medium saucepan, combine the broth, barley and bay leaf. Bring to a boil. Reduce the heat to medium-low, cover and cook for 15 minutes, or until the barley is tender and the liquid is absorbed. Remove and discard the bay leaf. Fluff the barley with a fork and set aside.

Meanwhile, in a large no-stick skillet over medium heat, warm the oil. Add the carrots, chestnuts, onions, scallions and garlic. Sauté for 5 minutes, or just until the vegetables are tender. Add the barley and toss to combine.

Makes 4 servings. Per serving: 227 calories, 2.7 g. fat (10% of calories), 8 g. protein, 44.7 g. carbohydrates, 8.4 g. dietary fiber, 0 mg. cholesterol, 51 mg. sodium

NOTES

• Peeled, chopped unsweetened chestnuts are availabe in jars at gourmet specialty stores. You can also mail-order them from gourmet catalogs.

• If using fresh chestnuts, cut an X into the flat part of the shell (to prevent the nuts from exploding) and place the nuts on a no-stick baking sheet. Bake in a 350° oven for 5 to 8 minutes. Using a kitchen towel or oven mitts, remove and discard the shells and rub off the inner brown skin while the nuts are still hot. Then chop the nut meat and use as directed.

Basic Risotto

- 2 teaspoons nondiet tub-style margarine or butter
- 1 teaspoon olive oil
- 1 cup chopped onions
- 1 cup Arborio rice
- 1 clove garlic, minced
- 4–5 cups defatted reduced-sodium chicken broth
  Salt and ground black pepper
- 2 tablespoons grated Parmesan cheese

In a large saucepan over medium-high heat, warm the margarine or butter and the oil. Add the onions and sauté for 8 minutes, or until soft and starting to brown. Stir in the rice and garlic and cook, stirring constantly, for 1 minute.

While the onions are cooking, bring the broth to a simmer in a medium saucepan over medium heat. Reduce the heat to low and maintain the simmer.

Slowly add ½ cup of the broth to the rice mixture, stirring constantly. Continue stirring until the broth is absorbed. Repeat with the remaining broth, adding ½ cup at a time and stirring constantly until each addition of broth is absorbed and the risotto is creamy but still firm to the bite. (You may not need to use all of the broth.)

Add the salt and pepper to taste. Stir in the Parmesan.

Makes 4 servings. Per serving: 255 calories, 5 g. fat (18% of calories), 7.3 g. protein, 44.1 g. carbohydrates, 0.9 g. dietary fiber, 2 mg. cholesterol, 150 mg. sodium

VARIATIONS

Microwave Risotto: Reduce the broth to 3 cups. After sautéing the rice, transfer the mixture to a 2½-quart microwave-safe dish. Stir in the broth. Cover and microwave on high power for a total of 15 minutes, or until the rice is thick and creamy; stop and stir every 5 minutes. Let stand, covered, for 5 minutes. If the rice is too firm, microwave for 1 to 2 minutes more; add more broth if necessary.

Mushroom Risotto: Add 1 cup sliced mushrooms along with the onions. Add 1½ teaspoons chopped fresh thyme toward the end of the cooking time.

Risotto with Greens and Beans: In a medium bowl, combine 1½ cups chopped tomatoes, 1½ cups seeded and chopped cucumbers, 1 cup cooked cannellini beans, ⅓ cup chopped red onions, 3 tablespoons chopped fresh basil, 1½ tablespoons minced fresh parsley, 2 teaspoons balsamic vinegar and ⅛ teaspoon ground black pepper; set aside. Prepare the risotto as directed. At the last minute, add ¾ cup chopped arugula and ¾ cup chopped radicchio. Cook and stir for 2 minutes, or until the greens are wilted. Spoon the risotto onto dinner plates and top each serving with an equal amount of the tomato mixture.

MAKING RISOTTO

For great risotto every time, follow these tips.

☞ Use a heavy saucepan of medium depth with a wide bottom. This type of pan will distribute the heat over a larger area and help speed cooking.

☞ Cook over medium-high heat.

☞ Always use hot, simmering broth so that the rice will cook properly. Keep a pot of simmering broth on the stove while you stir the risotto.

☞ Add no more than ½ cup of broth at a time. After each addition, stir the rice constantly until all of the liquid is absorbed. Constant stirring encourages the grains to release their starch, creating the creamy texture that is unique to risotto.

Sun-Dried Tomato and Goat Cheese Risotto

1 cup boiling water
½ cup dry-pack sun-dried tomatoes
6 cups reduced-sodium vegetable broth
1 tablespoon olive oil
¼ cup chopped scallions
¼ cup chopped shallots
1½ cups Arborio rice
3 tablespoons chopped fresh sage or 1 tablespoon rubbed sage
¼ teaspoon ground black pepper
2 ounces goat cheese, shredded

In a small bowl, combine the water and tomatoes. Let stand for 5 minutes, or until the tomatoes are soft. Drain, reserving the soaking liquid. Chop the tomatoes and set aside.

In a medium saucepan, bring the broth to a boil. Reduce the heat to low and maintain the simmer.

In a medium saucepan over medium heat, warm the oil. Add the scallions and shallots and sauté for 3 minutes, or until tender. Add the rice and sauté for 1 minute.

Slowly add ¼ cup of the broth to the rice mixture, stirring constantly. Continue stirring until the broth is absorbed. Continue adding the broth, ¼ cup at a time, stirring constantly after each addition until all of the broth is absorbed. When you have used half of the broth (about 15 minutes), stir in the tomatoes, sage, pepper and 2 tablespoons of the reserved soaking liquid. Continue adding broth for another 12 to 15 minutes, or until the rice is creamy but still firm to the bite (you may not need all of the broth).

Remove from the heat and stir in the goat cheese.

Makes 4 servings. Per serving: 439 calories, 9.2 g. fat (19% of calories), 11.9 g. protein, 76.4 g. carbohydrates, 0.5 g. dietary fiber, 15 mg. cholesterol, 316 mg. sodium

Chicken Risotto

This easy microwave risotto requires less stirring than the traditional stovetop version. Plus, the chicken, broccoli and sweet red peppers make it filling enough to serve as a one-dish meal.

Rice
¾ cup Arborio rice
2 teaspoons nondiet tub-style margarine or butter
2⅔ cups defatted reduced-sodium chicken broth
½ teaspoon dried thyme
½ teaspoon dried basil
¼ teaspoon ground black pepper

Chicken and Sauce
1 pound boneless, skinless chicken breast halves, cut into bite-size pieces
2 teaspoons nondiet tub-style margarine or butter
1 medium onion, chopped
⅓ cup defatted reduced-sodium chicken broth
1 clove garlic, minced
¼ teaspoon crushed saffron threads
1½ cups chopped broccoli florets and tender stems
½ sweet red pepper, chopped
2 tablespoons grated Parmesan cheese

To make the rice: In a 2½-quart microwave-safe dish, combine the rice and margarine or butter. Microwave on high power for 1 minute. Stir well.

Stir in the broth, thyme, basil and pepper. Cover and microwave for a total of 8 minutes; stop and stir after 4 minutes. Stir again after the full 8 minutes.

Microwave, uncovered, for 11 to 13 minutes, or until the rice is tender and most of the liquid is absorbed. Let stand for 3 minutes.

To make the chicken and sauce: While the rice is cooking, coat a large no-stick skillet with no-stick spray. Place over medium heat and add the chicken. Cook, stirring occasionally, for 3 minutes, or until the chicken is tender. Remove from the pan.

In the same skillet, melt the margarine or butter. Add the onions, broth, garlic and saffron and cook, stirring, for 5 minutes, or until the onions are tender.

Stir in the chicken, broccoli and peppers. Bring to a boil. Reduce the heat to medium-low, cover and simmer, stirring frequently, for 6 to 7 minutes, or until the broccoli is crisp-tender.

Stir the chicken mixture into the rice. Sprinkle with the Parmesan.

Makes 4 servings. Per serving: 364 calories, 8.7 g. total fat (22% of calories), 32.6 g. protein, 37.4 g. carbohydrates, 2.3 g. dietary fiber, 71 mg. cholesterol, 228 mg. sodium

NOTE
• To make this rice on the stove top, bring the broth to a boil in a medium saucepan. Reduce the heat to low and maintain the simmer. In another saucepan, warm the margarine or butter over medium heat. Add the rice and sauté for 2 minutes. Stir in the thyme, basil and pepper. Slowly add ¼ cup of the broth, stirring the rice constantly. Stir until the broth is absorbed. Continue adding the broth, ¼ cup at a time, stirring constantly after each addition until the broth is absorbed. Continue adding broth until the rice is creamy but still firm to the bite (you may not need all of the broth). Set aside while you prepare the chicken and sauce.

Paella

2 tablespoons olive oil
3 cloves garlic, minced
3 cups defatted reduced-sodium chicken broth

1 can (14½ ounces) peeled whole tomatoes (with juice)
¼ teaspoon ground saffron or 8 saffron threads
3 cups quick-cooking brown rice
5 scallions, sliced
1 small sweet red pepper, sliced
12 peeled baby carrots
½ cup frozen peas, thawed
½ cup cooked or canned chick-peas
4 water-packed artichoke hearts, halved
8 ounces chicken tenders
⅓ pound low-fat smoked turkey sausage, sliced ½" thick
8 littleneck clams, scrubbed
8 mussels, scrubbed and beards removed
½ pound large shrimp (15 to 20 shrimp), peeled and deveined

Preheat the oven to 425°.

In a medium saucepan over medium-high heat, warm the oil. Add the garlic and sauté for 1 minute. Add the broth, tomatoes (with juice) and saffron and bring to a boil.

Meanwhile, spread the rice evenly over the bottom of a 9" × 13" no-stick baking dish. Add the scallions, peppers, carrots, peas and chick-peas. Pour the broth and tomatoes over the rice and vegetables and stir to coat. Top with the artichokes, chicken and sausage.

Cover with foil and bake on the top rack of the oven for 10 minutes. Remove the foil and place the clams and mussels, hinge-side down, in the rice. Top with the shrimp. Cover with the foil and return the dish to the top rack of the oven. Bake, covered, for 15 minutes, or until the clams and mussels open. Discard any unopened clams or mussels.

Remove and discard the foil. Bake, uncovered, for 5 minutes. Remove from the oven and let stand for 5 minutes before serving.

Makes 8 servings. Per serving: 458 calories, 9.6 g. fat (19% of calories), 26.5 g. protein, 65.9 g. carbohydrates, 6.5 g. dietary fiber, 85 mg. cholesterol, 440 mg. sodium

Basic Polenta

Traditional polenta tends to be fatty because butter and cheese are added before serving. Here we've cut the fat and boosted the flavor by cooking the polenta in broth and using reduced amounts of margarine and Parmesan cheese. While the percentage of calories from fat is a bit high in the basic recipe, this percentage is lowered when you add almost any topping.

- 1 cup yellow cornmeal
- 1 cup water
- 2½ cups defatted reduced-sodium chicken broth
- 2 tablespoons nondiet tub-style margarine or butter
- 2 tablespoons grated Parmesan cheese

In a large bowl, whisk together the cornmeal and water.

In a medium saucepan, bring the broth to a rapid boil. Gradually add the cornmeal, stirring constantly with a wooden spoon. Cook, stirring constantly, for 25 to 30 minutes, or until the mixture thickens and begins to pull away from the sides of the pan.

Stir in the margarine or butter and Parmesan; mix well. Cover and cook, without stirring, for 3 minutes.

Serve immediately by spooning the hot polenta onto dinner plates.

Makes 4 servings. Per serving: 182 calories, 7.5 g. fat (36% of calories), 5 g. protein, 24.6 g. carbohydrates, 4.8 g. dietary fiber, 0 mg. cholesterol, 172 mg. sodium

NOTES

• For polenta with a smooth texture, use fine imported cornmeal. (Fine cornmeal tends to produce more lumps, so be sure to thoroughly whisk the cornmeal into the water.)

• For a grainy texture, use coarse imported cornmeal.

• To shape the polenta for later use, coat an 8½″ × 4½″ no-stick loaf pan with no-stick spray. Pour in the hot polenta. Cover with plastic and refrigerate for about 2 hours, or until firm. Unmold the chilled polenta onto a cutting board and cut into 1″ slices. Sauté, broil or bake the slices until hot.

VARIATIONS

Broccoli Polenta: Before stirring in the cornmeal, add ½ cup finely chopped broccoli to the boiling broth. Boil for 1 minute, then proceed with the recipe. As you stir, the broccoli will disperse into flecks of green in the polenta.

Polenta Pizza: Coat a no-stick baking sheet with no-stick spray. Pour hot polenta onto the baking sheet and spread out into a circle, forming a rim around the edge. Cover with plastic wrap and refrigerate for about 2 hours, or until set. Top with sauce and cheese and bake at 425° for about 12 minutes, or until the cheese is bubbly. For individual pizzas, cut the chilled polenta into squares or circles with a sharp knife. Top with sauce and cheese and bake at 425° for 10 minutes.

Polenta-Stuffed Peppers: Slice off the tops and remove the seeds and ribs from 3 sweet red, orange or green peppers. Cook for 2 minutes in boiling water. Fill each pepper with hot polenta. Arrange the peppers upright in an 8″ × 8″ no-stick baking dish and drizzle with a little olive oil. Bake at 350° for 30 minutes, or until the peppers are tender. Top with warmed tomato sauce.

Polenta with Mushroom-and-Asparagus Sauté: In a large no-stick saucepan over medium heat, warm 2 tablespoons defatted chicken broth and 1 teaspoon olive oil. Add 1 cup sliced mushrooms and ½ cup chopped shallots. Sauté for 4 minutes, or until the mushrooms are tender. Stir in 2 teaspoons snipped olives, ½ teaspoon dried tarragon and 2 cups steamed asparagus. Cook for 1 minute. Stir in ¼ cup shredded low-fat colby cheese. Serve over hot polenta or chilled, cut and baked polenta slices.

POLENTA TOPPERS

For the busy cook, polenta is simplicity itself. Made by cooking cornmeal in a little water, it can be jazzed up with almost any topping. Many cooks favor polenta with tomato sauce or other pasta toppings. Or you can try something a little more creative to transform this simple dish into something special.

Herbed Summer Vegetables

- 1 tablespoon olive oil
- 1 cup sliced onions
- 2 cups broccoli florets
- 1½ cups sliced mushrooms
- 1 cup sliced yellow summer squash
- 1 can (28 ounces) plum tomatoes, drained and chopped
- ¼ cup chopped fresh basil
- ½ teaspoon dried savory
- ¼ teaspoon dried thyme
- ¼ teaspoon hot-pepper sauce

In a large no-stick skillet over medium heat, warm the oil. Add the onions and sauté for 5 minutes, or until soft. Add the broccoli, mushrooms and squash and sauté for 5 minutes.

Add the tomatoes, basil, savory, thyme and hot-pepper sauce. Cover and cook for 20 minutes, or until the vegetables are tender.

Makes 4 servings. Per serving: 112 calories, 4.3 g. fat (35% of calories), 4.6 g. protein, 17.4 g. carbohydrates, 3.9 g. dietary fiber, 0 mg. cholesterol, 338 mg. sodium

Creamy Primavera Sauce

- 1 cup sliced carrots
- 1 cup sliced zucchini
- ½ cup sliced scallions
- 2 tablespoons all-purpose flour
- 1 tablespoon olive oil
- 1¼ cups skim milk
- 1 teaspoon Dijon mustard
- 1 teaspoon dried dill
- 2 tablespoons grated Sapsago or Parmesan cheese

In a large saucepan, bring 1″ of water to a boil. Place the carrots, zucchini and scallions on a steaming rack and set the rack in the pan. Cover and steam for about 4 minutes, or until tender.

Meanwhile, in a medium saucepan, combine the flour and oil. Stir over medium heat for 3 minutes. Whisk in the milk and cook, whisking constantly, until the sauce thickens and comes to a boil. Whisk in the mustard and dill. Remove from the heat and stir in the steamed vegetables and the Sapsago or Parmesan.

Makes 4 servings. Per serving: 98 calories, 3.8 g. fat (34% of calories), 5.3 g. protein, 11.3 g. carbohydrates, 1.5 g. dietary fiber, 1 mg. cholesterol, 173 mg. sodium

Couscous with Tomatoes and Lentils

2 teaspoons nondiet tub-style margarine or butter
½ cup sliced scallions
1½ cups defatted reduced-sodium chicken broth
1 cup spicy reduced-sodium vegetable juice cocktail
1 cup brown lentils, rinsed and drained
1 bay leaf
1 cup whole-wheat or regular couscous
1 medium tomato, coarsely chopped
½ cup chopped fresh basil
2 tablespoons grated Parmesan cheese

In a medium saucepan over medium heat, melt the margarine or butter. Add the scallions and sauté for 2 to 3 minutes, or until tender.

Stir in the broth, vegetable juice cocktail, lentils and bay leaf and bring to a boil. Reduce the heat to low, cover and simmer for 30 to 45 minutes, or until the lentils are soft but not mushy.

Remove the pan from the heat and discard the bay leaf. Stir in the couscous, tomatoes, basil and Parmesan. Cover and let stand for 5 minutes, or until the couscous is soft. Uncover and fluff with a fork before serving.

Makes 4 servings. Per serving: 379 calories, 4 g. fat (9% of calories), 20.1 g. protein, 66 g. carbohydrates, 7.7 g. dietary fiber, 2 mg. cholesterol, 133 mg. sodium

VARIATION

Bulgur with Tomatoes and Lentils: Replace the couscous with 1 cup bulgur. Place the bulgur in a medium bowl and add boiling water to cover. Cover the bowl and let stand for 30 minutes, or until the bulgur is tender. Drain well. Stir into the cooked lentils along with the tomatoes. Cover and let stand for 5 minutes. Uncover and fluff with a fork before serving.

Couscous-and-Zucchini Casserole

1 tablespoon olive oil
1 cup chopped onions
3 large cloves garlic, minced
3 cups thinly sliced zucchini
2 cups chopped sweet red peppers
1 cup chopped celery
1 teaspoon dried basil
2 cups canned reduced-sodium stewed tomatoes (with juice)
1 cup canned black beans, rinsed and drained
1 cup couscous
10 kalamata olives, pitted and chopped
2 tablespoons grated Parmesan cheese
½ cup shredded reduced-fat Cheddar cheese

Preheat the oven to 375°. Coat a 3-quart no-stick baking dish with no-stick spray and set aside.

In a large no-stick skillet over medium heat, warm the oil. Add the onions and sauté for 4 minutes. Add the garlic, zucchini, peppers, celery and basil and sauté for 6 minutes, or until tender.

Stir in the tomatoes (with juice), beans, couscous, olives and Parmesan and cook for 1 minute.

Spoon the mixture into the prepared baking dish. Sprinkle with the Cheddar. Cover and bake for 20 minutes, then uncover and bake for 20 minutes.

Makes 4 servings. Per serving: 393 calories, 9 g. fat (19% of calories), 18.5 g. protein, 66.5 g. carbohydrates, 14.9 g. dietary fiber, 8 mg. cholesterol, 470 mg. sodium

Couscous with Tomato, Fennel and Shrimp

QUICK!

1½ tablespoons olive oil
1 small onion, sliced
1 small fennel bulb, sliced
1 large clove garlic, minced
¼ teaspoon turmeric
2 cups water
⅓ pound cleaned raw salad shrimp
1 small tomato, peeled and chopped
2 tablespoons chopped fennel leaves
⅛ teaspoon ground black pepper
1½ cups couscous

In a large saucepan over medium heat, warm the oil. Add the onions, sliced fennel and garlic and sauté for 5 minutes, or until the onions are soft. Stir in the turmeric and sauté for 1 minute.

Add the water to the pan and bring to a boil. Add the shrimp, return to a boil and cook for 1 minute. Stir in the tomatoes, fennel leaves, pepper and couscous. Remove from the heat. Cover and let stand for 5 minutes. Fluff with a fork before serving.

Makes 4 servings. Per serving: 354 calories, 6 g. fat (16% of calories), 15.8 g. protein, 57.7 g. carbohydrates, 11.4 g. dietary fiber, 58 mg. cholesterol, 82 mg. sodium

VARIATION

Couscous with Tomato, Fennel and Scallops: Replace the shrimp with ⅓ pound small bay scallops.

Basic Granola

6 cups rolled oats
½ cup wheat germ
1 teaspoon ground cinnamon
¼ cup honey
2 tablespoons vegetable oil
2 tablespoons water or apple juice
1 cup raisins

Preheat the oven to 300°. Coat two 2-quart no-stick baking dishes with no-stick spray.

In a large bowl, combine the oats, wheat germ and cinnamon.

In a small microwave-safe bowl, combine the honey, oil and water or apple juice. Microwave on high power for 1 minute. Stir well and add to the oats. Mix well.

Spread the granola thinly and evenly in the prepared baking dishes and bake for 20 minutes, or until the granola is golden brown. Cool completely in the baking dishes.

Stir in the raisins. Store in an airtight container in a cool, dry place.

Makes 7 cups. Per ½ cup: 216 calories, 4.6 g. fat (18% of calories), 6.9 g. protein, 38.6 g. carbohydrates, 4.1 g dietary fiber, 0 mg. cholesterol, 4 mg. sodium

VARIATIONS

Fruited Granola: Replace the raisins with 1 cup chopped dried apples, apricots, figs, peaches, pears, pineapple or prunes, or a combination. Other possible additions include unsweetened shredded coconut, wheat bran, oat bran and sunflower or sesame seeds.

Nutty Granola: Along with the wheat germ, add ¼ cup coarsely chopped nuts, such as almonds, walnuts, pecans, cashews or peanuts, or a combination.

Legumes

Beans are truly international. Italian minestrone, French cassoulet, hummus from the Middle East and feijoada (black beans) from Brazil are just a few of the savory legume recipes that grace the world's tables.

Legumes are seeds harvested from pod-bearing plants. (Peanuts are also legumes, but for culinary purposes, they're generally grouped with nuts.) While Italian green beans, snap beans and a few other legumes are eaten fresh, most of us, when we think of beans, have in mind the many dried varieties, such as pintos, black beans and Great Northerns.

Inexpensive and easy to use, beans provide a double-barreled supply of nourishment. Loaded with complex carbohydrates, fiber and valuable vitamins and minerals, they're also low in fat and sodium and have no cholesterol. In addition, they take a while to digest, which means that they keep you feeling full for a long time after eating. Suffice it to say that, bite for bite, legumes offer one of the best nutritional packages of any staple in the kitchen.

SELECTING AND STORING LEGUMES

Legumes are among the longest-lasting foods that you can buy. Properly packed and stored, they will keep for years. At the supermarket, however, you want to shop carefully to avoid getting inferior beans.

☞ Dried beans should be whole and intact, with bright, vivid hues.

☞ When buying packaged legumes, inspect the contents by peering through the plastic package. If a large percentage of the contents seem to be chipped, broken or dull in color, try another package or another brand.

☞ It's best to buy your beans in a market where there is a high turnover rate. Whereas old beans don't go bad, they do take longer to cook and won't expand in water as readily as fresher beans.

☞ Beans should be free of insect damage. Look for pinhole-size holes on the beans that would suggest that you're not the only one doing the eating.

☞ Store dried legumes in airtight containers like mason jars in a place that's cool, dry and dark. Beans stored in warm, humid areas take longer to cook.

☞ Older beans cook more slowly than newer ones, so try not to mix the two in the same recipe.

COOKING LEGUMES

If you can boil water, you can cook beans. To make a truly wonderful batch, however—one that is perfectly cooked and tender but still has texture and a slight chewiness—here's what chefs advise.

Look for has-beans. Before cooking beans, spread them out in a shallow pan or bowl. Pick through and remove broken beans, pebbles, grit or other dirt. This will help ensure that your beans have an even, consistent texture—and also that your teeth don't receive an unpleasant shock while chewing.

Rinse them well. Beans can be extremely dusty, so it's best to rinse them thoroughly before soaking or cooking.

Soak them well. Soaking beans in water allows them to gradually rehydrate and expand, yielding tender, easily digested beans. Soaking also reduces the overall cooking time by as much as 30 to 60 minutes.

☞ When soaking beans, cover them with three to four times their volume of cold water. One cup beans, for example, should be covered with 3 to 4 cups water.

☞ Beans should be soaked for a minimum of 4 hours; overnight is better.

Give them room. When you're ready to start cooking, put the beans in a sturdy, large pot—the bigger the better. Beans swell to several times their dry size during cooking. It's better to have room left over in the pot than to have the beans crowded together or to have the pot boil over.

Cook them slowly. After bringing the water to a boil, lower the heat and simmer the beans uncovered. Occasionally give them a stir. Skim

MAKE BEANS FAST

When you have a taste for beans and don't feel like soaking them overnight, use the quick-soak method.

☞ Put the beans in a pot, cover with water and bring to a boil; cook for 2 minutes.

☞ Remove the beans from the heat and let stand, covered, for 1 hour.

☞ Drain and discard the soaking liquid. Cover the beans with fresh water and cook as usual.

Helpful Hint

You can quick-soak beans using the microwave. Put the beans in a large microwave-safe container, cover with water and put a lid on the container. Microwave on high power for 10 minutes, or until the water boils. Let stand for 1 hour. Drain, add new water and proceed with the recipe.

off any scum that rises to the top. Pour in hot water if the cooking liquid evaporates too quickly and exposes the beans; they should always be completely covered.

Add salt late. Adding salt early in the cooking process inhibits the absorption of liquid and can make beans tough. If you want salt, add it only after the legumes are tender. Then continue cooking for 10 to 15 minutes to allow the salt to be absorbed.

Hold the acids. Adding tomatoes, vinegar or other acidic foods to legumes during cooking causes them to toughen. It also may cause some beans to split. It's best to add acids only after the beans have finished cooking.

Add some flavor early. When you're seasoning beans with dried herbs, add them about halfway through the cooking process to give them time to release all their flavors.

For cold bean salads, add seasonings and other ingredients like vegetables and dressings at least a half-hour before serving. This will give the flavors time to mingle.

Use fresh herbs late. Fresh herbs aren't as hardy as the dried variety, and adding them to the pot too soon will cause their delicate flavors to dissipate. Add them only after the beans are almost done.

(continued on page 182)

THE BEAN SCENE

Beans have moved beyond basic. While healthy cooks haven't abandoned the old standbys like lentils and navy beans, they're also experimenting with exotic "designer" beans, like flageolet and Appaloosa beans. Here are cooking times and suggestions for some of the more common beans, and also for some that you may not have tried yet.

BEAN	CHARACTERISTICS	STOVE-TOP COOKING TIME	PRESSURE-COOKING TIME	RECOMMENDED USES
Adzuki (also called aduki)	Small, oval bean with an attractive burgundy color and a nutty flavor	1–1½ hours	15–20 minutes	Goes well with Asian desserts and red rice
Anasazi	Kidney-shaped bean that's mottled with reddish-purple and white	1½ hours	10–12 minutes	The firm texture is good for stews, chili and soups.
Black (also called turtle bean)	A medium, oval bean ranging from dark gray to jet-black; earthy, woodsy flavor	1½ hours	15 minutes	Complements Mexican, Brazilian and Cuban dishes
Black-eyed pea (also called cowpea)	A medium, oblong bean the color of creamy coffee, with a tiny dark eye on the ridge; mealy texture and slight sweetness	1½ hours	10 minutes	Often used for hoppin' John and for southern soups and salads
Chick-pea (also called garbanzo and ceci bean)	A beige, acorn-shaped bean with a tiny peak; nutty flavor and chewy texture.	2–3 hours	Not recommended	Used in hummus, falafels and other Middle Eastern and Spanish and Indian dishes
Cranberry (also called Roman bean and tongue of fire)	Mild kidney-shaped bean with a light, cranberry mottle that turns solid pink when cooked	1½ hours	12–15 minutes	Goes well with stews and Italian soups
Fava (also called broad bean)	Small, round or kidney-shaped light brown bean	1½ hours	Not recommended	Commonly used in Middle Eastern, Italian and South American stews and purees

Bean	Characteristics	Stove-Top Cooking Time	Pressure-Cooking Time	Recommended Uses
Flageolet	Pale green, kidney-shaped bean	1–1½ hours	10–15 minutes	A gourmet French bean, it's used in stews, soups and side dishes
Great Northern	An ivory white, kidney-shaped bean with a mild flavor	1½ hours	15–20 minutes	Can be used interchangeably with navy and cannellini beans; good for baked beans, cassoulet and European soups
Lentil	Thin and oval-shaped with a mild, earthy flavor; common colors are green, red, yellow and brown	30–45 minutes	Not recommended	Complements Indian, Middle Eastern and North African side dishes, soups and salads
Lima (also called butter bean)	Small, creamy white bean with a mild flavor and soft, mealy texture	1½–2 hours	Not recommended	Good in soups and stews; also good with garlicky sauces
Pigeon pea (also called Congo pea)	Pale, brownish pea with a tiny eye on the ridge; earthy flavor and soft, mealy texture	1–1½ hours	8–10 minutes	Often used in Caribbean and Hispanic soups and rice dishes
Pinto	Oval bean with pink and brown speckles	1½–2 hours	15–20 minutes	Good for refried beans, chili, burritos and side dishes
Red kidney	Large, kidney-shaped bean that ranges from pale to dark red; full-flavored with a chewy texture	1½–2 hours	20 minutes	Used in chili, soups, salads, Louisiana beans and rice, and Jamaican red-pea soup
White cannellini (also called white kidney or haricot blanc)	A creamy white bean with a large kidney shape; smooth, firm texture and nutty flavor	1½–2 hours	20 minutes	Often used in minestrone, salads, stews and side dishes

BEAN SEASONINGS

Beans traditionally have been cooked with high-flavored, high-fat ingredients, like salt pork, bacon, lard and meats. By using the right spices and ingredients, however, you can boost the flavor of beans without using fat.

BEAN	RECOMMENDED SEASONINGS
Black beans	Bay leaf, bell peppers, chili peppers, cilantro, cumin, garlic, onions, oregano, parsley, thyme, tomatoes
Chick-peas	Chili peppers, coriander, cumin, curry, garam masala, garlic, ginger, onions, paprika, parsley, tomatoes, turmeric
Lentils	Chili peppers, coriander, cumin, curry, garam masala, garlic, ginger, lemon, onions, parsley, turmeric
Red and pink beans	Bay leaf, bell peppers, celery, chili powder, cumin, garlic, onions, oregano, parsley, tomatoes
Split peas	Bay leaf, carrots, garlic, onions, oregano, parsley, root vegetables, thyme
White beans	Basil, garlic, leeks, marjoram, onions, oregano, rosemary, sage, thyme, tomatoes

Mix it up. Rather than making beans a solo act, you may want to add hearty vegetables to the pot.

☞ Dense vegetables like turnips, winter squash and carrots should be added early in the cooking time to ensure that they're done all the way through.

☞ More delicate vegetables like onions and peppers should be added toward the middle or end of the cooking time.

Try them without meat. While beans were traditionally made with such meaty additions as salt pork or bacon, you may want to try a healthier version. Adding roasted tofu or cubed seitan (flavored wheat gluten) to the beans during cooking will simulate the chewy texture of meat but without the saturated fat.

Make sure they're done. Few things are less appetizing than undercooked beans. They usually take anywhere from 1 to 3 hours to cook. (Split peas and lentils cook faster, usually in

Helpful Hint

Adding a few thin strips of kelp to a pot of beans will help them cook up tender as well as more quickly. You can find kelp at most health food stores and in most supermarkets.

about 45 minutes to an hour.) The beans should be doubled or tripled in size.

☞ To test for doneness, remove a spoonful of legumes from the pot and place them on a cutting board. Press the back of a spoon against the beans; they should mash easily.

☞ Another method is to place a few beans on a spoon and then blow on them. If the skins burst open, the beans are done.

GOURMET BEANS

Along with fancy coffee beans and imported chocolates, there has been a surge of interest in exotic beans. Many of these are heirloom varieties that are grown in small quantities. They often have colorful markings—and a gourmet price tag to boot. They're fun to try, though, and like all beans, they are veritable powerhouses of fiber, vitamins and minerals.

☞ **Appaloosa.** Named after the ponies with a similarly mottled appearance, Appaloosa beans have a mild, pintolike flavor and are good for making chili and bean salads.

☞ **Canary.** Pale yellow, pea-shaped beans popular in Peruvian cuisine, they have a mild flavor, somewhat between lima beans and chick-peas. They're often pureed for use in side dishes.

☞ **Christmas lima.** Brown and purple speckled beans with a roasted-chestnut flavor, these are often added to bean salads.

☞ **Jacob's cattle.** Similar to anasazi beans but with maroon markings, these have a mealy texture and mild flavor. Good in chili and stews.

☞ **Soldier.** European beans with reddish-brown markings that resemble little soldiers, these have a mild flavor similar to that of white kidney beans. They're often combined with pasta, added to soup or used with rice and aromatic spices.

Helpful Hint

Canned beans like chick-peas, cannellinis and kidney beans are often of excellent quality and provide a fast, convenient substitute for the dried kind. Rinse them thoroughly to remove excess sodium and thick canning liquid.

BEAN-DIP TIPS

Beans have a firm texture and smooth interior that makes them ideal for dips.

☞ Adding black beans to your favorite tomato salsa is an easy way to make a filling, chunky dip.

☞ To make a Southwestern dip, puree black or red beans, adding cumin, garlic, chili peppers and cilantro.

☞ To make hummus, mash up chick-peas with tahini, garlic, lemon juice and a hint of cumin.

CANNED BEANS

When you don't have time to cook beans from scratch, canned beans provide a fast, convenient alternative. In most recipes, canned beans are interchangeable with the cooked dried ones. And, like dried beans, canned beans can be stored a long time; they're always on your pantry shelf when you need them.

Read the label. While the quality of canned beans in some cases is comparable to fresh, you may want to avoid products with added sugar, corn syrup, monosodium glutamate (MSG) or meat products.

Many supermarkets stock reduced-sodium canned beans. Instead of being packed in a salt solution, they're packed in kombu, a seaweed that provides a salty flavor but that's naturally low in sodium.

Rinse them well. To remove the salty taste from canned beans, rinse them under cold running water until the taste is neutral, or just barely salty. Drain well.

Experiment with new combinations. You can make a quick bean salad simply by tossing together two or three varieties of canned beans, adding a handful of raw salad vegetables, then dressing with a vinaigrette. Let the salad marinate for 30 minutes before serving.

☞ When making rice, couscous or other grains, fold in a can of red kidney beans, black beans or chick-peas at the end of the cooking time. The beans will add exciting flavor to an otherwise bland grain. You'll also get an added jolt of fiber, vitamins and minerals.

☞ For a tasty, last-minute addition to soups or stews, add canned beans near the end of the cooking time. They'll provide a filling main meal.

For a long time, beans were neglected, even scorned, because of their reputation as being peasant food. The thinking was that people who couldn't afford meat made do with beans.

Today, the opposite is true: Many people prefer the delicious variety of beans over fatty, cholesterol-laden meat. Beans are a truly versatile ingredient that go with just about everything.

Bean Soups

For great taste, wonderful aroma and a genuine stick-to-your-ribs feeling, bean soup is

BEANS FROM THE GARDEN

The only thing that differentiates dry beans from fresh beans is time: Dry beans are allowed to grow to full size and dry in the pod, whereas fresh beans are picked at an earlier stage. Nutritionally, however, the differences are more substantial. Dry beans are high in protein, carbohydrates and fiber. Fresh beans, like many green plant foods, are higher in antioxidant nutrients like vitamin C.

The next time you're at the farmers' market, here are some fresh beans to look for.

☞ **Chinese long beans.** Measuring up to 18″ long, these thin, mild-tasting green beans are excellent for stir-fries.

☞ **Green beans.** These are sometimes still referred to as string beans, although most newer varieties don't have strings that need removal. Fresh-tasting and with a deliciously crispy snap, green beans are usually served as a side dish. They're also good in stir-fries, soups and stews.

☞ **Haricots verts.** Tender, very thin and expensive, these have a flavor similar to green beans and are prominently used in French cooking. The pods can be blanched and added to salads or lightly steamed and dressed with lemon for a tangy side dish.

☞ **Italian green beans.** Also known as Romano beans, these are wider and flatter than regular green beans.

☞ **Lima beans.** These are best when they're small and tender. Look for plump, firm, dark green pods. Shell and use them as a side dish or in salads.

☞ **Purple beans.** Often used for a beautiful garnish, these have a similar taste to their more common yellow kin, although they're somewhat chewier. The purple pod turns green during cooking.

☞ **Soybeans.** While these are usually sold dry, some Asian markets stock the fresh varieties. They have a mild flavor and are high in protein.

☞ **Yellow wax beans.** These are a pale yellow variety of green bean that are used in similar ways.

SPROUTING BEANS

It's interesting that foods as tough and durable as dried beans are used to produce their absolute opposite: the fragile, short-lived and fresh-tasting bean sprout. Made by soaking and rinsing dried beans for a number of days, bean sprouts make a wonderful addition to salads and stir-fries. Almost any whole unsprayed bean or pea can be used for sprouting. You can buy bean sprouts at the supermarket. Or you can make your own, either in a mason jar or in a special sprouter, which is available at kitchen supply stores.

You can also sprout seeds such as alfalfa, wheat, radish and others with the same technique.

Rinse the beans well, then soak them for 8 to 12 hours in a 1-quart jar, using four parts water to one part beans. Cover the jar with a piece of cheesecloth secured with a rubber band and place the jar in a cool, dark place.

After soaking the beans, pour off the water, straining it through the cheesecloth. Rinse and drain the beans twice a day with fresh cold water. Be sure to drain the beans very well; any water left standing in the jar can cause mold.

The pale green shoots should begin appearing in three to six days. When they're about an inch long, they're ready to harvest. But before harvesting, allow them a quick peak at the sun for just a few hours. This will cause them to produce additional chlorophyll, thus increasing their nutrient value.

hard to beat. What's more, it's so easy to make. Just combine beans, water, vegetables or other ingredients and some seasonings, then let the pot simmer.

☞ Virtually any bean is a candidate for the soup pot, although chick-peas, red beans, black beans, lentils and split peas are traditional favorites.

☞ People in Scandinavia and other Northern European countries typically prefer yellow split peas, which have a distinct nutlike flavor, over the green split peas that are commonly used in this country.

☞ While most dried beans require soaking, split peas and lentils need just a quick rinse before being added to the cooking liquid.

☞ When making chili or long-cooking stews, use large, firm-textured beans, like red kidney beans, cannellini beans or chick-peas, which hold their shape and retain texture through the long cooking process.

☞ For an interesting blend of tastes and textures, combine several varieties of beans. In minestrone, for example, you can mix white beans and cranberry beans. For chili, try black beans, pinto beans and red beans.

When mixing bean varieties, consider cooking them separately to ensure that the texture of the finished dish is consistent throughout.

☞ Since split peas and lentils fall apart quickly, they're generally recommended for soups with a smooth, bisquelike consistency, like the classic split pea soup.

☞ You can cook beans ahead for future use. Covered and stored in the refrigerator, cooked beans keep for about four or five days. For longer storage, freeze them.

BEANS WITHOUT BLOAT

Although legumes are one of the healthiest foods that you can eat, they have the unfortunate habit of bragging about it. Gas, cramping and general gastric distress can be particularly uncomfortable in people who are unaccustomed to eating a high-fiber diet.

With a little planning, however, you can enjoy your bowl of beans without enduring its noisy and sometimes painful epilogue.

Start with soaking. Soaking beans for at least 4 hours and preferably overnight is one way to reduce or eliminate their gas-causing potential. Soaking helps remove from the beans complex sugars, called oligosaccharides, which are responsible for bloating. When you pour out the rinse water, you eliminate the noise-causing compounds as well.

Change the water. An extension of this idea is to change the water once or twice during

---

GAS RATINGS

Despite their great taste and nutritional benefits, beans have a way of talking back. Here are some common offenders, ranked from the most volatile to the least.

☞ Soybeans
☞ Pea (navy) beans
☞ Black beans
☞ Pinto beans
☞ Great Northern beans
☞ Chick-peas
☞ Lima beans
☞ Black-eyed peas

---

the cooking period. As more of the oligosaccharides are leached into the water, they can be poured off.

Let them cook. Beans that are undercooked are tough and hard to digest. It's best to cook beans until they're tender enough to mash easily but still have some texture and firmness. Don't worry about overcooking beans; an extra 15 to 20 minutes in the water isn't likely to cause problems.

Try supplemental protection. An over-the-counter product called Beano contains an enzyme (alphagalactosidase) that breaks down the indigestible sugars in beans while they're still in your stomach. This causes the sugars to be absorbed into your bloodstream, where they can't cause uncomfortable or embarrassing problems.

To use Beano, add three to eight drops for every ½ cup of food. (Put the drops on your first bite of food.) If that doesn't do the trick, you can play around with the amount. Don't add Beano during cooking, however, as the high temperatures will render the enzyme ineffective.

Raji Jallepalli

*L*entils, peas and beans are common ingredients in French and Indian cooking, and Raji Jallepalli uses them to advantage in her popular Memphis restaurant, Raji.

"I think that the trend in the 1990s has been toward low-fat and vegetarian cooking, and lentils are very versatile in both," she says. "This recipe uses a homemade chutney as an accent. However, chutney is sautéed much less today than in the past, which helps preserve its color and texture."

The recipe calls for *urad dal*, which are split black lentils. Look for them in Indian or Middle Eastern groceries.

Lentil Blini with Red-Pepper Sauce

Red-Pepper Sauce
  1   teaspoon canola oil
  ¼   teaspoon ground cumin
  ¼   teaspoon ground red pepper
  ¼   teaspoon brown mustard seeds
      Pinch of turmeric
  2   large sweet red peppers, chopped
  2   tablespoons water
      Pinch of salt

Lentil Blini
  ½   cup split black lentils
  ½   cup water
  ¼   teaspoon salt
      Pinch of ground black pepper
  1   tablespoon canola oil
  ¼   cup chopped fresh cilantro

To make the red-pepper sauce: In a large no-stick skillet over medium heat, warm the oil. Add the cumin, ground red pepper, mustard seeds and turmeric. Sauté for 3 minutes, or until the mustard seeds begin to pop.

Add the sweet red peppers, water and salt. Cook, stirring occasionally, for 4 minutes, or until the peppers are soft. Increase the heat to evaporate any remaining liquid. Place the mixture in a food processor or blender and puree until smooth. Set aside.

To make the blini: Soak the lentils in water to cover for 2 to 4 hours. Drain. In a food processor or blender, puree the lentils until smooth. Continue to puree, gradually adding the water, until the mixture is the thickness of pancake batter. Add the salt and pepper.

In a large no-stick skillet over medium heat, warm 1 teaspoon of the oil. Drop rounded tablespoonfuls of the batter into the skillet, allowing room for them to spread. Cook for 3 minutes per side, or until the blini are lightly browned. Transfer the blini to a plate to keep warm. Repeat to use the remaining 2 teaspoons oil and batter. (You should have about 16 blini, each 2¼" in diameter.)

Divide the blini among 4 dinner plates and top with equal amounts of the sauce. Sprinkle with the cilantro.

Makes 4 servings. Per serving: 135 calories, 5.2 g. fat (34% of calories), 6 g. protein, 18.4 g. carbohydrates, 2.1 g. dietary fiber, 0 mg. cholesterol, 135 mg. sodium

Baked Beans

1 cup dried navy beans, soaked overnight
2 cups water
⅓ cup crumbled low-fat turkey sausage
½ cup diced onions
1 cup defatted reduced-sodium chicken broth
¼ cup molasses
2 tablespoons reduced-sodium ketchup
1½ teaspoons honey
1½ teaspoons brown sugar
1½ teaspoons brown mustard
1½ teaspoons Dijon mustard
½ teaspoon dry mustard
¼ teaspoon ground ginger
¼ teaspoon ground allspice
Pinch of ground cloves

Drain the beans and place them in a large saucepan. Add the water and bring to a boil. Reduce the heat to medium-low and simmer for 1 hour, or until the beans are tender. Drain the beans and transfer to a 2-quart no-stick baking dish.

Meanwhile, in a medium saucepan over medium heat, cook and break up the sausage for 2 to 3 minutes, or until almost cooked through. Add the onions and sauté for 3 to 4 minutes, or until the onions are tender. Stir the sausage mixture into the beans.

In the medium pan over medium heat, combine the broth, molasses, ketchup, honey, brown sugar, brown mustard, Dijon mustard, dry mustard, ginger, allspice and cloves. Bring to a simmer, stirring occasionally. Pour over the beans and mix well.

Preheat the oven to 300°. Cover and bake, stirring occasionally, for 1½ hours. Uncover and bake, stirring occasionally, for 45 minutes, or until the beans are tender.

Makes 4 servings. Per serving: 274 calories, 1.9 g. fat (6% of calories), 14.5 g. protein, 51.7 g. carbohydrates, 0.6 g. dietary fiber, 6 mg. cholesterol, 176 mg. sodium

NOTES
• You can use other beans, such as baby lima, Great Northern, pinto or pea beans or a combination.
• This recipe can be doubled to serve 8. Use a 3-quart no-stick baking dish and increase the initial baking time to 2 hours.

VARIATIONS
Baked Beans with Peppers: Sauté 1 cup diced sweet red or green peppers along with the onions.
Vegetarian Baked Beans: Replace the turkey sausage with tofu-based sausage. Or omit the sausage and sauté the onions in 2 teaspoons canola oil. Replace the chicken broth with vegetable broth.

QUICK!
Southwestern Black Beans

2 teaspoons canola oil
1 small red onion, chopped
1 clove garlic, minced
2 teaspooons chili powder
1 teaspoon ground cumin
2 cans (15 ounces each) black beans, rinsed and drained
¼ cup water or vegetable broth
¼ cup chopped fresh cilantro
2 tablespoons lime juice

In a large no-stick skillet over medium heat, warm the oil. Add the onions and sauté for 4 minutes, or until soft. Add the garlic, chili powder and cumin and sauté for 1 minute.

Stir in the beans and water or broth. Cook, stirring occasionally, for 5 minutes, or until the beans are heated through and most of the liquid has evaporated.

Remove from the heat and stir in the cilantro and lime juice.

Makes 4 servings. Per serving: 209 calories, 4.6 g. fat (20% of calories), 17.7 g. protein, 39.7 carbohydrates, 13.1 g. dietary fiber, 0 mg. cholesterol, 680 mg. sodium

Curried Red Lentils

- ¾ cup red lentils, sorted and rinsed
- 1 tablespoon olive oil
- ½ cup chopped onions
- ½ cup chopped scallions
- 1 green pepper, diced
- 1 tablespoon chopped canned mild green chili peppers
- 1 tablespoon all-purpose flour
- 2 teaspoons curry powder
  Pinch of ground red pepper
- ¾ cup defatted reduced-sodium chicken broth
- 1 teaspoon reduced-sodium soy sauce
- 1 teaspoon rice-wine vinegar
- 1 tablespoon chopped fresh cilantro

In a medium saucepan over medium-high heat, combine the lentils with 1¾ cups water and bring to a boil. Reduce the heat to low, cover and simmer for 25 to 30 minutes, or until the lentils are tender. Drain.

Meanwhile, in a large no-stick skillet over medium heat, warm the oil. Add the onions, scallions, green peppers and chili peppers. Cook, stirring frequently, for 2 to 3 minutes, or until the peppers are tender. Stir in the flour, curry powder and red pepper and cook for 1 minute.

Whisk in the broth, soy sauce and vinegar. Add the lentils and cook for 2 minutes, or until the mixture is heated through and begins to thicken. Sprinkle with the cilantro.

Makes 4 servings. Per serving: 169 calories, 4.1 g. fat (21% of calories), 9.8 g. protein, 24.7 g. carbohydrates, 1.3 g. dietary fiber, 0 mg. cholesterol, 85 mg. sodium

NOTE
• For a spicier dish, use 2 tablespoons chopped jalapeño peppers (wear plastic gloves when handling) and ⅛ teaspoon ground red pepper. Top each serving with 2 teaspoons chopped mango chutney.

Mexican Lentils with Peppers

- 2 teaspoons olive oil
- ¼ cup chopped scallions
- ¾ cup diced carrots
- 1 cup diced sweet red peppers
- 1 cup diced green peppers
- ½ cup long-grain white rice
- ½ cup brown lentils, sorted and rinsed
- ½ teaspoon chili powder
- ½ teaspoon ground cumin
- ½ cup chopped tomatoes
- 2 cups defatted chicken broth

In a medium saucepan over medium heat, warm the oil. Add the scallions, carrots, red peppers and green peppers and sauté for 5 minutes, or until the vegetables are tender. Add the rice, lentils, chili powder and cumin and sauté for 2 minutes.

Stir in the tomatoes and broth and bring to a boil. Stir once and reduce the heat to low. Cover and simmer, stirring occasionally, for 25 minutes, or until the rice is tender and the liquid is absorbed.

Makes 4 servings. Per serving: 240 calories, 3.2 g. fat (12% of calories), 11.5 g. protein, 43.5 g. carbohydrates, 3.4 g. dietary fiber, 0 mg. cholesterol, 185 mg. sodium

Cannellini Beans with Rosemary

2 teaspoons olive oil
½ cup chopped green peppers
¼ cup chopped onions
1 clove garlic, minced
1 can (19 ounces) cannellini beans, rinsed and drained
¼ cup reduced-sodium vegetable broth
½ cup chopped tomatoes
1 tablespoon orange juice
1 teaspoon grated orange rind
1 teaspoon chopped fresh rosemary
⅛ teaspoon ground black pepper

In a large no-stick skillet over medium heat, warm the oil. Add the green peppers, onions and garlic and sauté for 4 minutes, or until the peppers are soft.

Add the beans, broth, tomatoes, orange juice, orange rind and rosemary. Reduce the heat to low, cover and cook for 10 minutes. Uncover, sprinkle with the black pepper, and cook, stirring occasionally, for 4 minutes.

Makes 4 servings. Per serving: 140 calories, 3.4 g. fat (22% of calories), 10.4 g. protein, 28.4 g. carbohydrates, 9 g. dietary fiber, 0 mg. cholesterol, 273 mg. sodium

Simmered White Beans and Sweet Potatoes

1 tablespoon olive oil
1 Spanish onion, chopped
2 cloves garlic, minced
¼ cup long-grain white rice
1½ cups chopped tomatoes
1 cup cooked or canned Great Northern beans, rinsed and drained
1 sweet red pepper, chopped
2 sweet potatoes, peeled and cubed
1 cup water
½ teaspoon salt (optional)

In a large no-stick skillet over medium heat, warm the oil. Add the onions and garlic and sauté for 4 minutes, or until the onions are soft. Add the rice and sauté for 2 minutes.

Add the tomatoes, beans, peppers, sweet potatoes, water and salt (if using). Bring to a boil. Reduce the heat to low, cover and simmer for 30 minutes, or until the rice is tender.

Makes 4 servings. Per serving: 237 calories, 4.2 g. fat (15% of calories), 7.6 g. protein, 44.6 g. carbohydrates, 7 g. dietary fiber, 0 mg. cholesterol, 16 mg. sodium

Cuban Beans

8 ounces dried black beans, soaked overnight
1 small onion, finely chopped
⅛ teaspoon ground cloves
1 bay leaf
1 green pepper, finely chopped
2 teaspoons nondiet tub-style margarine or butter
1 small tomato, coarsely chopped
1 clove garlic, minced
2 tablespoons red-wine vinegar
1½ teaspoons tomato paste
½ teaspoon molasses

Drain the beans and place them in a large saucepan. Add the onions, cloves, bay leaf, half of the peppers and enough cold water to cover. Bring to a boil over high heat. Reduce the heat to low, partially cover and simmer for 1½ to 2 hours, or until the beans are tender and most of the liquid is absorbed. Drain any remaining liquid and discard the bay leaf.

Remove 1 cup of the beans and mash them to make a thick paste. Return them to the pan.

Meanwhile, in a large no-stick skillet over medium-high heat, melt the margarine or butter. Add the tomatoes, garlic and the remaining peppers. Sauté for 3 to 4 minutes, or until the peppers are tender.

Stir the tomato mixture into the bean mixture. Add the vinegar, tomato paste and molasses. Simmer, stirring often, for 10 minutes, or until the mixture thickens.

Makes 4 servings. Per serving: 235 calories, 2.9 g. fat (11% of calories), 13.1 g. protein, 41.3 g. carbohydrates, 1.2 g. dietary fiber, 0 mg. cholesterol, 49 mg. sodium

NOTES
• This dish can be made ahead and reheated before serving. Add a little broth or water to make reheating easier.
• You can replace half of the black beans with dried pinto or red kidney beans.

QUICK!
Red Beans and Rice

3 slices turkey bacon, diced
⅓ cup diced onions
1 clove garlic, minced
⅓ cup diced green peppers
1 cup water
½ cup long-grain white rice
1 can (16 ounces) kidney beans, rinsed and drained
1 bay leaf
½ teaspoon dried thyme
¼ teaspoon hot-pepper sauce
⅛ teaspoon ground black pepper

Coat a medium saucepan with no-stick spray. Heat the pan over medium heat until hot. Add the bacon and sauté for 3 minutes. Add the onions, garlic and green peppers and sauté for 2 minutes.

Add the water, rice, beans, bay leaf, thyme, hot-pepper sauce and black pepper. Bring to a boil. Reduce the heat to low, cover and cook for 15 to 20 minutes, or until the liquid is absorbed. Remove and discard the bay leaf before serving.

Makes 4 servings. Per serving: 223 calories, 3.3 g. fat (12% of calories), 13.4 g. protein, 42.6 g. carbohydrates, 7.9 g. dietary fiber, 7 mg. cholesterol, 371 mg. sodium

QUICK!
Tex-Mex Pinto Beans

2 teaspoons nondiet tub-style margarine or butter
1 medium onion, chopped
1 clove garlic, minced
1 can (15 ounces) reduced-sodium tomato sauce
1 tablespoon canned diced mild green chili peppers
2 teaspoons brown sugar
1 teaspoon chili powder
2–3 drops hot-pepper sauce
2 cans (15 ounces each) pinto beans, rinsed and drained

In a large saucepan over medium heat, melt the margarine or butter. Add the onions and garlic and sauté for 4 minutes. Add the tomato sauce, chili peppers, brown sugar, chili powder and hot-pepper sauce and mix well.

Stir in the beans. Cover and bring to a boil over medium heat. Reduce the heat to low and simmer, stirring occasionally, for 20 minutes.

Makes 4 servings. Per serving: 392 calories, 3.6 g. fat (8% of calories), 17.6 g. protein, 53.9 g. carbohydrates. 2.4 dietary fiber, 0 mg. cholesterol, 617 mg. sodium

Hoppin' John

1 teaspoon nondiet tub-style margarine or butter
½ cup chopped onions
½ cup chopped green peppers
1 small clove garlic, minced
½ cup diced cooked lean smoked ham
 Pinch of ground red pepper
2 cups frozen black-eyed peas
1 cup water
1 bay leaf
1 cup chopped tomatoes
½ cup long-grain white rice
¼ cup reduced-sodium tomato juice
¼ teaspoon dried thyme
⅛ teaspoon hot-pepper sauce

In a medium saucepan over medium heat, melt the margarine or butter. Add the onions and green peppers and sauté for 5 minutes, or until soft. Add the garlic, ham and red pepper and sauté for 2 minutes.

Stir in the black-eyed peas, water and bay leaf and bring to a boil. Reduce the heat to medium-low, cover and simmer for 15 minutes.

Stir in the tomatoes, rice, tomato juice, thyme and hot-pepper sauce. Bring to a boil. Reduce the heat to medium-low, cover and simmer for 20 minutes, or until the rice is tender and most of the liquid is absorbed. Uncover and simmer for 5 minutes. Remove and discard the bay leaf before serving.

Makes 4 servings. Per serving: 283 calories, 3 g. fat (10% of calories), 14.5 g. protein, 50.7 g. carbohydrates, 6.9 g. dietary fiber, 9 mg. cholesterol, 267 mg. sodium

VARIATION

Vegetarian Hoppin' John: Omit the ham and add 2 to 3 drops liquid smoke (available in the condiment section of most supermarkets) along with the tomatoes.

Savory Split Peas

1 cup green or yellow split peas, rinsed and drained
6 medium red potatoes
1 tablespoon olive oil
1 cup finely chopped onions
1 cup finely chopped sweet red peppers
1 teaspoon dried thyme
½ teaspoon crushed dried rosemary
¼ teaspoon ground black pepper
½ cup defatted reduced-sodium chicken broth

In a medium saucepan over medium-high heat, combine the split peas with 2½ cups water and bring to a boil. Reduce the heat to low, cover and simmer for 15 to 20 minutes, or until tender. Drain.

Meanwhile, place the potatoes in another medium saucepan with enough cold water to cover. Bring to a boil over medium-high heat and boil for 10 minutes. Drain. Cube the potatoes and set aside.

In a large saucepan over medium heat, warm the oil. Add the onions, red peppers, thyme, rosemary and black pepper. Cook for 5 minutes, or until tender.

Add the potatoes and cook, stirring frequently, for 8 to 10 minutes, or until the potatoes are tender. Stir in the broth and split peas and cook for 5 to 7 minutes.

Makes 4 servings. Per serving: 324 calories, 4.4 g. fat (12% of calories), 15.5 g. protein, 58.5 g. carbohydrates, 5.1 g. dietary fiber, 0 mg. cholesterol, 22 mg. sodium.

Frittata Florentine with White Beans

1 tablespoon olive oil
1 cup chopped onions
2 cloves garlic, minced
1 cup sliced mushrooms
1½ cups chopped fresh spinach
1½ cups fat-free egg substitute
¼ cup skim milk
¼ cup shredded reduced-fat Swiss cheese
½ teaspoon dried thyme
⅛ teaspoon ground black pepper
3 drops hot-pepper sauce
2 cups canned Great Northern beans, rinsed and drained
1 tablespoon grated Parmesan cheese

In a large ovenproof no-stick skillet over medium heat, warm the oil. Add the onions, garlic and mushrooms and sauté for 5 minutes, or until tender. Add the spinach and cook for 1 minute, or until wilted.

Meanwhile, in a medium bowl, whisk together the egg substitute, milk, Swiss, thyme, black pepper and hot-pepper sauce. Add the beans.

Gently stir the egg mixture into the skillet and combine well. Reduce the heat to low, cover and cook for 10 minutes, or until the egg mixture is almost set.

Preheat the broiler. Sprinkle the egg mixture with the Parmesan. Broil 4″ to 5″ from the heat for 1 to 2 minutes, or until the egg mixture is set and the cheese is golden brown.

Makes 4 servings. Per serving: 281 calories, 5.9 g. fat (18% of calories), 22.6 g. protein, 35.6 g. carbohydrates, 1.5 g. dietary fiber, 6 mg. cholesterol, 234 mg. sodium

NOTE
• To vary the flavor, replace the mushrooms with thinly sliced zucchini. Replace the Great Northern beans with cannellini or navy beans.

White Bean Soufflé

1 teaspoon olive oil
½ cup chopped scallions
½ cup chopped sweet red peppers
1 small shallot, minced
1 cup canned Great Northern beans, rinsed and drained
½ cup shredded reduced-fat Cheddar cheese
⅓ cup cornmeal
⅓ cup all-purpose flour
1½ teaspoons baking powder
1 cup buttermilk
½ cup fat-free egg substitute
2 tablespoons seasoned dry bread crumbs
4 large egg whites

In a medium no-stick skillet over medium heat, warm the oil. Add the scallions, peppers and shallots and sauté for 4 minutes, or until the peppers are soft; set aside.

In a large bowl, combine the beans, Cheddar, cornmeal, flour and baking powder.

In a small bowl, whisk together the buttermilk and egg substitute. Pour over the bean mixture. Add the scallion mixture, then gently mix and set aside.

Preheat the oven to 375°. Coat a 3-quart no-stick baking dish or soufflé dish with no-stick spray. Sprinkle the bottom and sides of the dish with the bread crumbs and set aside.

In a clean small bowl, beat the egg whites with an electric mixer until stiff but not too dry. Gently fold into the bean mixture.

Pour the batter into the prepared baking dish. Bake for 35 to 40 minutes, or until puffed and golden.

Makes 4 servings. Per serving: 322 calories, 6.8 g. fat (19% of calories), 18.5 g. protein, 46.3 g. carbohydrates, 3.4 g. dietary fiber, 17 mg. cholesterol, 622 mg. sodium

Chick-Pea, Eggplant and Tomato Casserole

1 eggplant, peeled and cubed
¼ cup defatted reduced-sodium chicken broth
1 medium onion, finely chopped
6 tomatoes, peeled, seeded and chopped
¼ cup chopped fresh parsley
½ teaspoon dried thyme
1 bay leaf
2 cans (16 ounces each) chick-peas, rinsed and drained
½ cup chopped fresh basil
2 teaspoons extra-virgin olive oil
½ teaspoon ground allspice
½ teaspoon red-pepper flakes
⅛ teaspoon ground black pepper
¼ cup grated reduced-fat Parmesan cheese

Lightly salt the eggplant and place in a colander for 15 minutes. Rinse and pat dry.

Preheat the oven to 400°. Coat a no-stick baking sheet with no-stick spray. Place the eggplant on the baking sheet and bake for 20 minutes, turning occasionally. Remove from the oven and set aside.

Reduce the oven temperature to 375°.

In a large no-stick skillet over medium heat, warm the broth. Add the onions and cook, stirring occasionally, for 5 minutes. Stir in the tomatoes, parsley, thyme and bay leaf. Cook and stir over medium-high heat until the liquid has evaporated. Remove from the heat. Remove and discard the bay leaf.

Stir in the eggplant, chick-peas, basil, oil, allspice, red-pepper flakes and black pepper.

Coat a 4-quart no-stick baking dish with no-stick spray. Spoon the eggplant mixture into the baking dish and sprinkle with the Parmesan. Bake for 30 minutes, or until bubbly and brown.

Makes 4 servings. Per serving: 466 calories, 5.7 g. fat (11% of calories), 14.2 g. protein, 93.2 g. carbohydrates, 8 g. dietary fiber, 0 mg. cholesterol, 600 mg. sodium

Chick-Pea and Potato Curry

2 teaspoons olive oil
1 large onion, chopped
1 green pepper, chopped
2 cloves garlic, minced
2 teaspoons minced fresh ginger
1 tablespoon curry powder
3 cups defatted reduced-sodium chicken broth
1 can (16 ounces) chick-peas, rinsed and drained
1 can (14 ounces) reduced-sodium tomatoes, drained and chopped
6 small new potatoes, quartered
3 tablespoons tomato paste

In a large saucepan over medium heat, warm the oil. Add the onions, peppers, garlic and ginger and sauté for 10 minutes, or until the vegetables are tender. Add the curry powder and sauté for 1 minute.

Stir in the broth, chick-peas, tomatoes, potatoes and tomato paste. Cover and simmer over medium heat for 30 minutes, or until the potatoes are tender.

Makes 4 servings. Per serving: 332 calories, 5.6 g. fat (14% of calories), 11.6 g. protein, 62.3 g. carbohydrates, 8 g. dietary fiber, 0 mg. cholesterol, 465 mg. sodium

NOTE

• For a boost of rich flavor, stir in 1 tablespoon tamarind paste along with the tomato paste. Tamarind paste is made from an exotic fruit and is available in large supermarkets and Indian grocery stores.

Casserole of Black-Eyed Peas and Collards

1 cup dried black-eyed peas
2½ cups water
2 teaspoons canola oil
1 small onion, chopped
½ green pepper, chopped
4 ounces mushrooms, sliced
2 cloves garlic, minced
12 ounces collards, coarsely chopped
½ cup reduced-sodium tomato sauce
¼ cup reduced-sodium ketchup
1 tablespoon molasses
3 tablespoons honey
1½ teaspoons dry mustard
¼ cup chopped fresh parsley
2–3 drops hot-pepper sauce

In a large saucepan, combine the black-eyed peas and water and let them soak overnight.

In the same pan over high heat, bring the beans and the soaking liquid to a boil. Reduce the heat to medium-low, cover and simmer for 50 minutes, or until the beans are tender. Transfer the beans and liquid to a 3-quart no-stick baking dish.

Rinse out the saucepan. Add the oil and warm over medium heat. Add the onions, green peppers and mushrooms and sauté for 5 to 6 minutes, or until the mushrooms begin to release their liquid. Add the garlic and collards. Cover and cook, stirring occasionally, for 5 minutes, or until the collards are just wilted.

Preheat the oven to 350°.

To the black-eyed peas and cooking liquid, add the collard mixture, tomato sauce, ketchup, molasses, honey, mustard, parsley and hot-pepper sauce. Mix well. Cover and bake for 20 minutes.

Makes 4 servings. Per serving: 273 calories, 3.4 g. fat (11% of calories), 7 g. protein, 56.5 g. carbohydrates, 10.3 g. dietary fiber, 0 mg. cholesterol, 38 mg. sodium

NOTE

• For a splash of zesty flavor, sprinkle this dish with a few drops of hot-pepper vinegar at the table.

QUICK!

Lima Bean Gratin

1 teaspoon olive oil
2 large shallots, minced
¾ teaspoon dried thyme
1 can (15 ounces) lima beans, rinsed and drained
½ cup buttermilk
4 ounces feta cheese, crumbled
⅛ teaspoon ground nutmeg
2 tablespoons seasoned dry bread crumbs
1 tablespoon shredded Monterey Jack cheese
½ teaspoon paprika

In a medium no-stick skillet over medium heat, warm the oil. Add the shallots and thyme and sauté for 1 minute. Stir in the beans and sauté for 2 minutes.

Preheat the oven to 350°. Coat a gratin dish or shallow 1-quart no-stick baking dish with no-stick spray and set aside.

Transfer half of the bean mixture to a food processor or blender and add the buttermilk, feta and nutmeg. Process until smooth. Spoon the whole beans and pureed beans into the prepared baking dish and mix well.

In a small bowl, combine the bread crumbs, Monterey Jack and paprika. Sprinkle over the casserole and bake for 8 to 10 minutes, or until golden.

Makes 4 servings. Per serving: 206 calories, 8.1 g. fat (35% of calories), 11.6 g. protein, 22.3 g. carbohydrates, 0 g. dietary fiber, 27 mg. cholesterol, 712 mg. sodium

Lentil, Mushroom and Spinach Gratin

- 2 teaspoons nondiet tub-style margarine or butter
- 1 cup sliced mushrooms
- ½ cup finely chopped onions
- 2¼ cups defatted reduced-sodium chicken broth
- ¼ cup brown lentils, sorted and rinsed
- ¼ cup long-grain white rice
- ¼ teaspoon dried oregano
- ¼ teaspoon dried thyme
- ⅛ teaspoon ground black pepper
- 1½ packages (10 ounces each) frozen chopped spinach, thawed and squeezed dry
- ⅓ cup skim milk
- ½ cup fat-free egg substitute
- ¾ cup shredded reduced-fat Monterey Jack cheese
- 2 tablespoons seasoned dry bread crumbs

In a large saucepan over medium heat, melt the margarine or butter. Add the mushrooms and onions and sauté for 4 minutes. Stir in the broth, lentils, rice, oregano, thyme and pepper. Reduce the heat to low, cover and simmer for 25 minutes.

Stir in the spinach. Cover and cook for 10 minutes. Remove from the heat and stir in the milk and egg substitute.

Preheat the oven to 350°. Coat a 2-quart no-stick baking dish with no-stick spray. Spoon the spinach mixture into the baking dish and sprinkle with the Monterey Jack and bread crumbs. Bake at 350° for 20 minutes, or until the gratin is set in the center and the cheese is bubbly.

Makes 4 servings. Per serving: 205 calories, 6.6 g. fat (28% of calories), 16.1 g. protein, 21.8 g. carbohydrates, 1.1 g. dietary fiber, 15 mg. cholesterol, 454 mg. sodium

Cassoulet

This classic French bean-and-meat casserole usually contains pork, lamb, duck and sausage. We've cut the fat considerably by using low-fat turkey sausage and smoked turkey breast.

- 6 ounces low-fat turkey sausage links
- 1 cup chopped onions
- 2 cloves garlic, minced
- 1 medium carrot, diced
- 1 cup chopped plum tomatoes
- ¼ cup nonalcoholic white wine or defatted chicken broth
- 2 tablespoons minced fresh parsley
- ½ teaspoon ground black pepper
  Pinch of ground cloves
- 2 cans (19 ounces each) Great Northern beans, rinsed and drained
- 3 ounces smoked turkey breast, diced
- ½ teaspoon dried thyme
- 1¼ cups defatted reduced-sodium chicken broth
- ¼ cup unseasoned dry bread crumbs

Coat a large no-stick skillet with no-stick spray. Add the sausage and brown over medium heat. Remove to a cutting board and slice into ½" pieces. Return the sausage to the pan and add the onions and garlic. Sauté for 4 minutes, or until the onions are soft.

Add the carrots, tomatoes, wine or broth, 1 tablespoon of the parsley, ¼ teaspoon of the pepper and the cloves. Cook for 10 minutes, or until the carrots are almost tender.

Stir in the beans, turkey, thyme and the remaining ¼ teaspoon pepper.

Preheat the oven to 350°. Coat a 3-quart no-stick baking dish with no-stick spray. Add the bean mixture to the baking dish and pour the broth over the mixture.

In a small bowl, combine the bread crumbs

and the remaining 1 tablespoon parsley. Sprinkle over the bean mixture. Bake for 1¼ hours, or until the crumbs are golden brown.

Makes 4 servings. Per serving: 470 calories, 5.1 g. fat (10% of calories), 35 g. protein, 73 g. carbohydrates, 1.9 g. dietary fiber, 36 mg. cholesterol, 700 mg. sodium

VARIATION

Cassoulet with Spinach: Add 1½ cups chopped fresh spinach to the carrot mixture and cook until the spinach wilts.

Chili con Carne

Lean ground beef gives this stew a hearty traditional flavor without the traditional fat.

12	ounces extra-lean ground beef
2	cups chopped onions
1	cup chopped green peppers
3	cloves garlic, minced
1½	tablespoons chili powder
1	teaspoon ground cumin
1	teaspoon dried oregano
3	cans (8 ounces each) reduced-sodium tomato sauce
1	can (15 ounces) red kidney beans, rinsed and drained
1	can (14 ounces) whole tomatoes (with juice), coarsely chopped
1	tablespoon light brown sugar
	Salt and ground black pepper
6	tablespoons shredded fat-free Cheddar cheese
2	scallions, thinly sliced

In a large saucepan over medium heat, brown the beef. Drain well, discarding the excess fat. Crumble the beef and set aside.

Return the pan to medium heat. Add the onions, green peppers and garlic and sauté for 5 minutes, or until the peppers are almost tender. Add the chili powder, cumin and oregano and sauté for 2 to 3 minutes.

Add the beef, tomato sauce, beans and tomatoes (with juice) and bring to a boil. Reduce the heat to medium-low, cover and simmer for 10 minutes. Uncover and simmer until the desired consistency is reached.

Stir in the brown sugar and add the salt and black pepper to taste.

Divide the chili among 6 serving bowls. Sprinkle each with the Cheddar and scallions.

Makes 6 servings. Per serving: 290 calories, 8.1 g. fat (25% of calories), 22.6 g. protein, 36.9 g. carbohydrates, 8.9 g. dietary fiber, 35 mg. cholesterol, 376 mg. sodium

NOTE

• Always cook beef separately so the fat can be drained off.

VARIATIONS

Chili Mole: Sauté 1 small seeded and minced jalapeño pepper (wear plastic gloves when handling) along with the green peppers. Replace the kidney beans with pinto or black beans. Stir in 2 to 3 tablespoons unsweetened cocoa powder along with the brown sugar. Omit the Cheddar cheese and scallions; garnish each serving with a dollop of nonfat sour cream and a sprinkling of finely chopped cilantro.

Eggplant Chili: Sauté 1 cup peeled, cubed eggplant and 1 cup sliced carrots along with the green peppers. Replace the beef with 1½ cups cooked bulgur, barley, millet, rice or crumbled firm tofu. Add to the mixture along with the tomatoes.

Mediterranean Chili con Carne: Replace the beef with lean ground lamb. Replace the kidney beans with chick-peas. Omit the Cheddar cheese and scallions; garnish each serving with crumbled feta cheese and a sprinkling of sliced ripe olives.

Lean
and Hearty
Main Courses

Poultry

Whether your tastes run to sautéed chicken, a regal holiday turkey or a tasty ragout of duck, there is always a place at the table for poultry. Inexpensive, versatile and easy to cook, poultry lends itself to virtually any cooking style, from stir-frying and roasting to grilling and slow-cooking.

For the healthy cook, poultry provides additional benefits. High in protein, it's also low in cholesterol and saturated fat. Once you remove the skin, it's nice and lean (some cuts more than others, and some birds more than others, of course). That's why nutritionists often recommend that people trying to lose weight or lower their overall fat intake would do well to make poultry a regular guest at the table.

COOKING POULTRY SAFELY

Proper food hygiene is of paramount importance when cooking poultry. This is because chicken, turkey and other birds are vulnerable to salmonella, a type of bacteria that can cause nausea, diarrhea and other digestive upsets. By taking a few simple precautions, however, infection is very easy to prevent.

Store it securely. When keeping poultry in the refrigerator, make sure that it's well-sealed in a plastic bag without leaks. Otherwise, juice from the poultry could drip on other foods, like lettuce or celery in the produce drawer. This in turn can cause infection, even when you haven't eaten the bird.

Health-conscious cooks are rightly concerned about recycling, but don't make the mistake of reusing a plastic bag that once contained poultry. Bacteria may remain even after careful washing, causing illness days or even weeks later.

Keep it wrapped. Bacteria on poultry is killed during cooking, so the bird itself is generally quite safe. Danger occurs when germs migrate from the poultry to nearby cooking areas, like countertops, knives and cutting boards, contaminating foods that won't be exposed to the same heat. Keeping poultry wrapped until just before you're ready to start cooking will help keep the rest of your kitchen safe.

Use a poultry board. Since salmonella is readily passed from poultry to other foods, chefs generally use two cutting boards: one that's only for poultry and other meats, and a second board for everything else, like produce. Be sure to clean the poultry board well with a solution of diluted bleach and then wash it well with hot, soapy water.

Wash up often. It doesn't take large amounts of salmonella to cause illness. Even slight contamination—on a cabinet handle, for example, or simply on your hands—can cause problems later on. Every time you handle poultry, you should wash your hands right away.

After washing your hands, quickly wash any surface that you may have touched, like cabinet doors, knife handles or even coffee mugs. A quick swipe with a sponge and hot, soapy water will keep things safe.

BUYING THE BEST

Unless you live on a farm, the days are past when having chicken for dinner meant wandering out to the backyard and picking your own. For most of us, the henhouses of yesteryear are the supermarkets of today. When you have a taste for chicken, turkey, guinea hen or some other kind of poultry, all you have to do is visit the meat aisle.

Inspect the skin. It should be smooth and clean-looking, without discoloration. Dark bruises mean that the bird was treated roughly during handling, and the meat will likely be tough.

Make sure that it's clean. Chicken that has been properly processed will not only be noticeably clean and fresh-looking but will also be free of pin feathers. (Pin feathers on wing tips are extremely hard to remove and are considered acceptable.) If the pin feathers are still in the skin, pass the bird by.

Check for freezer burn. U.S. Department of Agriculture guidelines call for "fresh" chicken to be processed at 26°F. Birds that have been frozen at too-low temperatures may develop freezer burn, which can cause meat to be dry and tough. This is more likely to occur in home freezers than in those used commercially, but if you happen to see a bird with dry-looking white or gray spots—a sign of freezer burn—choose another one.

DEFROSTING POULTRY

Poultry freezes well and stays fresh for up to two months in the freezer. When thawing it, however, special precautions are needed.

Fire up the microwave. To defrost poultry in a hurry, pop it into the microwave. With the microwave set on defrost, a whole chicken will thaw in about 20 minutes. Consult the manufacturer's directions for details. Use this method only if you intend to fully cook the bird immediately after thawing.

BIRD BASICS

Supermarkets stock a variety of chickens, which are classified according to size. Here's a look at what you'll find.

☞ **Broilers.** The smallest of the chickens, broilers are all-purpose birds that weigh less than 2½ pounds. They can be used in virtually any recipe and are often sold cut up.

☞ **Capons.** Young roosters that were castrated and then fattened up, capons usually weigh between 6 and 10 pounds each. A large percentage of their weight is in tender breast meat.

☞ **Cornish hens.** These are small hybrid chickens that weigh up to 2½ pounds. They have tender, delicate meat. The smaller Cornish hens tend to be enough to make a single serving. These birds are also called Cornish game hens and Rock Cornish hens.

☞ **Fryers.** Slightly larger than broilers, these weigh between 2½ and 3 pounds. Fryers are also considered all-purpose birds. They can be roasted whole, but they are more commonly cut into parts.

☞ **Roasters.** Young birds weighing between 3 and 5 pounds, roasters are sold whole and should be cooked that way, too. They can be roasted in the oven or grilled or smoked outdoors.

☞ **Stewers.** Older birds weighing between 4½ and 7 pounds, these are very flavorful. They are also the least tender and are used for making soups and stews.

Thaw it slowly. The easiest strategy for thawing poultry, albeit the slowest, is to put it in the refrigerator ahead of time. The cool temperature will inhibit the growth of bacteria as the meat slowly thaws. A whole chicken will defrost in the refrigerator in one day, while a large turkey might take two or three days.

ROASTING POULTRY

There is something naturally festive about having roast poultry, whether it's a Thanksgiving turkey or a Sunday-dinner chicken. What's more, the actual hands-on time is minimal. Apart from occasional basting, once the bird is in the oven, it essentially takes care of itself.

Season it first. Before putting the bird in the oven, rub it well with herbs, pepper or a little salt. For a more intense flavor, put the herbs under the skin. This causes them to steam and release their flavors into the meat throughout the cooking process.

Bend the wings. Bending the wings back behind the body serves to lift the back slightly off the baking dish. This allows for more thorough heat circulation, causing the meat to cook evenly.

You should close the cavity even if you're not stuffing the bird, in order to retain moisture.

Drain the oil. To prevent the bird from soaking in its own fat, use a roasting pan with a rack. This lifts the bird off the bottom of the pan, allowing fat to drain away. The rack also allows hot air to circulate, which will make an attractive brown crust.

Heat it fast. To brown the bird and lock in the juices, place it in a preheated 400° oven. After 20 to 30 minutes, reduce the heat to 325° and continue cooking for the recommended time.

Check for doneness. Properly cooked poultry is moist but not running with juice. The easiest way to test for doneness is to use a meat thermometer.

☞ Before putting the bird in the oven, insert a standard meat thermometer in the thickest part of the thigh muscle without

Chicken Skin
Is It GOOD for You?

The short answer, of course, is no: Chicken skin isn't good for you. It's high in saturated fat. But there's more than one way to skin a chicken. Contrary to popular belief, removing the skin after cooking instead of before is perfectly acceptable. And that technique will not raise the fat content of the meat.

Although meat may look fatty when you peel off the skin after cooking, what you're really seeing is moisture. Grilling and roasting chicken in the skin helps keep the meat insulated. This allows it to retain more of its natural moisture and flavors. Cooking chicken in the skin is particularly helpful for breast meat, which may otherwise become dry and tough.

The important thing to remember is to strip off the skin after the meat is cooked. There's no point in eating all the extra fat contained in the skin.

touching bone. Cook until the temperature reads 180°.

☞ When the bird is stuffed, cook until the center of the stuffing is 165°.

☞ Another way to test for doneness is to pierce the thickest part of a thigh with a fork. If the juices that seep out are clear, not pink, the bird is done.

ROASTING TIMES

Roasting poultry is easy. Once it's in the oven, you can almost forget it until it's done. The only hard part is knowing when that is. Here are approximate roasting times, with an initial temperature of 400° that's reduced to 325° after the amount of time indicated.

CHICKEN SIZE, STUFFED (LB.)	TIME AT 400° (MIN.)	TIME AT 325° (HR.)
4	30	1
5	30	1–1¼
6	30	1¼–1½
7	30	1½–2

TURKEY SIZE, STUFFED (LB.)	TIME AT 400° (HR.)	TIME AT 325° (HR.)
6–8	—	3–3½
8–12	—	3½–4¼
12–16	—	4–5
16–20	—	4½–5½

☞ Alternatively, cut the string holding the legs together and wiggle one of the legs. If it moves freely and without resistance, the bird is ready.

Baste it often. Even when cooking a self-basting bird, chefs recommend basting the meat with pan juices every 15 to 30 minutes (baste smaller birds more frequently than large ones) during cooking. This adds flavor to the bird, while at the same time browning the skin and making the meat moist and tender.

Stuffings and Dressings

Traditionally, stuffings were almost always cooked inside the bird. This helped lock in moisture and keep the meat moist and flavorful. The problem with this method is that the stuffing could absorb formidable amounts of fat. That's why many healthy cooks prefer to bake the stuffing in a separate container rather than inside the bird. Bake the following dressing at 350° for 30 minutes, or until cooked through.

Start simple. Although there are nearly as many stuffing or dressing recipes as there are cooks, all you really need are bread, chopped vegetables and herbs.

☞ In a bowl, combine crumbled or cubed bread with vegetables like minced onions, celery and carrots. Add fresh or dried herbs to taste; parsley, thyme, sage and rosemary are traditional favorites.

☞ Add enough water or chicken broth to moisten the bread. Mix well.

Stuff it late. If you cook the stuffing in the bird, leave the uncooked stuffing in the refrigerator until just before you place the bird in the oven. Stuffing poultry ahead of time gives germs a chance to migrate from the bird into the stuffing.

To prevent contamination after cooking, don't store stuffing inside the cavity of the bird. Scoop all of it out and into a bowl before you begin carving.

Give it room to move. All stuffings, and particularly those made with bread, expand during cooking. Don't pack the baking dish or bird cavity brim-full. Instead, spoon in the stuffing loosely.

Close the door. When baking stuffing in a separate dish, always use a cover to prevent moisture from escaping. When making stuffing inside the bird, seal the open cavity before putting the bird in the oven. While larger birds like turkeys should be trussed with string, chickens can usually be sealed by folding over the skin that hangs at the opening.

OTHER TECHNIQUES

Virtually no other main ingredient in the healthy cook's kitchen is used as often or in as many different recipes as poultry. In part, this is because poultry lends itself to a variety of cooking techniques. The flesh is tender yet firm, making it ideal for everything from grilling to long-cooking soups.

Sautéing

Perhaps the easiest method for preparing chicken breasts, turkey tenders and other poultry pieces is sautéing. It quickly browns the meat and locks in flavor. In some cases, it's used to cook poultry all the way through. More often, it's a first step in recipes requiring further cooking, as when sautéed chicken pieces are then cooked with vegetables.

☞ When sautéing poultry, first remove the skin. If desired, cut the pieces as needed. Then dredge the pieces in seasoned flour. The pieces should be lightly dusted, not thickly coated; shake off the excess.

☞ When sautéing a whole chicken cut into pieces, coat the pan with no-stick spray or use about a tablespoon of oil.

☞ To reduce the amount of fat, add a small amount of chopped onions to the pan. They'll release natural juices and help keep the bird lubricated.

☞ Heat the pan until hot. Add the larger, slower-cooking pieces first. Then add the smaller pieces. Cook for about 5 minutes per side to brown the meat. To cook it all the way through, cook for an additional 10 minutes per side. Exact times depend upon the cut and whether the bones have been removed.

☞ Remove the pieces from the pan and place on paper towels to drain. Then serve or continue with the recipe.

Microwaving

The great advantage of using the microwave for poultry is speed; you can cook a whole bird in almost half the time needed in a traditional oven. The drawback, of course, is that you won't get the same crispy skin or attractive browned appearance. That's why many cooks use the microwave as a way of precooking poultry prior to further preparation.

☞ Poultry is extremely moist, making it difficult to brown in the microwave. Many cooks brown the bird first on the stove top or in the oven, then transfer it to the microwave for final cooking. Or you can microwave it first, then move it to the broiler for quick browning.

☞ For even cooking, place the bird, breast down, in the microwave for about half the cooking time, then turn it over and continue cooking for the duration.

TRUSSING POULTRY

If you stuff a chicken or turkey, you need to close the cavity before putting the bird in the oven. Here are two easy methods.

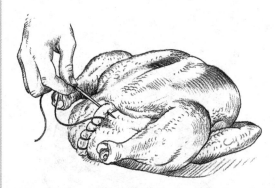

Using a large needle and cotton trussing thread or string, stitch the cavity closed. Loop one end around the legs to hold them close to the body.

Pull the drumstick ends close together and tie them closed with cotton string.

☞ To prevent wing tips or the ends of drumsticks from cooking too quickly and burning, cover them with small pieces of aluminum foil, carefully smoothed to eliminate creases.

☞ Food continues cooking for several minutes after being removed from the microwave, so remove poultry just before you think it should be done.

Broiling and Grilling

Whether done in the oven or on a grill, the high heats used in broiling and grilling quickly sear the flesh of poultry, sealing in moisture and flavor while requiring little or no added fats.

☞ The bird should be cut into serving pieces—or at least halved—to allow the meat to sear evenly.

☞ Since poultry is typically broiled with the skin on, you don't need to add extra oil.

☞ To season the bird, use your fingers to rub dried or fresh herbs between the skin and the meat underneath. Seasoning the skin itself is counterproductive, since you won't want to eat it.

☞ Poultry is typically oven-broiled for about 12 minutes per side. When grilling, give it about 15 minutes per side.

BASIC BIRDS

While chicken is the bird of choice in kitchens worldwide, there are many forms of poultry to try, from turkey, duck and goose to squab, pheasant and other game birds. Here are some favorites.

Turkey

A favorite guest at Christmas and Thanksgiving celebrations, the traditional holiday bird is both lean and inexpensive, making it a great choice all year long.

☞ To enjoy turkey without the mountain of leftovers that comes from a whole bird, try turkey breasts or legs. They can be roasted just like the whole bird, but they are done in a fraction of the time. They require a lot less cleanup time, too.

☞ Boneless, skinless turkey tenderloins and cutlets are readily available. They're lean, cook quickly and make a less-expensive

ARTFUL CARVING

Carving a holiday bird can be a nerve-wracking experience, particularly when you're the one at the head of the table. Once you master a few cuts, however, you'll do it right every time.

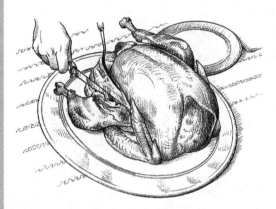

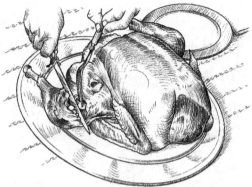

Using a carving knife and a two-tined carving fork, cut between the breast and thigh, pushing down on the leg until the joint separates.

Wriggle the leg to find the joint between the thigh and the drumstick. Slice downward through the joint. Slice meat off the bones as desired.

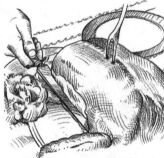

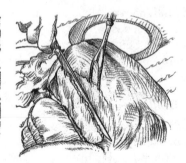

Bend the wings to find the joint, then cut straight downward.

Make a long incision along one side of the breastbone.

Carve meat from the breast, working toward the first cut in smooth, even slices.

substitute for veal in many recipes.

☞ Turkeys are often sold prebasted—that is, the meat has been injected with oil or butter before being frozen. While prebasting makes a bird somewhat easier to cook, it also loads it up with unnecessary saturated fat.

☞ Turkey labels may specify whether the bird is a tom or a hen, with the latter fetching a premium price. Chefs agree, however, that there is little appreciable difference between the two, either in taste or texture. Let the turkey's price, not its sex, be your guide.

LEAN PICKS

For the healthy cook, poultry is nearly the perfect meat: low in cost, cholesterol and saturated fat and high in protein. Of course, some cuts and types of poultry are considerably lower in fat than others. This chart will help you know exactly what you're getting. Figures are for 3 ounces of cooked lean meat (no bone or fat).

POULTRY	CALORIES	FAT (G.)	CALORIES FROM FAT (%)	CHOLESTEROL (MG.)
Chicken breast, broiler-fryer	142	3.1	19	73
Chicken drumsticks, broiler-fryer	151	5	30	82
Chicken wings, broiler-fryer	171	6.8	36	71
Chicken leg, broiler-fryer	181	8	40	89
Turkey, white meat	133	2.7	18	59
Turkey, dark meat	159	6.1	35	72
Duck, breast	132	2	14	153
Duck, leg	163	5	27	117
Goose	202	10.8	48	82

Ducks and Geese

One good thing about these extremely fatty birds is that they don't require basting. In fact, once they're in the oven, a veritable torrent of fatty fluid helps keep the meat moist and tender. Most of the fat is contained in the skin, however. Once the fat is removed after cooking, the meat itself is on the lean side, particularly the breast meat.

☞ Stuffing duck and goose before cooking will help lock moisture in and keep the meat tender. But because the stuffing will absorb a huge amount of strong-tasting fat, it's generally discarded rather than eaten.

☞ To add flavor to the meat, many cooks put fruit in the cavity along with—or instead of—the traditional bread stuffing. An easy way to do this is to put a peeled apple or onion or a cut orange inside the cavity.

☞ To prevent fat from pooling and being absorbed by the meat, duck and goose should be placed on a rack for roasting.

☞ Place duck in a 450° oven and immediately lower the temperature to 350°. Allow 20 minutes per pound for an unstuffed duck; for a stuffed duck, add 25 minutes total cooking time.

☞ For a goose weighing less than 14 pounds, allow 20 to 25 minutes per pound; geese larger than 14 pounds require 15 minutes per pound. If the goose is stuffed, add 25 minutes total cooking time.

☞ Pricking the skin every 10 to 15 minutes will release more fat and drain it away from the bird.

Other Birds

Although supermarkets rarely have more than the poultry basics, specialty stores often stock a variety of birds, including pheasant, squab (farm-raised pigeon) and guinea hens.

☞ **Squabs**. These are small birds that are usually cut in half, dredged in flour and broiled. Squabs under ¾ pound are known as doves;

DISJOINTING POULTRY

Your butcher can separate your bird into its component parts. However, it's also an easy enough task to do yourself. Here's how.

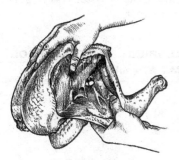

Cut the skin between the thigh and the lower body, bending the leg back until the hip joint pops.

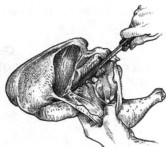

Remove the leg by cutting through the joint.

Separate the drumstick from the thigh by cutting straight down through the joint.

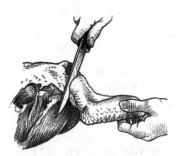

Pull the wings upward until the joint pops, then cut through the skin and meat and through the joint.

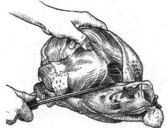

Place the bird on its back and make a diagonal cut from front to back just under the rib cage toward the wing joint.

Pry the body apart by pulling up on the back and pushing down on the breast.

larger birds are called pigeons. Plan on preparing two squabs per person.

☞ **Guinea hens.** These are almost chicken-size, although the meat tends to be more dry. The traditional cooking method includes barding—slathering them with a layer of lard or bacon to keep the meat moist. Barding really isn't necessary, however. Cooking the birds in the skin will provide plenty of moisture. To prevent them from drying, baste them frequently in a 350° oven for about 45 minutes.

☞ **Pheasants.** These are fast disappearing from the wild, but these colorful game birds are also raised commercially. The flavor is quite gamey and, like duck or goose, the bird is usually stuffed with apple, onion or potato to absorb the strong flavors.

Francesco Ricchi

Francesco Ricchi has been preparing traditional Tuscan cuisine since 1989, when he arrived in Washington, D.C.

Poultry dishes showcase his distinctive style of using simple, flavorful ingredients.

"Having been raised in the hillside area north of Florence, I always appreciated the simplicity of the country life," Ricchi says. "I still laugh when I think of Uncle Dante eating lemon chicken and saying, 'The problem was not in cooking this chicken; it was in catching it.'"

This is one of the juiciest and most flavorful chicken dishes you will ever try. Francesco serves it with potatoes roasted with rosemary and garlic.

Lemon Chicken

- 1 chicken (about 3 pounds)
   Pinch of salt
   Pinch of ground black pepper
- 1 sprig fresh sage
- 1 sprig fresh rosemary
- 2 cloves garlic
- 1 lemon, thinly sliced
- 1 tablespoon olive oil
- 2 cups dry white wine or nonalcoholic white wine
- 2 tablespoons lemon juice

Remove all visible fat from the chicken, especially from the cavity. Rinse the chicken, inside and out, with cold water. Pat dry with paper towels.

Sprinkle the cavity with the salt and pepper. Add the sage, rosemary and garlic. Reserve 2 of the lemon slices; place the remainder in the cavity.

Slide the reserved lemon slices under the skin, positioning one over each side of the breast.

Heat the oil in a heavy roasting pan or a large ovenproof no-stick skillet over medium-high heat. Add the chicken and brown it on all sides. Drain off any remaining fat.

Preheat the oven to 400°. Bake the chicken in the roasting pan for 30 to 35 minutes, or until the skin is golden brown.

Remove the pan from the oven and pour off any accumulated fat. Add the wine and lemon juice to the pan. Bake, basting occasionally with pan juices, for 10 to 20 minutes, or until the juices run clear when you pierce the thickest part of a thigh with a fork.

Transfer the pan to the stove top. Remove the chicken and keep it warm. Skim off and discard any visible fat from the liquid in the pan. Bring the liquid to a boil over high heat and cook for 10 minutes, or until reduced by half. Transfer to a small bowl or gravy boat.

Cut the chicken into quarters. Serve with the pan juices.

Makes 4 servings. Per serving: 278 calories, 9.6 g. fat (31% of calories), 24.5 g. protein, 5.1 g. carbohydrates, 0.3 g. dietary fiber, 74 mg. cholesterol, 78 mg. sodium

Chicken and Green Bean Stir-Fry

QUICK!

1⅓ cups long-grain white rice
½ cup minced scallions
1 tablespoon rice-wine vinegar
½ teaspoon sugar
1 teaspoon grated fresh ginger
1 large clove garlic, minced
2 tablespoons reduced-sodium soy sauce
1 pound boneless, skinless chicken breasts, cut into short strips
⅓ cup defatted chicken broth
1½ teaspoons cornstarch
½ teaspoon sesame oil
1 pound green beans, trimmed and cut on the diagonal into 1″ pieces
2 teaspoons canola oil

Cook the rice according to the package directions.

Meanwhile, place the scallions, vinegar, sugar, ginger, garlic and 1 tablespoon of the soy sauce in a large bowl and whisk to combine. Add the chicken and stir until coated. Let stand at room temperature for 5 minutes.

In a glass measuring cup, stir together the broth, cornstarch, sesame oil and the remaining 1 tablespoon soy sauce; set aside.

In a large no-stick skillet, bring ¼ cup water to a boil. Add the beans. Cover and cook over high heat for 3 to 4 minutes, or until bright green and crisp-tender. Drain and set aside.

Wipe the skillet dry. Add the canola oil and warm over medium-high heat. Add the chicken mixture and cook, stirring, for 3 minutes. Add the beans and cook, stirring, for 2 minutes.

Stir in the cornstarch mixture. Continue cooking and stirring until the sauce begins to thicken and just comes to a boil. Cook, stirring, for 2 minutes, or until the beans are hot. Serve over the rice.

Makes 4 servings. Per serving: 427 calories, 6.4 g. fat (14% of calories), 32.2 g. protein, 58.7 g. carbohydrates, 0.9 g. dietary fiber, 69 mg. cholesterol, 346 mg. sodium

VARIATION

Turkey-and-Asparagus Stir-Fry: Replace the chicken with turkey breast. Replace the green beans with asparagus.

Texas-Style Chicken Fajitas

1 clove garlic, minced
½ teaspoon ground cumin
½ teaspoon chili powder
¼ teaspoon reduced-sodium Worcestershire sauce
12 ounces boneless, skinless chicken breasts, cut into short strips
½ cup chopped fresh cilantro
3 medium sweet red or green peppers, cut into short strips
1 medium red onion, thinly sliced and separated into rings
3 tablespoons lime juice
8 warm corn tortillas (6″ diameter)
8 tablespoons nonfat sour cream
8 tablespoons salsa

In a medium bowl, stir together the garlic, cumin, chili powder and Worcestershire sauce. Stir in the chicken and cilantro until coated. Cover and refrigerate for 1 hour.

Coat a large no-stick skillet with no-stick spray and warm over medium-high heat until hot. Add the chicken mixture and cook, stirring, for 3 to 4 minutes, or until the chicken is no longer pink. Transfer to a large bowl and keep warm.

Add the peppers to the skillet. Cook, stirring, for 4 to 6 minutes, or until the peppers are crisp-tender. Transfer to the bowl with the chicken.

Add the onions to the skillet. Cook, stirring, for about 3 minutes, or until the onions are crisp-tender.

Return the chicken and peppers to the skillet. Drizzle the lime juice over the mixture and stir until combined. Remove from the heat.

To serve, place the mixture on the tortillas. Garnish each tortilla with 1 tablespoon of the sour cream and 1 tablespoon of the salsa. Roll up to enclose the filling. Serve immediately.

Makes 4 servings. Per serving: 312 calories, 4.1 g. fat (12% of calories), 27.2 g. protein, 44.5 g. carbohydrates, 4.3 g. dietary fiber, 52 mg. cholesterol, 377 mg. sodium

NOTE
• Fajitas come in many flavors. If you like, replace the chicken with lean flank steak, beef tenderloin, pork tenderloin, swordfish, halibut or medium shrimp. The cooking time for fish and shrimp is comparable to that for chicken. The meat cooking time will be 2 to 3 minutes longer.

QUICK!

Chicken Cacciatore

1½ pounds boneless, skinless chicken breast halves
½ teaspoon dried Italian seasoning
¼ teaspoon garlic powder
1 cup chopped onions
1 cup chopped green peppers
2 cloves garlic, minced
1 can (15 ounces) diced tomatoes with Italian herbs (with juice)
½ cup dry white or red wine or nonalcoholic white or red wine
2 cups halved or quartered mushrooms
   Salt and ground black pepper
3 cups hot cooked whole-wheat pasta
   Minced fresh parsley

Coat a large no-stick skillet with no-stick spray. Warm the skillet over medium heat.

Season both sides of the chicken with the Italian seasoning and garlic powder. Add to the skillet and cook over medium heat, turning once, for about 5 minutes, or until browned. Remove the chicken and set aside.

Add the onions, green peppers and garlic to the skillet and sauté for 5 to 8 minutes, or until the onions are tender. Add the tomatoes (with juice), wine and mushrooms. Return the chicken to the skillet and bring to a boil. Reduce the heat, cover and simmer for about 10 minutes, or until the chicken is no longer pink in the center.

If the sauce is too thin, transfer the chicken to a warm dish and set aside. Cook the sauce, uncovered, at a brisk simmer for about 5 minutes, or until thick. Season to taste with the salt and black pepper. Serve the chicken and sauce over the pasta. Sprinkle with the parsley.

Makes 4 servings. Per serving: 420 calories, 5.2 g. fat (11% of calories), 46.3 g. protein, 41.6 g. carbohydrates, 5.2 g. dietary fiber, 103 mg. cholesterol, 325 mg. sodium

VARIATIONS
Greek-Style Chicken: Replace the mushrooms with 1 cup halved artichoke hearts. Omit the pasta. Serve over cooked rice and sprinkle each serving with sliced ripe olives and feta cheese.
Meatballs Cacciatore: Omit the chicken. Instead, make meatballs using 1 pound extra-lean ground beef, 1 teaspoon dried Italian seasoning, 1 teaspoon salt and ½ teaspoon ground black pepper. Make the tomato sauce as above; add the meatballs and simmer, covered, for about 20 minutes, or until the meatballs are cooked through.
Sausage Sandwiches: Omit the chicken. Instead, coat a large no-stick skillet with no-stick spray and cook 4 reduced-fat Italian sausages (4 ounces each) until well-browned; drain well, discarding all fat. Make the tomato sauce as above, omitting the mushrooms and adding ½ teaspoon dried Italian seasoning. Add the sausages and simmer, covered, for 10 minutes, or until cooked through. Cook, uncovered, until the sauce thickens to the desired consistency. Serve in warm crusty buns.

Chicken Potpie

Chicken Filling
- 3 cups defatted reduced-sodium chicken broth
- 1 cup thinly sliced celery
- ⅔ cup thinly sliced carrots
- ⅔ cup frozen baby peas
- ⅔ cup diced green peppers
- ¼–½ cup 1% low-fat milk
- 1 tablespoon nondiet tub-style margarine or butter
- ½ cup chopped onions
- ⅓ cup whole-wheat flour
- 2 tablespoons minced fresh parsley
- 1 teaspoon reduced-sodium Worcestershire sauce
- ½ teaspoon hot-pepper sauce
- ½ teaspoon dried sage
- ½ teaspoon dried thyme
- Pinch of salt (optional)
- 2 cups cubed cooked chicken breast

Biscuits
- 1 cup all-purpose flour
- ¾ cup whole-wheat flour
- 2 teaspoons baking powder
- ½ teaspoon baking soda
- Pinch of salt (optional)
- 3 tablespoons nondiet tub-style margarine or butter
- ¾–1 cup buttermilk
- 1 teaspoon honey

To make the chicken filling: In a medium saucepan, combine the broth, celery, carrots, peas and green peppers and bring to a boil. Boil for 5 minutes. Strain the broth into a 4-cup glass measuring cup and add enough milk to make 3 cups; set aside. Reserve the vegetables.

In a medium saucepan over medium heat, melt the margarine or butter. Add the onions and sauté for 2 to 3 minutes. Add 3 tablespoons water and the flour and cook, stirring, for 1 minute. Gradually whisk in the broth mixture. Add the parsley, Worcestershire sauce, hot-pepper sauce, sage and thyme. Season to taste with the salt (if using). Cook, stirring constantly, over low heat until thick. Add the reserved vegetables and the chicken. Remove from the heat and set aside.

Coat four 2-cup no-stick baking dishes with no-stick spray. Divide the chicken mixture among them. Preheat the oven to 400°.

To make the biscuits: Sift the all-purpose flour, whole-wheat flour, baking powder, baking soda and salt (if using) into a large bowl. Using 2 knives, cut in the margarine or butter until the mixture resembles coarse crumbs.

In a small bowl, whisk together ¾ cup buttermilk and the honey. Pour over the flour mixture and toss gently with a fork to moisten the flour. If the dough is too dry, mix in a little more buttermilk. Turn the dough out onto a lightly floured surface and divide it into 4 pieces. Pat each piece into a circle. Place over the chicken. Bake for 20 minutes or until the biscuits are golden and the sauce bubbles.

Makes 4 servings. Per serving: 540 calories, 16.6 g. fat (27% of calories), 34.2 g. protein, 64.8 g. carbohydrates, 8 g. dietary fiber, 56 mg. cholesterol, 697 mg. sodium

VARIATION

Southwestern Chicken Potpie with Cheddar Biscuits: For the chicken filling, replace the sage with ½ teaspoon ground cumin and the thyme with ½ teaspoon dried oregano. For the biscuits, add ½ cup shredded fat-free sharp Cheddar cheese and ¼ teaspoon ground red pepper to the flour mixture before cutting in the margarine or butter.

Chicken Braised with 40 Cloves of Garlic

 1 medium bulb fennel with leaves attached
40 cloves unpeeled garlic (about 3 heads)
 2 large carrots, thinly sliced
1½ cups sliced leeks (white parts only)
 1 cup defatted chicken broth
 ½ teaspoon ground black pepper
 6 skinless whole chicken legs
 1 loaf French bread, warmed

Preheat the oven to 425°.

Cut the stems with leaves from the fennel bulb. Cut the bulb into quarters lengthwise; remove and discard the core sections. Cut each quarter into thin slices and set aside. Cut the dark green leaves from the stems and discard the stems. Chop 1 tablespoon of leaves and set aside.

In a shallow 3-quart no-stick baking dish, combine the garlic, chopped fennel bulb, carrots and leeks. Add the broth. Sprinkle the vegetables with ½ tablespoon of the fennel leaves and ¼ teaspoon of the pepper. Arrange the chicken in a single layer on top of the vegetables. Sprinkle the chicken with the remaining ½ tablespoon fennel leaves and ¼ teaspoon pepper. Cover the dish tightly with a double layer of foil.

Bake for about 1 hour, or until the chicken is cooked through and the garlic is soft. Serve the chicken and vegetables in shallow soup bowls with the pan juices. Squeeze the soft garlic from the skins and spread onto slices of the bread.

Makes 6 servings. Per serving: 458 calories, 10.7 g. fat (21% of calories), 35.3 g. protein, 54.1 g. carbohydrates, 1.7 g. dietary fiber, 89 mg. cholesterol, 628 mg. sodium

Chicken Paprikash with Broccoli

 4 boneless, skinless chicken breast halves (1 pound), cut into bite-size pieces
 ½ teaspoon salt (optional)
 ¼ teaspoon ground black pepper
 1 large onion, chopped
 1 clove garlic, minced
 ¾ cup defatted chicken broth
 2 teaspoons paprika
 1 large sweet red pepper, chopped
1½ cups broccoli florets
12 ounces egg (no-yolk) noodles
 1 cup nonfat sour cream

Sprinkle the chicken with the salt (if using) and black pepper.

Coat a large no-stick skillet with no-stick spray. Place over medium heat and add the chicken. Cook, stirring, for 7 to 8 minutes, or until the pieces begin to brown. Remove and set aside.

Add the onions, garlic and 3 tablespoons of the broth to the skillet. Cook, stirring, for 5 minutes, or until the onions are tender. (If necessary, add more broth to prevent sticking.)

Stir in the paprika and cook for 1 minute. Stir in the remaining broth, then add the chicken, red peppers and broccoli. Bring to a boil. Reduce the heat, cover and simmer for 20 minutes, or until the vegetables are tender.

Meanwhile, cook the noodles according to the package directions. Drain and cover the noodles to keep warm.

Stir the sour cream into the chicken mixture. Cook, stirring, over low heat for 1 to 2 minutes, or until heated through. (Do not boil.) Serve the chicken over the noodles.

Makes 4 servings. Per serving: 470 calories, 6.5 g. fat (12% of calories), 41.7 g. protein, 64.1 g. carbohydrates, 4.9 g. dietary fiber, 69 mg. cholesterol, 187 mg. sodium

Chicken-and-Bean Enchilada Casserole

¾ cup finely shredded reduced-fat Cheddar cheese

¾ cup finely shredded fat-free Cheddar cheese

4 boneless, skinless chicken breast halves (1 pound), cut into bite-size pieces

2 teaspoons olive oil

1 large onion, chopped

3 tablespoons defatted chicken broth

2 cloves garlic, minced

1 large green pepper, chopped

1 can (15 ounces) reduced-sodium tomato sauce

1 cup mild picante sauce

1½ teaspoons ground cumin

1 teaspoon chili powder

1 can (15 ounces) no-salt kidney beans, rinsed and drained

10 corn tortillas (6″ diameter)

½ cup nonfat sour cream

1 large tomato, chopped

Preheat the oven to 350°.

In a medium bowl, toss together the reduced-fat Cheddar and fat-free Cheddar.

Coat a large no-stick skillet with no-stick spray. Place over medium heat and add the chicken. Cook, stirring, for 10 minutes, or until the chicken is no longer pink. Remove and set aside.

Add the oil to the skillet and warm over medium heat. Add the onions, broth and garlic. Cook, stirring, for 5 minutes, or until the onions are tender.

Stir in the peppers, tomato sauce, picante sauce, cumin and chili powder. Add the chicken and beans and bring to a boil. Reduce the heat and simmer for 5 minutes.

Spread half of the chicken mixture evenly in a 9″ × 13″ no-stick baking dish. Place the tortillas on top, overlapping them to cover the entire surface. Sprinkle with half of the cheese mixture. Top with the remaining chicken mixture.

Cover with foil and bake for 30 to 35 minutes, or until heated through. Sprinkle with the remaining cheese mixture. Bake, uncovered, for 5 minutes, or until the cheese is partially melted.

To serve, use a sharp knife to cut the mixture into 8 pieces. Use a wide spatula to transfer the pieces to dinner plates. Top each serving with the sour cream and tomatoes.

Makes 8 servings. Per serving: 295 calories, 5.8 g. fat (17% of calories), 26 g. protein, 36 g. carbohydrates, 4.2 g. dietary fiber, 40 mg. cholesterol, 552 mg. sodium

QUICK!
Chicken Piccata with Rice

2 teaspoons olive oil

4 boneless, skinless chicken breast halves (1 pound)

1½ cups quick-cooking brown rice

1¼ cups defatted chicken broth

½ teaspoon dried oregano

¼ cup minced fresh parsley

¼ cup lemon juice

2 tablespoons capers, rinsed and chopped

2 tablespoons chopped toasted pine nuts or almonds (see note)

Coat a large no-stick skillet with no-stick spray. Add the oil and warm over medium heat. Add the chicken and cook for 5 minutes, or until lightly browned on both sides. Add the rice, broth, oregano, parsley, lemon juice and capers. Bring to a boil. Cover and simmer over medium-low heat for 10 minutes, or until the chicken is cooked through. Remove from the heat and let stand for 5 minutes. Sprinkle with the pine nuts or almonds.

Makes 4 servings. Per serving: 449 calories, 9.8 g. fat (20% of calories), 33.6 g. protein, 56.3 g. carbohydrates, 4.1 g. dietary fiber, 69 mg. cholesterol, 329 mg. sodium

NOTE

• To toast the nuts, place them in a dry no-stick skillet over medium heat. Toast the nuts, shaking the skillet often, for 3 to 5 minutes, or until fragrant and golden.

Grilled Chicken Breasts with Tomato-Basil Salsa

Tomato-Basil Salsa
    1 cup chopped ripe tomatoes
    ½ cup chopped scallions
    1 tablespoon finely chopped fresh basil
    2 teaspoons extra-virgin olive oil
    1 tablespoon balsamic vinegar or red-wine vinegar
    2 teaspoons minced serrano peppers or jalapeño peppers (optional); wear plastic gloves when handling
       Pinch of sugar (optional)

Chicken and Marinade
    ½ cup tomato juice
    1 tablespoon minced garlic
    1 teaspoon extra-virgin olive oil
    4 boneless, skinless chicken breast halves (1 pound)

To make the tomato-basil salsa: In a medium bowl, combine the tomatoes, scallions, basil, oil, vinegar, peppers (if using) and sugar (if using). Cover and refrigerate while preparing the chicken.

To make the chicken and marinade: Combine the tomato juice, garlic and oil in a shallow bowl large enough to hold the chicken. Place the chicken in the bowl and marinate for 15 minutes. Remove the chicken from the marinade and discard the marinade.

While the chicken is marinating, coat an unheated grill rack with no-stick spray. Light the grill according to the manufacturer's directions. Place the rack on the grill.

Place the chicken on the rack and grill 4″ to 6″ from the heat for 6 to 8 minutes, or until cooked through, turning once. Serve topped with the salsa.

Makes 4 servings. Per serving: 185 calories, 6.5 g. fat (32% of calories), 26 g. protein, 4.7 g. carbohydrates, 1 g. dietary fiber, 69 mg. cholesterol, 101 mg. sodium

Chicken Breasts Marrakesh

    1 can (28 ounces) plum tomatoes, seeded and chopped (with juice)
    1 large onion, quartered
    1 green pepper, quartered
    2 cloves garlic, minced
    1 teaspoon ground cumin
    ½ teaspoon ground coriander
    ¼ teaspoon ground cinnamon
    ½ teaspoon ground black pepper
    ¼ cup chopped fresh cilantro
    1½ pounds boneless, skinless chicken breasts
    2 cups defatted reduced-sodium chicken broth
    ⅓ cup raisins
    1 cup couscous
       Hot-pepper sauce

In a large no-stick Dutch oven over medium-high heat, combine the tomatoes (with juice), onions, green peppers, garlic, cumin, coriander, cinnamon, black pepper and 2 tablespoons of the cilantro. Bring to a boil. Place the chicken in the pot and spoon some of the sauce over it. Return to a boil, then immediately reduce the heat. Cover and simmer for 15 to 20 minutes, or until the chicken is no longer pink in the center. Transfer the chicken to a warm plate and set aside.

Increase the heat to high and boil the sauce, stirring frequently, for 10 minutes, or until thick. Reduce the heat to low. Return the chicken to the pot and spoon some of the sauce over it.

Meanwhile, in a medium saucepan over medium-high heat, bring the broth and raisins to a boil. Remove from the heat and stir in the couscous. Cover and let stand for 5 minutes, or until the liquid is absorbed. Fluff with a fork. Serve with the chicken and sauce.

Sprinkle with the remaining 2 tablespoons cilantro. Season to taste with the hot-pepper sauce.

Makes 4 servings. Per serving: 455 calories, 5.1 g. fat (10% of calories), 41.7 g. protein, 60 g. carbohydrates, 10.1 g. dietary fiber, 86 mg. cholesterol, 440 mg. sodium

NOTE
• In Morocco, couscous is often served with harissa, a fiery-hot pepper-garlic spice paste. Harissa complements the sweet and spicy flavors of this dish and is available at most Middle Eastern groceries. If it's unavailable, any hot-pepper sauce or Chinese chili paste will achieve a similar effect.

Baked Chicken Thighs with Peppers and Olives

1	teaspoon olive oil
1½	cups sliced onions
1	tablespoon minced garlic
1	green pepper, thinly sliced
1	sweet red or yellow pepper, thinly sliced
5	pitted black olives, sliced
¼	teaspoon dried thyme
¼	teaspoon dried rosemary
	Pinch of red-pepper flakes
1¼	pounds boneless, skinless chicken thighs, trimmed of all visible fat

2	teaspoons lemon juice
⅛	teaspoon ground black pepper
1	tablespoon grated Parmesan cheese
2	cups hot cooked rice

Preheat the oven to 425°. Coat a no-stick skillet with no-stick spray. Add the oil and warm over medium heat. Add the onions and garlic and sauté for 4 to 5 minutes, or until the onions are nearly tender.

Add the green peppers and red or yellow peppers and sauté for 5 to 6 minutes, or until tender. Add the olives, thyme, rosemary and red-pepper flakes and sauté for 1 minute.

Coat a shallow 3-quart no-stick baking dish with no-stick spray. Arrange the chicken in a single layer in the baking dish. Drizzle with the lemon juice and sprinkle with the black pepper. Spoon the vegetables over the chicken and sprinkle with the Parmesan.

Bake for 25 to 30 minutes, or until the chicken is cooked through. Serve with the rice.

Makes 4 servings. Per serving: 310 calories, 9.7 g. fat (28% of calories), 20.9 g. protein, 35.1 g. carbohydrates, 2.6 g. dietary fiber, 59 mg. cholesterol, 111 mg. sodium

NOTE
• When preparing skinless chicken thighs, be sure to use a sharp knife or kitchen scissors to remove the fatty deposits clinging to the meat.

VARIATION
Baked Chicken Thighs with Tomatoes and Pine Nuts: Omit the green peppers and sweet red or yellow peppers. Replace with 2 medium tomatoes, each cut into 8 wedges. Instead of sautéing, add the tomatoes to the baking dish after the chicken. Replace the olives, thyme and rosemary with 1 tablespoon toasted pine nuts (see note on page 215)and 1 tablespoon chopped fresh basil. Sprinkle over the chicken and tomatoes in the baking dish.

Chicken Thighs with Apricot Sauce

- 1 pound boneless, skinless chicken thighs, trimmed of all visible fat
- ¼ teaspoon ground cinnamon
- Pinch of ground red pepper
- 1 teaspoon canola oil
- 2 tablespoons defatted reduced-sodium chicken broth
- ⅓ cup apricot all-fruit spread
- 3 tablespoons lime juice
- Pinch of ground allspice
- ¼ teaspoon grated fresh ginger

Rinse the chicken and pat dry with paper towels. Lightly sprinkle with the cinnamon and pepper and set aside.

Coat a large no-stick skillet with no-stick spray. Add the oil and warm over medium-high heat. Add the chicken and cook for 3 to 4 minutes, or until lightly browned on all sides.

Push the chicken to the side of the skillet. Add the broth, fruit spread, lime juice, allspice and ginger and mix well. Push the chicken back to the center of the skillet. Cover and cook, stirring occasionally, over medium heat for about 15 minutes, or until the chicken is no longer pink.

Makes 4 servings. Per serving: 224 calories, 8.3 g. fat (34% of calories), 17.3 g. protein, 19.9 g. carbohydrates, 0.2 g. dietary fiber, 62 mg. cholesterol, 63 mg. sodium

NOTE

• This spicy-sweet main dish is delicious served with steamed couscous or quinoa, a super-nutritious ancient grain from South America.

New American Fried Chicken

Why give up fried chicken? In this recipe, we used a little American ingenuity to create a tastier and healthier version that contains less than 9 grams of fat per serving.

- ½ cup buttermilk
- ½ cup fresh white bread crumbs
- ½ cup fresh whole-wheat bread crumbs
- ½ teaspoon paprika
- 1 teaspoon ground black pepper
- ½ teaspoon dried thyme or sage
- 1 tablespoon minced fresh parsley
- Pinch of salt (optional)
- 4 skinless whole chicken legs

Coat a baking rack with no-stick spray. Place the rack on a foil-lined baking sheet and set aside. Preheat the oven to 425°.

Place the buttermilk in a shallow dish. Place the bread crumbs in another shallow dish. In a cup or small bowl, combine the paprika, pepper, thyme or sage, parsley and salt (if using). Add 1 teaspoon of the mixture to the bread crumbs and the remainder to the buttermilk.

Dip the chicken pieces in the buttermilk to coat, then roll them in the seasoned bread crumbs to coat. Place the chicken on the prepared rack and lightly coat with no-stick spray.

Bake for 15 minutes. Turn the chicken and coat again with no-stick spray. Bake for 15 minutes, or until the crust is golden brown and the juices run clear when the joint is pierced with a sharp knife.

Makes 4 servings. Per serving: 226 calories, 8.8 g. fat (36% of calories), 27.9 g. protein, 7.5 g. carbohydrates, 0.3 g. dietary fiber, 90 mg. cholesterol, 178 mg. sodium

QUICK!
Chicken Nuggets

- ¼ cup fat-free egg substitute
- 1 tablespoon water
- 1 pound boneless, skinless chicken breasts, trimmed of all visible fat and cut into 1" cubes
- ½ cup unseasoned dry bread crumbs
- ¼ cup rice bran
- 1 tablespoon minced fresh parsley
- ½ teaspoon dried basil
- 1 teaspoon dried thyme
- ½ teaspoon ground black pepper
- Pinch of ground red pepper

Coat a no-stick jelly-roll pan or no-stick baking sheet with no-stick spray and set aside. Preheat the oven to 425°.

In a medium bowl, mix the egg substitute and water. Add the chicken and stir to coat well.

In a plastic or paper bag, mix the bread crumbs, rice bran, parsley, basil, thyme, black pepper and red pepper.

Working in batches, remove the chicken from the egg mixture, shaking gently to remove any excess. Add to the bag and shake well to coat all of the pieces evenly with the crumbs.

Place the chicken pieces in a single layer on the prepared pan, leaving a little space between them. Coat generously with no-stick spray. Bake for 10 minutes. Turn the pieces and bake for 5 minutes, or until lightly browned and crisp.

Makes 8 servings. Per serving: 106 calories, 2.4 g. fat (20% of calories), 14.5 g. protein, 6.6 g. carbohydrates, 0.3 g. dietary fiber, 34 mg. cholesterol, 101 mg. sodium

NOTE

• Serve the nuggets with zippy low-fat dips such as honey mustard mixed with plain yogurt or salsa stirred into nonfat sour cream.

Roast Chicken with Winter Vegetables

- 1 broiler-fryer chicken (about 3 pounds)
- 1 clove garlic, minced
- 2 teaspoons crushed fennel seeds
- 4 small red potatoes, quartered
- 3 medium carrots, halved and quartered
- 2 small turnips, peeled and quartered
- 1 small onion, quartered
- ¼ teaspoon salt
- ½ cup defatted reduced-sodium chicken broth or water

Preheat the oven to 400°. Coat a roasting rack and a shallow roasting pan with no-stick spray and set aside.

Rinse the chicken and pat dry with paper towels. Remove and discard any excess fat from inside the chicken. Starting at the neck opening, use your fingers to gently loosen the skin from the meat and create a pocket on each side of the breast. Leave the skin attached to the breastbone.

Rub the garlic and ½ teaspoon of the fennel seeds onto the meat underneath the skin. Place the chicken, breast side up, on the prepared rack in the roasting pan.

In a shallow bowl, combine the potatoes, carrots, turnips and onions. Coat lightly with no-stick spray. Sprinkle with the remaining 1½ teaspoons fennel seeds and the salt and toss to coat. Loosely stuff some of the vegetables into the chicken cavity. Place the remaining vegetables in the pan around the chicken. Skewer the neck skin to the back of the chicken and tie the legs to the tail. Insert a meat thermometer in the thickest part of a thigh.

Roast for 30 minutes. Turn the vegetables and roast for about 30 minutes, or until the thermometer registers 180° to 185° and the chicken is no longer pink.

Transfer the vegetables from the pan to an ovenproof serving dish; keep warm in the oven on low heat. Let the chicken stand for 10 minutes before carving.

Meanwhile, discard all of the fat from the roasting pan. Add the broth or water to the pan, scraping with a pancake turner to remove browned particles. Pour the pan juices into a small saucepan and cook at a brisk simmer for 3 to 4 minutes, or until reduced slightly.

Remove the skin from the chicken and discard. Serve the chicken and vegetables with the pan juices.

Makes 6 servings. Per serving: 247 calories, 4.5 g. fat (16% of calories), 19.4 g. protein, 32.9 g. carbohydrates, 1.1 g. dietary fiber, 49 mg. cholesterol, 181 mg. sodium

NOTE

• The technique of seasoning poultry breast with garlic and herbs before roasting can also be applied to Cornish hens or bone-in chicken breasts. Another aromatic option is to place lemon, lime or orange slices under the skin.

Rinse the hens and pat dry with paper towels. Starting at the neck opening of each hen, use your fingers to gently loosen the skin from the meat over the breasts, thighs and legs. Use your index finger to reach the drumstick meat without tearing the skin.

In a small bowl, combine the garlic, cumin, oregano, paprika, salt and vinegar. Rub the seasoning mixture under the skin and over the meat of the hens.

Place the hens, breast side up, on the prepared rack in the roasting pan. Skewer the neck skin to the backs of the hens and tie the legs to the tails. Insert a meat thermometer in the thickest part of a thigh.

Roast, uncovered, for 45 to 60 minutes, or until the thermometer registers 180° to 185° and the meat is no longer pink.

Let stand for 10 minutes before carving. Remove and discard the skin before serving. Serve with the rice.

Makes 8 servings. Per serving: 351 calories, 14.5 g. fat (38% of calories), 30.2 g. protein, 24 g. carbohydrates, 0.1 g. dietary fiber, 52 mg. cholesterol, 133 mg. sodium

Spice-Rubbed Roast Cornish Hens

- 4 Cornish hens (1–1½ pounds each)
- 2 tablespoons minced garlic
- 1 teaspoon ground cumin
- ½ teaspoon dried oregano
- ½ teaspoon paprika
- ¼ teaspoon salt
- 2 teaspoons red-wine vinegar
- 4 cups hot cooked rice

Preheat the oven to 350°. Coat a roasting rack and a large shallow roasting pan with nostick spray and set aside.

Grilled Herbed Duck Breasts

- 1 teaspoon dried thyme
- 2 small bay leaves
- 1 large clove garlic, sliced
  Pinch of salt
  Pinch of ground black pepper
- 1 pound boneless duck breasts, excess fat removed (skin on)
- 2 cups hot mashed potatoes

In a large resealable plastic bag, combine the thyme, bay leaves, garlic, salt and pepper.

Rinse the duck and pat dry with paper

towels. With a sharp knife, score through the skin at 1″ intervals, taking care not to cut the meat. Add the duck to the bag. Seal the bag and turn to coat the meat. Refrigerate for 24 hours, turning the bag occasionally.

Coat an unheated grill rack with no-stick spray. Light the grill according to the manufacturer's directions. Place the rack on the grill.

Remove the duck from the bag and scrape off most of the seasonings. Place the duck, skin side up, on the rack. Cover with the grill lid and grill 4″ to 6″ from the heat for 4 minutes. Turn the duck. Cover and grill for 3 to 4 minutes, or until the juices run clear when the meat is pierced with a sharp knife. Transfer to a platter and let stand for 5 minutes. Remove and discard the skin. Serve with the potatoes.

Makes 4 servings. Per serving: 142 calories, 4.9 g. fat (32% of calories), 22.6 g. protein, 0.7 g. carbohydrates, 0 g. dietary fiber, 38 mg. cholesterol, 65 mg. sodium

NOTE

• For a special presentation, just before serving, cut the duck breasts diagonally across the grain into thin slices.

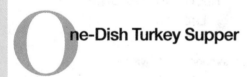

One-Dish Turkey Supper

1½	pounds turkey breast cutlets
1½	teaspoons dried thyme
½	teaspoon ground black pepper
2	teaspoons olive oil
1	large onion, chopped
1	large clove garlic, minced
2¾	cups defatted chicken broth
1¼	cups long-grain white rice
1	small sweet potato, peeled and chopped
1	cup chopped yellow summer squash
¼	cup chopped fresh parsley
1	large bay leaf
1	teaspoon dried sage
¼	teaspoon salt (optional)

Sprinkle the turkey with ½ teaspoon of the thyme and ¼ teaspoon of the pepper.

Coat a large no-stick skillet with no-stick spray. Place over medium heat and add the turkey. Brown the pieces on both sides. Remove and set aside.

In the same skillet, warm the oil. Add the onions, garlic and 3 tablespoons of the broth. Cook, stirring, over medium heat for 5 minutes, or until the onions are tender. Stir in the rice, sweet potatoes, squash, parsley, bay leaf, sage, salt (if using) and the remaining 1 teaspoon thyme, remaining ¼ teaspoon pepper and remaining broth.

Bring to a boil. Reduce the heat, cover and simmer for 12 minutes. Place the turkey on top of the rice mixture. Cover and simmer for 8 minutes, or until the rice is tender and the liquid is absorbed.

Remove and discard the bay leaf. Move the turkey to one side of the skillet. Stir the rice, then transfer it to a serving platter. Arrange the turkey on top.

Makes 6 servings. Per serving: 324 calories, 2.6 g. fat (7% of calories), 32.9 g. protein, 40.5 g. carbohydrates, 1.9 g. dietary fiber, 75 mg. cholesterol, 207 mg. sodium

Chinese Turkey Kebabs

½ cup orange juice
¼ cup thinly sliced scallions
2 tablespoons reduced-sodium soy sauce
1 tablespoon packed brown sugar
1 tablespoon cider vinegar
1 clove garlic, minced
½ teaspoon ground ginger
2–3 drops hot-pepper sauce (optional)
1 pound boneless, skinless turkey breast, cut into bite-size pieces
1 large green pepper, cut into 1½" pieces
1 large sweet red or yellow pepper, cut into 1½" pieces
12 small white onions, trimmed and peeled
12 chunks pineapple

In a medium bowl, stir together the orange juice, scallions, soy sauce, brown sugar, vinegar, garlic, ginger and hot-pepper sauce (if using). Add the turkey and stir until coated. Cover and marinate in the refrigerator for 30 minutes.

Bring a large saucepan of water to a boil. Carefully add the green peppers, red or yellow peppers and onions. Boil for 3 minutes, or until the vegetables are crisp-tender. Drain, rinse with cold water and drain again.

Drain the turkey and discard the marinade. Arrange the turkey and vegetables on 4 long metal skewers, alternating the pieces and leaving a small space between pieces. Thread the pineapple onto 4 separate skewers.

Coat an unheated grill rack with no-stick spray. Light the grill according to the manufacturer's directions. Place the rack on the grill.

Grill the turkey and vegetable kebabs 4" to 6" from medium-high heat, turning frequently, for 18 to 20 minutes, or until the turkey is cooked. During the last 5 minutes of cooking, add the pineapple kebabs to the grill and cook, turning frequently, until hot.

Makes 4 servings. Per serving: 180 calories, 1 g. fat (5% of calories), 28.7 g. protein, 14.1 g. carbohydrates, 1.9 g. dietary fiber, 75 mg. cholesterol, 138 mg. sodium

QUICK!

Sesame Turkey Cutlets

2 tablespoons hoisin sauce
2 tablespoons water
1 pound turkey breast cutlets
Ground black pepper
1 tablespoon toasted sesame seeds (see note)

In a small bowl, stir together the hoisin sauce and water; set aside.

Rinse the turkey and pat dry with paper towels. Sprinkle each cutlet with the pepper. Coat a large no-stick skillet with no-stick spray and warm over medium-high heat. Add the turkey and cook for 1 minute. Turn the cutlets and cook for 2 to 3 minutes, or until the turkey is no longer pink.

Pour the hoisin-sauce mixture over the turkey and cook until the mixture comes to a boil. Sprinkle with the sesame seeds.

Makes 4 servings. Per serving: 142 calories, 1.8 g. fat (12% of calories), 27.6 g. protein, 2.7 g. carbohydrates, 0.3 g. dietary fiber, 75 mg. cholesterol, 148 mg. sodium

NOTE
• To toast the sesame seeds, place them in a small no-stick skillet. Cook and stir over medium heat for 2 to 3 minutes, or until golden and fragrant.

Breaded Turkey Thighs with Mustard Sauce

¼ cup cider vinegar
2 tablespoons Dijon mustard
2 tablespoons brown sugar
1 teaspoon grated fresh ginger
½ teaspoon dried thyme
2 boneless, skinless turkey thighs
½ cup fresh bread crumbs

In a small bowl or cup, combine the vinegar, mustard, brown sugar, ginger and thyme; set aside.

Cut each turky thigh in half. Place the turkey between two sheets of wax paper and pound to equal thickness. Transfer the turkey to a shallow bowl and pour half of the mustard sauce over it. Cover and marinate for 15 minutes.

Preheat the broiler. Coat a baking rack with no-stick spray and place the rack on a foil-lined no-stick baking sheet. Remove the turkey from the marinade, gently shaking off the excess. Discard the marinade. Coat the turkey with the bread crumbs.

Place the turkey on the prepared rack and broil 8" from the heat for 6 to 8 minutes per side, or until the turkey is cooked through and the crumbs are golden.

In a small saucepan over low heat, warm the remaining half of the mustard sauce. Serve with the turkey.

Makes 4 servings. Per serving: 195 calories, 6.5 g. fat (30% of calories), 22.4 g. protein, 11.6 g. carbohydrates, 0.2 g. dietary fiber, 63 mg. cholesterol, 817 mg. sodium

Turkey-and-Bean Burritos

1 pound ground turkey breast
1 medium onion, chopped
1 clove garlic, minced
1 can (15 ounces) no-salt-added kidney beans, rinsed and drained
1 can (8 ounces) reduced-sodium tomato sauce
⅓ cup picante sauce
1½ teaspoons chili powder
⅛ teaspoon salt (optional)
1 cup shredded fat-free Cheddar cheese
¾ cup shredded reduced-fat sharp Cheddar cheese
10 flour tortillas (8″ diameter)

Preheat the oven to 375°.

Coat a large saucepan with no-stick spray and warm over medium heat. Add the turkey, onions and garlic and sauté for 8 to 10 minutes, or until the turkey is no longer pink. If necessary, add a small amount of water to the pan to prevent sticking.

Stir in the beans, tomato sauce, picante sauce, chili powder and salt (if using). Cover and cook, stirring occasionally, over low heat for 10 minutes.

In a small bowl, toss together the fat-free Cheddar and reduced-fat Cheddar.

Coat a no-stick baking sheet with no-stick spray.

Place a tortilla on a flat work surface. Spoon a generous ½ cup of the turkey mixture onto the tortilla, positioning it slightly off-center. Sprinkle with a scant 2 tablespoons of the cheese mixture. Carefully roll up the tortilla and place, seam side down, on the prepared baking sheet. Repeat with the remaining tortillas, turkey mixture and cheese.

Bake for 12 to 14 minutes, or until the cheese is mostly melted and the tortillas begin to crisp around the edges.

Makes 10 servings. Per serving: 231 calories, 4.3 g. fat (17% of calories), 20.9 g. protein, 26.6 g. carbohydrates, 1.4 g. dietary fiber, 34 mg. cholesterol, 445 mg. sodium

NOTES

• If you have extra picante sauce, it makes a delicious topping for the burritos.

• This recipe makes enough for a generous supply of leftovers. To reheat for lunch, a snack or a second dinner, place one burrito at a time on a microwave-safe plate. Cover it with wax paper and microwave on high power for 30 to 40 seconds, or until heated through.

Turkey Tetrazzini

Here's an American classic made healthy. For the cream sauce, we replaced the butter-flour roux and heavy cream with buttermilk and cornstarch. Garlic and parsley give it a fresh new taste.

4	ounces spaghetti
1	cup chopped fresh mushrooms
12	ounces diced cooked turkey
1¼	cups buttermilk
2	tablespoons cornstarch
1	small clove garlic, minced
½	teaspoon ground black pepper
	Pinch of nutmeg
¼	cup chopped fresh parsley
¼	cup grated Parmesan cheese
2	tablespoons fresh bread crumbs

Preheat the oven to 350°. Coat a 9″ × 9″ no-stick baking dish with no-stick spray and set aside.

In a large pot of boiling water, cook the spaghetti according to the package directions. Drain and set aside.

Meanwhile, coat a large no-stick skillet with no-stick spray and warm over medium heat. Add the mushrooms and cook for about 5 minutes, or until the mushroom liquid has evaporated. Stir in the turkey and set aside.

In a small bowl, stir together the buttermilk, cornstarch, garlic, pepper and nutmeg. Stir into the turkey mixture. Cook, stirring, over medium heat until the mixture slightly thickens and begins to gently boil. Cook and stir for 2 minutes. Remove from the heat and stir in the reserved spaghetti and the parsley and Parmesan.

Transfer the spaghetti mixture to the prepared baking dish. Sprinkle with the bread crumbs. Coat with no-stick spray. Bake for 12 to 15 minutes, or until the tetrazzini is golden and bubbly.

Makes 4 servings. Per serving: 325 calories, 3.9 g. fat (11% of calories), 35.6 g. protein, 34.9 g. carbohydrates, 0.4 g. dietary fiber, 79 mg. cholesterol, 252 mg. sodium

NOTES

• Tetrazzini makes a great party dish. This recipe can be doubled; bake in a 8″ × 12″ no-stick baking dish for 20 to 25 minutes.

• You can replace the spaghetti with any type of dry semolina-type pasta. Try shells, rotini or penne.

• You can replace the turkey with 12 ounces diced cooked chicken.

Roast Turkey Breast with Pineapple-Basil Sauce

1½ cups pineapple juice
1 tablespoon sugar
1 bone-in turkey breast (4–6 pounds)
1 cup water
1 tablespoon cornstarch
2 tablespoons shredded fresh basil
¼ cup minced scallions

Preheat the oven to 325°. In a medium saucepan, combine the pineapple juice and sugar. Bring to a boil. Reduce the heat to medium and simmer, uncovered, for 10 to 15 minutes, or until reduced to about 1 cup.

Rinse the turkey and pat dry with paper towels. Coat a roasting rack with no-stick spray and place the rack in a roasting pan. Place the turkey, skin side up, on the rack. Insert a meat thermometer in the thickest part of the breast.

Roast, uncovered, for 1¼ to 2 hours, or until the thermometer registers 170° to 175° and the turkey is no longer pink in the center. During the last 15 minutes of roasting, brush with ¼ cup of the pineapple mixture.

Remove the turkey from the oven and loosely cover with foil. Let stand for 10 minutes before slicing. Remove and discard the skin before serving.

Meanwhile, in a small bowl, stir together the water and cornstarch. Stir into the remaining ¾ cup of the pineapple mixture in the saucepan. Cook and stir over medium heat until the sauce thickens and begins to boil. Add the basil and scallions. Cook and stir for 2 minutes. Serve the sauce with the turkey.

Makes 10 to 12 servings. Per serving: 239 calories, 5.8 g. fat (23% of calories), 37 g. protein, 7.3 g. carbohydrates, 0.1 g. dietary fiber, 69 mg. cholesterol, 661 mg. sodium

NOTE
• To easily shred fresh basil, stack the leaves on top of one another, then roll into a tight tube. Cut the tube into thin slices and unfurl. This is also known as chiffonade-cut.

QUICK!
Barbecued Turkey Sandwich

1 pound turkey breast cutlets, pounded ¼" thick and cut into short, thin strips
¼ teaspoon dried thyme
¼ teaspoon ground black pepper
¼ teaspoon salt (optional)
2 teaspoons nondiet tub-style margarine or butter
1 medium onion, chopped
1 small green pepper, chopped
1 small clove garlic, minced
½ cup reduced-sodium ketchup
¼ cup water
1 tablespoon reduced-sodium Worcestershire sauce
1 tablespoon honey
¼ teaspoon dry mustard
  Pinch of ground allspice
4 Kaiser rolls

Season the turkey with the thyme, black pepper and salt (if using).

In a large no-stick skillet over medium heat, melt the margarine or butter. Cook the turkey for 2 minutes per side, or until lightly browned. Remove and set aside.

Coat a large no-stick skillet with no-stick

spray and warm over medium heat. Add the onions, green peppers and garlic and cook, stirring occasionally, for 5 to 6 minutes, or until the peppers are soft. If necessary, add 1 tablespoon water to the skillet to prevent sticking.

Stir in the ketchup, water, Worcestershire sauce, honey, mustard and allspice. Simmer for 10 minutes, or until the vegetables are tender.

Add the turkey, reduce the heat to very low and cook for 5 minutes, or until the turkey is heated through and flavored with the sauce. Spoon onto rolls just before serving.

Makes 4 servings. Per serving: 378 calories, 5.2 g. fat (13% of calories), 33.8 g. protein, 48.5 g. carbohydrates, 1.5 g. dietary fiber, 75 mg. cholesterol, 417 mg. sodium

NOTE

• For a Carolina-style accompaniment, top the turkey barbecue with coleslaw made with a reduced-fat oil-and-vinegar dressing.

QUICK!
Turkey-and-Sausage Jambalaya

Jambalaya is one of the most popular Cajun-Creole dishes. The variations are endless, but it usually contains chili peppers, green peppers, rice and chorizo, a high-fat spicy pork sausage. To trim the fat, we replaced the chorizo with low-fat turkey sausage.

- 2 teaspoons canola oil
- 1 cup chopped scallions
- 1 large stalk celery, sliced
- 1 small coarsely chopped sweet red or green pepper
- ⅓ cup chopped fresh parsley

- 1 pound boneless, skinless turkey breast, cut into ¾" cubes
- 2 cups defatted chicken broth
- 1¼ cups quick-cooking white rice
- ½ cup chopped low-fat smoked turkey sausage
- ½ teaspoon dried thyme
- ¼ teaspoon ground red pepper
- ⅛ teaspoon ground black pepper
- 1 large bay leaf
- 1 can (16 ounces) chopped tomatoes (with juice)

In a large no-stick skillet over medium heat, warm the oil. Add the scallions, celery, red or green peppers and parsley. Cook, stirring, for 3 minutes, or until the onions are tender.

Add the turkey and cook, stirring, for 4 minutes. Stir in the broth, rice, sausage, thyme, red pepper, black pepper and bay leaf. Bring to a simmer. Reduce the heat and gently simmer, stirring occasionally, for 3 minutes.

Stir in the tomatoes (with juice) and cook just until the mixture comes to a simmer. Turn off the heat, cover and let stand for 5 minutes.

Remove and discard the bay leaf. Stir well.

Makes 6 servings. Per serving: 231 calories, 3.3 g. fat (13% of calories), 24.4 g. protein, 25.1 g. carbohydrates, 2.3 g. dietary fiber, 56 mg. cholesterol, 415 mg. sodium

VARIATION

Chicken-and-Ham Jambalaya: Replace the turkey with boneless, skinless chicken breasts. Replace the sausage with good-quality lean smoked ham, trimmed of all visible fat.

Oven-Baked Stuffings

Traditional stuffings are loaded with fat. But why blow your fat budget on a side dish? Here's how to make rich and delicious stuffings that are also lean.

Skip the organ meats. Instead of using butter, let chicken broth, fruit juices or herbs provide the flavor. Bake the stuffing in a separate container so it won't soak up fat from the roasting bird. And to keep it moist, cover it with foil during baking. If you like a crunchy top on your stuffing, bake it, uncovered, for the last 5 to 10 minutes. Stuffings are incredibly easy to adapt, so let the recipes below get your creative juices flowing.

Chestnut Stuffing

- 1 tablespoon olive oil
- 2 onions, chopped
- 4 stalks celery, chopped
- 1 medium carrot, chopped
- 3 tablespoons chopped fresh parsley
- 1 teaspoon crushed dried rosemary
- ¼ teaspoon ground black pepper
- 3 cups canned peeled chestnuts, drained and coarsely chopped
- 6½ cups bread cubes
- 1 cup raisins
- 1¼ cups defatted reduced-sodium chicken broth
- ¼ cup fat-free egg substitute

Preheat the oven to 325°. Coat a 9″ × 13″ no-stick baking dish with no-stick spray; set aside.

In a large, deep no-stick skillet over medium-high heat, warm the oil. Add the onions, celery, carrots, parsley, rosemary and pepper. Sauté for 4 to 5 minutes, or until the vegetables are soft. Remove from the heat.

Stir in the chestnuts, bread cubes, raisins, broth and egg substitute.

Spoon the stuffing into the prepared dish. Cover with foil and bake for about 45 minutes, or until heated through.

Makes 8 servings. Per serving: 191 calories, 3 g. fat (14% of calories), 4.8 g. protein, 38.4 g. carbohydrates, 2.7 g. dietary fiber, 0 mg. cholesterol, 177 mg. sodium

Confetti Cornbread Stuffing

- 1 teaspoon canola oil
- 1 stalk celery, minced
- 1 carrot, minced
- 1 onion, minced
- 1 small sweet red or green pepper, minced
- ½ cup fresh or frozen corn
- 4 cups coarsely crumbled cornbread
- 2 teaspoons hot-pepper flakes
- ½ teaspoon dried sage
- ½ teaspoon dried thyme
- ¼ cup fat-free egg substitute
- 2–3 cups defatted reduced-sodium chicken broth

Coat a 3-quart no-stick baking dish with no-stick spray; set aside.

In a large no-stick skillet over medium heat, warm the oil . Add the celery, carrots, onions, red or green peppers and corn. Sauté for about 10 minutes, or until the vegetables are tender.

Add the cornbread, hot-pepper flakes, sage and thyme and toss to mix well. Add the egg substitute and 2 cups of the broth and stir well. If the bread is dry, add enough of the remaining broth to moisten it.

Preheat the oven to 350°. Spoon the stuffing into the prepared dish. Cover with foil and bake for 20 minutes. Uncover and bake for 5 minutes, or until golden.

Makes 6 servings. Per serving: 265 calories, 7.9 g. fat (27% of calories), 7.7 g. protein, 41.3 g. carbohydrates, 1.5 g. dietary fiber, 41 mg. cholesterol, 569 mg. sodium

Wild Rice and Cranberry Stuffing

- 1 cup defatted reduced-sodium chicken broth
- ½ cup orange juice
- ⅔ cup wild rice, rinsed and drained
- 2 teaspoons canola oil
- 4 ounces sliced cremini or portobello mushrooms
- ½ cup chopped onions
- 1 stalk celery, chopped
- ½ teaspoon dried thyme
- ½ teaspoon dried sage
- ½ cup dried cranberries
- ¼ cup chopped pecans

Coat a 1-quart no-stick baking dish with no-stick spray; set aside.

In a medium saucepan, bring the broth and orange juice to a boil.

Stir the rice into the broth mixture and return to a boil. Reduce the heat, cover and simmer for 45 to 50 minutes, or until the rice is tender and the liquid is absorbed.

Meanwhile, in a large no-stick skillet, warm the oil. Add the mushrooms, onions, celery, thyme and sage. Cook, stirring occasionally, over medium heat for about 4 minutes, or until the vegetables are tender. Add the cranberries and pecans. Cook and stir for 2 minutes. Add the rice and toss until well-mixed.

Preheat the oven to 325°. Spoon the stuffing into the prepared dish. Cover with foil and bake for about 30 minutes, or until heated through.

Makes 8 servings. Per serving: 105 calories, 3.7 g. fat (30% of calories), 3.4 g. protein, 15.9 g. carbohydrates, 1.5 g. dietary fiber, 0 mg. cholesterol, 48 mg. sodium

VARIATION

Wild Rice Stuffing with Dried Apricots and Pistachios: Replace the dried cranberries with diced dried apricots. Replace the pecans with unsalted natural (undyed) pistachios.

Wild Mushroom–Barley Stuffing

- 1 ounce dried porcini mushrooms
- 1½ cups hot water
- 2 teaspoons olive oil
- 1 cup chopped scallions
- 2 cloves garlic, minced
- ½ teaspoon dried thyme
- 2 cups sliced fresh button mushrooms
- 2 cups pearl barley
- 3 cups defatted reduced-sodium chicken broth
- ¼ cup chopped fresh parsley
- 2 tablespoons grated Romano cheese
- ¼ teaspoon salt
- ¼ teaspoon ground black pepper

Coat a 3-quart no-stick baking dish with no-stick spray; set aside.

In a small bowl, combine the porcini mushrooms and water and let stand for about 20 minutes, or until the mushrooms are soft. Using a slotted spoon, remove the mushrooms; chop and set aside. Strain the liquid into a small bowl through a fine sieve lined with cheesecloth or a coffee filter; set aside.

Coat a medium saucepan with olive oil no-stick spray. Add the oil and warm over medium heat. Add the scallions, garlic, thyme and button mushrooms. Cook over medium heat for 7 to 10 minutes, or until the mushroom liquid has evaporated.

Add the reserved porcini mushrooms and the barley. Cook, stirring often, for 3 to 4 minutes to coat the barley with the vegetables. Add the reserved mushroom liquid and the broth and bring to a boil. Remove from the heat. Stir in the parsley, Romano, salt and pepper.

Preheat the oven to 400°. Spoon the stuffing into the prepared dish. Cover with foil and bake for 35 to 40 minutes, or until the barley is tender.

Makes 8 servings. Per serving: 231 calories, 2.6 g. fat (10% of calories), 7.5 g. protein, 43.3 g. carbohydrates, 8.5 g. dietary fiber, 2 mg. cholesterol, 120 mg. sodium

Fish and Shellfish

For great taste, ease of preparation and a wide range of cooking options, fish and other seafood are a welcome addition to the healthy cook's table. Seafood certainly delivers an almost infinite variety to the diet. You can serve a snow-white fillet of sole one day and a thick coral-colored salmon steak the next. You can turn any meal into a celebration with the addition of shrimp, crab or lobster. You can enjoy the light essence of albacore tuna in summer salads. Or you can savor the hearty goodness of clam, oyster or fish chowder in the dead of winter.

As a bonus, fish and shellfish are among the healthiest foods that you can eat. They're high not only in protein but also in a type of fat called omega-3 fatty acids, which may help reduce the risk of stroke and heart disease. And since seafood is very low in saturated fat, it's a perfect replacement for red meat or other high-fat fare.

FIND THE BEST CATCH

While fresh fish delivers some of the most delicate flavors imaginable, it can turn very quickly; a single day may be all it takes to transform a beautiful, aromatic fish into a stinker. Careful shopping is essential.

Tom Ney, director of the Rodale Test Kitchen in Emmaus, Pennsylvania, recommends that you literally introduce yourself to the various fishmongers in your area. Forming a personal relationship with the experts is the best way to get good advice and the freshest catch. Your efforts will be rewarded with compliments when your family sits down to eat a truly tasty fish dinner.

One question that you should always ask is, "What's running today?" Fish like wild salmon are freshest during their annual "runs" to spawn during the spring and summer.

Although wild fish are freshest only at certain times of the year, most of the seafood that you buy, like trout, mussels and shrimp, is farm-raised. This means that it's available—and fresh—all year long.

To make sure that you get the best catch, here's what chefs recommend.

Shop around. Since fish and seafood perish so quickly, it's important to find a merchant who buys the freshest fish. He should also have sufficient turnover, so that the fish doesn't sit out too long. Shop around until you find a clean-looking and clean-smelling seafood counter with an appealing display. The raw fish should be kept on ice, and the cooked fish in a separate, chilled display.

Make it personal. Being comfortable with your local fishmonger can make the difference between a meal that's memorable and one that's best forgotten. So get to know the expert behind the counter. Tom Ney recommends bringing in a recipe and asking for advice. Better yet, bring in a sample of your creation the next day. You'll have a friend for life.

Follow your nose. Fish should smell fresh and just slightly briny. Off odors develop in the gut cavity first. If at all possible, take a sniff in that area to make sure that the fish is clean and fresh.

HEALTHY FISHING

Fish are high in omega-3 fatty acids, which may help reduce the risk of stroke and heart disease. To get helpful amounts of omega-3's, experts recommend eating fish two to four times a week. In the chart below, the amounts of omega-3's are based on 3 ounces of seafood.

SEAFOOD	OMEGA-3'S (G.)
Anchovies, canned in olive oil	1.8
Atlantic herring, cooked	1.8
Pink salmon, canned	1.5
Atlantic sardines, canned in oil	1.3
Bluefin tuna, cooked	1.3
Atlantic mackerel, cooked	1.1
Sockeye salmon, cooked	1.1
Swordfish, cooked	0.9
Eastern oysters, steamed	0.8
Rainbow smelts, cooked	0.8
Rainbow trout, cooked	0.8
Tilefish, cooked	0.8
Whiting, cooked	0.8
Albacore tuna, canned in water	0.7
Blue mussels, cooked	0.7
Carp, cooked	0.7
Sea bass, cooked	0.7
Shark, uncooked	0.7
Striped bass, cooked	0.7
Eel, cooked	0.6
Halibut, cooked	0.5
Atlantic ocean perch, cooked	0.4
Blue crab, cooked	0.4
Chinook salmon (lox), smoked	0.4
Pollack, cooked	0.4
Sturgeon, smoked	0.3
Haddock, cooked	0.2

☞ At a fish counter, ask to sniff the fish after it has been weighed for you.

☞ If that's not possible, open the package after it has been handed to you. Hand it right back if it doesn't suit you—and consider finding another place to get your fish.

☞ Beware of fish that has been prewrapped in plastic. It goes bad quickly.

Check the eyes. The eyes of whole fish should be clear, bright and bulging. If the eyes are slightly milky, it generally means that freshness is waning. Sunken, opaque white or gray eyes indicate an old fish. Move on to something fresher.

Inspect the gills. They should be moist and bright red, almost burgundy. Pink gills are acceptable. Gray or brown gills, however, mean that the fish is old and unacceptable.

Examine the skin. The skin and scales should be bright and shiny. Loose, dried scales indicate an old or poorly handled fish.

Press the flesh. The flesh should be firm. When you press it with your finger, it should spring right back. If a dent remains, the fish is old and should be avoided.

When it's time to take your fish home, ask the fishmonger to throw a handful of ice in a plastic bag along with your packaged fish. (You don't want the fish to come into direct contact with melting ice, since this can cause the flesh to get soggy.) When the weather is warm, even a short trip from the store to your home can spoil your precious purchase, so careful handling at this point is a must.

COLD FACTS

Given its perishable nature, fish bought at the store should always be eaten within 24 hours. If the fish was previously frozen (ask if it was), don't even think of refreezing it, since that can give bacteria the opportunity to colonize. Freshly caught fish, however, can be safely frozen.

☞ If you have a whole fish, fillet it and rinse the fillets in cold water.

STANDARD SERVINGS

A little seafood goes a long way, so you generally don't need to cook a lot. Here are some recommended serving sizes.

FISH	APPETIZER	MAIN DISH
FINFISH		
Pan-dressed	3½–5 ounces	6–8 ounces
Skinless fillet	1½–3 ounces	4–6 ounces
Steaks	3½–5 ounces	6–8 ounces
Whole, dressed	3–6 ounces	8–12 ounces
BIVALVES		
Clams, oysters or mussels (small)	4–10	12–20
Clams, oysters or mussels (medium)	3–8	9–16
Clams, oysters or mussels (large)	2–6	7–12
Scallops	1½–3 ounces	4–6 ounces
CRABS		
Blue (whole)	1–3	4–8
Dungeness (whole)	6–10 ounces	12–16 ounces
King and snow (clusters, legs and claws)	4–8 ounces	8–12 ounces
Soft-shell (whole)	1	2–3
Stone (claws)	4–8 ounces	8–12 ounces
CRAWFISH		
Whole	3–5	6–10
LOBSTER		
Tail	3–5 ounces	6–8 ounces
Whole	½–¾ pound	1–1½ pounds
SHRIMP		
Medium	5–10	12–20
Large	3–6	8–12
SQUID		
Whole	3½–5 ounces	6–8 ounces

☞ Lay the fillets flat on a wide tray covered with wax paper.

☞ Put the tray in the freezer for 2 to 3 hours. When the fillets are solid, wrap them individually with freezer paper and seal with freezer tape. Label well.

☞ Place the wrapped fillets in a tightly sealed container or freezer bag and store in the coldest part of the freezer. Frozen fish will generally keep for up to four months.

Preparing Frozen Fish

It isn't necessary or even desirable to completely thaw frozen fish before cooking. Once a fish is frozen, individual cells in the flesh burst from the crystallization of the liquids inside. As long as the fish stays frozen, the juice stays in the fish. If you thaw it completely, however, you will soon discover a puddle of liquid forming under the fish. This means that the flesh has lost its moisture and is going to cook up tough and dry, no matter how careful you are.

With care, however, frozen fish will cook up as moist and tender as fresh. Here's what you need to do.

☞ Place the frozen fish on a flat dish on the countertop. Allow it to thaw for 30 minutes (no longer).

☞ Begin cooking when the fish has lost its rigid hardness but still remains in a frosted, half-frozen state.

☞ Cook the fish for approximately 50 percent longer than the time given in the recipe, which is based on fresh—or at least thawed—fish.

FISH WITHOUT ODORS

While the delicate taste of fish is downright delicious, the smell of cooking fish can be daunting. To enjoy your catch without catching a noseful, here's what chefs recommend.

Add some acid. When cooking fish, pour in a small amount of an acidic aromatic flavoring, such as lemon juice or flavored vinegar. This will help subdue the pungent odors and keep your kitchen smelling fresh.

Watch the time. Cooking fish too long is guaranteed to send a pungent, penetrating aroma wafting through your house. The best way to limit cooking odors is to watch the time carefully and remove fish from the heat the instant that it's done.

MARINATING FISH

Briefly bathing fish in a flavorful aromatic liquid is a great way to add taste and make the flesh wonderfully moist and tender. Fish that take well to marinades include striped bass, bluefish, catfish, mackerel, mahimahi, marlin, monkfish, salmon, sea trout, shark, skate, snapper, swordfish and tuna. Market cuts that marinate well are fillets and steaks.

But unlike beef or chicken, which often require long marinating times, fish is too delicate for this sort of rough treatment. Marinating it briefly will enhance the flavor; leaving it in too long will only make it mushy.

☞ Limit marinating time to 1 hour.

☞ Fish at room temperature can turn very quickly, so never marinate it on the counter. Put it in the refrigerator instead.

COOKING FISH

For the healthy cook who is short on time—these days, this applies to just about everyone—fish is the ideal meal. Most simple fish dishes can be completely cooked and ready for the table in 15 minutes.

Regardless of your technique, the secret to cooking perfect fish is to never overcook it. Fish flesh is a soft, delicate protein that needs quick and gentle cooking. Cooking it too long makes it dry and hard. The odor becomes stronger, too.

Although people have traditionally drenched fish in butter or other fats, it really isn't necessary. By making good use of herbs, spices, vinegars or other flavored foods, you can enhance the fresh, healthy taste of fish without overwhelming it.

Baking

A 400° oven cooks fish quickly and gives it just a hint of crust. The oven's dry heat can quickly remove moisture from the flesh, however, so be sure to watch the time carefully.

☞ Chefs advise baking fish on the top rack of the oven, as the heat there is generally more even than on racks lower down.

☞ While fatty fish like salmon can easily withstand the oven's dry heat, leaner cuts like sole may require a brushing with a flavored liquid, like broth, to keep them from drying out.

Broiling

As with baking, broiling cooks fish quickly and evenly. Also like baking, the dry heat will quickly dry out your catch if you're not careful, so keep an eye on the time.

SEAFOOD COOKING TIMES

When cooking seafood, the time between "just right" and "whoops" is measured in minutes—or less. Here are some approximate cooking times for a variety of finny fare. Actual times may vary, depending on the thickness and freshness of the fish, the cookware being used and the type of microwave or steamer.

SEAFOOD	MICROWAVE TIME (MIN.)	STEAMING TIME (MIN.)
Fish fillet, ¾"–1" thick	4–6	4–5
Fish fillet, 1" thick	4–7	7–8
Fish steak	4–7	7–9
Whole fish	4–5 per inch of thickness	10 per inch of thickness
Shrimp, medium, shelled	3–5	2
Clams, 1 pound, in the shell	3–5, or until shells open	5–10, or until shells open
Mussels, 1 pound, in the shell	2–4, or until shells open	5–10, or until shells open
Scallops, 1 pound	5–8 on medium-high power	4–6
Lobster tails, 2, in the shell	7–11 on medium power, until bright red	10–12, wrapped in parchment paper

COOKING WITH PARCHMENT

Cooking fish allows little latitude for mistakes. When fish overcooks by even a minute, the flesh starts getting dry and tough. Cooking in parchment, however, locks in moisture, making it easy to have great fish every time.

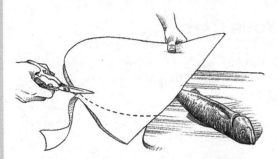

Cut a piece of parchment about four times the size of the fish. Fold the paper in half, then cut out a large heart-shaped piece.

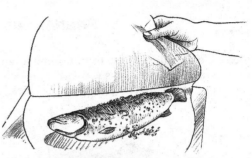

Place the fish on one half of the heart. Add any herbs, seasonings or vegetables that the recipe calls for. Fold the parchment over to cover the fish.

Starting at the top of the heart—at the crease—begin making a series of small double folds all the way around. Make sure that you overlap them as you go to seal the package tightly.

When you get to the tip of the heart, fold the paper several times to keep it tightly closed.

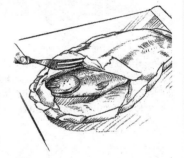

After baking, cut the browned parchment and carefully lift the fish out. Serve immediately.

☞ To prevent the intense overhead heat of broiling from drying the fish, baste it with chicken or vegetable broth or with a little lemon juice added to water. Chefs advise basting once at the beginning of cooking and again halfway through.

☞ Delicate seafood like sole and crabmeat are best broiled 4″ to 6″ from the heat.

☞ Fatty fish like bluefish and salmon are essentially self-basting. To prevent them from burning or drying, however, they should be cooked about 4″ from the heat.

Grilling

For making great seafood every time, it's hard to beat the outdoor grill. Grills generate very hot, intense heat that is ideal for searing fish and locking in moisture. And unlike cooking in the oven, where hot spots form directly over (or under) the gas jets or electric elements, the cooking area on the grill is potentially as large as the grate itself. You can cook two fillets or a dozen, and they'll all be done at the same time.

PREPARING YOUR CATCH

The only thing worse than finding a bone in your fish is not finding it—until it's too late. And chewing scales is no pleasure either. Here's how to scale and bone fish so that you don't have unpleasant surprises later.

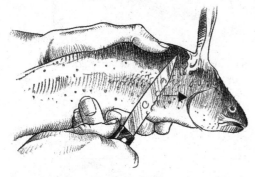

Using the back edge of a knife, scrape away the scales, moving forward from the tail to the head. (Hold the fish under water while you work will prevent the scales from scattering.)

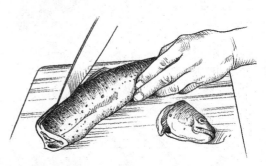

With the fish on a cutting board, remove the head and make a ½"-deep cut from nape to tail along the back, next to the dorsal fin. Flip the fish over and make an identical cut on the other side.

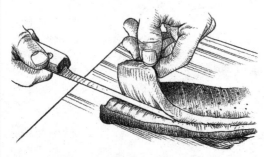

Using a fillet knife, remove the meat from each side of the fish, peeling back the flesh as you go. To avoid leaving too much flesh on the bones, scrape the knife against the bones as you work. (Save the bones to make fish stock.)

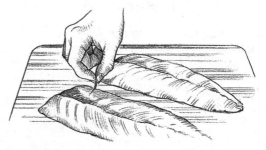

Lay the fillet flat, skin side down, and feel for the pinbones along the edge. You can pull them out one at a time. (Clean tweezers or needle-nose pliers reserved for cooking work great.) Or you can cut out the entire row by removing a thin strip of flesh the entire length of the fillet.

HELP FOR CHOKING

A fish bone caught in your throat can cause choking or even damage to your throat or esophagus.

If you accidentally swallow a fish bone, experts say, the traditional advice is still the best: Immediately chew and swallow a small piece of bread, followed by plenty of water. This can help dislodge the bone and move it out of harm's way. If the choking or discomfort continues, see a doctor right away.

While many cooks "grill" fish by wrapping it in foil and laying it on the heat, this technique is really more like steaming. It won't impart the delicate smoky taste that makes grilled fish superb.

☞ Marinating fish for an hour before cooking will help keep the flesh moist and tender.

☞ A grill's intense heat can quickly dry fish, so you'll want to baste it several times during cooking.

☞ To prevent fish from falling through the grate, lay it on a rectangular quarry tile that has been coated with a spray of vegetable oil or no-stick spray. This will allow the fish to gently cook while the aromas of hardwood or charcoal swirl around it.

☞ One of the easiest ways to grill fish is with a grilling basket, which sandwiches the fish between wire meshes. The basket makes it easy to turn fish during cooking and helps prevent it from falling apart—and into the fire.

Poaching

The moist, steamy heat of poaching is the most gentle and delicate method for cooking fish and is perfect for fillets, steaks and whole or pan-dressed fish.

If you cook fish often, you may want to invest in a poacher—an elongated pot with a lowering platform and lid. Or you can use a soup pot or deep roasting pan with a wire rack on the bottom.

☞ When poaching, always keep the liquid at a simmer; the vigorous action of boiling will literally tear a fish apart.

☞ A rule of thumb is to poach fish for approximately 10 minutes for every inch of thickness.

☞ A skimmer can be used to lower the fish into the liquid and to lift it out when it's done.

Steaming

Cooking fish with moist heat virtually guarantees that it will be moist and tender. Steaming is particularly recommended for lean fish like sole and flounder, which may get tough with other forms of cooking.

☞ Since steaming provides its own moisture, there's no need to add butter, oil or other forms of fatty protection to the cooking fish.

☞ Steam is extremely hot and cooks food quickly, so check the fish often.

☞ A wok makes an excellent steamer. Pour in a cup of water with aromatic herbs and spices. Place the fish on a metal or bamboo steaming rack above the liquid. Cover and cook.

Sautéing

When you're cooking for one, or when you're preparing a small fillet that needs simple treatment, a sauté pan may be all that you need. Cooking on the stove top is fast and easy. And for small, delicate fillets that dry out easily, sautéing is more gentle than oven cooking. Plus, you don't have to heat the entire oven—no small favor in the warm months.

☞ Sautéing in a no-stick skillet allows you to enjoy the speed and convenience of stove-top cooking without the addition of large amounts of fat.

☞ Chefs have traditionally sautéed fish in butter, but they are increasingly turning to

POACHING BASICS

Poaching is the gentlest method for cooking fish and is perfect for fillets, steaks and whole or pan-dressed fish. Best of all, it's among the healthiest of all cooking techniques, requiring little or no added fat.

Fish Poaching Liquid

   2   quarts water
   ¼   cup white-wine vinegar
   3   bay leaves
  12   sprigs fresh parsley
  12   peppercorns
   1   teaspoon mustard seeds
   6   slices lemon

In a large pot, combine the water, vinegar, bay leaves, parsley, peppercorns, mustard seeds and lemon slices. Bring to a boil over high heat. Reduce the heat to medium, cover and simmer for 15 minutes. If not using immediately, remove from the heat and let stand for 15 minutes. Strain and reserve the liquid for poaching fish.

Provides enough liquid to poach about 4 whole 8-ounce fish.

Prepare the poaching liquid by putting fresh herbs or seasonings in enough water to cover the fish. (See the accompanying recipe for an idea of ingredients and amounts.) Simmer for 15 minutes.

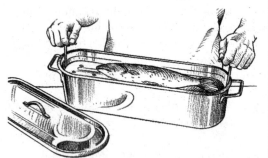

Using an insert rack or skimmer, lower the fish into the liquid. Make sure that it's completely submerged. When the fish is done—plan on cooking about 10 minutes for every inch of thickness—remove it from the liquid with the skimmer.

olive oil. The advantage of olive oil is that it imparts a more delicate flavor and is lower in saturated fat.

☞ To add extra flavor, splash a little broth or citrus juice into the sauté pan during cooking.

☞ To avoid breaking the fish during turning, cook it for one-third of the recommended time on one side. Then flip it and cook it for the remaining time.

Stews and Chowders

Fish stews and chowders are a delicious way to put seafood on the menu. It's important, however, not to add fish or shellfish at the beginning of the cooking time. Otherwise, they'll be overdone and fall apart.

☞ Cook all the other ingredients in the liquid until they are tender. Then add raw boneless fish pieces or shelled shellfish.

STEAMING FISH

Steaming is one of the best low-fat cooking methods for fish. The moist heat of the steaming liquid both tenderizes the food and flavors it. You can create a wide variety of steaming liquids to impart different flavors to the food. The techniques used in this steamed sole recipe work equally well with other types of fish.

Steamed Sole with Creamy Dill Sauce *QUICK!*

Dill Sauce

- ¼ cup 1% low-fat cottage cheese
- ¼ cup nonfat plain yogurt
- 2 teaspoons Dijon mustard
- 1 teaspoon lemon juice
- 1 teaspoon minced shallots
- ⅛ teaspoon reduced-sodium soy sauce (optional)
- 1 tablespoon minced fresh dill

Sole

- 4 sole fillets (4 ounces each)
- 1 sweet red pepper, thinly sliced
- 1 stalk celery, thinly sliced on the diagonal
- 1 carrot, halved lengthwise and thinly sliced on the diagonal
- ¾ cup green beans split lengthwise and halved
- 1 tablespoon lemon juice
- 2 teaspoons olive oil
- 2 teaspoons minced fresh dill
- 1 teaspoon minced onions
- ⅛ teaspoon reduced-sodium soy sauce

To make the dill sauce: In a food processor or blender, process the cottage cheese, yogurt, mustard, lemon juice, shallots and soy sauce until smooth. Transfer to a small bowl and stir in the dill. Cover and refrigerate until serving time.

To make the sole: Bring about 1" of water to a boil in a large saucepan. Place the sole in a steamer basket and add to the saucepan. Cover and steam for 3 to 4 minutes.

Add the peppers, celery, carrots and beans to the steamer basket. Cover and steam for 3 to 5 minutes, or until the vegetables are tender. Remove from the heat and set aside.

In a large bowl, combine the lemon juice, oil, dill, onions and soy sauce. Using a spoon or metal spatula, transfer the cooked vegetables to the bowl. Toss to coat well.

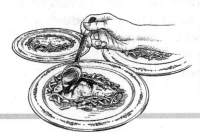

Divide the vegetables among 4 dinner plates, forming them into nests. Place a piece of fish in each nest. Top each piece with dill sauce.

Makes 4 servings. Per serving: 183 calories, 4.2 g. fat (21% of calories), 25.7 g. protein, 10.7 g. carbohydrates, 2.1 g. dietary fiber, 61 mg. cholesterol, 216 mg. sodium

☞ Immediately stir and remove from the heat. Allow the soup to steep for 5 to 10 minutes, then serve.

Pan Smoking

While smoking fish to preserve it for long periods is a complicated process, it's easy to hot-smoke fish to impart a savory, smoky taste to your evening's meal.

☞ Spread 2 to 4 tablespoons hardwood sawdust or chips (such as mesquite, hickory, maple or apple) in the bottom of a wok.

☞ Lay the fish on a steaming rack and place it in the wok. Cover the wok with a dome lid. Heat over high heat for 1 minute, then reduce the heat to medium-high and smoke for 10 to 15 minutes. Do not lift the lid. Turn off the heat and let the wok stand for 10 more minutes to allow the smoke to subside.

☞ Hot-smoked fish can be served warm or hot. Or it can be chilled and served with a savory sauce.

Microwaving

This is perhaps the simplest method for turning out healthful, perfectly cooked seafood with no added fat.

☞ Arrange the seafood in a single layer around the edges of a dish. (Microwave ovens typically cook fastest around the edges.) Brush the fish with broth, water or juice and cover.

☞ Cook finfish like cod or salmon on high power for 3½ to 7 minutes, depending on the thickness of the cut. Cook shelled scallops and shrimp on medium power for 4 to 6 minutes per pound.

☞ If your microwave isn't equipped with a carousel, rotate the dish several times during cooking to help the fish cook evenly.

☞ Do not overcook your fish or shellfish. As with other items, seafood continues cooking for a few minutes after being removed from the microwave. As a rule, let the fish stand, covered, for 2 to 5 minutes after cooking before serving.

TESTING FOR DONENESS

Fish needs to be cooked just right to achieve perfect taste and texture. Chefs have devised a number of strategies for telling, almost to the second, when to remove fish from the heat.

Test with your fingers. As fish cooks, it gradually becomes firmer. To educate your fingers, press on the thickest part of the fish before you cook it. Then press again when you're sure that it's done. Once you know how a cooked fish is supposed to feel, you'll be able to trust your fingers in the future.

Check the color. Fish that is properly cooked is generally an opaque white or light gray; salmon, with its pink-orange color, is an exception. To check the color during cooking, slip the tip of a knife into the thickest part of the flesh. If the center flesh is still dark and translucent, continue cooking for a few more minutes. Then check again.

SHELLFISH

Shellfish fall into two categories: Mollusks include clams, oysters, mussels, scallops, conch, squid and octopus. Crustaceans include shrimp, crayfish, crab and lobster.

When buying shellfish, take advantage of your fishmonger's expertise and ask for cooking tips before leaving the store. In addition, here are some guidelines for getting started.

Helpful Hint

To purge sand from clams, give them a quick rinse, then soak them for about 3 hours in water to which you've added a handful of cornmeal. Rinse the clams well, then cook as directed.

Shellfish

Is It Good for You?

For years, healthy cooks were nervous about using shellfish. They worried that various crustaceans and mollusks, such as shrimp, squid, crab, oysters and lobster, were too high in cholesterol to be included in a healthful diet.

Researchers now agree that a diet including shellfish is unlikely to raise cholesterol levels by any significant extent. Since shellfish contain virtually no saturated fat, they're a better dietary choice, from the heart's point of view, than even the leanest red meats.

What's more, improvements in testing methods show that shellfish contain less cholesterol than previously thought. One caveat, though: Preparing these goodies with extra fat, such as butter, negates their health advantage.

Find them fresh. Shellfish deteriorate extremely quickly, so it's critical to find a merchant who stocks them live. An exception may be made for shrimp, which freeze well and are rarely found fresh in any event.

Check the shells. Before buying clams, mussels or oysters, make sure that the shells are closed tightly. When they're beyond freshness, the shells will gape open. If a few shells are just slightly open, tap them with your finger. They should snap shut.

Test for mudders. Occasionally, a batch of

PREPARING LOBSTER

With its armored appearance, lobster can be a daunting treat. Here's how to get to the meat.

Placed the cooked lobster, back side down, on the cutting board. Use a sharp knife to cut the body in half lengthwise.

Cut away the membrane on the underside of the tail to expose the meat. If it suits your taste, spoon up the tomalley (liver) and, in females, the coral-colored roe.

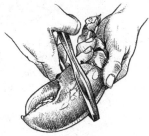

Twist the claws away from the body. Use a nutcracker to break the shell.

FRESH FROM THE DEEP

Few shellfish are as easy to prepare as shrimp. Once you get past the hard armorlike shell, all you have to do is devein and butterfly the shrimp to reveal the wonderfully tender white flesh inside.

SHELL GAMES

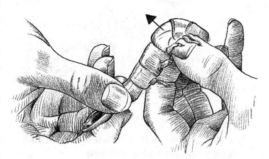

Holding the shrimp by the tail, grab the legs and peel the shell up and over with your thumb.

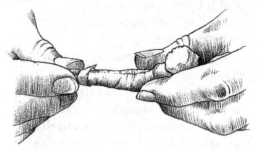

To remove the tail, hold the shrimp meat with one hand and pull straight back on the tail.

BUTTERFLYING SHRIMP

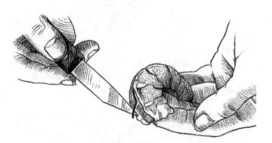

Start by deveining the shrimp. Take a peeled shrimp and use a sharp knife to carefully make a shallow slit along the back, just deep enough to expose the vein. With the tip of the knife, pry up and pull out the vein.

To butterfly the shrimp, extend the cut a little deeper so that you can spread the sides and flatten the shrimp. Be careful not to cut all the way through.

PREPARING SQUID

Squid (also known as calamari) has a sweet taste and attractive snow-white, boneless flesh. To prepare it for the pan, here's what you need to do.

Rinse well and firmly pull the head and innards from the body. Discard.

Cut away the edible tentacles and set aside.

Carefully squeeze the transparent backbone out of the body. With your finger, clean out any remaining membrane and rinse the body well.

Slice the body into rings. Cook very quickly (or slow-simmer until tender). Overcooking squid will cause it to turn rubbery.

mussels will harbor a mudder—a closed shell packed with dark, inklike mud that can ruin an entire recipe. To root out mudders, simply twist the two shells of every mussel in opposite directions. Mud mussels will open at the slightest pressure.

Cook them quickly but gently. Clams and mussels in the shell don't take long to cook—about 10 minutes is usually enough. You'll know that they're done when the shells gape open. Shelled oysters cook more quickly, usually in about 5 to 6 minutes; when the edges start curling, they're about done. Shrimp, whether shelled or not, cook in about 3 minutes.

☞ Just before cooking unshelled mussels, remove the beards (the dark threads protruding from the shell). Either snip them off or pull them.

☞ Scrub the shells of clams, mussels and oysters with a stiff brush and cold water.

☞ Raw shrimp are easier to peel than cooked ones.

☞ No matter what type of shellfish you're preparing, use gentle heat and don't overcook them, or they'll get tough.

Don't delay. Once you get shellfish home, it's important to eat it quickly, preferably within 24 hours.

Thaw them well. Frozen shrimp can be thawed in the refrigerator 5 to 8 hours before cooking. Or you can thaw them quickly in a colander held under cold running water.

Plan ahead. Shrimp continue cooking even after being removed from the heat. To keep them from turning tough and rubbery, always undercook them slightly.

Jimmy Sneed

*L*ocal products and straightforward preparations are what Jimmy Sneed is known for at his Richmond, Virginia, restaurant, The Frog and the Redneck. He takes pride in using only the freshest fish available. His recipes are simple and uncluttered, so it's critical that the natural flavors of the fish come through loud and clear.

One of his favorite dishes is baked rockfish in a mussel-and-tomato broth. (On the East Coast, rockfish is also called striped bass.)

"My chef, Dale, and I created this recipe in an effort to have a dish that was rich-tasting without using butter and cream," he says.

When shopping, ask your fishmonger for farm-raised mussels, which contain less grit and are easier to clean than the wild variety. If rockfish is unavailable, substitute snapper or grouper. For this recipe, use a large sweet onion such as a Vidalia or Walla Walla.

Baked Rockfish with Mussels

1   large sweet onion, thickly sliced
    Salt
    Ground black pepper
¾   cup dry white wine or nonalcoholic white wine
½   cup sliced shallots
    24 mussels, scrubbed and beards removed
½   cup diced tomatoes
1   tablespoon chopped fresh basil
2   teaspoons minced garlic
4   rockfish fillets (8 ounces each)
1   tablespoon extra-virgin olive oil

Place the onions in a medium saucepan and cover with cold water. Bring to a boil over high heat. Cover, reduce the heat to medium and simmer for 30 minutes, or until soft. Drain, reserving the liquid. Process the onions in a food processor or blender, adding only enough of the liquid to make a thick puree.

Discard the remaining liquid. Season lightly with the salt and pepper.

Place the wine and shallots in a large pot. Bring to a boil over high heat. Add the mussels, cover and cook, shaking the pot from time to time, for 5 minutes, or until the mussels open.

Remove the mussels and strain the liquid into a medium saucepan; discard the shallots. Remove the mussels from the shells and add them to the saucepan. Add the tomatoes, basil and garlic. Bring to a boil over medium heat and simmer for 2 minutes.

Preheat the oven to 350°. Season the rockfish lightly with salt and pepper. Brush with the oil and place in a single layer in a no-stick baking dish. Bake for 8 to 10 minutes, or until the fillets just begin to flake when tested with a fork.

To serve, divide the onion puree among 4 shallow bowls. Top with the rockfish, then with the mussels and broth.

Makes 4 servings. Per serving: 384 calories, 9 g. fat (22% of calories), 54 g. protein, 12.1 g. carbohydrates, 1 g. dietary fiber, 102 mg. cholesterol, 388 mg. sodium

Blackened Catfish

- 1 cup quick-cooking white or brown rice
- 2 cups water
- 1 medium tomato, diced
- ¼ cup minced scallions
- ¼ teaspoon salt
  Pinch of dried thyme
- 4 catfish fillets (4 ounces each and ½" thick)
- 2 tablespoons Cajun Spice (page 33)

In a medium saucepan, combine the rice, water, tomatoes, scallions, salt and thyme. Bring to a boil. Cover, reduce the heat to low and cook for about 10 minutes, or until the rice is tender and the liquid is absorbed.

Meanwhile, heat a large cast-iron skillet on high heat for about 8 minutes, or until it is very hot (see note).

Coat the catfish with no-stick spray. Rub in the Cajun Spice, coating each piece well. Place the catfish in the skillet and cook for about 2 minutes per side, or until the fish is opaque and flakes easily when tested with a fork. Serve over the rice.

Makes 4 servings. Per serving: 236 calories, 7.5 g. fat (29% of calories), 19.2 g. protein, 21.6 g. carbohydrates, 0.9 g. dietary fiber, 58 mg. cholesterol, 487 mg. sodium

NOTE

• The blackening process creates some smoke, so use an exhaust fan or cook the fish outdoors on a very hot grill. Be careful when handling the skillet after cooking, because it will take considerable time to cool down.

VARIATION

Oven-Blackened Catfish: Bake the seasoned catfish at 400° for about 20 minutes, or until the fish is opaque and flakes easily when tested with a fork. Serve with hot cooked orzo pasta.

Skinny Shrimp Scampi

- 1 cup quick-cooking brown rice
- 1 pound extra-large shrimp (26 to 30 shrimp per pound), peeled and deveined, tails attached
- 1 tablespoon olive oil
- 8 slices lemon
- 8 scallions, trimmed and cut into ½" pieces
- 4 cloves garlic, minced
- ½ cup freshly squeezed orange juice
- ½ cup minced fresh parsley
- ¼ teaspoon ground black pepper

Cook the rice according to the package directions. Set aside and keep warm.

Meanwhile, cut a 1" lengthwise slit in each shrimp, starting at the head; set aside.

In a large no-stick skillet over medium-high heat, warm the oil for 1 minute. Add the lemon slices and scallions and sauté for 3 minutes. Add the garlic and cook for 1 minute. Transfer the mixture to a small bowl; set aside.

Add the shrimp to the skillet and cook for 2 to 3 minutes, or until they start to turn opaque. Add the orange juice, parsley and pepper and bring to a boil. Return the lemon mixture to the skillet and cook for 2 minutes. Serve hot over the rice.

Makes 4 servings. Per serving: 318 calories, 5.9 g. fat (17% of calories), 23.4 g. protein, 43.3 g. carbohydrates, 3.4 g. dietary fiber, 175 mg. cholesterol, 207 mg. sodium

VARIATION

Sea-Scallop Scampi: Replace the shrimp with sea scallops.

QUICK!
Shrimp-and-Vegetable Stir-Fry

1 small head bok choy
¾ cup fish stock or defatted chicken broth
1 tablespoon reduced-sodium soy sauce
1 teaspoon toasted sesame oil
12 ounces large shrimp (23 to 30 shrimp), peeled, deveined and tails removed
1 clove garlic, minced
1 cup baby carrots, halved lengthwise
4 scallions, trimmed and sliced on the diagonal into 1" pieces
1 sweet red pepper, cut into strips
½ cup canned sliced water chestnuts, drained
8 ears canned baby corn
2 teaspoons cornstarch
3 cups hot cooked brown rice

Trim and discard the root end of the bok choy. Cut off and discard most of the green leaves. Cut into diagonal slices and set aside.

In a measuring cup, combine the stock or broth, soy sauce and oil. Stir to blend thoroughly.

Heat a dry wok or large no-stick skillet over high heat for 5 minutes. Add 2 tablespoons of the broth mixture and heat for 1 minute. Add the shrimp and stir-fry briskly for 30 seconds. Cover and cook for 2 minutes, or until the shrimp start to turn opaque. Transfer the shrimp and pan juices to a bowl and set aside.

Return the wok or skillet to high heat for 1 minute. Add 2 tablespoons of the broth mixture. Add the garlic and cook for 30 seconds.

Add the bok choy, carrots, scallions and peppers. Stir-fry for 3 minutes, or until the vegetables are just crisp-tender. Add the water chestnuts and corn and stir-fry for 30 seconds. Add the reserved shrimp and pan juices.

Combine the cornstarch with the remaining ½ cup of the broth mixture and mix well. Add to the wok or skillet and stir-fry to coat all of the ingredients. Cover and cook, stirring once, for 3 minutes, or until thick. Serve immediately with the rice.

Makes 4 servings. Per serving: 319 calories, 3.7 g. fat (10% of calories), 22.6 g. protein, 50 g. carbohydrates, 5.5 g. dietary fiber, 131 mg. cholesterol, 469 mg. sodium

VARIATION
Scallop-and-Vegetable Stir-Fry: Replace the shrimp with sea scallops.

QUICK!
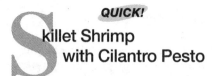
Skillet Shrimp with Cilantro Pesto

Cilantro Pesto
1 cup packed fresh cilantro leaves
2 tablespoons fish stock or defatted chicken broth
1 tablespoon olive oil
1 teaspoon minced garlic
½ teaspoon lemon juice
¼ teaspoon hot-pepper sauce

Shrimp
1 teaspoon olive oil
2 small zucchini, thinly sliced
1 carrot, thinly sliced
1 pound extra-large shrimp (26 to 30 shrimp per pound), peeled, deveined and tails removed
2 tablespoons fish stock or defatted chicken broth
1 teaspoon lemon juice
½ teaspoon grated lemon rind
½ teaspoon minced garlic

To make the cilantro pesto: In a food processor or blender, combine the cilantro, stock or broth, oil, garlic, lemon juice and hot-pepper sauce. Process until smooth and set aside.

To make the shrimp: In a large no-stick skillet over medium heat, warm the oil. Stir in the zucchini and carrots. Cover and cook, stirring occasionally, for 5 to 6 minutes, or until the vegetables begin to soften. Uncover and cook, stirring occasionally, for 4 to 5 minutes, or until the carrots are cooked. Transfer to a platter and set aside.

Increase the heat to medium-high. Add the shrimp and cook for about 1 minute per side. Add the stock or broth, lemon juice, lemon rind, garlic and reserved zucchini and carrots. Cook for 1 minute, or until the shrimp are cooked through. Serve with the pesto.

Makes 4 servings. Per serving: 166 calories, 5.8 g. fat (32% of calories), 20.7 g. protein, 5.5 g. carbohydrates, 1.1 g. dietary fiber, 176 mg. cholesterol, 217 mg. sodium

NOTES

• The shrimp tastes great served over cooked spaghettini, angel hair or any other long, thin cooked pasta. Toss the pasta with the cilantro pesto and 1 to 2 tablespoons of reserved pasta cooking water.

• To vary the flavor, replace the cilantro with fresh basil or fresh tarragon leaves.

Crab Cakes

These moist and tender crab cakes have just 4 grams of fat per serving. Enjoy them with a side dish of rice to reduce the meal's total percentage of calories from fat.

8	ounces lump or backfin crabmeat, flaked
1	cup fresh white or whole-wheat bread crumbs
1	tablespoon minced onion
1	tablespoon minced celery
1	tablespoon minced sweet red pepper
1	tablespoon minced fresh parsley
1	egg, lightly beaten

1	egg white, lightly beaten
2	teaspoons reduced-sodium Worcestershire sauce
1	teaspoon lemon juice
½	teaspoon hot-pepper sauce
⅛	teaspoon ground black pepper
2	teaspoons canola oil

In a medium bowl, combine the crabmeat, bread crumbs, onions, celery, red peppers, parsley, egg, egg white, Worcestershire sauce, lemon juice, hot-pepper sauce and black pepper. Cover and refrigerate for 30 minutes to make handling easier.

Shape the crab mixture into 4 cakes.

In a large no-stick skillet over medium-high heat, warm the oil. Add the crab cakes and cook for 5 to 7 minutes per side, or until golden.

Makes 4 servings. Per serving: 87 calories, 4.1 g. fat (43% of calories), 5.3 g. protein, 6.9 g. carbohydrates, 0.5 g. dietary fiber, 62 mg. cholesterol, 134 mg. sodium

NOTE

• Mustard mayonnaise makes an excellent topping for these crab cakes. Combine 2½ teaspoons Dijon mustard with ¼ cup fat-free mayonnaise.

VARIATION

Fish Cakes: Replace the crab with cooked and flaked catfish, cod, haddock or salmon. Or you may used canned (water-packed) chunk white tuna, drained and flaked.

Fish and Chips with Tartar Salsa

QUICK!

Fish and Chips

- 12 whole-grain unsalted melba toasts, broken into chunks
- 1 cup fat-free egg substitute
- 1½ pounds skinless catfish fillets, cut into 8 thick sticks
- 1 teaspoon salt-free lemon-pepper seasoning
- 2 large baking potatoes, peeled and cut lengthwise into ½"-thick sticks

Tartar Salsa

- ⅓ cup mild thick-and-chunky salsa
- ⅓ cup fat-free mayonnaise
- 1 tablespoon lemon juice

To make the fish and chips: Preheat the oven to 450°. Coat a no-stick baking sheet with no-stick spray and set aside.

Place the melba toasts in a food processor or blender and process with on/off turns to make fine crumbs. Transfer to a shallow bowl and set aside.

Pour the egg substitute into another shallow bowl. Dip the catfish into the egg substitute to coat completely, then dip in the crumbs, pressing to coat evenly on all sides. Place the catfish in a single layer on half of the prepared baking sheet, leaving space between them.

Add the lemon-pepper seasoning to the remaining egg substitute in the bowl. Add the potatoes and toss gently to coat.

Place the potatoes in a single layer on the other half of the baking sheet, leaving space between them.

Bake on the top oven rack for 20 minutes, or until the potatoes are tender and the catfish is opaque and flakes easily when tested with a fork.

To make the tartar salsa: In a small bowl, combine the salsa, mayonnaise and lemon juice and mix well. Serve with the hot fish and chips.

Makes 4 servings. Per serving: 375 calories, 11 g. fat (27% of calories), 35.4 g. protein, 31.9 g. carbohydrates, 3.2 g. dietary fiber, 87 mg. cholesterol, 654 mg. sodium

NOTE
• You can replace the catfish with cod or haddock.

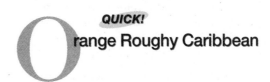

Orange Roughy Caribbean

QUICK!

- 1 cup fish stock or defatted chicken broth
- 1 yellow pepper, cut into thin strips
- 8 scallions, sliced on the diagonal into 1" pieces
- 4 slices lime
- 1 tablespoon minced fresh cilantro
- ¼ teaspoon curry powder
- 4 skinless orange roughy fillets (4 ounces each and ½" thick)
- 4 cups hot cooked rice

In a large no-stick skillet, combine the stock or broth, peppers, scallions, lime, cilantro and curry powder. Cover and bring to a boil.

Carefully add the orange roughy. Reduce the heat to medium-low, cover and gently simmer for 5 to 6 minutes, or until the orange roughy is opaque and flakes easily when tested with a fork. Discard the lime.

Serve with the rice and top with the pepper-and-scallion sauce.

Makes 4 servings. Per serving: 305 calories, 1.4 g. fat (4% of calories), 22.3 g. protein, 49.2 g. carbohydrates, 0.3 g. dietary fiber, 22 mg. cholesterol, 156 mg. sodium

NOTE
• You can replace the yellow pepper with a sweet red, orange or green pepper, or a colorful combination.

All-American Bouillabaisse

1 tablespoon olive oil
1 cup sliced carrots
1½ cups sliced celery
1 cup sliced onion
1 large leek (white part only), thinly sliced
1 pound plum tomatoes, peeled, seeded and chopped
1 large clove garlic, minced
¼ teaspoon saffron threads
2 quarts fish stock or defatted chicken broth
2 bay leaves
1 teaspoon crushed fennel seeds
½ teaspoon dried thyme
⅛ teaspoon ground black pepper
1 strip orange rind, 2″ long
1¼ pounds ocean perch or red snapper
¾ pound bay scallops
12 medium-large shrimp, peeled, deveined and tails removed
12 whole crawfish
2 tablespoons minced fresh parsley

In a large saucepan over medium-high heat, warm the oil for 30 seconds. Add the carrots, celery, onions and leeks and sauté for 5 minutes. Add the tomatoes, garlic and saffron and sauté for 5 minutes.

Add the stock or broth, bay leaves, fennel seeds, thyme, pepper and orange rind. Bring to a boil. Reduce the heat to low, cover and simmer for 30 minutes.

Add the ocean perch or snapper, scallops, shrimp, crawfish and parsley. Cover and simmer for 5 to 7 minutes, or until the fish is opaque and flakes easily when tested with a fork. Discard the bay leaves and orange rind before serving.

Makes 6 servings. Per serving: 258 calories, 5.5 g. fat (19% of calories), 36.8 g. protein, 15.5 g. carbohydrates, 3 g. dietary fiber, 137 mg. cholesterol, 338 mg. sodium

NOTES
• You can replace the crawfish with medium shrimp.
• Serve with a loaf of hot crusty bread to dip in the broth.

Roast Swordfish with Herbed Crust

4 swordfish steaks (5 ounces each)
1 tablespoon lemon juice
⅓ cup fine unseasoned dry bread crumbs
1½ teaspoons dried Italian herb seasoning
1 tablespoon minced fresh parsley
½ teaspoon salt
¼ teaspoon ground black pepper

Preheat the oven to 400°. Coat a 9″ × 13″ no-stick baking dish with no-stick spray and set aside.

Sprinkle the swordfish with the lemon juice and set aside for 10 minutes.

In a shallow bowl, combine the bread crumbs, Italian seasoning, parsley, salt and pepper. Dip the swordfish into the bread-crumb mixture and press gently to coat both sides.

Place the swordfish in a single layer in the prepared baking dish. Generously coat the surface of the fish with no-stick spray. Bake for 20 to 25 minutes, or until the swordfish is opaque and flakes easily when tested with a fork.

Makes 4 servings. Per serving: 210 calories, 6.2 g. fat (26% of calories), 29.2 g. protein, 7.2 g. carbohydrates, 0 g. dietary fiber, 56 mg. cholesterol, 474 mg. sodium

NOTE
• You can replace the swordfish with tuna, shark or mahimahi.

Poached Salmon with Horseradish-Dill Sauce

QUICK!

Poached Salmon
- 1 salmon fillet (1 pound), skin attached
- 4 cups water
- 1 lemon, thinly sliced
- 1 small leek (white part only), thinly sliced
- 1 stalk celery, thinly sliced
- 2 teaspoons peppercorns

Horseradish-Dill Sauce
- ½ cup low-fat sour cream
- ½ cup nonfat plain yogurt
- 2 scallions, minced
- 1 tablespoon prepared horseradish
- 1 tablespoon minced fresh dill

To make the poached salmon: Place the salmon in a large no-stick skillet. Add the water, lemon, leeks, celery and peppercorns. Bring to a simmer over high heat; do not boil. Reduce the heat to medium-low, cover and simmer for 10 minutes. Remove from the heat and let stand for 8 minutes.

Carefully remove the salmon from the poaching liquid and place on a layer of paper towels; gently pat dry. Discard the poaching liquid. With a pancake turner or broad knife, carefully separate the skin from the salmon; discard the skin. Cut the salmon into 4 equal portions.

To make the horseradish-dill sauce: In a small bowl, combine the sour cream, yogurt, scallions, horseradish and dill. Serve over the salmon.

Makes 4 servings. Per serving: 181 calories, 5.8 g. fat (30% of calories), 24.7 g. protein, 5.2 g. carbohydrates, 0.2 g. dietary fiber, 67 mg. cholesterol, 119 mg. sodium

NOTE
• To serve the salmon chilled, let it cool in the poaching liquid in the refrigerator.

Mustard-Glazed Salmon with Cucumber Relish

- ½ cup diced red onions
- 2 medium cucumbers, peeled, seeded and diced
- ½ cup rice-wine vinegar
- 2 teaspoons sugar
- ¼ teaspoon salt
- ⅛ teaspoon ground black pepper
- 4 salmon steaks (6 ounces each)
- 2 teaspoons olive oil
- 2 tablespoons honey mustard

Rinse the onions with cold water to remove any sharpness. Drain, then pat dry with paper towels and set aside.

In a small bowl, combine the vinegar, sugar, salt and pepper. Whisk to dissolve the salt and sugar. Stir in the onions and cucumbers. Cover and refrigerate for 1 hour.

Coat an unheated grill rack with no-stick spray. Light the grill according to the manufacturer's directions. Place the rack on the grill.

Rub the salmon with the oil. Place on the rack and grill for 4 to 5 minutes per side, or until the salmon flakes easily when tested with a fork. Remove from the grill. With the back of a spoon, spread the mustard in a thin layer over the steaks. Drain the cucumber relish and serve on the side.

Makes 4 servings. Per serving: 256 calories, 8.5 g. fat (30% of calories), 34.6 g. protein, 9.5 g. carbohydrates, 0.4 g. dietary fiber, 86 mg. cholesterol, 235 mg. sodium

NOTES
• For a hotter dish, replace the honey mustard with jalapeño honey mustard.
• You can replace the salmon with catfish, swordfish or tuna.

Flounder Florentine

QUICK!

1 package (10 ounces) frozen spinach, thawed and squeezed dry
2 shallots, minced
⅓ cup fish stock or defatted chicken broth
⅛ teaspoon ground nutmeg
1 pound skinless flounder fillets
½ cup buttermilk
½ cup fat-free egg substitute
⅛ teaspoon hot-pepper sauce
2 tablespoons grated Romano cheese

In a medium saucepan over medium heat, combine the spinach shallots, stock or broth and nutmeg. Stir, then cover and cook for 5 minutes, stirring once more.

Coat a medium ovenproof no-stick skillet or large pie plate with no-stick spray. Spread the spinach mixture in an even layer in the skillet or pie plate. Place the flounder on top of the spinach in a single layer.

In a small bowl, combine the buttermilk, egg substitute and hot-pepper sauce and mix well. Spoon evenly over the flounder. Sprinkle with the Romano.

Preheat the broiler. Broil 8″ from the heat for 15 minutes, or until the sauce is evenly browned and the flounder is opaque and flakes easily when tested with a fork. Remove from the heat and let stand for 5 minutes. Cut into portions with a spatula and serve hot.

Makes 4 servings. Per serving: 161 calories, 2.7 g. fat (15% of calories), 28.1 g. protein, 5.6 g. carbohydrates, 0 g. dietary fiber, 65 mg. cholesterol, 289 mg. sodium

NOTE
• You can replace the flounder with scrod, sole or orange roughy.

Teriyaki Tuna

¼ cup reduced-sodium soy sauce
3 tablespoons dry sherry or nonalcoholic white wine
1 tablespoon toasted sesame oil
2 teaspoons packed brown sugar
¾ teaspoon ground ginger
2–3 drops hot-pepper sauce
4 tuna steaks (4 ounces each and ½″–¾″ thick)

In a shallow bowl, combine the soy sauce, sherry or wine, oil, brown sugar, ginger and hot-pepper sauce. Add the tuna and turn to coat both sides. Cover with plastic wrap and marinate in the refrigerator, turning the pieces occasionally, for at least 1 hour.

Preheat the broiler. Coat the rack of a broiling pan with no-stick spray. Remove the tuna from the marinade and place on the rack. Drizzle with a few tablespoons of the marinade.

Broil 4″ from the heat for 3 minutes. Using a wide spatula, turn the tuna and drizzle with a few more tablespoons of the marinade. Discard the remaining marinade. Broil for 2 to 5 minutes, or until the tuna is opaque and flakes easily when tested with a fork.

Makes 4 servings. Per serving: 152 calories, 2.8 g. fat (17% of calories), 26.5 g. protein, 2.3 g. carbohydrates, 0 g. dietary fiber, 49 mg. cholesterol, 306 mg. sodium

NOTES
• You can replace the tuna with swordfish or mahimahi.
• The tuna is also delicious grilled.

Grilled Sea-Scallop Kebabs

2 tablespoons barbecue sauce
1 tablespoon lemon juice
2 teaspoons olive oil
1 teaspoon reduced-sodium Worcestershire sauce
2 cloves garlic, minced
1 pound sea scallops

In a medium bowl, combine the barbecue sauce, lemon juice, oil, Worcestershire sauce and garlic. Add the scallops and stir to coat. Cover and marinate in the refrigerator for 35 to 40 minutes.

On 4 long skewers, thread the scallops, piercing them through the sides so the round parts face outward. Leave some space between them. Discard any leftover marinade.

Coat an unheated grill rack with no-stick spray. Light the grill according to the manufacturer's directions. Place the rack on the grill.

Place the kebabs on the rack and grill about 5" from the heat for 3 to 5 minutes per side, or until the scallops are opaque and cooked through.

Makes 4 servings. Per serving: 112 calories, 2.1 g. fat (17% of calories), 21.2 g. protein, 2.3 g. carbohydrates, 0 g. dietary fiber, 48 mg. cholesterol, 265 mg. sodium

NOTE

• For a main-course salad, remove the scallops from the skewers and serve them on a bed of mixed greens tossed with low-fat creamy garlic dressing.

VARIATION

Grilled Shrimp Kebabs: Replace the scallops with 1 pound large shrimp (31 to 40 shrimp per pound).

Mussels Marinara

1 tablespoon olive oil
1 medium onion, chopped
1 tablespoon chopped garlic
8 medium tomatoes, chopped
2 tablespoons lemon juice
2 cups fish stock or water
2 bay leaves
½ teaspoon dried thyme
¼ cup minced fresh parsley
2 tablespoons minced fresh basil
4 dozen mussels, scrubbed and beards removed
   Ground black pepper (optional)

In a large saucepan over medium heat, warm the oil. Add the onions and sauté for 8 to 10 minutes, or until soft. Add the garlic and sauté for 1 minute. Stir in the tomatoes, lemon juice, stock or water, bay leaves and thyme. Cover and simmer, stirring occasionally, over medium heat for 35 to 40 minutes, or until the mixture is thick and chunky. (If you prefer a less chunky sauce, mash some of the tomatoes with the back of a wooden spoon.) Stir in the parsley and basil.

Add the mussels and cook for about 3 to 5 minutes, or until the shells open. Discard the bay leaves and any unopened mussels. Serve immediately. Season to taste with the pepper (if using).

Makes 4 servings. Per serving: 185 calories, 6.2 g. fat (30% of calories), 15.2 g. protein, 19.6 g. carbohydrates, 3.8 g. dietary fiber, 48 mg. cholesterol, 269 mg. sodium

NOTE

• This dish is wonderful served over hot cooked pasta with French or Italian bread on the side to soak up the tomato sauce.

Meats

Although meat has gotten a lot of bad press, you don't have to give it up entirely in order to be a healthy cook. Meats such as beef, pork and lamb are wonderful sources of vitamins, minerals and protein. Meat also delivers a variety of satisfying tastes and textures, whether you're preparing lean hamburger, grilled steak or lamb stew.

While red meat often looms large in our daily diets, moderation is the only way to keep saturated fat under control. Health experts advise eating no more than 6 to 9 ounces of protein a day. This includes not only meat but also fish, poultry and eggs. In addition, you should always buy the leanest cuts of meat that you can find. Good health begins not at the table but in your shopping cart. Here's what to look for.

Good Buys

Consumers have begun demanding healthier, leaner meats, and producers have responded. Some cuts of beef, for example, are up to 27 percent leaner than they were in the 1970s.

In addition, butchers now routinely trim away much of the excess fat before the meat even goes on display.

To get the leanest, freshest meat available, here's what you need to do.

Watch out for marbling. When you look at a piece of beef, lamb or pork and see lots of marbling—streaks of white fat running through it—

pass it by. Marbled meats are the most tender, but they're also the fattiest.

Check the grade. All meat is graded by government inspectors. The different grades indicate the degree of marbling present.

☞ **Prime.** The most expensive, tender and flavorful meat, prime has the highest amount of fat.

☞ **Choice.** Not quite as tender as prime, choice meat is what you usually see in the supermarket. It can be quite fatty, although less so than prime.

☞ **Select.** The leanest, least tender meat, select is often packaged as a store or economy brand. For the healthy cook, select is often the best choice, although it may require a slower cooking process to make it tender.

Look for name cuts. Anything that has "loin" or "round" in the name is going to be a fairly lean meat. Good choices include eye of round, top round, tip round, top sirloin, top loin and tenderloin.

☞ Labels like "lean ground beef" or "extra-lean ground beef" can mean anything that the supermarket wants them to. Look for packages with a percent figure on the label, such as 92 percent lean.

Buy it whole. While it's often convenient (and inexpensive) to use prepackaged stew meat, in many cases the pieces aren't well-trimmed and are high in fat. An easy alternative is to buy a larger piece, then trim and cube it

BEST CUTS

In today's super-size markets, there may be scores of packages of meat to choose from. Some cuts of meat are quite low in fat, whereas others are unacceptably high. In the chart below, you'll find some of the leanest cuts—although some, like the pork center rib roast, have a fair amount of fat. All the figures are for 3 ounces of cooked lean meat with no bone or fat.

MEAT	NUTRIENT INFORMATION	MEAT	NUTRIENT INFORMATION
BEEF		**PORK**	
Top round steak 	4.2 g. fat 25% cal. from fat 71 mg. cholesterol	Tenderloin	4.1 g. fat 26% cal. from fat 79 mg. cholesterol
Eye of round roast 	4.2 g. fat 26% cal. from fat 59 mg. cholesterol	Ham, cured	6.5 g. fat 42% cal. from fat 48 mg. cholesterol
Shank cross cuts 	5.4 g. fat 29% cal. from fat 66 mg. cholesterol	Canadian bacon	7.8 g. fat 41% cal. from fat 54 mg. cholesterol
Tip round steak 	5.9 g. fat 34% cal. from fat 69 mg. cholesterol	Center rib 	11.7 g. fat 51% cal. from fat 67 mg. cholesterol
Sirloin steak	6.1 g. fat 33% cal. from fat 76 mg. cholesterol	**LAMB**	
Bottom round roast	7 g. fat 35% cal. from fat 82 mg. cholesterol	Shank 	5.7 g. fat 33% cal. from fat 74 mg. cholesterol
		Stew meat 	6.2 g. fat 35% cal. from fat 77 mg. cholesterol
Pot roast, arm	7.1 g. fat 35% cal. from fat 86 mg. cholesterol	Leg 	6.6 g. fat 36% cal. from fat 76 mg. cholesterol

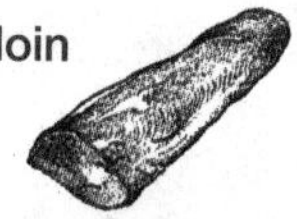

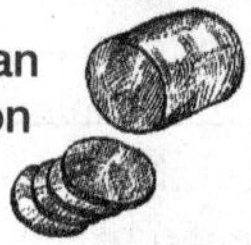

yourself. That way, you'll know exactly what you're getting. In addition, the larger size means that less of the meat was exposed to air, which in turn means extra freshness.

Check the date. Meats in the supermarket are labeled with a sell date. Unless you'll be freezing the meat as soon as you get it home, be sure to cook it before the sell date expires. You might also want to check with someone behind the meat counter to see if that date has an extra day or two built in for storing the meat at home.

Get expert advice. Even though you probably pick your meat from among dozens of identical packages, somewhere behind the display counter is the butcher who got it all ready. Don't hesitate to ask his advice. He can tell you which meats are freshest and leanest. He'll also prepare custom cuts on request.

Start with a trimming. Once you're ready to cook, trim away any visible fat that you can find. It takes just a minute and can dramatically reduce the amount of saturated fat in your diet.

☞ When making stews and pot roasts, remove any excess fat that floats to the surface during cooking.

☞ When time permits, chill soups or stews to make it easy to remove even more fat without altering the taste.

TENDERIZING MEATS

The one advantage of using high-fat meats is that they require almost no help from you; fat is nature's tenderizer. But lean meats can also be tender and exquisitely full of flavor—if you treat them right.

Marinades

Meat that is stewed or braised doesn't need marinating; the slow simmering in liquid makes it tender and flavorful. Meat that is cooked over dry heat, however, can often use a bit of help. Traditional marinades combine an acidic ingredient, such as vinegar, with oil and herbs and

spices. Here are a few ways to make marinades healthier.

Reduce the oil. Since it's the acidic ingredient in marinades that helps tenderize meat, you can reduce or even eliminate the added oil without noticeably affecting the outcome.

Vary the flavors. While most marinades are made with vinegar or wine, you can vary the taste by using other acidic ingredients, such as fruit juice, mashed papaya or nonfat plain yogurt.

☞ An easy way to make a marinade is to combine an acidic ingredient like vinegar in equal proportion with water or low-fat broth.

☞ Depending on the size of the meat, you'll want anywhere from ½ to 1½ cups marinade.

Use a safe pan. Marinating meats in an aluminum or cast-iron pan may discolor both the pan and the meat. It can also give an off taste to the meat. Chefs advise marinating meat in a nonreactive pan, such as glass or stainless steel.

Coat it well. When marinating meat, turn it several times to coat the entire surface. There should be enough marinade so that the bottom of the meat is completely covered.

☞ After coating the meat, cover the pan loosely and place it in the refrigerator. Turn the meat several times while it is marinating so that all sides of the meat absorb the marinade.

☞ Tender cuts like lamb chops or rib-eye steaks can marinate for as little as 1 hour. Larger pieces of meat or tougher cuts like bottom round may need to marinate for 24 hours or longer.

Spice Rubs and Herb Crusts

A popular way to flavor meat is by rubbing the surface with a generous amount of spices or herbs. In Cajun cooking, this technique has led to the creation of blackened steak; in French cuisine, the result is *steak au poivre*. Many cooks have had wonderful success with recipes like rosemary-crusted lamb chops.

The main difference between rubs and crusts

is that rubs use dried herbs and crusts use fresh ones. Otherwise, the technique is the same.

☞ In a small bowl, combine the spices or herbs and mix to blend completely. (For a selection of rubs and crusts, see "Spice Rubs and Herb Crusts.")

☞ A dry rub won't readily adhere to meat, so you may want to add a little broth or water to give it more sticking power. Or moisten the meat with a little liquid or nonfat plain yogurt.

☞ Coat the meat thoroughly with the mixture, rubbing or patting it into the meat. You can cook the meat right away or store it in the refrigerator for 1 to 2 hours so the flavors can meld.

COOKING TECHNIQUES

Meat is a versatile ingredient in the healthy cook's kitchen. It can be sautéed, stir-fried, grilled, roasted, braised and pan-broiled. Although meat can be steamed and poached, these techniques don't bring out its best qualities.

Sautéing

Done in a skillet over medium heat, this is a quick method for cooking tender cuts of meat, like steaks, chops and burgers.

☞ Large cuts of meat can't be sautéed to completion, because they won't cook all the way through. However, you can briefly sauté large cuts—a pot roast, for example—in order to seal in the juices prior to further cooking and give the meat an attractive brown color.

☞ When sautéing meat, preheat the pan over medium heat for a minute before adding oil. Once the oil is added, let it heat for an additional 30 to 60 seconds before adding the meat.

☞ To keep the amount of fat to a minimum, replace cooking oil with a misting of no-stick spray and use a no-stick skillet.

☞ Another way to "sauté" without fat is to pour a couple tablespoons of broth into the pan. The drawback to this method is that meat won't brown as it will when using oil.

Stir-Frying

Like sautéing, this is a very quick method for preparing meat. Unlike sautéing, however, the meat is generally cut into small cubes or strips. In addition, the meat isn't allowed to brown on one side before turning; it's constantly stirred and moved about from one place of high heat to another.

☞ Use medium-high heat and let the pan get hot for a couple of minutes before adding the meat.

☞ You can stir-fry meat in a wok or large skillet, replacing added oil with a misting of no-stick spray.

CHECKING DONENESS

Whether you like your meat rare, medium or well-done, it's not always easy to tell when it's ready. The easiest way is to use a meat thermometer. Insert it into the thickest part of the meat (but not touching bone) for an accurate temperature reading in less than a minute.

☞ **Rare.** The meat should be pink at the edges and quite red in the center; the temperature will be 140°F.

☞ **Medium-rare.** The meat should be pink on the edges and dark pink in the center; the temperature will be 145° to 150°F.

☞ **Medium-well.** Beef and lamb should be brown at the edges; pork should be white. All three should be slightly pink in the center; the temperature will be 155° to 160°F.

☞ **Well-done.** No pink should be visible; the temperature will be above 160°F.

Spice Rubs and Herb Crusts

One of the easiest ways to increase the flavor of meat while cutting back on fat is to slather the surface with spices or herbs. Rubs can be put on dry, though adding a teaspoon of water or broth will help them spread more evenly. Always use fresh herbs, unless otherwise indicated.

Cajun Spice Rub

- 1 tablespoon paprika
- 1 teaspoon garlic powder
- 1 teaspoon onion powder
- ½ teaspoon dried thyme
- ½ teaspoon dried oregano
- ⅛ teaspoon ground black pepper
- ⅛ teaspoon ground red pepper

Makes about 2½ tablespoons

Mexican Spice Rub

- 1 tablespoon chili powder
- 1 tablespoon fresh chopped cilantro
- 2 cloves garlic, minced
- ½ teaspoon ground cumin
- ⅛ teaspoon ground red pepper

Makes about 2½ tablespoons

Moroccan Spice Rub

- 1 tablespoon chopped fresh mint
- 2 cloves garlic, minced
- 2 teaspoons grated fresh ginger
- ½ teaspoon ground cinnamon
- ½ teaspoon ground cumin

Makes about 2 tablespoons

Thai Spice Rub

- 2 tablespoons chopped fresh lemongrass
- 1 tablespoon grated fresh ginger
- 2 cloves garlic, minced
- ⅛ teaspoon ground red pepper

Makes about 3½ tablespoons

French Herb Crust

- 3 tablespoons chopped fresh parsley
- 1 tablespoon chopped fresh chives
- 2 teaspoons chopped fresh thyme
- 2 cloves garlic, minced
- 2 teaspoons grated orange rind

Makes about 5 tablespoons

Greek Herb Crust

- 2 tablespoons chopped fresh parsley
- 1 tablespoon chopped fresh oregano
- 1 tablespoon grated lemon rind
- 2 cloves garlic, minced

Make about 4 tablespoons

Italian Herb Crust

- 3 tablespoons chopped fresh parsley
- 2 tablespoons chopped fresh basil
- 2 cloves garlic, minced
- 2 teaspoons grated lemon rind

Makes about 5½ tablespoons

Traditional Herb Crust

- 2 tablespoons chopped fresh parsley
- 1½ tablespoons chopped fresh rosemary
- 2 cloves garlic, minced

Makes about 3½ tablespoons

Liver

Is It GOOD for You?

Liver is a food of extremes. kids—and more than a few adults—hate it. Gourmets adore it. Doctors—well, they can't quite make up their minds about it.

On the plus side, liver is packed with vitamins and minerals, particularly iron. One 3-ounce serving of beef liver, for example, contains 5.8 milligrams of iron, whereas most other cuts of beef have less than half that. Liver is also high in vitamins A and B$_{12}$.

Anyone worried about heart health, however, may have good reason for avoiding liver. A single serving of beef liver contains 331 milligrams of cholesterol—over the 300-milligram-a-day limit recommended by most doctors. Pork liver has 302 milligrams, lamb liver has 426 milligrams and chicken liver, 536 milligrams.

So what's the bottom line? If your blood cholesterol levels are on the low side (under 200 milligrams of cholesterol per deciliter of blood, or mg/dl) and you generally eat a low-fat, low-cholesterol diet, having liver once or twice a month shouldn't be a problem. If your blood cholesterol is on the high side of 200 mg/dl, however, you'd be wise to leave the liver behind.

Pan-Broiling

Done in a skillet or no-stick pan over medium-high heat, pan-broiling is used for very thin, tender cuts of meat, like cube steaks, cutlets and burgers. The advantage of pan-broiling is that it calls for no added fat.

☞ Since the meats used in pan-broiling are often fairly fatty, be sure to drain fat from the pan several times during cooking.

☞ When pan-broiling sausage, bacon or other high-fat meats, using a stove-top grill or ridged pan will allow the fat to drain away from the meat, so that it won't be reabsorbed.

☞ Transfer the cooked meat to a triple thickness of paper towels and pat well to remove excess fat clinging to it.

Grilling and Broiling

Two of the most popular methods for cooking meat, grilling and broiling differ from each other only in the direction of the heat. Grilling—whether it's done outdoors or in a special stove-top pan—supplies heat from the bottom. Broiling, by contrast, directs the heat downward. Both methods are perfect for healthy cooking, since they cause fat to drip downward and away from the food.

☞ Since grilling and broiling are quick cooking methods, they're usually used for tender meats, such as steaks, chops, burgers or tenderloins.

☞ Placing food about 4" from the heat creates a nice crust and seals in juices, helping the meat stay tender and flavorful.

☞ Since grilling usually cooks more slowly than broiling, marinating meat beforehand, or basting the meat during cooking, will help keep it moist and tender. (For more on grilling, see page 67.)

Braising

The only moist heat method recommended for cooking meats is braising, which involves simmering meat for long periods of time in a flavorful liquid. The long cooking time makes the meat fork-tender. It's used for stews and for cooking pot roasts, rump roasts and shanks.

☞ Since braising is often used for large cuts of meat, it's generally done in a Dutch oven or stew pot.

☞ To seal in the juices, meat should be browned before braising. For one-pot cooking, browning can be done in the Dutch oven or stew pot; after the meat is browned, additional ingredients or liquids can be added.

☞ Once ingredients are added, cover the pot and cook over medium-low heat, keeping the liquid at a gentle simmer. Cook until the meat is fork-tender.

Roasting

Used for cuts like leg of lamb, beef rib roasts, sirloin tip roasts and ham, roasting is among the easiest techniques for cooking meats. Once the meat is in the oven, all you have to do is keep an eye on the time.

☞ Always preheat the oven before roasting, since the times given in recipes are based on the oven being at the proper temperature before the meat goes in. Also, the high initial heat sears the meat, sealing in flavor and juices.

☞ Putting meat on a roasting rack will cause the fat to run off and away from the meat.

☞ Roasts can be marinated or rubbed with spices or herbs. They can also be surrounded by vegetables, such as carrots, parsnips, onions, potatoes, turnips, fennel or celery root, which impart their flavors to the meat during roasting.

☞ Vegetables generally take an hour to cook in the oven. When preparing a small roast, you can add vegetables at the beginning of the cooking time; for larger pieces of meat, add the vegetables later on.

☞ Most roasting recipes call for the meat to be cooked uncovered. If the meat is browning too rapidly, however, loosely cover the meat with aluminum foil to slow it down.

☞ Use a meat thermometer to ensure that the roast is properly done. It should read 140°F for rare meat, 145° to 150°F for medium-rare, 155° to 160°F for medium-well and over 160°F for well-done.

☞ Allow a roast to rest for about 15 minutes after removing it from the oven. This give juices time to be reabsorbed, so that they don't all run out during carving.

BEEF

From succulent roasts and hearty stews to grilled kebabs and steaks, beef is one of our favorite meats. Extremely versatile, it can be used as a main dish or a supporting ingredient, and it works well with an enormous variety of flavor combinations.

The problem with beef, of course, is that it's high in saturated fat and cholesterol. While beef is considerably leaner than it used to be, it should still be eaten in fairly small quantities, preferably no more than once or twice a week.

Buy it bright. Meat in the supermarket should have a bright red color, which indicates that it hasn't been exposed to air. If the meat is purplish or even brown, it may not have been properly packaged.

Get good ground. As with whole pieces of meat, ground beef should be bright red. Ideally, it will have only a small amount of visible fat.

Wrap it well. When properly wrapped, fresh beef will keep in the refrigerator for up to four days.

☞ Ground beef is more perishable than whole pieces and will generally keep for about two days.

☞ Put meat in the coldest part of the refrigerator, preferably in the meat drawer. If your refrigerator doesn't have meat compartment, store it as far away from the door as possible.

☞ When freezing meat, remove it from the original packaging. Otherwise, air that is trapped in the package will cause crystals to form,

INSTANT FLAVOR

One of the easiest ways to add flavor to roasts is to introduce some garlic. Cooks who prefer a milder taste will simply crush a clove and rub it over the surface of the meat. For more assertive flavors, you can put the flavor into the meat instead.

With a sharp knife, slice 3 to 5 cloves garlic into lengthwise slivers. Try to get about 5 slivers per clove.

Make shallow slits (no more than 1" deep) in the meat, about 3" to 5" apart, all around the surface.

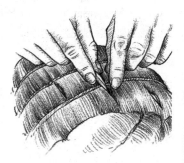

Insert a garlic sliver into each of the slits. The flavor will permeate the meat, getting mellower and richer as it cooks.

causing freezer burn. Rewrap the meat in heavy-duty freezer foil or freezer paper.

☞ Roasts and steaks will last between six and nine months in the freezer. Ground beef will keep for up to four months.

☞ Meat should be thawed slowly in the refrigerator to prevent bacterial growth. For large cuts, allow 5 to 7 hours per pound for complete thawing. Don't thaw meat on the counter.

Helpful Hint

Cutting leftover cooked meat into small pieces allows it to cool quickly and reheat very quickly, preventing it from drying out.

Cook it right. Not every cut of meat is created equal; more tender cuts like sirloin benefit from fast, light cooking, while tougher meats like rump roast need long cooking to break down tough tissues.

☞ Back ribs can be braised or roasted.
☞ Beef strips can be sautéed or stir-fried.
☞ Cube steak can be sautéed or pan-broiled.
☞ Eye of round can be braised or roasted.
☞ Ground beef can be sautéed, broiled or grilled.
☞ Rib roast can be roasted.
☞ Round steak can be sautéed or braised.
☞ Rump roast can be braised or roasted.
☞ Sirloin steak can be sautéed, pan-broiled, broiled or grilled.
☞ Tenderloin can be sautéed, roasted, broiled or grilled.

PORK

Like beef, pork is a versatile meat. We eat it fresh in the forms of roasts and chops. It can also be smoked or cured, as with ham and bacon. A tender and flavorful meat, pork can also be quite lean. Many cuts of pork have less saturated fat than beef and about the same amount of cholesterol.

Buy it lean. The leanest cuts of pork are those from the loin area: loin roast, tenderloin, rib roast, rib chop and loin chop.

☞ When buying pork, make sure that it is pink and fresh-looking; even the bones should have a pinkish tinge to them. Meat that is gray or dull-looking has probably passed its peak.

Cook it safe. Because of better means of raising hogs, trichinosis is no longer a real threat. (In the rare case where contamination is present, cooking the pork to 137°F will destroy the trichanae.) So you can cook pork to a medium-well state—an internal temperature of 155° to 160°F—to give you tender, juicy results.

☞ Pan-frying works for pork chops, tenderloin slices or pork patties less than 1″ thick. Larger pieces of pork should be broiled or roasted.

☞ When roasting pork, always position the meat fat side up. This causes it to self-baste

---

MAKING PAN GRAVY

Nothing is easier, or quicker, than making gravy to accompany a roast of beef, pork or lamb. To make your gravy extra lean, you can replace virtually all the pan drippings with broth or water. A general rule of thumb is to use 2 tablespoons flour and 1 cup liquid for a medium-thick gravy.

Tip the pan so that all the fat and drippings collect in the corner. Spoon out and discard all but 1 tablespoon or less of the fat. Retain the browned bits of pan drippings.

Place the pan over medium heat and whisk in flour, a little at a time, until a thin paste forms.

Cook for 1 to 2 minutes, stirring constantly. Whisk in hot broth or water and continue cooking until thick. Transfer to a gravy boat and serve.

☞ When cooking regular bacon, broil it on a rack so that the fat drips away from the meat.

☞ Microwaving is an excellent method for preparing bacon. Use plenty of paper towels both under and over the bacon to absorb the copious amounts of fat that drain off during microwaving. Pat dry with clean paper towels.

LAMB

Many healthy cooks enjoy lamb mainly as a holiday treat. Yet this flavorful, tender meat is lean enough to be enjoyed all year long.

The most tender lamb, called baby or milk-fed lamb, is brought to market when it's between six and eight weeks old. Other varieties include spring lamb (five to six months old), yearling lamb (one to two years old) and mutton (older than two years). Mutton can be tough, but other varieties of lamb are very tender.

Look for lean. When buying lamb, the cuts that are lowest in fat come from the loin and rib areas.

The meat should be bright pink; even the bones should be tinged with pink. If the meat and bones are bright red, the lamb is somewhat old and may be markedly tough.

Put the fat up. When roasting lamb, put it in the oven with the fat side facing up. This causes juices to run downward over the meat, keeping it moist and tender.

Many cooks remove the tough, fatty skin (the fell), because it can lend a gamey taste to the meat. Leaving the fell in place, however, helps keep the meat moist as it cooks.

while it cooks; all you have to do is remove the layer of fat on top before serving.

☞ Putting the meat on a roasting rack allows fat to drip down into the pan and away from the meat, so less gets reabsorbed.

☞ Meat continues cooking even after it's removed from the oven. To prevent pork from being overdone, remove it from the oven when the temperature is 5 degrees lower than the final recommended temperature.

Enjoy a holiday ham. While fresh hams are high in fat, preserved, precooked hams can be quite lean. Some are 95 percent fat-free. They can be very high in sodium, however, so they aren't recommended for those on salt-restricted diets.

Go north for your bacon. Although regular bacon is really too fatty for everyday use, Canadian bacon, which is taken from the loin area, is considerably leaner than the traditional kind.

Benjamin Cevelo

As chef at Spago Cicago, Benjamin Cevelo has combined classical cooking techniques with the best of regional ingredients.

"Meat doesn't have to be the only focus of a dish," he says. "We increase the importance of side dishes by maximizing their flavor."

Cevelo serves this rack of lamb with a Chinese version of the traditional French ratatouille. He accompanies it with cooked noodles, such as angel hair or capellini. The noodles reduce the total percent of calories from fat in the meal.

Lamb with Chinese Ratatouille

1   small eggplant, cut into ¾″ slices
½   teaspoon salt
3   teaspoons olive oil
9   fermented black beans, rinsed (see note)
2   teaspoons minced fresh ginger
1   clove garlic, minced
1   small red onion, sliced
10   plum tomatoes, peeled, seeded and diced
2   summer squash, diced
2   zucchini, diced
2   sweet red peppers, roasted, peeled and diced
2   green peppers, roasted, peeled and diced
1   tablespoon chopped fresh parsley
1   tablespoon chopped fresh cilantro
1   teaspoon reduced-sodium soy sauce
½   teaspoon sesame oil
¼   teaspoon chili sauce
2   racks of lamb (7 bones each), meat removed and trimmed of all fat

Sprinkle the eggplant with the salt and let stand for 20 minutes. Rinse off the salt and pat dry with paper towels. Brush the eggplant with 1 teaspoon of the olive oil and grill or broil until tender. Dice and set aside.

Warm the remaining 2 teaspoons olive oil in a large no-stick skillet over medium-low heat. Add the beans, ginger and garlic. Cook for 5 minutes. Add the onions and eggplant and cook for 3 minutes. Add the tomatoes, squash and zucchini. Increase the heat to medium and cook for 5 minutes, or until the mixture is thickened.

Stir in the red peppers, green peppers, parsley, cilantro, soy sauce, sesame oil and chili sauce. Keep warm.

Preheat the oven to 450°.

Place a large cast-iron skillet over medium-high heat for 2 minutes. Add the lamb and sear on all sides. Place the skillet in the oven and roast for 5 to 10 minutes, or until a meat thermometer inserted in the center registers 130°. Remove from the oven and allow to rest for a few minutes. Slice and serve with the vegetable mixture.

Makes 4 servings. Per serving: 456 calories, 20.4 g. fat (40% of calories), 35.8 g. protein, 37.6 g. carbohydrates, 7.9 g. dietary fiber, 92 mg. cholesterol, 170 mg. sodium

NOTE
• Fermented black beans are sold in Asian groceries. Before using, thoroughly rinse the beans to remove any grit.

All-American Meat Loaf

Makes 6 servings. Per serving: 165 calories, 7.2 g. fat (39% of calories), 13.5 g. protein, 11.5 g. carbohydrates, 1.8 g. dietary fiber, 35 mg. cholesterol, 261 mg. sodium

Here's a moist meatloaf that boasts great flavor and is good for you, too. The secret is using the leanest possible ground beef in combination with healthy vegetables and rice. Serve with mashed potatoes and peas to lower the total percentage of calories from fat.

- 2 cups shredded cabbage
- 1 cup chopped onions
- 1 cup shredded carrots
- ½ cup chopped green peppers
- 2 cloves garlic, minced
- 1 cup cooked brown rice or barley
- 1 teaspoon dried basil
- ½ teaspoon dried savory
- ¼ teaspoon dried thyme
- 1 pound extra-lean ground beef
- 3 egg whites, lightly beaten
- ¾ teaspoon salt
- ¼ teaspoon ground black pepper
  Horseradish mustard

Preheat the oven to 350°. Coat an 8½″ × 4½″ no-stick loaf pan with no-stick spray.

Coat a large no-stick skillet with no-stick spray and warm over medium heat. Add the cabbage, onions, carrots, green peppers and garlic. Cover and cook, stirring occasionally, for 8 to l0 minutes, or until the carrots are tender. Stir in the rice or barley, basil, savory and thyme. Let stand for 5 to l0 minutes, or until cool.

Add the beef, egg whites, salt and black pepper. Mix with your hands to combine. Pack the mixture into the prepared loaf pan.

Bake for about 1 hour, or until the juices run clear. Remove from the oven and to cool for 5 minutes. Turn out of the pan onto a platter and slice. Serve with the horseradish mustard.

VARIATIONS

Chili Sauce Meat Loaf: Add ¼ cup chili sauce to the meat mixture. Spread 2 to 3 tablespoons chili sauce over the top of the loaf.

Cheesy Meat Loaf: Add ½ cup shredded fat-free Cheddar cheese to the meat mixture. Sprinkle ¼ cup shredded fat-free Cheddar cheese over the top of the loaf during the last 10 minutes of baking.

Tofu Meat Loaf: Replace the rice or barley with 1 cup pressed and crumbled tofu.

Ham Loaf: Replace 8 ounces of the ground beef with 8 ounces ground lean baked ham. Replace the basil and savory with ¾ teaspoon crushed caraway seeds.

Pork-and-Beef Loaf: Replace 8 ounces of the ground beef with 8 ounces ground pork tenderloin.

QUICK!
Better Beef Burgers

A better-for-you burger is pretty simple. Start with the leanest ground beef. Add meaty sautéed mushrooms and pungent seasonings. Then grill the burger so that excess fat drains away.

- ¼ cup minced onions
- ½ cup finely chopped shiitake or portobello mushrooms
- 1½ tablespoons chopped fresh parsley or thyme
- 1 tablespoon reduced-sodium Worcestershire sauce
- ¼ teaspoon hot-pepper sauce
- 12 ounces extra-lean ground beef
- 4 kaiser rolls, toasted
- 4 leaves lettuce (optional)
- 4 slices tomato (optional)

Coat a medium no-stick skillet with no-stick spray and warm over medium heat. Add the onions and mushrooms. Cook, stirring frequently, for 4 to 5 minutes, or until the mushrooms are lightly browned. Place in a medium bowl and set aside to cool.

Stir in the parsley or thyme, Worcestershire sauce and hot-pepper sauce. Add the beef and mix quickly with your hands to combine. Shape into 4 burgers, ¾″ thick.

Coat an unheated grill rack with no-stick spray. Light the grill according to the manufacturer's directions. Place the rack on the grill.

Place the burgers on the rack and grill about 6″ from the heat for 5 to 6 minutes per side, or until browned and cooked through. Serve on the rolls with the lettuce (if using) and tomatoes (if using).

Makes 4 servings. Per serving: 108 calories, 2.8 g. fat (24% of calories), 15.9 g. protein, 4.1 g. carbohydrates, 0.5 g. dietary fiber, 41 mg. cholesterol, 63 mg. sodium

NOTES

• Top the burgers with grilled onions or a mixture of grilled onions and grilled sweet red or yellow peppers.

• For a delicious horseradish sauce, combine ½ cup nonfat plain yogurt, 1 tablespoon snipped fresh dill, 2 teaspoons prepared horseradish and 1 teaspoon sweet pickle relish. Add a dollop to the burgers just before serving.

VARIATIONS

Beef-and-Tofu Burgers: Replace the mushrooms with ½ cup reduced-fat silken (soft) tofu, drained and patted dry with paper towels. Combine with the onions, Worcestershire sauce and hot-pepper sauce in the bowl.

Beef-and-Bulgur Burgers: Replace the mushrooms with ½ cup cooked and cooled bulgur. Combine with the onions, Worcestershire sauce and hot-pepper sauce in the bowl.

Pepper Steak

2 cups sliced mushrooms
1 cup sliced sweet red peppers
1 cup sliced green peppers
2 cups sliced onions
4 cloves garlic, minced
1 pound boneless beef eye of round or sirloin tip steak, trimmed of all visible fat and cut into ¼″-thick strips
2 teaspoons all-purpose flour
1½ cups defatted reduced-sodium beef broth
½ cup water
½ teaspoon dried thyme
½ cup tomato sauce
1 tablespoon cornstarch
¼ cup dry white wine or nonalcoholic white wine
1 tablespoon reduced-sodium Worcestershire sauce
Salt and ground black pepper
3 cups cooked brown rice
Chopped fresh parsley

Coat a Dutch oven with no-stick spray and warm over medium heat. Add the mushrooms, red peppers and green peppers and sauté for 3 to 5 minutes, or until the peppers are tender. Remove the vegetables from the pan and set aside.

Add the onions and garlic to the pan and sauté for 2 to 3 minutes, or until the onions are tender. Coat the beef lightly with the flour. Add to the pan and cook over medium heat, stirring constantly, for 3 to 5 minutes. Add the broth, water and thyme and bring to a boil. Reduce the heat, cover and simmer for 30 to 35 minutes, or until the beef is tender. Add the tomato sauce and the reserved vegetables and cook for 5 to 10 minutes, or until the mixture is heated through.

(continued)

In a small bowl, dissolve the cornstarch in the wine. Bring the beef mixture to a boil. Add the cornstarch mixture and boil, stirring constantly, until the mixture thickens. Add the Worcestershire sauce. Season to taste with the salt and pepper. Serve over the rice and garnish with the parsley.

Makes 4 servings. Per serving: 456 calories, 9.1 g. fat (18% of calories), 34.7 g. protein, 56.7 g. carbohydrates, 6.9 g. dietary fiber, 56 mg. cholesterol, 258 mg. sodium

VARIATIONS

Asian Pepper Steak: Replace the green peppers with 1 cup snow peas, steamed until crisp-tender. Add the snow peas, ½ cup sliced water chestnuts and 1 teaspoon minced fresh ginger to the beef mixture along with the reserved mushrooms and red peppers. Replace the Worcestershire sauce with reduced-sodium soy sauce or teriyaki sauce.

Italian Pepper Steak: Replace the green peppers and mushrooms with 1 cup chopped tomatoes and 1 cup sliced zucchini. Add ¾ to 1 teaspoon dried Italian herb seasoning. Serve over cooked fettuccine instead of rice. Garnish with chopped fresh basil instead of parsley.

Sweet and Sour Pepper Steak: Stir ¼ cup apricot all-fruit spread and 3 to 4 teaspoons cider vinegar into the mixture at the end of the cooking time. Serve over steamed couscous instead of rice. Garnish with chopped fresh cilantro instead of parsley.

Peppers Stuffed with Beef and Spanish Rice

6	large green peppers
12	ounces extra-lean ground beef
1	large onion, finely chopped
⅔	cup chopped sweet red peppers
1	can (8 ounces) tomato sauce
⅓	cup reduced-sodium ketchup
1½	cups cooked white rice
1	tablespoon reduced-sodium Worcester-shire sauce
2½	teaspoons chili powder

1¼	teaspoons dried marjoram
1	teaspoon paprika
½	teaspoon dry mustard
½	teaspoon dried thyme
¼	teaspoon celery salt

Cut the tops off the peppers, about 1″ down. Remove the seeds and ribs, being careful not to tear or rip the peppers. If necessary, trim the bottoms so that the peppers stand upright.

Choose a round, microwave-safe baking dish large enough to hold the peppers upright in a circle around the edge. Coat the dish with no-stick spray. Arrange the peppers upright in the dish and loosely cover with wax paper. Microwave on high power for a total of 4 minutes; stop and rotate the dish a quarter-turn after 2 minutes.

Coat a large no-stick skillet with no-stick spray. Add the beef, onions and red peppers. Cook over medium-high heat, breaking up the beef with a spoon, until the beef is no longer pink and the peppers are tender. Drain the mixture in a strainer or colander, then transfer to a large plate lined with paper towels. Blot the top of the mixture with additional paper towels, then return to the skillet.

In a small bowl, combine the tomato sauce and ketchup. Add all but ¼ cup to the beef mixture. Stir the rice, Worcestershire sauce, chili powder, marjoram, paprika, mustard, thyme and celery salt into the beef mixture.

Spoon equal amounts of the rice mixture into the green peppers. Drizzle the reserved tomato mixture on top of each pepper. Loosely cover with wax paper.

Microwave on high power for 4 to 6 minutes, or until the green peppers are just tender when pierced with a fork. Let stand for 5 minutes before serving.

Makes 6 servings. Per serving: 234 calories, 7.6 g. fat (29% of calories), 14.3 g. protein, 28.3 g. carbohydrates, 3.5 g. dietary fiber, 35 mg. cholesterol, 335 mg. sodium

Sloppy Joes from the Microwave

12 ounces extra-lean ground beef
1 cup finely chopped onions
1 large green pepper, chopped
1 clove garlic, minced
1 carrot, grated or finely shredded
1 can (8 ounces) reduced-sodium tomato sauce
⅓ cup reduced-sodium ketchup
2 teaspoons packed brown sugar
2 teaspoons lemon juice
1 teaspoon dried thyme
¼ teaspoon ground black pepper
 Pinch of ground cinnamon
¼ teaspoon salt (optional)
4 English muffins or hamburger buns, split and toasted

In a 3-quart microwave-safe baking dish, combine the beef, onions, green peppers and garlic. Cover and microwave on high power for a total of 7 to 8 minutes, or until the beef is no longer pink; stop and stir every 3 minutes to break up the beef.

Break up any remaining large pieces of beef. Drain the mixture in a strainer or colander, then transfer to a large plate lined with paper towels. Blot the top of the mixture with additional paper towels. Return the mixture to the baking dish.

Stir in the carrots, tomato sauce, ketchup, brown sugar, lemon juice, thyme, black pepper, cinnamon and salt (if using).

Cover and microwave on high power for 3 minutes, then stir. Microwave for 4 to 5 minutes, or until hot.

Serve over the English muffins or hamburger buns.

Makes 4 servings. Per serving: 381 calories, 11.5 g. fat (27% of calories), 22.6 g. protein, 46.4 g. carbohydrates, 2.7 g. dietary fiber, 53 mg. cholesterol, 339 mg. sodium

Savory Beef Tenderloin

1 pound new potatoes, cut into 1" pieces
2 tablespoons minced shallots
3 tablespoons minced fresh tarragon
3 tablespoons minced fresh parsley
1 tablespoon cracked mustard seeds
1 tablespoon cracked coriander seeds
1 tablespoon minced garlic
1 teaspoon extra-virgin olive oil
1 pound lean beef tenderloin, trimmed of all visible fat

Preheat the oven to 375°. Coat a 2-quart no-stick baking dish with no-stick spray. Add the potatoes and roast for 10 minutes.

Meanwhile, in a small bowl, combine the shallots, tarragon, parsley, mustard seeds, coriander seeds, garlic and oil. Rub the mixture over the beef to coat well.

Coat a large no-stick skillet with no-stick spray and warm over medium-high heat. Sear the beef for 2 minutes, turning to brown it evenly on all sides.

Remove the baking dish from the oven and shake or stir the potatoes to prevent sticking. Place the beef on top of the potatoes and roast for 15 minutes. Reduce the heat to 350°. Roast for 10 minutes, or until the internal temperature registers 140° (rare) or 145° to 150° (medium) on a meat thermometer.

Remove the beef from the oven and let stand for at least 10 minutes before slicing. If the potatoes are not brown enough, return them to the oven while the beef is standing.

Makes 4 servings. Per serving: 303 calories, 9.1 g. fat (27% of calories), 25.7 g. protein, 29.7 g. carbohydrates, 0.1 g. dietary fiber, 53 mg. cholesterol, 59 mg. sodium

Skillet Goulash

12	ounces extra-lean ground beef
1	large red onion, finely chopped
2	stalks celery, sliced
1	large clove garlic, minced
1½	cups defatted reduced-sodium beef broth
⅓	cup dry red wine or nonalcoholic red wine
1	can (15 ounces) reduced-sodium tomato sauce
2	cups thinly sliced red cabbage
2	large carrots, sliced
2	teaspoons paprika
1	teaspoon dried thyme
¼	teaspoon dry mustard
¼	teaspoon ground black pepper
1	large bay leaf
12	ounces thin egg (no-yolk) noodles
¾	cup nonfat sour cream
2	tablespoons chopped fresh parsley

Coat a large no-stick skillet with no-stick spray and warm over medium heat. Add the beef and cook over medium-high heat, breaking up the beef with a spoon, for 7 to 8 minutes, or until no longer pink. Remove to a plate lined with paper towels. Blot the top with additional paper towels and set aside.

Drain any fat from the skillet and warm the skillet over medium-high heat. Add the onions, celery and garlic and cook for 6 to 8 minutes, or until the celery is tender.

Stir in the broth, wine and tomato sauce and mix well. Add the cabbage, carrots, paprika, thyme, mustard, pepper and bay leaf. Bring to a boil. Reduce the heat to medium-low, cover and simmer for 30 minutes, or until the carrots are tender. Remove and discard the bay leaf.

Meanwhile, in a large pot of boiling water, cook the noodles according to package directions. Drain.

Reduce the heat under the skillet to the lowest possible setting. Stir in the sour cream and gently heat through; do not boil. Serve over the noodles. Sprinkle with the parsley.

Makes 6 servings. Per serving: 365 calories, 9.3 g. fat (22% of calories), 22.3 g. protein, 48.1 g. carbohydrates, 4.2 g. dietary fiber, 35 mg. cholesterol, 128 mg. sodium

VARIATION

Skillet Pork Goulash: Replace the ground beef with ground pork tenderloin that has been trimmed of all visible fat before grinding.

Braised Beef Rump Roast

1	tablespoon minced fresh parsley
½	teaspoon dried thyme
1	large clove garlic, minced
¼	teaspoon crushed dried rosemary
2	pounds boneless beef rump roast, trimmed of all visible fat
½	cup finely chopped leeks (white parts only)
¼	cup finely chopped carrots
¼	cup finely chopped celery
½	cup defatted reduced-sodium beef broth
½	cup apple cider
½	cup coarsely chopped tomatoes
1	bay leaf
	Salt and ground black pepper
2	pounds hot cooked new potatoes

In a small bowl, stir together the parsley, thyme, garlic and rosemary. Using the tip of a small, sharp knife, make ½"-deep slits about 2" apart in the beef. Fill the slits with equal amounts of the parsley mixture.

Preheat the broiler.

Place the beef on the rack of a broiling pan. Broil 4" from the heat for about 4 minutes per side, or until the surface is browned. Drain the beef, then pat dry with paper towels.

Preheat the oven to 325°.

While the beef is cooking, coat a medium no-stick skillet with no-stick spray and warm over medium heat. Add the leeks, carrots and celery. Cook, stirring occasionally, for about 5 minutes, or until the carrots start to soften. Transfer the mixture to a large ovenproof Dutch oven. Place the beef on top of the vegetables.

In the same skillet, combine the broth, cider, tomatoes and bay leaf. Bring to a boil. Reduce the heat to low, cover and simmer for 5 minutes. Pour over the beef. Cover tightly and bake for about 2 hours, or until the beef is tender.

To serve, remove and discard the bay leaf. Skim and discard the fat from the top of the vegetable mixture. Thinly slice the beef. Season to taste with the salt and pepper. Transfer the beef to a serving platter along with the potatoes. Spoon the vegetable mixture over the beef.

Makes 8 servings. Per serving: 335 calories, 6.7 g. fat (18% of calories), 27.6 g. protein, 41.8 g. carbohydrates, 2.8 g. dietary fiber, 57 mg. cholesterol, 93 mg. sodium

NOTE
• You can replace the new potatoes with spaetzle or egg (no-yolk) noodles. Or serve the braised rump roast with warm French or Italian bread.

Marinated London Broil with Gravy

Marinated London Broil
- 3 cloves garlic, halved
- 2 pounds beef top round, about 2" thick
- 3 tablespoons balsamic vinegar
- 1 teaspoon dried thyme
- 1 teaspoon ground coriander
  Ground black pepper

Gravy
- 2 tablespoons cornstarch
- ¼ teaspoon dry mustard
- 2 cups defatted reduced-sodium beef broth

To make the marinated London broil: Pierce the flat side of each half of the garlic cloves and rub the garlic over the beef. Set the garlic and beef aside.

In a large glass baking dish, combine the vinegar, thyme and coriander. Add the beef and garlic halves. Turn the meat to coat both sides evenly with the marinade. Set aside to marinate, turning once, for 30 minutes. Discard the marinade.

Coat an unheated grill rack with no-stick spray. Light the grill according to the manufacturer's directions. Place the rack on the grill.

Place the meat on the rack and grill about 6" from the heat for about 8 minutes per side for rare meat. (Cook 1 to 2 minutes longer per side for medium doneness.) Remove and let stand for 5 minutes. Carve into thin slices. Season with the pepper.

To make the gravy: While the London broil is marinating, in a medium saucepan, dissolve the cornstarch and mustard in ¼ cup of the broth. Whisk in the remaining 1¾ cups broth and cook over medium heat until the gravy comes to a boil and thickens. Serve over the London broil.

(continued)

Makes 8 servings. Per serving: 168 calories, 3.6 g. fat (20% of calories), 29.4 g. protein, 2.7 g. carbohydrates, 0.1 g. dietary fiber, 70 mg. cholesterol, 52 mg. sodium

VARIATION

Marinated London Broil with Mushroom Gravy: To make the gravy, warm 1 teaspoon olive oil in a medium saucepan. Add ½ cup chopped shiitake, portobello or button mushrooms. Sauté for 5 to 7 minutes, or until the mushrooms begin to release their liquid. Stir in the cornstarch and mustard until dissolved. Add the broth and cook, stirring constantly, until thick.

Beef Fajitas

- 2 tablespoons reduced-sodium Worcestershire sauce
- 2 tablespoons lime juice
- 1 teaspoon ground cumin
- ½ teaspoon dried oregano
- ¼ teaspoon ground red pepper
- 1 large clove garlic, thinly sliced
- 12 ounces flank steak, trimmed of all visible fat
- 1 teaspoon olive oil
- 1 bunch scallions (white and light green stems only), halved lengthwise and cut into 2″ pieces
- 1 large sweet red or yellow pepper, cut into strips
- 8 warm corn tortillas (6″ diameter)
- 8 tablespoons nonfat sour cream
- 8 tablespoons chunky salsa
- 4 tablespoons chopped fresh cilantro

In a 9″ × 13″ glass or ceramic baking dish, combine the Worcestershire sauce, lime juice, cumin, oregano, ground red pepper and garlic. Place the flank steak in the dish, turning to coat both sides with the marinade. Set aside to marinate, turning once, for 30 minutes.

In a medium no-stick skillet over medium heat, warm the oil. Add the scallions and red or yellow peppers and sauté for 5 to 7 minutes, or until the peppers are soft. Set aside.

Preheat the broiler. Coat the rack of a broiler pan with no-stick spray. Remove the flank steak from the marinade, scraping off any garlic pieces, and place on the broiler pan. Discard the marinade. Broil 6″ from the heat for 3 to 5 minutes per side for medium doneness. Remove from the broiler and let stand for 5 minutes. Carve into thin slices across the grain.

To serve, lay the tortillas on a work surface. Place the beef strips just below the center of each tortilla. Top with the peppers, scallions, sour cream, salsa and cilantro. Fold the bottom edge of each tortilla over the filling, then fold in the sides and roll up to enclose the filling.

Makes 4 servings. Per serving: 323 calories, 8.7 g. fat (24% of calories), 28.7 g. protein, 33.1 g. carbohydrates, 1.9 g. dietary fiber, 37 mg. cholesterol, 380 mg. sodium

QUICK!

Polynesian-Style Pork

- 1 pound boneless pork loin, trimmed of all visible fat and cut into ¾″ cubes
- 2 medium onions, each cut into 8 wedges
- 1 medium green pepper, cut into 1″ pieces
- ¼ cup reduced-sodium soy sauce
- 1 teaspoon canola oil
- 1½ tablespoons cider vinegar
- 1 tablespoon sugar
- 1 tablespoon cornstarch
- 1 tablespoon minced fresh ginger
- 1 can (20 ounces) pineapple chunks (packed in juice)
- 3 cups hot cooked rice

In a medium bowl, combine the pork, onions, peppers and 3 tablespoons of the soy sauce.

In a large no-stick skillet over medium-high heat, warm the oil until hot but not smoking. Add the pork mixture. Cook and stir for 3 to 4 minutes, or until the pork is lightly browned. Transfer to a large bowl and set aside.

In the same skillet, whisk together the vinegar, sugar, cornstarch, ginger and the remaining 1 tablespoon of the soy sauce.

Drain the juice from the pineapple and stir the juice into the skillet. Cook and stir over medium heat until the mixture comes to a boil and thickens.

Stir in the reserved pork mixture and the pineapple chunks and heat through. Serve over the rice.

Makes 4 servings. Per serving: 436 calories, 7.6 g. fat (16% of calories), 23.9 g. protein, 68.8 g. carbohydrates, 2.4 g. dietary fiber, 50 mg. cholesterol, 565 mg. sodium

Sesame Pork-and-Broccoli Stir-Fry

QUICK!

1½ cups defatted reduced-sodium chicken broth
2 tablespoons cornstarch
1 tablespoon reduced-sodium soy sauce
½ teaspoon toasted sesame oil
4 scallions, finely diced
1 teaspoon canola oil
1 pound pork tenderloin, trimmed of all visible fat and cut into bite-size pieces
1 large clove garlic, minced
2 teaspoons grated fresh ginger
1½ pounds broccoli, cut into bite-size pieces
4½ cups hot cooked rice
1 tablespoon sesame seeds, lightly toasted (see note)

In a small bowl, combine the broth, cornstarch, soy sauce and sesame oil and mix well. Stir in the scallions and set aside.

In a wok or large no-stick skillet over medium-high heat, warm the oil. Add the pork, garlic and ginger. Stir-fry for 3 to 4 minutes, or until the pork is no longer pink. Transfer to a bowl and set aside.

Add the reserved broth mixture to the wok or skillet. Cook, stirring constantly, for 2 to 3 minutes, or until thick. Add the broccoli, cover and simmer over low heat for 8 minutes, or until the broccoli is bright green and crisp-tender. Add the reserved pork. Cook for 1 to 2 minutes, or until the pork is hot. Serve over the rice. Top with the sesame seeds.

Makes 6 servings. Per serving: 314 calories, 5.5 g. fat (16% of calories), 23.9 g. protein, 41.8 g. carbohydrates, 0.2 g. dietary fiber, 39 mg. cholesterol, 169 mg. sodium

NOTES
• For a spicier stir-fry, add 1 seeded and minced serrano or cayenne pepper to the pork, garlic and ginger (wear plastic gloves when handling).
• For an herbal accent, add ¼ cup shredded Thai or Italian basil leaves along with the reserved cooked pork.
• To toast the sesame seeds, place them in a small no-stick skillet. Cook and stir over medium heat for 2 to 3 minutes, or until golden and fragrant.

VARIATIONS
Sesame Beef-and-Cauliflower Stir-Fry:
Replace the pork with 1 pound beef top round or sirloin. Replace the broccoli with 1½ pounds cauliflower.
Sesame Chicken-and-Broccoflower Stir-Fry:
Replace the pork with 1 pound boneless, skinless chicken breasts. Replace the broccoli with 1½ pounds broccoflower.

Indian-Style Pork

2 tablespoons reduced-sodium tamari or soy sauce

⅓ cup defatted reduced-sodium chicken broth

1 slice fresh ginger (about ¼" thick)

¼ teaspoon ground allspice

1 bay leaf

1 clove garlic, halved

12 ounces pork loin roast, trimmed of all visible fat and cut into ¼" strips

¾ cup thinly sliced onions

¾ cup thinly sliced sweet red peppers

1 teaspoon cornstarch

1 teaspoon honey

3 cups hot cooked basmati or white rice

In a large bowl, combine the tamari or soy sauce, broth, ginger, allspice, bay leaf and garlic. Add the pork and toss to coat. Cover and marinate in the refrigerator, turning several times, for at least 4 hours.

Remove and discard the bay leaf. Remove the pork from the bowl, reserving the marinade. Coat a wok or large no-stick skillet with no-stick spray and warm over medium heat. Add the pork and stir-fry for 3 to 5 minutes, adding a bit of marinade if necessary to prevent sticking. Remove the pork and set aside.

Wipe the pan clean with paper towels. Coat with no-stick spray and warm over medium heat. Add the onions, peppers and 1 tablespoon of the marinade. Stir-fry for 1 minute. Continue stir-frying, adding a tablespoon of water at a time if necessary to prevent sticking, for 3 to 4 minutes, or until the peppers are tender.

In a small bowl, combine the cornstarch, honey and the remaining marinade. Add to the wok or skillet and stir until thick. Add the pork, tossing to coat with the sauce.

Makes 4 servings. Per serving: 288 calories, 5.7 g. fat (18% of calories), 19.1 g. protein, 41.8 g. carbohydrates, 1.3 g. dietary fiber, 37 mg. cholesterol, 324 mg. sodium

NOTE

• Plantains (Caribbean cooking bananas) or ripe but firm eating bananas are an excellent side dish with the pork. To prepare, peel 2 plantains or bananas, then cut them in half crosswise. Cut each half lengthwise into two pieces. Coat a no-stick skillet with no-stick spray. Add 1 teaspoon canola oil and warm over medium-high heat. Sauté the plantains or bananas for 2 to 3 minutes per side, or until golden and tender when pierced with a fork. Lightly sprinkle with ground cinnamon.

Chinese Pork with Noodles

¾ cup cellophane noodles

4 ounces green beans, trimmed

2 tablespoons fermented black beans, rinsed and chopped (see note on page 261)

1 tablespoon mirin (see note)

2 teaspoons cornstarch

5 tablespoons defatted reduced-sodium chicken broth

1 clove garlic, minced

2 teaspoons minced fresh ginger

¾ pound lean pork, trimmed of all visible fat and sliced paper-thin

2 scallions, cut into short strips

½ small sweet red pepper, cut into short strips

In a medium bowl, cover the noodles with hot water and let stand for 20 minutes. Drain. Using kitchen scissors, cut the noodles into 1" pieces; set aside.

Meanwhile, bring a medium saucepan of water to a boil. Add the green beans and boil for 3 to 4 minutes, or until the beans are tender but still firm. Drain and plunge into a bowl of ice water for 30 seconds to stop the cooking process. Drain and pat dry. Cut the beans in half lengthwise and then into 1″ pieces; set aside.

In a small bowl, combine the black beans, mirin, cornstarch and 2 tablespoons of the broth; set aside.

Coat a wok or large no-stick skillet with no-stick spray. Add the remaining 3 tablespoons of the broth and warm over medium heat. Add the garlic and ginger and cook over medium-high heat for 1 minute. Add the pork and noodles. Stir-fry for 3 minutes, or until the pork is no longer pink. Add the scallions, peppers and the reserved green beans and stir-fry for 30 seconds. Add the reserved black-bean mixture and stir-fry for 1 to 2 minutes, or until the sauce thickens.

Makes 4 servings. Per serving: 231 calories, 5.1 g. fat (20% of calories), 15 g. protein, 31 g. carbohydrates, 0.7 g. dietary fiber, 37 mg. cholesterol, 349 mg. sodium

NOTES
• Mirin is sold in Asian grocery stores and some supermarkets. If it is unavailable, substitute 1 tablespoon rice-wine vinegar mixed with 1 teaspoon sugar.
• To make the pork easier to slice paper-thin, place it in the freezer for about 20 minutes.

Barbecued Pork Sandwiches

Replacing the traditional pork shoulder with lean pork tenderloin significantly reduces the fat in this classic sandwich. For an authentic look, pull the pork barbecue apart with two forks instead of slicing it.

    1   chipotle pepper (wear plastic gloves
        when handling; see note)
   12   ounces pork tenderloin, trimmed of all
        visible fat
    ¼   teaspoon ground red pepper
    ⅔   cup diced onions
    1   tablespoon minced garlic
    ¾   cup reduced-sodium barbecue sauce
    ¼   cup apple cider
    1   teaspoon brown sugar
    4   sandwich buns, toasted

In a small bowl, cover the chipotle pepper with hot water and let stand for 5 minutes. Drain. Remove the stems and seeds. Coarsely chop the pepper and set aside.

Coat a large no-stick skillet with no-stick spray and warm over medium-high heat. Sear the pork, turning as necessary, for about 5 minutes, or until browned on all sides. Remove the pork and place on a large piece of triple-layered foil. Season with the red pepper and set aside.

Coat a medium no-stick saucepan with no-stick spray and warm over medium heat. Add the onions and cook, stirring occasionally, for 5 minutes. If necessary, add 1 to 2 teaspoons of water to prevent sticking. Add the garlic and cook for 1 minute. Add the barbecue sauce, cider, brown sugar and the reserved chipotle peppers. Bring to a boil and simmer for 10 minutes.

Preheat the oven to 350°.

Pour one-third of the sauce over the pork, reserving the remainder. Tightly seal the foil over the pork. Bake for 25 minutes, or until the pork is very tender.

Using 2 forks, shred the pork. Add the pork to the remaining sauce and cook over medium heat until the sauce is hot. Serve the pork and sauce with the buns.

Makes 4 servings. Per serving: 291 calories, 5.7 g. fat (18% of calories), 22.4 g. protein, 37.2 g. carbohydrates, 0.7 g. dietary fiber, 49 mg. cholesterol, 235 mg. sodium

NOTE
• Chipotle peppers are mesquite-smoked, dried jalapeño peppers. They are also available canned. Omit the soaking if using a canned pepper.

Pork Chops with Apple-Raisin Relish

4 pork chops (3 ounces each), trimmed of all visible fat
½ cup chopped sweet onions
¼ cup apple cider
Pinch of ground cinnamon
Pinch of ground nutmeg
2 large red or green cooking apples, diced
2 tablespoons golden raisins
2 teaspoons cider vinegar
1 teaspoon maple syrup
Pinch of salt

Coat a large no-stick skillet with no-stick spray and warm over medium-high heat for 2 minutes. Sear the pork chops for about 2 minutes per side, or until browned. Reduce the heat to medium and cook until the chops have only a trace of pink in the center (check by inserting the tip of a sharp knife into 1 chop).

Meanwhile, in a medium saucepan, combine the onions, cider, cinnamon and nutmeg. Simmer over low heat for 10 minutes. Add the apples and raisins and simmer for 5 minutes. Remove from the heat and stir in the vinegar, maple syrup and salt. Serve with the pork chops.

Makes 4 servings. Per serving: 226 calories, 8.3 g. fat (33% of calories), 18.9 g. protein, 19.7 g. carbohydrates, 2 g. dietary fiber, 40 mg. cholesterol, 43 mg. sodium

VARIATION

Chicken Thighs with Onion-Cranberry Relish: Replace the pork chops with 8 boneless, skinless chicken thighs. Replace the raisins with 2 tablespoons dried cranberries. Increase the maple syrup to 2 teaspoons.

Honey-Mustard Pork Tenderloins

4 pieces pork tenderloin (4 ounces each), trimmed of all visible fat
1 teaspoon canola oil
½ cup diced shallots or onions
½ cup defatted reduced-sodium chicken broth
1 tablespoon honey mustard

Using your palm or the flat side of a large knife, press the tenderloins to ½" thickness.

Coat a large no-stick skillet with no-stick spray and warm over medium-high heat for 2 minutes. Sear the pork for about 2 minutes per side, or until browned. Remove from the skillet and set aside.

In the same skillet, warm the oil over medium heat. Add the shallots or onions and sauté for 4 to 5 minutes, or until soft. Add the broth and cook at a brisk simmer for 2 to 3 minutes, or until slightly reduced. Whisk in the mustard.

Return the pork to the skillet, spooning some of the mustard glaze over the top. Reduce the heat to low and cook for 4 to 5 minutes, or until the pork is hot and only slightly pink in the center (check by inserting the tip of a sharp knife into 1 tenderloin). Serve the pork topped with the mustard glaze.

Makes 4 servings. Per serving: 167 calories, 5.3 g. fat (30% of calories), 24.3 g. protein, 3.6 g. carbohydrates, 0 g. dietary fiber, 65 mg. cholesterol, 106 mg. sodium

NOTE

• For a more zesty sauce, replace the honey mustard with stone-ground mustard.

VARIATION

Honey-Mustard Catfish: Replace the pork tenderloins with 4 catfish fillets, ½" thick.

Orange-Braised Pork Tenderloins

QUICK!

4 pieces pork tenderloin (4 ounces each), trimmed of all visible fat
½ cup thinly sliced red onions
1 tablespoon red-wine vinegar
1 navel orange, peeled and sectioned
½ cup orange juice
½ cup defatted chicken broth
  Pinch of dried sage, crumbled
  Pinch of dried thyme
  Pinch of salt

Coat a large no-stick skillet with no-stick spray and warm over medium-high heat. Sear the pork for 2 to 3 minutes per side, or until browned. Remove from the skillet and set aside.

Add the onions to the skillet and sauté for 2 minutes, or until soft. Add the vinegar and toss to coat. Add the oranges, orange juice, broth, sage, thyme and salt. Reduce the heat to medium-low.

Return the pork to the skillet. Cover and cook for 8 to 10 minutes, or until the pork is only slightly pink in the center (check by inserting the tip of a sharp knife into 1 tenderloin).

Uncover and cook for 1 minute, or until the liquid is slightly reduced. Serve the pork with the oranges and sauce spooned over it.

Makes 4 servings. Per serving: 180 calories, 4.1 g. fat (21% of calories), 24.9 g. protein, 10.1 g. carbohydrates, 1.3 g. dietary fiber, 65 mg. cholesterol, 89 mg. sodium

Italian-Style Pork over Linguine

QUICK!

1 pork tenderloin (12 ounces), cut into ¼"–½"-thick slices
1 teaspoon crushed dried rosemary
¼ teaspoon ground black pepper
1 teaspoon olive oil
½ cup chopped onions
1 large clove garlic, chopped
2 cups seeded and chopped plum tomatoes
¼ cup defatted reduced-sodium chicken broth
1 tablespoon grated lemon rind
4 cups hot cooked linguine
2 tablespoons chopped fresh Italian parsley
2 tablespoons grated Parmesan cheese

Sprinkle both sides of the pork slices with the rosemary and pepper and set aside.

In a large no-stick skillet over medium heat, warm the oil. Sear the pork for 2 to 3 minutes per side, or until browned. Remove from the skillet and set aside.

Add the onions and garlic to the skillet and sauté for 2 minutes. Add the tomatoes, broth and lemon rind. Cook and stir for 4 to 5 minutes, or until the liquid has evaporated. Return the pork to the skillet. Spoon some of the sauce over the pork and simmer for 1 to 2 minutes, or until the pork is heated through.

Serve the pork and sauce over the linguine. Sprinkle with the parsley and Parmesan.

Makes 4 servings. Per serving: 371 calories, 8.8 g. fat (21% of calories), 28.3 g. protein, 45.5 g. carbohydrates, 3.3 g. dietary fiber, 128 mg. cholesterol, 133 mg. sodium

Moroccan Lamb and Vegetables with Couscous

1 teaspoon ground cumin
¾ teaspoon ground coriander
¼ teaspoon ground cinnamon
¼ teaspoon ground ginger
¼ teaspoon salt
12 ounces lean lamb, trimmed of all visible fat and cut into 1" cubes
1 green pepper, cut into 8 wedges
1 large onion, cut into 8 wedges
1 large carrot, cut into ½"-long pieces
1 medium tomato, peeled and diced
2 cloves garlic, minced
2 cups defatted reduced-sodium chicken broth
1 cup couscous
2 tablespoons chopped fresh cilantro
Hot-pepper sauce

In a small bowl, combine the cumin, coriander, cinnamon, ginger and salt. Place the lamb in a large bowl and season with half of the spice mixture. Toss to coat.

Coat a Dutch oven with no-stick spray and warm over medium heat. Add the lamb and cook, stirring occasionally, for 6 to 7 minutes, or until browned.

Add the peppers, onions, carrots, tomatoes, garlic and the remaining spice mixture. Pour in the broth and gently stir to combine. Cover and cook, gently stirring occasionally, over medium heat for about 25 minutes, or until the carrots are tender when pierced with a sharp knife.

Sprinkle the couscous over the lamb and vegetables, tilting the pan if necessary to moisten all the couscous. Sprinkle with the cilantro. Cover, remove from the heat and let stand for 5 minutes, or until the couscous is tender and most of the liquid is absorbed. Season to taste with the hot-pepper sauce.

Makes 4 servings. Per serving: 302 calories, 4.2 g. fat (13% of calories), 19.9 g. protein, 45.1 g. carbohydrates, 9 g. dietary fiber, 36 mg. cholesterol, 210 mg. sodium

Lamb with Lemon Rice and Mint Sauce

Lamb
2 teaspoons minced garlic
1 teaspoon crushed dried rosemary
4 boneless lamb leg center steaks or loin lamb chops (4 ounces each), trimmed of all visible fat
Salt and ground black pepper

Lemon Rice
1½ cups defatted reduced-sodium chicken broth
¾ cup long-grain white rice
2 teaspoons grated lemon rind
1 tablespoon finely chopped fresh mint
Salt and ground black pepper

Mint Sauce
¼ cup packed light brown sugar
¼ cup mint jelly
2–3 teaspoons finely chopped fresh mint

To make the lamb: In a small bowl, mash the garlic with the rosemary to make a paste. Rub evenly over the lamb and set aside to marinate for 30 minutes.

Coat a large no-stick skillet with no-stick spray and warm over medium heat. Add the lamb and cook for about 4 minutes per side for medium doneness. Remove the lamb and place on a plate lined with paper towels. Blot the top with additional paper towels. Season the lamb to taste with the salt and pepper and set aside.

To make the lemon rice: While the lamb is marinating, in a medium saucepan, bring the broth to a boil. Stir in the rice and lemon rind. Reduce the heat to low, cover and simmer for about 25 minutes, or until the rice is tender and the liquid is absorbed. Stir in the mint. Season to taste with the salt and pepper.

To make the mint sauce: While the rice is cooking, combine the brown sugar and jelly in a small saucepan. Cook over medium heat until melted. Remove from the heat and stir in the mint. Serve warm with the lamb and rice.

Makes 4 servings. Per serving: 397 calories, 6.2 g. fat (14% of calories), 27.4 g. protein, 56.4 g. carbohydrates, 0.5 g. dietary fiber, 74 mg. cholesterol, 91 mg. sodium

VARIATIONS

Lamb with Jalapeño Mint Sauce: To make the lamb, replace the rosemary with finely chopped fresh cilantro. Omit the mint sauce. Instead, in a small saucepan, melt ½ cup jalapeño pepper jelly. Remove from the heat and stir in 2 teaspoons finely chopped fresh mint and 2 teaspoons finely chopped fresh cilantro. Serve the jalapeño mint sauce warm or at room temperature with the lamb and lemon rice.

Lamb with Mint Chutney: Omit the mint sauce. Instead, in a small saucepan, combine ½ cup finely chopped fresh mint leaves, ¼ cup minced onions, 2 tablespoons chopped dried apples, 2 tablespoons raisins, 1 teaspoon Dijon mustard, ¼ cup cider vinegar, ¼ cup packed light brown sugar and ⅛ teaspoon salt. Cook over medium heat for 5 to 8 minutes, or until the liquid is absorbed. Serve the chutney warm or at room temperature with the lamb and lemon rice.

Pork Tenderloin with Honey-Mint Sauce: Replace the lamb with 1 pound boneless pork tenderloin. Rub with the garlic-rosemary paste and let stand for 30 minutes. Cut into scant ½"-thick slices. Coat a medium no-stick skillet with no-stick spray and warm over medium heat. Cook the pork for 3 to 4 minutes per side, or until browned. To make the honey-mint sauce, replace the brown sugar with honey.

Greek-Style Lamb-and-Vegetable Kebabs

Marinade

⅓ cup chopped fresh parsley
1 tablespoon dried oregano
3 cloves garlic, minced
2 tablespoons lemon juice
½ cup nonfat yogurt
½ teaspoon ground cinnamon
Pinch of ground black pepper
12 ounces lean lamb leg, trimmed of all visible fat and cut into 1" cubes

Kebabs

1 large onion
1 sweet red pepper, cut into 1" pieces
1 yellow pepper, cut into 1" pieces
1 zucchini, cut lengthwise into quarters and sliced ½" thick
8 medium mushrooms
4 cups hot cooked rice

To make the marinade: In a medium bowl, combine the parsley, oregano, garlic, lemon juice, yogurt, cinnamon and pepper. Add the lamb and mix well. Cover and marinate in the refrigerator, stirring occasionally, for 2 to 3 hours.

To make the kebabs: Peel the onion and carefully trim off the root hairs, leaving the root attachment intact. Cut lengthwise into 1" wedges, leaving the root attachment on each wedge so the layers don't separate. Add the onions, red peppers, yellow peppers, zucchini and mushrooms to the marinade. Toss to coat.

Thread the lamb and vegetables onto 4 metal skewers.

Coat an unheated grill rack with no-stick spray. Light the grill according to the manufacturer's directions. Place the rack on the grill.

Place the kebabs on the rack and grill

about 6″ from the heat, turning to cook on all sides, for 15 to 20 minutes, or until the lamb is cooked through. Serve with the rice.

Makes 4 servings. Per serving: 405 calories, 5.4 g. fat (12% of calories), 26.9 g. protein, 62.3 g. carbohydrates, 2.6 g. dietary fiber, 56 mg. cholesterol, 71 mg. sodium

NOTES

• These kebabs can be broiled instead of grilled. Place on a broiler pan and broil 6″ from the heat.

• You can replace the lamb with lean beef and the rice with cooked bulgur or couscous.

QUICK!
Basic Meat Marinade

Here's an oil-free marinade that lends great flavor to beef, pork and lamb. It's perfect for grilling or broiling. Try it on vegetables, too.

⅓ cup red-wine vinegar
1 tablespoon Dijon mustard
1 tablespoon reduced-sodium Worcester-shire sauce
1 clove garlic, crushed
1 tablespoon chopped fresh parsley
¼ teaspoon ground black pepper
1 bay leaf, broken in half

In a small bowl, whisk together the vinegar, mustard, Worcestershire sauce, garlic, parsley and pepper. Add the bay leaf.

Makes ½ cup. Per tablespoon: 5 calories, 0.1 g. fat (19% of calories), 0.2 g. protein, 1.1 g. carbohydrates, 0 g. dietary fiber, 0 mg. cholesterol, 39 mg. sodium

NOTES

• To use, pour the marinade over 1 pound of beef, pork or lamb in a heavy-duty resealable plastic bag or rectangular glass or ceramic baking dish. Seal or cover and refrigerate, turning occasionally. For meat that is cut into small pieces, refrigerate for 1 hour before cooking. For meat in one large piece, refrigerate for up to 3 hours before cooking. After marinating is complete, remove and discard the bay leaf.

• To tenderize meat during cooking, baste occasionally with the marinade.

• To ensure food safety, discard any leftover unheated marinade.

• For a spicier marinade, add 1 minced serrano or jalapeño chili pepper (wear plastic gloves when handling) or ½ teaspoon hot-pepper sauce or ground red pepper to the mixture.

VARIATIONS

Citrus Herb Marinade for Meat: Omit the mustard and Worcestershire sauce. Replace the vinegar with 3 tablespoons orange juice and 3 tablespoons lemon juice. Add 1 tablespoon chopped fresh rosemary, cilantro, tarragon or thyme.

Tropical Spice Marinade for Meat: Omit the mustard, Worcestershire sauce, parsley and bay leaf. Replace the vinegar with pineapple juice, apple cider or apricot nectar. Add 1 teaspoon ground cumin, ½ teaspoon ground coriander, ¼ teaspoon ground ginger and a pinch of allspice.

Vegetarian Entrées

Did you ever see a fat squirrel? Or a rabbit with heart disease? Probably not. Squirrels, rabbits, chipmunks and many other animals usually eat a slimming vegetarian diet. Human animals would do well to follow their lead.

Many healthy cooks are already doing so. Experts estimate that there are nearly 12.5 million vegetarians in this country. And some of the most highly respected doctors advocate a low-fat, meatless—or reduced meat—diet for both weight control and heart health. The evidence is compelling. In one large study, for example, researchers found that the Chinese, who eat little meat and derive fewer than 15 percent of their calories from fat, are extremely unlikely to get diseases such as cancer, heart disease and diabetes.

Even if you have no desire to go vegetarian, chances are that you still crave the occasional meatless meal, with an abundance of vegetables, grains or legumes. With just a few simple techniques, and with the enormous variety of fresh ingredients available in supermarkets today, you'll never tire of this delicious, healthful cuisine.

NATURALLY HEALTHY

The great thing about meatless cuisine is that vegetables, grains and other plant-based ingredients are naturally low in fat. As long as you don't inundate them with high-fat cheese, cook them in pools of oil or drench them with butter at the table, it's almost impossible to prepare vegetarian entrées that will raise your cholesterol or threaten your waistline.

Vegetarian meals provide an abundance of fiber, vitamins and minerals. Getting enough protein, however, can be a challenge, particularly if you're a strict vegetarian who avoids eggs, milk, cheese and other dairy products. The reason is that the proteins found in plants may not be as complete as those found in meats.

Some vegetarians go to great lengths to combine a variety of foods at every meal in order to achieve a complete protein balance. A typical meal might consist of grains and dairy products (pasta and a little low-fat Parmesan cheese, for example) or grains and legumes (tabbouleh followed by a black-bean main dish). Once you start thinking in terms of combinations rather than simply eating a plateful of steamed zucchini or plain boiled rice, you will have no trouble getting enough protein.

While many vegetarians or near-vegetarians strive to mix and match proteins on a daily basis, most experts say that this level of planning really isn't necessary. As long as you consistently eat a variety of grains, legumes and vegetables—not necessarily at every meal, but on an ongoing, daily basis—you'll almost certainly get all the key nutrients that you need, including protein.

CUTTING BACK THE FAT

Since meats are one of the main sources of saturated fats, cutting back on meat will almost certainly reduce the amount of fat in your diet.

A Vegetarian Diet

Is It GOOD for You?

Nutritionists have long debated whether or not a vegetarian diet is as healthy as the traditional omnivorous kind, at least in adults. (Children have different needs than adults, and you should talk to a doctor before putting any young child on a strict vegetarian diet.)

Research has shown that people who don't eat meat tend to have fewer instances of stroke and heart attack than nonvegetarians. They may also have a lower risk of colon cancer. Yet the proteins found in plant foods are not as high-quality as those in meats. That's why vegetarians are advised to eat a wide variety of legumes, grains and nuts or seeds.

One nutrient that requires special attention is vitamin B_{12}. Found only in meat and dairy products, B_{12} is needed for the production of healthy blood cells and certain nerve-related tissues. Many vegetarians play it safe and take B_{12} supplements.

It's possible, however, to eat no meat at all and still get unhealthy amounts of fat in your diet. The reason is that many people, in their efforts to eliminate meat from their diets, substitute unacceptably high amounts of nuts, cheeses and dairy products, many of which are

MIX AND MATCH

Most plant proteins are not as high in quality as animal proteins. To get the proper protein balance, some vegetarians combine a variety of foods with every meal. Here are some delicious combinations.

LEGUMES	GRAINS	NUTS OR SEEDS
Dried beans	Rice	Cashews
Lentils	Corn	Sunflower seeds
Tofu	Rice	Sesame seeds
Split peas	Bulgur	Walnuts

extremely high in fat. A 1-ounce chunk of Cheddar cheese, for example, contains more fat than a 3-ounce cut of T-bone steak and almost as much as 3 ounces of fresh ham.

To enjoy the benefits of vegetarian cuisine without loading up on fat, here's what experts advise.

Turn up the flavors. To replace the rich taste of meat, don't hesitate to compensate by raiding the spice cabinet. Go for big flavors—with dry and fresh herbs, spice mixtures or flavored liquids, such as herbal or balsamic vinegar. Once you amplify the flavor of your favorite foods, you'll be surprised at how little you miss the meat.

Be wary of dairy. Cheese, sour cream and other dairy products can add good taste and a wonderfully creamy texture to many meals. At the same time, however, they can add unacceptably high levels of dietary fat. To get the taste and texture of dairy without the fat, try to use ingredients that are lower in fat than their traditional counterparts.

☞ Substitute skim milk or 1% low-fat milk for whole.

To thicken soups and sauces without using a fattening roux (a cooked combination of fat and flour used as a thickening agent), puree cooked vegetables in a food processor or blender and use as a flavorful base.

☞ Swap buttermilk for whole milk. Despite the name, buttermilk is a low-fat product. Read the label, though; some buttermilk is fat-free while other brands aren't.

☞ Neufchâtel cheese is a good substitute for cream cheese and has about one-third less fat.

☞ Rather than using full-fat ricotta or cottage cheese, use homemade yogurt cheese or reduced-fat ricotta and cottage cheese.

☞ Substitute big-flavored cheeses like sharp Cheddar for milder varieties. Even when they're higher in fat than milder cheeses, they have a stronger taste, so you can get by with using less.

VEGETARIAN COOKING

In some ways, meat cuisine is more forgiving than cooking with vegetables. The strong flavors of meat, whether you're broiling, baking or deep-frying, come through loud and clear, regardless of the seasonings that you use. Meat

MAKING YOGURT CHEESE

For the flavor and texture of cheese without the fat, many healthy cooks substitute yogurt cheese. It's fresh-tasting, low in fat and a breeze to make. One pound of yogurt makes about 1 cup of yogurt cheese. When you buy the yogurt, however, make sure that it doesn't contain gelatin, because this may prevent drainage of the whey.

If you're unsure if your yogurt is suitable for draining, scoop out a large spoonful, leaving a depression. If the hole starts to fill with liquid within 10 to 15 minutes, you'll be able to drain excess whey from the yogurt.

Line a colander with three to four layers of cheesecloth and set it over a bowl.

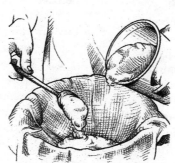

Spoon nonfat or low-fat plain yogurt in the colander. Refrigerate and allow to drain.

After 3 to 4 hours, the yogurt will have turned into soft curds; after 10 to 12 hours, the curds will be very firm. Use in place of other fresh cheeses in salads, spreads and sauces.

EGG SAFETY

A type of food poisoning caused by salmonella bacteria has been the subject of a number of alarming headlines. According to the Centers for Disease Control and Prevention in Atlanta, these bacteria struck more than 18,000 people between 1985 and 1993. In many of those cases, experts say, eggs were to blame.

Even though the risk of contracting salmonella from eggs is extremely low—experts estimate that only about 1 in 10,000 eggs may be contaminated—a bout with salmonella is sufficiently unpleasant to warrant taking a few precautions. For the most part, this boils down to cooking: Heating an egg to 140°F for about 3½ minutes will kill virtually all the bacteria.

☞ When cooking eggs over easy, fry them for about 3 minutes on one side and 1 minute on the other.

☞ When making scrambled eggs, make sure you cook them just past the runny stage.

☞ When making soft-boiled eggs, bring the eggs and water to a boil, cover the pan and turn off the heat. Let stand for about 5 minutes.

☞ If you make Caesar salad at home, either omit the egg from the recipe or use egg substitute, which has been pasteurized. In restaurants, Caesar salads are generally made with pasteurized egg products, so they are quite safe. If you are in doubt, ask the waiter to verify the preparation technique.

☞ Discard eggs with cracked shells, since these provide a doorway for bacteria to get inside.

is also filling, and you can make an entire meal by broiling a chicken thigh and adding a little salad as an afterthought.

Vegetarian entrées, by contrast, typically have a more delicate, uncluttered flavor. It's important to prepare them in such a way that their basic good taste and texture aren't lost in the process. Here are some tips on managing the kitchen, vegetarian-style.

☞ **Blanching.** This involves plunging a vegetable very briefly into boiling water and then immersing it in cold water, which sets the color, enhances the flavor and makes it slightly tender but crisp.

Chefs often blanch tender vegetables like snap peas and young asparagus before adding them to salads.

Blanching is often used to partially cook a vegetable as a prelude to further cooking. For example, vegetables are often blanched before being moved to the grill.

☞ **Grilling.** The venerable backyard grill does more than just char burgers. Grilling also caramelizes the natural sugars in vegetables, giving them a smoky, slightly sweet taste.

You don't need to marinate vegetables before grilling. Before putting them on the heat, drizzle on a little extra-virgin olive oil or splash on some herbal vinegar.

To make sure that dense vegetables cook all the way through, chefs advise blanching or parboiling them first, then putting them on the grill.

☞ **Microwaving.** This is perhaps the fastest, easiest way to cook vegetables. Despite the high technology, cooking in the microwave essentially steams vegetables quickly, so they're tender, yet crisp.

☞ **Simmering.** For tough vegetables like turnips and potatoes or for dense, long-cooking items like legumes simmering at just below the boiling point will make them tender without damaging their delicate textures.

☞ **Steaming.** Done on the stove top or in the microwave, steaming cooks food quickly, making it crisp-tender without leaching out the valuable nutrients.

☞ **Stir-frying.** A popular technique in vegetarian cooking, this requires a wok or high-sided no-stick sauté pan that allows plenty of room for stirring. The goal is to use very high heats, which cook vegetables quickly and help sear in flavors and moisture.

When stir-frying, add just a little oil (about 1 tablespoon) to the pan after it's already hot. When the oil is almost to the smoking point, begin adding vegetables.

Add slow-cooking vegetables like carrots or cauliflower first, then add the more tender ingredients toward the end of the cooking time.

VEGETARIAN SEASONINGS

When you start cooking without meat, you may find the results somewhat flat. This is because meat naturally adds a lot of flavor. When you eliminate meat, you'll need to add more seasonings in order to compensate for the flavor.

☞ Use fresh herbs whenever possible, as their flavor is superior to that of dried. To maintain their delicate flavors, however, always add fresh herbs near the end of the cooking time.

☞ Dried herbs are more convenient than fresh. They're also much more potent. Use about 1 teaspoon of a dried herb for every 1 tablespoon that you'd use of fresh.

☞ It's best to add dried herbs early in the cooking process to give them time to release their flavors. Before adding to food, rub the herbs well to release the flavorful oils.

☞ Flavored liquids like hot sauces and herbal vinegars add a startling splash of excitement to rice, legumes and other vegetarian fare.

DELICIOUS STRATEGIES

Many of us took our first tastes of vegetarian cuisine in the 1960s and early 1970s, when "healthy" was all too often a euphemism for "tasteless." As a result, many cooks continue to regard meatless meals with suspicion, if not outright disdain.

But things have changed. Vegetarian cooking has been a popular cultural phenomenon for more than 30 years. Chefs are well-versed in the glorious tumbles of colors, textures and shapes available at supermarkets and farmers markets nationwide. In short, there's nothing dull about today's meatless meals. On the contrary, they represent an exciting journey of discovery, good taste and vibrant good health.

Here are some basic strategies.

Go for the whole. Whenever possible, use whole-grain foods. The less milling or processing a food undergoes, the more natural fiber and nutrients—as well as textures and tastes—it's likely to contain.

Fill up on rice. Even though whole grains are preferable, white rice can play a valuable role in the healthy cook's kitchen. White rice turns out fluffy and light, with the additional advantage of cooking quickly. For more fiber and a nutty flavor, opt for brown rice. Let your taste buds—and the recipe—be your guide.

Whereas rice is perhaps our most familiar grain, many cooks are exploring other varieties, such as corn, oats, bulgur, amaranth and quinoa.

Put up some pasta. It's nutritious, filling and a breeze to cook. Plus, it's available in an enormous variety of interesting shapes and flavors. It can be tossed into salad, added to soup or used as a base for a delicious sauce or topping.

Explore the produce bin. Many of today's supermarkets stock dozens or even hundreds of varieties of vegetables and leafy greens. Variety is good not only for nutritional balance but also for creating an exciting culinary palette.

☞ Since vegetables and greens typically get star billing in vegetarian meals, it's important to find the freshest ingredients available. Chefs agree that it's best to use fresh ingredients within a few days of buying them.

☞ Frozen vegetables will do in a pinch, but they lack the texture of fresh.

☞ Canned vegetables have an even softer texture than frozen and can be extremely salty. Always rinse canned vegetables thoroughly to remove at least some of the excess sodium.

☞ Don't hesitate to create your own vegetable recipes. Steamed vegetables are good; so are vegetable sautés and stir-fry medleys. Feel like pasta but don't want the sauce? Just sauté a little bit of garlic and onion in a spoonful of olive oil for an instant aromatic pasta topping.

☞ For extra flavor, try steaming vegetables over water that's been infused with herbs, spices, garlic or shallots.

Go dark. As a rule, the darker the vegetable—dark orange, dark red or dark green—the more nutrients it contains.

Turn over a new leaf. Here's a tip about iceberg lettuce: Mom may have bought it religiously, but the fact is, iceberg is pretty devoid of nutrients and fiber. Since salads often play a big part in no-meat meals, go for the nutritious darker leaves, such as romaine, Swiss chard, endive, watercress, spinach, arugula and turnip greens.

Toast for the most. To boost the flavors of spices, nuts or seeds, toast them in a dry no-stick skillet over medium heat, shaking the skillet often, for 3 to 5 minutes before adding them to your recipe. This will help release the essential oils that give these items their flavor—and that make meatless meals a flavor treat.

BRING ON THE BEANS

High in fiber, protein, complex carbohydrates and a vast assortment of vitamins and minerals, beans make a perfect entrée at the meatless table. Best of all, with the wide variety of beans available—from pintos and kidney beans to Jacob's cattle and soldier beans—it's almost impossible to get bored.

For a more detailed look at beans, see page 178. Here are a few bean basics to get you started.

☞ With the exception of lentils, split peas and black-eyed peas, most dried beans should be soaked before cooking. Soaking reduces the cooking time. In addition, changing the soaking liquid several times can help reduce uncomfortable "bean bloat."

Helpful Hint

To tell when beans are done, press one (after it has cooled) against the roof of your mouth with your tongue. It should be easy to crush but still have a firm texture.

☞ If you're not in a hurry, you can simply rinse the beans, cover them with water and let them stand for at least 4 hours, changing the water several times.

☞ To hasten the soaking time, rinse and drain the beans, then cover them with water in a large pot. Bring the water to a boil over high heat. Reduce the heat to a simmer and continue cooking for 2 to 3 minutes, skimming the foam that rises to the surface. Remove from the heat, cover and let stand for 1 hour.

☞ After soaking, drain the beans, put them in a pot and add enough cold water to cover by 2 to 3 inches. Bring to a boil over high heat, reduce the heat to a low simmer and cook for 1 to 2 hours, or until tender.

☞ To give extra flavor to cooked beans, add onions, carrots, celery or other vegetables or herbs to the beans during cooking.

☞ When drained, cooled and packed in a plastic bag, beans can be frozen for two months.

☞ While canned beans offer a convenient alternative to the dried kind, they're typically high in sodium. Rinse and drain them well before using them, to help remove some of the sodium. Or look for beans processed with little or no salt.

MASTERING MUSHROOMS

When creating a summery salad, creamy soup or hearty barley casserole, many cooks reach first for the mushrooms. They provide a delicate flavor while lending a bit of elegance and visual excitement. They also have a firm, slightly chewy texture that's a perfect substitute for meat.

Wild mushrooms have been gaining in popularity. Because of their brief growing seasons, limited availability and relatively high cost, however, wild mushrooms are still something of a specialty item. Domestic mushrooms, on the other hand, are as much an everyday staple as rice and fresh vegetables.

To get the most from mushrooms, here's what chefs advise.

Use them quickly. The quality of mushrooms declines rapidly, even with refrigeration, so it's important to use them quickly, preferably within a week after bringing them home.

Mushrooms need to breathe, so don't store them in sealed plastic containers. Instead, store them in the produce drawer—loose or in a paper bag.

Wash them well. Mushrooms grow close to the ground in loose soil, so they tend to accumulate a lot of grit that needs to be washed off. Kitchen supply stores sell mushroom brushes, but all you really need is running water. Use your fingers or a damp paper towel to rub the grit away.

EXPLORING TOFU

Although tofu (bean curd) has long been a staple in Asian cooking, here in America, it's often seen more as a health food joke than as the truly versatile ingredient that it is.

Helpful Hint

The one problem with mushrooms is that they often turn brown, sometimes in as little as a few hours. To keep white mushrooms white, wipe them gently with water mixed with a little lemon juice.

PREPARING DRIED MUSHROOMS

How many times have you bought a bag of fresh mushrooms only to have most of them go bad in the produce bin? Unlike fresh varieties, dried mushrooms last virtually forever. Rehydrated in water, they plump up nice and fresh and make a delicately flavored, nicely textured addition to soups, casseroles and stir-fries.

Put the dried mushrooms in a bowl and add enough hot water to cover by about an inch. Let them soak for at least 30 minutes, until soft, then drain. (You can strain the soaking liquid through cheesecloth to remove any grit and use it in soups or sauces.)

Trim away the stem, thinly slice the cap and use as though fresh.

MAKE THE MOST OF MUSHROOMS

When you're tired of the common white button mushroom and would like an exciting change, try eating exotic mushrooms instead. Found in large supermarkets and some specialty shops, exotics add a rich, deeply layered taste to meals.

NAME	DESCRIPTION	PREPARATION
Chanterelle	Has a golden or orange-yellow wide-gilled cap that resembles an inside-out umbrella; delicately flavored with a slight hint of apricot	Often combined with creamy sauces and served over pasta
Cremini	A firm, meaty, brown mushroom with a hearty flavor	Excellent with strong-flavored foods like pizzas, stuffings or casseroles
Enoki	Long but tiny white mushrooms with caps; sold in clumps; have a very delicate taste and texture	Can work well in salads, clear soups and other delicate foods that won't conceal their light flavor
Morel	Distinctive, honey-combed, cone-shaped cap, with a delicate, earthy taste	Can be sautéed in olive oil or served in a creamy sauce
Oyster	Light colored and delicate; the gilled, spreading cap resembles a white or gray calla lily; has a mild taste and soft texture	Can be substituted for white button mushrooms in soups or sauces
Porcini (also known as cèpes)	Large, meaty mushroom with a broad brown cap; has a deep, smoky flavor.	To bring out the "wild" flavor, sauté, broil or grill, then drizzle with olive oil.
Portobello	Large and intensely flavored; perhaps the meatiest of the mushrooms; a giant version of the cremini	Can be grilled, baked or sautéed; because of the strong flavor, it should be served with other assertive ingredients
Shiitake	Ranges in color from tan to dark brown; has a strong flavor and meaty texture	Often used as a meat substitute in vegetarian dishes; also excellent in soups, stews and casseroles

In the past, unfortunately, tofu was often served up overcooked, rubbery and devoid of flavor; its negative reputation was often well-deserved.

But tofu, properly prepared, is an infinitely versatile ingredient. Often used in aromatic stir-fries or spicy hot-and-sour dishes, it absorbs flavors and helps bring them together in a smooth blend. At the same time, it stays true to its own mellow character.

Since tofu is high in protein and also adds body to dishes, many cooks use it as a substitute for meat—in lasagna, for example, or other baked casseroles. It can also be used instead of, or to augment, the eggs in egg salad.

There are several forms of tofu. The firm and extra-firm varieties are used for grilling and stir-frying. They can also be used for crumbling into salads or lasagna, just as you might crumble chopped meat into a marinara sauce. Soft tofu is often used for making desserts like cheesecake. Silken tofu, which has a soft, creamy texture, is often used for things like salad dressings and smooth sauces.

☞ Although tofu is high in protein as well as calcium, it's not necessarily low in fat; regular versions get anywhere from 30 to more than 50 percent of their calories from fat. It's best to use full-fat tofu in relatively small quantities—to add substance to a soup, for example, or to beef up a stir-fry.

☞ Tofu is extremely perishable. Be sure to store it in the refrigerator submerged in water. Changing the water daily will help keep the tofu fresh.

☞ When using tofu for stir-fries, rinse it well, then cut it into cubes and add it to the pan near the end of the cooking time.

☞ For a slightly smoky taste, brush tofu lightly with olive oil or a marinade of your choice, then grill it as you would meat. It takes only minutes to cook.

☞ Many healthy cooks crumble tofu and add it to scrambled eggs or egg salad.

☞ When making creamy soups, you can blend a little tofu with broth for a natural thickener and for added nutrients.

PREPARING TOFU

Tofu is ready to use straight from the package, but because it contains so much water, it tends to fall apart during cooking. That's why you may want to press it first.

Cut the tofu in half and lay the pieces side by side. Cover the tofu with wax paper and place it on a cutting board that's been propped at a slight angle.

Place a heavy object on top of the tofu; a large skillet will do nicely. Let it stand for about half an hour, or until water oozes from the tofu and runs off.

A quick way to press water from tofu that's going to be crumbled—for use in a meat loaf, for example—is to place it in a clean, nonterry dish towel, twist the ends and firmly ring it dry.

Patrick Clark

Patrick Clark is executive chef at Tavern on the Green in Central Park. He always makes it a point to include a number of meatless entrées on his menu. "Vegetarian entrées are exciting to create," he says. "I heighten the flavoring of the vegetables by combining them with herbs that complement them, like combining thyme with zucchini or basil with peppers.

When serving his vegetarian shepherd's pie, Clark layers the mixtures in four ring molds. (A simpler strategy is given below.)

Ratatouille Shepherd's Pie

- 4 teaspoons olive oil
- 2 Japanese eggplants, diced
- ½ cup + 1 tablespoon water
-   Salt and ground black pepper
- 2 small zucchini, diced
- 1 small fennel bulb, diced
- 1 sweet red pepper, roasted and diced
- 1 red onion, diced
- 2 medium Italian tomatoes, diced
- 3 cloves garlic, chopped
- 3 tablespoons chopped fresh basil
- 1½ teaspoons chopped fresh thyme
- 1 pound spinach
- ⅔ cup fresh bread crumbs
- ¼ cup grated Parmesan cheese
- 1 pound potatoes, cooked and mashed

Heat 1 teaspoon of the oil in a large no-stick skillet over medium-high heat. Add the eggplant and sauté for 30 seconds. Add ¼ cup of the water. Cook and stir for 4 minutes, or until the water has evaporated and the eggplant is tender. Season with the salt and black pepper. Transfer to a bowl and set aside.

Add 1 teaspoon of the remaining oil to the skillet. Add the zucchini, fennel and red peppers and sauté for 30 seconds. Add ¼ cup of the remaining water. Season lightly with the salt and pepper. Add to the bowl with the eggplant.

Add 1 teaspoon of the remaining oil to the skillet. Add the onions and the remaining 1 tablespoon water. Cook for 4 minutes, or until soft. Add the tomatoes and half of the garlic. Cook over low heat for 3 minutes, or until all the liquid is evaporated. Add to the bowl with the eggplant. Stir in the basil and 1 teaspoon of the thyme. Allow to cool.

Wash the spinach, shake off excess water and remove the stems. Cut the leaves into thin strips. Place the wet leaves in a large skillet. Cover and cook over medium-high heat for 5 minutes, or until wilted. Add the remaining 1 teaspoon oil and sauté for 3 minutes, or until the water has evaporated.

In a small bowl, mix the bread crumbs, Parmesan and the remaining ½ teaspoon thyme.

In another small bowl, mix the potatoes and the remaining garlic.

Press the spinach evenly into the bottom of a 4-cup gratin dish. Spoon the eggplant mixture evenly over the spinach. Top with the mashed potatoes. Sprinkle with the bread-crumb mixture.

Preheat the oven to 350°. Bake for 20 minutes. Place under a broiler and allow the crumbs to brown.

Makes 4 servings. Per serving: 276 calories, 7.8 g. fat (24% of calories), 11.7 g. protein, 45 g. carbohydrates, 6.3 g. dietary fiber, 5 mg. cholesterol, 266 mg. sodium

Vegetable Potpie

Vegetable Filling

- 1 cup chopped onions
- ½ cup sliced sweet red pepper
- 2 cloves garlic, minced
- 2 cups reduced-sodium vegetable broth
- 1 medium baking potato, scrubbed and cubed
- 2 small zucchini, sliced ½" thick
- 1 large carrot, sliced
- 1 medium parsnip, sliced
- ½ cup fresh or frozen peas
- ½ cup fresh or frozen corn
- ½ teaspoon dried rosemary
- ½ teaspoon dried tarragon
- ¼ teaspoon dried thyme
- 3 tablespoons all-purpose flour
- ⅓ cup cold water
- 2 tablespoons dry white wine (optional)
  Salt and ground black pepper

Crust

- 1 cup all-purpose flour
- ¼ teaspoon baking powder
- ¼ teaspoon salt
- 3 tablespoons vegetable oil or cold margarine, cut into pieces
- 4-4½ tablespoons ice water
- 1½ teaspoons skim milk
- 2 teaspoons grated reduced-fat Parmesan cheese

To make the vegetable filling: Coat a large saucepan with no-stick spray; warm over medium heat until hot. Add the onions, red peppers and garlic. Sauté for 5 minutes, or until the vegetables are tender.

Add the broth, potatoes, zucchini, carrots, parsnips, peas, corn, rosemary, tarragon and thyme. Bring to a boil over high heat. Reduce the heat to low, cover and simmer for 10 minutes, or until the vegetables are tender.

Return to a boil over medium-high heat. In a small bowl, whisk together the flour and water. Stir into the vegetable mixture and cook, stirring constantly, until thickened. Stir in the wine (if using) and season to taste with the salt and black pepper. Spoon the mixture into a 2-quart baking dish or soufflé dish.

To make the crust: Preheat the oven to 425°. In a small bowl, combine the flour, baking powder and salt. Cut in the oil or margarine with a fork or pastry blender until coarse crumbs form. Mix in the water, 1 tablespoon at a time, until a dough forms.

Transfer to a lightly floured surface and roll to ¼" thickness. Carefully place the rolled dough over the baking dish. Trim the edges and flute or press with the tines of a fork. Cut several steam vents in the top of the crust. If desired, roll pastry scraps and cut into designs for the top of the crust.

Bake for 10 minutes. Lightly brush the top of the crust with the milk and sprinkle with the Parmesan. Bake for 5 to 10 minutes longer, or until the crust is lightly browned. Cool on a wire rack for 5 minutes before serving.

Makes 4 servings. Per serving: 391 calories, 11.2 g. fat (26% of calories), 9.6 g. protein, 65.6 g. carbohydrates, 6.4 g. dietary fiber, 0 mg. cholesterol, 246 mg. sodium

VARIATIONS

Pennsylvania Dutch Potpie: Omit the crust. Instead, serve the vegetable mixture over hot cooked egg (no-yolk) noodles.

Vegetable Casserole and Biscuits: Omit the crust. Instead, top the vegetables with biscuits. Arrange the biscuits over the vegetable mixture and bake at 400° for 15 minutes, or until the biscuits are lightly browned.

Winter Potpie: Replace the peas and corn with 1 cup halved brussels sprouts. Replace the zucchini with 1 medium turnip or sweet potato, cubed. Increase the dried thyme to ½ teaspoon and replace the dried rosemary and tarragon with ½ teaspoon dried sage.

Vegetarian Moussaka

Traditional Greek moussaka contains ground lamb or beef. In this low-fat vegetarian version, barley creates a hearty, flavorful dish without a lot of fat.

Vegetable Filling

- 1 large eggplant, sliced ½" thick
- 3 cups cubed unpeeled scrubbed potatoes
- 2 cups chopped onions
- 2 cups chopped carrots
- 3 cloves garlic, minced
- 1 teaspoon ground cinnamon
- 1 teaspoon dried oregano
- 1 teaspoon dried mint
- ¾ cup reduced-sodium vegetable broth
- 1 can (14½ ounces) diced tomatoes with roasted garlic
- 1 can (8 ounces) tomato sauce
- 2 cups sliced mushrooms
- 2 cups cooked barley
- Salt and ground black pepper

Custard Topping

- 5½ tablespoons margarine
- ½ cup all-purpose flour
- 3 cups skim milk
- 1 egg
- 2 egg whites
- ¼ teaspoon salt
- ⅛ teaspoon ground black pepper
- Pinch of ground nutmeg

To make the vegetable filling: Preheat the oven to 400°. Line a no-stick jelly-roll pan with foil. Coat the pan with no-stick spray.

Arrange the eggplant on the prepared pan and spray the tops with no-stick spray. Bake for 20 minutes, or until the eggplant is tender. Coat a 9" × 13" no-stick baking dish with no-stick spray. Arrange the slices in the bottom of the dish; set aside.

Coat a large no-stick skillet with no-stick spray. Warm over medium heat until hot. Add the potatoes, onions, carrots and garlic. Cover and cook for 5 minutes. Add the cinnamon, oregano, mint and broth. Bring to a boil over high heat. Reduce the heat to low and simmer, uncovered, for 5 minutes.

Add the tomatoes, tomato sauce, mushrooms and barley. Cook, stirring occasionally, for 10 minutes, or until the mixture is thick. Season to taste with the salt and pepper. Spoon the mixture evenly over the eggplant.

To make the custard topping: Preheat the oven to 350°. In a large saucepan over medium-low heat, melt the margarine. Stir in the flour and cook, stirring constantly, for 2 to 3 minutes. Stir in the milk and bring to a boil. Cook and stir until thickened.

In a small bowl, whisk together the egg and egg whites. Whisk 1 cup of the milk mixture into the eggs. Whisk back into the milk mixture in the saucepan. Cook over low heat for 2 minutes, or until thickened. Stir in the salt and black pepper.

Pour the topping over the vegetable mixture. Sprinkle with the nutmeg. Bake for 45 minutes, or until bubbly and browned on top. Cool for 5 minutes before cutting and serving.

Makes 8 servings. Per serving: 362 calories, 9.4 g. fat (23% of calories), 11.3 g. protein, 60.4 g. carbohydrates, 6.8 g. dietary fiber, 28 mg. cholesterol, 564 mg. sodium

VARIATIONS

Mixed-Grain Moussaka: Replace 1 cup of the barley with 1 cup cooked brown rice.

Squash Moussaka: Replace the potatoes with 3 cups peeled and cubed butternut squash. Replace the carrots with 2 cups chopped yellow squash.

Tofu Moussaka: Replace 1 cup of the barley with 1 cup crumbled firm tofu.

Winter Moussaka: Replace 1½ cups of the potatoes with 1½ cups parsnips or rutabagas. Replace 1 cup of the carrots with 1 cup halved brussels sprouts. Replace the cinnamon and mint with 1 teaspoon dried basil and 1 teaspoon dried savory.

Three-Layer Tortilla Casserole

1 can (15 ounces) pinto beans, rinsed and drained
¼ cup vegetable broth or water
2 cloves garlic
½ cup packed fresh cilantro leaves
2 teaspoons olive oil
2 cups thinly sliced onion
2 cups diced zucchini
1½ cups frozen corn
1 teaspoon ground cumin
Pinch of salt
3 flour tortillas (8″ diameter)
¾ cup reduced-sodium salsa
¾ cup shredded reduced-fat hot-pepper Monterey Jack cheese

Preheat the oven to 350°.

Coat a 10″ pie plate with no-stick spray. Set aside.

In a food processor or blender, combine the beans, broth or water, garlic, cilantro and 1 teaspoon of the oil. Process until smooth. Set aside.

In a large no-stick skillet over medium-high heat, warm the remaining 1 teaspoon oil. Add the onions. Sauté for 3 minutes, or until soft. Add the zucchini, corn, cumin and salt. Cook over medium-high heat, stirring occasionally, until the zucchini is tender.

Place 1 tortilla in the prepared pie plate. Spread a third of the bean mixture over the tortilla. Using a slotted spoon, lift a third of the vegetable mixture out of the skillet and scatter over the beans. Top with ¼ cup of the salsa and ¼ cup of the Monterey Jack. Repeat this layering process twice to make a total of 3 layers.

Bake, uncovered, for 25 to 30 minutes. Cut into wedges and serve hot.

Makes 4 servings. Per serving: 378 calories, 9.1 g. fat (20% of calories), 20.6 g. protein, 58.9 g. carbohydrates, 3.4 g. dietary fiber, 15 mg. cholesterol, 624 mg. sodium

NOTE

• Substitute black beans for the pinto beans. Or use a combination of black and pinto beans.

Vegetable Strudel

2 tablespoons finely chopped shallots or onions
1 cup sliced shiitake or cremini mushrooms
¼ cup dry sherry or vegetable broth
1½ teaspoons lemon juice
½ teaspoon dried tarragon
1 cup vegetable broth
1 tablespoon cornstarch
1 leek (white part only), thinly sliced
1 medium sweet red pepper, chopped
2 cloves garlic, minced
1 medium sweet potato, cubed and steamed until tender
1 cup broccoli florets, steamed until crisp-tender
½ cup shredded reduced-fat Swiss cheese
¼ cup grated reduced-fat Parmesan cheese
Salt and ground black pepper
4 sheets phyllo dough, thawed
1 tablespoon melted margarine (optional)
Fresh tarragon or parsley sprigs

Coat a medium saucepan with no-stick spray and warm over medium heat. Add the shallots or onions and the mushrooms. Sauté for 2 minutes. Stir in the sherry or broth, lemon juice and tarragon. Bring to a boil. Reduce the heat to low, cover and simmer for 2 minutes. Uncover and cook over medium heat until mixture is almost dry.

(continued)

Add ¾ cup of the broth and bring to a boil. Dissolve the cornstarch in the remaining ¼ cup broth and stir into the boiling mixture. Cook and stir for 1 minute, or until thickened. Remove from the heat, set aside and keep warm.

Coat a large no-stick skillet with no-stick spray. Warm over medium heat until hot. Add the leeks, red peppers and garlic. Sauté for 3 to 5 minutes, or until the peppers are tender. Add the sweet potatoes, broccoli and reserved mushroom sauce. Cook over medium heat for 1 minute, or until hot. Stir in the Swiss and Parmesan. Season to taste with the salt and pepper. Remove from the heat and set aside.

Preheat the oven to 350°. Coat a no-stick baking sheet with no-stick spray.

On a clean work surface, lay down 1 sheet of the phyllo with the long end facing you. Coat generously with no-stick spray. Top with a second sheet and coat with no-stick spray. Repeat with the remaining 2 sheets of phyllo.

Spoon the vegetable filling in a 4″ strip along the long end of the prepared phyllo, about 4″ from the edge. Fold that edge over the filling and continue to roll up in the same direction until completely rolled. (There is no need to fold up the short ends.) Place, seam side down, on the prepared baking sheet.

Brush the top of the phyllo with the margarine (if using) or spray generously with no-stick spray. Bake for 30 minutes, or until lightly browned and crisp. Remove from the oven and let stand for 5 minutes.

Cut the strudel into 4 equal pieces and arrange on serving plates. Garnish with the tarragon or parsley.

Makes 4 servings. Per serving: 193 calories, 3.7 g. fat (17% of calories), 10.6 g. protein, 28.2 g. carbohydrates, 3.9 g. dietary fiber, 10 mg. cholesterol, 171 mg. sodium

NOTE
• For a tasteful accompaniment, serve the strudel with Mushroom Gravy (page 510).

VARIATIONS
Ratatouille Strudel: Replace the leeks, sweet potato and broccoli with 1½ cups chopped peeled eggplant, 1 cup sliced onion, 1 cup sliced zucchini and 1 cup chopped tomatoes. Cook until most of the liquid from the tomatoes has evaporated. Add ½ teaspoon dried basil and ½ teaspoon dried tarragon to the vegetable mixture.

Summer Vegetable Strudel: Replace the sweet potato and broccoli with 1 cup sliced yellow summer squash, 1 cup sliced carrots, 1 cup sliced mushrooms, 1 cup chopped tomatoes and ½ cup corn or peas. Cook until most of the liquid from the tomatoes has evaporated. Add ½ teaspoon dried marjoram and ½ teaspoon dried savory to the vegetable mixture.

Vegetable and Wild Rice Strudel: Add 1¼ cups cooked wild rice to the vegetable mixture.

Barbecued Tofu with Onions and Peppers

1 pound firm tofu, drained, frozen and thawed
½ cup reduced-sodium ketchup
¼ cup Dijon mustard
3 tablespoons water
1 tablespoon safflower or canola oil
1 tablespoon minced garlic
¼ teaspoon ground black pepper
¼ teaspoon liquid smoke
　 Hot-pepper sauce
2 cups thinly sliced onions
2 medium green peppers, seeded and cut into strips
3 cups hot cooked brown rice

Preheat the oven to 375°.

Set the tofu between two plates and place a heavy pot on top. Set aside for 10 minutes to release excess water.

Meanwhile, in a shallow 2-quart no-stick baking dish, combine the ketchup, mustard, water, oil, garlic, black pepper, liquid smoke and hot-pepper sauce to taste.

With the long side of the tofu facing you, cut the tofu into ½″ slices starting from the short end. Dip the slices on both sides in the ketchup mixture. Remove to a plate and set aside.

Toss the onions in the ketchup mixture. Remove to a plate and set aside.

Toss the green peppers in the remaining ketchup mixture and leave on the bottom of the baking dish. Arrange the tofu in one layer on top of the peppers. Top with the onions.

Cover with foil and bake for 15 minutes. Uncover and bake for 15 minutes more. Serve over the rice.

Makes 4 servings. Per serving: 453 calories, 15.9 g. fat (30% of calories), 24.7 g. protein, 59.4 g. carbohydrates, 6.7 g. dietary fiber, 0 mg. cholesterol, 234 mg. sodium

Set the tofu between two plates and place a heavy pot on top. Set aside for 10 minutes to release excess water. Cut into ¾″ cubes and set aside.

In a large saucepan over medium-high heat, warm the oil. Add the onions, ginger, garlic, coriander, cumin seeds, turmeric and red pepper. Sauté for 2 minutes.

Add the broth or water, salt, squash and tofu. Bring to a boil. Reduce the heat to medium-low, cover and cook, stirring occasionally, for 15 to 20 minutes, or until the squash is tender.

Mash some of the squash against the sides of the pan to create a thick sauce. Add the beans and stir well. Cover and simmer for 2 to 3 minutes, or until the beans are tender and heated through. Season with the black pepper. Serve over the rice.

Makes 4 servings. Per serving: 464 calories, 14.6 g. fat (26% of calories), 28.2 g. protein, 63.4 g. carbohydrates, 11.2 g. dietary fiber, 0 mg. cholesterol, 486 mg. sodium

Curried Tofu with Squash and Lima Beans

1	pound firm tofu, drained
1	tablespoon safflower or canola oil
1½	cups coarsely chopped onion
1½	tablespoons minced fresh ginger
1	teaspoon minced garlic
2½	teaspoons ground coriander
1½	teaspoons whole cumin seeds
1½	teaspoons turmeric
⅛	teaspoon ground red pepper
1	cup vegetable broth or water
¾	teaspoon salt
1	medium butternut squash, peeled, seeded and cut into ¾″ chunks
10	ounces frozen lima beans, defrosted
	Ground black pepper
2	cups hot cooked basmati rice

Black Bean Casserole with Cornbread Topping

Black Bean Casserole

1	tablespoon olive oil
1	cup chopped onions
1	large clove garlic, minced
1	large green pepper, seeded and diced
1	large stalk celery, finely chopped
1	medium carrot, finely chopped
1	can (15 ounces) black beans, rinsed and drained
1	cup drained canned diced tomatoes with green chilies
½	teaspoon dried oregano
½	cup packed minced fresh cilantro

(continued)

Cornbread Topping

    1   cup yellow cornmeal
    ⅓   cup unbleached white flour
    ½   teaspoon baking powder
    ¼   teaspoon baking soda
    ¼   teaspoon salt
    ½   cup fresh or frozen corn
    1   cup buttermilk
    1   tablespoon canola oil
    1   tablespoon maple syrup

To make the black bean casserole: Preheat the oven to 400°. Coat a shallow 3-quart baking dish (approximately 8″ round by 2″ deep) with no-stick spray. Set aside.

In a large nonreactive no-stick skillet over medium heat, warm the oil. Add the onions and garlic. Sauté for 2 minutes. Add the peppers, celery and carrots. Sauté for 5 minutes. Add the beans, tomatoes and oregano. Cook for 5 minutes, or until the vegetables begin to soften. Remove from the heat, stir in the cilantro and transfer to the prepared baking dish. Set aside.

To make the cornbread topping: In a large bowl, combine the cornmeal, flour, baking powder, baking soda and salt. Stir in the corn.

In a separate bowl, whisk together the buttermilk, oil and maple syrup. Add to the cornmeal mixture and stir just until blended. Pour over the bean mixture and bake for 30 to 35 minutes, or until a toothpick inserted in the center of the cornbread comes out clean. Cut into wedges and serve.

Makes 4 servings. Per serving: 393 calories, 9.8 g. fat (20% of calories), 16.4 g. protein, 69.6 g. carbohydrates, 13.7 g. dietary fiber, 2 mg. cholesterol, 678 mg. sodium

NOTES

• For a spicier dish, add ¼ to ½ teaspoon hot-pepper sauce along with the celery and carrots.
• If desired, puree half of the cooked bean mixture in a food processor or blender. Stir into the remaining bean mixture and mix well before transferring to the prepared baking dish.

Stuffed Eggplant

    2   eggplants (about 1 pound each), halved
    2   tablespoons olive oil
        Salt and ground black pepper
 1½   cups fresh whole-wheat bread crumbs
    2   teaspoons minced garlic
    1   cup finely chopped onions
    4   ounces mushrooms, finely chopped
    1   cup finely diced sweet red peppers
    ½   teaspoon dried oregano
    ½   teaspoon dried rosemary
    ½   teaspoon fennel seeds
    ¾   cup tomato sauce
    2   tablespoons minced fresh parsley

Preheat the oven to 375°.

Using a paring knife, carefully cut away the flesh of each eggplant half, leaving about ½″ of flesh adhering to the skin. Discard any large clumps of seeds and finely chop the flesh; set aside. (If there are no seeds, discard about ⅓ of the flesh anyway.)

Lightly brush the insides of each eggplant half with a small amount of the oil. Sprinkle with the salt and black pepper to taste; set aside.

In a large bowl, combine the eggplant flesh with the bread crumbs, garlic, onions, mushrooms, red peppers, oregano, rosemary, fennel seeds, 2 tablespoons of the tomato sauce and the remaining oil. Stir in additional salt to taste.

Divide the filling equally among the eggplant halves. Spoon 2 heaping tablespoons tomato sauce over each half.

Arrange the eggplant halves in a 9″ × 13″ baking dish. Add ¼″ water to the bottom of the dish. Cover tightly with foil and bake for 30 minutes. Uncover and add more water to the bottom of the baking dish, if necessary.

Bake, uncovered, for 15 minutes, or until the eggplant is tender. Sprinkle with the parsley before serving.

Makes 4 servings. Per serving: 224 calories, 8.4 g. fat (31% of calories), 6.4 g. protein, 35.6 g. carbohydrates, 2.9 g. dietary fiber, 0 mg. cholesterol, 309 mg. sodium

NOTES
• You can bake the eggplants in two 10″ pie plates.
• To make fresh bread crumbs, tear any type of bread into large chunks. Place them in a food processor and process with on/off turns.
• For a tasty flavor boost, sprinkle the eggplant with grated Parmesan cheese before baking.

Pilaf-Stuffed Peppers

1⅔	cups reduced-sodium vegetable broth
¾	cup long-grain white rice
¼	cup wild rice
4	sweet red, yellow or green peppers
1	tablespoon olive oil
½	cup chopped onions
1	clove garlic, minced
½	cup fresh or frozen peas
½	cup fresh or frozen corn
½	cup shredded carrots
½	cup shredded reduced-fat mozzarella cheese
1½	teaspoons chopped fresh basil
4	thin slices reduced-fat mozzarella cheese
2	cups tomato sauce, warmed

In a small saucepan, combine the broth, white rice and wild rice. Bring to a boil over medium heat. Cover, reduce the heat to low and simmer for 20 minutes, or until the rice is tender and the broth has been absorbed. Set aside.

Cut the tops off the peppers, about 1″ down. Remove the seeds and ribs, being careful not to tear or rip the peppers. If necessary, trim the pepper bottoms so that they stand upright. Blanch the peppers in gently boiling water for 6 minutes, or until the peppers are soft but still retain their shape. Drain well and set aside.

In a large no-stick skillet over medium heat, warm the oil. Add the onions and sauté for 4 minutes, or until tender. Add the garlic, peas, corn and carrots. Reduce the heat to low, cover and cook for 5 minutes. Remove from the heat. Stir in the rice, shredded mozzarella and basil.

Preheat the oven to 375°.

Stuff the peppers with the rice mixture; top each with a slice of mozzarella. Place the peppers upright in an 8″ × 8″ no-stick baking dish. Pour ¼″ water into the dish. Bake for 15 minutes, or until heated through. Turn on the broiler and broil about 6″ from the heat for 3 minutes, or until the cheese is lightly browned and bubbly. Serve with the tomato sauce.

Makes 4 servings. Per serving: 515 calories, 11.4 g. fat (20% of calories), 23.4 g. protein, 81.7 g. carbohydrates, 8.4 g. dietary fiber, 19 mg. cholesterol, 140 mg. sodium

Stuffed Spaghetti Squash

2	small spaghetti squash, halved lengthwise
1	tablespoon olive oil
1	large sweet red pepper, chopped
1	cup fresh or frozen peas
½	cup chopped scallions
2	cloves garlic, minced
1	teaspoon dried oregano
1	teaspoon dried mint
1½	cups tomato juice
1	cup couscous
4	ounces crumbled feta cheese

(continued)

Place the squash halves, cut side down, on a microwave-safe plate. Microwave on high power for 10 to 12 minutes, or until the squash is easily pierced with a fork. Cool until easy to handle. Spoon out and discard the seeds. With a fork, separate the flesh into strands and place in a large bowl. Reserve the squash shells.

Preheat the oven to 350°.

In a large no-stick skillet over medium heat, warm the oil. Add the peppers, peas, scallions, garlic, oregano and mint. Sauté for 5 minutes, or until the vegetables are tender.

Stir in the tomato juice and bring to a boil. Stir in the couscous. Cover, remove from the heat and let stand for 5 minutes, or until the couscous is soft. Fluff with a fork.

Add the couscous mixture and the feta to the bowl with the squash. Toss to mix well. Divide among the reserved squash shells. Cover each shell with foil, place in a 9″ × 13″ no-stick baking dish and bake for 15 to 20 minutes, or until heated through.

Makes 4 servings. Per serving: 369 calories, 10.4 g. fat (25% of calories), 14.7 g. protein, 56.1 g. carbohydrates, 11 g. dietary fiber, 25 mg. cholesterol, 366 mg. sodium

Casserole in a Cabbage

1   large head green cabbage (2–2¼ pounds)
1   tablespoon olive oil
⅔   cup sliced carrots
⅓   cup chopped onions
⅓   cup chopped green peppers
2   cloves garlic, minced
1   cup sliced yellow summer squash
1   cup chopped tomatoes
¾   teaspoon caraway seeds, crushed
½   teaspoon dried oregano
2   cups cooked brown or white rice
1   cup cooked or canned red kidney beans, rinsed and drained
⅔   cup shredded reduced-fat sharp Cheddar cheese
1   egg, beaten
¼   cup minced fresh parsley
    Salt and ground black pepper

Place the cabbage in a large saucepan. Pour in enough water to cover. Bring to a boil over high heat. Reduce the heat to low, cover and simmer for 10 minutes. Drain the cabbage and let stand in a colander for 10 minutes, or until cool enough to handle.

Transfer the cabbage to a large piece of double-layer cheesecloth (large enough to be wrapped around the entire cabbage). Spread and flatten as many of the soft outer cabbage leaves as possible, without breaking them off. Cut out the inner leaves of the cabbage and discard the core. (Leave the very bottom of the cabbage to which the outer leaves are attached.) Chop the inner leaves to make 2¼ cups; set aside.

In a large no-stick skillet over medium heat, warm the oil. Add the carrots, onions, green peppers and garlic. Sauté for 2 to 3 minutes. Reduce the heat to medium-low, cover and cook for 5 minutes. Add the chopped cabbage, squash, tomatoes, caraway seeds and oregano. Cook, covered, for 5 to 8 minutes, or until the vegetables are tender. Stir in the rice, beans, Cheddar, egg and parsley. Season to taste with the salt and black pepper.

Mound the vegetable mixture in the center of the hollowed-out cabbage. Fold the outer leaves firmly around the mixture, reshaping the cabbage. Gather up the cheesecloth tightly around the filled cabbage and tie the top of the cheesecloth with kitchen string.

Carefully transfer the filled cabbage to a large saucepan. Add 2″ water. Bring to a boil over high heat. Reduce the heat to low, cover and simmer for 20 to 30 minutes, or until the cabbage is tender. Carefully remove the cabbage from the saucepan; let stand for 10 minutes. Remove and discard the cheesecloth. To serve, place the cabbage on a serving plate and cut into wedges.

Makes 6 servings. Per serving: 231 calories, 6.3 g. fat (24% of calories), 10.4 g. protein, 35.5 g. carbohydrates, 4 g. dietary fiber, 42 mg. cholesterol, 223 mg. sodium

NOTE
• Serve with your favorite tomato sauce.

VARIATIONS
Garden-Stuffed Cabbage: Replace the carrots, onions, green peppers, squash and tomatoes with 4 cups sliced or chopped vegetables such as broccoli, mushrooms, zucchini, corn or green beans. Sauté until the vegetables are tender. Replace the caraway seeds and oregano with ¾ teaspoon dried rosemary and ½ teaspoon dried marjoram. Add enough of the rice or other cooked grain to make a 4-cup mixture.
Mexican-Style Stuffed Cabbage: Add ½ minced jalapeño pepper (wear plastic gloves when handling) along with the carrots and onions. Replace the red kidney beans with pinto or black beans and replace the caraway seeds with ½ to ¾ teaspoon ground cumin.
Wild Mushroom and Barley Stuffed Cabbage: Replace the carrots, onions, green peppers, squash and tomatoes with 6 cups sliced wild mushrooms such as shiitake, portobello, oyster or cremini. Sauté until the mushrooms are just tender. Replace the rice with cooked barley and add enough to make a 4-cup mixture. Omit the beans. Replace the caraway seeds and oregano with 1 teaspoon dried thyme.

QUICK!
Vegetarian Paella

Here is a vegetarian version of the classic Spanish rice dish. The saffron gives it a distinctive flavor and a gorgeous golden hue. This paella is an elegant dish to serve company.

1	tablespoon olive oil
1	cup chopped onions
1	teaspoon minced garlic
2	cups water
¾	teaspoon salt
¼	teaspoon saffron threads
1	cup long-grain white rice
1	cup diced carrots
1½	cups frozen peas, thawed
1	cup cooked or canned chick-peas, rinsed and drained
¼	cup roasted red peppers, cut into thin strips
	Ground black pepper

In a large, heavy saucepan over medium heat, warm the oil. Add the onions and garlic. Sauté for 1 minute.

Add the water, salt and saffron. Bring to a boil. Stir in the rice and carrots. Return to a boil. Reduce the heat to low, cover and simmer for about 18 minutes, or just until the rice is tender.

Uncover and quickly sprinkle the peas, chick-peas and red peppers over the rice. Cover and continue to simmer for 2 minutes, or until the rice is cooked and the liquid has been absorbed. Stir gently to fluff up the rice and distribute the vegetables. Season with the black pepper.

Makes 4 servings. Per serving: 374 calories, 7.9 g. fat (19% of calories), 11.3 g. protein, 64.9 g. carbohydrates, 7.5 g. dietary fiber, 3 mg. cholesterol, 616 mg. sodium

NOTE
• Store saffron in the refrigerator to maintain maximum freshness.

Broccoli and Red Pepper Stir-Fry

QUICK!

½ cup reduced-sodium vegetable broth
1½ tablespoons black bean garlic sauce (see note)
1 tablespoon reduced-sodium soy sauce
1 tablespoon cornstarch
2 teaspoons rice-wine vinegar
1 teaspoon toasted sesame oil
¼ teaspoon red-pepper flakes
1 tablespoon peanut oil
3 cups broccoli florets
1 tablespoon water
1 medium sweet red pepper, cut into small strips
2 cloves garlic, minced
1 teaspoon minced fresh ginger
4 cups hot cooked rice

In a small bowl, whisk together the broth, garlic sauce, soy sauce, cornstarch, vinegar, sesame oil and red-pepper flakes. Set aside.

Warm a wok or large no-stick skillet over high heat. Add the peanut oil and tilt the pan in all directions to coat the pan. Add the broccoli and stir-fry for 10 seconds. Add the water, cover and steam, shaking the pan occasionally, for 30 to 45 seconds, or until the broccoli is just crisp-tender.

Add the red peppers, garlic and ginger; stir-fry for 30 seconds, or until the peppers are just crisp-tender.

Quickly whisk the sauce and pour it into the pan. Cook and stir for 20 seconds, or just until thickened. Serve over the rice.

Makes 4 servings. Per serving: 304 calories, 5.6 g. fat (16% of calories), 7.7 g. protein, 56.6 g. carbohydrates, 3.3 g. dietary fiber, 0 mg. cholesterol, 173 mg. sodium

NOTE

• Black bean garlic sauce is a delicious prepared sauce available in the Oriental section of most supermarkets.

VARIATIONS

Asparagus Stir-Fry: Omit the broth, black bean garlic sauce and cornstarch. Increase the rice-wine vinegar to 2 tablespoons and add 1 teaspoon sugar. Replace the broccoli and water with ½ cup thinly sliced scallions, 1 large carrot (thinly sliced), 1 cup asparagus (cut into 1″ pieces), 5 cups coarsley shredded savoy cabbage and 3 ounces fresh oyster mushrooms. Reduce the sweet red pepper to 1 cup small strips. Stir in 4 ounces mung bean sprouts before serving.

Mixed Vegetable Stir-Fry: To make the sauce, reduce the broth to ⅓ cup. Omit the black bean garlic sauce, cornstarch, rice-wine vinegar and sesame oil. Add 2 teaspoons hoisin sauce and 1 teaspoon brown sugar. To make the vegetables, replace the broccoli, water and sweet red pepper with 1 cup thinly sliced red onions, 1 cup sliced celery, 1 cup sliced mushrooms, 1 cup trimmed snow peas and ½ cup sliced water chestnuts. Along with the sauce, add 1 cup baby corn (rinsed and halved lengthwise) and 2 tablespoons chopped fresh cilantro.

Wild Mushroom Stir-Fry over Couscous: Replace the black bean garlic sauce with 2 tablespoons hoisin sauce. Omit the rice-wine vinegar. Replace the broccoli and water with 3 ounces sliced fresh shiitake mushrooms (stems removed), 3 ounces fresh oyster mushrooms, 3 sliced scallions and 3 ounces trimmed snow peas. Use 2 sweet red peppers instead of 1. Replace the rice with hot cooked couscous.

Stir-Fry with Tofu and Vegetables

1 pound firm tofu, drained
2 tablespoons reduced-sodium soy sauce
1½ teaspoons peanut or canola oil
2 tablespoons minced fresh ginger
1 tablespoon minced garlic
½ teaspoon crushed red-pepper flakes
6 ounces mushrooms, sliced
1 large sweet red pepper, seeded and cut into thin strips
6 scallions, cut into 1½" diagonal slices
1 pound bok choy, coarsely chopped
1 can (15 ounces) baby corn, drained
1½ teaspoons toasted sesame oil
3 cups hot cooked white or brown rice

Set the tofu between 2 plates and place a heavy pot on top. Set aside for 10 minutes to release excess water. Cut into ½" cubes and place in an airtight container or plastic bag. Add the soy sauce and marinate, shaking occasionally, for 10 minutes.

Warm a wok or large no-stick skillet over medium-high heat. Add the oil and tilt the pan in all directions to coat the pan. Add the ginger and garlic. Stir-fry for 10 seconds. Add the red-pepper flakes, mushrooms and red peppers. Stir-fry for 2 to 3 minutes, or until the mushrooms release their liquid and the liquid has evaporated.

Stir in the scallions, bok choy, tofu and tofu marinade. Cover and cook for 1 to 2 minutes, or until the bok choy is crisp-tender.

Stir in the baby corn, sesame oil and additional soy sauce to taste. Serve over the rice.

Makes 4 servings. Per serving: 444 calories, 15.2 g. fat (30% of calories), 27.8 g. protein, 57.4 g. carbohydrates, 5.9 g. dietary fiber, 0 mg. cholesterol, 646 mg. sodium

Curried Potatoes and Peas

¼ cup sliced almonds
1 teaspoon cumin seeds
½ teaspoon canola oil
3 medium yellow-flesh potatoes, scrubbed and cubed
1 medium onion, chopped
1 clove garlic, chopped
½ teaspoon minced fresh ginger
1 teaspoon turmeric
½ teaspoon ground coriander
2 cups reduced-sodium vegetable broth
1 package (10 ounces) frozen peas, thawed
1 tablespoon grated lemon rind
2 tablespoons chopped fresh cilantro
4 cups hot cooked basmati rice

In a large, dry no-stick skillet over medium heat, toast the almonds, shaking the skillet for 3 to 5 minutes, or until the almonds are fragrant. Remove from the skillet and set aside.

In the same skillet over medium heat, toast the cumin seeds, shaking the skillet for 2 to 4 minutes, or until the seeds are fragrant. Add the oil and warm for 30 seconds.

Add the potatoes and onions. Sauté for 3 minutes, or until the onions are soft. Stir in the garlic, ginger, tumeric and coriander. Cook, stirring frequently, for 3 to 5 minutes.

Add the broth, peas and lemon rind. Continue cooking for 15 minutes, or until the potatoes are tender. Stir in the cilantro 5 minutes before the end of cooking time.

Serve over the rice and sprinkle with the almonds.

Makes 4 servings. Per serving: 425 calories, 6.2 g. fat (13% of calories), 13.2 g. protein, 82.1 g. carbohydrates, 5.2 g. dietary fiber, 0 mg. cholesterol, 151 mg. sodium

Black Bean Pie

1 can (16 ounces) black beans, rinsed and drained
¼ cup reduced-sodium vegetable broth
2 teaspoons olive oil
1 cup diced red onions
3 cloves garlic, minced
¼ teaspoon chili powder
2 teaspoons ground cumin
1 teaspoon chopped canned green chili peppers
2–3 drops hot-pepper sauce
½ cup fat-free egg substitute
1 prebaked pie crust (9″)
½ cup salsa
½ cup shredded reduced-fat Monterey Jack cheese

In a food processor, puree ½ cup of the beans and the broth until smooth. Set aside.

In a medium no-stick skillet over medium heat, warm the oil. Add the onions. Sauté for 4 minutes, or until soft. Add the garlic, chili powder, cumin, chili peppers, hot-pepper sauce and pureed beans. Bring to a simmer. Stir in the remaining beans, cover and simmer for 5 minutes, or until heated through. Remove from the heat and set aside to cool. Stir in the egg substitute.

Preheat the oven to 400°.

Pour the bean mixture into the pie crust and bake for 10 minutes. Spread the salsa evenly over the bean mixture. Sprinkle with the Monterey Jack.

Reduce the oven temperature to 325° and bake for 15 minutes, or until the cheese is bubbly. Remove from the oven and cool for 5 minutes. Cut into wedges and serve.

Makes 6 servings. Per serving: 253 calories, 11.9 g. fat (39% of calories), 13.3 g. protein, 28.8 g. carbohydrates, 5.9 g. dietary fiber, 7 mg. cholesterol, 722 mg. sodium

Red Lentil Burritos

10 dry-pack sun-dried tomatoes
1 cup boiling water
2½ cups water
1 cup red lentils, sorted and rinsed
1 tablespoon olive oil
½ cup chopped onions
½ cup chopped broccoli florets
½ cup chopped cauliflower florets
½ cup thinly sliced carrots
1½ cups tomato sauce
1 teaspoon curry powder
½ teaspoon ground cinnamon
4 whole-wheat tortillas (8″ diameter), warmed

Place the tomatoes in a small bowl and cover with the boiling water. Let soak for 10 minutes, or until the tomatoes are soft. Drain, reserving ½ cup of the soaking liquid. Chop the tomatoes and set aside.

In a medium saucepan, combine the 2½ cups water, lentils and reserved soaking liquid. Bring to a boil over medium-high heat. Reduce the heat to low and simmer for 6 to 10 minutes, or just until the lentils are tender. Drain and set aside.

In a large no-stick skillet over medium heat, warm the oil. Add the onions, broccoli, cauliflower and carrots. Sauté for 4 to 5 minutes, or until the vegetables are tender. Stir in the tomato sauce, curry powder and cinnamon. Add the lentils and tomatoes. Simmer for 15 to 20 minutes, or until slightly thickened.

Divide the lentil mixture evenly among the tortillas. Roll to enclose the filling.

Makes 4 servings. Per serving: 391 calories, 5.6 g. fat (12% of calories), 18.1 g. protein, 72.6 g. carbohydrates, 5.3 g. dietary fiber, 0 mg. cholesterol, 481 mg. sodium

Spinach-Cheese Enchiladas

2 cups reduced-sodium vegetable broth
1 cup chopped canned green chili peppers
2 tomatoes, peeled and diced
2 tablespoons finely chopped scallions
2 cloves garlic, minced
2 tablespoons cornstarch
2 tablespoons water
1¼ pounds fresh spinach, coarsely chopped
½ cup shredded reduced-fat Monterey Jack cheese
8 corn tortillas (6″ diameter)

Preheat the oven to 400°. Coat a 9″ × 13″ no-stick baking dish with no-stick spray and set aside.

In a medium saucepan, combine the broth, peppers, tomatoes, scallions and garlic. Bring to a boil over high heat. Reduce the heat to medium and simmer for 15 minutes.

In a glass measuring cup, whisk together the cornstarch and water. Add to the tomato mixture. Cook and stir until thickened. Remove from the heat.

While the sauce is cooking, place the spinach in a large saucepan with about 2 tablespoons water. Cover and steam over medium heat for 2 to 4 minutes, or until the spinach is wilted. Divide the spinach and Monterey Jack evenly among the tortillas. Roll up to enclose the filling.

Place the enchiladas, seam side down, in a single layer in the prepared baking dish. Top with the tomato mixture. Bake for 10 minutes, or until the filling is hot.

Makes 4 servings. Per serving: 240 calories, 4.5 g. fat (16% of calories), 12.8 g. protein, 41.3 g. carbohydrates, 5.1 g. dietary fiber, 10 mg. cholesterol, 749 mg. sodium

Black Bean Burritos

QUICK!

4 flour tortillas (12″ diameter)
2 teaspoons olive oil
½ cup chopped onions
1 large clove garlic, minced
1 can (16 ounces) reduced-sodium black beans (with liquid)
1 teaspoon chili powder
2 tablespoons finely chopped fresh cilantro (optional)
½ cup salsa
¼ cup nonfat or low-fat plain yogurt
¼ cup nonfat or low-fat sour cream
6 tablespoons shredded reduced-fat Monterey Jack or Cheddar cheese

Preheat the oven to 350°. Wrap all 4 tortillas in one piece of foil. Place on a no-stick baking sheet and bake for 10 minutes to heat through.

Meanwhile, in a medium no-stick skillet over medium heat, warm the oil. Add the onions and garlic. Sauté for 3 minutes. Stir in the beans (with liquid) and chili powder. Simmer, stirring occasionally, for 10 minutes. Stir in the cilantro (if using).

In a small saucepan, combine the salsa, yogurt and sour cream. Stir over very low heat just until warm. (Do not boil.)

To assemble the burritos, divide the bean mixture evenly among the tortillas. Sprinkle each with the Monerey Jack or Cheddar and roll to enclose the filling.

Place the burritos, seam side down, in a 1-quart microwave-safe baking dish. Top with the salsa mixture. Microwave on high power for a total of 3 minutes, or until the burritos are heated through; stop and rotate the dish after 2 minutes.

Makes 4 servings. Per serving: 346 calories, 7.4 g. fat (19% of calories), 18.8 g. protein, 52.2 g. carbohydrates, 5.8 g. dietary fiber, 8 mg. cholesterol, 503 mg. sodium

Garden Vegetable Kebabs

Apricot-Fennel Basting Sauce
- ¾ cup apricot all-fruit spread
- 3 teaspoons Dijon mustard
- 2 teaspoons fennel seeds, crushed
- 3 tablespoons water

Vegetables
- 2 medium sweet potatoes
- ½ small eggplant
- 1 medium yellow summer squash
- 1 medium zucchini
- 1 medium sweet red or green pepper
- 1 medium yellow pepper
- 8 medium mushrooms
- 8 cherry tomatoes

To make the apricot-fennel basting sauce: In a small bowl, whisk together the all-fruit spread, mustard, fennel seeds and enough of the water to make a saucy, spreadable consistency.

To make the vegetables: Cut the sweet potatoes, eggplant, squash, zucchini, red or green peppers and yellow peppers into bite-size pieces. Place the sweet potatoes in a small saucepan. Add 1″ of water, cover and simmer for 5 to 8 minutes, or until the sweet potatoes are crisp-tender. Drain, rinse with cold water and drain again.

Thread the sweet potatoes, eggplant, squash, zucchini, red or green peppers, yellow peppers, mushrooms and tomatoes on 8 long metal or wooden skewers to make kebabs.

Preheat the broiler. Broil the kebabs 5″ from the heat or grill over medium-hot coals for a total of 8 to 10 minutes, or until the vegetables are tender. Baste several times with the basting sauce. Turn the kebabs halfway through the cooking time.

Makes 4 servings. Per serving (2 kebabs): 292 calories, 1.2 g. fat (3% of calories), 4.5 g. protein, 71.1 g. carbohydrates, 4.4 g. dietary fiber, 0 mg. cholesterol, 70 mg. sodium

NOTE
• Almost any combination of vegetables can be used in this recipe. To complete the meal, serve the kebabs on a bed of herbed couscous or rice.

VARIATIONS
Balsamic Barbecue Kebabs: Omit the basting sauce. Place the cut vegetables in a large plastic bag. In a glass measuring cup, whisk together ⅔ cup tomato sauce, ¼ cup balsamic vinegar, ¼ cup honey, ½ teaspoon minced roasted garlic and 1½ to 2 teaspoons dried basil. Pour over the vegetables, seal and let stand for 20 to 30 minutes, shaking the bag occasionally. Drain, reserving the marinade. Thread the vegetables onto skewers as directed. Baste the kebabs occasionally with the marinade during cooking. Serve with cornbread.

Southwestern-Style Kebabs: Omit the basting sauce. Place the cut vegetables in a large plastic bag. In a glass measuring cup, whisk together ½ cup lime juice, 3 cloves minced garlic, 3 teaspoons dried oregano and 1½ teaspoons ground cumin. Pour over the vegetables, seal and let stand for 20 to 30 minutes, shaking the bag occasionally. Drain, reserving the marinade. Thread the vegetables onto skewers as directed. Baste the kebabs occasionally with the marinade during cooking. Serve with cooked black beans, rice and warm tortillas.

Spicy Sesame Kebabs: Omit the basting. Place the cut vegetables in a large plastic bag. In a glass measuring cup, whisk together 6 tablespoons orange juice, 3 tablespoons reduced-sodium tamari soy sauce, 1½ tablespoons honey, ¾ teaspoon toasted sesame oil, 2 teaspoons minced fresh ginger and ⅛ teaspoon red-pepper flakes. Pour over the vegetables, seal and let stand for 20 to 30 minutes, shaking the bag occasionally. Drain, reserving the marinade. Thread the vegetables onto skewers as directed. Baste the kebabs occasionally with the marinade during cooking. Serve with cooked brown rice.

Chick-Pea Burgers

1 can (16 ounces) chick-peas, rinsed, drained and mashed
½ cup finely chopped red onions
½ cup finely chopped celery
1 cup unseasoned dry bread crumbs
½ cup reduced-sodium tomato sauce
1 tablespoon Dijon mustard
1 tablespoon Worcestershire sauce (see note)
1 egg white
½ teaspoon liquid smoke (optional)
2 teaspoons olive oil
1 teaspoon dried thyme
¼–¾ teaspoon salt
¼ teaspoon ground black pepper
½ cup minced fresh parsley

Preheat the oven to 350°. In a large bowl, combine the chick-peas, onions, celery, bread crumbs, tomato sauce, mustard, Worcestershire sauce, egg white, liquid smoke (if using), olive oil, thyme, salt, pepper and parsley. Mix well. Using your hands, shape the mixture into 4 patties.

Coat a no-stick baking sheet with no-stick spray. Place the patties on the baking sheet. Cover with aluminum foil and bake for 30 minutes. Uncover and bake for 5 to 10 minutes, or until the patties are lightly browned.

Makes 4 servings. Per serving: 266 calories, 6 g. fat (20% of calories), 10.6 g. protein, 43.3 g. carbohydrates, 6.3 g. dietary fiber, 0 mg. cholesterol, 789 mg. sodium

NOTES
• Serve these burgers hot on toasted whole-wheat buns with traditional toppings, such as sliced tomatoes and onions, ketchup and mustard.
• Traditional Worcestershire sauce contains anchovies. Vegetarian versions may be found in health food stores.

Garden Burgers with Mustard Sauce

QUICK!

Vegetables, grains and reduced-fat cheeses make these burgers moist, delicious and low in fat.

Garden Burgers
1 cup finely chopped cremini, shiitake or button mushrooms
½ cup finely chopped broccoli florets and stalks
¼ cup finely chopped scallions
2 cloves garlic, minced
¼ cup pecan pieces (optional)
½ teaspoon dried marjoram
½ teaspoon dried savory
¼ teaspoon dried thyme
½ cup quick-cooking oats
½ cup cooked brown rice
½ cup shredded reduced-fat Cheddar cheese
⅓ cup reduced-fat cottage cheese
3 egg whites
¼ teaspoon ground black pepper
  Pinch of salt

Mustard Sauce
¼ cup fat-free mayonnaise
4 teaspoons Dijon mustard
4 whole-wheat or multigrain buns

To make the garden burgers: Coat a medium no-stick skillet with no-stick spray. Warm over medium heat until hot. Add the mushrooms, broccoli, scallions, garlic, pecans (if using), marjoram, savory and thyme. Cover and cook for 5 minutes, or until the mushrooms are soft and the broccoli is crisp-tender.

Stir in the oats and rice. Cook, uncovered, for 2 to 3 minutes, stirring occasionally. Remove from the heat and cool to room temperature.

Stir in the Cheddar, cottage cheese, egg

whites, pepper and salt. Mix well. Form the mixture into four ½"-thick patties, using about ½ cup mixture for each. (The patties will be soft, but will firm up when cooked).

Coat a large no-stick skillet with no-stick spray. Warm over medium heat until hot. Add the burgers and cook for 5 minutes on each side, or until browned.

To make the mustard sauce: In a small bowl, combine the mayonnaise and mustard. Spread on the bottoms of the buns. Top with the burgers and serve.

Makes 4 servings. Per serving: 262 calories, 4.5 g. fat (15% of calories), 15.2 g. protein, 42.5 g. carbohydrates, 4.5 g. dietary fiber, 8 mg. cholesterol, 770 mg. sodium

NOTE
• These burgers can be broiled about 3″ from the heat on a no-stick baking sheet coated with no-stick spray. Broil for 3 to 4 minutes on each side, or until browned.

VARIATIONS
California Burger: For the burgers, replace the marjoram, savory and thyme with ½ teaspoon dried basil and ½ teaspoon dried tarragon. For the sauce, replace the mustard with 2 tablespoons finely chopped fresh basil or tarragon. Replace the whole-wheat buns with toasted sourdough bread. Top the burgers with sliced fresh tomatoes and whole fresh basil leaves.
Indian Burger: For the burgers, replace the marjoram, savory and thyme with ¾ teaspoon curry powder. Omit the mustard sauce. Spread the bottom of each bun with 1 to 1½ tablespoons coarsely chopped chutney.
Mediterranean Burger: For the burgers, replace the marjoram, savory and thyme with ½ teaspoon dried oregano and ½ teaspoon dried mint. Omit the mustard sauce. In a small bowl, combine ½ cup nonfat plain yogurt, ¼ cup chopped cucumber, ¼ teaspoon dried oregano and ¼ teaspoon dried mint. Serve the patties in pita breads. Top with the yogurt mixture.

Meatless Sloppy Joes

Frozen and thawed tofu gives these sloppy joes a delicious meatlike texture and flavor.

1	pound firm tofu, drained, frozen and thawed
1½	teaspoons canola oil
⅔	cup chopped onions
⅔	cup chopped green peppers
⅓	cup thinly sliced celery
1	can (16 ounces) reduced-sodium tomato sauce
4	teaspoons cider vinegar
2½	teaspoons prepared mustard
¾	teaspoon Worcestershire sauce (see note)
1	teaspoon sugar
	Salt and ground black pepper
4	whole-wheat or multigrain buns

Set the tofu between 2 plates and place a heavy pot on top. Set aside for 10 minutes to release excess water. Pat dry. Coarsely mash or crumble the tofu with a fork.

In a medium no-stick skillet over medium heat, warm the oil. Add the tofu, onions, green peppers and celery. Sauté for 8 minutes, or until the tofu is well-browned and the vegetables are tender.

Stir in the tomato sauce, vinegar, mustard, Worcestershire sauce and sugar. Cook, stirring frequently, for 5 minutes. Season to taste with the salt and black pepper. Mound equal amounts of the mixture onto the buns.

Makes 4 servings. Per serving: 344 calories, 12.9 g. fat (31% of calories), 24.3 g. protein, 39 g. carbohydrates, 6.2 g. dietary fiber, 0 mg. cholesterol, 307 mg. sodium

NOTES

• Traditional Worcestershire sauce contains anchovies. Vegetarian versions can be found in health food stores.

• This mixture tastes great as a baked potato topping. Then top it with shredded reduced-fat Cheddar cheese.

VARIATIONS

Taco Joes: To the tofu mixture, add 1 cup cooked or canned black beans (rinsed and drained, if canned) and 1 to 2 teaspoons chili powder or taco seasoning. Roll up in warm corn or flour tortillas instead of the whole-wheat buns.

Vegetable Sloppy Joes: Add ⅓ cup each sliced carrots and zucchini along with the onions and green peppers. Stir in ⅓ cup cooked or canned black beans.

Vegetarian Chili

1½   cups dried red kidney beans, soaked overnight

2   teaspoons olive oil

1   teaspoon whole cumin seeds

1   tablespoon chopped garlic

1½   cups coarsely chopped onions

1   large sweet red pepper, seeded and diced

1   large green pepper, seeded and diced

1   jalapeño pepper, seeded and diced (wear plastic gloves when handling)

1½   tablespoons mild chili powder

1   teaspoon dried oregano

⅛   teaspoon ground cinnamon

3   cups water

2   tablespoons tomato paste

½–1   teaspoon salt

½   cup chopped fresh cilantro

Drain and rinse the beans. Set aside.

In a large saucepan over medium-high heat, warm the oil. Add the cumin seeds and sizzle for 5 seconds. Add the garlic, onions, red peppers, green peppers, jalapeño peppers, chili powder, oregano and cinnamon. Sauté over medium-high heat for 3 minutes, stirring frequently. Add the beans and water.

Bring to a boil. Reduce the heat to low, cover and simmer for 30 minutes. Uncover and simmer for 30 to 45 minutes, or until the beans are tender. (Add more water if the mixture becomes too dry during cooking.)

Stir in the tomato paste and salt. Cook for 2 minutes. Just before serving, stir in the cilantro.

Makes 4 servings. Per serving: 328 calories, 4.1 g. fat (11% of calories), 18.6 g. protein, 58.4 g. carbohydrates, 3.9 g. dietary fiber, 0 mg. cholesterol, 391 mg. sodium

NOTES

• Serve over polenta or steamed brown rice.

• Replace the dried red kidney beans with 2 cans (19 ounces each) kidney beans, rinsed and drained.

• Use a combination of black, pinto and kidney beans.

• Add 1 cup fresh or frozen corn along with the peppers.

• This chili will thicken considerably upon standing or overnight refrigeration. Thin as needed with water or vegetable broth.

Moroccan Vegetable Stew

1 cup chopped onions
1 cup sliced celery
1 medium sweet red pepper, sliced
4 cloves garlic, minced
1 tablespoon all-purpose flour
1 teaspoon ground cinnamon
½ teaspoon curry powder
½ teaspoon ground cumin
¼ teaspoon ground cloves
¼ teaspoon turmeric
¼ teaspoon ground red pepper
1 small eggplant, cubed
½ medium butternut squash, peeled and cubed
1 can (16 ounces) whole tomatoes, drained and coarsely chopped
½ cup reduced-sodium vegetable broth
8 ounces fresh or frozen and thawed whole small okra, stems trimmed
1 can (16 ounces) chick-peas, rinsed and drained
¼ cup raisins
¼ cup blanched whole almonds, toasted (optional); see note
  Salt and ground black pepper

Coat a Dutch oven with no-stick spray. Warm over medium heat until hot. Add the onions, celery, sweet red peppers and garlic. Sauté for 5 minutes, or until the vegetables are tender.

Stir in the flour, cinnamon, curry powder, cumin, cloves, turmeric and ground red pepper. Cook and stir over medium-low heat for 2 minutes.

Stir in the eggplant, squash, tomatoes and broth. Bring to a boil over high heat. Reduce the heat to low, cover and simmer for 10 minutes.

Stir in the okra, chick-peas, raisins and almonds (if using). Simmer for 10 to 15 minutes, or until the okra is tender. Season to taste with the salt and black pepper. Serve in shallow bowls.

Makes 6 servings. Per serving: 187 calories, 2.1 g. fat (9% of calories), 7.3 g. protein, 39.1 g. carbohydrates, 6.9 g. dietary fiber, 0 mg. cholesterol, 446 mg. sodium

NOTES

• To toast almonds, place them in a dry no-stick skillet over medium heat. Toast the nuts, shaking the skillet often, for 3 to 5 minutes, or until fragrant.

• This stew is wonderful served over cooked couscous or turmeric rice. To make turmeric rice, cook 1 cup white rice according to package directions, adding ½ teaspoon ground turmeric to the cooking water.

VARIATIONS

Eggplant Chili: Replace the chick-peas with red kidney or pinto beans. Replace the okra with 1 cup cooked rice or barley and add ½ cup corn. Omit the cinnamon, curry powder, cloves, raisins and almonds. Add 1 to 2 tablespoons chili powder.

Greek-Style Vegetable Stew: Replace the okra with 1¾ cups cubed zucchini and the squash with 1 can (15 ounces) water-packed artichoke hearts, drained and quartered. Replace the cinnamon, curry powder, cumin, cloves, turmeric and ground red pepper with 1 to 2 teaspoons dried oregano. Add 1 can (4 ounces) ripe olives, drained and sliced.

Italian-Style Vegetable Stew: Replace the okra with 1¾ cups cubed zucchini and the squash with 1¾ cups sliced carrots. Replace the cinnamon, curry powder, cumin, cloves, turmeric and ground red pepper with 1½ to 2 teaspoons Italian seasoning.

Vegetarian Jambalaya

This Cajun dish traditionally contains shrimp and fatty sausage. We cut the fat and cooking time by using beans instead of meat and bulgur instead of rice and omitting the butter-and-flour roux (a cooked combination of flour and fat used as a thickening agent).

1 tablespoon canola oil
1 cup chopped onions
½ cup chopped celery
½ cup chopped green peppers
2 cloves garlic, minced
1 cup salsa
1 cup reduced-sodium tomato sauce
1 cup bulgur
¾ teaspoon dried thyme
¼ teaspoon ground red pepper
½ cup vegetable broth
1 can (19 ounces) red kidney beans, rinsed and drained
1 cup drained canned corn

In a large no-stick skillet over medium heat, warm the oil. Add the onions, celery, green peppers and garlic. Sauté for 5 minutes, or just until the vegetables are tender.

Stir in the salsa, tomato sauce, bulgur, thyme, red pepper and ¼ cup of the broth. Bring to a boil. Reduce the heat to low, cover and simmer for 10 minutes.

Stir in the beans, corn and the remaining ¼ cup broth. Cover and simmer for 5 to 10 minutes longer, or until the bulgur is soft.

Makes 4 servings. Per serving: 369 calories, 5 g. fat (11% of calories), 18.8 g. protein, 74.2 g. carbohydrates, 20.5 g. dietary fiber, 0 mg. cholesterol, 674 mg. sodium

NOTES
• This dish is wonderful with low-fat meatless sausage. Several brands are available near the regular sausage or frozen food sections of most supermarkets. Brown the sausage according to the package directions. Then cut it into bite-size pieces and add along with the tomato sauce.
• For a taste of shrimp without the meat, add ½ teaspoon dulse sea vegetable flakes. Dulse is a common sea vegetable available in Asian grocery stores, health food stores and large supermarkets.

QUICK!
Spinach-and-Mushroom Frittata

Frittata is the Italian version of an omelet. By combining egg whites and whole eggs, we cut the fat and cholesterol without compromising taste. Serve the frittata with toasted bread to reduce the total percent of calories from fat.

½ cup chopped onions
4 ounces mushrooms, sliced
5 ounces frozen chopped spinach, thawed and squeezed dry
4 eggs
6 egg whites
2 teaspoons water
1 tablespoon chopped fresh thyme
1 tablespoon chopped fresh oregano or marjoram
½ teaspoon salt
Pinch of ground black pepper

Coat a large ovenproof no-stick skillet with no-stick spray. Warm over medium heat until hot. Add the onions and mushrooms. Sauté for 4 minutes, or until the mushrooms begin to release their liquid.

Add the spinach to the skillet and cook, stirring frequently, for 5 minutes, or until most of the liquid has evaporated.

Meanwhile, in a medium bowl, beat

together the eggs, egg whites, water, thyme, oregano or marjoram, salt and pepper. Add to the skillet and swirl to evenly distribute the mixture. Cook over medium heat for 5 minutes, gently lifting the egg mixture from the sides of the skillet with a spatula as it becomes set. Cook until the eggs are set on the bottom but still moist on the top. Remove from the heat.

Wrap the handle of the skillet with 2 layers of heavy foil. Broil 4″ from the heat for 1 minute, or until the top is golden.

Use a spatula to loosen the frittata from the skillet and slide it onto a serving plate. Cut into wedges and serve.

Makes 4 servings. Per serving: 123 calories, 5.2 g. fat (39% of calories), 13.1 g. protein, 5.7 g. carbohydrates, 0.7 g. dietary fiber, 213 mg. cholesterol, 434 mg. sodium

NOTE

• For an extra boost of flavor, sprinkle the frittata with 1 tablespoon grated reduced-fat Parmesan cheese just before broiling.

VARIATION

Summer Vegetable Frittata: Increase the onions to ⅔ cup. Replace the mushrooms and spinach with ⅔ cup quartered and sliced zucchini and ⅔ cup chopped sweet red peppers. Sauté until the vegetables are soft. Replace the thyme and oregano with 2 tablespoons chopped fresh basil.

Quiche Florentine

We've reduced the fat of traditional quiche by replacing the pastry crust with bread crumbs and using reduced-fat cheeses and evaporated skim milk.

 3 tablespoons unseasoned dry bread crumbs
 1 tablespoon minced fresh parsley
 ¼ teaspoon ground black pepper
 1 cup sliced cremini or button mushrooms
 2 tablespoons chopped onions
 ¼ teaspoon dried thyme
 5 ounces frozen spinach, thawed and squeezed dry
 1 tablespoon all-purpose flour
 ⅓ cup reduced-fat cottage cheese
 ¼ cup shredded reduced-fat Swiss cheese
 1 can (12 ounces) evaporated skim milk
 3 eggs
 ⅛ teaspoon ground nutmeg
 ¼ teaspoon salt

Preheat the oven to 350°. Coat a 9″ no-stick pie pan with no-stick spray. In a small bowl, mix together the bread crumbs, parsley and ⅛ teaspoon of the pepper. Sprinkle evenly over the bottom and sides of the pan; set aside.

Coat a large no-stick skillet with no-stick spray. Warm over medium heat until hot. Add the mushrooms, onions and thyme. Cover and cook for 3 minutes, or until the mushrooms are soft.

Add the spinach to the skillet and cook, uncovered, for 3 to 4 minutes, or until the mixture is quite dry. Stir in the flour and cook for 1 minute. Remove from the heat and stir in the cottage cheese and Swiss.

In a medium bowl, beat together the milk, eggs, nutmeg, salt and remaining ⅛ teaspoon pepper. Stir in the spinach mixture. Pour the mixture into the prepared pie pan. Bake for 35 minutes, or until the quiche is lightly browned and a knife inserted in the center comes out clean. Remove from the oven and cool on a wire rack for 5 minutes. Cut into wedges and serve.

Makes 4 servings. Per serving: 216 calories, 5.8 g. fat (24% of calories), 18.2 g. protein, 23.1 g. carbohydrates, 0.9 g. dietary fiber, 168 mg. cholesterol, 440 mg. sodium

NOTE
• To serve this quiche with a more traditional crust, replace the bread-crumb mixture with a prebaked Basic Pie Crust (page 449).

VARIATIONS
Wild Mushroom Quiche: Replace the spinach and mushrooms with 3 cups sliced wild mushrooms, such as shiitake, portobello, oyster or cremini. Sauté until soft, adding 2 tablespoons dry white wine or nonalcoholic dry white wine. Replace the Swiss cheese with reduced-fat mozzarella cheese.

Wild Rice and Cheddar Quiche: Use only ½ cup mushrooms and 2½ ounces spinach. Stir ¾ cup cooked wild and/or white rice into the milk mixture. Replace the Swiss cheese with reduced-fat Cheddar cheese.

Broccoli-Cheese Quiche: Replace the spinach with ¾ cup broccoli florets and finely chopped stalks. Place the broccoli in a steamer basket and blanch in a pot of boiling water for 45 seconds, or until crisp-tender. Drain and stir the broccoli into the egg mixture along with the mushrooms. Replace the Swiss cheese with reduced-fat Cheddar cheese. Omit the nutmeg.

Mushroom-Asparagus Quiche: Replace the spinach with 1 cup 1" asparagus pieces. Blanch the asparagus in a pot of boiling water for 45 seconds, or until crisp-tender. Drain and stir the asparagus into the egg mixture along with the mushrooms. Omit the nutmeg.

Eggplant Parmesan

2	medium eggplants, peeled
4	egg whites, lightly beaten
½	cup unseasoned dry bread crumbs
½	teaspoon dried basil
½	teaspoon dried oregano
½	teaspoon garlic powder
¼	teaspoon ground black pepper
3	cups reduced-sodium tomato sauce
2	cups shredded reduced-fat mozzarella cheese
¼	cup grated reduced-fat Parmesan cheese
2	tablespoons chopped fresh parsley

Coat a no-stick baking sheet with no-stick spray; set aside.

Cut the eggplants crosswise into ½" slices.

Place the egg whites in a shallow bowl. In another shallow bowl, mix the bread crumbs, basil, oregano, garlic powder and pepper.

Dip each eggplant slice first into the egg whites, then into the crumb mixture.

Place the eggplant on the prepared baking sheet and broil about 4" from the heat for 5 minutes per side, or until lightly browned.

Preheat the broiler.

Spread about ½ cup of the tomato sauce in the bottom of a 9" × 13" baking dish. Arrange a layer of eggplant on top of the sauce. Sprinkle with ½ cup of the mozzarella and 1 tablespoon of the Parmesan. Repeat the layers of sauce, eggplant and cheese—ending with tomato sauce—until all the ingredients have been used up. Sprinkle with the parsley and cover with foil.

Reduce the oven temperature to 350°. Bake for 30 minutes.

Makes 4 servings. Per serving: 376 calories, 10 g. fat (24% of calories), 28.4 g. protein, 40.9 g. carbohydrates, 2.8 g. dietary fiber, 30 mg. cholesterol, 725 mg. sodium

Hot

from the Oven

YEAST BREADS, PAGE 310

QUICK BREADS, MUFFINS AND BISCUITS, PAGE 336

Yeast Breads

If you ever doubt the value of fresh-baked bread, consider this trick from the annals of real estate: When potential buyers are due to come knocking, savvy sellers put a loaf of bread in the oven. The aroma is as irresistible as a low down payment. Baking bread smells like warmth, sustenance and home sweet home.

Healthy cooks have long known that home-baked bread is often better than store-bought kinds. Even so-called healthy breads are often loaded with refined sugar, hydrogenated fat and other additives. When you make bread yourself, you know exactly what goes into the mix. You can even add ingredients to boost its already high nutritional content.

Best of all, home-baked bread is wonderfully easy to make. With the right ingredients and just a few basic techniques, you can have fresh bread as often as you like. It's almost impossible to go wrong.

GEARING UP

Great bread doesn't require expensive cookware; you can get by with little more than a large mixing bowl and a wooden spoon. (Wood is preferable to metal, since it's less likely to rip the dough and release the yeasty gases.) If you bake often, however, you may find yourself wanting special equipment to make your life easier. The basics include:

☞ **Bread board.** Having a large surface to work on, whether it's made of wood or plastic, is really indispensable for kneading and shaping dough. Experienced bread bakers prefer wood, but a kitchen counter will do.

☞ **Oven thermometer.** Many home ovens have considerable variation between the temperature in the oven and the number on the dial. Oven thermometers are inexpensive and let you know what the real temperature is, so that you can make adjustments. At the very least, if you can't get the temperature exact, you can increase or decrease your baking time accordingly.

☞ **Bread pans.** Good bread pans last forever, so buy the best ones that you can find. Quality pans help produce a nice crust and can withstand plenty of wear. Don't forget: Glass pans cook more quickly than metal. Either reduce the temperature by 25° or decrease the baking time.

☞ **Baking tiles.** These help achieve a crispier crust by wicking moisture away from the loaves.

☞ **Parchment paper.** This no-stick paper can be used in lieu of oiling or greasing the pan. Laid on baking sheets or in pans, it prevents rolls and bread from sticking.

☞ **Dough scraper.** Made of curved plastic, this is handy for releasing dough from the bowl.

☞ **Heavy-duty mixer.** While hands-on bread making is a sensual delight, there are times when you'll want to get the job done faster and with less strain. When buying a standing mixer, get the most powerful one that you can afford; less expensive models don't always have enough power to mix heavy doughs. They also have a tendency to skate across the counter—and sometimes off the countertop. Make sure that the machine comes with a dough hook.

☞ **Food processor.** Like a mixer, this does a fine job of mixing dough. These machines tend to overheat quickly, so when making large quantities of bread, you may want to knead the dough in batches.

☞ **Bread machine.** These gee-whiz wonders really can do it all: mixing, kneading, rising and baking. They make it easy to have fresh bread as often as you like. However, some machines may have trouble handling heavier doughs, like those containing whole-grain flours. In addition, a machine can't make last-minute adjustments—a little less flour, say, or a little more liquid—the way you can. The quality of machine-made bread may vary somewhat from day to day.

There's probably no other food as universally loved as bread. Virtually every culture and country has its favorites, from classic French baguettes to the dense, 6-pound Austrian pumpernickels. Yet for all this variety, yeast breads consist of just four basic elements: flour, yeast, salt and liquid.

F*lour*

Most yeast breads are made with refined wheat flour. Why wheat? Wheat flour contains a mixture of plant proteins called gluten, which stretches to capture the gases produced by the yeast. This is what causes breads to rise. While all wheat flours contain gluten, they aren't quite interchangeable.

☞ **All-purpose flour.** Made by combining soft and hard wheats, this is the most common type of flour. It's really not ideal for bread making because it permits relatively little rise.

FLOURS FOR FLAVOR

Who says that bread has to be all white . . . or all anything? Many bakers add small amounts of specialty flours to give their breads a unique taste. Substitute the amounts given below for the main flour in your recipe. Be aware that these flours don't contain enough gluten—the protein in flours that gives them their stretch—to be used as the sole base for a loaf.

FLOUR	ADD THIS MUCH (cup)	WHAT IT DOES
Amaranth	⅛	Gives a slightly sweet taste
Barley	¼	Gives a sweet, maltlike taste
Brown rice	¼	Gives a sweet taste
Buckwheat	¼	Gives a nutty taste
Cornmeal	¼–½	Gives a slightly sweet, cornbready taste
Rye	½–1	Gives a tangy, slightly sour taste
Soy	¼	Gives a slightly bitter taste
Triticale	½	Gives a tangy taste

White Flour

Is It GOOD for You?

It wasn't so many years ago that the only flour in common use was whole-wheat flour. After all, white flour required extensive milling and processing. It was expensive; only the rich could indulge.

How times have changed. Today, white flour is in every kitchen, and it's one of the cheapest foods we can buy. Is it good for you? Yes—but nowhere near as good as it should be.

White flour is made by removing wheat's nutritious bran and germ. What remains is the starchy heart of the grain (the endosperm), which is ground into flour. In the process, many of the original nutrients are lost, along with most of the fiber. Even though most flours are enriched, the final mix loses some of its natural goodness.

So even though white flour isn't exactly bad for you, a better choice is to use flours made with whole grains, which retain their natural nutrients and fiber. A compromise for many recipes is to use a mixture of the two, with the white flour lightening the heavy texture of the whole-grain flour.

☞ **Bread flour.** This is a hard-wheat, high-gluten flour that produces a fast-rising, puffy loaf.

☞ **Self-rising flour.** Often used for making quick breads, this type of flour contains baking powder and sometimes salt. It's never used for making yeast breads.

☞ **Unbleached flour.** This is the flour of choice for baking bread. High in protein, unbleached flour generally produces a fine, elastic dough.

☞ **Whole-wheat flour.** Unlike all-purpose flour, whole-wheat flour retains the nutritious bran and germ. This produces a denser, nuttier loaf that's also higher in fiber.

Yeast

Yeast is the secret ingredient that makes bread rise. It's an astonishingly small form of plant life; a single ounce of yeast consists of approximately half a trillion individual cells.

When you mix yeast with flour, liquid and other ingredients, the yeast cells rapidly grow and divide, all the while releasing clouds of carbon dioxide gas. The gas gets trapped in the muscular strands of gluten, which causes the loaf to rise. The high heat of baking eventually kills the yeast, leaving behind a wonderfully light, airy bread.

There are several types of yeast available to home bakers. Whichever one you use, always check the expiration date on the package to ensure that it's still fresh. For extra measure, proof the yeast by mixing it with warm water and seeing if it bubbles up, which indicates that it's still usable.

☞ **Active dry yeast.** Available in scant-tablespoon packets, small jars or large cans, active dry yeast is the most common variety. It's extremely durable and keeps for two to four years when stored in the refrigerator or freezer in a tightly sealed or unopened container.

☞ **Rapid-rise yeast.** A variety of active dry yeast, rapid-rise yeast dissolves more readily

TROUBLESHOOTING BREAD PROBLEMS

When you consider that the key ingredient for making bread—yeast—is a living organism, it's really not surprising that bread sometimes takes on a life of its own. The dough doesn't rise; it rises too much; the bread is overdone today and underdone tomorrow. What's the problem? And, more important, what can you do to fix it?

PROBLEM	POSSIBLE CAUSE	SOLUTIONS
Dough doesn't rise	Yeast is inactive	Make sure that the yeast hasn't passed the expiration date. The proofing water should be warm, not hot. Cut back on flour, eggs or oil. Check the oven temperature with a thermometer.
Bread has a yeasty taste	Too much yeast in the recipe	Check the amount of yeast. Make sure bread rises only until doubled. Let the dough rise in a cooler place.
Bread is dense and heavy	Too much liquid in the recipe	Adjust the amount of liquid. Let the bread rise more fully.
Bread is bland and coarse	Salt was omitted	Use salt—it's really indispensable.
Crumb is uneven	Not enough salt or the oven temperature is too low	Add a little more salt to the recipe. Check the oven temperature with a thermometer.
Bread is crumbly	Not enough gluten developed	Use a higher-gluten flour. Knead the dough a little longer. Allow more time for rising.
The crust splits	The dough has more rise than the crust can accommodate	Make slashes across the top before baking to release the pressure.
Bread is pale	Bread is undercooked	Remove the baked loaf from the pan and place it directly on the oven rack for several minutes, or until brown. Use nonshiny pans, which make a darker crust.
Bottom is burned	Oven rack is too low	Make sure that the baking dish is in the middle of the oven, where the heat is most even. Decrease the oven temperature or the baking time when using glass bakeware.

and raises dough in about half the time. It can give the bread a slightly yeasty taste that some people find unappealing.

☞ **Compressed fresh yeast.** A more fragile, more perishable form of yeast, this is found in the refrigerated sections of supermarkets. It can be used interchangeably with active dry yeast, although some people say that it gives a slightly more authentic flavor than the dry kind.

☞ **Bread-machine yeast.** This type of yeast differs from other forms in that the individual cells have thinner walls; it dissolves readily without being mixed with water first.

Salt

Many healthy cooks are concerned about adding unnecessary salt to their food. When making bread, however, salt isn't an optional ingredient. It helps regulate the activity of the yeast, preventing it from overrising. In addition, salt keeps bread from tasting flat.

☞ To make sure that salt gets evenly dispersed, dissolve it in liquid before adding it to the mix.

☞ If you're on a sodium-restricted diet, you may want to cut the salt in half, then boost the flavor of the bread by adding seasonings like anise seeds, cinnamon or herbs.

☞ Don't use salt substitutes, since they won't regulate the natural rising of the yeast.

Liquids

If yeast is the soul of bread, liquid is the spirit; bread won't rise without it. Which liquid you add depends on the recipe.

☞ **Water.** Used in making French bread, water creates a loaf that's light and airy on the inside, with a crispy crust on the outside. Plain water works well, although many healthy cooks prefer to reserve the water used for boiling potatoes and use that in their breads. Dissolved nutrients from the potatoes make a wonderful, nutrient-rich broth for the yeast.

☞ **Milk.** While not recommended for hard-crust breads like French bread, milk gives the loaf a moist, tender crumb that many people like. To reduce the amount of fat in recipes, it's best to use low-fat or skim milk; buttermilk, nonfat plain yogurt, evaporated milk and powdered milk can also be used.

☞ **Juices.** Both fruit and vegetable juices can be used in bread making. Which juice you use is entirely up to you. Juices add a touch of flavor and color as well as nutrients to your recipes.

Other Ingredients

A basic bread dough is like a blank slate: It can be refined, embellished or even changed entirely by adding or subtracting certain ingredients.

☞ **Sugars.** Yeast thrives on sugars, both the kind found naturally in wheat flour and the ones you add. Adding honey, molasses or white or brown sugar to a recipe will slightly change the taste and also the color, as the sugars partially caramelize during baking. Molasses adds iron, minerals and a distinctive rustic flavor to dark breads. Maple syrup makes an excellent sweetener for loaves with pumpkin or cornmeal.

☞ **Fats.** Butter, margarine, shortening and vegetable oil soften a dough's gluten, making it pleasantly tender. Of course, adding fat also adds calories, so you're wise to keep added fat to a minimum. When you do add fat, choose a heart-healthy kind, like canola, olive, safflower, sunflower or corn oil.

☞ **Eggs.** Used both for color and flavor, eggs have the additional advantage of giving an almost cakelike texture to breads. Unfortunately, they also add cholesterol. If that's a concern for you, chefs advise replacing each whole egg with two egg whites or an appropriate amount of egg substitute.

☞ **Seasonings.** To transform a basic bread recipe into a world of flavors, all you have to do is add herbs or spices. Ingredients like grated raw carrots, mashed potatoes, sun-dried tomatoes or sprouted grains, like wheat or rye berries, also add flavors that you may enjoy.

MAKING THE DOUGH

In this age of store-bought bread and automatic bread machines, many cooks have never tried baking their own. Making bread may seem time-consuming, but most of that time is taken up by the bread rising and doesn't require attention from you. The actual hands-on time rarely exceeds half an hour.

Here's how to make great bread every time.

Start warm. Dough mixes best when all the ingredients are at room temperature or warmer. Using cool ingredients inhibits yeast, slowing the rising time.

☞ Although warm is good, hot is not. Any ingredients that you have scalded or otherwise heated should be cooled to lukewarm before using, so that they don't kill the yeast.

☞ Quick-rising yeast can withstand higher temperatures than regular active dry yeast or compressed fresh yeast. Recipes created for quick yeast often call for liquids as hot as 130°F.

Proof the yeast. Since yeast is a living organism, it occasionally gives up the ghost before you have a chance to use it.

☞ Start by checking the expiration date on the package. Don't waste your time with yeast that's past its prime.

☞ Most recipes call for the yeast to be proofed before adding other ingredients. That serves as a double check on the yeast's viability. Mix 1 package or cake of yeast with ½ cup warm

Helpful Hint

For a lighter, better-textured bread, combine the yeast, liquid and about half the flour. Mix well and set aside to rise, covered, for between 30 and 60 minutes. The resulting "sponge" helps the dough get off to a fast start.

Helpful Hint

Sometimes dough becomes so elastic that it fights you as you try to shape it. Letting it rest in a covered bowl for about 10 minutes will allow the gluten to relax so that the dough is more manageable.

water, 1 teaspoon sugar and 1 teaspoon flour. Stir, then set aside. If the yeast is still fresh, froth and bubbles will appear in about 10 minutes. If nothing happens, the yeast has died and should be replaced with a fresh batch.

☞ Water used to proof yeast should be warm—preferably between 105° and 115°F. If using compressed fresh yeast, make sure that the temperature is no higher than 95°F.

Mix liquids first. To ensure even mixing, combine all the liquid ingredients first, along with the salt and any oil or melted butter that the recipe calls for.

Once the liquids are well-mixed, start adding the flour, stirring briskly. Continue adding flour, mixing with a wooden spoon (or, if you're using an electric mixer, the dough hook) until the dough gets stiff. At this point, use your hands to finish incorporating the flour into the dough.

Knead it well. The importance of proper kneading can't be overstated. Knead it too little and the bread won't rise properly. Improper kneading will also cause the bread's texture to be coarse and uneven.

☞ When all the flour has been mixed in, turn the dough out onto a lightly floured bread board and work in additional flour as needed to keep it pliable.

☞ To keep dough from sticking to your hands, dip them frequently in flour. A small mound kept in a corner of the bread board works well for this.

KNEADING DOUGH

Kneading is exercise for both bread and baker. Just as exercise strengthens the muscles, kneading develops gluten in the wheat, helping the finished bread achieve a pleasant texture and the necessary rise. Don't be too gentle; the harder you work dough, the better the gluten develops. It's almost impossible to overknead dough by hand. Every once in a while, lift the dough off the counter and slam it back down. This is a quick, time-honored way to exercise the dough even more.

To prepare for kneading, wash and dry your hands to keep them from sticking to the dough. If you're using a bread board, make sure that it rests securely on the counter; putting a damp towel underneath will provide a good anchor. Dust the dough and board lightly with flour.

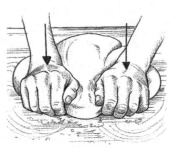

With your hands side by side, press down with the heels, flattening the dough to about ½" thick.

With your hands still together, reach to the far end of the dough and fold it back on itself.

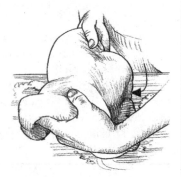

Rotate the dough a quarter-turn, then flatten it again. Repeat for 7 to 10 minutes, or until the dough feels elastic and pliable. As needed, incorporate more flour into the dough to keep it from sticking, but try not to add too much, or the bread will be heavy.

☞ On humid days, you may need more flour than the recipe calls for; on dry days, add less. Trust your hands: When the dough is firm and holds its shape, you've added enough flour.

☞ Bread baking is a forgiving craft. At almost any stage in the process, you can knead in more liquid or flour to get the texture that you want. This goes for other ingredients as well. If you forget to add salt or sugar during mixing, you can always dissolve them in a little warm water, then knead them directly into the dough.

☞ Knead for 7 to 10 minutes, or until the dough is soft and satiny smooth. Poke the dough with your finger: If it bounces nearly all the way back, it's ready for rising.

Let it rise. Breads that are made with baking soda or baking powder get their rise during mixing and baking. Yeast breads, however, require more of a prolonged resting time, usually about 1 to 2 hours, during which the yeast multiplies, produces gases and causes the dough to rise.

Helpful Hint

One difficulty with making homemade bread is that wet dough can have the sticking power of paste. To clean sticky dough from your hands or utensils, rub them well with flour until the dough comes off.

☞ To prevent the dough from sticking, place it in a lightly oiled bowl prior to rising. Or mist the bowl with no-stick spray.

☞ Turn the dough to coat it on all sides with the oil and keep the top from drying out.

☞ Cover the bowl with a sheet of plastic wrap or a damp dishcloth and place in a warm, draft-free place. Leave until doubled in size, usually about 1 to 1½ hours.

☞ Ideal rising places include the oven with a pilot light on, a cabinet close to the water heater, on top of a still-warm (but not hot) range or floating in a larger bowl of warm water.

Take the air out. When the dough has doubled in size, punch it with your fist to remove excess gas bubbles, then knead it briefly until it's smooth.

Give it shape. Now's the time to shape the dough and put it into a bread pan or on a baking sheet. Cover the shaped dough with a cloth and let it rise a second time. The second rising occurs more quickly than the first; the dough usually doubles in 30 to 60 minutes.

☞ Near the end of the rising time, preheat the oven to the temperature called for in the recipe. When the bread has doubled in size, put it in the oven and bake.

☞ To test for doneness, remove baked bread from the pan and firmly rap the bottom. A hollow sound means that the bread is ready. If all you get is a dull thud, put the bread back in the oven for another 5 minutes, then check it again.

☞ Another way to test for doneness is to insert a quick-read thermometer into the center of the loaf. Bread is done when the temperature reads 185° to 190°F.

A WORLD OF GOODNESS

From the pitas of the Middle East and the black breads of Russia to the sourdoughs of San Francisco and the baguettes of France, it is literally possible to travel all around the globe without ever being deprived of bread. We've included recipes in this chapter for some of the most common and best-loved breads. In addition, here are a few variations that you may want to try.

Sourdough Bread

The process of making sourdough bread is as ancient as bread itself. As early as 4000 B.C., the

(continued on page 320)

WHEN YOU'RE IN A HURRY

Experienced bread bakers recommend long, slow rises for the best texture and overall results. But when you need to speed things up, look to your microwave.

☞ Place the dough in a microwave-safe bowl and cover loosely with plastic wrap.

☞ Microwave on low power for 5 minutes. Repeat once or twice, always on low power, until the dough doubles in volume.

☞ Punch down the dough, shape and place in a glass loaf pan or other microwave-safe container. Microwave on low power for 5 minutes. Repeat until the dough doubles in volume.

SHAPING DOUGH

It's not uncommon for busy cooks to give considerable attention to mixing and kneading the dough, then slap together the final loaf. The resulting shape, more often than not, looks more like an accident than a polished piece of work.

Forming the dough into its final shape requires some care. Most important, you want to work the dough as little as possible so as not to reactivate the gluten. Here are a few simple ways to shape your bread so that it delights the eyes as well as the taste buds.

LOAF

 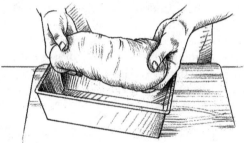

After forming the dough into an oval shape, roll it into a cylinder slightly longer than the pan, with the seam side up.

Flip the ends toward the center so that the loaf is the same length as the pan. Turn the dough so that the seam faces down and lower the loaf into the pan.

BAGUETTE

Roll the dough into a lengthy, narrow cylinder, then transfer it to a no-stick baking sheet.

BRAID

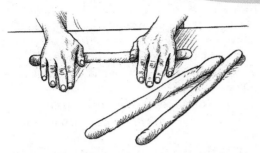

Divide the dough into 3 equal parts and roll each part into a cylinder.

Line up the cylinders so that the ends face you. Braid from the middle to the ends. Be sure to slightly stretch the strands as you braid so that it tapers at the end. Then pinch the ends together.

PINWHEEL

Roll or press the dough into a rectangle about ¼" thick. Spread or sprinkle with filling, leaving a border of about 1" on all sides.

Roll into a cylinder. Press on the seam to seal, then transfer to a no-stick baking dish, seam side down.

BREADSTICKS

Using your palms, roll golf ball–size portions of dough into ropes about 6″ to 8″ long. Sprinkle with seeds, kosher salt or grated Parmesan cheese to flavor.

Egyptians discovered that when ground grain and water were combined and left exposed to air, they naturally attracted airborne spores of yeast. The resulting fermentation not only caused the bread to rise but also provided a mother lode of fermentation to get the next loaf started.

Quite a few years later, the same method was used in the famous bakeries of San Francisco during the Gold Rush. Even today, in the best French bakeries, a piece of sourdough, or *levain*, is added to every one of that day's loaves.

Since airborne yeasts are literally everywhere, it's easy to make your own sourdough. You can also use a little store-bought yeast to help get the process started.

Make a starter. To get the process underway, combine 2 cups whole-wheat flour with 1½ cups warm water and 1 tablespoon active dry yeast in a large glass or stainless-steel bowl. Stir well and cover lightly. Let the mix rest in a warm spot for about 24 hours. Briefly stir the mix, then set it aside again. At this point, it should look like a soft, spongy batter.

On the third day, refrigerate the starter in a tightly capped quart jar for six days. During that time, the flavor will deepen as the yeast continues to multiply. After six days, the starter will be ready to use. Just follow the instructions in the recipe.

Traditional yeast breads typically rise in about 1 to 2 hours. Sourdough takes a little longer, usually about 2 to 3 hours or even more.

Fortify the starter. As time goes by, you should periodically rejuvenate the starter by "feeding" it. Remove 1 cup of the mix (you can either discard it or use it to make bread) and re-place it with ½ cup whole-wheat flour and ½ cup water. Stir well. Let the jar stand at room temperature overnight, then refrigerate. Do not add more yeast. At this point, the starter is ready to use again. You can repeat this process virtually forever.

Rolls

Made from the same dough as bread, rolls are simply smaller versions. Because they're smaller, they take less time to rise and also to bake, making them an ideal choice for busy bakers.

When making rolls, first form the risen dough into a long cylinder. Cut off even portions, about 3″ long. Then form the dough into one of the following shapes.

☞ **Round.** Using the curved palm of your hand, roll dough in a circular motion to form a round ball.

☞ **Hamburger buns.** After forming a round ball, flatten the dough slightly with your hand.

☞ **Twist.** Roll the dough into a rope about 8″ long. Fold the rope in half, then twist the ends, one over the other. Place the twists on a no-stick baking sheet, pressing down the ends so that they don't unravel.

☞ **Bow knot.** Roll the dough into a rope, then tie a single knot.

☞ **Snails.** Roll the dough into a thin rope, about ½″ around. Then wind the dough into a spiral, tucking the end underneath to prevent it from unraveling.

Bagels

Of obscure origin but enduring popularity, bagels have surpassed even doughnuts in popularity. They're a wonderful boon for the healthy cook, being low in calories and containing little fat or cholesterol. Alone or with the addition of whole grains and seeds, bagels make a filling, very nutritious snack.

Shape the dough. After the dough has risen once, divide it into even, ball-shaped portions. Flatten each ball into a 3½″ disk.

With your finger, poke a hole through the center of each disk. Lift the bagel slightly and twirl it on your index finger until the hole is about 1½″ around. Set aside and let rise for about 20 minutes.

Put them in hot water. The secret to great bagels is to simmer them for just a few seconds in a large pot of water. This is what gives bagels their traditional glossy appearance and chewy crust.

For even cooking, don't add more than two bagels at a time. Let simmer for a few seconds on each side, then remove with a slotted spoon. Set on lightly oiled wax paper to drain.

Make the final preparations. After the bagels have drained, transfer them to a lightly oiled no-stick baking sheet.

To keep fat to a minimum, coat a baking sheet with no-stick spray. Brush the top of each bagel with egg whites beaten with a little water. Bagels can be plain or lightly sprinkled with sesame seeds, poppy seeds, onions, garlic or other favorite toppings before baking.

TIME SAVERS

We tend to think of baking bread as being an all-day activity, but the amount of time that you actually spend in the kitchen is often less than it takes to put together a simple stir-fry. The only really time-consuming part is the rising, and that takes place without any help from you.

Still, there are ways to make bread faster and easier than ever. For busy cooks, here's what chefs advise.

Plan ahead. Although most recipes call for dough to be set aside in a warm place for rising, this step can also be done in the refrigerator, although at a much slower pace. This is helpful when you want to make dough today for tomorrow's bread.

☞ After mixing the dough, put it in a large, lightly oiled bowl or pot. Cover the container tightly, either with its lid or with plastic wrap.

☞ Put the bowl in the refrigerator and let the dough rise overnight. In the morning, punch it down, shape it and continue with the recipe.

☞ Storing dough in the freezer in individual packages means that you'll always have fresh bread ready for baking. When you want bread for the next day, remove the dough from the package and put it in a covered bowl at room temperature. Leave it until morning, then continue with the recipe.

A CUT IN TIME

Those deep cuts across the loaves of fine French and Italian breads aren't there just for decoration. Scoring the top allows bread to expand without busting out the side or cracking on top. Chefs advise slicing the bread just after glazing and before placing it in the oven.

Using a sharp knife or a razor blade, slash the dough about ½" deep. The cuts can be parallel, cross-hatched or in a checkerboard pattern. The deeper the cuts, the more the bread will "blossom."

It's difficult for home bakers to duplicate the ethereal, crispy crusts created by the finest commercial, tile-lined, steam-injected ovens—or even your great-grandmother's wood-fired stove. But there are a few ways to get great crusts at home. Here's how.

Hold the fat. Recipes that include a lot of oil and milk produce softer crusts and crumbs. A simple dough of water, unbleached flour, salt and yeast is the best way to get a crackly crust.

Choose the right pan. Bread crusts can vary tremendously depending upon the pan you use. For hard rolls, cooks recommend using a metal pan lined with parchment paper. Or, if you prefer a thick crust, you'll probably want to use a glass or darkened metal pan.

Lay some tiles. A tile-lined oven is perhaps *the* secret for crispy crusts; the tiles absorb moisture from the dough and also retain tremendous amounts of heat, making the crust crisp.

Home bakers can partially duplicate this effect by making bread on baking stones, available in kitchen supply stores. Or you can buy unglazed terra-cotta tiles at a kitchen supply store and use them to line the baking rack.

When using tiles, place them in a cold oven. Preheat the oven, then sprinkle the tiles with cornmeal. Carefully transfer the shaped dough to the tiles and bake until done.

Helpful Hint

One difficulty with making round loaves is that they often flatten during rising. To help them hold their shape, wrap a 1″ strip of foil around each loaf. Remove the strip about halfway through the baking time.

Turn on the steam. The trick to getting a firm, crisp crust is to put steam inside the oven during baking. The easiest way to do this is by placing a shallow pan of boiling water in the oven on the lowest rack just prior to baking. Let it steam for the first 10 minutes of baking, then remove it as the bread continues baking.

Another method is to spritz the baking loaves often with water. Use a clean spray bottle that you reserve for this purpose.

Add a little salt. Yet another way to get a slightly hard crust is to brush the loaf with saltwater, using about a teaspoon of salt in ½ cup water. Brush the loaf about halfway through the baking time.

FINISHING TOUCHES

Glazes and toppings are more than just afterthoughts to a good loaf of bread. They can add flavor and eye appeal along with pleasing amounts of texture or crunch, depending on the topping. Just be sure to use a light hand; since glazes and toppings go on when the dough is still soft, the bread can easily lose its shape if you press too hard.

Tasty toppings include:

☞ **Nuts and seeds.** Sprinkle the loaf with sesame, poppy, anise or caraway seeds or crushed walnuts, sliced almonds or other nuts. Brush on some beaten egg white beforehand, so that the seeds and nuts adhere to the dough.

☞ **Shiny glazes.** Brushing on a little beaten egg gives bread that bakery-window sheen. Egg yolk alone gives the shiniest appearance. For more subtle color—and less cholesterol and fat—brush the dough with milk or water.

☞ **Rolled oats.** As do cornmeal and flour, these lend a rustic effect when lightly sprinkled on the dough. Brush on a little egg white beforehand to help the topping stick.

☞ **Sugar.** Both granulated and confectioners' sugar lend a delicious finish and are recommended for sweet breads and rolls like cinnamon-raisin.

David Burke

The breads alone make dining at David Burke's Park Avenue Cafe worth the trip.

Burke, who has restaurants in New York and Chicago, believes that bread is much more then just filler food. It's as important, in it's own way, as the main course.

"Bread is usually the first thing you eat at a meal, and it can excite or disappoint you for what comes next," he says. "I have always enjoyed baking bread. Here is a favorite."

Potato Rye Bread

1½ cups finely diced potatoes
¼ cup diced onions
½ teaspoon canola or olive oil
1¼ cups warm water (about 110°F)
⅓ cup skim milk
1½ tablespoons active dry yeast
1 tablespoon sugar
2 cups unbleached flour
¾ cup coarse rye flour
2½ cups white rye flour
1½ teaspoons salt

Place the potatoes in a medium saucepan and cover with cold water. Bring to a boil over high heat. Reduce the heat to medium and cook for 10 minutes, or until tender. Drain and cool. If desired, reserve the liquid for another use.

In a medium no-stick skillet over medium heat, sauté the onions in the oil for 10 minutes, or until slightly caramelized.

In a medium bowl, mix the water and milk. Stir in the yeast and sugar. Let stand for 5 minutes, or until the yeast becomes foamy.

In a large bowl, mix the unbleached flour, coarse rye flour, white rye flour and salt. Stir in the onions. Add the yeast mixture. Mix by hand or with an electric mixer fitted with a dough hook until a dough forms.

Place the dough on a lightly floured surface. Knead the potatoes into the dough until distributed throughout, being careful not to mash the potatoes.

Coat an 8″ × 4″ no-stick loaf pan with no-stick spray. Form the dough into a loaf and place in the pan. Cover and set in a warm, draft-free place until doubled in size.

Preheat the oven to 375°. Bake for 45 to 50 minutes. Remove the bread from the pan and return to the oven for 10 minutes, or until the bottom is browned and the loaf sounds hollow when tapped.

Makes 1 loaf; 8 slices. Per slice: 325 calories, 1.4 g. fat (4% of calories), 9.7 g. protein, 69 g. carbohydrates, 3.6 g. dietary fiber, 0.2 mg. cholesterol, 410 mg. sodium

Healthy White Bread

Yes! You can have good-tasting and good-for-you white bread. We've reduced the fat and cholesterol by replacing whole milk with skim milk and replacing shortening with a reduced amount of canola oil. This everyday favorite is perfect for sandwiches and toast.

2	packages (¼ ounce each) active dry yeast
½	cup warm water (105°–115°F)
1	tablespoon sugar
2	cups skim milk, warmed
1	tablespoon canola oil
2	teaspoons salt
5–6	cups bread flour

In a large bowl, dissolve the yeast in the water. Stir in 1 teaspoon of the sugar and let stand for 5 minutes until the yeast begins to bubble.

Add the remaining 2 teaspoons sugar, milk, oil, salt and 4 cups of the flour. Beat until the mixture is smooth and satiny. Gradually stir in enough of the remaining flour to make a dough that forms an irregular ball. Cover with a damp cloth and let stand for 15 minutes.

Turn the dough out onto a lightly floured surface. Knead until the dough is smooth and satiny, only adding enough of the remaining flour to keep the dough from being sticky.

Coat a clean large bowl with no-stick spray. Place the dough in the bowl, cover with a damp cloth and let rise in a warm place for 45 to 60 minutes, or until the dough is light and doubled in bulk.

Coat two 9″ × 5″ or 8″ × 4″ no-stick loaf pans with no-stick spray. Gently deflate the dough with your fist and knead to eliminate air bubbles. Divide the dough into 2 equal-size pieces and shape into oblong loaves. Place in the prepared pans, cover with a damp cloth and let rise in a warm place for 30 to 35 minutes, or until the dough fills the pans and the tops of the loaves are about 1″ above the pan edges.

Preheat the oven to 375°. Uncover the dough and bake for 30 to 40 minutes, or until a toothpick inserted in the center comes out clean.

Makes 2 loaves; 18 slices each. Per slice: 80 calories, 1 g. fat (11% of calories), 2.6 g. protein, 15.8 g. carbohydrates, 0.6 g. dietary fiber, 0.2 mg. cholesterol, 126 mg. sodium

VARIATIONS

Cinnamon-Swirl Loaf: After dividing the risen dough into 2 equal-size pieces, roll each piece into a 14″ × 7″ rectangle. Brush each with 1 teaspoon melted butter. Mix together ½ cup sugar and 2 teaspoons cinnamon. Sprinkle over the dough. Starting with the short side, roll up each loaf jelly-roll style. Seal the edges with a little water and place the loaves, seam side down, into the prepared pans. Let rise and bake as directed above.

Hamburger Buns: Coat 2 no-stick baking sheets with no-stick spray. Divide the risen dough into 16 equal-size pieces and shape into balls. Place on the prepared sheets and flatten each ball into a bun about ½″ thick. Cover with a warm cloth and let rise in a warm place for 30 minutes. Bake at 400° for 15 minutes, or until golden. Makes 16.

Herbed Mini Loaves: Add 2 teaspoons dried Italian seasoning to the liquid ingredients. Coat six 3″ × 5″ small no-stick loaf pans with no-stick spray. Divide the risen dough into 6 equal-size pieces and shape each into an oblong loaf about 5″ long. Place in the prepared pans, cover with a warm cloth and let rise in a warm place for 45 minutes, or until the dough doubles in bulk. Brush each loaf with water and sprinkle with sesame seeds. Bake at 375° for 20 to 25 minutes, or until the loaves sound hollow when tapped. Makes 6 small loaves.

Whole-Wheat Bread

Makes 2 loaves; 16 slices each. Per slice: 89 calories, 0.8 g. fat (8% of calories), 3.2 g. protein, 18.5 g. carbohydrates, 3 g. dietary fiber, 0 mg. cholesterol, 135 mg. sodium

2 packages (¼ ounce each) active dry yeast
2½ cups warm water (105°–115°F)
¼ cup honey
2 teaspoons salt
1 tablespoon canola oil
About 6 cups whole-wheat bread flour (see note)

In a large mixing bowl, dissolve the yeast in the water. Stir in the honey and let stand for 5 minutes, or until the yeast is foamy. Stir in the salt, oil and 2 cups of the flour. Beat until smooth. Stir in enough of the remaining flour to form a soft dough. Cover with a damp cloth and let the dough rest for 15 minutes.

Turn the dough out onto a lightly floured surface and knead for 10 to 15 minutes, or until the dough is smooth and elastic.

Coat a clean large bowl with no-stick spray. Place the dough in the bowl, cover with a damp towel and let rise in a warm place for 35 to 45 minutes, or until the dough is light and doubled in bulk.

Coat two 9″ × 5″ or 8″ × 4″ no-stick loaf pans with no-stick spray. Gently deflate the dough with your fist and knead to eliminate air bubbles. Divide the dough into 2 equal-size pieces and shape into oblong loaves. Place in the prepared pans, cover with a damp cloth and let rise in a warm place for 40 to 45 minutes, or until the dough is light and almost doubled in bulk.

Preheat the oven to 375°. Bake the loaves for 30 minutes. Reduce the oven temperature to 350° and bake for 10 to 15 minutes longer, or until a toothpick inserted in the center comes out clean. Immediately remove from the pans and cool on a wire rack.

NOTE

• The 100% whole-wheat bread flour makes a great-textured light loaf in this recipe. This type of flour is available in health food stores and some supermarkets. For an easy substitution, see the Light Wheat Bread variation below.

VARIATIONS

Light Wheat Bread: Replace the whole-wheat bread flour with 3 cups whole-wheat flour and 3 to 3½ cups white bread flour.
Whole-Wheat Raisin Bread: Add ½ teaspoon cinnamon to the dough along with the salt. Stir in 1 cup raisins after 2 cups of the flour have been added.

Herb Dinner Rolls

½ cup water
½ cup + 1 tablespoon skim milk
1 package (¼ ounce) quick-rising yeast
1 tablespoon olive oil
1 teaspoon honey
About 1¾ cups unbleached flour
½ cup whole-wheat flour
½ teaspoon dried thyme
½ teaspoon crushed dried rosemary
½ teaspoon salt
¼ teaspoon ground black pepper

In a small microwave-safe bowl, combine the water and ½ cup of the milk. Microwave on high power for 30 seconds, or until lukewarm. Mix in the yeast, oil and honey. Let stand for 5 minutes, or until the yeast is foamy.

In a food processor, add the unbleached

flour, whole-wheat flour, thyme, rosemary, salt and pepper. Process briefly to mix well. With the machine running, pour in the yeast mixture through the feed tube. Process for about 1 minute, or until the mixture forms a ball of dough that sits on top of the blade.

Turn the dough out onto a lightly floured surface. Knead for 5 minutes, or until the dough is smooth. (If necessary, add a little more flour to keep the dough from sticking.)

Coat a clean large bowl with no-stick spray. Place the dough in the prepared bowl. Cover with a damp cloth and let rise in a warm place for 30 minutes, or until the dough doubles in bulk.

Gently deflate the dough with your fist and turn out onto a lightly floured surface. Knead for 1 minute. Form into a rope about 18″ long. Cut into 12 equal-size pieces. Form each piece into a ball.

Preheat the oven to 400°. Coat a no-stick baking sheet with no-stick spray. Place the balls on the sheet, leaving about 2″ between them. Cover with a damp towel and let rise in a warm, draft-free place for 15 minutes, or until the balls double in bulk. Uncover and lightly brush the balls with the remaining 1 tablespoon milk.

Bake for 15 to 20 minutes, or until the rolls are lightly browned.

Makes 12. Per roll: 101 calories, 1.4 g. fat (13% of calories), 3.2 g. protein, 18.9 g. carbohydrates, 1.3 g. dietary fiber, 0.2 mg. cholesterol, 95 mg. sodium

NOTE

• To save time, let the dough rise in the microwave. Microwave on low power for 5 minutes. (Do not use a higher power, because the heat may kill the yeast.) Give the bowl a quarter-turn, then microwave on low power for another 5 minutes. If the dough has not doubled in bulk, microwave on low power for another 5 minutes.

VARIATIONS

Dinner Bread Twists: Form each ball of risen dough into a 12″ rope. Twist into a coil shape.

Garlic Knots: Form each ball of risen dough into an 8″ rope. Loosely tie it into a knot. Instead of brushing with the milk, coat the knots with butter-flavored no-stick spray. Sprinkle with minced garlic.

Braided Dinner Rolls: Divide each ball of risen dough into thirds and form each third into a 6″ rope. Braid the pieces together.

Clover Rolls: Divide each ball of risen dough into thirds and form each third into a small ball; group the balls together to form a clover.

Vienna Breadsticks: Form each ball of risen dough into an elongated loaf about 3″ long. Use a sharp knife to make 3 diagonal slashes ¼″ deep in the top.

Cottage Dinner Rolls: Divide each ball of risen dough into 2 pieces, with one twice the size of the other, and stack the small piece on top of the larger one. Flour your finger and press it straight down through both pieces to form a small hole in the center.

Sourdough Bread

Sourdough Starter

    1   package (¼ ounce) active dry yeast
    1   teaspoon sugar
1–1½   cups warm water (105°–115°F)
    2   cups all-purpose flour

Bread Dough

    1   cup warm water (105°–115°F)
    2   teaspoons salt
4½–5   cups bread flour

To make the sourdough starter: In a large plastic bowl with a tight-fitting lid, combine the yeast, sugar, water and flour. Loosely cover and let stand in a warm place for 5 days, stirring at least once a day. When the starter is ready for use, it will be bubbly and may have a layer of yellow liquid on top. Stir well before using.

To make the bread dough: Add the water, salt and 1 cup of the flour into the starter and stir. Gradually stir in enough of the remaining flour to make a very stiff dough. Turn the dough out onto a lightly floured surface and knead until the dough is smooth and elastic, adding flour as needed. (You may also turn the dough into the bowl of a heavy-duty mixer with a dough hook and knead for 8 to 10 minutes, or until the dough is smooth and elastic.)

Coat a clean large bowl with no-stick spray. Place the dough in the bowl, cover with a damp towel and let rise in a warm place for 2 hours, or until the dough is doubled in bulk.

At this point, you may use all of the dough to make one loaf of bread or remove some of the dough to repeat the starter process (so you can make more loaves of bread in the future). To repeat the starter process, remove 1 cup of the risen dough and place it into the plastic starter bowl. Pour 1½ cups warm water over the starter dough. Stir in 1 cup all-purpose flour. Cover and let stand at room temperature until the starter has doubled in bulk. Then, refrigerate the starter until you are ready to bake again (see note).

Shape the remaining bread dough into a round loaf about 2½" thick. Coat a no-stick baking sheet with no-stick spray. Place the loaf on the sheet. Loosely cover with a damp cloth and let rise for 1 to 2 hours, or until the dough is doubled in bulk.

Preheat the oven to 400°. With a sharp knife, make three ¼"-deep slits on the top of the loaf. Bake for 20 to 25 minutes, or until golden and crusty. Remove the bread from the baking sheet and cool on a wire rack.

Makes 1 large loaf; 24 slices. Per serving: 106 calories, 0.3 g. fat (2% of calories), 3.1 g. protein, 22.2 g. carbohydrates, 0.9 g. dietary fiber, 0 mg. cholesterol, 178 mg. sodium

NOTES

• It takes 5 days to develop the sourdough flavor in this starter. Once the starter is made, you can keep making bread from it by repeating the directions under "to make the bread dough."

• If you don't plan to make bread again within a week, you can refrigerate the starter indefinitely by refreshing it once a week. To do this, remove 1 cup of the starter. Into the remaining starter, stir 1½ cups warm water and 1 cup all-purpose flour. Cover and let stand at room temperature until the starter has doubled in bulk. Refrigerate and repeat until you are ready to make bread.

VARIATIONS

Sourdough Hard Rolls: Divide the risen dough into 12 equal-size pieces. Coat a no-stick baking sheet with no-stick spray. Place the dough pieces on the baking sheet. Cover with a damp cloth and let rise in a warm place for 1 to 2 hours, or until doubled in bulk. Bake at 400° for 12 to 15 minutes, or until golden.

Sourdough Breadsticks: Divide the risen dough in half. Divide each half into 32 equal-size pieces. Shape each piece into an 8"-long bread-stick. Coat 2 no-stick baking sheets with no-stick spray. Place the dough pieces on the baking sheets. Lightly brush the breadsticks with beaten egg white and sprinkle with sesame seeds. Cover with a damp cloth and let rise in a warm place for 30 minutes, or until doubled in bulk. Bake at 400° for 15 minutes, or until golden. Makes 64.

Milwaukee Pumpernickel Bread

This dark and tasty bread contains no shortening and is very low in fat. Mashed potatoes add tenderness and moistness to the dough.

1	cup mashed potatoes
½	cup rolled oats
1	cup rye flour
½	cup stone-ground cornmeal
⅓	cup wheat germ
⅓	cup dark molasses
2	teaspoons salt
2	cups boiling water
1	teaspoon instant coffee powder
½	cup warm water (105°–115°F)
2	packages (¼ ounce each) active dry yeast
2	cups whole-wheat flour
2½–3	cups bread flour

In a large mixing bowl, combine the potatoes, oats, rye flour, cornmeal, wheat germ, molasses, salt, boiling water and coffee powder. Stir well and set aside until the mixture has cooled to 105° to 115°F.

Place the warm water in a small bowl. Sprinkle with the yeast and set aside for 2 minutes, or until the yeast is foamy. Stir the yeast mixture into the cooled potato mixture. Stir in the whole-wheat flour and beat well. Add the bread flour gradually to make a stiff dough that clears the edge of the bowl. Let the dough rest for 15 minutes.

Turn the dough out onto a lightly floured surface and knead for 10 minutes, or until the dough is smooth and free of any dry flour lumps. (The dough will not be as springy as a white-flour dough, but should feel well-mixed. It may be slightly sticky, but do not add too much additional flour.)

Coat a clean large bowl with no-stick spray. Place the dough in the bowl and cover with a damp cloth. Let rise in a warm place for 1 to 1½ hours, or until the dough doubles in bulk.

Turn the dough out onto a surface coated with no-stick spray and divide into 2 equal-size pieces. Shape each piece into an oblong loaf about 12″ long.

Coat a no-stick baking sheet with no-stick spray. Place the loaves on the prepared sheet, cover with a damp cloth and let rise for 45 to 60 minutes, or until puffy.

Preheat the oven to 375°. Bake the loaves for 30 to 40 minutes, or until deep golden brown. Cool on a wire rack.

Makes 2 loaves; 22 slices each. Per slice: 76 calories, 0.4 g. fat (5% of calories), 2.6 g. protein, 16 g. carbohydrates, 1.5 g. dietary fiber, 0 mg. cholesterol, 115 mg. sodium

NOTES

• For a less sweet pumpernickel, reduce the molasses to ¼ cup.

• For best results, wait until the second day to cut this loaf into thin slices.

Molasses Rye Bread

2	packages (¼ ounce each) active dry yeast
2	cups warm water (105°–115°F)
1	cup instant nonfat dry milk powder
⅓	cup light or dark molasses
2	tablespoons canola oil
2	teaspoons salt
3–3½	cups bread flour
3	cups light or medium rye flour

In a large bowl, dissolve the yeast in the water. Stir in the milk powder and molasses. Let stand for 5 minutes, or until the yeast begins to bubble.

Mix in the oil and salt. Add 2 cups of the bread flour and beat until the mixture is smooth and satiny. (If using an electric mixer, beat at medium speed for 5 minutes.) Stir in the rye flour and ¾ to 1 cup of the remaining bread flour until the dough pulls away from the sides of the bowl in an irregular ball. Cover with a damp cloth and let rest for 15 minutes.

Turn the dough out onto a lightly floured surface and knead until the dough is smooth and satiny, adding more bread flour as necessary to prevent stickiness.

Coat a clean large bowl with no-stick spray. Place the dough in the bowl, cover with a damp cloth and let rise in a warm place for 45 to 60 minutes, or until the dough doubles in bulk.

Coat 2 no-stick baking sheets with no-stick spray. Gently deflate the dough with your fist and turn out onto a surface lightly coated with no-stick spray. Divide into 2 equal-size pieces and shape into round or oblong loaves. Place on the prepared baking sheets, cover with a damp cloth and let rise in a warm place until almost doubled.

Preheat the oven to 350°. Brush the loaves with water. Using a sharp knife, make four ¼"-deep diagonal slashes on the top of each loaf. Bake for 35 to 45 minutes, or until a toothpick inserted in the center comes out clean. Remove from the pans and cool on a wire rack.

Makes 2 loaves; 22 slices each. Per slice: 75 calories, 0.8 g. fat (10% of calories), 2.4 g. protein, 14.8 g. carbohydrates, 0.4 g. dietary fiber, 0.3 mg. cholesterol, 108 mg. sodium

NOTE

• For a less sweet rye bread, reduce the molasses to ¼ cup.

VARIATIONS

Caraway Rye Bread: Add 1 tablespoon caraway seeds to the dough along with the salt.
Swedish Rye Bread: Add 1 teaspoon caraway seeds, 1 teaspoon anise seeds, 1 teaspoon fennel seeds and 1 tablespoon freshly grated orange rind to the liquid ingredients.

Crusty French Baguette

This bread's delightfully crisp crust and tender interior are developed when the bread is baked in an oven with steam. You can easily create this environment in a conventional home oven by using a baking stone or unglazed quarry tiles and a large pan of water.

2	packages (¼ ounce each) active dry yeast
2¼	cups warm water (105°–115°F)
2	teaspoons salt
½	cup whole-wheat flour
4½–5½	cups bread flour

In a large bowl, dissolve the yeast in the water. Let stand for 5 minutes, or until the yeast is foamy.

Add the salt, whole-wheat flour and 2 cups of the bread flour; beat with a wooden spoon until smooth and satiny. Slowly stir in enough of the remaining bread flour to make a dough that forms a ball. Let rest for 15 minutes.

Turn the dough out onto a lightly floured surface and knead for 10 to 15 minutes, or until very smooth and satiny. (Or, mix the dough in a heavy-duty electric mixer using a dough hook for 5 minutes.)

Coat a clean large bowl with no-stick spray. Place the dough in the bowl and cover with a damp cloth. Let rise in a warm place for 1 hour, or until the dough doubles in bulk.

Divide the dough into 3 equal-size pieces. Shape each piece into a very narrow loaf about 15″ long. Coat a bread board or no-stick baking sheet with no-stick spray. Place the loaves, at least 3″ apart, on the prepared board. Cover with a damp cloth and let rise for 30 minutes, or until puffy.

Meanwhile, place a baking stone or unglazed quarry tiles on the center oven rack. On the lower oven rack, place a large empty pan (about 12″ × 15″). Preheat the oven to 450°.

With a sharp knife, cut 3 or 4 crosswise slashes in each loaf. Place each loaf, one at a time, onto the preheated baking stone or tiles, leaving at least 3″ between them. Pour a cup of water into the pan below to create steam. Bake for 15 minutes, or until golden brown and crusty. Remove from the oven and cool on a wire rack.

Makes 3 loaves; 6 slices each. Per slice: 118 calories, 0.4 g. fat (3% of calories), 3.7 g. protein, 24.7 g. carbohydrates, 1.4 g. dietary fiber, 0 mg. cholesterol, 238 mg. sodium

NOTES

• Baking stones are widely available in kitchen supply stores. Unglazed quarry tiles are available at tile stores or kitchen supply stores.

• To make the shaped loaves easier to handle, you can place them on a large piece of foil (leave room for expansion). Let them rise on the foil, then slash the tops of the loaves with a sharp knife. Carefully transfer the loaves, foil and all, onto the preheated stone or tiles.

• To bake the loaves without a baking stone or tiles, place the 3 shaped loaves onto a no-stick baking sheet coated with no-stick spray instead of a bread board. Cover and let rise for 30 minutes, or until puffy. Slash in 3 or 4 places with a sharp knife and brush or spray with water. Preheat the oven to 375° and omit the preheated pan of water. Instead, bake for 20 to 30 minutes, brushing or spraying occasionally with water.

VARIATIONS

Crusty French Braid: Replace the whole-wheat flour with bread flour. After dividing the dough into 3 equal-size pieces, shape into ropes. Braid the ropes together and seal the ends. Cover and let rise for 20 to 30 minutes, or until doubled in bulk. Preheat the oven to 375°. Coat a no-stick baking sheet with no-stick spray and place the braided loaf on the sheet. Brush the loaf with water and bake for 25 to 30 minutes, or until golden brown.

Vienna Bread: Replace the whole-wheat flour with bread flour and the warm water with warm 1% low-fat milk. Add 2 tablespoons sugar and 2 tablespoons melted nondiet tub-style margarine or butter to the dough. After the initial rising, divide the dough into 2 equal-size pieces and shape each into an oblong loaf, 14″ long. Coat a no-stick baking sheet with no-stick spray. Place the loaves on the sheet. Using kitchen scissors or a sharp knife, cut five 1″-deep slits in the tops of the loaves. Cover and let rise for 30 to 40 minutes, or until doubled in bulk. Preheat the oven to 350°. Brush the loaves with beaten egg white and sprinkle with sesame seeds. Bake for 40 to 50 minutes, or until golden and a toothpick inserted in the center comes out clean.

Honey-Oatmeal Bread

1	cup + 2 tablespoons quick rolled oats
2	cups boiling skim milk
1	tablespoon canola oil
⅓	cup + 1 tablespoon honey, warmed
1	teaspoon salt
1	package (¼ ounce) active dry yeast
¼	cup warm water (105°–115°F)
4½–5	cups bread flour

Place 1 cup of the oats in a large mixing bowl. Stir in the milk, oil, ⅓ cup of the honey and salt; set aside to cool to lukewarm.

In a small bowl, dissolve the yeast in the water and let stand for 5 minutes, or until the yeast is foamy. Add to the cooled oat mixture. Gradually stir in the flour until the dough comes together in an irregular ball and cleans the sides of the bowl. Cover with a damp cloth and let rest for 15 minutes.

Turn the dough out onto a lightly floured surface and knead for 10 minutes, or until smooth and satiny. Coat a clean large bowl with no-stick spray. Place the dough in the bowl, cover with a damp cloth and let rise in a warm place for 45 to 60 minutes, or until the dough doubles in bulk.

Coat 2 no-stick baking sheets with no-stick spray. Divide the dough into 2 equal-size pieces and shape into balls. Place the balls, smooth side up, onto the prepared sheets. Press the balls down until they are about 1″ thick. Let rise for 45 minutes, or until puffy.

Preheat the oven to 350°. Pierce the loaves all over with a fork. Brush the tops of the loaves with the remaining 1 tablespoon honey and sprinkle with the remaining 2 tablespoons oats.

Bake the loaves for 30 to 35 minutes, or until golden. Remove from the pans and cool on a wire rack.

Makes 2 loaves; 22 slices each. Per slice: 71 calories, 0.6 g. fat (7% of calories), 2.1 g. protein, 14.2 g. carbohydrates, 0.6 g. dietary fiber, 0.2 mg. cholesterol, 55 mg. sodium

VARIATION

Oat Dinner Rolls: Divide the risen dough into 16 equal-size pieces instead of 2 equal-size pieces. Shape into balls and place, smooth side up, on the prepared baking sheets. Let rise for 45 minutes, or until puffy. Brush with the warmed honey and sprinkle with the remaining 2 tablespoons oats. Bake at 350° for 15 to 20 minutes, or until the rolls are lightly browned.

Peasant Bread

1	cup warm water (105°–115°F)
1	cup whole-wheat flour
3½–4	cups unbleached flour
1	package (¼ ounce) quick-rising yeast
1	teaspoon honey
1	cup buttermilk
2½	teaspoons salt
2	teaspoons olive oil
	Cornmeal

In a large bowl, whisk together the water, whole-wheat flour, ½ cup of the unbleached flour, yeast and honey. Beat hard until creamy and smooth. Cover loosely with a damp cloth and allow to rest at room temperature for 5 minutes.

Add the buttermilk, salt, oil and 1 cup of the remaining flour. Beat until smooth. Add the remaining 2 to 2½ cups flour, ½ cup at a time, until the mixture gathers into a ball and forms a soft dough. Coat a clean medium bowl with no-stick spray. Turn the dough into the prepared bowl. Cover with a damp cloth and let rise in a warm place for 30 minutes.

Preheat the oven to 400°.

Gently deflate the dough with your fist and turn out onto a lightly floured surface. Form into two oblong loaves and roll lightly in flour. Sprinkle a no-stick baking sheet with the cornmeal and place the loaves on it. Let rise for 10 minutes, or until puffy. Slash the tops of the loaves with a sharp knife. Bake for 30 to 35 minutes, or until the loaves are golden brown and sound hollow when tapped.

Makes 2 loaves; 8 slices each. Per slice: 139 calories, 1.1 g. fat (7% of calories), 4.5 g. protein, 27.6 g. carbohydrates, 1.8 g. dietary fiber, 1 mg. cholesterol, 350 mg. sodium

Basic Bagels

Because this is a relatively small batch of dough, you can mix and knead it in the food processor to save time.

3–3½	cups all-purpose flour
2	teaspoons + 1 tablespoon sugar
1	teaspoon salt
1	package (¼ ounce) active dry yeast
1¼	cups very warm water (125°–135°F)
8	cups + 1 tablespoon cold water
1	egg, beaten
2	tablespoons poppy seeds, sesame seeds or caraway seeds

In a food processor, combine 3 cups of the flour, 2 teaspoons of the sugar, salt and yeast. Turn the processor on and gradually add the warm water through the feed tube, processing until the dough forms a smooth ball that cleans the sides of the bowl. If the dough is too sticky to clean the sides of the bowl, add the remaining ½ cup flour, a tablespoon at a time. Cover the bowl with a damp cloth and let the dough rise until it doubles in bulk.

Coat 2 no-stick baking sheets with no-stick spray. Turn the dough out onto a surface lightly coated with no-stick spray and gently knead to eliminate air bubbles. Divide the dough into 16 equal-size pieces. Roll each piece into a ball and press your thumb into the center to make a hole. Using your thumbs and fingers, gently stretch and pull the dough from the center to widen the hole. Place the bagels on the prepared baking sheets. Cover with a damp cloth and let rise in a warm place for 10 minutes, or until puffy. (Do not let overrise, or the dough will flatten when cooked.)

Preheat the oven to 375°.

In a large saucepan, combine 8 cups of the cold water and the remaining 1 tablespoon sugar. Bring to a boil over high heat. Reduce the heat to medium-high and maintain a gentle boil. Place 2 of the shaped bagels in the boiling water for 30 seconds, turning once. Using a slotted spoon, remove the bagels from the water and return to the baking sheets. Repeat with the remaining bagels.

In a small bowl, combine the egg and remaining 1 tablespoon cold water. Brush over the bagels and sprinkle with the seeds.

Bake for 20 to 25 minutes, or until light golden brown. Immediately transfer the bagels to wire racks to cool.

Makes 16. Per bagel: 101 calories, 0.8 g. fat (7% of calories), 3 g. protein, 20.2 g. carbohydrates, 0.9 g. dietary fiber, 0 mg. cholesterol, 134 mg. sodium

NOTE

• To make the bagels without a food processor, combine 2 cups of the flour, the sugar, salt and yeast in a large bowl. Beat in the warm water until the mixture is smooth. Gradually add the remaining flour to make a stiff but smooth dough. Turn out onto a floured surface and knead until the dough is smooth and satiny. Return to the bowl, cover and let rise until the dough doubles in bulk.

VARIATIONS

Raisin Rye Bagels: Replace ½ cup of the all-purpose flour with ½ cup rye flour. Add ½ cup raisins to the dough.

Cinnamon Bagels: Add 2 teaspoons ground cinnamon and 2 teaspoons sugar to the dough along with the first cup of flour. If desired, add ½ cup raisins.

Focaccia

1 cup warm water (105°–115°F)
1 package (¼ ounce) quick-rising yeast
1 teaspoon honey
2½–3 cups unbleached flour
3 tablespoons extra-virgin olive oil
1 tablespoon chopped fresh basil
1 tablespoon chopped fresh thyme
1½ teaspoons salt

Preheat the oven to 400°.

In a large bowl, stir together the water, yeast and honey. Add 1 cup of the flour. Beat with a wire whisk until smooth and creamy. Let rest at room temperature for 5 minutes.

Add 2 tablespoons of the oil, basil, thyme, salt and 1 cup of the remaining flour. Whisk hard for 3 minutes or until smooth. Add the remaining ½ to 1 cup flour, a little at a time, with a wooden spoon until a soft, sticky dough is formed.

Turn the dough out onto a lightly floured surface and knead gently for 3 minutes.

Coat a no-stick baking sheet with no-stick spray. Place the dough on the baking sheet and shape into a 9″ round that is 1″ thick. Brush with the remaining 1 tablespoon oil.

Bake for 20 to 25 minutes, or until golden brown.

Makes one 9″-round loaf; 8 wedges. Per wedge: 193 calories, 5.5 g. fat (26% of calories), 4.4 g. protein, 31 g. carbohydrates, 1.3 g. dietary fiber, 0 mg. cholesterol, 401 mg. sodium

VARIATIONS

Whole-Wheat Focaccia: Replace ¾ cup of the unbleached flour with whole-wheat flour.
Savory Focaccia: Replace the basil with 1 tablespoon chopped fresh sage and 1 tablespoon chopped fresh rosemary.

Tomato-Basil Focaccia: Sauté 1 cup chopped tomatoes and 2 cloves minced garlic until most of the liquid has evaporated. Then stir in 1 tablespoon chopped fresh basil. After brushing the dough with the oil, use your fingers to make several deep indentations in the dough. Sprinkle the tomato mixture over the dough and bake.
Focaccia with Mediterranean Vegetables: In a small saucepan, sauté 1 minced clove garlic for 2 minutes, or until fragrant. Add 2 roasted and chopped red peppers, 1 tablespoon pitted and chopped kalamata olives and 1 teaspoon capers; heat through. Remove from the heat and stir in 2 tablespoons balsamic vinegar, 1 tablespoon extra-virgin olive oil and salt and black pepper to taste. After brushing the dough with the oil, use your fingers to make several deep indentations in the dough. Sprinkle the vegetable mixture over the dough and bake.

Cinnamon Buns with Coffee Glaze

Dough

2 packages (¼ ounce each) active dry yeast
½ cup warm water (105°–115°F)
1 cup skim milk, scalded and cooled to lukewarm
1 large egg, beaten
¼ cup sugar
1 teaspoon salt
3½–4 cups all-purpose flour

Filling

1 cup packed brown sugar
2 teaspoons cinnamon
3 tablespoons softened butter

(continued)

Coffee Glaze
- 1 cup confectioners' sugar
  Pinch of salt
- 1 teaspoon vanilla
- 1–3 teaspoons strong hot coffee

To make the dough: In a large bowl, dissolve the yeast in the water. Let stand for 5 minutes, or until the yeast is foamy. Stir in the milk, egg, sugar and salt. Stir in 2 cups of the flour and beat until the batter is smooth and elastic. Gradually stir in enough of the remaining 1½ to 2 cups flour to make a dough that forms an irregular ball. Let the dough rest for 15 minutes.

Turn the dough out onto a lightly floured surface and knead, adding flour as necessary, until the dough is smooth and satiny.

Coat a clean large bowl with no-stick spray. Place the dough in the bowl, cover with a damp cloth and let rise for 1 hour, or until the dough doubles in bulk.

To make the filling: Coat a 9″ × 13″ no-stick baking dish with no-stick spray; set aside. In a small bowl, combine the brown sugar and cinnamon; set aside.

Roll the dough out to make a 24″ × 14″ rectangle. Spread the butter over the dough. Sprinkle with the brown-sugar mixture. Starting with the long end, tightly roll the dough. When completely rolled, pinch the edges to seal. Cut into 1″ slices and place the slices, cut side down, close together in the prepared pan. Let rise for 45 minutes, or until puffy and almost doubled in bulk.

Preheat the oven to 350°. Bake the buns for 25 to 30 minutes, or until golden.

To make the glaze: In a small bowl, mix the confectioners' sugar, salt and vanilla. Stir in the coffee, 1 teaspoon at a time, until the mixture is smooth and pourable. Drizzle over the warm rolls.

Makes 24. Per bun: 149 calories, 1.9 g. fat (11% of calories), 2.8 g. protein, 30.4 g. carbohydrates, 0.7 g. dietary fiber, 13 mg. cholesterol, 114 mg. sodium

Fruit-Stuffed Stollen with Almond Glaze

Stollen is a traditional German sweet yeast bread that's filled with fruit and nuts. The almond glaze on this version makes it extra special. Try it at your next holiday get-together.

Stollen
- ½ cup dark raisins
- ½ cup golden raisins
- ¾ cup red glacé cherries (see note)
- ¼ cup sliced almonds
- ¼ cup candied orange rind
- 2 tablespoons dark rum or ½ teaspoon rum extract + 1½ tablespoons orange juice
- ½ cup warm water (105°–115°F)
- ¼ cup sugar
- 2 packages (¼ ounce each) active dry yeast
- ½ cup skim milk, warmed
- 1 tablespoon grated lemon rind
- ¼ cup butter, softened
- ½ teaspoon salt
- 1 egg, lightly beaten
- ½ teaspoon almond extract
- 3–3¼ cups all-purpose flour
- 1 tablespoon melted butter

Almond Glaze
- 1   cup confectioners' sugar
- 1–2 tablespoons skim milk
- ½   teaspoon almond extract

To make the stollen: In a small bowl, mix the dark raisins, golden raisins, cherries, almonds, orange rind and rum or rum extract with orange juice; set aside.

In a large bowl, combine the water and 1 tablespoon of the sugar. Sprinkle with the yeast and set aside for 5 minutes, or until the yeast is foamy. Add the remaining 3 tablespoons sugar, milk, lemon rind, ¼ cup butter, salt, egg, almond extract and 1 cup of the flour. Beat until smooth and satiny. Stir in the fruit mixture and enough of the remaining 2 to 2¼ cups flour to make a dough that forms a ball and cleans the sides of the bowl. Cover and let rest for 15 minutes.

Turn the dough out onto a lightly floured surface and knead until well-mixed and satiny.

Coat a clean large bowl with no-stick spray. Place the kneaded dough in the bowl. Cover and let rise in a warm place for 1 hour, or until the dough doubles in bulk.

Turn the dough out onto a surface lightly coated with no-stick spray and gently knead to eliminate air bubbles.

Coat a no-stick baking sheet with no-stick spray. Place the dough on the prepared sheet and pat it into a 7″ × 9″ oblong loaf. Brush with the 1 tablespoon butter. Using the handle of a wooden spoon, make a lengthwise crease, just off the center of the dough. Fold lengthwise, bringing the small section over the large one. Loosely cover with a damp cloth and let rise in a warm place for 45 minutes, or until the dough is almost doubled in bulk.

Preheat the oven to 350°. Uncover the dough and bake for 35 to 40 minutes, or until a toothpick inserted in the center comes out clean. Remove from the baking sheet and transfer to a wire rack to cool.

To make the almond glaze: In a small bowl, combine the confectioners' sugar, milk and almond extract. Brush over the stollen.

Makes 1 large loaf; 24 slices. Per slice: 152 calories, 3.5 g. fat (20% of calories), 2.7 g. protein, 28.4 g. carbohydrates, 1.1 g. dietary fiber, 14 mg.cholesterol, 52 mg. sodium

NOTES
- This recipe makes a large stollen that is perfect for special occasions. To make two smaller stollens, divide the dough and shape into 2 equal-size oblong loaves.
- The stollen can be wrapped in plastic and stored for up to 5 days.
- Red glacé cherries are available in the bulk or baking section of most supermarkets. If they are unavailable, you can substitute raisins, dried cherries or dried tropical fruit, such as papaya.

VARIATION
Fruit-Stuffed Stollen with Vanilla Glaze: Replace the almond extract in the stollen with ½ teaspoon vanilla extract. Replace the almond extract in the glaze with ½ teaspoon vanilla extract. If desired, omit the almonds in the stollen or replace them with ¼ cup coarsely chopped hazelnuts or pecans (toasted). To toast the nuts, place them in a dry no-stick skillet over medium heat. Toast the nuts, shaking the pan often, for 3 to 5 minutes, or until fragrant.

Quick Breads, Muffins and Biscuits

There's nothing like the taste and aroma of homemade quick breads, muffins, biscuits and batter products like pancakes, waffles and crêpes. They're delicious and nutritious, and they're ready in a flash. You don't need special skills or equipment, either. Just mix the ingredients and bake or cook. They're ready when you are.

QUICK BREADS

Traditional quick breads were almost always full of butter, cream or other high-fat ingredients. But by cutting back the amount of fat, replacing whole eggs with egg whites and using low-fat versions of milk, yogurt and sour cream, you can enjoy quick breads every day without worrying about your health or your waistline.

Unlike yeast breads, which depend on the slow-rising action of live organisms (yeast), quick breads get their rise from faster-acting leavens, such as baking soda and baking powder. These work by releasing bubbles of carbon dioxide, which inflate the dough or batter. Beaten egg whites, which incorporate large volumes of air into the batter, are another quick-acting leaven.

Baking Soda

A vigorous leaven, baking soda has about four times the rising power of baking powder. It's an alkaline ingredient; used alone, it would impart a slightly soapy taste to food. That's why baking soda is used in recipes that also call for an acidic ingredient, like buttermilk or yogurt. The acid neutralizes the alkaline, smoothing the taste.

☞ Since baking soda readily absorbs odors and flavors—hence the open box placed at the back of refrigerators and freezers—it should be stored in a sealed container.

☞ Baking soda starts working as soon as it comes into contact with liquid ingredients. The batter won't hold, so use it right away.

Baking Powder

This versatile leaven comes in two forms: double-acting and single-acting. Double-acting baking powder, the type that you usually see in stores, literally rises twice: once when the dry and liquid ingredients are mixed together and again when the food goes into the oven. Single-acting baking powder, by contrast, rises only in the oven. It's the leaven of choice for people who, for taste reasons, want to avoid the aluminum sulfate in the double-acting kind.

☞ Baking powder contains baking soda, an alkaline, and cream of tartar, an acid. Since the two ingredients essentially neutralize each other, baking powder can be used in recipes that don't call for acidic ingredients like buttermilk.

☞ Batters or doughs made with double-acting baking powder get a second rise on exposure to heat, so they can be refrigerated for a day or two and still be light and airy when baked.

HIGH-ALTITUDE BAKING

The air at high altitudes is thinner than it is at sea level, and the atmospheric pressure is lower. This combination causes batter to rise more quickly and cook more slowly. There's also a tendency for liquids to evaporate, causing a drier product.

If you live above 3,000 feet, you'll want to raise the oven temperature 25°. To reduce excessive rise, you'll also want to beat eggs and batters less vigorously and keep eggs chilled until just before using. Other adjustments will depend on the altitude. Here are some suggestions.

ALTITUDE	ADJUSTMENTS
Above 3,000 feet	Increase the amount of liquid by 1 to 2 tablespoons per cup.
Above 5,000 feet	Reduce the amount of baking soda or baking powder by ⅛ to ¼ teaspoon per teaspoon called for. Increase the amount of liquid 3 to 4 teaspoons per cup. Decrease the amount of sugar 1 to 2 teaspoons per cup.
Above 7,000 feet	Reduce the amount of baking soda or baking powder ¼ teaspoon per teaspoon called for. Decrease the amount of sugar about 2 teaspoons per cup. Increase the amount of liquid 3 to 4 teaspoons per cup.

☞ Baking powder becomes ineffective with age, so be sure to check the expiration date before buying.

☞ To make your own single-acting baking powder, combine 2 parts cream of tartar with 1 part baking soda. The mix loses its effectiveness quickly, so use it right away.

Egg Whites

Although whole eggs are used to provide strength and body to a variety of quick breads, it's the whites that make them light and airy. And since egg whites don't contain fat or cholesterol, you can use them freely.

☞ Egg whites achieve the most volume at room temperature, so remove them from the refrigerator at least 15 minutes before using.

☞ Even a speck of egg yolk will inhibit the whites' rising action. Separate the eggs carefully, and if yolk does get into the whites, scoop it out with a spoon or a piece of eggshell.

☞ Adding cream of tartar to the egg whites helps them whip up easier and hold their shape better. Chefs usually recommend adding ¼ teaspoon cream of tartar for every 3 whites.

☞ An alternative is to add 1 teaspoon lemon juice or a pinch of salt.

Helpful Hint

Baking powder loses its potency over time. To test it, add 1 teaspoon baking powder to ½ cup hot water. If it fizzes, it's okay. If not, buy a new container.

WHIPPING EGG WHITES

Egg whites, when properly beaten, incorporate a tremendous amount of air into batter, making the finished product wonderfully light and airy. It's important, however, to handle the whites properly. Getting bits of yolk into the whites will keep them from beating up properly.

When separating eggs, chefs recommend using three bowls: one to catch the white, a second for the yolk and a third to hold all the finished whites together. This way, if you accidentally break one yolk, it won't ruin the entire lot.

Crack an egg over a small bowl. Holding half of the shell in each hand, shift the contents back and forth until the white has flowed out into the bowl.

Collect all the yolks in another small bowl.

Transfer all the whites to a larger bowl for beating.

Beat the whites well until they're about quadrupled in volume. They should stand up in peaks and have a slight sheen.

Baking with Ease

The great thing about quick breads, unlike those made with yeast, is that they're incredibly simple and fast to prepare. It's possible to have fresh bread every day with only minutes of preparation time.

Get the pans ready. To maximize the rise, quick breads should go into the oven as soon as the batter is prepared. Chefs recommend preparing your pans before you start the batter.

☞ If you want bread that's tender and has a light crust, shiny metal pans are best.

☞ For a darker crust with more crunch, use dark-colored pans.

☞ When using a glass baking dish or custard cups, decrease the oven temperature by 25° to prevent burning.

Measure with care. Much of cooking is improvisation, but when it comes to baking, even slight changes in amounts can substantially alter the finished product, usually for the worse.

☞ Always use the proper spoons and cups for measuring liquid and dry ingredients. Using a dry measuring cup for liquids (or vice versa) will skew the amounts—and the results.

☞ Flour and other dry ingredients naturally compress during storage. To make sure that the ingredients are accurately measured, sift or stir the dry ingredients before measuring.

Keep them lean. Although traditional quick breads are high in fat, an easy way to cut back is to replace half the oil, butter or margarine with an equal amount of pureed bananas, apples, pears or prunes.

☞ When using pureed fruit as a replacement for fat, try to match the color of the fruit with the final product. A carrot cake, for example, could be matched with an apricot puree, whereas a dark, molasses-sweetened muffin or a chocolate cake might call for a prune puree.

☞ Before adding dried fruit to quick-bread batter, soak it briefly in hot water. This will help prevent it from drawing moisture out of the batter.

Mix it lightly. Overmixing dough causes the development of too much gluten, which makes the bread tough and chewy. With batters, overmixing causes tunneling—tiny holes in the batter that make the final product tough. A light touch is needed when making quick breads; you want the finished dough or batter to be suffici-

---

COOKING CHEMISTRY

Healthy cooks are always looking for ways to replace cream and whole milk with low-fat or nonfat equivalents. When substituting ingredients, however, it's important to keep the equation constant. This is particularly true when swapping whole milk for a lower-fat but acidic ingredient, like buttermilk or yogurt.

There's no hard-and-fast rule, but when adding an acidic ingredient like buttermilk to a recipe normally calling for milk, try adding ¼ teaspoon baking soda for each teaspoon of baking powder. This will help neutralize the mix, reducing the acid taste and enabling the batter to rise correctly.

Eggs
Is It GOOD for You?

Ever since cholesterol started making headlines, eggs have taken a beating. Egg yolks are among the most concentrated sources of cholesterol, with about 212 milligrams each. If you're trying to lower your cholesterol levels, the thinking goes, cutting back on hen fruit just makes sense.

Well, maybe not. Researchers have learned that even though eggs are high in cholesterol, for most people, they play little role in raising the amount of cholesterol in the bloodstream. Why? Because our bodies naturally make their own cholesterol and regulate the supply; extra cholesterol in the diet can have little effect on cholesterol in the blood.

Not so with saturated fat, however. Eating foods high in saturated fats does raise cholesterol. So go ahead and enjoy an egg now and then. Just don't fry it in butter or eat it with a mound of greasy hash browns.

---

ently mixed but not whipped or kneaded smooth.

Start it hot. Putting quick breads into a cold oven will impede the rising process and cause uneven cooking. To get the best rise and texture, always put quick bread in an oven that has been preheated.

Go for the middle. Chefs recommend baking quick breads in the middle of the oven, where air circulation is most even.

☞ When using more than one oven rack, stagger the pans so that the air will circulate evenly between them.

☞ When placing two or more pans on one rack, separate the pans so that they don't touch.

Check the heat. Since quick breads cook, well, quickly, even a slight difference between your oven's actual temperature and the temperature called for in the recipe can skew the results. Chefs recommend using an oven thermometer to doublecheck what the dial or digital readout says.

☞ Many ovens have hot zones—areas where the heat is most intense. To ensure that the bread cooks evenly, turn the pans 180° midway through baking.

☞ If the top is browned before the bread is done, cover loosely with foil and continue baking for the required time.

Test for doneness. Before removing quick breads from the oven, insert a toothpick, skewer or sharp knife into the center; if it comes out clean, the bread is done.

When you're in a hurry, putting dough or batter in mini loaf pans can help speed the cooking time by as much as 50 percent.

MUFFINS

Ranging in size from petite to mammoth, muffins are essentially mini bread loaves that can generally be made in less than a half-hour. Whether you like them sweet or savory, muffins are a terrific way to start the day. And because they're so compact, they make a perfect carry-along in a lunch box or briefcase.

Mix the batter gently. It's almost impossible to undermix muffin batter, while even a few strokes too many can cause the muffins to be tough and chewy. After mixing the dry ingredients, add the liquids and stir until the mix is just moistened.

Put on protection. Muffin tins are usually coated with oil or a no-stick spray to prevent sticking. Lining the cups with paper liners will reduce the amount of fat, while at the same time helping speed cleanup time.

Plan for expansion. Muffins expand during cooking, so don't fill the cups more than two-thirds full of batter.

When you want your muffins to have a large cap on top, fill the cup all the way. Be sure to increase the cooking time to allow for the extra batter.

Fill the tray. If you run out of batter before filling all the cups, put a little water in the empty cups. This will prevent them from scorching and also help the muffins bake more evenly.

Cool them well. Muffins come out of the oven with soft, crumbly centers. To help them set, put the pan on a wire rack and allow it to cool for at least 10 minutes.

Wrap them up. Muffins freeze well and will keep for up to three months when carefully wrapped in a plastic bag or plastic wrap and stored in the freezer.

COFFEE CAKES

With a cakelike texture and sweet taste, coffee cakes are wonderful for breakfast, brunch and mid-afternoon snacks as well as after-dinner desserts. They can be plain or fancy. The fancy ones are often filled with fruit or jam and topped with a sugar glaze or streusel. By using low-fat or nonfat dairy products, it's now possible to make coffee cakes that are extremely low in fat.

Although some coffee cakes are made with yeast, the easiest and quickest kinds are leavened with baking powder, baking soda or egg whites. Here are some quick tips for getting started.

Replace the fat. There's no reason anymore to depend on unhealthy saturated fats for taste and satisfying mouthfeel when making coffee cakes. It's easy to use lower-fat versions of sour cream, margarine, butter or milk.

☞ To get the body of eggs without the fat, replace each egg yolk with two egg whites.

☞ Replace a cream cheese filling with a lower-fat equivalent. Or replace the cream cheese with a healthy fruit filling.

Whip it well. Unlike the batters used in most quick breads, coffee cake batter requires vigorous beating, preferably with an electric mixer. This helps incorporate the maximum amount of air into the mix, which gives it a lighter, cakelike texture.

Combine the wet ingredients first and beat until fluffy. Then combine the dry ingredients and beat them into the liquid. Extras like raisins or nuts should be added last.

Check for doneness. To prevent coffee cakes from overbaking, it's important to check them about 10 to 15 minutes before the time recommended in the recipe.

☞ Insert a toothpick into the thickest part of the cake. If it comes out clean, the cake is done and should be removed from the oven.

☞ To prevent the cake from sticking, let it cool on a wire rack for at least 15 minutes before removing it from the pan.

Plan ahead. Coffee cake reheats well and can be enjoyed for days after baking. To reheat, wrap it loosely in foil and place it in a 250° oven for about 15 minutes.

To freeze coffee cake, wrap it well in plastic wrap. It can then be defrosted at room temperature before reheating. Or put it in the microwave for a quick snack.

Coffee Cake Toppings

Coffee cakes are delicious plain, but many cooks prefer adding a slightly sweet topping, either before or after cooking.

☞ Toppings that are added before baking are called streusel. Streusel is made by combining a little bit of butter or oil with sugar, cinnamon or cardamom and nuts or bread crumbs. The mix is then sprinkled on top of the batter.

☞ When the topping is added after baking, it's called a glaze. Also consisting of spices, sugar and sometimes nuts, glazes usually have a finer consistency than streusel and add an attractive sheen.

☞ Don't add a glaze until after the coffee cake has cooled to barely warm. Otherwise, the glaze will be absorbed by the cake, resulting in a soggy texture.

BISCUITS

Unlike most other quick breads, biscuits are made from a soft dough rather than a batter. The perfect accompaniment to almost any meal, they can be plain or embellished with such added ingredients as raisins, herbs or cheese.

There are two basic techniques for making biscuits. The taste and texture of each are nearly the same, although the appearance of the finished product will be quite different.

☞ **Rolled and cut biscuits.** The most popular style, these are made by rolling dough on a floured board and then cutting out shapes with a knife, a biscuit cutter or simply a juice glass that's pressed into the dough.

When making rolled biscuits, roll out the dough on a floured board to a thickness of ½" to ¾". Cut as many biscuits as you can. Then gather up the scraps and roll out the dough again.

☞ **Drop biscuits.** Rougher and more irregular than rolled biscuits, drop biscuits are made with a soft dough that is closer in consistency to a very thick batter. They are made by dropping spoonfuls of dough onto a baking sheet.

It's easy to get good results when making biscuits, as long as you don't overwork the dough. Overworking the dough causes additional gluten to develop, making the biscuits tough and chewy rather than flaky.

Biscuits get increasingly tough the more the dough is handled, so try to get as many biscuits as you can out of the first rolling.

Choose your texture. If you like biscuits with soft sides, place them in a baking dish rather than on a baking sheet and arrange them so that the sides of the biscuits are in contact with each other. For a little bit of crunch, put the biscuits on a baking sheet and spread them about an inch apart.

Check the color. When you think the biscuits are done, lift one with a spatula and check the color underneath. Biscuits are done when the top and the bottom are golden brown.

Pack them away. Once biscuits have cooled, put them in a plastic bag or container and store at room temperature for three days. In the freezer, they'll keep for up to three months.

PANCAKES, WAFFLES AND CRÊPES

The quickest of the quick breads are pancakes, waffles and crêpes. All use baking soda or baking powder (or both) for their rising action. And since they're typically topped with

CUTTING IN SHORTENING

Recipes for biscuits (as well as pie crusts) usually call for the butter or other solid fat to be cut into the flour. The purpose of this is to create layers of fat separated by pockets of air, which is what makes a delicate, tender crust.

Pastry blenders are inexpensive and quickly meld fat and flour without overmixing. Keep cutting the fat into the flour until the resulting mix has the consistency of coarse cornmeal. You will have to periodically run your finger between the blades to remove clumps of shortening and return them to the bowl for more thorough mixing.

You can also use two table knives to cut in fat. Hold a knife in each hand, with your arms in a crisscross fashion. Repeatedly pull the knives outward in a slicing motion until all the fat is in very small pieces.

syrup or fruit or stuffed with filling, they provide a taste treat that's generally very low in fat.

Use the right pan. When making crêpes, chefs recommend a small skillet. For pancakes, use a medium or large skillet. It doesn't really matter what the pan is made of, as long as it's heavy and heats evenly across the entire surface.

Cook them hot. Putting batter on a cold pan guarantees that the finished product will be pale and lifeless. To get an attractive brown crust, always get the pan hot before adding batter. You know that it's hot enough when water sprinkled on the surface dances and beads up.

☞ When making pancakes, cook until the top is riddled with bubbles and the bottom is lightly browned. Then flip and cook the other side.

☞ For crêpes, pour about ¼ cup batter into the center of the hot pan, then tilt the pan so

that the batter lightly covers the bottom. Pour the excess batter back into the bowl and let the crêpe cook for about 30 seconds, or until the bottom is brown. Flip it over and cook the other side for about 15 to 20 seconds.

☞ Since waffle irons cook both sides simultaneously, flipping isn't required. To ensure even cooking, don't open the iron until all the steaming has stopped.

Cook ahead. Pancakes and waffles will stay fresh for about 30 minutes when kept on a baking sheet placed in a 300° oven.

Crêpes keep well when they're allowed to cool in a single layer, then stacked, wrapped in plastic and refrigerated or frozen.

To defrost crêpes, briefly heat one at a time in a pan coated with no-stick spray. Or spoon on a warm sauce—applesauce, for example—to help them thaw.

Sarabeth Levine

Orange-apricot marmalade might seem like a small beginning, but for Sarabeth Levine, it was the key to big success—an entire line of fresh-tasting jams and bakery products, as well as three Sarabeth's restaurants in New York City.

Among Sarabeth's baked specialties is a variety of quick breads. "Quick breads have earned their name for just that reason—they are fast and easy," she says. "This light, fluffy banana-nut bread is rich in flavor, and its smell lingers long after the loaf leaves the oven."

The recipe calls for sunflower seeds, but you can substitute the nuts of your choice. If you prefer margarine instead of butter, use regular stick margarine rather than reduced-calorie.

Banana-Nut Bread

½ cup butter, softened
1 cup sugar
1 teaspoon vanilla
6 egg whites
3 cups unbleached flour
1½ teaspoons baking powder
½ teaspoon salt
½ cup skim milk
2 cups mashed bananas
½ teaspoon grated lemon rind
¾ cup sunflower seeds

Preheat the oven to 400°. Butter and flour two 8″ × 4″ no-stick loaf pans; set aside.

Using an electric mixer and a large bowl, beat together the butter, sugar and vanilla on medium speed until light and fluffy. Slowly add the egg whites and beat well.

In a medium bowl, mix the flour, baking powder and salt with a wire whisk until combined.

Alternately add the flour mixture and milk to the egg mixture, starting and ending with the flour. Mix the batter until it is just smooth. Be careful not to overmix.

Use a spatula to gently fold in the bananas, lemon rind and sunflower seeds.

Place the batter in the prepared pans, smoothing the top with a rubber spatula.

Bake for 50 to 60 minutes, or until the top is golden brown and a toothpick inserted in the bread comes out clean. (If the bread browns too quickly as it bakes, lay a sheet of aluminum foil lightly over the top.) Remove from the oven and cool on a wire rack for 10 to 15 minutes before removing from the pan.

Makes 2 loaves; 10 slices each. Per slice: 208 calories, 7.5 g. fat (32% of calories), 4.7 g. protein, 31.4 g. carbohydrates, 1.3 g. dietary fiber, 12 mg. cholesterol, 145 mg. sodium

Basic Muffins

2 cups all-purpose flour
1 tablespoon baking powder
¼ teaspoon salt
2 tablespoons honey
1 cup skim milk
3 tablespoons canola oil
3 egg whites

Preheat the oven to 375°. Coat a 12-cup no-stick muffin pan with no-stick spray or line the cups with paper liners.

In a medium bowl, combine the flour, baking powder and salt; set aside.

In a small bowl, stir together the honey, milk, oil and egg whites. Using a fork, quickly stir the honey mixture into the flour mixture just until a lumpy batter forms.

Divide the batter evenly among the prepared muffin cups, filling them two-thirds full. Bake for 25 minutes, or until the muffins are lightly browned and a toothpick inserted in the center comes out clean.

Cool in the pan on a wire rack for 10 minutes. Remove from the pan and serve warm or cool completely.

Makes 12. Per muffin: 129 calories, 3.6 g. fat (26% of calories), 3.7 g. protein, 20 g. carbohydrates, 0.6 g. dietary fiber, 0 mg. cholesterol, 151 mg. sodium

VARIATIONS

Banana-Nut Muffins: Stir 2 tablespoons chopped walnuts, pecans or hazelnuts and ⅛ teaspoon ground nutmeg into the dry ingredients. Reduce the amount of canola oil to 2 tablespoons. Stir ⅔ cup mashed bananas into the wet ingredients.
Blueberry Muffins: Gently stir 1 cup fresh or frozen blueberries into the dry ingredients.
Cranberry-Orange Muffins: Gently stir 1 cup frozen cranberries and 1 tablespoon freshly grated orange rind into the dry ingredients. Replace the honey with ⅓ cup sugar.

Corn Muffins

1 cup all-purpose flour
1 cup cornmeal
2 tablespoons sugar
2½ teaspoons baking powder
¼ teaspoon baking soda
¼ teaspoon salt
2 tablespoons canola oil
2 tablespoons unsweetened applesauce
2 egg whites, lightly beaten
1 cup buttermilk

Preheat the oven to 400°. Spray a 12-cup no-stick muffin pan with no-stick spray or line the cups with paper liners.

In a medium bowl, combine the flour, cornmeal, sugar, baking powder, baking soda and salt; set aside. Using a fork, stir in the oil, applesauce and egg whites until well-distributed. Stir in the buttermilk just until a lumpy batter forms.

Divide the batter evenly among the prepared muffin cups, filling them two-thirds full. Bake for 20 minutes, or until the muffin tops are lightly browned and a toothpick inserted in the center comes out clean.

Cool in the pan on a wire rack for 10 minutes. Remove from the pan and serve warm or cool completely.

Makes 12. Per muffin: 116 calories, 2.9 g. fat (23% of calories), 3.2 g. protein, 19.4 g. carbohydrates, 1.9 g. dietary fiber, 1 mg. cholesterol, 174 mg. sodium

VARIATIONS

Blueberry Corn Muffins: Add 1 cup fresh or frozen blueberries to the dry ingredients.
Jalapeño Corn Muffins: Add ¼ cup chopped, drained, canned jalapeño peppers (wear plastic gloves when handling) to the dry ingredients.

Bran Muffins

For a so-called health food, bran muffins tend to be high in fat. In our version, skim milk and egg whites keep the muffins light, while whole-wheat flour and all-bran cereal give them a hearty texture and delicious flavor.

½ cup all-purpose flour
½ cup whole-wheat flour
1 tablespoon baking powder
¼ teaspoon salt
¼ teaspoon cinnamon
1 cup skim milk
2 tablespoons canola oil
2 tablespoons honey
3 egg whites
1 cup all-bran cereal

Preheat the oven to 400°. Spray a 12-cup no-stick muffin pan with no-stick spray or line the cups with paper liners.

In a medium bowl, combine the all-purpose flour, whole-wheat flour, baking powder, salt and cinnamon; set aside.

In a small bowl, stir together the milk, oil, honey and egg whites. Stir in the cereal and let sit for 10 minutes. Gently stir the milk mixture into the flour mixture just until a lumpy batter forms.

Divide the batter equally among the prepared muffin cups, filling them two-thirds full. Bake for 20 to 25 minutes, or until the muffin tops are lightly browned and a toothpick inserted in the center comes out clean.

Cool in the pan on a wire rack for 10 minutes. Remove from the pan and serve warm or cool completely.

Makes 12. Per muffin: 97 calories, 2.6 g. fat (22% of calories), 3.8 g. protein, 17.1 g. carbohydrates, 2.9 g. dietary fiber, 0.3 mg. cholesterol, 231 mg. sodium

VARIATIONS

Carrot Bran Muffins: Add ½ cup grated carrots to the dry ingredients.
Raisin Bran Muffins: Add ½ cup raisins to the dry ingredients.
Spice-Nut Muffins: Add ½ cup chopped walnuts or pecans and ½ teaspoon ground nutmeg to the dry ingredients.

Basic Scones

QUICK!

1 cup + 2 tablespoons all-purpose flour
1 cup cake flour
½ cup rolled oats
2 tablespoons sugar
2½ teaspoons baking powder
¼ teaspoon salt
3 tablespoons nondiet tub-style margarine or butter
½ cup skim milk
2 egg whites

Preheat the oven to 425°. Coat a no-stick baking sheet with no-stick spray.

In a medium bowl, combine the all-purpose flour, cake flour, oats, sugar, baking powder and salt; set aside.

Using 2 table knives or a pastry blender, cut the margarine into the flour mixture until coarse crumbs form. Using a fork, stir in the milk and egg whites until a dough forms.

Turn the dough out onto a lightly floured surface and gently knead for 1 minute. Using a floured rolling pin, gently roll the dough into a ½"-thick rectangle or pat into shape using your hands. Using a 2" biscuit cutter, cut the dough into rounds. Reroll as necessary to cut 12 scones.

Place the scones on the prepared baking sheet. Lightly coat the top of the scones with no-stick spray. Bake for 12 to 15 minutes, or until the bottoms of the scones are lightly browned and the tops are golden.

Makes 12. Per scone: 129 calories, 3.3 g. fat (23% of calories), 3.5 g. protein, 21.1 g. carbohydrates, 0.8 g. dietary fiber, 0.2 mg. cholesterol, 166 mg. sodium

NOTES

• For wedge-shaped scones, roll the dough into a ½"-thick circle, then place the dough onto the prepared baking sheet. Using a sharp knife, cut the dough like a pizza to make 12 wedges. Separate the wedges, leaving a 1" space between each.

• Wrap extra scones in plastic or place in freezer bags and freeze for later use.

VARIATIONS

Lemon-Thyme Scones: Add ¾ teaspoon dried thyme and 1 teaspoon grated lemon rind to the dry ingredients. Reduce the sugar to 1 tablespoon.

Raisin or Currant Scones: Add ½ cup raisins or currants to the dry ingredients.

Apricot Scones: Add ½ cup chopped dried apricots to the dry ingredients.

Basic Dessert Crêpes

- ¾ cup skim milk
- 1 egg, beaten
- 1 tablespoon sugar
- 1½ teaspoons canola oil
  Pinch of salt
- ½ cup unbleached flour

In a medium bowl, whisk together the milk, egg, sugar, oil and salt. Gradually stir in the flour. Beat well.

Coat a small no-stick skillet with no-stick spray and warm over medium heat until hot.

Spoon 2 tablespoons of the batter into the pan. Quickly tilt the pan in all directions to spread the batter into an even circle. Cook for 1 to 2 minutes, or until the bottom is lightly browned and the top is set.

Loosen the crêpe with a spatula and invert it onto a plate. Cover to keep warm. Repeat with the remaining batter.

Makes 4 servings. Per serving (2 crêpes): 119 calories, 3.2 g. fat (24% of calories), 4.7 g. protein, 17.4 g. carbohydrates, 0.4 g. dietary fiber, 54 mg. cholesterol, 40 mg. sodium

NOTES

• For lighter, fluffier crêpes, cover the batter and let sit at room temperature for 2 hours.

• These crêpes may be frozen for up to 4 months. Place the cooked crêpes between layers of wax paper and tightly wrap in plastic. Completely thaw before using.

VARIATIONS

Asparagus-Cheese Crêpes: Omit the sugar and fill the crêpes with steamed asparagus and Cheddar Cheese Sauce (page 510). To serve these crêpes for Easter supper (menu on page 562), double the recipe.

Basic Crêpes: Omit the sugar. (Without sugar, the crêpes can be used for savory fillings.)

Berry-Banana Crêpes: Fill the crêpes with sliced fresh bananas and strawberries, blueberries or raspberries. Drizzle with maple syrup and sprinkle with cinnamon or confectioner's sugar.

Buckwheat Crêpes: Replace ¼ cup of the unbleached flour with ¼ cup buckwheat flour.

Cherry-Cheese Crêpes: In a food processor or blender, puree ⅓ cup nonfat cottage cheese, ⅓ cup nonfat plain yogurt, ½ teaspoon honey and ½ teaspoon vanilla until smooth. Add 1 cup pitted dark sweet cherries and process using on/off turns until the cherries are chopped but not pureed. Fill the crêpes with the cherry-cheese filling. (You can replace the cherries with ¾ cup peeled, pitted and chopped peaches, sliced strawberries or blueberries).

Whole-Wheat Crêpes: Replace ¼ cup of the unbleached flour with ¼ cup whole-wheat flour.

Basic Pancakes

Omitting the butter significantly reduced the fat in these delicious, fluffy pancakes.

1½	cups all-purpose flour
2½	teaspoons baking powder
2	teaspoons sugar
¼	teaspoon salt
1	cup skim milk
¼	cup fat-free egg substitute

In a medium bowl, combine the flour, baking powder, sugar and salt; set aside.

In a small bowl, whisk together the milk and egg substitute. Gently stir the milk mixture into the flour mixture just until a lumpy batter forms.

Coat a griddle or large no-stick skillet with no-stick spray. Warm over medium heat for 1 minute.

For each pancake, pour ¼ cup of the batter onto the hot griddle. Cook for 2 to 3 minutes, or until the top of the pancake bubbles and the bottom is lightly browned. Turn the pancake over and cook for 2 minutes, or until the bottom is lightly browned. Transfer to a serving plate and cover to keep warm.

Repeat with the remaining batter.

Makes 12. Per serving (3 pancakes): 209 calories, 0.6 g. fat (2% of calories), 8.2 g. protein, 41.6 g. carbohydrates, 1.3 g. dietary fiber, 1 mg. cholesterol, 397 mg. sodium

NOTES
• For thinner pancakes, use up to 1¼ cups skim milk.
• For thicker pancakes, use only ¾ cup skim milk.

VARIATIONS
Banana Pancakes: Stir ½ cup mashed bananas into the wet ingredients.

Buckwheat Pancakes: Replace ¾ cup of the all-purpose flour with ¾ cup buckwheat flour.
Buttermilk Pancakes: Replace the baking powder with ½ teaspoon baking soda. Replace the skim milk with buttermilk.
Cornmeal Pancakes: Replace ¾ cup of the all-purpose flour with ¾ cup yellow cornmeal.
Whole-Wheat Pancakes: Replace ½ cup of the all-purpose flour with ½ cup whole-wheat flour.

Basic Coffee Cake

1½	cups all-purpose flour
2	teaspoons baking powder
½	teaspoon baking soda
¼	teaspoon cinnamon or ⅛ teaspoon ground cardamom
½	cup packed light brown sugar
2	tablespoons nondiet tub-style margarine or butter
¾	cup fat-free egg substitute
½	cup nonfat sour cream

Preheat the oven to 350°. Spray an 8″ × 8″ no-stick baking dish with no-stick spray. In a medium bowl, combine the flour, baking powder, baking soda and cinnamon or cardamom.

In another medium bowl, beat together the brown sugar and margarine or butter until smooth. Beat in the egg substitute until well-blended. Add the sour cream and continue beating for 2 minutes.

Beat in half of the flour mixture until blended; then beat in the remaining flour mixture for about 1 minute, or until the batter is smooth.

Spread the batter evenly in the prepared dish. Top as desired with coffee-cake topping or leave plain. Bake for 35 to 40 minutes, or until a toothpick inserted in the center comes out clean.

Cool the cake on a wire rack for 10 minutes. Serve warm or at room temperature.

Makes 9 servings. Per serving: 162 calories, 2.7 g. fat (15% of calories), 4.7 g. protein, 29.6 g. carbohydrates, 0.6 g. dietary fiber, 0 mg. cholesterol, 225 mg. sodium

VARIATIONS

Pecan Coffee Cake: Stir in ⅓ cup chopped pecans to the finished batter.
Berry Coffee Cake: Stir in 1 cup frozen blueberries or raspberries to the finished batter.
Apple Coffee Cake: Add ⅛ teaspoon nutmeg and ¼ teaspoon ground ginger to the dry ingredients. Stir in 1¼ cups chopped peeled apples to the finished batter. Increase the baking time to 40 to 45 minutes.

COFFEE CAKE TOPPINGS

The crowning touch of any good coffee cake is the topping. Toppings can be put together in a flash, and we've kept fat and calories to a minimum. Whether you prefer a streusel, crumb or glaze, you'll find it here. These toppings work on muffins, too.

Nut Streusel

- 3 tablespoons chopped walnuts, pecans, almonds or hazelnuts
- 2 tablespoons brown sugar
- 1 teaspoon cinnamon

In a small bowl, combine the walnuts, pecans, almonds or hazelnuts, brown sugar and cinnamon. Sprinkle the topping over the coffee-cake batter. Bake as recipe directs.

Makes enough for 1 coffee cake (9 servings). Per serving: 28 calories, 1.5 g. fat (45% of calories), 0.6 g. protein, 3.5 g. carbohydrates, 0.1 g. dietary fiber, 0 mg. cholesterol, 1 mg. sodium

Citrus Glaze

- 1 cup sifted confectioners' sugar
- 1 tablespoon finely grated orange or lemon rind
- ⅛ teaspoon ground ginger (optional)
- 2 tablespoons orange or lemon juice

In a small bowl, combine the confectioners' sugar, orange or lemon rind, ginger (if using) and orange juice or lemon juice. Stir until smooth. Drizzle the glaze over the completely cooled coffee cake.

Makes enough for 1 coffee cake (9 servings). Per serving: 45 calories, 0 g. fat (0% of calories), 0 g. protein, 11.6 carbohydrates, 0.1 g. dietary fiber, 0 mg. cholesterol, 0 mg. sodium

Oat Crumb Streusel

- 1 tablespoon all-purpose flour
- 2 tablespoons rolled oats
- 2 tablespoons brown sugar
- ½ teaspoon cinnamon
- ⅛ teaspoon nutmeg
- 1 tablespoon nondiet tub-style margarine or canola oil

In a small bowl, combine the flour, oats, brown sugar, cinnamon and nutmeg. Using a fork, stir in the margarine or oil until well-distributed. Sprinkle the topping over the coffee-cake batter. Bake as recipe directs.

Makes enough for 1 coffee cake (9 servings). Per serving: 31 calories, 1.4 g. fat (39% of calories), 0.3 g. protein, 4.5 g. carbohydrates, 0.1 g. dietary fiber, 0 mg. cholesterol, 18 mg. sodium

Basic Waffles

QUICK!

To keep waffles from going to your waist, we replaced half of the oil with applesauce and used fat-free egg substitute in place of whole eggs.

1½ cups all-purpose flour
2 teaspoons baking powder
1 teaspoon baking soda
½ teaspoon cinnamon
2 tablespoons canola oil
3 tablespoons unsweetened applesauce
1¼ cups buttermilk
½ cup fat-free egg substitute or 4 egg whites

PANCAKE AND WAFFLE TOPPINGS

Pancakes are an American classic. But the traditional butter-and-syrup topping adds a wallop of fat and calories to your breakfast. Try these simple fruit toppings to add sweet flavor without the fat.

Apple or Peach Topping

3 cups thinly sliced peeled apples or peaches
2 tablespoons apple juice or white grape juice
2 tablespoons honey
⅛ teaspoon ground nutmeg

In a medium saucepan over low heat, combine the apples or peaches, apple juice or grape juice, honey and nutmeg. Cook, stirring occasionally, for 3 minutes.

Cover the pan and cook for 5 minutes, or until the fruit is softened. Cool slightly before serving.

Makes 2 cups. Per ½ cup: 85 calories, 0.3 g. fat (3% of calories), 0.2 g. protein, 22 g. carbohydrates, 1.9 g. dietary fiber, 0 mg. cholesterol, 1 mg. sodium

NOTE
• This topping can be reheated on top of the stove or in the microwave.

Berry Sauce

2¼ cups fresh or frozen blueberries, strawberries or raspberries
2 tablespoons water
2 tablespoons honey
¼ teaspoon freshly grated orange rind or lemon rind (optional)

In a small saucepan over low heat, combine the berries, water, honey and orange or lemon rind (if using). Cook, stirring occasionally, for 8 minutes, or until the berries are softened and their juices are released.

Transfer the mixture to a food processor or blender. Puree until smooth. Pass the mixture through a sieve to remove the seeds.

Return the mixture to the saucepan. Cook over medium heat for 3 minutes, or until the sauce is reduced to about 1 cup. Cool slightly before serving.

Makes 1 cup. Per ¼ cup: 78 calories, 0.3 g. fat (3% of calories), 0.5 g. protein, 20 g. carbohydrates, 2.2 g. dietary fiber, 0 mg. cholesterol, 5 mg. sodium

Coat a waffle iron with no-stick spray. Preheat the waffle iron according to the manufacturer's directions.

In a medium bowl, combine the flour, baking powder, baking soda and cinnamon; set aside.

In a small bowl, combine the oil, applesauce, buttermilk and egg substitute or egg whites. Pour the oil mixture into the flour mixture, stirring just until blended.

Spoon enough batter onto the bottom grids of the waffle iron to cover two-thirds of it. Close the waffle iron and bake according to the manufacturer's directions. Do not open during baking.

Using a fork, carefully remove the waffle from the iron. Transfer to a serving plate to keep warm.

Repeat with the remaining batter.

Makes 8. Per waffle: 141 calories, 4 g. fat (26% of calories), 5 g. protein, 20.9 g. carbohydrates, 0.7 g. dietary fiber, 1 mg. cholesterol, 306 mg. sodium

NOTES

• Wrap extra waffles in plastic or place in freezer bags and freeze for later use.

• For waffles and ice cream, sandwich your favorite low-fat ice cream or frozen yogurt between 2 warm waffles.

VARIATIONS

Strawberry Waffles: Stir ¼ cup strawberry all-fruit spread into the wet ingredients. Serve with Berry Sauce on the opposite page.

Whole-Wheat Waffles: Replace ¾ cup of the all-purpose flour with ¾ cup whole-wheat flour.

Pecan Waffles: Sprinkle 2 teaspoons finely chopped pecans over each waffle before closing the waffle iron to bake.

QUICK! French Toast

Egg substitute cuts both fat and cholesterol in this cinnamon-scented breakfast treat.

- ¾ cup skim milk
- ¾ cup fat-free egg substitute
- 1 teaspoon canola oil
- ½ teaspoon vanilla
- ¼ teaspoon ground cinnamon
- 8 slices oat-bran or whole-wheat bread

In a 9″ × 13″ no-stick baking dish, combine the milk, egg substitute, oil, vanilla and cinnamon. Add the bread in a single layer and soak until most the liquid is absorbed. Using a spatula, turn the bread slices to coat both sides with the egg mixture.

Coat a griddle or large no-stick skillet with no-stick spray. Place over medium heat until hot. Using a spatula, transfer the bread slices to the griddle, working in batches if necessary. Brown on both sides.

Makes 4 servings. Per serving: 190 calories, 3.8 g. fat (18% of calories), 11.6 g. protein, 27 g. carbohydrates, 0 g. dietary fiber, 1 mg. cholesterol, 345 mg. sodium

NOTE

• For a delicious tropical fruit topping, toss 2 cups mixed fruit (raspberries, kiwi, mangoes, strawberries, melon) with ¼ cup pineapple juice.

VARIATION

Crunchy French Toast: Place 2 cups crushed Grape-Nuts flakes in a shallow dish. Carefully dip the soaked bread slices in the crushed flakes to coat both sides. Place on a baking sheet coated with no-stick spray. Bake at 375° for 7 minutes per side.

Cornbread

1 cup low-fat buttermilk
⅓ cup water
1 egg white
3 tablespoons canola oil
3 tablespoons brown sugar
1¼ cups cornmeal
1 cup all-purpose flour
1¾ teaspoons baking powder
½ teaspoon baking soda
½ teaspoon salt

Preheat the oven to 425°. Coat an 8″ × 8″ no-stick baking dish with no-stick spray; set aside.

In a medium bowl, whisk together the buttermilk, water, egg white, oil and brown sugar.

In a large bowl, stir together the cornmeal, flour, baking powder, baking soda and salt. Add the buttermilk mixture and stir just until a lumpy batter forms.

Spoon the batter evenly into the prepared dish. Bake for 15 minutes, or until the cornbread is lightly browned and a toothpick inserted in the center comes out clean. Cut into squares.

Makes 9 servings. Per square: 181 calories, 5.3 g. fat (26% of calories), 4.1 g. protein, 29.6 g. carbohydrates, 3 g. dietary fiber, 0.5 mg. cholesterol, 295 mg. sodium

NOTE
• For wedge-shaped cornbread, use a round 9″ pie plate or cast-iron skillet in place of the 8″ × 8″ baking pan. After baking, cut the cornbread like a pizza to make wedges.

VARIATIONS
Savory Cornbread: Add ½ teaspoon dried thyme and ½ teaspoon onion flakes to the dry ingredients.
Jalapeño Cornbread: Add ¼ cup chopped, drained, canned jalapeño peppers (wear plastic gloves when handling) to the dry ingredients.

Pumpkin Bread

1 egg
1 egg white
6 tablespoons sugar
¼ cup packed brown sugar
1 cup canned pumpkin
6 tablespoons low-fat buttermilk
1½ tablespoons canola oil
½ teaspoon vanilla
1½ cups all-purpose flour
2 tablespoons cornstarch
¾ teaspoon baking powder
½ teaspoon baking soda
¼ teaspoon salt
⅛ teaspoon ground allspice
⅛ teaspoon ground cloves
¼ teaspoon ground cinnamon
¼ teaspoon ground nutmeg

Preheat the oven the 350°. Coat a 9″ × 5″ no-stick loaf pan with no-stick spray; set aside.

In a food processor or blender, process the egg, egg white, sugar and brown sugar until smooth. Add the pumpkin, buttermilk, oil and vanilla. Blend until smooth.

In a large bowl, combine the flour, cornstarch, baking powder, baking soda, salt, allspice, cloves, cinnamon and nutmeg. Add the pumpkin mixture. Stir just until a lumpty batter forms.

Spoon the batter evenly into the prepared pan. Bake for 45 minutes, or until the bread is golden brown. Cool in the pan for 10 minutes. Remove the bread from the pan and cool on a wire rack.

Makes 18 slices. Per slice: 91 calories, 1.6 g. fat (15% of calories), 1.9 g. protein, 17.4 g. carbohydrates, 0.7 g. dietary fiber, 12 mg. cholesterol, 92 mg. sodium

Zucchini Bread

1½ cups shredded zucchini
⅔ cup sugar
¼ cup skim milk
¼ cup fat-free egg substitute
2 tablespoons canola oil
2 tablespoons honey
1 teaspoon vanilla
1 teaspoon ground cinnamon
½ teaspoon ground cloves
1⅓ cups all-purpose flour
¾ teaspoon baking powder
½ teaspoon baking soda
⅛ teaspoon salt

Preheat the oven to 350°. Coat an 8″×4″ no-stick loaf pan with no-stick spray; set aside.

Place the zucchini on paper towels and pat dry.

In a medium bowl, whisk together the sugar, milk, egg substitute, oil, honey, vanilla, cinnamon and cloves.

In a large bowl, stir together the flour, baking powder, baking soda and salt. Add the zucchini and the milk mixture. Using a large wooden spoon, stir just until the ingredients are thoroughly combined (do not overmix).

Spoon the batter into the prepared pan. Bake for 35 to 45 minutes, or until a toothpick inserted in the center comes out clean. Cool in the pan for 10 minutes. Remove the bread from the pan and cool on a wire rack.

Makes 10 slices. Per slice: 159 calories, 2.9 g. fat (17% of calories), 2.7 g. protein, 30.9 g. carbohydrates, 0.6 g. dietary fiber, 0.1 mg. cholesterol, 129 mg. sodium

VARIATION

Chocolate Zucchini Bread: Add ½ cup cocoa powder to the dry ingredients. If desired, add ½ cup mini chocolate chips along with the zucchini.

QUICK!
Rolled Biscuits

We cut the fat but retained the flaky texture of classic rolled biscuits by replacing butter and whole milk with margarine and buttermilk.

2 cups all-purpose flour
2½ teaspoons baking powder
½ teaspoon baking soda
3 tablespoons nondiet tub-style margarine
⅔ cup buttermilk

Preheat the oven to 425°. Coat a no-stick baking sheet with no-stick spray.

In a medium bowl, combine the flour, baking powder and baking soda. Using 2 table knives or a pastry blender, cut in the margarine until coarse crumbs form. Gently stir in the buttermilk until a dough forms.

Turn the dough out onto a lightly floured surface and gently knead for 1 minute.

Using a floured rolling pin, gently roll the dough into a ½″-thick rectangle, or flour your hands and pat into shape. Using a 2″ biscuit cutter, cut the dough into rounds, rerolling as necessary to cut 12 biscuits.

Place the biscuits on the prepared baking sheet. Lightly coat the top of the biscuits with no-stick spray. Bake for 12 to 15 minutes, or until the bottoms of the biscuits are browned and the tops are lightly golden.

Makes 12. Per biscuit: 107 calories, 3.2 g. fat (27% of calories), 2.6 g. protein, 16.8 g. carbohydrates, 0.6 g. dietary fiber, 0.5 mg. cholesterol, 174 mg. sodium

Fresh

from the
Garden

SPRING AND SUMMER VEGETABLES, PAGE 356

WINTER VEGETABLES, PAGE 376

Spring and Summer Vegetables

The warm months bring out the garden's most wholesome bounty. String beans, spinach, green peas, tomatoes, summer squash—these and other spring and summer vegetables offer a refreshing and healthful way to begin the season.

It's not merely that spring and summer vegetables are high in fiber, vitamins, minerals and complex carbohydrates. They're also colorful, easy to prepare and versatile enough that you can enjoy them every day of the week.

Unlike their hardy winter kin, warm-weather vegetables aren't long keepers. To get the best tastes and textures, you need to buy or pick the freshest vegetables available and then use them as soon as possible after bringing them home.

Buy them young. Oversize vegetables may appear to give more value for the money (unless you're paying by the pound), but smaller, younger vegetables usually have more flavor and sweetness.

Look for smooth skin. Vegetables that have wrinkles, blemishes, cracks or breaks in the skin may have been damaged in picking or transport. Or they may be too old to make the best eating. When shopping, always look for vegetables with smooth skins and a taut appearance, without obvious marks or blemishes.

Don't neglect the freezer case. You needn't forgo summer vegetables in the off-season. While frozen vegetables lose a little in texture and taste, they're an excellent alternative to fresh. They're quick to prepare and, in many cases, have just as many nutrients

as fresh (possibly more, if the fresh ones took a long time to get to your table).

Store them dry. Excessive moisture hastens decay, so don't rinse vegetables before storing them in the refrigerator. Instead, put them away in plastic bags. If they've been misted in the store, blot up excess moisture with paper towels. Clean the vegetables thoroughly before you start cooking.

Spare the skin. While some vegetables are waxed and always require peeling, most spring and summer vegetables can be enjoyed with the skin on. This adds another dimension of taste and flavor.

TOMATOES

For providing an almost limitless range of exciting tastes, the tomato is in a class by itself. There are literally hundreds of varieties of tomatoes, ranging from the jewel-like tiny red or yellow currant tomatoes to robust monsters the size of a softball. They can be sweet or tart, tender or tough. The colors vary, from the traditional red to yellow, orange, green or pink. There are even striped varieties.

For the healthy cook, tomatoes are more than just a delicious and versatile ingredient. They're also high in vitamins, particularly A and C, low in sodium and decidedly nonfattening. One medium tomato contains only 35 calories.

Unless you're lucky enough to have your own greenhouse or winter access to vine-ripened

TENDER VEGETABLES

The bounty of the warm months is highly perishable and at its flavor and nutrient peak when fresh. Use the storage and preparation tips below to reap the very best from your produce.

VEGETABLE	STORAGE AND PREPARATION
Artichokes	Refrigerate in plastic bags and use within a week. Trim leaf tips with scissors; boil whole in a large pot of water until a leaf pulls out easily.
Asparagus	Refrigerate in plastic bags. Use within three days. To use, break off or peel tough stem ends. Steam or cook, covered, in simmering water.
Beans: green, yellow wax, Italian, purple	Refrigerate in plastic bags and use within three days. Rinse, snap off ends and remove strings, if any. Leave whole, julienne or cut into 1" pieces. Steam or cook, covered, in a small amount of simmering water.
Corn	Refrigerate in husks; use within one day. To use, remove silk and husks; cook whole cobs, covered, in simmering water. Or microwave, grill or bake unhusked ears, with the silks removed. Or cut kernels from ears and cook in a small amount of simmering water.
Cucumbers	Refrigerate in plastic bags and use within two weeks. Rinse and peel (if waxed). Slice as desired. Use raw or sauté.
Eggplant	Refrigerate in plastic bags and use within a few days. Rinse; peel if skin is tough. Slice as desired and cook or microwave in a small amount of simmering water, or steam, bake or broil.
Mushrooms	Refrigerate in paper bags and use within three days. Wipe with damp paper towels before using. Leave whole or slice. Use raw or sauté.
Okra	Choose small pods. Refrigerate in plastic bags and use within three days. Rinse and cut off stems. Best sautéed whole; otherwise, slice and cook, covered, in a small amount of simmering water.
Peas: snow, sugar snap	Refrigerate in plastic bags and use within three days. Rinse, snap off ends and remove strings, if any. Cook, covered, in a small amount of simmering water.
Peas: sweet green	Refrigerate in plastic bags and use within two days. Shell and cook, covered, in a small amount of simmering water.
Peppers: sweet green, red, yellow, orange, purple	Refrigerate in plastic bags and use within a week. Wash, pat dry. Slice as desired; eat raw or sauté. To stuff, halve or leave whole; remove seeds and inner membranes; parboil in water to cover; drain, fill and bake.
Summer squash: zucchini, yellow, pattypan	Refrigerate in plastic bags and use within four days. Wash and pat dry just before using; cut off stem and blossom end. Slice as desired. Cook or microwave, covered, in a small amount of simmering water, or steam or stir-fry.
Tomatoes	Store at room temperature and use within one week. Wash and slice as desired. Use raw or cook as recipe directs (if desired, peel before chopping).

PEELING TOMATOES

Whether you're making a sauce for spaghetti or preparing a blender full of bracing gazpacho, you'll get more pleasing results if you peel the tomatoes first. Here's an easy way to do it.

Core the tomato with a paring knife, removing the stem and white middle.

Carefully cut an X in the bottom of the tomato, trying to cut only the skin.

Immerse the tomato in a large pot of boiling water for 20 seconds. Then remove it with a slotted spoon and dunk it in a bowl of ice water.

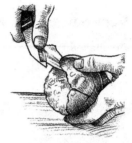

Using the edge of the knife, carefully slip off the skin.

Florida tomatoes, the best are available only during the warm months. While cold-weather supermarket tomatoes might serve in a pinch, they can't meet the sweet taste and nearly explosive juiciness of summer tomatoes.

Many out-of-season tomatoes are picked green and artificially ripened without natural sunlight. The result is a woolly texture and almost no taste.

☞ When buying supermarket tomatoes, look for those labeled "hothouse," "green-house" or "vine-ripened." These terms tell you that the tomato was picked and shipped when it was almost, but not quite, ripe.

☞ During the winter, it's best to avoid globe tomatoes, which have little taste and texture. Go with cherry tomatoes instead.

☞ For cooking, canned tomatoes are preferable to substandard fresh ones. They were picked and processed at their peak.

☞ To hasten ripening, place underripe tomatoes in a brown bag or wrap them in newspaper and keep them at room temperature. As the fruit ripens, it emits a natural gas (ethylene) that speeds the ripening process.

☞ Plum tomatoes have thicker walls and a fuller flavor than globe or cherry tomatoes,

Helpful Hint

For an instant tomato sauce, chop ripe tomatoes along with a few cloves of garlic and cook in the microwave for about three minutes. If you have a lot of tomatoes, put extra sauce in freezer bags for future use.

SEEDING TOMATOES

It's almost impossible to scrape away a tomato's tiny seeds without sacrificing the tasty flesh as well. Here's a better way, which also removes a little of the juice that can dilute your finished product.

Cut the tomato in half crosswise and gently squeeze each half. This will cause the seeds in the middle to bulge out, making them easy to remove with a swipe of your finger.

meaning that their flavor and texture aren't likely to dissipate during cooking. They're typically used for sauces, stews and other cooked dishes.

☞ Globe and cherry tomatoes have a firm texture and deliciously sweet taste, making them ideal for salads or just eating raw.

☞ Whole tomatoes should be stored in a cool, dark place with plenty of air circulation to prevent them from going bad. Don't refrigerate them, as chilling diminishes their flavor. (Once they've been cut, however, they should be refrigerated and will keep for a day or two.)

☞ Don't stack tomatoes; store them in a single layer, stem end up. When stored with the bumpy "shoulders" down, the weight of the tomato will cause this delicate portion to bruise.

Dried Tomatoes

Although nothing can match the full, refreshing taste of a vine-picked tomato at the peak of freshness, dried tomatoes provide a wonderfully concentrated flavor. Stored in an airtight container out of direct light or in the refrigerator, they'll keep for up to one year. Best of all,

they're never out of season.

☞ To rehydrate dried tomatoes, cover them with boiling water and let them stand about two minutes.

☞ Dried tomatoes that have been packed in oil don't need to be soaked in water. Simply remove them from the container and blot them.

ASPARAGUS

Available from spring to early summer, this tender, crunchy shoot is among the easiest vegetables to prepare and cook. What's more, its natural freshness means that you don't need butter or added sauces to bring out or augment its flavors.

The asparagus that most of us are familiar with is the green variety. White asparagus, however, has also become popular for its delicate flavor and mild taste.

☞ To keep asparagus fresh, wrap the bottom ends of the spears in moist paper towels and place them unwashed in a plastic (preferably perforated) bag and store in the vegetable bin.

DRYING TOMATOES

Gardeners pray for success, but a prolific tomato plant can give too much of a good thing. Drying Italian tomatoes (also known as plum or Roma tomatoes) takes just a few minutes of your time and turns summer's surplus into a yearlong treat. Besides, making your own saves considerable money.

Slice the tomatoes lengthwise almost in half so that they lie open, cut side up, like a book. Put them on a no-stick baking sheet and sprinkle them lightly with salt.

Place the sheet in a 120° to 140° oven for about 24 hours, or until shrivelled. They should feel dry but still be pliable.

Pack into small jars, cover with olive oil and refrigerate or freeze until you're ready to use them.

☞ To remove the tough part of each spear, simply bend a stalk. Asparagus naturally snaps off at the point where the woody, tough end stops and the tender top end begins.

☞ If the spears are thick, the snap method can waste perfectly good flesh. In that case, use a vegetable peeler to peel the bottom area of each spear. Use a knife to find the point where the flesh turns woody (it will be tough to slice) and cut the bottom off there.

☞ Asparagus tips cook more quickly than the stalks. One way to prevent overcooking is to stand the spears upright in a tall, narrow pot. Add a few inches of water to the bottom, cover with a lid and bring to a boil.

☞ Tying the spears together with string will prevent them from toppling over during cooking. Plus, it makes them easier to fish out later.

☞ If you don't have a suitable asparagus pot, bring an inch or so of water to a boil in a large skillet. Add the loose spears and cook, uncovered, until just tender (test with the tip of a paring knife).

AVOCADOS

These tender, pear-shaped fruits are treated as vegetables. They have a soft, oily flesh that's almost always eaten raw—alone or in salads—or as an appetizer marinated in oil or vinegar. There are two main varieties: the pebbly black Haas and the smooth green Fuerte. The Haas has a more buttery texture.

☞ Since avocados ripen quickly at room temperature, you can buy them green and place them on a sunny ledge for several days until they're ready.

☞ When an avocado is almost but not quite ripe, you can speed the softening process by putting it in a loosely closed paper bag and

Avocado

Is It Good for You?

Avocados are great for guacamole, and they are super in salads, too. But that's not all that these fleshy, pear-shaped fruits—which are treated as vegetables—are known for. Unfortunately, avocados also have the dubious distinction of being extremely high in fat.

Fortunately, it's good fat. Avocados contain mostly monounsaturated fat—the kind that doesn't clog your arteries. (This is the same fat that's also found in heart-friendly olive oil and canola oil.) What's more, most of the fat in avocados comes from oleic acid, which researchers suspect may actually help reduce cholesterol levels.

In addition, avocados are higher in fiber than you would guess. The exact amount depends on the variety and the size of the fruit, but a hefty Florida avocado can have nearly 18 grams of dietary fiber. Plus, avocados contain all of the B vitamins and are particularly high in folate.

letting it stand at room temperature for one or two days.

☞ A ripe avocado yields slightly to gentle pressure. An alternate ripeness test: Insert a wooden toothpick into the stem end; if it goes in easily, the avocado is ready to use.

☞ Putting avocados in the refrigerator stops the ripening process and keeps them fresh for up to one week.

☞ To remove the pit, cut the avocado in half lengthwise and gently twist the halves apart. Take a chef's knife and firmly whack the seed with it (the knife should embed itself into the pit). Give the knife a twist and the pit should come right out.

☞ Rubbing lemon or lime juice over a cut avocado helps prevent browning and keeps the flesh fresh.

EGGPLANT

This fruit (yes, technically it is a fruit) is a member of the nightshade family and, as such, is related to tomatoes, potatoes and peppers. Choose eggplants that are plump, glossy and heavy for their size. Although most are of the familiar large purple-black variety, other types are showing up in markets. They include large white, baby white, baby purple and the elongated purple Japanese.

☞ When preparing young eggplant, the skin typically is tender enough not to require peeling. With older eggplant, however, the peel is really too tough to eat and should be discarded.

☞ Eggplant discolors quickly when the peel is removed, so delay this step until just prior to cooking.

☞ Some people like to salt cut eggplant before cooking to draw out potentially bitter juices. If you do this, salt the pieces generously, place them in a colander and let them drain for about 30 minutes. Rinse very well to remove the salt. If you will be sautéing or roasting the pieces, pat them dry with paper towels.

☞ Eggplant's biggest shortcoming is its ability to soak up cooking oil like a sponge. One way to prevent this is to microwave the pieces first to soften them, then sauté them in a small amount of oil in a hot no-stick skillet. You can also lightly brush slices with oil and bake until tender.

☞ You can make an excellent dip, like the Middle Eastern baba ghanoush, by first roasting a whole eggplant until tender. Place it on a no-stick baking sheet, prick the eggplant in several places to keep it from exploding and broil it until the skin is well-charred all over and the eggplant is quite soft. Split the skin and scrape out the flesh.

THE GOURD FAMILY

This extended family of vegetables includes cucumbers as well as summer squashes like zucchini and yellow crookneck. Unlike winter squash, which typically require long cooking times to tenderize the dense flesh, the spring and summer gourds are tender and require only the lightest cooking.

Perhaps the most popular of the summer squash is zucchini. Although the name is Italian (meaning "little squash"), zucchini actually originated in America. Occasionally, you'll see in stores a similarly shaped squash with white stripes and pale green skin. This is coccozelle; it can be used interchangeably with zucchini.

Other popular summer squash include the golden zucchini, various pattypan types (white, green and yellow), chayote (also known as mirlitons), yellow straightneck and baby versions of zucchini and yellow scallop squash.

☞ All summer squash have tender skin that's fine for eating. However, they should be washed vigorously under running water before eating.

☞ Some farmers markets sell bright yellow zucchini flowers. They don't keep long but are extremely delicious when sautéed or steamed lightly. You can also stuff and bake them.

The two main types of cucumbers are the familiar regular ones, which have seeds, and the thin, elongated English cukes that are virtually seedless. The small pickling cucumbers (also known as Kirbys) are, as their name implies, used mostly for pickles.

☞ When buying cucumbers, look for those that are hard, medium-size and dark green. A large cucumber, or one with a yellowish cast, is likely old, bitter and tough.

☞ To seed a regular cucumber, slice it in half lengthwise. Use a spoon to scoop out the seed area.

☞ Cucumbers are often coated with wax to prevent the loss of moisture. If the ones that you buy are, peel them before using.

FANCY CUCUMBERS

To make your salads really stand out, try adding decorative cucumber slices.

Drag a fork or citrus zester all the way along the length of the cucumber, making shallow furrows through the skin. Continue to work your way around the cuke.

Slicing the cucumber crosswise produces attractive fluted slices.

THE LEAFY GREENS

Virtually all of the leafy greens can do double duty. They're equally good cooked as a side dish or served raw in the salad bowl. (To learn more about salad greens, see page 83.)

However they're prepared, colorful leafy greens like Swiss chard, radicchio, escarole, chicory, mustard greens, collard greens, spinach, kale, turnip greens, beet greens, arugula, dandelion greens, sorrel and watercress are among the best sources for beta-carotene. Experts say that this heart-healthy nutrient may play a powerful role in reducing the threat of stroke, heart disease, high cholesterol and some forms of cancer.

☞ Greens grow close to the ground and have an abundance of nooks and crevices where grit can hide, so it's important to wash them thoroughly before serving. Put the greens in a sink filled with cold water. Toss them with your hands to help loosen grit, which will fall to the bottom. Remove the greens from the water, inspecting them as you go. Do not let the greens soak, or they'll lose water-soluble nutrients.

☞ Before storing, dry the greens in a salad spinner or by blotting them dry with paper towels. Then wrap them in a towel, place the towel in a plastic bag and store in the vegetable bin.

☞ If you'll be cooking the greens, wash them just before using. For most recipes, you can just shake off some of the excess water and place the greens right in a pan. You'll have enough moisture to generate steam and for the greens to cook down without sticking to the pan.

☞ Greens shrink considerably in volume when cooked. What looks like an impressive mound on the kitchen counter may not fill a small bowl when cooked. As a rule, one pound of greens is enough for about two servings.

MUSHROOMS

Both cultivated and wild mushrooms have become increasingly popular. When cooking with wild varieties, however, always get them from a reliable and reputable source to avoid getting poisonous ones.

☞ Shop for mushrooms with smooth, unblemished skins that are dry to the touch. The gills beneath the cap should be fresh-looking. Tightly closed gills indicate fresher

FLUTING MUSHROOMS

When serving whole mushrooms, you can add a bit of flare by fluting the caps.

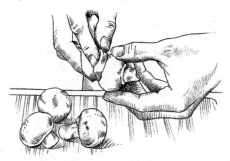

Wipe off the cap with a damp paper towel. If you want the mushroom to be white, peel it by removing the stem, then gently pulling away strips of skin until the entire cap is bare.

Using a traditional punch-type can opener, make a series of impressions around the edge of the cap. The indented areas will darken slightly, making an attractive fluted pattern.

mushrooms, but ones that are open somewhat may have more flavor.

☞ Store mushrooms in the refrigerator, unwashed, in an open container or paper bag. Loosely cover the mushrooms with a dry paper towel.

☞ When preparing mushrooms, trim away any stems that are woody, sticky or discolored. When stems are tender, however, only the very bottom needs trimming.

☞ Wash mushrooms well with a slightly damp cloth or mushroom brush. Do not soak mushrooms, because they tend to absorb water.

☞ When sautéing mushrooms, be aware that they will first give off a lot of liquid. Let it cook away, then continue with the sautéing until the mushrooms brown as needed.

POD AND SEED VEGETABLES

From the mild days of early spring to the fierce heat of summer, pod and seed vegetables—like fresh green peas, green beans, yellow wax beans, snow peas, snap peas, okra and corn—can be key players in virtually every meal. High in fiber, minerals and vitamins, these vegetables are at their best when young. As they get older, they get increasingly tough.

☞ Buy corn still in the husk, as this serves as a natural wrapper that keeps moisture in. Look for husks with that bright green, just-picked look. Bypass ones that are ragged or dried out.

☞ Pod vegetables lose their sweetness within days after being picked, and the texture quickly turns mealy as natural sugars in the pod turn to starch. They should be bought and eaten within two or three days of being picked.

☞ When buying fresh green peas, you can test their freshness by opening a pod and tasting a pea. If it tastes starchy instead of sweet, it's getting too old.

☞ To shell green peas, snap off the stem and pull the string. Then press on the seam of

CUTTING CORN

Corn cobs don't give up their kernels easily. Kitchen stores sell push-down devices that "automatically" strip kernels from the cob, but this one-size-fits-all approach doesn't always work. An easier way is simply to use a sharp knife.

Hold the cob upright in a wide bowl. With a sharp knife, cut stright down, slicing the kernels from the cob. Don't get too close to the cob, or you'll end up with tough pieces in the mix.

Once the kernels are removed, reverse the knife and rub the dull side down the cob to extract the "milk," which will make the recipe more creamy.

the pod to pop it open. Gently push the exposed peas out of the shell.

☞ The outer shell of English green peas is inedible and should be removed. Snap peas are an entirely different variety and are meant to be eaten pod and all.

☞ When buying green beans or yellow wax beans, bend one over sharply. It should snap crisply. If it's rubbery, pass it by.

☞ In some modern varieties, the string has been bred out of green and yellow beans. For aesthetic reasons, you'll want to snip off the stem end. Whether or not you remove the tail is up to you.

☞ Some varieties of okra have a fuzzy skin, which can be removed by rubbing the unwashed pods with a towel. Okra can get really tough as it grows, and the pods do grow quickly.

☞ Sautéing small okra pods whole is the best way to avoid the slimy quality many people find objectionable about this vegetable. Trim off the stem end before cooking.

SWEET PEPPERS

Unlike their more fiery counterparts, sweet peppers can be safely munched right off the vine or added to soups, stews or stir-fries for a sweetly smoky taste.

Sweet peppers come in a variety of colors, from green or red to orange, yellow, ivory and purple (which mysteriously turns green when cooked). All are similar in flavor, although the red, orange and yellow varieties tend to be somewhat sweeter. In addition, all are rich in vitamins A, C and E.

Italian peppers, or frying peppers, are longer and narrower than the sweet peppers and have a somewhat more assertive flavor.

☞ At the store, look for sweet peppers that are heavy for their size and crisp-firm to the touch. They should also have a peppery fragrance; where there is little scent, there is generally little or no flavor.

☞ Store green peppers, unwashed, in plastic bags in the crisper drawer of your refrigerator for up to one week. Other peppers are fur-

USES FOR ROASTED PEPPERS

What can you do with roasted peppers? Here are a few simple ideas that you can try.

☞ **Pepper-and-cheese canapés.** Puree roasted peppers with mild goat cheese, scallions and curry powder. Spread on split pitas. Broil for 1 to 2 minutes, then cut the pitas into wedges; serve hot.

☞ **Pepper fritters.** Cut roasted peppers into strips and dredge them in flour that has been seasoned with oregano and thyme. Dip the coated strips in beaten egg, then sauté in a small amount of olive oil on both sides until golden.

☞ **Pepper-and-shrimp salad.** Cut roasted peppers into strips and toss with watercress, steamed and peeled shrimp, olive oil, lemon juice and ground toasted cumin seeds. (To toast cumin seeds, place them in a heavy, dry no-stick skillet over medium heat. Toast the seeds, shaking the skillet often, until fragrant. Then powder in a spice grinder or with a mortar and pestle.)

☞ **Antipasto.** Cut roasted peppers into strips and toss them with blanched mushrooms, minced garlic, artichoke hearts, spinach, lemon juice and olive oil.

☞ **Peppers parmigiana.** Place roasted pepper halves on a no-stick baking sheet and top each with a strip of reduced-fat mozzarella cheese. Sprinkle with grated Parmesan cheese and snipped fresh chives. Serve with crusty bread.

ROASTING PEPPERS

You don't need to go to a fancy restaurant to enjoy the smoky, full-bodied flavor of roasted peppers. Here's an easy way to do it at home.

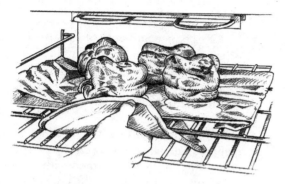

Preheat the broiler. Put whole peppers on a no-stick baking sheet covered with aluminum foil. Position the sheet so that the peppers are about 3″ below the heat source. Broil, turning the peppers often, until the skin is charred black all over and is bubbling loose from the flesh.

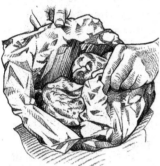

Remove from the oven. Wrap the foil loosely around the peppers and allow them to cool for about 10 minutes.

When the peppers are cool enough to handle, remove the stem and seed core. Peel off the skin with your fingers or the edge of a knife.

Scrape away remaining seeds and the ribs from the inside. Store the peppers, covered, in the refrigerator. Roasted peppers will keep for about one week.

ther along in ripeness than the green kind and won't keep as long.

☞ To prepare sweet peppers, cut them in half through the stem end. Pull out the seed area and snap off the stem. Rinse out any remaining seeds and trim away the interior ribs, using a small paring knife.

☞ When preparing peppers for stuffing, try to choose peppers that are blocky and will stand upright. If necessary, cut a sliver from the bottom of each pepper to steady it. Then cut off a slice from the top of each pepper for a lid; snap the stem out of the center. Use your fingers to remove the interior seed area and ribs.

ENUOYING ARTICHOKES

In the tender, fast-cooking world of summer vegetables, the artichoke is a tough case. Undercooked, it resembles leather; overcooked, it's a gray, mushy mess. Even when cooked to perfection, the sharp leaves or hidden choke may get you. To gain control over artichokes, follow these tips.

Lay the artichoke flat on a cutting board and slice the stem flush with the base.

Rub all cut surfaces with a piece of lemon or frequently dip the artichoke in a bowl of cold water containing a few tablespoons of lemon juice to keep it from turning dark. Reverse the artichoke and cut about 1" from the top.

Using scissors, cut off the sharp point from each leaf. Peel away the loose bottom leaves; they have a bitter taste and little meat.

Place the artichoke in a pot half-full of simmering water. (The water should cover about one-third to one-half of the artichoke.) Cook for 20 to 30 minutes, or until the lower leaves pull off easily.

To eat an artichoke, take one leaf at a time and place it between your teeth; scrape off the delectable meat that lines the inside, especially at the base. Discard the rest of the leaf and pick another one.

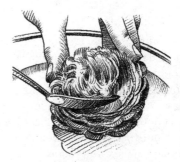

After eating the fleshy leaves, break off the thin inner leaves. You'll expose the fuzzy choke. Scoop it out with a spoon and discard it. What remains at this point is the heart—the best part.

COOKING VEGETABLES

Whereas the cold-weather crops typically require long cooking times to get even remotely tender, spring and summer vegetables are more obliging. They cook quickly and can be made crunchy-tender in just a few minutes.

Here are guidelines for the more common cooking techniques.

Steaming

Steaming is often considered the best cooking method for tender, lightweight vegetables like peas and summer squash. Steam cooks quickly and evenly, helping to retain important nutrients.

☞ Putting fresh herbs, flavored liquids like herbal vinegars or other aromatic ingredients in the cooking water lends a delicate nuance to steamed foods.

☞ Steaming is most effective when the pressure inside the pot reaches suitably high levels, so practice patience and keep the number of peeks to a minimum.

☞ Steamed food continues to cook even after you turn off the heat. Make it a point to slightly undercook food. By the time it reaches the table, it should be just right.

Boiling

Boiling is really too vigorous for many of the more delicate spring and summer vegetables. For heavier vegetables like corn on the cob, however, boiling is a good choice.

☞ For all but the toughest vegetables, it's best not to cut them into pieces smaller than an inch or two. Otherwise, you'll expose too great a surface to the rolling action of the water, leaching out nutrients and possibly leaving the food mushy and tasteless.

☞ As with steaming, boiled vegetables can be embellished by putting aromatic herbs, spices or flavorful liquids into the water.

Baking and Roasting

Cooking vegetables in the oven caramelizes their sugars, bringing out all their richness.

Baking and roasting are often recommended for firm-fleshed vegetables, such as peppers and corn on the cob, which take on a slightly smoky flavor.

Grilling

As with roasting, grilling enhances a vegetable's natural sweetness and distinctive flavors. Since grilling is a dry heat, vegetables will quickly toughen if left on too long. Cut them into slices no more than ½″ thick and turn them as soon as they turn just slightly brown.

Blanching

Blanching is used when preparing summer vegetables, such as green beans, for the freezer. To blanch a vegetable is to plunge it briefly into boiling water, then immediately into very cold water. The process kills certain enzymes that would hasten the spoilage of vegetables during freezer storage.

The technique is also helpful for intensifying the color of green vegetables that you want to serve raw. Green beans, snow peas, snap peas and asparagus turn beautifully bright when blanched for a minute.

Stir-Frying

This method of cooking, which is similar to sautéing, is both fast and healthy, as it requires very little oil.

☞ Cut vegetables into small enough pieces so that they cook rapidly. If you're mixing in heavier, denser vegetables, cut them smaller or thinner so that they'll be done in the same amount of time.

☞ Start by heating a wok or large skillet over high or medium-high heat. Add just a little bit of oil and let warm for a minute until the oil is almost but not quite at the smoking point.

☞ Add slow-cooking vegetables first, followed by those that cook more quickly.

☞ Adding a few tablespoons water and then covering the pan with a lid will cause an almost instant burst of steam, which will help speed the cooking time.

Jody Adams

Having grown up in a family where food was celebrated and everyone cooked, Jody Adams decided early on to spend much of her life in the kitchen. Now an owner of Boston's Rialto Restaurant in the Charles Hotel, she takes particular pleasure in working with summer's bounty.

"In the summer, restaurant kitchens become full of color," she says. "This crêpe-and-vegetable recipe is rich in flavor but not in fat."

Summer Corn Crêpes

Corn Crêpes
½ cup unbleached flour
3 tablespoons cornmeal
½ cup skim milk
2 eggs, lightly beaten
3 tablespoons olive oil
½ teaspoon salt
½ teaspoon pepper
2 tablespoons water

Scallion Filling
1 pound baking potatoes, peeled and chopped
⅓ cup skim milk
2 tablespoons nonfat plain yogurt
1 scallion, thinly sliced
4 black olives, pitted and chopped
2 teaspoons chopped fresh parsley
2 teaspoons chopped fresh basil
   Salt and ground black pepper
6 thin slices part-skim mozzarella cheese
12 cherry tomatoes, cut into quarters
6 long fresh chives or thin slices scallion greens

To make the corn crêpes: In a large bowl, mix the flour and cornmeal. Whisk in the milk, eggs, oil, salt and pepper. Refrigerate for at least 2 hours. Then, bring the batter to room temperature. Whisk in the water.

Coat a large no-stick skillet with no-stick spray. Warm over medium heat until hot. Add ¼ cup of the batter and tilt the skillet to coat the bottom. Cook for 2 minutes, or until the crêpe is golden on the bottom. Flip and cook for 30 seconds. Transfer to a covered plate to keep warm. Repeat with the spray and batter to make 6 crêpes.

To make the scallion filling: Place the potatoes in a large saucepan and add cold water to cover. Bring to a boil over high heat. Cook for 15 minutes, or until the potatoes are soft. Drain and mash. Stir in the milk, yogurt, scallions, olives, parsley, basil, salt and pepper.

Put a spoonful of the potato mixture in the center of each of 6 crêpes. Top each with a piece of the mozzarella and 8 tomato quarters. Pull up the sides of the crêpes to form beggars' purses (tie them shut with the chives or scallion greens).

Preheat the oven to 400°. Coat an 8″ × 8″ no-stick baking dish with no-stick spray. Add the bundles. Bake at 400° for 10 minutes.

Makes 6 servings. Per serving: 290 calories, 12.3 g. fat (38% of calories), 12.3 g. protein, 33.9 g. carbohydrates, 2.6 g. dietary fiber, 84 mg. cholesterol, 344 mg. sodium

NOTE
• Serve the crêpes with summer vegetables. In a pot of boiling salted water, blanch 2 ounces each corn kernels, peas, diced zucchini and green beans cut into 1″ pieces for 1 to 2 minutes. Drain all but 2 tablespoons of the water and stir in ½ teaspoon each chopped fresh basil and thyme. Sprinkle around the crêpes.

Stuffed Tomatoes

½ cup fresh whole-wheat bread crumbs
¼ cup grated Parmesan cheese
3 tablespoons chopped fresh basil
1 tablespoon chopped fresh parsley
⅛ teaspoon ground black pepper
2 teaspoons extra-virgin olive oil
3 medium tomatoes
2 cups hot cooked white rice

In a small bowl, combine the bread crumbs, Parmesan, basil, parsley and pepper. Mix well. Add the oil and stir until well-combined.

Slice the tomatoes in half crosswise and squeeze gently to remove the seeds. Place 2 tablespoons of the bread-crumb stuffing into each tomato, mounding slightly. Place on a broiling pan or a no-stick baking sheet coated with no-stick spray. Broil 4″ from the heat for 1 to 2 minutes, or until lightly browned. Serve with the rice.

Makes 6 servings. Per serving: 124 calories, 3.3 g. fat (24% of calories), 4 g. protein, 19.8 g. carbohydrates, 0.9 g. dietary fiber, 3 mg. cholesterol, 103 mg. sodium

NOTES

• To make fresh bread crumbs, cut bread into cubes and place the cubes in a food processor. Process with on/off turns until crumbs form.

• For a twist of flavor, try fresh lemon, cinnamon or Thai basil in place of regular basil.

Grilled Marinated Tomatoes

8 plum tomatoes
2 tablespoons rice vinegar
2 teaspoons olive oil
2 bay leaves
1 large clove garlic, minced
1½ teaspoons minced fresh thyme or basil
½ baguette, sliced

Make a lengthwise cut in each tomato, being careful not to cut the tomato in half. Gently seed and drain the tomatoes.

Coat an unheated grill rack with no-stick spray. Light the grill according to the manufacturer's directions. Place the rack on the grill. Grill or broil the tomatoes about 6″ from the heat for a total of 7 minutes. Turn them over after 5 minutes. The skins will be blistered and slightly charred.

Meanwhile, in a 9″ or 10″ round nonreactive shallow dish, combine the vinegar, oil, bay leaves, garlic and thyme or basil. Place the tomatoes in a single layer in the marinade, spooning some marinade over the tomatoes. Cover and marinate for at least 1 hour.

Serve each tomato on a slice of the baguette.

Makes 4 servings. Per serving: 87 calories, 3.2 g. fat (30% of calories), 2.6 g. protein, 14.6 g. carbohydrates, 3.3 g. dietary fiber, 0 mg. cholesterol, 46 mg. sodium

NOTES

• The tomatoes can be broiled instead of grilled.

• The marinated tomatoes can be refrigerated for up to 5 days.

Sautéed Spinach and Mushrooms

- 1 teaspoon olive oil
- 1 teaspoon toasted sesame oil
- 1½ cups sliced mushrooms
- 1 Vidalia onion, thinly sliced
- 2 cloves garlic, sliced
- 1 package (10 ounces) frozen chopped spinach, thawed and squeezed dry
- ½ teaspoon minced ginger
- 2 teaspoons reduced-sodium soy sauce

In a medium saucepan over low heat, warm the olive oil and sesame oil. Add the mushrooms, onions and garlic. Sauté for 15 to 20 minutes, or until the onions and mushrooms are soft.

Add the spinach, ginger and soy sauce. Cover and cook for 10 minutes, or until the spinach is hot.

Makes 4 servings. Per serving: 67 calories, 2.6 g. fat (31% of calories), 3.1 g. protein, 9.6 g. carbohydrates, 1.4 g. dietary fiber, 0 mg. cholesterol, 132 mg. sodium

QUICK!
Green Beans with Peppers and Artichokes

- 12 ounces small red potatoes
- 8 ounces green beans
- 1 cup chopped roasted red peppers
- 8 water-packed artichoke hearts, halved
- ⅓ cup tarragon vinegar
- 1 tablespoon olive oil
- 1 teaspoon Dijon mustard
- 1 clove garlic, minced
- ½ teaspoon dried marjoram
- ¼ teaspoon ground black pepper
- ¼ teaspoon Worcestershire sauce

In a large saucepan, bring 1″ water to a boil. Place the potatoes on a steaming rack and set the rack in the pan. Cover and steam for 15 minutes, or until tender; set aside to cool. When cool enough to handle, slice thinly and place in a large bowl.

Blanch the beans in boiling water for 5 minutes. Drain and add to the bowl with the potatoes.

Add the peppers and artichoke hearts. Toss to combine.

In a small bowl, whisk together the vinegar, oil, mustard, garlic, marjoram, black pepper and Worcestershire sauce. Pour over the vegetables and toss to combine.

Makes 4 servings. Per serving: 172 calories, 5.8 g. fat (30% of calories), 3.7 g. protein, 30.5 g. carbohydrates, 2.1 g. dietary fiber, 0 mg. cholesterol, 113 mg. sodium

QUICK!
Mediterranean Green Beans

- 1 pound green beans, cut into 1″ pieces
- 2 teaspoons butter-flavored sprinkles
- 2 teaspoons minced fresh rosemary or basil
- 1 teaspoon grated lemon rind
- 1 teaspoon olive oil
- ⅛ teaspoon ground black pepper

In a large saucepan, bring 1″ water to a boil. Place the beans on a steaming rack and set the rack in the pan. Cover and steam for 5 minutes, or until tender. Place in a large bowl. Sprinkle with the butter-flavored sprinkles, rosemary or basil, lemon rind, oil and pepper. Toss to coat well.

Makes 4 servings. Per serving: 39 calories, 1.3 g. fat (30% of calories), 1.4 g. protein, 6.5 g. carbohydrates, 0.01 g. dietary fiber, 0 mg. cholesterol, 43 mg. sodium

Minted Snap Peas with Peppers

QUICK!

1 teaspoon olive oil
1 sweet red pepper, cut into strips
¼ cup chopped fresh mint
1 clove garlic, minced
1 pound snap peas
½ cup defatted chicken broth
¼ teaspoon ground black pepper

In a medium saucepan over low heat, warm the oil. Add the red peppers, mint and garlic. Sauté for 3 minutes, or until the peppers are soft.

Stir in the snap peas, broth and black pepper. Bring to a boil over high heat. Reduce the heat to medium-low. Cover and cook for 4 minutes, or just until the peas are tender.

Makes 4 servings. Per serving: 126 calories, 1.6 g. fat (11% of calories), 7.3 g. protein, 21.9 g. carbohydrates, 1.1 g. dietary fiber, 0 mg. cholesterol, 46 mg. sodium

Sauté of Peas and Mushrooms

QUICK!

2 teaspoons olive oil
2 scallions, thinly sliced
1 clove garlic, minced
6 ounces mushrooms, sliced
2 cups fresh or frozen peas
2 teaspoons water
½ teaspoon dried thyme
⅛ teaspoon salt
⅛ teaspoon ground black pepper
¾ teaspoon balsamic vinegar

In a large no-stick skillet over medium heat, warm the oil. Add the scallions and garlic. Sauté for 3 minutes. Stir in the mushrooms. Cover and cook for 3 minutes. Add the peas, water and thyme. Reduce the heat to medium-low. Cover and cook for 5 minutes, or until the peas are tender.

Stir in the salt, pepper and vinegar.

Makes 4 servings. Per serving: 101 calories, 2.6 g. fat (22% of calories), 5.3 g. protein, 15.2 g. carbohydrates, 3.4 g. dietary fiber, 0 mg. cholesterol, 71 mg. sodium

Spicy Southwest Corn

QUICK!

1 teaspoon olive oil
2 scallions, thinly sliced
½ cup chopped sweet red peppers
3 cloves garlic, minced
2 cups fresh or frozen corn
2 cups peeled, seeded and chopped tomatoes
1 teaspoon chili powder
½ teaspoon ground cumin
½ teaspoon ground coriander
½ teaspoon dried oregano
⅛ teaspoon hot-pepper sauce

In a medium saucepan over medium heat, warm the oil. Add the scallions and red peppers. Sauté for 2 minutes.

Stir in the garlic, corn, tomatoes, chili powder, cumin, coriander, oregano and hot-pepper sauce. Bring to a boil. Reduce the heat to low and cook, stirring occasionally, for 20 minutes, or until the mixture is thickened.

Makes 4 servings. Per serving: 118 calories, 1.8 g. fat (12% of calories), 4.2 g. protein, 25.7 g. carbohydrates, 3.9 g. dietary fiber, 0 mg. cholesterol, 22 mg. sodium

Succotash

QUICK!

Traditional succotash is cooked with salt pork and whole milk. We slimmed down this American classic by replacing the salt pork with margarine or butter and omitting the milk. Fresh dill, parsley and a pinch of paprika add wonderful flavor—without the fat!

2	teaspoons nondiet tub-style margarine or butter
½	cup thinly sliced scallions
1	clove garlic, minced
¾	cup cooked green beans, cut into 1″ pieces
½	cup frozen baby lima beans, thawed
½	cup cooked or canned navy beans, rinsed and drained
½	cup fresh or frozen corn, thawed
2	teaspoons chopped fresh dill
2	teaspoons chopped fresh parsley
⅛	teaspooon paprika
⅛	teaspoon ground black pepper

In a large no-stick skillet over medium heat, melt the margarine or butter. Add the scallions and sauté for 1 minute.

Stir in the garlic, green beans, lima beans, navy beans and corn. Sauté over medium heat for 3 minutes, or until the vegetables are cooked and the mixture is hot. Stir in the dill, parsley, paprika and pepper.

Makes 4 servings. Per serving: 102 calories, 2.2 g. fat (18% of calories), 4.8 g. protein, 17.4 g. carbohydrates, 4 g. dietary fiber, 0 mg. cholesterol, 35 mg. sodium

NOTE
• If you like your succotash with milk, add ¼ cup skim milk after sautéing the vegetables. Cook for 3 minutes, or until the liquid is slightly reduced.

Asparagus and Couscous

¾	cup couscous
1½	cups defatted chicken broth
¼	cup chopped fresh basil
2	tablespoons toasted pine nuts (see note)
1	teaspoon olive oil
2	small leeks, thinly sliced (white part only)
1	small shallot, minced
8	ounces trimmed asparagus, cut into 1″ pieces
½	teaspoon ground black pepper
¼	teaspoon hot-pepper sauce

Preheat the oven to 350°.

Place the couscous in a 2-quart no-stick baking dish with a tight-fitting lid. Stir in 1¼ cups of the broth, basil and pine nuts. Set aside, uncovered, for 15 minutes. Cover and bake for 20 minutes.

Meanwhile, in a large no-stick skillet over medium heat, warm the oil. Add the leeks and shallots. Sauté for 5 minutes, or until the leeks are soft. Add the asparagus, black pepper, hot-pepper sauce and the remaining ¼ cup broth. Bring to a boil. Reduce the heat to medium-low, cover and simmer for 5 minutes, or until the asparagus is just tender and all of the liquid has been absorbed. Remove from the heat.

Add the asparagus to the couscous and fluff with a fork.

Makes 4 servings. Per serving: 227 calories, 4.2 g. fat (16% of calories), 9.8 g. protein, 39.5 g. carbohydrates, 6.7 g. dietary fiber, 0 mg. cholesterol, 149 mg. sodium

NOTE
• To toast pine nuts, place them in a dry no-stick skillet over medium heat. Toast the nuts, shaking the skillet often, for 3 to 5 minutes, or until fragrant and golden.

Eggplant Caponata

1 eggplant, peeled and cut into 1" cubes
½ teaspoon salt
1 teaspoon olive oil
1 cup chopped fresh or canned tomatoes, drained
1 sweet red pepper, chopped
1 green pepper, chopped
1 onion, chopped
3 cloves garlic, minced
15 imported black olives, pitted and chopped
¼ cup drained capers
¼ cup chopped fresh parsley
2 tablespoons chopped fresh marjoram
1 tablespoon red-wine vinegar

Place the eggplant in a colander and sprinkle with the salt. Set aside to drain for 20 minutes. Rinse and pat dry with paper towels.

In a large no-stick skillet over medium-high heat, warm the oil. Add the eggplant and sauté for 2 minutes. Add the tomatoes, red peppers, green peppers, onions and garlic. Reduce the heat and simmer for 10 minutes, stirring occasionally. Stir in the olives, capers, parsley, marjoram and vinegar. Transfer to a large bowl. Cover and let sit for at least 2 hours before serving, or refrigerate overnight.

Makes 4 servings. Per serving: 115 calories, 4.4 g. fat (34% of calories), 3.5 g. protein, 20.4 g. carbohydrates, 3.1 g. dietary fiber, 0 mg. cholesterol, 400 mg. sodium

Zucchini Marinara

QUICK!

1 small onion, thinly sliced
2 medium tomatoes, seeded and chopped
1 clove garlic, minced
1 tablespoon minced fresh parsley
1 tablespoon minced fresh basil
½ teaspoon minced fresh marjoram or ¼ teaspoon dried
⅛ teaspoon cracked black pepper
1½ cups zucchini sliced ¼"-thick on the diagonal
2 tablespoons shredded reduced-fat mozzarella cheese (optional)

Coat a large no-stick skillet with no-stick spray. Warm the skillet over medium heat. Add the onions and sauté for 4 minutes. Stir in the tomatoes, garlic, parsley, basil, marjoram and pepper. Cook, stirring occasionally, for 2 minutes, or until heated through.

Stir in the zucchini. Cover and cook, stirring occasionally, for 5 minutes more, or until the zucchini is crisp-tender.

Transfer the mixture to a serving dish. Sprinkle with the mozzarella (if using).

Makes 4 servings. Per serving: 29 calories, 0.3 g. fat (8% of calories), 1.4 g. protein, 6.4 g. carbohydrates, 1.6 g. dietary fiber, 0 mg. cholesterol, 8 mg. sodium

Stuffed Zucchini

- 4 medium zucchini
- 1 small onion, chopped
- 8 medium mushrooms, chopped
- ⅔ cup unseasoned dry bread crumbs
- 1½ cups reduced-sodium tomato sauce
- ½ cup chopped canned water chestnuts
- 2 teaspoons dried oregano
- ⅛ teaspoon ground black pepper
- 1 tablespoon shredded reduced-fat Parmesan cheese

Cut the zucchini in half lengthwise. Remove and discard the pulp and seeds, leaving a ½″ shell. Set aside.

Coat a medium no-stick skillet with no-stick spray. Warm the skillet over medium heat. Add the onions and sauté for 4 minutes, or until soft. Transfer to a large mixing bowl.

To the bowl, add the mushrooms, bread crumbs, tomato sauce, water chestnuts, oregano and black pepper. Mix well.

Stuff each zucchini half with an equal amount of the filling. Sprinkle with the Parmesan.

Preheat the oven to 350°. Coat an 9″ × 13″ no-stick baking dish with no-stick spray. Place the filled zucchini in the dish. Cover and bake for 30 minutes. Uncover and bake for 10 minutes, or until the cheese is lightly browned.

Makes 4 servings. Per serving: 153 calories, 1.5 g. fat (9% of calories), 6.8 g. protein, 29.5 g. carbohydrates, 3.8 g. dietary fiber, 0 mg. cholesterol, 209 mg. sodium

Turkey Sausage–Stuffed Peppers

- 4 sweet red, yellow or orange peppers
- 4 ounces turkey sausage patties
- 1 cup chopped onions
- 1 cup chopped mushrooms
- 1 clove garlic, minced
- ¼ teaspoon dried thyme
- 1 cup unseasoned dry bread crumbs
- 1 tablespoon minced fresh parsley
- 1 tablespoon grated Parmesan cheese
- 2 cups hot cooked white rice

Cut the tops off the peppers, about 1″ down. Remove the seeds and ribs, being careful not to tear or rip the peppers. In a medium saucepan, blanch them in gently boiling water for 6 minutes, or until they are soft but still retain their shape. Drain well.

Meanwhile, crumble the sausage into a no-stick skillet over medium-high heat. Brown for 5 minutes, or until the sausage is no longer pink, stirring occasionally. Remove the sausage and set aside. Wipe the pan clean.

Set the pan over medium-high heat. Add the onions and mushrooms. Sauté for 1 minute. Add the garlic and thyme. Cover; cook for 3 minutes, or until soft. Remove from the heat. Stir in the sausage, bread crumbs and parsley.

Preheat the oven to 375°.

Stuff the peppers with the sausage mixture. Sprinkle with the Parmesan. Place the peppers upright in an 8″ × 8″ no-stick baking dish. Pour ¼″ water into the dish. Bake for 15 minutes, or until heated through. Turn on the broiler and broil about 6″ from the heat for 3 minutes, or until the Parmesan is lightly browned. Serve over the rice.

Makes 4 servings. Per serving: 359 calories, 7.2 g. fat (17% of calories), 14.3 g. protein, 61.7 g. carbohydrates, 3.0 g. dietary fiber, 17 mg. cholesterol, 447 mg. sodium

Winter Vegetables

The so-called winter vegetables include root crops like potatoes, carrots, parsnips, onions, turnips and rutabagas as well as broccoli, celery, cauliflower, winter squash and more. They're not necessarily grown in the winter, but they're the items that keep well and that traditionally carried people through the cold months until tender greens, ripe tomatoes, fresh asparagus and other perishables made their appearance in the spring and summer.

These vegetables are enormously versatile and, in most cases, remarkably easy to prepare. Squash and potatoes, for instance, can be baked in their skins and served whole; carrots, fennel, turnips and parsnips can be steamed or boiled; broccoli and cauliflower florets can be stir-fried as part of a main course or kept raw for munching.

Like other vegetables, these hearty varieties are high in fiber, complex carbohydrates and various vitamins. Some, like deep orange squashes, carrots and sweet potatoes, are excellent sources of beta-carotene, which may help prevent heart disease and certain types of cancer. Others, including broccoli, cauliflower, cabbage, brussels sprouts and turnips, are cruciferous vegetables and, as such, also have cancer-preventing properties. Like other vegetables, all have no cholesterol and hardly any sodium or fat. For healthy, low-calorie eating, they can't be beat.

FROM STORE TO KITCHEN

Whether you do most of your harvesting in your garden, at a well-stocked farmers market or at the nearest supermarket, remember that even the hearty winter vegetables won't stay fresh forever. To keep your produce in peak condition, here's what chefs advise.

Store them dry. It's best not to wash winter vegetables until you're ready to prepare them. Otherwise, the moisture from washing will hasten their decay during storage. This applies to both vegetables that are stored in the refrigerator and those kept at room temperature.

Cater to individual needs. While it's true that most winter vegetables are best kept dry during storage, there are exceptions. Radishes, for example, have a very short shelf life. To keep them from withering, store them, uncovered, in a bowl of water in the refrigerator.

Take a little off the top. When storing root vegetables like beets and carrots, always remove any green tops first. Otherwise, the growing part of the plant will rob the root of its moisture, taking away crunch and freshness.

Don't smother them. Store stalk and leaf vegetables like fennel and cabbage in the refrigerator and keep them in perforated plastic bags in the vegetable bin. This will help them retain moisture, while at the same time allowing fresh air to circulate.

Turn out the lights. Winter squash and root vegetables like potatoes will keep longest—months, in some cases—when stored in a cool, dark, dry place. If you don't have an appropriate basement or storage closet, put them in a hanging basket in a dark corner to help keep them fresh. Darkness will help prevent potatoes from sprouting or getting a bitter-tasting green tinge to them. Do not store potatoes in the refrigerator, because they'll turn inappropriately sweet and the flesh may darken when you cook them.

Give them breathing room. Even when root vegetables are put into dark storage, they still need ample air circulation in order to stay fresh. Spread such things as squash, potatoes and onions in a single layer, far enough apart so that they're not touching. Piling them in a heap will save space, but when vegetables are stored for a long time, this will also restrict air flow, increase dampness and hasten decay.

Don't let them fraternize. Some fruits and vegetables simply aren't meant to reside together. Stored apples, for example, release ethylene gas, which will cause carrots to turn bitter. Similarly, storing onions and potatoes together will cause the potatoes to spoil faster.

PREPARING VEGETABLES

Autumn and winter vegetables in their whole states are exceptionally hardy, but once they've been cut, they lose freshness fast. As with other vegetables, it's best to cut them just before you're ready to cook.

While each vegetable must be cut to fit the recipe that you're preparing, here are a few guidelines to keep in mind.

For cooking speed, cut them small. Since many hardy vegetables consist of dense, fibrous

Helpful Hint

To prevent onions from going bad, store them in the leg of an old stocking, knotted at the bottom and hung in a dark, cool place. When you need a fresh onion, cut the knot, remove the bottom onion, then tie the stocking shut again.

Helpful Hint

To keep onions from reducing you to tears as you chop, don't cut off the root end until the last minute, because that's where most of the tear-causing compounds are stored. Alternatively, freeze onions for about 20 minutes before chopping.

tissue, you can substantially hasten their cooking times by cutting them into pieces that are smaller than 1″.

For healthy cooking, cut them large. Cutting vegetables into small pieces exposes large surface areas, which in turn increases the amount of nutrients that might be lost during cooking. When time permits, try cutting vegetables larger rather than smaller in order to preserve valuable vitamins along with texture and crunch.

For convenience, look for packaged. While canned and frozen vegetables don't quite have the pizzazz of their fresher counterparts, they still work well in a pinch and provide valuable minerals and vitamins as well as color and variety to your meal.

Frozen vegetables can pretty much be used straight from the bag or box. With canned, however, always drain and rinse well to remove some of the sodium that was added during processing. Check labels when buying both frozen and canned vegetables to make sure that you're not getting butter sauces, heavy syrup or other ingredients that you don't want.

Potatoes

While most of us give scant thought to the lumpy, humble little spud, there are many varieties of potatoes. They aren't necessarily interchangeable; potatoes that work well for one

(continued on page 381)

Hearty Vegetables

Unlike their warm-weather counterparts, winter vegetables tend to keep well. But since they may already have spent time in transit and on the grocer's shelf, try to use them within a reasonable period. That applies especially to those vegetables that require refrigeration; use them within a week.

The following storage and preparation tips will help you preserve the fresh flavors and nutrients of your vegetables.

Vegetable	Storage and Preparation
Beets	Cut off tops 2˝ above root (save greens, if desired, to steam, sauté or eat raw); refrigerate in plastic bags. Scrub and boil whole in water to cover until easily pierced with a skewer; drain, cool and slip off skin. Alternatively, bake or microwave until tender.
Bok choy (pak choi)	Refrigerate in plastic bags. To use, cut off the bottom of the bunch; wash well. Remove the leafy tops and shred or chop them; cut stems into slices. Stir-fry, sauté or microwave both parts until tender.
Broccoflower	Refrigerate in plastic bags. To use, remove and discard any leaves. Break or cut florets from woody core; discard the core. Cook until just tender. Good methods: steam; cook, covered, in a small amount of water; cook, uncovered, in a large pot of water; stir-fry; microwave.
Broccoli	Refrigerate in plastic bags. Soak in cold water for 10 minutes to remove insects, especially if grown without pesticides. Remove tough outer leaves and cut tough ends off stalks. Slice or split stalks for quicker cooking. If desired, separate florets from stalks. Cook until just tender. Good methods: steam; stir-fry; cook, uncovered, in a large pot of water; microwave.
Broccoli rabe (broccoli raab, rapini)	Refrigerate in plastic bags. To use, rinse; trim off tough stem ends; if necessary, remove strings from large stalks as with celery. Cut stalks into small sections; shred or otherwise cut leaves; leave florets whole. Steam, stir-fry or boil in a small amount of water until tender.
Brussels sprouts	Refrigerate in plastic bags. Trim the bottoms and peel away discolored outer leaves. Halve large sprouts lengthwise; otherwise, cook whole (cut an X in the bottom for more even cooking). Cook until easily pierced with a sharp knife. Good methods: steam; boil, covered, in a small amount of water; boil, uncovered, in a large pot of water; microwave.
Cabbage: green, red, savoy, Chinese	Remove and discard tough or ragged outer leaves. Refrigerate in plastic bags. Halve or quarter and cut out inner core. Shred, slice or cut into wedges. Use raw or steam, sauté or microwave until just tender.
Carrots	Cut off any green tops; refrigerate in plastic bags. Either scrub with a vegetable brush or peel. Cut as desired. Serve raw or cook until just tender. Good methods: steam; cook, covered, in a small amount of water; cook, uncovered, in a large pot of water; stir-fry; roast; microwave.
Cauliflower	Remove and discard leaves; refrigerate in plastic bags. Break or cut florets from woody core of head; discard the core. Serve raw or cook until just tender. Good methods: steam; cook, covered, in a small amount of water; cook, uncovered, in a large pot of water; stir-fry; microwave.
Celery	Refrigerate in plastic bags. Break ribs from the bunch and wash. If desired, remove leaves; trim tough ends from ribs. Slice as desired; serve raw, sauté or cook, covered, in a small amount of water.

Vegetable	Storage and Preparation
Fennel (Florence fennel sweet anise)	Remove coarse or ragged outer layers; trim off stalks and feathery tops. Refrigerate in plastic bags. May be eaten raw. Halve or quarter for oven or stove-top braising. Cut as desired to steam or cook, covered, in a small amount of water.
Jícama	Buy firm, dry tubers with unblemished brown skin. Refrigerate in plastic bags. Peel just before using. Eat raw or cut as desired and steam or cook, covered, in a small amount of water until just tender but still crunchy.
Kale	Refrigerate in plastic bags. Wash just before using. Remove thick stems; tear or cut the leaves as desired. Eat raw, stir-fry or cook or microwave until just wilted in only the water that clings to the leaves from washing.
Kohlrabi: green or purple	Choose small, firm bulbs less than 3″ in diameter. Refrigerate in plastic bags. Peel; save crisp, tender greens for salads. Steam or cook bulbs, covered, in a small amount of simmering water until tender.
Leeks	Refrigerate in plastic bags. To use, remove damaged outer leaves, trim off tough green tops, trim root end. Halve lengthwise and wash under cold running water, fanning the layers to remove sandy grit from between them. Cut as desired. Braise, sauté, stir-fry or microwave until tender.
Onions	Store in net bags in a cool, dry, dark place. Peel and slice or chop as desired. Eat raw or bake, braise, stir-fry, sauté, steam or microwave until tender.
Parsnips	Refrigerate in plastic bags. Wash well, peel and cut off ends. Cut as desired; if inner core is woody, remove it. Bake, braise, microwave or cook, covered, in a small amount of water until tender.
Potatoes	Store in a cool, dry, dark place; do not refrigerate. Scrub well and remove any sprouts. Bake, steam or microwave whole and unpeeled. Or peel, cut as desired and cook until easily pierced with a fork: boil, steam, sauté or microwave.
Radishes: red, icicle, daikon, black	Refrigerate in plastic bags or in a bowl of water. Scrub and trim tops and roots. Peel if desired. Cut or slice as desired. Eat raw or cook, covered, in a small amount of water until tender.
Rutabagas	Store in a cool, dry, dark place. Peel to remove thick waxy coating. Cut or slice as desired. Cook until tender. Good methods: boil, steam or microwave.
Sweet potatoes	Store in a cool, dry, dark place. Scrub and bake whole until easily pierced with a sharp knife. Or peel, cut as desired and boil until tender.
Turnips	Cut off roots and greens. Refrigerate in plastic bags. Scrub; peel thinly, if desired. Leave whole or cut as desired and boil until tender.
Winter squash	Store in a cool, dry place. Scrub and cut in half lengthwise; remove seeds and stringy pulp. If size warrants, cut into smaller pieces. Bake, steam or microwave large pieces until tender. If desired, cut raw flesh into cubes (peel if desired); steam, microwave, bake or boil.

PROPER PEELING

While the thick-skinned winter vegetables are easy to peel with a paring knife or swivel-bladed peeler, some of their thin-skinned kin—like onions, garlic and shallots—can confound the nimblest of hands. Plus, their pungent oils will bring the strongest chef to tears. To peel quickly and without pain, here's what food experts recommend.

ONIONS

Cut off the top. Leave the root end intact to minimize tear-producing power.

Make a shallow cut lengthwise through the top layer of skin. Repeat on the other side.

Grip the skin near the cut and peel away.

GARLIC

Place a clove on a cutting board. With your hand, press the flat side of a wide knife blade down on the clove to split the skin.

Grip the loose skin near the split and gently peel it away.

SHALLOTS

Cut off the tops but not the root end.

Using the edge of a knife or your fingers, pull away the topmost layer of skin, taking the first layer of flesh along with it.

SPUD SECRETS

Potatoes are the perfect food. Inexpensive, long-keeping and easy to cook, they're packed with energy-rich carbohydrates. For super baked spuds every time, follow these tips.

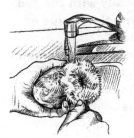

With a stiff brush, scrub the potatoes under running water.

Prick the skin with a fork or knife to prevent steam from building up inside during cooking.

Bake the potatoes at 375° for about 1 hour. When done, the flesh will yield to slight finger pressure, and a sharp knife will easily pierce the potatoes.

Roll each potato on the counter to crumble the flesh inside. Then use a fork to pierce an X into the skin. Squeezing the potato at both ends will cause it to pop open.

recipe may be totally wrong for another. Here are the major types.

☞ **Waxy potatoes.** Generally known as round whites or round reds, waxy potatoes are low in starch and contain more moisture than some other varieties. Because they hold their shape well, waxy potatoes are often used in soups and salads.

☞ **Mealy or starchy potatoes.** Spuds like russet potatoes are high in starch and have a somewhat mealy, or floury, interior. Because of their fluffy texture, they are ideal for mashed or baked potatoes.

☞ **All-purpose potatoes.** When you're not sure what's on the menu, buying a long white or other all-purpose potato is a good compromise. As a rule, all-purpose potatoes work for boiling, sautéing, steaming and roasting. But as with other jacks-of-all-trades, they don't excel in any single area.

In addition, there are a lot of interesting new varieties, with flesh that can range from yellow or pink to blue or purple. They vary as to what they're best suited for; ask for clarification when you buy them.

No matter what kind of potatoes you're buying, make sure that they're firm and free of blemishes. Avoid any that are sprouted, cracked or wrinkled. A green tinge is a sign of overexposure to light; greenish flesh is bitter. If potatoes that you have at home develop green areas, cut the green areas off.

All potatoes discolor quickly when exposed to air, so careful preparation is important. When peeling or slicing potatoes, quickly submerge the pieces in a bowl of cold water until you're ready to begin cooking. Then drain them well. Unless you'll be cooking them in liquid, blot up excess moisture with paper towels.

Cabbages

The cabbage family consists not only of the familiar red and green heads—which often seem raised for the sole purpose of ending up in coleslaw—but also of broccoli, broccoli rabe, brussels sprouts, cauliflower, kohlrabi and many more.

☞ When preparing cabbage, slice the head in half lengthwise and use a sharp knife to cut out the inner core, which is too tough to eat. Don't cook cabbage—or other cruciferous vegetables—too long. Prolonged exposure to heat causes essential oils to break down, which results in a powerful, sulfury smell.

☞ For bok choy, cut off the leafy top from the celery-like stalk. The greens cook more quickly than the stalks, so add them later in the cooking process or prepare them separately.

☞ When preparing napa cabbage, separate the tough, central part of the leaf from the frilly, delicate leaf surrounding it. Again, remember that the thin parts cook more quickly.

Helpful Hint

When preparing red cabbage, always use a stainless steel knife, because carbon steel interacts chemically with the red pigment and turns the leaves an unappealing blue.

Adding a little acid, like lemon juice or vinegar, to the cooking water will also keep red cabbage from turning blue.

☞ Brussels sprouts possess a combination of tender leaves and tough stalks, which makes it difficult to coordinate cooking times. Cook them too long, and the leaves lose their crunch; not long enough, and the core area stays tough.

To cook brussels sprouts evenly, first remove

TRIMMING BRUSSELS SPROUTS

It takes a little work to transform these tough, tightly packed little knobs into a tasty—and fork-tender—treat.

With a sharp knife, carefully trim the bitter bottom.

Peel off any dry or yellowing leaves.

Cut a shallow X in the bottom of each stem. This will allow the stem area to cook at about the same rate as the more delicate leaves.

PREPARING SQUASH

With their robust flavors and lushly colored flesh, winter squash will liven up any meal.

Cut the squash in half lengthwise. The smooth, tough skin resists the knife, so be sure to hold it firmly so that it doesn't slip.

With a metal spoon, remove the seeds and stringy membranes from the center.

To bake the squash, place it, cut side down, in a large no-stick baking dish. Add ¼" of water to the dish to prevent the flesh from drying. Bake at 350° for 45 to 60 minutes, or until easily pierced with a knife or fork.

any damaged outer leaves. Trim the bottom even with the leaves. Then use a sharp paring knife to pierce an X about ¼" deep in the bottom of each stem, which will help the stem area cook more rapidly.

Squash

Squash are extremely versatile and work equally well as side dishes or main courses. They make great additions to hearty stews and can even be pureed and used as a soup base.

☞ Squash have rigid shells, making them difficult to peel raw. Types with an irregular surface, like acorn, are especially hard to deal with. An easier method is to cook them in the shell and scoop out the flesh afterward.

☞ To bake squash, cut it in half, scoop out the seeds and place the pieces, cut side down, in a baking dish. Add a little water to prevent scorching and bake at 350° for 45 to 60 minutes, or until easily pierced with a knife or fork.

☞ Acorn squash can be microwaved whole. Pierce one several times with a sharp knife. Microwave on high power, rotating the squash occasionally, for 12 to 15 minutes, or until easily pierced with a knife. Let stand a few minutes before cutting and removing the seeds.

☞ To speed cooking times, winter squash can be cut into smaller pieces and either baked in the oven, steamed or microwaved.

Root Vegetables

Some of the foods commonly known as root vegetables aren't roots at all, but are actually swollen stems and food storage organs (called corms) that grow underground—buried in earth or submerged in water. Jerusalem artichokes are an example. Even onions are technically bulbs.

Still, the root vegetables have one thing in common. Since they function as nutrient reservoirs for the leafy plants, they're rich sources of starches, sugars, vitamins and minerals. Plus, their earthy flavors are among the glories of cold-weather dining.

☞ When buying fresh parsnips, especially if you get them directly from the grower at a farmers market or roadside stand, wait until the weather really turns nippy. The sweetest parsnips come to market after the first frost or even after a hard freeze.

☞ With the exception of carrots and young vegetables, most root vegetables that you buy at the store have peels that are tough and bitter. These should be removed before cooking.

☞ For thin-skinned vegetables like young carrots or potatoes, a vigorous rubbing with a vegetable brush under cold running water is really all the processing that they need.

☞ An obvious exception to the peel-first rule is the baking potato. The peel is left on during baking, not only to provide additional fiber, nutrients and flavor but also to trap heat and steam. Essentially, the skin acts like a miniature oven during cooking.

☞ Peeling root vegetables too deeply can remove valuable nutrients. To prevent this, chefs recommend using a swivel peeler. This removes the outer skin without taking too much of the nutritious flesh beneath.

COOKING VEGETABLES

Few ingredients are both as versatile and as easy to cook as winter vegetables. The only real challenge is judging how long to cook them.

Steaming

Steaming is a wonderful way to preserve the vital, fresh flavor and nutrients of winter vegetbles like baby carrots, young beets and new potatoes.

☞ Heavier vegetables, like whole or halved winter squash, can be steamed, although their larger size and dense flesh can make the cooking time prohibitively long. To speed things along, cut them into 1″ pieces before steaming. Where relatively easy and practical, as with butternut squash, peel the pieces before cooking.

CORING CARROTS

Unless you have the teeth of Bugs Bunny and the bite of Jaws, some supermarket carrots are simply too big, thick and tough to munch. Removing the woody core will take the toughness out while leaving the tenderness in.

Trim off the ends, then slice the entire carrot in half lengthwise. The fibrous core should be clearly visible.

Slip a small paring knife beneath the core and carefully pry it free.

☞ When steaming young, tender vegetables, leave them whole to help retain nutrients as well as their characteristic texture.

☞ Don't overload the steamer. It's best to spread vegetables in a shallow, even layer. This allows the cooking steam to reach each piece easily and evenly.

Boiling

Since this method completely immerses food in rolling, high-temperature liquid, it's often preferred for heavy, dense vegetables like beets and brussels sprouts or for large whole vegetables like potatoes that would otherwise take too long to cook if sautéed.

☞ When boiling, use just enough water to cover the vegetables.

☞ As soon as vegetables are tender, pour them into a colander to drain, then serve at once.

☞ When cooking vegetables for later use, put them in a colander, then rinse well with cold water. This stops the cooking process, so that the vegetables don't get mushy.

Baking and Roasting

Few things are as satisfying as the hearty, full flavor of a vegetable that's been baked or roasted. Roasting tends to use a higher temperature that caramelizes the exterior of the vegetable, giving it a crisp golden skin, moist interior and sweet, rich taste (most of the water of the vegetable evaporates, so the natural sugars are concentrated).

Vegetables that are especially wonderful when roasted include russet and other nonwaxy potatoes, sweet potatoes, onions, garlic, carrots, beets, squash, parsnips, rutabagas and turnips.

Baking is the simplest method for preparing any vegetable that can be cooked in its skin. It is also the method used to prepare vegetable gratins, and it is the last step for cooked stuffed vegetables like acorn squash.

Parboiling

The term *parboiling* is sometimes used interchangeably with blanching, but the techniques

Helpful Hint

Leave beets unpeeled during cooking. Also, avoid trimming the root end and leave about 1″ of the tops in place. Otherwise, the red inside will bleed out, depleting the vibrant color.

aren't the same. Both involve immersing vegetables in boiling water for brief periods. Blanching is followed by plunging the food into cold water to stop the cooking process.

Parboiling takes longer and partially cooks the vegetable. This technique is often used to ready a vegetable for another cooking treatment. For example, it's used to tenderize a dense vegetable like a potato before finishing it on the grill or a carrot before adding it to a stir-fry.

To parboil a vegetable, reduce its typical boiling time by a third.

Grilling

As with roasting, grilling brings out the essence of winter vegetables. It enhances their natural sweetness and distinctive flavors. However, these vegetables are often too dense for the rapid cooking that occurs during grilling. To prevent them from being burnt on the outside and raw on the inside, parboil or microwave them first. Then transfer them to the grill for final cooking.

Microwaving

This can save a lot of time, especially for slow-cooking squash, beets and other dense vegetables. However, microwaving tends to leave the skin soggy, much the way steaming does, so it is better not to use this method for vegetables that are typically served in a dry skin, like baked or sweet potatoes. One way around this dilemma is to partially cook the vegetable in the microwave, then transfer it to the oven to finish cooking and to crisp the skin.

Johanne Killeen and George Germon

Most of the cooking at Al Forno Restaurant in Providence, Rhode Island, is done in wood-burning ovens or on open-flame grills. (The name *Al Forno* means "from the oven.") For owners Johanne Killeen and George Germon, simplicity—both in ingredients and cooking

techniques—is the key to great cooking.

"Though we hate to say good-bye to summer, we look forward to fall, when the farmers' stands are filled with rutabagas, beets, Westport turnips and all sorts of potatoes," says Killeen. For this recipe she recommends

roasting the potatoes in a sturdy ceramic baking dish with a tight-fitting lid.

Or you can wrap the potatoes in heavy-duty aluminum foil. You can use any combination of your favorite fresh herbs; plan on using about 1½ ounces, including the tender stems.

Herb-Infused Roasted Potatoes

- 2 pounds small red potatoes (about 16)
- 3 sprigs fresh rosemary
- 2 sprigs fresh sage
- 1 sprig fresh fennel
- 2 bay leaves
- 2 sprigs fresh parsley
- 3 sprigs fresh oregano
- 2 sprigs fresh basil
- 1 teaspoon coarse sea salt or table salt

Preheat the oven to 400°.

Place a layer of the potatoes in a 2-quart baking dish. Top with a layer of the rosemary, sage, fennel, bay leaves, parsley, oregano, basil and a sprinkle of the salt. Repeat to make 1 or 2 more layers and to use all the potatoes, herbs and salt. Cover tightly.

Roast for 1¼ hours, or until the potatoes are tender when pierced with a fork.

Makes 6 servings. Per serving: 224 calories, 0.3 g. fat (1% of calories), 4.8 g. protein, 51.8 g. carbohydrates, 0 g. dietary fiber, 0 mg. cholesterol, 372 mg. sodium

Mashed Potatoes

QUICK!

These mashed potatoes are as creamy as the ones Mom used to make. Low-fat milk and nonfat sour cream replace the traditional butter and whole milk.

   1½   pounds potatoes, peeled and cubed
   1½   teaspoons nondiet tub-style margarine
   1½   teaspoons butter-flavored sprinkles
  ½–¾   cup 1% low-fat milk, warmed
   ¼   cup nonfat sour cream
   ½   teaspoon salt
   ¼   teaspoon ground black pepper
   ¼   teaspoon paprika

    Place the potatoes in a large saucepan and cover with cold water. Bring to a boil over medium-high heat. Boil for 10 to 15 minutes, or until the potatoes are tender when pierced with a fork. Drain well.

    Return the potatoes to the pan or transfer to a large bowl. Add the margarine and butter-flavored sprinkles. Using a potato masher or an electric mixer, mash the potatoes thoroughly. Beat in the milk and sour cream, ¼ cup at a time, until the desired consistency is reached. Beat in the salt, pepper and paprika.

Makes 4 servings. Per serving: 169 calories, 1.9 g. fat (10% of calories), 4.6 g. protein, 34.1 g. carbohydrates, 0 g. dietary fiber, 1 mg. cholesterol, 341 mg. sodium

NOTE

• Serve the potatoes plain or topped with snipped fresh chives, minced parsley or paprika.

VARIATIONS

Buttermilk Mashed Potatoes: Replace the low-fat milk and sour cream with ¾ cup buttermilk.
Garlic Mashed Potatoes: Add 5 cloves peeled garlic to the saucepan along with the potatoes. Mash with the potatoes.

Golden Mashed Potatoes: Use yellow-flesh potatoes, such as Yukon Gold, Yellow Finnish or Yellow Gold. These potatoes have a buttery texture and color. Their thin skins do not need to be peeled. Simply scrub them before use.
Mashed Potatoes with Horseradish: Replace the margarine, butter-flavored sprinkles and sour cream with 1¼ cups low-fat small-curd cottage cheese. Process the cottage cheese in a food processor or blender until smooth. Beat into the potatoes with the milk. Stir in 1 tablespoon prepared horseradish and 3 minced scallions.
Mashed Potatoes with Root Vegetables: Add 8 ounces carrots, turnips, parsnips or rutabagas, peeled and cut into ½″ pieces, to the saucepan along with the potatoes. Increase the cooking time to 20 minutes, or until the vegetables are tender when pierced with a fork. When mashing the vegetables, add enough reserved cooking liquid to achieve the desired texture. To serve these potatoes for Christmas dinner (menu on page 560), double the recipe.
Roasted Garlic Mashed Potatoes: Place peeled garlic cloves in a custard cup and drizzle with a little olive oil. Roast at 400° for 40 minutes, or until the garlic is soft and golden brown. Mash with the potatoes.

Twice-Baked Potatoes

   4   medium new potatoes
   2   tablespoons minced onions
   2   tablespoons finely chopped mushrooms or sweet red peppers
  ¼   teaspoon dried thyme
   2   tablespoons buttermilk
   2   tablespoons nonfat sour cream
   1   tablespoon snipped fresh chives
      Pinch of ground black pepper
   1   tablespoon shredded reduced-fat sharp Cheddar cheese

Preheat the oven to 375°.

Pierce the potatoes in several places with a fork. Bake the potatoes for about 1 hour, or until they yield to light pressure and are easily pierced with a fork. Set aside to cool.

Meanwhile, coat a small no-stick skillet with no-stick spray. Warm the skillet over medium heat until hot. Add the onions, mushrooms or red peppers and thyme. Sauté for 4 minutes, or until the onions are soft.

Slice ¼" off the top of each potato and scoop out the centers with a spoon, leaving ¼"-thick shells. Place the centers in a medium bowl and mash with a potato masher or fork. Add the onion mixture, buttermilk, sour cream, chives and black pepper. Stir well.

Spoon the filling into the potato shells and top with the Cheddar. Place the potatoes in an 8" pie plate.

Increase the oven temperature to 475°. Bake the potatoes for 5 minutes, or until the filling is hot and the Cheddar has melted.

Makes 4 servings. Per serving: 234 calories, 0.5 g. fat (2% of calories), 5.9 g. protein, 52.8 g. carbohydrates, 5.2 g. dietary fiber, 1 mg. cholesterol, 53 mg. sodium

NOTES

• To cut the baking time, microwave the potatoes on high power for a total of 7 to 10 minutes, or until tender. Turn the potatoes over halfway through the cooking time.

• To freeze the potatoes, place the stuffed potatoes on a no-stick baking sheet and freeze until firm. Wrap them in freezer wrap or foil or place in freezer bags. To serve, unwrap the potatoes and place them on the baking sheet. Bake at 350° for 30 to 40 minutes, or until heated through and lightly browned. Or, microwave 1 potato on high power for 5 to 7 minutes, or until hot.

VARIATIONS

Twice-Baked Broccoli Potatoes: Replace the thyme with dried dill. Steam 1 cup bite-size broccoli florets. Stir into the potato mixture with the sour cream. If desired, stir in ½ cup shredded carrots.

Twice-Baked Garlic Potatoes: Place 4 large cloves peeled garlic in a no-stick baking 2-cup dish. Drizzle with a little olive oil and roast in the oven with the potatoes. Mash with the potatoes.

Scalloped Potatoes

⅓ cup all-purpose flour
½ teaspoon salt
¼ teaspoon paprika
¼ teaspoon ground black pepper
4 baking potatoes, peeled and thinly sliced
1 small onion, thinly sliced
4 teaspoons nondiet tub-style margarine or butter
1⅔ cups skim milk, scalded

Preheat the oven to 350°. Coat a 2-quart no-stick baking dish with no-stick spray.

In a small bowl, combine the flour, salt, paprika and pepper.

Arrange the potatoes and onions in 4 layers in the prepared baking dish, sprinkling each layer with a quarter of the flour mixture and dotting each with 1 teaspoon of the margarine or butter.

Pour the milk over the potatoes. Cover and bake for 30 minutes. Uncover and bake for 50 to 60 minutes, or until the potatoes are tender when pierced with a fork and the tops are crisp. Remove from the oven and let stand for a few minutes before serving.

Makes 4 servings. Per serving: 336 calories, 4.3 g. fat (12% of calories), 9.5 g. protein, 65.8 g. carbohydrates, 5.7 g. dietary fiber, 2 mg. cholesterol, 387 mg. sodium

VARIATION

Creamy Scalloped Potatoes: In a small saucepan over medium heat, melt the margarine.

Whisk in the flour mixture. Cook and stir for 2 to 3 minutes. Add the milk and cook, stirring constantly, until the mixture thickens and begins to boil. Remove from the heat and pour over the potatoes and onions. Bake as directed.

Spicy Oven Fries: Replace the thyme and black pepper with 1 tablespoon coarse mustard, 1 clove minced garlic, 1 teaspoon dried tarragon, ¼ teaspoon paprika and ⅛ teaspoon ground red pepper.

O ven Fries

QUICK!

Why give up french fries? Here's a low-fat version to satisfy those cravings.

  1   tablespoon extra-virgin olive oil
1½   tablespoons chopped fresh thyme or rosemary
  ¼   teaspoon ground black pepper
  3   large baking potatoes

Preheat the oven to 475°.

In a large bowl, combine the oil, thyme or rosemary and pepper.

Cut each potato lengthwise to make several ½"-thick wedges. Add to the oil mixture and toss to coat.

Coat a 15" × 10" no-stick jelly-roll pan with no-stick spray. Place the potatoes in a single layer on the prepared pan. Bake, turning occasionally, for 15 to 20 minutes, or until the potatoes are lightly browned and tender.

Makes 4 servings. Per serving: 196 calories, 3.6 g. fat (16% of calories), 3.5 g. protein, 38.6 g. carbohydrates, 3.8 g. dietary fiber, 0 mg. cholesterol, 12 mg. sodium

VARIATIONS

Old Bay Oven Fries: Replace the thyme and black pepper with 1 tablespoon Old Bay crab boil seasoning.

Southwest Oven Fries: Replace the thyme and black pepper with 1 teaspoon each ground cumin, chili powder, paprika and dried oregano. Add ¼ teaspoon ground red pepper.

M aple-Stuffed Sweet Potatoes

  4   large sweet potatoes
  ¼   cup nonfat plain yogurt
  3   tablespoons maple syrup
  3   tablespoons orange juice
  ½   teaspoon ground nutmeg

Preheat the oven to 375°.

Place the potatoes on a no-stick baking sheet. Bake for 1¼ hours, or until easily pierced with a fork. Slice them in half lengthwise. Scoop out the pulp, leaving a ¼" shell. Set aside the shells and transfer the pulp to a large bowl.

Using a potato masher or fork, mash the pulp. Stir in the yogurt, maple syrup, orange juice and nutmeg. Mix well. Spoon the filling into the reserved shells.

Return to the oven and bake for 5 minutes, or until heated through.

Makes 4 servings. Per serving: 168 calories, 0.3 g. fat (1% of calories), 2.8 g. protein, 39.4 g. carbohydrates, 3.5 g. dietary fiber, 0.2 mg. cholesterol, 23 mg. sodium

NOTE

• To cut the baking time, microwave the potatoes on high power for a total of 8 to 10 minutes, or until tender; turn the potatoes over halfway through the cooking time.

Savory Simmered Carrots

QUICK!

5 medium carrots, sliced on the diagonal
¼ cup defatted beef broth
¼ cup chopped fresh parsley
⅛ teaspoon salt
⅛ teaspoon ground black pepper

Place the carrots in a medium saucepan. Pour in the broth and bring to a boil over high heat. Reduce the heat to medium-low, cover and simmer, stirring occasionally, for 15 to 20 minutes, or until the carrots are tender. Drain any remaining broth. Sprinkle with the parsley, salt and pepper.

Makes 4 servings. Per serving: 41 calories, 0.2 g. fat (4% of calories), 1.3 g. protein, 9.4 g. carbohydrates, 2.3 g. dietary fiber, 0 mg. cholesterol, 104 mg. sodium

VARIATIONS

Basil-Garlic Carrots: Steam the carrots for 5 to 8 minutes, or just until tender. Omit the broth and parsley. In a large no-stick skillet over medium-high heat, warm 1 teaspoon olive oil. Add the carrots, 2 cloves minced garlic, ¼ cup chopped fresh basil and 1 teaspoon lemon juice. Sauté for 2 to 3 minutes, or until heated through. Sprinkle with black pepper.

Ginger-Glazed Carrots: Steam the carrots for 5 to 8 minutes, or just until tender. Omit the broth and parsley. In a medium saucepan, combine ⅔ cup orange juice, 1 teaspoon toasted sesame oil and 1¼ teaspoons cornstarch. Stir until dissolved. Stirring constantly, add 1 tablespoon honey and bring to a boil over medium heat. Cook and stir for 2 minutes, or until thickened. Stir in ¼ teaspoon ground ginger, a pinch of ground nutmeg and a pinch of ground cinnamon. Add the carrots and stir to coat.

Glazed Acorn Squash Rings

2 small acorn squash
⅓ cup orange juice
1 seedless orange, peeled and sliced ¼" thick
3 tablespoons maple syrup
Pinch of ground cinnamon
Pinch of ground nutmeg

Preheat the oven to 400°.

Cut the squash into ½"-thick rings. Remove and discard the seeds.

Coat a large no-stick jelly-roll pan with no-stick spray. Place the squash in a single layer on the prepared pan. Pour the orange juice over the squash.

Cover with foil. Bake for 10 minutes, or until the squash is almost tender when pierced with a fork.

Remove the squash from the oven and add the orange slices in a single layer. Drizzle with the maple syrup. Sprinkle with the cinnamon and nutmeg.

Cover the pan and return it to the oven. Bake for 10 minutes. Remove the foil and bake for another 15 minutes, or until the squash is lightly caramelized and tender. (Flip the oranges and squash at least twice as they bake, basting them with pan juices each time.)

Makes 4 servings. Per serving: 118 calories, 0.2 g. fat (2% of calories), 1.6 g. protein, 30.3 g. carbohydrates, 3.1 g. dietary fiber, 0 mg. cholesterol, 6 mg. sodium

NOTES

• To make slicing easier, wrap the squash in wax paper and microwave it on high power for about 2 minutes.

• To serve these squash rings for Christmas Dinner (menu on page 560), double the recipe.

Potato-Parsnip Skillet Cakes

4 potatoes, shredded
2 parsnips, shredded
1 cup frozen corn, thawed
½ cup finely chopped sweet red peppers
1 small scallion, thinly sliced
½ teaspoon ground nutmeg
½ teaspoon ground black pepper
¼ teaspoon salt
½ cup fat-free egg substitute
2 teaspoons all-purpose flour
3 egg whites
1 tablespoon canola oil
¼ cup maple syrup or applesauce (optional)

Working in batches, squeeze the potatoes to remove excess moisture. Pat dry with paper towels. Place the potatoes in a large bowl.

Add the parsnips, corn, red peppers, scallions, nutmeg, black pepper and salt. Stir in the egg substitute and flour.

In a medium bowl, using an electric mixer, beat the egg whites until stiff. Fold into the vegetable mixture.

In a large no-stick skillet over medium heat, warm 1 teaspoon of the oil until hot. Drop large spoonfuls (2 level tablespoons) of the batter into the skillet and flatten slightly into rounds. Cook for 2 to 3 minutes, or until the tops bubble and the bottoms are lightly browned. Turn the cakes over and cook for 2 minutes, or until the bottom is lightly browned. Transfer to a serving plate and cover to keep warm.

Repeat with the remaining 2 teaspoons oil and remaining batter.

Serve with the maple syrup or applesauce (if using).

Makes 4 servings; about 6 cakes each. Per serving: 307 calories, 4 g. fat (11% of calories), 11.1 g. protein, 59.9 g. carbohydrates, 4.9 g. dietary fiber, 0 mg. cholesterol, 243 mg. sodium

NOTE

• These skillet cakes are delicious served with Roasted Red-Pepper Sauce (see recipe on page 512).

Roasted Root Vegetables

1 carrot, sliced on the diagonal
½ turnip, cut into 1″ pieces
½ small parsnip, cut into 1″ pieces
2 yellow-flesh potatoes, cut into 1″ pieces
2 cloves garlic, sliced
2 tablespoons extra-virgin olive oil
1½ teaspoons chopped fresh rosemary
1 teaspoon chopped fresh thyme
½ teaspoon ground black pepper
½ teaspoon salt
5 cherry tomatoes, halved

Preheat the oven to 400°.

Place the carrots, turnips, parsnips, potatoes and garlic in a large shallow 2-quart no-stick baking dish (a metal dish works best). Drizzle with the oil. Add the rosemary, thyme, pepper and salt. Toss to coat.

Bake for 15 minutes, stirring occasionally. Add the tomatoes and bake, stirring occasionally, for 25 minutes more, or until the vegetables are tender and the potatoes are lightly browned.

Makes 4 servings. Per serving: 208 calories, 7.1 g. fat (30% of calories), 3.4 g. protein, 34.6 g. carbohydrates, 4.9 g. dietary fiber, 0 mg. cholesterol, 296 mg. sodium

VARIATION

Roasted Root Vegetables over Pasta: Double the roasted vegetable recipe and increase the total cooking time to 50 minutes. Cook 8 ounces short pasta (such as rotelli or penne) according to the package directions. Toss with 2 teaspoons extra-virgin olive oil. Serve the vegetables over the pasta. Makes 4 servings.

Wild Rice–Stuffed Squash

Stuffed squash is the perfect winter dish. It's hearty, flavorful and warm. Plus, the variations are endless, so you can use whatever ingredients you have on hand. Simply replace the stuffing in this recipe with your favorite rice pilaf or bread stuffing.

Squash

    2   large butternut, buttercup or acorn squash
    ⅓   cup water

Wild-Rice Stuffing

    1½ tablespoons nondiet tub-style margarine or butter
    1   cup fresh bread crumbs
    1   teaspoon dried thyme
    2   cups sliced mushrooms
    ½   cup chopped onions
    ½   cup chopped celery
    1   cup chopped sweet red peppers
    2   cups cooked wild rice
    ½   cup reduced-sodium vegetable broth
    ½   cup nonfat sour cream
    2   tablespoons grated Parmesan cheese
    1   teaspoon no-salt herb blend

To make the squash: Preheat the oven to 375°. Cut the squash in half lengthwise; remove and discard the seeds. Coat a 4-quart no-stick baking dish with no-stick spray. Place the squash, cut side down, in the dish. Pour the water into the dish and bake for 45 minutes, or just until the squash is tender.

To make the wild-rice stuffing: Meanwhile, in a large no-stick skillet over medium heat, melt the margarine or butter. Add the bread crumbs and thyme. Cook, stirring frequently, for 4 to 5 minutes, or until the bread crumbs are golden. Transfer to a small bowl and set aside.

In the same skillet, cook the mushrooms, onions, celery and peppers for 8 to 10 minutes, or until tender. Stir in the rice and broth. Cook for 4 minutes. Remove from the heat and stir in the sour cream and Parmesan.

Sprinkle the flesh of the squash with the herb blend. Spoon equal amounts of the stuffing into each squash half, mounding the filling as necessary to use all of it. Sprinkle with the bread crumbs. Bake for 10 to 15 minutes, or until heated through.

Makes 4 servings. Per serving: 308 calories, 6.5 g. fat (18% of calories), 11.4 g. protein, 57.1 g. carbohydrates, 7.2 g. dietary fiber, 2 mg. cholesterol, 231 mg. sodium

NOTE

• If using small squash, such as delicata or sweet dumpling, allow 1 per person.

Fruit-and-Nut Stuffed Squash

    1   cup bulgur
    2½ cups boiling water
    1   tablespoon nondiet tub-style margarine or butter
    1   Granny Smith apple or pear, peeled, cored and cubed
    1   cup raisins
    ⅔   cup coarsely chopped walnuts
    ¾   cup orange juice
    ¼   cup orange all-fruit preserves
    1   teaspoon ground cinnamon
    ¼   teaspoon ground nutmeg
    2   large squash, cooked (see Wild Rice–Stuffed Squash)

Place the bulgur in a large bowl. Add 2 cups of the water, cover and set aside for 20 minutes, or until the bulgur is softened. Drain and set aside.

Meanwhile, in a large no-stick skillet over medium heat, melt the margarine or butter. Add the apples or pears, raisins and walnuts. Sauté for 5 minutes. Stir in the orange juice, preserves, cinnamon and nutmeg. Cook for 2 to 3 minutes.

Remove the skillet from the heat and stir in the bulgur. Mix well and set aside.

Scoop out the flesh from the cooked squash, leaving a ½″ shell. Reserve the flesh for another use. Mound equal amounts of the stuffing in the cooked squash cavities.

Place the squash in a 4-quart no-stick baking dish. Pour the remaining ½ cup water into the dish around the squash. Cover with foil and bake at 350° for 20 to 25 minutes, or until the squash is tender when pierced with a fork. Uncover and bake for 5 minutes longer.

Makes 4 servings. Per serving: 558 calories, 15.7 g. fat (23% of calories), 12.9 g. protein, 103.4 g. carbo-hydrates, 14.8 g. dietary fiber, 0 mg. cholesterol, 60 mg. sodium

Cornbread-Stuffed Squash

- ¾ cup yellow cornmeal
- ½ cup all-purpose flour
- 1½ teaspoons baking powder
- ½ cup skim milk
- ¼ cup fat-free egg substitute
- 1 tablespoon honey
- ¼ cup chopped toasted walnuts (see note)
- 2 large squash, cooked (see Wild Rice–Stuffed Squash on opposite page)
- 1 tablespoon olive oil
- 1 teaspoon dried basil
- 1 teaspoon ground nutmeg
- ½ cup apple juice

Preheat the oven to 350°. Coat a 9″ × 5″ no-stick loaf pan with no-stick spray and set aside.

In a large bowl, combine the cornmeal, flour and baking powder.

In a small bowl, whisk together the milk, egg substitute and honey. Add to the cornmeal mixture and mix just until moist-ened. Fold in the walnuts.

Spoon the batter into the pan and bake for 15 minutes, or until a toothpick inserted in the center comes out clean.

Scoop out the flesh from the cooked squash, leaving a ½″ shell. Transfer the flesh to a large bowl and mash lightly with a fork.

Crumble the cornbread and add to the bowl. Stir in the oil, basil and nutmeg. Add the apple juice and mix just until moistened. If necessary, add more juice, 1 tablespoon at a time, until the stuffing holds together.

Mound equal amounts of the stuffing in the squash shells. Place the squash in a 4-quart no-stick baking dish. Pour ⅓ cup hot water into the dish around the squash. Bake at 350° for 15 minutes, or until heated through.

Makes 4 servings. Per serving: 353 calories, 9.3 g. fat (22% of calories), 9.6 g. protein, 62.4 g. carbohy-drates, 7.8 g. dietary fiber, 0.5 mg. cholesterol, 183 mg. sodium

NOTE

• To toast walnuts, place them in a dry no-stick skillet over medium heat. Toast the nuts, shaking the skillet often, for 3 to 5 minutes, or until fragrant.

Luscious
Fruit
Favorites

FRESH FRUITS AND PRESERVES, PAGE 396

BAKED FRUIT, COMPOTES, SAUCES AND SOUFFLÉS, PAGE 419

Fresh Fruits and Preserves

Nothing shows off Mother Nature's beneficence like fruits. Compact, inexpensive and perfectly wrapped in their own skins, fruits give the satisfying sweetness of sugar without the empty calorie load found in many other sweets. Plus, they contain virtually no fat and deliver a dividend of fiber, vitamins and minerals.

We often think of fruits as snack foods to be dropped into a purse or briefcase for a mid-morning or lunch snack. But fruits also make great side dishes and flavorful desserts—a crunchy fruit salad, for example, or an elegant treat of berries and angel food cake.

It wasn't so many years ago that the only fruits available were those currently in season or those that had been canned or frozen. Today, thanks to a healthy global economy and refrigerated trucking, you can enjoy most fruits all year long, from strawberries in December and peaches in February to apples just about any time.

Of course, fruit that's out of season is more expensive than its seasonal counterpart. It's typically less tasty and possibly lower in vitamins. That's why many healthy cooks try to buy only fruits that are naturally ripe.

BUY SMART

Fruit is at its juiciest and most flavorful when it's stored at room temperature—the nearest thing to just-picked. The problem is that fruit may deteriorate quickly without refrigeration.

To have the best of both worlds—great taste plus keeping power—here's what chefs advise.

Buy it as you need it. Although we often think of fruit as being a packaged food, like dried beans or rice, it doesn't have a long shelf life. (Fruit will stay fresh in the refrigerator, but only at the expense of its natural full-flavored taste.) It's best to buy a few day's worth of fruit at a time. If you find that it's going bad before you have a chance to use it, buy less in the future.

Plan ahead. Unless you're lucky enough to have a farmers market or produce store nearby, you may not be able to buy fruit more than once or twice a week. That's why chefs advise purchasing it in various stages of ripeness. With bananas, for example, get one bunch that's ready to eat and another bunch that needs several days to ripen. That way, they won't all be ripe—or all go rotten—on the same day.

Shop for heft. Fruit that seems heavy for its size usually has the most juice and the tenderest flesh inside, making it the best buy. By contrast, fruit that's surprisingly light may be old and somewhat dry.

Stock up on dried. While dried fruit doesn't have the moisture of fresh, it retains virtually all the vitamins and minerals. It was picked at its prime and is long-lasting, high in fiber and packed with concentrated sugar. So you may want to stock up the next time you're at the store. It will last for months in the refrigerator and makes a great high-energy snack.

We often think of fruits as being the peel-and-eat variety, like apples, oranges and bananas. And in fact, these remain among our most popular snacks. Yet supermarkets stock dozens of other varieties as well. Here are a few of our favorites, both traditional and exotic, along with hints for getting the most flavor out of each one.

Apples

Apples are nature's gold mine. With some 300 varieties, many of which are available year-round, apples are loaded with fiber and potassium. They're also a lean snack, with about 80 calories each. They keep well, so you can load up whenever you go shopping.

Preserve the color. When making fruit salad or other snacks using apple wedges, dip

THE APPLE CART

You can eat apples all week without ever having the same kind twice. Some are sugary-sweet and best for munching, while others are mouth-puckering tart and used only for baking. Here are some common varieties and their best uses.

APPLE	FLAVOR	USES
Braeburn	Tangy-sweet	All-purpose
Cortland	Mildly tart	Eating, baking
Crispin	Sweet	All-purpose
Criterion	Sweet and crisp	All-purpose
Elstar	Tart-sweet	All-purpose
Empire	Mildly tart	Eating, salads
Fuji	Sweet	All-purpose
Gala	Sweet	Eating, salads
Golden Delicious	Mellow, sweet	All-purpose
Granny Smith	Tart, crisp	All-purpose
Jonagold	Sweet-tart	All-purpose
Jonathan	Mildly tart	All-purpose
McIntosh	Sweet-tart	Eating, cooking
Newtown-Pippin	Tart and firm	Eating, cooking
Northern Spy	Mildly tart	Eating, baking
Red Delicious	Sweet, crunchy	Eating, salads
Rome Beauty	Sweet and firm	Baking, cooking
Stayman	Mildly tart	Eating, cooking
Winesap	Tart, slightly winy	All-purpose
York Imperial	Mildly tart	Baking, cooking

QUICK APPLESAUCE

Once you've made your own applesauce, you'll never want store-bought again. This version may be a little nontraditional, but it's much quicker than the standard applesauce recipes.

Peel, core and quarter 8 medium apples (about 3 pounds). A combination of McIntosh and Granny Smith provides just the right mix of tart and sweet.

Put the apples in a large pot. Add ½ cup water, about ⅓ cup sugar and ⅛ teaspoon ground nutmeg or cinnamon. Bring to a boil over high heat. Reduce the heat to medium, cover and simmer for 10 minutes, or until the apples are very tender. If needed, add a little more water to keep the apples from sticking.

Let cool slightly, then mash the apples in a large bowl, run them through a food mill or puree in a food processor. If desired, leave some of the pieces a little chunky for an interesting consistency.

the cut pieces in lemon or orange juice. The acid in citrus fruits stops the oxidation that causes the exposed flesh to turn brown.

Make a near-instant dessert. To enjoy the freshness of apples with just a touch of sweetness, try microwave-baked apples.

☞ Pare a strip from the top of a large cored apple. Place the apple in a 10-ounce glass custard cup.

☞ Fill the center of the apple with a mixture of 1 tablespoon brown sugar and ½ teaspoon ground cinnamon. (If desired, add raisins for extra fiber.) Microwave, uncovered, on high power for 3 to 5 minutes, or until tender.

Try an apple cracker. When you want a quick snack, slice an apple and top the slices with nonfat yogurt cheese, nonfat cream cheese or reduced-fat peanut butter.

Bananas

Even though the banana wasn't imported into the United States until the 1830s, it quickly became one of our most popular fruits. A good source of potassium, bananas can be peeled and eaten on the spot. They can also be grilled, baked or sautéed, which adds smoky sweetness to a variety of recipes.

Buy ahead. Bananas readily ripen at room temperature, so you can buy them in varying stages of ripeness.

☞ Refrigerated bananas quickly turn black and look unappealing. But don't throw them out, at least not for a few days. Despite the ugly outside, the inside will still be white and sweet.

☞ If you can't use the bananas in a timely manner, peel and slice or puree them. Then freeze for future use in muffins, breads or snacks.

Look for variety. There's more to bananas than the familiar peel-and-eat Cavendish variety.

☞ **Finger bananas.** These bananas-in-miniature have a sweet, slightly tangy flavor that is good plain or with ice cream or yogurt. They must be fully ripe for the best flavor.

☞ **Manzanos.** Short bananas that develop black spots on the skin when ripe, this fruit is more tart and crunchy than Cavendish bananas.

☞ **Red bananas.** These are short, fat bananas that are sweeter than regular yellow ones and are usually eaten raw. The fruit may have a slight pink hue, and the skin turns purple-red as the bananas ripen.

☞ **Plantains.** These have a starchy taste, nearer a potato than the bananas we're most accustomed to. They're served as a cooked vegetable—most often baked or sautéed.

PREPARING PLANTAINS

Unlike regular bananas, which are enjoyed mainly as a snack, plantains can be sautéed or cooked on the grill; they're often served with fish, seafood or chicken. Also unlike bananas, which peel with the slightest pressure, plantains require a bit more effort. The riper a plantain is, the easier it peels. Really ripe plantains are almost black on the outside.

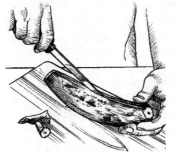

Cut off the ends and use a paring knife to slit through the skin from top to bottom on either side.

Use your thumbs to lift the skin and peel it off.

Gently rinse the peeled plantain under cold running water to remove the sticky juice. Pat dry.

Slice and bake on a baking sheet at 350° for about 40 minutes, or until fork-tender; slice or mash. (Another way to cook them is to slice the plantains and sauté them in a small amount of oil until golden on both sides and cooked through. Prepared this way, they resemble french fries but contain less fat.)

Berries

Except for cranberries, which need both cooking and sweetening, fresh berries in season can be enjoyed with little adornment. Indeed, one of life's great pleasures is popping sweet, juicy berries into your mouth, one by one. Berries are highly perishable, though, and need special handling to maintain peak freshness.

Shop with care. Mold can grow on berries in the store, especially if they're not handled properly. To make sure that the ones you buy are fresh, inspect them carefully—both on the top and bottom of the package—to make sure that they're not discolored.

Watch for leakage. Berries that are leaking from the bottom of the package are either old or have been crushed and are giving up their juice. Look for a fresher, drier batch.

Give them room. Berries that are crowded together deteriorate rapidly. It's best to store them, unwashed and uncovered, in a large bowl or spread out on a platter.

Use cranberries for cooking. Unlike most berries, the tart cranberry is usually cooked before serving.

☞ Place the berries, which are usually sold in 12-ounce packages, in a saucepan. For a whole bag, add about ½ cup sugar and ½ cup water. Bring to a boil over medium heat.

☞ When the cranberries start to burst, reduce the heat and cook for 5 minutes more, stirring frequently. Be sure to cover the pot to prevent spattering the stove top.

Plan ahead. Berries freeze well, so you can enjoy their fresh taste all year long.

Spread unwashed berries in a single layer on a rimmed baking sheet. Place in the freezer until the berries are solidly frozen, then transfer to plastic bags and return to the freezer. This two-stage process helps prevent the berries from clumping together, so that you can easily remove the amount that you need.

Help them float. The problem with adding berries to muffin and other batters is that they often sink to the bottom. Tossing fresh berries

Helpful Hint

To lift berry stains from table linens or clothing, apply straight lemon juice until the stain starts to disappear—usually within about 5 minutes. Then rinse out the juice and wash the item as you usually would.

with about 1 tablespoon flour per pint will suspend them in the mixture so that they stay evenly distributed throughout.

Cherries

This is one our most prized fruits, probably because its season is so short; you really have to rush to have your share.

Bing and Lambert cherries are very sweet, with colors ranging from dark red to mahogany. They're best eaten at room temperature—preferably straight from the tree. Rainier cherries are lighter colored, usually golden with a pink blush. Exceptionally sweet, they're often hard to find—and therefore expensive.

Sour cherries are especially perishable. Pit and use them quickly or freeze them for pies, preserves or crisps.

Washing cherries prior to storing hastens decay. Store them in the refrigerator dry in a loosely closed bag and wash them prior to using.

Citrus

For many of us, it's just not morning without orange juice or a grapefruit half to wake up our palates. But that's just the beginning of the charm of citrus. These fruits are unusual in that the skin is often as prized as the flesh. Indeed, the rinds are not only grated and added to foods as a seasoning but also candied and enjoyed as a sweet.

Buy them heavy. Citrus fruits that seem heavy for their size are the ones with the most juice. If you pick up an orange, grapefruit or other fruit that seems particularly light, it will probably be dry and tough.

Experiment with tartness. Lemons and limes are used for more than just making juice. Adding a squirt of juice or a bit of grated rind during or even after cooking will make any recipe sparkle.

☞ Lemon juice has a sharp, intense flavor that makes a great substitute for salt in many foods.

☞ Lime juice can be used in the same way, although it isn't quite as tart as lemon juice.

☞ To get the most juice from lemons or limes, microwave them on high power for about 30 seconds. Or roll them with the heel of your hand on the countertop before juicing.

☞ To remove the rind, rub the fruit lightly over a grater, removing only the colored, outer part. Or use a special tool called a zester. Don't grate the white layer underneath, which is unpleasantly bitter.

Try key limes. Small and yellow, these have a flowery flavor that's somewhat less tart than the familiar green kind. Fresh key limes are not easy to find, but they're worth seeking out. Bottled key lime juice is available for use in recipes.

Reach for variety. There's more to the citrus family than navel oranges, lemons and limes. Try some of these more unusual varieties.

☞ **Blood oranges.** Available in late winter, they have distinctive reddish-orange pulp and skin that's tinged with a bright orange blush. The flavor is more intense than that of a regular orange.

☞ **Clementines.** These are small, sweet, seedless oranges with easily removed skin. They're classified as mandarins, as are dancy oranges, satsuma oranges and tangerines.

☞ **Kumquats.** These are miniature versions of oranges with thin skin that's sweeter than the bittersweet-orange flesh contained inside. They can be eaten whole.

☞ **Pomelo** (also called pummelo). Larger than a grapefruit, this fruit has a taste that can vary from sweet to tart. It can be juicy to slightly dry.

MAKING A CITRUS GARNISH

An easy way to liven up a plate is with a twist of lemon or orange.

Cut the fruit into thin slices, then cut halfway through each slice.

Twist the slice so that it forms an S shape.

☞ **Tangelos.** These are a cross between tangerines and pomelos. There are many hybrids, which vary in size, color and sweetness. The Minneola has a distinctive knob at the end and deep orange to red-orange skin.

☞ **Ugli fruit.** A cross between a grapefruit and a tangerine, the skin is thick and yellow-green, and the flesh is juicy, acid-sweet and yellow-orange.

Figs

Dried figs have long been used in stuffings, preserves and fig bar cookies. Until recently, however, the only people lucky enough to have fresh figs were those living in fig-growing areas. Figs have become increasingly popular, however, and now are more readily available.

☞ Ripe figs are very soft and may be slightly sticky on the bottom.

☞ Although figs are at their best when picked fully ripe, slightly underripe ones can be left at room temperature for a few days to sweeten up.

☞ Figs are both fragile and expensive. To get your money's worth, chefs advise eating them the same day that they're purchased.

☞ For a perfect summer appetizer, cut figs in half and serve with curls of aged Parmesan cheese.

Grapes

The jewels of the fruit kingdom, grapes come in several seasonal varieties, making them available all year long. Popular varieties include:

☞ **Champagne.** Tiny and very sweet, these grapes are somewhat rare and are found mostly in gourmet and specialty shops.

☞ **Concord.** These purple slipskin grapes are prized for jelly making.

☞ **Red flame.** A green- to red-blush grape, these are seedless and quite sweet, with a firm texture.

☞ **Ribiers.** These large, round purple grapes have large seeds and tend to be very sweet.

☞ **Thompson seedless.** The most popular grape, these are green and elongated, ranging from extremely sweet to just slightly tart.

When buying grapes, look for firm, unbruised fruit that's firmly attached to the stems. Avoid bunches with stems that look withered or stringy or that have lots of fruit missing.

To store grapes, remove them from the plastic bag and place them in a bowl in the refrigerator, where they'll keep for about one week; on the counter, they'll last a few days.

Melons

Whether your tastes run to cantaloupe, honeydew, watermelon or any of the myriad other melons, you're assured of fine flavor, fiber and vitamin C. Some, like cantaloupe and watermelon, also have lots of vitamin A. Melons are

---

FRUIT SALADS—A FEAST FOR THE EYES

Eating an apple, orange or banana features a solo performance. A fruit salad, however, is a medley of colors, contrasts and textures. How you direct this show is up to you. Here are some ideas that you may want to try.

☞ To create an attractive salad, layer five different fruits in a large glass bowl. The beautiful colors and shapes will enliven any table.

☞ Make a platter of concentric circles of cantaloupe, honeydew and casaba melon, then heap blueberries in the center.

☞ Toss a variety of chopped, sliced and diced fruits together in a large bowl and garnish with sprigs of mint and slices of starfruit.

most plentiful in summer and early fall, although a few varieties are typically available all year.

Trust your nose. Thumping melons is a time-honored technique for testing their ripeness, but your nose is a more accurate guide. Melons have a sweet, lovely fragrance when ripe. If you can't smell it, pass it by.

Check the stem. Another test is to examine the stem area; it should be shriveled, dry and smooth. If it looks firm and fresh, the melon was probably picked too early.

Look for halves. Although it's cheaper to buy melons whole, many chefs advise buying them cut, so that you can see exactly what you're getting.

Pears

There are many varieties of pears, and although they are technically interchangeable, chefs have their favorites for different uses.

☞ **Anjou.** These have a buttery texture and a slightly spicy taste that's terrific when added to salads. Since they hold their shape well, they're also used for poaching and baking.

☞ **Bartlett.** A sweet, mild pear, it's perfect for canning and making preserves.

☞ **Bosc.** Juicy and sweet, its firm flesh holds up well for poaching.

☞ **Comice.** A large, delicate pear with a wonderfully fragrant flavor, this is often viewed by chefs as being the perfect pear. It scars easily, however, so it's often less attractive than other varieties.

☞ **Forelle.** A small pear with freckled golden skin and a red blush, it's good for eating out of hand.

☞ **Seckel.** A very small pear that's available in the late summer and fall, it's sweet and is good for snacks.

Pineapple

The pineapple has long been a symbol of hospitality. Despite its name, it's not related to either pine trees or apples. When ripe, fresh pineapple gives off a sweet, aromatic fragrance that puts the canned variety to shame. Pineapples are best picked ripe and don't get sweet if picked before they're ready.

☞ Choose pineapple that's slightly soft with good yellow color. The stem end should have a sweet, aromatic fragrance and not smell fermented.

☞ Look for leaves that are crisp and green without yellowed or browned tips. Contrary to popular wisdom, ease of pulling a leaf from the crown does not indicate ripeness.

☞ An interesting way of determining ripeness is to thump the inside of your wrist and then thump the pineapple. The two sounds should match. If you don't get a solid thump from the pineapple, pass it by.

☞ A variety known as golden pineapple has markedly golden yellow skin, deep yellow flesh and exceptional flavor.

☞ Fresh pineapple contains an enzyme called bromelain that prevents gelatin from setting up properly. The enzyme is destroyed by heat, so using canned pineapple or cooking fresh pineapple will take care of the problem.

Rhubarb

A vegetable that thinks it's a fruit, rhubarb has been called the pie fruit because it is often used in pies and crisps—especially paired with strawberries. Rhubarb is an excellent source of fiber. It needs to be cooked and sweetened.

Leave the leaves. Rhubarb leaves are not edible because of their high oxalic acid content. In supermarkets, the leaves are usually removed before it's put on display. If you grow your own, be sure to discard the leaves before cooking.

Make a sweet treat. Rhubarb makes a wonderful topping for frozen yogurt, angel food cake and other desserts.

☞ Wash and dry the stalks, then remove the strings as you would with celery. Slice into 1″ pieces.

☞ Place in a saucepan with ¾ cup sugar, ¼ cup water, a cinnamon stick and small sections of orange and lemon peel.

PREPARING PINEAPPLE

With its tough skin and formidable sharp edges, the pineapple turns a tough face to the world. To get to its heart of gold, here's what you need to do.

Place the pineapple on its side. Using a sharp knife, cut it into ½" slices.

Next, trim away the rind.

Use the tip of a sharp knife or a cookie cutter to remove the tough, bitter core.

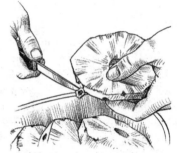

Rotate each slice, using a knife to flick away the woody eyes.

☞ Bring to a boil, then cover and simmer for 10 minutes, or until tender. Cool slightly; remove and discard the peels and cinnamon stick. Serve warm. Makes about 1½ cups.

Stone Fruits

Apricots, nectarines, peaches and plums are collectively known as stone fruit because of the large center pit, or stone. Great as snacks, they can also be enjoyed in pies and compotes.

Keep them warm. Refrigeration causes peaches and other stone fruit to get dry, mealy and unappealing. They're best stored at room temperature and eaten as soon as they're ripe.

To easily remove the skins from peaches and other stone fruit, place them one by one in a saucepan of boiling water. Leave them in for 10 to 20 seconds, remove them with a slotted spoon and plunge them into a bowl of cold water. Slit the skin with a paring knife and peel.

Use them as fat substitutes. To reduce the amount of butter or oil in baked goods, replace some of it with pureed, skinned fruit.

☞ To make a puree, combine 8 ounces fresh peeled and pitted fruit with ⅓ cup water in a food processor; blend until smooth.

☞ Plum or prune-plum puree works best with full-flavored desserts, like those containing

FRESH FROM THE TROPICS

There's an incredible array of tropical and other unusual fruits now available at supermarkets and specialty stores. Some of these fruits, like kiwifruit, have been widely embraced; others are waiting to catch on. Here are some up-and-comers.

☞ **Asian pear.** It looks like an apple but tastes like a pear, only crisper. It's best eaten chilled. Or sauté it to release more of the pear flavor.

☞ **Atemoya.** Also called custard apple, this artichoke-shaped fruit has a creamy white, custardy interior. It also has a sweet taste, something between a pineapple and a mango.

☞ **Carambola.** With waxy skin and deep ribs, it resembles a long, yellow pepper. When sliced, it looks like yellow stars, hence the nickname "starfruit." It can be used as a garnish or to add pizzazz to fruit salads with an apple-grape-citrus taste.

☞ **Guava.** Pebbly-green on the outside and pink on the inside, guava is great in salads. It can also be pureed and made into delicious tutti-frutti yogurt by combining it with nonfat plain yogurt, freezing it until firm and then running it through the food processor.

☞ **Kiwifruit.** This fuzzy, egg-shaped fruit is one of the most familiar of the unusual tropical fruits. Kiwifruit tastes like a cross between strawberry and pineapple.

☞ **Lychee.** This comes encased in a barklike brown shell that peels off, revealing a pearly white fruit with a grapelike appearance and taste.

☞ **Mango.** As sweet as it is fragrant, the mango is as close to paradise as you can get without getting on a plane. It looks rather like a large misshapen pear, ranging in color from green (unripe) to orange-red.

☞ **Papaya.** On the outside, it almost looks like a yellow or orange avocado. On the inside, however, is a beautiful orange-pink flesh with edible peppery black seeds. The seeds can be used to give crunch to a salad. The flesh is good in salsas or fruit salads. It also makes a good meat tenderizer.

☞ **Passion fruit.** Despite the heady name, passion fruit is ready to eat only when it's purple, shriveled and ugly. Inside you'll find a gelatinous mass of crunchy seeds and juice. The taste is a delightful combination of citrus, honey and floral.

☞ **Persimmon.** This is a smooth orange fruit that comes in two varieties. Hachiya persimmons are acorn shaped and must be quite soft to be eaten. They have a smooth, creamy texture. Smaller, tomato-shaped Fuyus can be eaten when still firm, even crisp.

☞ **Tamarillo.** Also called tree tomato, it actually looks more like a plum with either golden yellow or scarlet skin and has a slightly tart taste. It must be peeled with a vegetable peeler or blanched before using. To serve, slice and drizzle it with honey and a dusting of nutmeg.

CUTTING A MANGO

A luscious and highly nutritious tropical fruit, the mango comes in all shapes and sizes, from oblong and pear-shaped to long and skinny. Skin color ranges from greenish-yellow to red blushed. The one drawback to this juicy package of edible paradise is the large, difficult-to-remove seed. To successfully seed a mango, follow these steps.

Stand the mango upright on a cutting board. Using a sharp paring knife or serrated knife, slice through the flesh on one side, curving around the seed. Repeat on the other side. You will now have two disklike portions of fruit plus a third center section with the seed.

With the curved side down, score the flesh all the way down to the skin in a checkerboard pattern. Be careful not to slit the outer skin.

Working from the skin side, gently push up the center to expose the cubes of flesh. Use a paring knife to cut them away from the peel.

To extract flesh from the remaining center (seed) section, cut the fleshy sides away from the center. Then score these pieces as before and cut them away from the skin.

chocolate, whole wheat or bran, because of their dark color and strong flavors. A puree of dried prunes is also good. Make your own or use baby-food prunes or a commercial puree.

☞ If your baked goods are made from carrot or pumpkin, you'll want a milder fat substitute; a puree of apricots or peaches is a good choice.

PRESERVING THE HARVEST

We all want good things to last forever—or at least for a long time. By making your own preserves, you can enjoy the fruits of the harvest well into the future. Jams, jellies and other preserves are rich and satisfying—so much so that you can use a teaspoonful in place of the butter or margarine that you would normally slather on toast, pancakes or waffles.

When making preserves at home, you're in charge of the ingredients from start to finish. You can control not only the amount of sweetener but also the type that you use.

*F*lavorful Varieties

There are many types of preserves, all of which have different textures and are prepared in different ways.

☞ **Conserves.** These are a mixture of more than one fresh fruit, often including citrus, plus dried fruit or nuts.

FRUIT BUTTER

Although apple butter is probably the most familiar of the fruit butters, you can turn cherries, strawberries, raspberries and other fruits into smooth, rich-tasting spreads. Here's how.

Coarsely chop fruit and place it in a large heavy pot. Add cider, fruit juice or water to cover. Cover the pot and cook until very tender.

Press through a fine sieve or food mill into a bowl.

Return the puree to the pot; stir in sweetener—brown sugar, honey or maple syrup is good— and add spices to taste. Simmer until quite thick, being careful not to let the fruit scorch.

Let cool, then ladle into storage containers; cover and refrigerate. This mixture will keep for about three weeks.

☞ **Fruit butter**. Smooth and creamy, this is made by pureeing fruit and cooking it with spices and sweetener. Apple butter is the most common form.

☞ **Jam.** This consists of whole, chopped or crushed fruit, which is combined with sweetener and sometimes pectin, then cooked until thickened. Small pieces of fruit will be visible in the final mix.

☞ **Jelly**. Made from the juice of the fruit, it should be clear and firm enough to hold its shape, yet soft enough to be spreadable.

☞ **Marmalade**. Made from citrus fruits, it includes the flesh and the peel. Marmalades are translucent and thick yet spreadable.

Safety First

Whether you're preserving a chunky grape jam or the clearest apple jelly, be sure to follow the proper procedures.

Use the right glass. Most supermarkets and hardware stores stock tempered glass jars, in sizes ranging from 1 cup to 1 quart, that are made specially for preserving. Don't use leftover jars from the kitchen, because they may not hold up to the high heats used in canning.

Keep them clean. To prevent preserves from spoiling, first sterilize the jars in a water-bath canner—a large metal pot with a removable rack and a cover. Or fill the jars three-quarters full with water and place them in a metal or glass baking dish partly filled with water. Simmer the water on the stove top for 15 to 20 minutes; keep the jars hot and filled with water right up to the time when you're ready to add the preserves.

☞ Placing lids loosely on the jars while they simmer in the water will ensure that the metal is as well-sterilized as the glass beneath.

☞ As a final precaution, wipe the tops of the jars with a clean, damp cloth before screwing on the lids.

☞ Paraffin wax, once used to seal jams and jellies, isn't recommended, because it's relatively porous and may allow contamination of the preserves. It's also highly flammable and dangerous to work with.

Do the press test. To ensure that there's a solid seal after filling the jars, press down on the center of the lids. If they won't push down, the jar is properly sealed.

Jellies and jams expand once they've been put into the jar. It's important to leave a little empty space at the top of each jar to prevent pressure from building up and breaking the jar. Jams need about ¼″ headspace. For jellies, leave about ½″.

Store them well. Preserves that are stored in a cool, dark place will keep for a year or more. Once opened, however, they should be refrigerated and used promptly, preferably within three weeks.

The Role of Pectin

A natural carbohydrate found in fruits, pectin makes it possible for jellies, jams and preserves to hold together and jell. Some fruits, like apples and plums, are naturally high in pectin, while others, like blueberries and grapes, are quite low.

☞ When making jams with low-pectin fruits, it may be necessary to add commercial liquid or powdered pectin to aid jelling.

☞ Another way to promote jelling is to combine low-pectin fruits with those that are higher in pectin. Apples are a common addition to many jams, not just for their flavor but because of their higher pectin content.

Making Jelly

Unlike other types of preserves that utilize pieces of fruit, jellies are made from the juice itself. They are nearly clear, easy to spread and have a refreshing, clean taste. The one drawback is that the jelly process takes a little bit of time.

Begin by juicing. After washing the fruit, put it in a large pot and crush it well using a large wooden spoon. The best jellies are made without adding water, although relatively dry fruits, like apples, may require several cups of water to thoroughly draw the juices from the fruit. When adding water, bring it almost to the top of the fruit but not covering it.

Cook until tender. Using a low to moderate heat, cook the fruit, uncovered, until soft.

Strain it well. Put the cooked fruit into a metal strainer or a jelly bag—a strainer made from porous material like muslin—and let it drain into a bowl. Discard the fruit pieces when draining is complete.

Wetting the jelly bag with cold water before straining will help prevent it from absorbing precious flavors.

Start the thickening. Once you've collected the juice, pour it into a large enamel or stainless steel pan. (Don't use an aluminum pan, since it reacts with some fruit juices.) Bring to a simmer and cook for about 5 minutes, skimming off any scum or foam that forms.

Add the sweetener. Add the amount of sweetener called for in the recipe. If using sugar, stir until it dissolves. Cook until the mixture is at the point of jelling, or until the liquid is about 8° above the boiling point. (Adding sugar raises the boiling point of water.)

Check for doneness. Jelly is usually at the right stage in 8 to 10 minutes. To test for doneness, spoon up some of the mixture, then let it drip back into the pan. When it falls in a steady sheet, rather than dripping, remove it from the heat and transfer it to the waiting jars.

Making Jam and Preserves

Unlike jelly, which requires two distinct operations—juicing and cooking—jams and preserves need only be cooked and, to various degrees, strained.

☞ Crush the fruit and cook, uncovered, until soft. Add sugar or other sweetener and stir until dissolved. Bring to a boil and continue stirring.

☞ Reduce the heat and continue cooking until the mixture is thick, usually between 15 and 20 minutes.

☞ While a number of manufacturers make reduced-sugar spreads, it's difficult for the home cook to reduce the amount of sugar by more than ½ cup and still have the jam thicken. An exception is if you're using a no-sugar-needed packaged pectin, which allows jams to jell without sugar.

USING A JELLY BAG

When making jelly, use a jelly bag to separate juices from the crushed fruit.

To get a clear jelly, it's important to let the juices drip through at their own pace. Squeezing the bag to hurry things along will force out fruit residue, causing a muddy juice.

Sugar
Is It GOOD for You?

Sugar has long been considered the bad boy of the kitchen. Reviled by dieters ("too many calories"), teachers ("makes kids hyperactive") and doctors ("hurts blood sugar levels"), sugar is one food that we all love to hate.

Yet many of the negative claims about sugar fall somewhat short of the truth. For example, children given high-sugar meals don't become hyperactive. They may get excited—but that's because of the thrill of the treat and not the sugar itself.

In addition, research has shown that while eating sugar can cause blood sugar to temporarily rise, this is unlikely to cause symptoms. In fact, the American Diabetes Association's guidelines acknowledge that sugar is no more upsetting to the body's sugar balance than other carbohydrates.

The one area in which sugar appears to deserve its negative reputation is inside your mouth. Eating sugar can allow cavity-causing bacteria to thrive. To reduce the risk, experts advise eating sugar as part of meals. The high levels of saliva present during meals help neutralize tooth-damaging acids resulting from the sugar.

Making Freezer Jam

Water-bath canning is a surefire way to keep preserves fresh for long periods of time. But because it takes so much time, many cooks prefer making freezer jam instead. By taking cooked fruit and storing it in the freezer, the risk of contamination is virtually eliminated. This means that the water-bath process can be skipped entirely.

☞ When making freezer jam, choose fruits that are very ripe and free of bruises and mold. Berries work best, followed by stone fruits like cherries, peaches, apricots and plums.

☞ Try mixing up fruits for interesting flavors. Raspberries and cherries, for instance, make a good match. Hard fruits, like apples and pears, however, do not. Cook the fruit as you normally would, adding ingredients required in the recipe.

☞ When the fruit is properly thickened, ladle it into 8-ounce freezer jars or jelly jars, leaving ½" headspace at the top.

☞ Let the jars stand at room temperature until the preserves are set, no more than 24 hours.

☞ Store the jars in the freezer, leaving one in the refrigerator for immediate use. The preserves will stay fresh in the refrigerator for about three weeks. In the freezer, they'll keep for six months to a year.

Helpful Hint

The brilliant colors of homemade jams and jellies are fleeting when the jars are stored in bright light. Storing them in a cool, dark place will keep them looking—and tasting—good.

Charlie Trotter

Charlie Trotter's is an intimate restaurant located in a two-story renovated townhouse in Chicago. It has been attracting serious diners nationwide who are eager to sample Charlie's innovative and healthful cuisine. Fruits in season play an important role on the menu, and this unique fruit soup is an excellent example.

"There is nothing more glorious than walking through an orchard and finding that perfect piece of fruit—peach, apricot or cherry, it doesn't matter—still on the tree," he says. "This warm peach soup tries to capture that experience—and dress it up a bit."

Feel free to experiment with other fruit combinations, depending on what's available. The recipe can be simplified by using fewer fruits. Just be sure to look for a contrast in colors—both with the fruits and the sorbets—to maintain visual excitement.

In winter, unsweetened frozen fruits, such as peaches, work well. You can buy a high-quality sorbet or make your own by pureeing frozen fruit.

Warm Peach Soup with Fruit Sorbets

- 1 pound ripe peaches, peeled and coarsely chopped
- ¼ cup peeled and diced apples
- ¼ cup diced pineapple
- 2 cups water
- ¼ cup sugar
- 2 tablespoons diced pears
- 2 tablespoons diced strawberries
- 2 tablespoons diced mango
- 1 cup pear sorbet
- 1 cup strawberry sorbet
- 1 cup mango sorbet

In a large saucepan, place the peaches, apples, pineapple, water and sugar. Bring to a boil over high heat. Remove from the heat and let cool for 30 minutes. Puree in a food processor or blender and strain. Rewarm just before serving.

In a small bowl, mix the pears, strawberries and mango. Divide among 4 soup bowls.

Place a scoop of the pear sorbet, strawberry sorbet and mango sorbet in each bowl. Ladle in the soup.

Makes 4 servings. Per serving: 267 calories, 0.2 g. fat (1% of calories), 0.9 g. protein, 60.2 g. carbohydrates, 2.5 g. dietary fiber, 0 mg. cholesterol, 30 mg. sodium

Tropical Fruit Salad

QUICK!

- 1 cup sliced bananas
- 1 tablespoon orange or pineapple juice
- 2 tangerines, peeled and sectioned
- 1 Golden Delicious apple, cored and cubed
- 1 cup red seedless grapes
- 2 tablespoons unsweetened shredded coconut
- ½ teaspoon finely shredded lemon rind
- ⅛ teaspoon ground cinnamon
- ⅛ teaspoon ground nutmeg

Place the bananas in a medium bowl. Add the orange juice or pineapple juice and gently toss to coat.

Cut the tangerine sections in half crosswise; remove and discard the seeds. Add the sections to the bowl.

Add the apples, grapes, coconut, lemon rind, cinnamon and nutmeg. Gently toss to mix.

Cover and refrigerate for at least 20 minutes to allow the flavors to blend.

Makes 4 servings. Per serving: 132 calories, 1.6 g. fat (10% of calories), 1.3 g. protein, 31.7 g. carbohydrates, 3.2 g. dietary fiber, 0 mg. cholesterol, 3 mg. sodium

Sparkling Fruit Salad with Mint

QUICK!

- 1 cup sliced peaches
- 1 cup white seedless grapes
- 1 cup blueberries
- ½ cup honeydew melon balls
- ½ cup small strawberries, hulled
- 1½ teaspoons chopped fresh mint
- ¼ cup frozen apple juice concentrate
- ¼ cup sparkling water or club soda

In a medium bowl, gently toss the peaches, grapes, blueberries, melon balls, strawberries and mint.

In a measuring cup, combine the frozen juice concentrate and sparkling water or club soda. Pour over the fruit. Serve immediately.

Makes 4 servings. Per serving: 115 calories, 0.6 g. fat (4% of calories), 1.1 g. protein, 28.8 g. carbohydrates, 2.7 g. dietary fiber, 0 mg. cholesterol, 10 mg. sodium

VARIATION

Fresh Fig Salad with Kiwi-Lime Dressing: Replace the peaches and grapes with 2 cups halved fresh figs. Omit the mint, frozen juice concentrate and sparkling water or club soda. Instead, toss the fruit with 1 tablespoon lime juice. In a food processor or blender, process 1 small peeled and chopped kiwi, 2 tablespoons fat-free mayonnaise, 2 tablespoons nonfat sour cream, 1 tablespoon honey and 1 tablespoon lime juice. Serve the fruit over torn lettuce; top with the dressing. Sprinkle with chopped pecans.

Pineapple Ambrosia

QUICK!

- 1 container (16 ounces) nonfat vanilla yogurt
- 1 cup applesauce
- 1 can (8 ounces) crushed pineapple in juice, well-drained
- 1 cup blueberries
- 1 banana, thinly sliced
- ¼ cup toasted unsweetened coconut
- 2 tablespoons toasted slivered almonds (see note)

In a large bowl, whisk together the yogurt and applesauce. Fold in the pineapple, blueberries, bananas, coconut and almonds. Chill for at least 20 minutes.

Makes 6 servings. Per serving: 166 calories, 2.6 g. fat (13% of calories), 3.1 g. protein, 34.5 g. carbohydrates, 2.4 g. dietary fiber, 0 mg. cholesterol, 39 mg. sodium

NOTE

• If desired, sprinkle with low-fat granola before serving.

• To toast almonds, place them in a dry no-stick skillet over medium heat. Toast the nuts, shaking the skillet often, for 3 to 5 minutes, or until fragrant.

pplesauce

12 medium apples, peeled, cored and sliced
1 cup water
½ cup sugar
¼ cup lemon juice (optional)
½ teaspoon ground cinnamon (optional)
¼ teaspoon ground cloves (optional)
⅛ teaspoon ground nutmeg (optional)

In a large stainless steel saucepan, combine the apples, water and sugar. Stir in the lemon juice, cinnamon, cloves and nutmeg (if using). Cook over medium heat, occasionally mashing the apples with the back of a wooden spoon, for 20 to 30 minutes, or until the apples are tender and the liquid is reduced. If necessary, drain in a colander lined with cheesecloth.

Cool the sauce and serve immediately. Or pour into freezer containers, seal and freeze.

Makes about 5 cups. Per ½ cup: 126 calories, 0.5 g. fat (3% of calories), 0.2 g. protein, 32.8 g. carbohydrates, 2.3 g. dietary fiber, 0 mg. cholesterol, 0.1 mg. sodium

NOTES

• To make a wonderful topping for pancakes or waffles, leave the sauce slightly chunky and warm.

• For a smoother sauce, put the apples through a food mill.

• This sauce can be stored in the refrigerator for up to 5 days or in the freezer for up to 6 months. Thaw frozen sauce in the refrigerator.

• To can the sauce, pour the hot sauce into hot, scalded preserving jars, leaving ½″ headspace. Wipe the rims clean, attach the lids and tightly screw on the caps. Invert the jars for 10 seconds. Store in the refrigerator.

pple Butter

1½ cups apple cider
8 medium apples, unpeeled, uncored and thinly sliced
2 tablespoons honey (optional)
¼ teaspoon ground cinnamon (optional)
⅛ teaspoon ground allspice (optional)
⅛ teaspoon ground cloves (optional)

In a large stainless steel saucepan, bring the cider to a boil. Carefully add the apples to avoid splattering. Return to a boil. Reduce the heat to medium-low and simmer, stirring frequently, until the mixture begins to thicken.

When the apples start to break up and fall apart, remove from the heat. Put the mixture through a food mill or fine sieve, discarding the peels, seeds and stems. Return the mixture to the saucepan and add the honey, cinnamon, allspice and cloves (if using). Cook, stirring occasionally, over medium-low heat for about 4 hours, or until the mixture is thick and dark.

When the desired thickness is reached, bring the mixture to a boil. Pour the hot apple butter into hot, scalded preserving jars, leaving ½″ headspace. Wipe the rims clean, attach the lids and tightly screw on the caps. Invert the jars for 10 seconds.

Cool on a wire rack. Store in the refrigerator.

Makes 2 cups. Per tablespoon: 26 calories, 0.1 g. fat (4% of calories), 0.1 g. protein, 6.9 g. carbohydrates, 0.8 g. dietary fiber, 0 mg. cholesterol, 0.6 mg. sodium

Strawberry Jam

2 pounds fresh strawberries, hulled
1½ cups sugar
1 tablespoon fresh lemon juice

Halve or quarter the strawberries to make equal-size pieces.

In a large stainless steel saucepan, combine the strawberries and 1 cup of the sugar. Bring to a simmer and cook over medium heat, stirring frequently, for 15 minutes, or until the mixture thickens.

Occasionally mash the berries with the back of a wooden spoon.

Add the remaining ½ cup sugar and cook for 5 minutes, or until the jam thickens again. Remove from the heat and stir in the lemon juice.

Pour the jam into hot, scalded preserving jars, leaving ⅛″ headspace. Wipe the rims clean, attach the lids and tightly screw on the caps. Invert the jars for 10 seconds.

Cool on a wire rack. Store in the refrigerator.

Makes 3 cups. Per tablespoon: 30 calories, 0.1 g. fat (2% of calories), 0.1 g. protein, 7.6 g. carbohydrates, 0.3 g. dietary fiber, 0 mg. cholesterol, 0.3 mg. sodium

VARIATION

Strawberry Jam with Chamomile: Add 2 bags chamomile tea to the hot jam along with the lemon juice. Let steep for 5 minutes, stirring and pressing down on the bag once or twice. Remove and discard the tea bags.

Blueberry Jam with Mint

2 pints fresh blueberries, rinsed and drained
1 cup sugar
2 sprigs fresh mint (each 6″ long)

In a large stainless steel saucepan, combine the blueberries and ½ cup of the sugar. Bring to a simmer. Reduce the heat to low, cover loosely and simmer for 10 minutes. Using the back of a wooden spoon, crush about half of the blueberries against the bottom and sides of the pan while they cook.

Uncover, increase the heat to medium-high and cook, stirring frequently, for 5 minutes, or until almost all of the liquid has evaporated.

Add the remaining ½ cup sugar and cook for 1 to 2 minutes, or until the jam thickens.

Remove from the heat and stir in the mint. Using the back of a wooden spoon, crush the mint against the bottom and sides of the pan. Let steep for 5 minutes.

Remove and discard the mint. Pour the jam into hot, scalded preserving jars, leaving ⅛″ headspace. Wipe the rims clean, attach the lids and tightly screw on the caps. Invert the jars for 10 seconds.

Cool on a wire rack. Store in the refrigerator.

Makes 3 cups. Per tablespoon: 23 calories, 0.04 g. fat (2% of calories), 0.1 g. protein, 5.9 g. carbohydrates, 0.3 g. dietary fiber, 0 mg. cholesterol, 1 mg. sodium

VARIATION

Blueberry-Rhubarb Jam: To the blueberries, add 1 pound rhubarb (rinsed, trimmed and cut into 1″ pieces), ¼ cup water and ½ cup sugar. Loosely cover and simmer for 20 minutes. Add 2 cups more sugar, ½ cup at a time. Stir in ½ tablespoon lemon juice and the continuous rind of 1 lemon. Continue cooking until the jam thickens, stirring often and leaving the pan loosely covered to avoid splattering. Remove the lemon rind befor canning. Makes about 2½ cups.

Raspberry-Cherry Jam

1½ cups fresh or frozen pitted cherries, pureed
1½ cups fresh or frozen blueberries, pureed
1 cup fresh or frozen raspberries, pureed
⅓ cup apple juice
2 tablespoons lemon juice
⅔ cup sugar

In a food processor or blender, puree the cherries, blueberries, raspberries, apple juice and lemon juice until smooth. Transfer to a medium stainless steel saucepan and bring to a boil over high heat, stirring frequently. Stir in the sugar and return to a full boil. Cook, stirring occasionally, for 25 minutes, or until the jam is thick and sticky.

Pour into hot, scalded preserving jars, leaving ¼″ headspace. Wipe the rims clean, attach the lids and tightly screw on the caps. Invert the jars for 10 seconds.

Cool on a wire rack. Store in the refrigerator.

Makes 3 cups. Per tablespoon: 18 calories, 0.1 g. fat (5% of calories), 0.1 g. protein, 4.6 g. carbohydrates, 0.3 g. dietary fiber, 0 mg. cholesterol, 0.5 mg. sodium

Strawberry Preserves

2 pints fresh strawberries, hulled
½ cup water
2 tablespoons commercial fruit pectin
2 tablespoons lemon juice
1¾ cups sugar

Halve the strawberries to make equal-size pieces. Leave smaller berries whole.

In a large stainless steel saucepan, combine the strawberries and water. Bring to a simmer. Cover and simmer gently for 5 minutes. Uncover and cook for 5 minutes, or until all the berries are soft.

Strain the juice through a fine sieve for 5 minutes. Return the juice to the saucepan and cook over medium-high heat until reduced to 1 cup. Stir in the pectin and lemon juice. Bring to a simmer and add the sugar, ½ cup at a time, returning the mixture to a boil before each addition.

Boil until the liquid falls in a single sheet from a metal spoon. (A quick test for the jell is to drop a small amount of the hot liquid on a cold plate and place it in the freezer for 1 minute. At the jell point, the surface of the cooled preserve will wrinkle when pushed with a finger. For the most accurate test of a jell, use a canning thermometer. The jelling point will be about 220°F, or 8°F above the temperature reading in boiling water.)

Remove from the heat and stir in the strained strawberries. Let steep for 5 minutes. Return the mixture to a boil and cook for 1 to 2 minutes more.

Remove from the heat and let stand for 5 minutes in the pan. Stir any fruit pieces and pour the jam into hot, scalded preserving jars, leaving ⅛″ headspace. Wipe the rims clean, attach the lids and tightly screw on the caps. Invert the jars for 10 seconds.

Cool on a wire rack. Store in the refrigerator.

Makes 3 cups. Per tablespoon: 33 calories, 0.1 g. fat (3% of calories), 0.1 g. protein, 8.6 g. carbohydrates, 0.2 g. dietary fiber, 0 mg. cholesterol, 1 mg. sodium

VARIATION
Strawberry-Blackberry Preserves: To the strawberries, add 1 pint fresh whole blackberries and 2 cups sugar.

LIGHT JAMS

Traditional jellies, jams and preserves call for loads of sugar. But you can make them without all those empty calories. We've cut the sugar by as much as 75 percent in some recipes; others don't need any sugar at all. The results are rich and fruity with just the right amount of sweetness. These jams are perfect for spreading on your favorite toast. They're even chunky enough to use as a topping for pancakes or frozen yogurt. Remember to always store no-sugar jams in the refrigerator to prevent spoilage.

No-Sugar Apple-Blackberry Jam

- 3 McIntosh or Golden Delicious apples (about 1¼ pounds), peeled, cored and chopped
- 1 can (12 ounces) unsweetened apple juice concentrate
- 1 pound fresh blackberries

In a stainless steel saucepan, combine the apples and apple juice concentrate. Bring to a gentle simmer, cover and cook for 10 minutes.

Add the blackberries. Return the mixture to a gentle simmer, cover and cook for 5 minutes.

Uncover the pan and increase the heat to medium-high. Cook, stirring frequently, for 15 minutes, or until all of the liquid is almost evaporated. (At this point, a spoon drawn across the bottom of the pan should create a hissing sound.)

Pour the jam into hot, scalded preserving jars, leaving ⅛″ headspace. Wipe the rims clean, attach the lids and tightly screw on the caps. Invert the jars for 10 seconds.

Cool on a wire rack. Store in the refrigerator.

Makes 3 cups. Per tablespoon: 23 calories, 0.1 g. fat (4% of calories), 0.1 g. protein, 5.9 g. carbohydrates, 0.8 g. dietary fiber, 0 mg. cholesterol, 2 mg. sodium

NOTE

• For a seedless jam, strain the mixture through a fine sieve after cooking the blackberries and before cooking down the liquid.

No-Sugar Pear-Grape Jam

- 8 ripe Bartlett pears, peeled (about 3 pounds), cored and chopped
- 1 can (12 ounces) unsweetened grape juice concentrate
- 4 sprigs fresh thyme (optional)

In a large stainless steel saucepan, combine the pears, grape juice concentrate and 2 of the thyme sprigs (if using).

Bring to a simmer and cook, stirring frequently, for 35 to 40 minutes, or until the liquid is reduced.

Remove from the heat. Remove and discard the thyme. Add the remaining 2 sprigs thyme (if using). Using the back of a wooden spoon, press the sprigs against the bottom and sides of the pan. Let steep for 5 minutes. Remove and discard the thyme.

Pour the jam into hot, scalded preserving jars, leaving ⅛″ headspace. Wipe the rims clean, attach the lids and tightly screw on the caps. Invert the jars for 10 seconds.

Cool on a wire rack. Store in the refrigerator.

Makes 3 cups. Per tablespoon: 29 calories, 0.1 g. fat (4% of calories), 0.2 g. protein, 7.4 g. carbohydrates, 0.8 g. dietary fiber, 0 mg. cholesterol, 0.5 mg. sodium

VARIATION

No-Sugar Apple-Grape Jam: Replace the pears with 3 pounds McIntosh apples.

Peach-Orange Preserves

1   small navel orange, quartered and seeded
2   cups fresh or frozen peaches, coarsley chopped
2   tablespoons apple juice
1½ teaspoons lemon juice
⅓   cup sugar

Cut the orange into quarters; remove and discard the seeds. In a food processor or blender, combine the oranges and peaches. Process until the orange rind is finely chopped. Transfer to a medium stainless steel saucepan and add the apple juice and lemon juice.

Bring to a boil over high heat, stirring frequently. Stir in the sugar and return to a full boil. Cook, stirring occasionally, for 8 to 10 minutes, or until the jam is thick and sticky.

Pour into hot, scalded preserving jars, leaving ¼″ headspace. Wipe the rims clean, attach the lids and tightly screw on the caps. Invert the jars for 10 seconds.

Cool on a wire rack. Store in the refrigerator.

Makes 3½ cups. Per tablespoon: 9 calories, 0 g. fat, (0% of calories)0.1 g. protein, 2.3 g. carbohydrates, 0.1 g. dietary fiber, 0 mg. cholesterol, 0 mg. sodium

Orange Marmalade

3   navel oranges (about 1½ pounds)
1   cup orange juice
1   cinnamon stick
⅓   cup sugar

Scrub one of the oranges under running water. Using a vegetable peeler or citrus zester, remove and mince enough of the rind to measure 2½ tablespoons. Remove and discard the rind from the remaining oranges. Quarter the peeled oranges lenthwise, then slice them and remove the seeds.

In a large stainless steel saucepan, combine the oranges, orange rind, orange juice and cinnamon stick. Bring to a simmer and cook, stirring occasionally, for 15 minutes.

Add the sugar and increase the heat to medium-high. Cook, stirring frequently, for 15 minutes, or until the marmalade has thickened.

Remove from the heat. Remove and discard the cinnamon stick.

Pour the marmalade into a hot, scalded preserving jar, leaving ⅛″ headspace. Wipe the rim clean, attach the lid and tightly screw on the cap. Invert the jar for 10 seconds.

Cool on a wire rack. Store in the refrigerator.

Makes 1¼ cups. Per tablespoon: 34 calories, 0.1 g. fat (1% of calories), 0.4 g. protein, 8.7 g. carbohydrates, 0.7 g. dietary fiber, 0 mg. cholesterol, 0.4 mg. sodium

Sweet Cherry Conserve

- 4 cups sweet cherries
- 2 medium navel oranges, peeled, seeded and chopped
- ½ cup lemon juice
- ½ cup sugar
- 2 tablespoons grated orange rind
- ¾ teaspoon ground cinnamon
- ⅛ teaspoon ground cloves

In a large stainless steel saucepan, combine the cherries, oranges, lemon juice, sugar, orange rind, cinnamon and cloves. Bring to a boil. Reduce the heat to medium-low and simmer for 20 minutes, stirring occasionally. Return to a boil and boil for 5 minutes, or until thickened.

Pour into hot, scalded preserving jars, leaving ¼" headspace. Wipe the rims clean, attach the lids and tightly screw on the caps. Invert the jars for 10 seconds.

Cool on a wire rack. Store in the refrigerator.

Makes 3 cups. Per tablespoon: 21 calories, 0.1 g. fat (5% of calories), 0.2 g. protein, 5.3 g. carbohydrates, 0.3 g. dietary fiber, 0 mg. cholesterol, 0.1 mg. sodium

Raspberry-Apple Conserve

- 5 strips lemon rind (each 3" long)
- 1 cup sugar
- 3 tart apples (about 1 pound) quartered and cored
- 2 pints red raspberries
- ½ cup hazelnuts, skins on and roasted (see note)
- 2 tablespoons hazelnut liqueur or Frangelico (optional)

In a food processor or blender, combine the lemon rind and sugar. Process with on/off turns until the lemon rind is minced and well-blended with the sugar. Add the apples and process until the apples are coarsely chopped.

Transfer the mixture to a large saucepan. Cover and cook over medium heat for 10 minutes.

Remove from the heat. Stir in the raspberries and let them steep in the mixture for 15 minutes.

Cook the mixture over medium heat for 5 to 10 minutes, or just long enough to evaporate excess moisture.

Meanwhile, rub the warm hazelnuts gently against the mesh of a strainer to remove as much of the brown skin as possible. Coarsely crush the nuts.

Remove the raspberry mixture from the heat. Stir in the liqueur (if using) and the crushed nuts.

Pack the conserve into hot, scalded preserving jars, leaving ⅛" headspace. Wipe the rims clean, attach the lids and tightly screw on the caps. Invert the jars for 10 seconds.

Cool on a wire rack. Store in the refrigerator.

Makes 4 cups. Per tablespoon: 28 calories, 0.8 g. fat (25% of calories), 0.2 g. protein, 5.3 g. carbohydrates, 0.6 g. dietary fiber, 0 mg. cholesterol, 9 mg. sodium

NOTE
• To roast hazelnuts, place them on a no-stick baking sheet. Roast in a 350° oven for 10 minutes. Or place them in a paper bag and microwave on high power for 4 minutes.

Baked Fruit, Compotes, Sauces and Soufflés

The warm summer months entice us with luscious fresh peaches, nectarines, apricots and cherries. Berry farms with hand-painted "U-Pick" signs beckon to inveterate shortcake lovers. And what would the Fourth of July be without ice-cold wedges of watermelon to sink our teeth into?

Fruits are wonderfully versatile. They can be baked, poached, stewed, pureed or frozen into countless delectable confections. Here's how.

BAKED FRUIT

Served warm, baked fruit makes a wonderful comfort food. Firm, round fruits such as apples, pears and peaches are the best candidates. Baking causes the fruits' natural sugars to caramelize and intensify, giving extra sweetness and flavor. At the same time, the heat causes the flesh to soften and become tender while still remaining whole; it gains a satisfying soft texture while delivering just a hint of crunch.

Remove the skin. It isn't essential to peel fruits prior to baking, but removing the skin unveils the elegant flesh beneath and also allows the fruit to absorb flavors during cooking.

☞ Pears can be peeled completely and cored from the bottom up, leaving the stem attached.

☞ Apples are most attractive with only the top half of the skin pared away, leaving intact a short "jacket" to protect the bottom half of the fruit.

☞ Peaches and nectarines can be baked with the skin on, but they should be sliced in half and pitted. The wonderful indentation left behind cries out for a flavorful stuffing.

Baste before baking. To prevent fruit from drying during baking, brush each piece with about 2 tablespoons thawed apple juice concentrate, maple syrup, strained apricot jam or honey.

☞ Put the fruit in a 350° oven. After about 10 minutes, the fruit will begin releasing its natural juices, which can be used for further basting.

☞ Apples are generally done in about 45 to 60 minutes. Pears cook more quickly, usually in about 30 minutes.

☞ To tell when baked fruit is done, pierce the flesh with a toothpick; it should pass through with almost no resistance.

Choose your flavors. Although baked fruits can be enjoyed plain, the heavily caramelized sugar is naturally complemented by sweet, pungent spices like cinnamon and cloves.

☞ For a delicious spice mixture that works with any fruit, combine 1 teaspoon ground cinnamon, 1 teaspoon ground nutmeg, ⅛ teaspoon ground cloves, ⅛ teaspoon ground cardamom, 1 teaspoon grated lemon rind and 1 teaspoon grated orange rind. Sprinkle the mixture over fruit prior to putting it in the oven.

☞ Fruit can be glazed and baked with honey, jams or jellies.

☞ For a milder taste, top plain baked fruit with low-fat yogurt (regular or frozen). Or top it

HIGH-SPEED BAKING

Although baked fruit has a wonderfully intense flavor that's hard to match, many healthy cooks simply don't have time after dinner to wait around for dessert. You can speed things up by preparing fruit in the microwave.

A large apple that would take 45 to 60 minutes to bake in the oven is ready in 4 to 5 minutes in the microwave. And while microwave-baked fruit has a somewhat milder flavor, it typically holds its color better and stays juicier and sweeter, thus requiring less added sugar. When microwaving fruit:

☞ Peel and core the fruit prior to microwaving, but don't core it all the way through. When baking pears, leave the stem attached and core from the bottom. When preparing apples, work from the top down; leaving the bottom intact will help the fruit hold its shape better.

☞ When preparing a single piece of fruit, use a small microwave-safe bowl or custard cup. For two or more pieces, put them in an 8″ × 8″ no-stick baking dish.

☞ For each piece of fruit, combine 1 or 2 teaspoons brown sugar or maple syrup with a little apple juice or other juice and spread over the top.

☞ Cover the dish loosely with plastic wrap and cook on medium-high power until just tender. For one apple or pear, microwave for 3½ to 4½ minutes; for two, 7 to 8 minutes; for four, 13 to 14 minutes.

with ricotta cheese and sprinkle it with cinnamon sugar.

Try a stuffing. Apples and pears are delicious baked with a flavorful stuffing. Core the fruit and fill the cavity with several tablespoons stuffing, such as the ones below (each makes enough for four to six pieces of fruit).

☞ ¼ cup fine fresh bread crumbs, ¼ cup chopped walnuts and ¼ cup brown sugar

☞ ½ cup coarsely crumbled amaretti or ginger snaps and ¼ cup diced dried fruit

☞ ¼ cup coarsely chopped golden raisins, ¼ cup chopped almonds and ¼ cup dark brown sugar

POACHED FRUIT

Poaching is a wonderful way to prepare fresh and dried fruit. Poaching allows fruit to retain its natural shape and texture, while making it tender and intensely flavored.

Many fruits take well to poaching, including fresh pears, apples, peaches, sweet and sour cherries, figs, rhubarb and pineapple. Dried fruits such as figs, peaches, pears, apricots, prunes, raisins and cherries also poach well.

Poached fruit can be served warm or cold, alone or as an ingredient in another dessert. Dried fruit, when diced and poached, makes a delicious stuffing for baked apples, pears or peaches. Whole poached pears are gorgeous served cold standing in a pool of raspberry sauce.

Cut it up. Fruit should be peeled and seeded before poaching. Large fruits, like pineapple, should be peeled, cored and cut into 2″ chunks; smaller fruits, like apples, pears and peaches, can be peeled and cut in half and then cored or pitted before poaching. Cherries are best pitted and poached whole.

Simmer it sweet. For fruit to retain its sweetness and flavor during poaching, it should be cooked in a liquid such as fruit juice, cider or a light sugar syrup.

Y ou don't have to struggle to remove the hard little stone that's at the heart of a fresh cherry. A cherry pitter, which is essentially a kitchen hole punch, pops out the seed with one swift motion.

The advantage of using a cherry pitter is that it punches out the seed without damaging the tender flesh in the process.

☞ Place the liquid in a large, shallow saucepan. Bring the mixture to a boil over medium heat. Add fruit, arranging it in a single layer. Reduce the heat to low and simmer the fruit, uncovered, until tender.

☞ The cooking time will depend on the ripeness and density of the fruit. Delicate fruits, such as cherries, apricots, peaches and fresh figs can be added to a hot liquid, immediately removed from the heat and then allowed to stand until cool. Apples and pears take about 20 minutes to poach; dried fruit usually takes about 30 minutes.

Boost the flavor. For added flavor and color, use fruit juice for the poaching liquid. Raspberry or orange juice is wonderful with figs, pears and peaches. Cranberry juice gives pears and apples a gorgeous ruby color. Some cooks enjoy adding a squeeze of pomegranate juice or even a sprinkling of the pomegranate's tart, rubylike seeds.

☞ Putting tea bags in the poaching liquid lends a pleasant flavor to the fruit. Chamomile, mint, Darjeeling and jasmine all are good choices. Steep the tea until you have the desired strength, then add sugar and fruit.

☞ Many cooks add aromatic spices to the poaching liquid. Fresh herbs like thyme and bay leaf are delicious with fresh figs, dates and dried fruit. Fresh lemon balm and mint marry well with pears, peaches and apricots.

FRUIT COMPOTES

Despite the fancy name, fruit compotes are simply a combination of fruits, fresh or cooked, that have been moistened with a flavorful liquid or poaching syrup. Compotes can be prepared with both dried and fresh fruits and served either hot or cold. Compotes can be enjoyed alone or served as a topping for ice cream, sorbet or angel food cake.

Start with a syrup. To add flavor to dried fruits while making them suitably soft, they need to be simmered in juice or a light sugar syrup. For more pizzazz, flavor the liquid with a vanilla bean, a few thin slices of fresh ginger, a thick strip of lemon rind, a cinnamon stick, a few whole cloves or a single star anise.

Cook until tender. Simmering fills the dried fruit with moisture while also softening tough tissues. Cook, uncovered, over low heat until tender, usually about 20 minutes.

For a truly elegant parfait, prepare a compote of dried apricots, figs, peaches, pears and dried sour cherries. Flavor the poaching liquid with lemon and orange rind. Layer spoonfuls of the simmered compote with scoops of vanilla ice milk or frozen yogurt. Garnish with candied orange rind or chopped walnuts.

HOW TO PEEL A POMEGRANATE

The pomegranate is nature's fortress, concealing its brilliant, ruby red seeds within a tough, leathery skin. Here's an easy way to mine the wonderful flavors within.

Using a sharp knife, cut a thin slice from the stem end, revealing the seeds.

Make about six slices through the skin, without cutting into the seeds beneath.

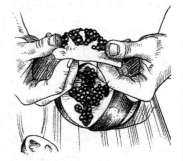

Open up the pomegranate by breaking apart the scored sections. Gently free the seeds from their surrounding pithy membranes. Because juice from the seeds stains easily, protect your clothing as you work.

Enjoy them fresh. When preparing a fresh fruit compote, peel the fruit, then cut it into bite-size pieces. Tender fruits like strawberries don't require cooking, whereas firm-fleshed fruits like apples or pears can be cooked or not, as you prefer.

Here are two fresh fruit compotes that you may want to try.

☞ Peel and pit one ripe peach; slice it into thick wedges and combine it with a handful of pitted Bing cherries in a medium bowl. Drizzle the fruit with 1 or 2 tablespoons of juice flavored with a sprinkling of chopped fresh mint. Serve topped with a scoop of raspberry sherbet or sorbet.

☞ Slice 2 pints fresh strawberries and marinate in the juice of 2 oranges or tangerines. Sweeten to taste. Top with a mixture of equal parts nonfat sour cream and nonfat plain yogurt sweetened with brown sugar and grated orange rind.

FRUIT SOUPS

Cold fruit soups have always been popular desserts in northern Europe. They are light, refreshing and low in fat and calories. Plus, they're a snap to prepare in a food processor or blender.

Fruit soups combine fresh or poached fruit with a flavorful liquid, like fruit juice or sweetened tea. Some cooks add a little sour cream or buttermilk to enrich the flavor and give the soup a creamy consistency.

Soft fruits such as berries, papaya, mango and melon can be pureed fresh. If you are using firmer fruits such as cherries, apples and pears should be simmered first in juice or a light sugar syrup, then pureed with the remaining soup ingredients.

☞ Only berry purees really need to be sieved of their seeds before being combined with the remaining ingredients; other fruits can be used straight out of the blender.

☞ When making fruit soup with mango, papaya, melon or other easily seeded fruits, cut the flesh into small pieces and combine with the remaining soup ingredients in a food processor or blender. Puree until smooth. The resulting soup can be poured straight from the blender to the serving bowl, or it can be covered and chilled a few hours to blend flavors.

Fruit soups can be thick as a bisque or as thin as a consommé. Bisquelike fruit soups are made by combining a fruit puree with buttermilk or low-fat or nonfat sour cream or yogurt (use a quarter to half the amount of fruit puree). The resulting mixture is then thinned down with a little fruit juice until the soup has the consistency of heavy cream.

Unlike bisque-style fruit soup, fruit consommé is made without adding buttermilk or other dairy products. Also, it contains a greater

proportion of liquid to fruit puree. Tea or fruit juice is used as the soup base, which is then flavored with a little strained fruit puree.

Just enough puree is added to give the final consommé a little body—about ½ cup puree to every 2 or 3 cups liquid. Fresh berries, slices of poached pear or apple and thin strips of fresh mint are all good garnishes for the consommé and give it a little texture and variety of flavor.

Almost any fruit can be pureed and used to make fruit soup. Here are sample recipes.

☞ **Cold berry bisque.** Puree equal parts strawberries, raspberries and blackberries. Using a wooden spoon, press the puree through a mesh sieve into a bowl; discard the seeds. Add sweetener to taste. For every 2 cups puree, add ½ cup buttermilk. If the soup is too thick, thin it with sparkling mineral water or a little orange, cranberry or apple juice. Top with a dollop of low-fat or nonfat raspberry yogurt and a few fresh raspberries.

☞ **Tropical fruit soup.** Puree a mixture of pineapple juice and chunks of fresh mango, papaya and banana until smooth. Garnish with a drizzle of kiwi puree and a few shavings of fresh coconut.

FRUIT SMOOTHIES

Thick, sweet and deliciously low in fat, fruit smoothies are essentially fresh fruit milkshakes. Made by blending fruit juices, yogurt (regular or frozen) and chunks of fresh fruit, smoothies can be enjoyed at any time of day.

Here's an easy recipe: Blend together 1 cup apple juice, 1 cup watermelon chunks, 1 cup strawberries and ½ cup strawberry yogurt.

To make a smoothie that's particularly thick and cold, use frozen fruit (alone or in addition to fresh). For convenience, keep small plastic bags filled with fruit in the freezer. Peeled and sliced bananas, peaches and pineapple work well; so do different types of berries.

FRUIT BRÛLÉE

Crème brûlée means "burnt cream" in French. This traditional favorite is luxuriously rich, consisting of sweetened heavy cream and egg yolks flavored with vanilla and topped with a thin, brittle shell of caramelized sugar.

To get the pleasure of crème brûlée without the fat, healthy cooks turn to fruit brûlée. It can be made in just a few minutes and combines the sweetness of fruit with the wonderfully rich texture of the best desserts. When you taste this delicious treat, you'll never guess it's good for you.

☞ Fill 6-ounce ramekins or custard cups halfway with lightly sweetened fresh fruit, such as raspberries, mango chunks, papaya chunks or poached diced fresh pineapple.

☞ Top the fruit with ¼ cup low-fat or nonfat vanilla yogurt (or low-fat or nonfat plain yogurt or sour cream flavored with honey and a few drops of vanilla).

☞ Sprinkle 2 tablespoons superfine sugar over the topping and smooth it flat with the back of a spoon.

☞ Put the custard cups under the broiler for 1 to 2 minutes, or until the sugar starts to turn brown and melts into a thin, crisp sheet.

☞ Pop the cups into the freezer for about 5 minutes to chill the ramekins. Serve immediately, before the caramelized sugar topping has a chance to soften.

FRUIT SAUCES

When most of us think about fruit sauces, we imagine the pale, thin ghost of applesauce that comes in a jar. Yet homemade fruit sauces—which can be made with virtually every fruit under the sun—deliver a thick texture and robust taste that's perfect for low-fat desserts. What's more, you can mix and match different fruits to get exactly the taste that you want.

Get it ready. Wash, peel, core and chop the fruit.

Flavor to taste. Fruit sauces are traditionally flavored with ground cinnamon, cloves, nutmeg and fresh or dried ginger. Some cooks add a split vanilla bean and perhaps a little orange or lemon rind.

It's best to add seasonings at the beginning of the cooking process, so that the flavors have a chance to mellow and permeate the fruit.

Cook it well. Combine the fruit and spices with sugar or honey in a heavy-bottomed saucepan. Try starting with 1 tablespoon sweetener per 1 cup fruit, adjusting for taste. Add enough water to prevent the fruit from sticking; usually a few tablespoons is all that you need, since the fruit will release its own juices during cooking. For added flavor, replace the water with a small amount of citrus or another fruit juice.

Start cooking the fruit over very low heat. As the fruit softens and begins releasing juices, increase the heat, stirring to break up the fruit, until it resembles a thick, slightly lumpy puree. Remove the sauce from the heat and cool completely, then refrigerate. The sauce is now ready to serve.

Applesauce is by far the most common type of fruit sauce on America's tables. But virtually any fruit can be used to make a rich and wonderfully healthy dessert. For example:

☞ **Gingered pear sauce.** Peel, core and dice ripe pears and cook with a little pear nectar, cinnamon, nutmeg, a dash of cloves, a few slices fresh ginger and a squeeze of fresh lemon juice. Cook over low heat until the sauce is soft and slightly lumpy. Serve warm over gingerbread, vanilla ice milk or frozen yogurt. Or serve alone topped with low-fat or nonfat plain yogurt and sprinkled with diced candied ginger.

☞ **Tropical fruit sauce.** Combine chunks of fresh papaya, mango, banana and pineapple with mango, papaya nectar, fresh lime juice and honey. Cook until soft and lumpy. Chill and layer with nonfat vanilla, lemon or strawberry-banana yogurt, frozen yogurt or sorbet for a festive fat-free parfait. Garnish with slices of fresh kiwi and pineapple.

☞ **Apricot-strawberry sauce.** Combine chopped dried or fresh apricots, sliced strawberries, orange juice and sweetener. Cook until the sauce is thick and lumpy. For a smoother sauce, puree in a food processor or press through a food

Eye-Catching Desserts

A smooth sauce made from lightly sweetened pureed fresh or frozen fruit is a wonderful low-fat way to add color and flavor to desserts. All you have to do is puree fruit in a food processor or blender. If you're using raspberries, strawberries or other fruit that contain small seeds, strain the puree through a fine sieve. Sweeten to taste. For a dramatic visual effect, place the sauce on a plate and then add fresh fruit, angel food cake, pound cake or whatever else you're serving with the sauce. Here are some simple ideas for presentation.

Spread about ¼ to ½ cup of the sauce on a dessert plate, lightly coating the entire bottom. This is called mirroring the plate.

For simple elegance, place a plain poached pear in the middle of the vibrant pool.

To create a "ring of hearts," fill a small squirt bottle with whisked yogurt or sauce of a contrasting color. Squirt small dots from the bottle in a circle about 1″ in from the edge.

Using a toothpick, pull through the center of each dot to form a heart shape. Place the dessert in the center of the ring.

mill. This sauce is delicious served alone or over slices of angel food cake. It can also be layered between two pieces of sponge cake to create a sensational low-fat shortcake.

Sorbets, Sherbets and Granitas

When you're craving a flavorful frozen dessert that is virtually fat-free, three classics come to mind: sorbets, sherbets and granitas.

Nowadays, frozen desserts are a snap to create at home. Electric ice cream makers are smaller and less expensive than ever before. Some models use regular ice cubes and table salt instead of large quantities of crushed ice and rock salt. Others don't use any ice at all; a metal insert is simply placed in the freezer a few hours before you're ready to make your frozen dessert.

Unlike ice cream, sorbets, sherbets and granitas contain little or no milk or cream, so they are much lower in fat.

☞ **Sorbet.** Lighter than a sherbet, it combines a sugar syrup with a fruit puree.

☞ **Sherbet.** This is the creamiest of the three. Fruit sherbet combines a sugar syrup with fruit juice, a fruit puree or both. A little milk can be added to create an even creamier texture.

☞ **Granita.** This is a glistening icy dessert

that resembles a snowcone rather than traditional ice cream. Unlike sorbets and sherbets, granitas aren't made in ice cream makers but in a pan in the freezer.

Each of these frozen desserts can be made with practically any type of fruit. It's easy to prepare a variety of frozen desserts in a rainbow of colors and flavors. For sorbets and sherbets:

Prepare the fruit. While soft fruits like berries require almost no preparation, others should be peeled and poached until soft.

Make a puree. Puree the fruit in a food processor, blender or food mill. To make 1 pint sorbet or sherbet, you will need 3 cups fruit puree.

Combine the fruit puree with chilled sugar syrup. The amount of syrup needed will depend on the acidity of the fruit that you are using. Start with 1 cup and add more if needed.

Brighten the flavor. Add the juice of half a lemon. At this point you can create a creamier texture—and transform the sorbet into a sherbet—by adding ¼ cup buttermilk or condensed skim milk to the mixture.

Put it on ice. Chilling the mixture in the freezer prior to putting into the ice cream maker will make it freeze more readily and also give it a smoother texture.

To make granita, place sweetened fruit juice (a mixture of citrus juices is good) in a shallow metal pan and place it in the freezer. Stir with a fork every 15 to 20 minutes to break up the ice crystals. Continue until the mixture is fairly well frozen.

FRUIT SOUFFLÉS

There's a mystique about soufflés, those heavenly puffs of egg white that are so astonishingly light that they seem to defy gravity and float up from the plate. Yet despite their elegance and rarefied appeal, soufflés are remarkably easy to prepare. What's more, they're relatively low in fat, making them a healthful dessert as well as a dramatic way to end a meal.

A soufflé is a fruit, cream or custard base that has been lightened with beaten egg whites. When popped into a hot oven, the air trapped in the egg whites rapidly expands, forming a fragile crown an inch or two above the rim of the dish.

☞ Bake soufflés in a straight-sided soufflé dish, which allows the mixture to rise straight up during baking.

☞ Most recipes call for a soufflé dish holding 1½ quarts. You can also use individual soufflé dishes, which hold 8 ounces (1 cup).

☞ Before filling a soufflé dish, coat it with butter or no-stick spray. If the recipe calls for it, sprinkle the inside of the dish with sugar or fine crumbs.

☞ For fruit soufflés, make a thick puree of raspberries, strawberries, prunes, peaches, cooked pears, cooked apples or other fruit.

☞ Using room-temperature egg whites, beat them until opaque and foamy.

☞ Add cream of tartar to the whites after they begin to foam to help them maintain their peaks.

☞ Slowly beat in sugar. Do not overbeat the whites; they should reach firm, but not stiff, peaks.

☞ Gently fold the whites into the base and then use a rubber spatula to scrape the mixture into the soufflé dish.

☞ Don't put a soufflé into a cold oven. Always preheat the oven for 15 minutes.

☞ When the soufflé is baking, never open the oven door during baking.

☞ A soufflé is done when the "crown" is puffed about an inch above the rim of the dish and the top feels firm when lightly touched. The edges will look firm and dry.

Emily Luchetti

Emily Luchetti was the longtime pastry chef at San Francisco's Stars restaurant and Stars Cafe. Her interpretations of classic American and European desserts have been praised by critics and home cooks alike. Many of her desserts call for the most flavorful fruits that she can find.

"Fruit marinated in champagne was popular in the 1940s and 1950s. It tastes so good that you won't even realize it's fat-free."

This variation on her classic recipe can use either sparkling cider or dry champagne. The cider is sweet enough that you probably won't need any sugar. With the champagne, sweeten the berries to taste with a syrup made by boiling equal parts sugar and water until the sugar dissolves; pour over the fruit while still hot.

There is no need to mask the clean flavors of great berries with whipped cream or ice cream. If you want to add something creamy, try serving the fruit with low-fat or nonfat frozen vanilla yogurt.

Marinated Summer Berries

1   pint raspberries
1   pint blueberries
1   pint blackberries, olallieberries or boysenberries
4   cups sparkling cider or dry champagne

Place the raspberries, blueberries and blackberries, olallieberries or boysenberries in a medium bowl. Pour the cider or champagne over the berries and let stand for about an hour.

Makes 6 servings. Per serving: 135 calories, 0.6 g. fat (4% of calories), 1.1 g. protein, 19.3 g. carbohydrates, 6.1 g. dietary fiber, 0 mg. cholesterol, 3 mg. sodium

NOTES

• This recipe works well with almost any combination of berries. Try replacing the raspberries with strawberries and/or loganberries.

• For a hint of spice, sprinkle the marinated berries with a pinch of ground cinnamon.

• These berries make a wonderful filling for Basic Dessert Crêpes (page 347). Top the filled crêpes with a dollop of nonfat frozen vanilla yogurt.

• For a colorful addition, use the berries to fill the center of Glazed Golden Bundt Cake (page 484).

QUICK!

Sauté of Sliced Apples and Almonds

4	Granny Smith apples, peeled and cored
2	tablespoons lemon juice
1	teaspoon canola oil
¼	cup apple cider
1	tablespoon maple syrup
¼	teaspoon lemon rind
¼	teaspoon vanilla
¼	teaspoon ground cinnamon
¼	teaspoon ground cloves
2	tablespoons sliced almonds, toasted (see note)

Slice the apples and toss them with the lemon juice in a large bowl.

In a large no-stick skillet over medium-high heat, warm the oil. Add the apples and sauté for 2 minutes. Reduce the heat to low, cover and simmer, stirring occasionally, for 5 to 8 minutes, or until the apples are just tender. Using a slotted spoon, carefully remove the apples and divide among 4 dessert dishes.

To the skillet, add the apple cider, maple syrup, lemon rind, vanilla, cinnamon and cloves. Cook over medium-high heat, stirring constantly, until syrupy. Spoon over the apples. Sprinkle with the almonds.

Makes 4 servings. Per serving: 128 calories, 3.5 g. fat (22% of calories), 1 g. protein, 25.9 g. carbohydrates, 2.3 g. dietary fiber, 0 mg. cholesterol, 2 mg. sodium

NOTE
• To toast almonds, place them in a dry no-stick skillet over medium heat. Toast the nuts, shaking the skillet often, for 3 to 5 minutes, or until fragrant and golden.

VARIATION
Sauté of Sliced Pears and Almonds: Replace the apples with 5 pears, the apple cider with ¼ cup orange juice and the lemon rind with 1 teaspoon orange rind.

QUICK!

Poached Pears

1	cup apple cider or red wine
1	cup water
3	tablespoons sugar
½	teaspoon vanilla
3	thin strips lemon rind
6	ripe but firm pears, peeled, halved and cored (leave the stems on)

In a large saucepan or Dutch oven, combine the cider or wine, water, sugar, vanilla and lemon rind. Add the pears and submerge as much as possible.

Over high heat, bring the mixture almost to a boil, or until the liquid is steaming vigorously. Reduce the heat to medium-low, cover and simmer for 15 to 20 minutes, or until the pears are just tender when pierced with a fork. Turn the pears occasionally for even cooking.

Using a slotted spoon, carefully remove the pears and divide among 6 dessert dishes.

Increase the heat under the pan to high. Boil the liquid until it is reduced by half. Cool slightly.

Spoon the reduced poaching liquid over the pears.

Makes 6 servings. Per serving: 144 calories, 0.7 g. fat (4% of calories), 0.7 g. protein, 37.2 g. carbohydrates, 4.7 g. dietary fiber, 0 mg. cholesterol, 1 mg. sodium

VARIATIONS
Orange Poached Pears: Replace the apple cider with 1 cup red wine or nonalcoholic red wine and 1 cup orange juice. Replace the lemon rind with orange rind.

Poached Pears in Vanilla Yogurt Sauce: After cooling the reduced poaching liquid, stir in ¼ cup nonfat vanilla yogurt.

Spiced Poached Pears with Cranberries: Before poaching the pears, add 1 cinnamon stick, 8 whole cloves, ½ teaspoon star anise pieces and 2 lemon tea bags to the poaching liquid. After removing the poached pears, strain the liquid and discard the solids. Measure out 1 cup liquid and return to the pan. Add 1 cup cranberries and cook over medium heat for 10 minutes, or until the cranberries pop. If desired, top the pear halves with nonfat frozen vanilla yogurt. Spoon the cranberries and liquid over the pears. To serve this dessert for Thanksgiving dinner (menu on page 558), double the recipe.

QUICK!
Poached Bananas in Vanilla Sauce

2   cups apple juice
3   tablespoons raisins
1   teaspoon vanilla
¾   teaspoon ground cinnamon
⅛   teaspoon ground nutmeg
4   bananas, sliced
¼   cup nonfat vanilla yogurt

In a medium saucepan, combine the apple juice, raisins, vanilla, cinnamon and nutmeg. Bring to a boil. Reduce the heat to low and simmer for 5 minutes.

Add the bananas, cover and simmer for 10 minutes, or until the bananas are plump and softened. Remove the pan from the heat. Using a slotted spoon, carefully remove the bananas and divide among 4 dessert bowls. Set aside.

Stir the yogurt into the juice mixture to make a sauce. Spoon over the bananas. Serve warm.

Makes 4 servings. Per serving: 196 calories, 0.8 g. fat (3% of calories), 2.3 g. protein, 48.4 g. carbohydrates, 2.5 g. dietary fiber, 0.3 mg. cholesterol, 16 mg. sodium

Spiced Dried Fruit Compote

2   cups water
1   Earl Grey tea bag
6   ounces dried apricots, halved
4   ounces dried figs, halved
4   ounces dried cherries
1   tablespoon honey
1   slice fresh ginger (about ¼" thick)
1   strip lemon rind (about 2" long)
1   small cinnamon stick

In a medium saucepan, bring the water to a boil. Remove from the heat. Add the tea bag and let steep for 5 minutes. Remove the bag, pressing to extract the liquid. Discard the bag.

Add the apricots, figs, cherries, honey, ginger, lemon rind and cinnamon stick. Bring to a boil. Reduce the heat to low and simmer, stirring occasionally, for 15 to 20 minutes, or until the fruit is tender.

Remove and discard the ginger, lemon rind and cinnamon stick. Serve warm or chilled.

Makes 6 servings. Per serving: 194 calories, 0.8 g. fat (3% of calories), 2.9 g. protein, 49.1 g. carbohydrates, 4.2 g. dietary fiber, 0 mg. cholesterol, 11 mg. sodium

NOTE
• The apricots can be replaced with other dried fruit, such as peaches or nectarines.

Cherry Compote with Vanilla Custard

QUICK!

Cherry Compote

- 4 cups fresh or frozen pitted sour cherries
- 5 tablespoons orange juice
- 2 tablespoons sugar
- ¾ teaspoon ground cinnamon
- ¼ teaspoon ground nutmeg
- ½ teaspoon grated orange rind

Vanilla Custard

- 2 tablespoons cornstarch
- 2 cups skim milk
- 2 tablespoons sugar
- ¼ cup fat-free egg substitute
- 2 teaspoons vanilla

To make the cherry compote: In a medium saucepan, combine the cherries, orange juice, sugar, cinnamon, nutmeg and orange rind. Bring to a boil over medium heat. Cover and simmer for 5 minutes. Set aside.

To make the vanilla custard: In a small saucepan, dissolve the cornstarch in a small amount of the milk. Whisk in the sugar and remaining milk. Cook over medium heat, stirring constantly, for 5 to 10 minutes, or until the mixture comes to a boil and thickens.

Remove from the heat and whisk in the egg substitute and vanilla. Return to the heat and cook, stirring constantly, for 1 minute. Transfer to a bowl. Serve warm or chilled over the compote.

Makes 6 servings. Per serving: 138 calories, 0.5 g. fat (3% of calories), 4.8 g. protein, 29.6 g. carbohydrates, 1.4 g. dietary fiber, 1 mg. cholesterol, 63 mg. sodium

NOTES

• To use dried sour cherries, reduce the amount to 1 cup and simmer them in water until plumped. Drain and proceed with the recipe.

• This compote also makes a delicious low-fat topping for waffles, pancakes, cooked cereal and frozen yogurt.

VARIATION

Blueberry Compote with Vanilla Custard: Replace the cherries with 4 cups fresh or frozen blueberries.

Raspberry Dessert Sauce

QUICK!

- 1 package (10 ounces) frozen raspberries in syrup, thawed
- 1 teaspoon lemon juice
- ¼ teaspoon almond extract
- ½ teaspoon unflavored gelatin

Press the raspberries through a fine sieve into a small saucepan. Discard the seeds.

Add the lemon juice, almond extract and gelatin to the pan. Set aside for 5 minutes, or until the gelatin is softened.

Cook over medium heat, stirring constantly, until the gelatin is dissolved and the mixture is hot. Remove from the heat and cool slightly.

Refrigerate any leftover sauce in an airtight container.

Makes 2 cups. Per ¼ cup: 38 calories, 0.1 g. fat (2% of calories), 0.4 g. protein, 9.4 g. carbohydrates, 1.6 g. dietary fiber, 0 mg. cholesterol, 0.6 mg. sodium

NOTE

• This smooth sauce works beautifully on ice cream and cakes. For a decorative presentation, try swirling it on the dessert plate before topping with the dessert.

VARIATION

Strawberry Dessert Sauce: Replace the raspberries with 1 package (10 ounces) frozen strawberries in syrup, thawed.

Creamy Strawberry Sauce

⅓ cup white grape juice
1 tablespoon honey
2 cups strawberries, hulled
½ cup nonfat vanilla yogurt

In a food processor or blender, combine the grape juice, honey and 1 cup of the strawberries. Process until smooth.

Slice the remaining 1 cup strawberries. Gently fold into the sauce along with the yogurt.

Refrigerate any leftover sauce in an airtight container.

Makes 2 cups. Per ¼ cup: 33 calories, 0.2 g. fat (4% of calories), 1 g. protein, 7.2 g. carbohydrates, 0.7 g. dietary fiber, 0 mg. cholesterol, 11 mg. sodium

NOTE

• This chunky sauce is perfect for shortcake or angel food cake.

Peach-and-Blueberry Sauce

1 tablespoon cornstarch
1 cup orange juice
3 tablespoons maple syrup
½ teaspoon ground cinnamon
⅛ teaspoon ground nutmeg
¼ teaspoon almond extract
2 cups peeled and sliced peaches
¼ cup blueberries

In a medium saucepan, dissolve the cornstarch in a small amount of the orange juice.

Stir in the maple syrup, cinnamon and nutmeg. Bring to a boil over medium heat, stirring constantly. Cook and stir for 2 minutes, or until the sauce thickens. Stir in the almond extract, peaches and blueberries.

Refrigerate any leftover sauce in an airtight container.

Makes 2½ cups. Per ¼ cup: 46 calories, 0.1 g. fat (2% of calories), 0.4 g. protein, 11.5 g. carbohydrates, 0.8 g. dietary fiber, 0 mg. cholesterol, 1 mg. sodium

VARIATION

Orange and Blueberry Sauce: Add ½ teaspoon minced fresh ginger along with the maple syrup. Replace the peaches with 2 cups seeded and chopped orange segments.

Banana-Mango Mousse

2 ripe mangoes, peeled and coarsely chopped (about 2½ cups)
½ cup nonfat vanilla yogurt
1 small banana
2 teaspoons honey
2 drops vanilla
3 ice cubes
4 sprigs mint

In a food processor or blender, combine the mangoes, yogurt, banana, honey, vanilla and ice cubes. Process with on/off turns until the ice is broken up. Process until smooth. Remove any remaining large pieces of ice.

Divide the mixture among 4 dessert dishes. Garnish with the mint. Serve immediately.

Makes 4 servings. Per serving: 127 calories, 0.4 g. fat (3% of calories), 2.2 g. protein, 31.5 g. carbohydrates, 2.9 g. dietary fiber, 0 mg. cholesterol, 20 mg. sodium

NOTE

• Serve with Raspberry Dessert Sauce (opposite page) for a delicious and colorful accompaniment.

Melon Sorbet

4 cups frozen cantaloupe, honeydew or watermelon chunks, slightly thawed
1 frozen banana, sliced
1 teaspoon lemon juice

In a food processor or blender, combine the melon, bananas and lemon juice. Process until smooth.

Transfer the mixture to a metal or plastic container. Cover and freeze for 4 hours or overnight. Remove from the freezer and break up the mixture with a knife. Process briefly in a food processor or blender. Return to the container, cover and freeze for at least 30 minutes before serving.

Makes 6 servings. Per serving: 55 calories, 0.4 g. fat (6% of calories), 1.1 g. protein, 13.5 g. carbohydrates, 1.1 g. dietary fiber, 0 mg. cholesterol, 10 mg. sodium

VARIATIONS

Pineapple Sorbet: Replace the melon with 4 cups frozen pineapple chunks.

Mango Sorbet: Replace the melon with 2¼ cups peeled and coarsely chopped fresh or frozen mangoes. Omit the banana and lemon juice. Instead, in a food processor or blender, process the mangoes with ½ cup carbonated water, ⅓ cup honey and 1 tablespoon lime juice. Freeze as directed.

Blueberry-Buttermilk Sorbet

1 package (12 ounces) frozen blueberries
½ cup frozen white grape juice concentrate
⅓ cup sugar
1 teaspoon grated lemon rind
1 cup buttermilk

In a small saucepan, combine the blueberries, frozen juice concentrate, sugar and lemon rind. Bring to a boil over high heat. Reduce the heat to medium-low and simmer for 5 minutes, or until the blueberries are thawed and begin to pop. Remove the pan from the heat; set aside to cool.

In a food processor or blender, combine the buttermilk and the blueberry mixture. Puree until smooth.

Transfer the mixture to a metal or plastic container. Cover and freeze for 4 hours or overnight. Remove from the freezer and break up the mixture with a knife. Process briefly in a food processor or blender.

Return to the container, cover and freeze for at least 30 minutes before serving.

Makes 4 servings. Per serving: 197 calories, 1.2 g. fat (5% of calories), 2.6 g. protein, 46 g. carbohydrates, 2.7 g. dietary fiber, 2 mg. cholesterol, 68 mg. sodium

VARIATION

Cranberry Sorbet: Replace the blueberries with 1 package (12 ounces) cranberries. In a small saucepan, bring the cranberries and 2 cups water to a boil. Reduce the heat to low and simmer for 5 minutes, or until the berries pop. Press the mixture through a sieve to extract the juice. Transfer the juice to a food processor or blender. Replace the the frozen grape juice concentrate with frozen apple juice concentrate and the sugar with brown sugar. Add these to the food processor and blend until smooth. Omit the lemon rind and buttermilk. Freeze as directed.

Raspberry Sorbet: Replace the blueberries with 1 package (12 ounces) raspberries and the lemon rind with 1 teaspoon lemon juice. Mash the berries against the bottom and sides of the pan. Press the cooked berry mixture through a fine sieve. Discard the seeds. Freeze as directed. (For *Minted Raspberry Sorbet*, add 1 tablespoon crème de menthe liqueur to the pan with the frozen juice concentrate.)

Strawberry Sorbet: Replace the blueberries with 1 package (12 ounces) strawberries and the lemon rind with 1 teaspoon lemon juice. Mash the berries against the bottom and sides of the pan. Press the cooked berry mixture through a fine sieve. Discard the seeds. Freeze as directed.

Peach Soufflé

3 peaches, peeled, pitted and chopped (about 1½ cups)
¼ cup sugar
2 egg yolks
1 tablespoon lemon juice
½ teaspoon ground nutmeg
5 egg whites, at room temperature
½ teaspoon cream of tartar
Pinch of ground cinnamon

Preheat the oven to 300°.

In a blender or food processor, puree the peaches. Transfer to a medium bowl and gently stir in the sugar, egg yolks, lemon juice and nutmeg. Set aside.

In a large clean bowl, using an electric mixer, beat the egg whites at high speed until foamy. Add the cream of tartar and beat until stiff peaks form.

Gradually stir ¼ of the egg-white mixture into the peach mixture. Gently fold the peach mixture back into the remaining egg-white mixture.

Spoon the mixture into a 1½-quart soufflé dish. Sprinkle with the cinnamon.

Place the soufflé dish in a baking dish large enough to hold the soufflé dish, then place it on the bottom rack of the oven. Pour 1″ hot water into the baking dish. Bake for 50 to 60 minutes, or until the soufflé is puffed and lightly browned. (Do not open the oven door until near the end of baking time. Otherwise, the soufflé may fall.)

Serve immediately.

Makes 4 servings. Per serving: 126 calories, 2.7 g. fat (19% of calories), 6.3 g. protein, 20.4 g. carbohydrates, 1.1 g. dietary fiber, 107 mg. cholesterol, 90 mg. sodium

NOTE
• You can replace the fresh peaches with 1½ cups frozen and thawed peaches or well-drained canned peaches (packed in juice).

Banana Ice Cream

2 large frozen bananas, sliced
2 tablespoons sugar
1½ cups skim milk
½ teaspoon cinnamon
½ teaspoon vanilla
Pinch of ground nutmeg

In a food processor or blender, combine the bananas, sugar and ½ cup of the milk. Puree until smooth. Add the cinnamon, vanilla and remaining 1 cup milk. Puree until smooth.

Transfer the mixture to a metal or plastic container. Cover and freeze for 4 hours or overnight. Remove from the freezer and break up the mixture with a knife. Process briefly in a food processor or blender.

Return to the container, cover and freeze for at least 30 minutes before serving. Sprinkle with the nutmeg and serve.

Makes 4 servings. Per serving: 111 calories, 0.4 g. fat (3% of calories), 3.7 g. protein, 24.5 g. carbohydrates, 1 g. dietary fiber, 1 mg. cholesterol, 48 mg. sodium

NOTE
• Top the ice cream with Chocolate Sauce (page 472)

VARIATION
Berry-Banana Ice Cream: Add 1 cup frozen blueberries, strawberries or raspberries along with the bananas.

Peach Sherbet Parfaits

5 peaches, peeled and coarsely chopped
½ cup peach-blend juice
1 teaspoon unflavored gelatin
3 tablespoons sugar
1 tablespoon lemon juice
1 teaspoon vanilla
¼ teaspoon almond extract
1½ cups nonfat peach yogurt with fruit on the bottom, well-mixed
2 tablespoons slivered almonds, toasted (see note on page 428)
6 peach slices

In a food processor or blender, process the peaches until smooth. Measure out 2 cups puree and set aside.

Place the peach-blend juice in a small saucepan. Sprinkle in the gelatin and set aside for 5 minutes, or until the gelatin is softened.

Add the sugar to the pan. Cook over medium heat, stirring constantly, until the gelatin is dissolved and the mixture is hot. Remove from the heat and stir in the lemon juice, vanilla and the 2 cups reserved peach puree.

Transfer the mixture to a metal or plastic container. Cover and freeze for 2 hours.

Meanwhile, in a small bowl, stir the almond extract into the yogurt and set aside.

Remove the mixture from the freezer and break it up with a knife. Process briefly in a food processor or blender. Divide half of the sherbet among 6 parfait glasses. Spoon in the yogurt and sprinkle with half of the almonds. Top with the remaining sherbet. Cover the parfaits and freeze for at least 2 hours, or until set. Before serving, garnish with the peach slices and remaining almonds.

Makes 6 servings. Per serving: 107 calories, 1.3 g. fat (11% of calories), 3.4 g. protein, 21.3 g. carbohydrates, 1.4 g. dietary fiber, 0 mg. cholesterol, 38 mg. sodium

NOTE
• To serve these parfaits for Easter supper (menu on page 562), double the recipe and use large parfait glasses.

VARIATIONS
Orange Sherbet Parfaits with Walnuts: Replace the peach sherbet with prepared orange sherbet, the peach yogurt with vanilla yogurt and the almonds with chopped toasted walnuts.
Raspberry Sherbet Parfaits with Pecans: Replace the peach sherbet with prepared raspberry sherbet, the peach yogurt with raspberry yogurt and the almonds with chopped toasted pecans.

QUICK!
Apricot Smoothie

10–12 pitted canned apricot halves (packed in juice), drained
1 cup skim milk
⅔ cup nonfat vanilla frozen yogurt
⅛ teaspoon almond extract

In a food processor or blender, combine the apricots, milk, frozen yogurt and almond extract. Process until smooth.

Spoon the mixture into 2 tall glasses. Serve immediately.

Makes 2 servings. Per serving: 286 calories, 1.6 g. fat (5% of calories), 11.1 g. protein, 61.3 g. carbohydrates, 6.7 g. dietary fiber, 2 mg. cholesterol, 103 mg. sodium

VARIATION
Peach Smoothie: Replace the apricots with 10 to 12 pitted canned peaches (packed in juice).

S

trawberry-Banana Shake

2 cups sliced strawberries
1 large banana, sliced
½ cup orange juice
½ cup nonfat vanilla yogurt
4 ice cubes

In a blender, combine the strawberries, bananas, orange juice, yogurt and ice cubes. Blend until thick and smooth.

Makes 4 servings. Per serving: 85 calories, 0.5 g. fat (5% of calories), 2.3 g. protein, 19.5 g. carbohydrates, 2.1 g. dietary fiber, 0 mg. cholesterol, 19 mg. sodium

NOTE
• For a thicker shake, use frozen fruit.

VARIATIONS
Banana-Mango Shake: Replace the strawberries with 2 cups peeled and coarsely chopped mangoes.
Blueberry-Banana Shake: Replace the strawberries with 2 cups fresh or frozen blueberries.
Blueberry-Peach Shake: Replace the strawberries with 2 cups fresh or frozen blueberries and the banana with 1 cup peeled and sliced peaches. Replace the yogurt and ice cubes with 1 cup nonfat frozen vanilla or peach yogurt.
Strawberry-Apricot Shake: Replace the banana with 1 cup sliced apricots. Replace the yogurt and ice cubes with 1 cup nonfat frozen vanilla or strawberry yogurt.

C

old Melon Soup

1 ripe cantaloupe or honeydew melon, seeded and cut into cubes
¼ teaspoon ground cinnamon (optional)
2½ cups orange juice
2 tablespoons lime juice
1 tablespoon honey
1 teaspoon chopped fresh mint

In a food processor or blender, combine the cantaloupe or honeydew, cinnamon (if using), orange juice, lime juice and honey. Process until smooth.

Pour the mixture into a bowl. Stir in the mint, cover and refrigerate for at least 1 hour.

Makes 4 servings. Per serving: 186 calories, 0.7 g. fat (3% of calories), 3.8 g. protein, 45.7 g. carbohydrates, 4.8 g. dietary fiber, 0 mg. cholesterol, 64 mg. sodium

C

hilled Strawberry-Apricot Soup

2 cups strawberries, hulled
2 cups ripe fresh apricot halves
1 cup nonfat vanilla yogurt
1½ teaspoons lemon juice
1 tablespoon sugar

In a food processor or blender, combine the strawberries and apricots. Process until smooth. Transfer to a medium bowl and stir in the yogurt, lemon juice and sugar. Cover and refrigerate for 20 minutes.

Makes 4 servings. Per serving: 113 calories, 0.5 g. fat (4% of calories), 4.1 g. protein, 25 g. carbohydrates, 0.9 g. dietary fiber, 0 mg. cholesterol, 39 mg. sodium

Classic
Homestyle
Desserts

Pies, Crisps and Other Sweets

When you're craving a simple, homey dessert, pies, crisps, cobblers and their kin fit the bill. Not only do they provide delectable good flavors, but they can also be made without the sky-high fat and calories of traditional after-meal delights.

These crusty desserts can be as simple as fresh-baked apple slices embraced in a no-fuss shell or as elaborate and lovely as a latticework cherry pie. For the most part, however, these flavorful desserts are eminently easy to make.

The biggest difference between pies and members of the crisps-cobblers-bettys family is the type and placement of the crust material. Pies typically have a bottom shell and maybe a top one; either shell can be made of pastry dough or crumbs. The other fruit desserts generally have only a top crust, which can be pastry, biscuit dough or a crumb-type mixture. Occasionally, the crumbs are layered in with the fruit.

CRUMB CRUSTS

When you have a taste for pie but don't feel like starting from scratch on a traditional crust, a crumb crust is a wonderful alternative. Rather than creating a dough, you simply line the bottom of a pan with moistened crumbs, pat them firm and add the filling of your choice.

Crumb crusts are frequently used for custard and cream pies. The crumbs can be made from graham crackers, cookies or dry bread. You can even make granola-based crusts; choose a low-fat granola to make a healthy dessert.

Although traditional crumb crusts can be as fatty as pastry ones, there are ways to lighten them up. If you really want to save time, look for ready-made reduced-fat crumb crusts in the store. But if you want a homemade crust, follow these tips.

☞ Put low-fat cookies, graham crackers or stale bread in a food processor or blender. Process to make crumbs. You'll need about 1½ cups crumbs for a 9″ pie shell.

☞ Mix 2 tablespoons melted butter or margarine, 1½ tablespoons water and 1 tablespoon light corn syrup in a cup. Add to the crumbs and mix well. The mixture should hold together when you press it; if needed, add a little more water.

☞ You can replace the butter or margarine with vegetable oil to reduce saturated fat.

☞ A fat-free alternative to bind the crust is to mix in enough melted preserves or jelly, such as apricot, to thoroughly moisten the crumbs.

☞ Spread the crumb mixture evenly in the bottom and up the sides of a pie pan. Pack it firmly with your fingers or press the bottom of a second pie pan into the crust to evenly distribute the crumbs.

PASTRY CRUSTS

While chefs have had great success in reducing the amount of fat in cakes, ice cream and many other wonderful desserts, they've had a harder

BEYOND PIES

You're familiar with pies and tarts, but what about crumbles, slumps and grunts? Here's a glossary of a few favorite homespun desserts. All but the slumps and grunts are traditionally prepared in the oven.

☞ **Brown betty.** A betty is similar to a crisp, but the crumbly topping is layered in with the fruit rather than sprinkled on top.

☞ **Cobbler.** A cobbler has fruit filling that's topped with a biscuit crust.

☞ **Crisp.** Like the cobbler, a crisp is made with baked fruit. But it's covered with a crumbly mixture that's sprinkled on top.

☞ **Crumble.** This is similar to a crisp but has a crunchier texture, because oats are included in the topping.

☞ **Grunts and slumps.** These are cobblers that are made on top of the stove, often in a cast-iron skillet, rather than in the oven. The names stem from the cooking process: When steam softens the crust, for example, it slumps. Similarly, when the sizzling fruit filling expands and releases liquid, it emits a soft grunt.

☞ **Pandowdy.** This is a form of cobbler made with very ripe fruit, which becomes so juicy that the topping is pushed down into it to absorb the juice.

time putting pastry dough on a diet. This is because fat—such as butter, lard, margarine and vegetable shortening—simply makes the flakiest pie crusts. While it's possible to make a crust with virtually no fat, it will likely be unpleasantly tough, with a flat, unsatisfying flavor.

You can't eliminate all fat from pastry crust, but there are ways to make it leaner.

To achieve light, flaky pie crusts, it's important to work quickly. Handling the mixture too much causes gluten in the flour to develop. While this stretchy protein is helpful when making bread, it can turn pastry crust unpleasantly tough.

Subtract some fat. While pastry recipes tend to be exact and balanced formulas, it's often possible to cut out about one-third the amount of shortening without seriously affecting the texture. To enhance the flavor, add a pinch of grated lemon or orange rind or a little vanilla or almond extract.

Mix it up. Rather than making crusts with pure butter or shortening, try replacing some of the solid fat with oil. While this won't significantly lower the calories or total fat count, at least it will replace some of the saturated fat with a more heart-healthy, polyunsaturated kind.

There isn't an exact formula when it comes to substituting liquid fat for solid fat. Chefs recommend experimenting—substitute just a little bit at a time until you find a combination that gives the desired texture and taste. Keep in mind that crusts made with oil tend to be more crumbly and, therefore, harder to handle.

When rolling out a crust that contains oil, put it between sheets of wax paper. Or simply press the crust into the pie plate with your fingers.

Skim the toughness. Using some cooking oil in place of shortening can make crusts tough and chewy. Adding a few tablespoons skim milk along with the oil will help keep the crust tender.

Switch to low-gluten flour. Using oil or other liquid activates the gluten in flour, making crusts tough. To prevent this, chefs advise using cake flour, which has less gluten than all-purpose flour.

THE CRUST DOCTOR

Yot read the recipe, worked carefully and followed directions to the letter. So what went wrong? Here are some common pie problems—and the usual causes.

PROBLEM	LIKELY CAUSES
PIE DOUGH	
Too stiff	Not enough shortening Not enough liquid Wrong flour was used
Too crumbly	Too much shortening Not enough liquid Dough was overmixed
Too tough	Not enough shortening Wrong flour was used Dough was overmixed
BAKED CRUST	
Crust shrinks	Not enough shortening Dough was overmixed
Tough crust	Not enough shortening Dough was overmixed
Soggy crust	Oven temperature was too low Not baked long enough Filling seeped through holes in dough
Crumbly crust	Dough was too dry Too much shortening
Crust edges lost shape	Oven temperature was too low Dough was too warm before baking

Try a new mix. If you don't have cake flour, mix a little cornstarch or oat flour with regular flour to help keep gluten levels down to manageable levels. Replace 2 tablespoons of the flour with an equal amount of cornstarch or oat flour.

Keep it cool. Since heat activates gluten, make it a point to chill all your ingredients before adding them to the mix.

Take a hands-off approach. Since gluten responds to heat, the more you handle the dough, the tougher the resulting crust is likely to be.

Make it tender. Adding a small amount of lemon juice, vinegar or yogurt to the dough inhibits the production of gluten and helps tenderize the crust.

Baking Flours

We often think that flour, as it says on the label, really is all-purpose. But different types of flour work best for specific types of baking.

☞ **All-purpose.** This is the kind of flour that most people use every day. Although it's fairly high in gluten (from 10 to 13 percent), it has been formulated to work well for a variety of baked goods, including pastries, cakes, cookies and breads. For pies and tarts, it's not necessarily the best choice but will still give adequate results.

☞ **Cake flour.** Because of its extremely low gluten content (usually between 6 and 10 percent), cake flour works well for pastry crusts. Do not hesitate to substitute cake flour for pastry flour. Make sure, however, that you don't

FIGHT FAT WITH PHYLLO

A traditional Middle Eastern dough called phyllo (or filo) is very low in fat—as long as you don't slather the paper-thin sheets with lots of butter. Found in the freezer section of supermarkets, it resembles strudel dough and can be used to replace traditional crusts for pies and tarts. However, phyllo is fragile and tends to break apart rather than flake.

When using phyllo:

☞ Defrost it in the refrigerator overnight rather than at room temperature. This makes it easier to separate and work with the papery leaves.

☞ Keep the leaves well-wrapped until you're ready to use them. To use, unroll and cover the stack with plastic wrap under a dampened kitchen towel. This will prevent the dough from drying and cracking.

☞ Most recipes call for phyllo leaves to be stacked four or five deep. Using a pastry brush, lightly flick melted butter on the surface to provide needed moisture. Healthy cooks sometimes combine a little vegetable oil with the butter. For less fat, use a light coating of no-stick spray over each layer.

☞ Phyllo refreezes well. Wrap leftover sheets tightly with plastic wrap and store them in the freezer for up to three months.

☞ **Pastry flour.** Lower in gluten (from 8 to 12 percent) than all-purpose flour, pastry flour is finely milled and is generally the first choice for making pie and tart crusts. It's sometimes hard to find, however, which is why many cooks routinely substitute the all-purpose kind.

☞ **Whole-wheat flour.** While its gluten content equals that of all-purpose flour, the additional presence of the germ and bran makes whole-wheat flour heavy and dense—not the best choice for making tender crusts.

☞ **Whole-wheat pastry flour.** More finely milled than plain whole-wheat flour, it can be used in pastry recipes, although the resulting crust will be somewhat heavier than one made from all-purpose flour.

Shortening

Healthy cooks are always looking for new ways to reduce or eliminate fat from their diets without sacrificing good taste and satisfying textures. This is particularly challenging when making pie crusts, which depend on fat for taste and fork-tender flakiness.

A flaky pastry is composed of many layers of gluten, each separated by bits of fat. A good crust can never be fat-free. It is possible to reduce the amount of shortening you use. These are the fats generally used for pastry.

☞ **Vegetable shortening.** This type of shortening produces the flakiest crust, while imparting little flavor. It keeps well and is easy to use, making it the fat of choice for many bakers. Because shortening is hydrogenated—and therefore saturated—it's not considered a healthy fat.

☞ **Butter.** The grande dame of baking, butter gives crusts a rich taste. Unfortunately, it also delivers large amounts of saturated fat. To get the flavor of butter with a somewhat lighter texture, many cooks combine it half-and-half with vegetable shortening.

☞ **Margarine.** This produces a slightly oily crust with little flavor, so it isn't most chefs'

inadvertently use self-rising cake flour. This type of flour contains baking soda or baking powder that would make pastry crust rise in an undesirable way.

choice for pastry crusts. If you do use margarine, however, use the stick type rather than the tub variety. Margarine in a tub contains more moisture, which can throw off the balance of fluids in the recipe.

☞ **Vegetable oil.** Although oils like safflower or canola contain none of the rich taste of butter, they contain little saturated fat. The drawback to using oil is that it makes dough difficult to work, and the resulting crust will likely be tough. Some cooks compromise and use a combination of oil, shortening and butter.

Mixing Pastry Dough

The golden rule for making a good pastry crust is to handle the dough as little—and as quickly—as possible. Otherwise, you could lose the necessary layering of fat and moisture that makes a crust flaky and fork-tender.

To get a good crust every time, here's what chefs recommend.

Keep it cold. When making pastry dough, chilling the ingredients and even the utensils will help prevent gluten from developing and making the crust tough.

If you've started work and the dough seems unresponsive to rolling or shaping, chill it for an additional 15 to 20 minutes. This will relax the gluten that has already developed, making it easier to work.

Helpful Hint

Pastry dough freezes well, so you can always have some on hand. Rolled into rounds, stacked between sheets of wax paper and sealed in a plastic bag, the frozen dough keeps for several months.

Handle it gently. Overworking the dough causes it to heat up, melting some of the fat particles inside. This reduces flakiness and causes additional gluten to develop, which will further toughen the crust.

To prevent this from occurring, most recipes call for shortening to be cut into the flour. The purpose of this is to mix the ingredients fairly well, without going so far as to cause the shortening to melt or break down. (For more on cutting fat into flour, see the illustrations on page 343.)

Cut the chilled shortening, butter or margarine into pieces and sprinkle it over the flour. Use a pastry blender, two forks or two knives to quickly cut the fat into smaller and smaller pieces. Make pieces that are pea-size or smaller.

Add liquid sparingly. Once the dough mixture is crumbly, you need to add a little liquid to hold it all together. Don't add too much, however; 2 to 3 tablespoons is generally all that you need. Chefs advise using ice water to prevent the mix from overheating.

Sprinkle the liquid over the flour and use a fork to toss the flour to moisten it without activating the gluten. When you're done, the dough should hold together when pressed but not be wet or sticky.

Let it rest. When you've formed the dough into a ball, wrap it in wax paper or plastic wrap and refrigerate it for at least 30 minutes. The chilling stops gluten development, keeping the dough soft and pliable. It will also help reduce shrinkage of the crust during baking.

Go easy on the flour. Putting too much flour on the work surface or rolling pin will also toughen the dough. Use only as much flour as absolutely necessary to prevent the dough from sticking.

Let a machine help out. Although pastry dough is easy enough to mix by hand, a food processor can make the whole process even easier. It's important to remember, however, that the machine's speed and efficiency make it easy to overmix the dough. So always mix it a little bit less than you think necessary.

☞ Put the flour and other dry ingredients in the bowl and give it a quick whirl. It's best to fit the processor with a metal blade, which will cut the solid fat quickly and smoothly. Using a plastic blade could cause the shortening to be mashed rather than cut.

☞ Add small pieces of chilled solid fat to the bowl and process with on/off turns just until the mixture resembles coarse meal.

☞ With the processor running, add 2 to 3 tablespoons ice water. Immediately turn it off and then process with on/off turns until the dough masses on the mixing blade. Add more water as necessary.

☞ When the dough holds together, gather it into a ball and wrap and refrigerate it until it is cool and firm. Then proceed to roll the dough.

Rolling Dough

How you roll your pastry dough helps determine whether the crust turns out tender and flaky or whether it's tough, heavy and dense. As with mixing, the less you handle the dough, the less that gluten has a chance to develop.

☞ Take the dough from the refrigerator and place it on a lightly floured work surface. Let the dough rest for a minute to warm up very slightly. This will make it easier to roll.

ROLLING PINS

Perhaps no other image is so evocative of the home kitchen as the rolling pin. How many cartoons have shown irate cooks chasing the object of their displeasure with an upright pin? We can only hope that they never connect; rolling pins are substantial pieces of equipment, the main job of which is flattening pie and pastry dough to an even thickness.

American rolling pins are fitted with handles, and the center section rolls freely. European pins, slightly longer and tapered at both ends, do without handles. Both types work well; the kind that you choose is entirely a matter of personal preference. For specific tasks, however, certain rolling pins have distinct advantages.

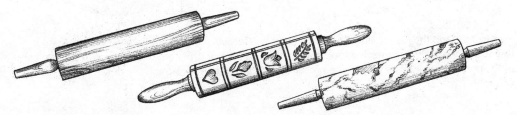

Baker's rolling pins. Made of hardwood, these heavy-duty rolling pins have a steel rod inserted in the cylinder that makes them extra heavy.

Springerle rolling pins. Carved with decorative patterns, these are used for making German Christmas cookies.

Marble rolling pins. Heavy, smooth and cold, marble rolling pins are often used for pastries that must be kept cold to maintain their light and flaky texture.

CREATIVE CRUSTS

W hen you want your homemade pies to look spectacular, spend a few extra minutes gussying up the crusts. Here are some ways to give a professional-looking, picture-perfect finish to your pies.

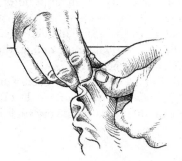

Fluted edge. Place the thumb of one hand flat against the inside edge of the pie. Then press the dough around your thumb using the thumb and index finger of your other hand.

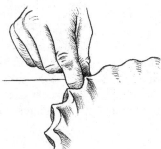

Rickrack flute. First make a fluted edge, then press each "flute" into a point.

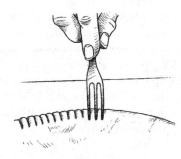

Fork-edged rim. Use the tines of a fork to make a decorative pattern around the edge of the crust.

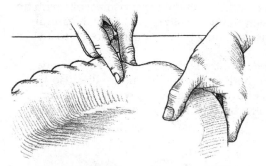

Rope edge. Grip the pie rim firmly between your thumb and index finger, pressing toward the side of the pan with your thumb. Continue pressing as you rotate the pan all the way around.

Cutouts. Cut small triangles, circles, hearts, leaves or other shapes from leftover dough and arrange them around the rim.

☞ Using a rolling pin and applying even pressure, roll out the dough with short strokes. Work from the center outward. Lift and turn it every few strokes. This promotes even rolling and prevents the dough from sticking to the work surface. Try not to roll over the edge of the dough, which will make the edges too thin.

☞ For soft, oily or crumbly doughs, roll out the dough between sheets of wax paper. To prevent the wax paper from skating, lightly flour the paper and dampen the work surface with a sprinkle or two of water.

☞ Recipes vary, but in most cases, you'll want to roll the dough to about ⅛" thickness.

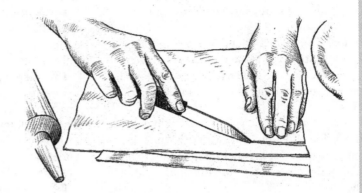

Lattice top. Roll leftover pastry dough into a rectangle about 12″ long. Then cut strips about ½″ wide.

Cross the two longest strips over the center of the pie. Then cover the top strip with another long strip.

Fold back every other strip and lay the cross strips in place. Then return the folded-back strips to their original position.

When all the strips are in place, trim off the overhang with kitchen scissors. Brush the edges of the pastry with water and seal them with a pinch.

Filled or Not?

Pastry dough can be baked either filled or un-filled. Most traditional fruit pies are baked filled—the fruit is placed in uncooked dough and the whole thing bakes at once.

Some types of custard pies start with a partially baked crust. Prebaking the crust keeps it from getting soggy when a wet filling is added. And partial baking prevents delicate fillings from overbaking while the crust gets properly done.

Pies that don't require the filling to be baked use a blind-baked shell—that is, a shell that is baked and cooled, then filled afterward.

Filled crusts. Since most of the fat in a pie resides in the crust, filled pies made with fruit are a great way to enjoy your dessert and not load up on unhealthy calories. For success with a filled crust:

☞ Use a deep pie pan with a channeled rim. This helps prevent the filling from bubbling over.

☞ Don't prick the bottom before filling. Unlike with a blind-baked or partially baked crust, pricking the shell of a filled pie allows liquids to penetrate the crust, making a soggy bottom.

☞ When you're using a moist filling, brush the inside of the pie crust with egg white or sprinkle the crust lightly with flour before filling. This prevents any moisture from penetrating the crust.

☞ Adding hot filling to the uncooked shell causes it to begin cooking immediately, making it less likely to get soft and soggy.

Unfilled crust. Whether you're completely baking an unfilled crust or only partially cooking it, follow these steps.

☞ Prick the bottom of the dough with the tines of a fork before baking to allow steam to escape and also to relax the gluten. This in turn will help reduce shrinkage during baking.

☞ To prevent the shell from bubbling, first line it with aluminum foil or parchment paper. Then add a layer of weights. You can buy pie weights in kitchen supply stores. Or use dried beans or uncooked rice reserved for this purpose. The point is simply to prevent the bottom of the pie from swelling up during baking.

☞ Bake the crust in the center of a preheated oven at 425° for about 10 minutes. Then remove the weights and lining.

☞ For a partially baked shell, bake it for about 3 to 5 minutes longer. Add filling and complete baking according to your recipe.

☞ For a blind-baked shell, bake it for 10 to 15 minutes after removing the weights, or until golden brown. Cool on a wire rack before filling.

Glazing the Crust

The secret to a great-looking two-crust pie is simple: Brush the top with a bit of glaze before baking. An egg-wash glaze will give your pie a beautiful golden shine. For more of a homestyle, country look, use a milk-and-sugar glaze.

The following glazes can be used on a 9″ pie, whether topped with pastry cutouts, latticework or a full top crust.

☞ **Egg-wash glaze.** Whisk together 1 egg and 1 tablespoon water. Brush this mixture on the top crust, then sprinkle with 1 teaspoon sugar, if desired.

☞ **Milk and sugar glaze.** Brush the top crust with 2 teaspoons low-fat milk. Sprinkle with 1 to 2 teaspoons sugar.

MAKING THE MOVE

Perhaps the diciest moment in making pastry is transferring the thin, delicate dough from the counter to the pie pan. Here's an easy way to get it there in one piece.

Loosely wrap the dough around a rolling pin. Then unwrap the dough directly into a no-stick pie pan.

FILLING AND BAKING

The hardest part of making any pie is preparing the crust. Once that's completed, all that remains is to add a filling, pop it into the oven (if it's a cooked filling) and sit back with satisfaction as wonderful smells fill the house.

Fruit fillings are commonly used for pies and tarts. Generally, they are prepared by peeling and slicing fresh fruit, which is then either poached first or put directly into the crust and allowed to bake. Reduced-fat custards also make delicious fillings.

☞ Fruit fillings usually cook down during baking, so what seemed like too much going into the pan may turn out to be too little. Always mound the filling about an inch or two over the rim, measuring from the center where the mound is highest.

☞ Fruit pies are usually done when the filling bubbles up around the edges of the pie. In addition, the crust should be golden brown.

☞ Cutting vents in the upper crust of a double-crust pie allows steam to vent. This helps prevent the filling from bubbling over.

☞ It's normal for custard fillings to first rise during baking and then fall. You can't prevent them from falling, so don't even try.

☞ Custard pies firm up during cooling, so they are usually baked until they are nearly firm but still a little jiggly in the center. To test a custard filling for doneness, stick a toothpick in the center. It should come out dry or, at most, slightly moistened.

Helpful Hint

When the edge of a pie is browning too quickly, cover the rim with strips of aluminum foil. The foil deflects heat and helps the crust cook more slowly while the filling has a chance to get done.

MAKING MERINGUE

Like billowing clouds of airy sweetness, meringues provide the perfect topping for cream, custard or chiffon pies. For the healthy cook, they're also a dream come true: Made with egg whites and just a little sugar, they contain few calories and zero fat.

☞ Begin with a clean, dry bowl and clean electric beaters or a wire whisk. Any oil or egg yolk present on the bowl or beaters will keep the whites from beating up properly.

☞ Beat the whites on low speed until they are opaque and foamy.

☞ Add a pinch of salt or cream of tartar to stabilize the whites. Continue mixing until soft, white peaks form.

☞ Add sugar steadily and slowly, beating all the while on medium speed, until the meringue forms peaks that are firm but not stiff or dry.

☞ Spoon the meringue onto the pie and smooth it into graceful waves with the back of the spoon.

☞ Put the pie into a preheated 350° oven and bake for 20 minutes. This time and temperature are sufficient to destroy any salmonella bacteria. For extra measure, use a quick-read thermometer to check that the temperature in the middle of the meringue has reached 160°.

Jim Dodge

After spending ten years as pastry chef at the Stanford Court in San Francisco, Jim Dodge opened The American Pie Restaurant and Pastry Shop in Hong Kong. Currently with the New England Culinary Institute in Montpelier, Vermont, Dodge has taken the best of American baking and created delicious new recipes—both in the Unites States and abroad.

"The demand for tasty low-fat baked goods is amazing," he says. "The cobbler below is simple to prepare, is filled with great flavor and has a terrific crust."

Although the recipe calls for a combination of delicious summer fruits, it can be made out of season by using unsweetened frozen fruits. Try serving it warm or at room temperature with low-fat vanilla yogurt.

Peach-and-Cherry Cobbler

- 5 large peaches, peeled and pitted
- 3 cups cherries, pitted and halved
- ½ cup + 1 teaspoon sugar
- 1 cup unbleached flour
- 2 tablespoons dark brown sugar
- 1 teaspoon baking powder
- ¼ teaspoon ground nutmeg
- 6 tablespoons cold butter or margarine
- ⅓ cup nonfat sour cream

Preheat the oven to 375°.

Cut each peach into 8 wedges, then cut each wedge in half crosswise. Place in a shallow 3-quart no-stick baking dish. Sprinkle with the cherries and ½ cup of the sugar; toss to coat the fruit with the sugar.

In the bowl of a food processor, place the flour, brown sugar, baking powder and nutmeg. Cut the butter or margarine into 6 pieces and distribute the pieces on top of the flour mixture. Process with on/off turns until the butter or margarine is in pea-size pieces.

Add the sour cream and process with on/off turns until the dough is soft and crumbly. Remove the dough from the food processor and press it together with your hands. Place on a lightly floured surface.

Roll the dough out to fit the top of your baking dish. Carefully lift and place it over the fruit. Tuck in any edges that stick out; the dough doesn't have to lie smooth.

Brush the top lightly with water and sprinkle on the remaining 1 teaspoon sugar. Make four slashes in the dough to allow steam to escape. Bake for 50 minutes, or until the top is firm and lightly browned and the fruit is bubbling around the edges.

Makes 6 servings. Per serving: 339 calories, 11.9 g. fat (31% of calories), 4.4 g. protein, 56.7 g. carbohydrates, 2.6 g. dietary fiber, 31 mg. cholesterol, 184 mg. sodium

Basic Pie Crust

The key ingredient in a tender, flaky pie crust is shortening. We successfully lowered the fat in this tasty pie crust by using less shortening and a bit of low-fat cream cheese.

- 1½ cups all-purpose flour
- ¼ teaspoon salt
- 4 tablespoons vegetable shortening
- 2 ounces low-fat cream cheese
- 2 teaspoons lemon juice
- 4–5 tablespoons ice water

Preheat the oven to 425°.

In a large bowl, combine the flour and salt. Cut in the shortening and cream cheese until the mixture resembles coarse crumbs.

In a cup, combine the lemon juice with 2 tablespoons of the ice water. Sprinkle over the crumbs and mix until the crumbs are moistened. Mix in the remaining ice water, 1 tablespoon at a time, until the crumbs resemble the texture of cottage cheese and can be pressed into a firm ball. Gather the mixture into a ball and press into a thick disk. Cover and refrigerate for 15 to 30 minutes before rolling out.

For a 9″ single-crust pie, roll the dough out to a 12″ circle. Gently lay the dough in a 9″ no-stick pie pan. Firmly press the dough against the bottom and sides of the pan. Fold the edges under and crimp to form a rim. Using a fork, pierce the bottom of the crust all over to prevent it from puffing up during baking. Bake for 10 to 12 minutes, or until lightly browned. Remove from the oven and cool on a wire rack.

Makes one 9″ pie crust; 8 servings. Per serving: 156 calories, 7.5 g. fat (44% of calories), 3.2 g. protein, 18.5 g. carbohydrates, 0.6 g. dietary fiber, 2.5 mg. cholesterol, 107 mg. sodium

NOTES

• To speed preparation, combine the flour and salt in the bowl of a food processor. Add the remaining ingredients as directed, using on/off turns to mix.

• For an unbaked crust, omit the baking step. Tightly wrap the crust in plastic and refrigerate until ready to use.

• For a 9″ double-crust pie, double the ingredients and divide the dough into two thick disks. Roll the second disk into a 12″ circle. Lay over the filled crust and crimp to form a rim.

• For an 8″ single-crust pie with pastry cut-outs or lattice top crust, set aside ⅓ cup of the dough. Roll the remaining dough out to a 10″ circle and press into an 8″ no-stick pie pan. Roll the reserved dough out to ⅛″ thickness. Using a cookie cutter or sharp knife, cut out decorative shapes and gently lay them over the pie filling before baking. For a lattice, follow the directions on page 445.

VARIATION

Whole-Wheat Pie Crust: Replace the all-purpose flour with 1½ cups whole-wheat pastry flour.

Graham Cracker Crust

QUICK!

- 1½ cups broken reduced-fat graham crackers
- 1 egg white

Preheat the oven to 375°. Generously coat a 9″ no-stick pie pan with no-stick spray; set aside.

In medium bowl, crush the crackers with a spoon until fine crumbs form. Add the egg white and stir vigorously until the crumbs are well-moistened and the dough holds together.

Turn the crumb mixture into the pie pan. Using a large spoon, press the crumb mixture into the bottom and up the sides of the pan.

Bake for 5 to 8 minutes, or until the crust is just beginning to brown. Cool completely on a wire rack before filling.

(continued)

Makes one 9″ pie crust; 8 servings. Per serving: 68 calories, 0 g. fat (0% of calories), 3.1 g. protein, 15.3 g. carbohydrates, 2 g. dietary fiber, 0 mg. cholesterol, 27 mg. sodium.

NOTES

• This crisp, crumbly crust works best with cream fillings.

• To speed preparation, place the crackers in the bowl of a food processor. Process using on/off turns until fine crumbs form. Add the egg white and process, using on/off turns, until the dough holds together.

• If the crumb mixture doesn't quite hold together after mixing in the egg white, stir in apricot or other all-fruit spread, 1 teaspoon at a time, until it does.

• If the crumb mixture sticks to the spoon while pressing it into the pan, place a piece of wax paper on top of the crumb mixture. Then press against the wax paper to prevent sticking.

VARIATIONS

Vanilla-Nut Crumb Crust: Replace the graham crackers with 1¼ cups broken reduced-fat vanilla-wafer cookies and ¼ cup finely chopped toasted nuts, such as pecans or walnuts.

Chocolate Crumb Crust: Replace the graham crackers with 1½ cups broken chocolate graham crackers or chocolate wafer cookies.

Gingersnap Crumb Crust: Replace the graham crackers with 1½ cups broken gingersnap cookies.

Basic Tart Crust

1½ cups all-purpose flour
1 tablespoon sugar
¼ teaspoon salt
4 tablespoons vegetable shortening
2 ounces low-fat cream cheese
2 teaspoons lemon juice
3–4 tablespoons ice water

Preheat the oven to 425°.

In a large bowl, combine the flour, sugar and salt. Cut in the shortening and cream cheese until the mixture resembles coarse crumbs.

In a cup, combine the lemon juice with 2 tablespoons of the ice water. Sprinkle over the crumbs and toss with a fork until the crumbs resemble the texture of cottage cheese. Mix in the remaining ice water, 1 tablespoon at a time, until the dough holds together. Gather the mixture into a ball and press into a thick disk. Cover and refrigerate for 30 minutes before rolling out.

For an 11″ tart, roll the dough out to a 12″ circle. Gently lay the dough in a no-stick tart pan. Firmly press the dough against the bottom and sides of the pan. Fold the edges under. Using a fork, pierce the bottom of the crust all over to prevent it from puffing up during baking. Bake for 10 to 12 minutes, or until lightly browned. Remove from the oven and cool on a wire rack.

Makes one 11″ tart crust; 8 servings. Per serving: 162 calories, 7.5 g. fat (42% of calories), 3.2 g. protein, 20.1 g. carbohydrates, 0.6 g. dietary fiber, 3 mg. cholesterol, 107 mg. sodium

NOTES

• To speed preparation, combine the flour, sugar and salt in the bowl of a food processor. Add the remaining ingredients as directed, using on/off turns to mix.

• For an unbaked crust, omit the baking step. Tightly wrap the crust in plastic and refrigerate until ready to use.

• After baking, this tart crust is perfect for your favorite fruit filling.

VARIATION

Basic Whole-Wheat Tart Crust: Replace the all-purpose flour with 1½ cups whole-wheat pastry flour.

Meringue Pie Shell

 3 large egg whites, at room temperature
 ¼ teaspoon cream of tartar
 ⅛ teaspoon salt
 ⅔ cup superfine sugar
 ½ teaspoon vanilla

Preheat the oven to 275°. Coat a 9″ no-stick pie pan with no-stick spray; set aside.

In a medium bowl, combine the egg whites, cream of tartar and salt. Using an electric mixer at high speed, beat until foamy. Gradually add 5 tablespoons of the sugar. Beat for 30 seconds. Gradually add the remaining sugar. Beat for 30 seconds. Add the vanilla and beat for 7 to 10 minutes, or until stiff peaks form.

Spoon the meringue into the prepared pie pan. Spread evenly over the bottom and up the sides. (Do not allow the meringue to extend more than ½″ over the rim of the pie pan.)

Place on a baking sheet and bake for 1¼ hours, or until the shell is lightly golden, firm and crisp. Do not open the oven door during baking. If the meringue is golden but not firm at the end of the baking time, turn off the oven and leave the meringue in the oven for 1 hour. Remove from the oven and cool on a wire rack. Before filling, loosen the shell from the pie pan but leave it in the pan for support.

Makes one 9″ pie shell; 8 servings. Per serving: 72 calories, 0 g. fat (0% of calories), 1.3 g. protein, 16.9 g. carbohydrates, 0 g. dietary fiber, 0 mg. cholesterol, 54 mg. sodium

NOTE
• This sweet and crunchy meringue shell is fat-free and just right for cooked fruit fillings. Try one of the chunky fruit sauces on page 424.

Cherry Pie

 1 unrolled Basic Pie Crust (page 449)
 4 cups fresh tart cherries, pitted
 ⅔ cup maple syrup
 3 tablespoons quick-cooking tapioca
 ½ teaspoon grated lemon rind
 ½–1 teaspoon ground cinnamon

Preheat the oven to 425°.

Reserve ⅓ cup of the pie dough. Roll the remaining dough out to an 11″ circle. Gently lay the dough in a 9″ round no-stick pie pan. Firmly press the dough against the bottom and sides of the pan. Fold the edges under and crimp to form a rim. Using a fork, pierce the bottom of the crust all over to prevent it from puffing up during baking. Bake for 8 to 10 minutes, or until lightly browned. Remove from the the oven and cool on a wire rack.

Reduce the oven temperature to 375°.

Roll the reserved dough out to ⅛″ thickness. Using a cookie cutter or sharp knife, cut out decorative shapes, such as hearts or stars; set aside.

Meanwhile, in a large saucepan, combine the cherries, maple syrup, tapioca, lemon rind and cinnamon. Let the mixture stand for 5 minutes. Place over medium heat. Cook and stir for 10 minutes, or until thickened.

Pour the cherry filling into the prebaked pie crust. Gently lay the cut-outs over the filling. Bake for 20 to 30 minutes.

Makes 8 servings. Per serving: 271 calories, 7.7 g. fat (25% of calories), 4 g. protein, 47.8 g. carbohydrates, 1.6 g. dietary fiber, 2 mg. cholesterol, 112 mg. sodium

NOTES
• The fresh tart cherries can be replaced with frozen and thawed tart cherries.
• For a lattice top, use the reserved ⅓ cup dough. Follow the lattice directions on page 445.

Apricot-Blackberry Pie

¼ cup cornstarch
3 tablespoons quick-cooking tapioca
½ teaspoon cinnamon
⅔ cup sugar
2 cups sliced apricots
2 cups fresh or frozen unsweetened black-berries
1 tablespoon lemon juice
1 prebaked Basic Pie Crust (page 449)

Preheat the oven to 375°.

In a small bowl, combine the cornstarch, tapioca and cinnamon. Add the sugar and mix well.

In a large bowl, gently toss the apricots and blackberries with the lemon juice. Fold in the sugar mixture.

Pour the fruit into the pie crust. Place the pie on a baking sheet to catch any drips. Bake for 35 minutes, or until the filling is bubbly and the crust is lightly browned. Cool before serving.

Makes 8 servings. Per serving: 284 calories, 7.7 g. fat (24% of calories), 3.9 g. protein, 50.8 g. carbohydrates, 3.9 g. dietary fiber, 2 mg. cholesterol, 43 mg. sodium

VARIATION

Peach-Berry Pie: Replace the apricots with 2 cups sliced peaches and the blackberries with 2 cups fresh or frozen blueberries, strawberries or raspberries.

Apple Crumb Pie

Crumb Topping
¾ cup all-purpose flour
2 tablespoons nondiet tub-style margarine or butter
¼ cup packed brown sugar
¼ teaspoon ground cinnamon
⅛ teaspoon ground nutmeg

Apple Filling
6 Granny Smith apples, peeled, cored and sliced
1 tablespoon lemon juice
½ cup sugar
2½ tablespoons quick-cooking tapioca
½ teaspoon ground cinnamon
⅛ teaspoon ground cloves
1 Basic Pie Crust (page 449)

Preheat the oven to 425°.

To make the crumb topping: Place the flour in a medium bowl. Using a pastry blender or table knives, cut in the margarine or butter until the mixture resembles coarse crumbs. Add the brown sugar, cinnamon and nutmeg. Mix until well-blended; set aside.

To make the apple filling: In a large bowl, combine the apples and lemon juice; set aside.

In a small bowl, combine the sugar, tapioca, cinnamon and cloves. Sprinkle over the apples and gently toss to coat.

Spoon into the prepared pie crust. Sprinkle with the crumb topping.

Bake for 10 minutes. Reduce the oven temperature to 350° and bake for 30 minutes, or until golden brown.

Makes 8 servings. Per serving: 364 calories, 10.8 g. fat (26% of calories), 4.6 g. protein, 63.9 g. carbohydrates, 2.4 g. dietary fiber, 2 mg. cholesterol, 148 mg. sodium

VARIATIONS

Pear Pie: Replace the apples with 8 Anjou pears.

Phyllo-Top Apple Pie: Omit the crumb topping. Instead, coat one sheet of thawed phyllo dough with no-stick spray. Sprinkle with ½ teaspoon cinnamon and ½ teaspoon sugar. Top with a second sheet of phyllo. Coat with no-stick spray. Place the phyllo topping over the filling. Using your hands, gently wrinkle and fit the topping into the pan without going over the edges. Using a sharp knife, cut slashes into the top.

Raspberry-Apple Pie: Add 1 package (10 ounces) frozen raspberries to the apples and lemon juice.

Fresh Blueberry Pie

2⅓	cups unbleached flour
3	teaspoons baking powder
⅓	cup canola oil
½	cup skim milk
1	cup sugar
½	teaspoon grated lemon rind
½	teaspoon cinnamon
4	cups fresh blueberries

Preheat the oven to 425°. Coat a 9″ no-stick pie pan with no-stick spray. Set aside.

In a medium bowl, whisk 2 cups of the flour with the baking powder. Alternately add the oil and milk, stirring until the dough forms a ball.

Divide the dough in half. Place one half of the dough on a large piece of wax paper. Top with another large sheet of wax paper. Roll out to a 12″ circle. Remove the top sheet of paper and gently invert the dough into the prepared pan. Remove the remaining sheet of wax paper. Firmly press the dough against the bottom and sides of the pan. Trim the dough that extends beyond the edge of the pan. Add the trimmed pieces to the remaining dough. Roll the dough out to a 12″ circle between the wax paper; set aside.

In a large bowl, gently mix the sugar, lemon rind, cinnamon, blueberries and the remaining ⅓ cup flour. Pour the filling into the pie shell.

Remove the top sheet of wax paper and carefully invert the top crust over the pie filling. Fold the edges under. Seal and crimp to form a rim. Using a sharp knife, make slits in the top.

To prevent overbrowning, cover the edge of the crust with a 1½″-wide strip of foil. Bake for 20 minutes. Remove the foil and bake for 15 to 20 minutes, or until golden brown and bubbly. Cool slightly before serving.

Makes 8 servings. Per serving: 357 calories, 9.7 g. fat (24% of calories), 4.8 g. protein, 64.3 g. carbohydrates, 2.9 g. dietary fiber, 0.2 mg. cholesterol, 137 mg. sodium

Lemon Meringue Pie

1½	cups water
6	tablespoons cornstarch
¾	cup sugar
½	cup lemon juice
1	cup fat-free egg substitute
2	teaspoons grated lemon rind
6	egg whites, at room temperature
⅛	teaspoon cream of tartar
½	teaspoon vanilla
1	prebaked Basic Pie Crust (page 449)

Preheat the oven to 350°.

In a medium saucepan, whisk the water and cornstarch until the cornstarch is dissolved. Whisk in ½ cup of the sugar and the lemon juice. Place over medium heat and cook, whisking constantly, until the mixture comes to a boil. Whisk until the mixture turns clear and begins to thicken.

(continued)

Remove from the heat and gradually whisk in the egg substitute. Return to medium heat and cook, whisking constantly, until thickened. Whisk in the lemon rind. Set aside to cool to room temperature.

Place the egg whites in a large, clean, dry bowl. Beat until foamy. Add the cream of tartar and beat until soft peaks form. Beat in the remaining ¼ cup sugar, 1 tablespoon at a time. Add the vanilla and beat until the whites are stiff but not dry.

Spoon the cooled lemon filling into the prebaked crust. Smooth the top. Spread the meringue over the pie so that it covers the filling and touches the crust around the edge. Using the spoon, make peaks in the meringue.

Bake for 6 to 8 minutes, or until the meringue is golden brown. Cool completely before serving.

Makes 8 servings. Per serving: 282 calories, 7.5 g. fat (24% of calories), 8.5 g. protein, 45 g. carbohydrates, 0.7 g. dietary fiber, 2 mg. cholesterol, 201 mg. sodium

Pumpkin Pie

1 cup canned mashed pumpkin
1 egg
¾ cup fat-free egg substitute
1 cup evaporated skim milk
¾ cup packed brown sugar
½ teaspoon ground cinnamon
½ teaspoon ground ginger
⅛ teaspoon ground nutmeg
⅛ teaspoon ground allspice
1 prebaked Basic Pie Crust (page 449)

Preheat the oven to 375°.
In a large bowl, whisk together the

pumpkin, egg, egg substitute, milk, brown sugar, cinnamon, ginger, nutmeg and allspice. Pour into the prebaked crust.

Bake for 40 to 45 minutes, or until the center of the filling is set. Cool before serving.

Makes 8 servings. Per serving: 288 calories. 8.3 g. fat (26% of calories), 8.7 g. protein, 45.3 g. carbohydrates, 1.5 g. dietary fiber, 30 mg. cholesterol, 200 mg. sodium

VARIATION

Praline Pumpkin Pie: Before baking the pie crust, add a layer of praline. To make the praline, cut 2 teaspoons nondiet tub-style margarine or butter into ¼ cup packed brown sugar. Stir in 1 tablespoon maple syrup and ⅓ chopped toasted pecans. Press the praline mixture evenly into the bottom of the unbaked pie crust. Bake at 425° for 10 minutes. Remove from the oven, allow to cool, then fill with the pumpkin mixture. Bake as directed.

Shoofly Pie

Crumb Topping
1½ cups all-purpose flour
2 tablespoons nondiet tub-style margarine or butter
½ cup packed brown sugar
1 teaspoon ground cinnamon

Filling
1 cup boiling water
1 teaspoon baking soda
1 cup Barbados molasses or regular light molasses
¼ teaspoon ground ginger
1 unbaked Basic Pie Crust (page 449)

To make the crumb topping: Place the flour in a medium bowl. Using a pastry blender or table knives, cut in the margarine or butter until the mixture resembles coarse crumbs.

Mix in the brown sugar and cinnamon until well-blended. Set aside.

To make the filling: Preheat the oven to 450°.

In another medium bowl, whisk the water and baking soda until the baking soda dissolves. Stir in the molasses and ginger. Mix well. Allow the mixture to cool slightly. Pour into the unbaked pie crust. Sprinkle evenly with the crumb mixture.

Bake for 10 minutes. Reduce the heat to 350° and bake for 30 to 40 minutes, or until the center of the filling is set and the crumbs are golden brown.

Makes 8 servings. Per serving: 430 calories, 10.6 g. fat (22% of calories), 5.6 g. protein, 78.8 g. carbohydrates, 1.3 g. dietary fiber, 2 mg. cholesterol, 315 mg. sodium

NOTE

• For a tasty fat-free topping, spoon a dollop of nonfat vanilla frozen yogurt over each slice of pie.

QUICK!
Apricot Tart

- 2 tablespoons apricot brandy or reserved apricot juice
- ¾ cup apricot all-fruit spread, warmed
- 1 prebaked Basic Tart Crust (page 450)
- 4 cans (16 ounces each) apricot halves, drained and juice reserved (if using juice in place of brandy)
- 2 tablespoons toasted slivered almonds (see note)

Preheat the oven to 350°.

Stir the brandy or apricot juice into the all-fruit spread.

Using a pastry brush, brush a thin layer of the fruit spread mixture over the prebaked tart crust.

Arrange a single layer of the apricot halves, cut side down, in the crust. Brush the apricots with fruit spread. Continue layering with apricot halves and brushing with fruit spread until they are all used. Sprinkle with the almonds.

Bake for 15 minutes. Cool on a wire rack before serving.

Makes 8 servings. Per serving: 374 calories, 8.5 g. fat (20% of calories), 5.1 g. protein, 70.5 g. carbohydrates, 3.6 g. dietary fiber, 2 mg. cholesterol, 119 mg. sodium

NOTE

• To toast almonds, place them in a dry no-stick skillet over medium heat. Toast the nuts, shaking the skillet often, for 3 to 5 minutes, or until fragrant.

Blueberry Custard Tart

It *is* possible to make good-tasting low-fat custard. This tangy blueberry custard tart is full of flavor. Don't worry if it rests a little lower in the pan than most tarts; that's because of the low-fat ingredients used.

- 2 eggs
- ½ cup fat-free egg substitute
- ½ cup sugar
- 1 can (12 ounces) evaporated skim milk
- 1 teaspoon vanilla
- 1 teaspoon almond extract
- 1 chilled prebaked Basic Tart Crust (page 450)
- 1 cup fresh blueberries
- ¼ teaspoon ground nutmeg

Preheat the oven to 325°.

Place the eggs and egg substitute in a medium bowl. Using an electric mixer, beat the mixture until fluffy. Add the sugar and beat until thick. Add the milk, vanilla and almond extract. Beat just until combined.

Pour the filling into the tart crust. Top with

the blueberries, distributing them evenly. Sprinkle with the nutmeg.

Place the tart on a no-stick baking sheet. To prevent the rim of the tart from over-browning during baking, cover it with foil (avoid touching the filling with the foil). Bake for 1 hour, or until the filling is set and a knife inserted in the center comes out clean. Cool on a wire rack, then refrigerate until chilled.

Makes 8 servings. Per serving: 282 calories, 8.9 g. fat (29% of calories), 9.4 g. protein, 40.7 g. carbohydrates, 1.1 g. dietary fiber, 57 mg. cholesterol, 199 mg. sodium

NOTE
• If you prefer a more brown crust, remove the foil for the last 10 minutes of baking.

VARIATION
Cherry Custard Tart: Replace the blueberries with 1 cup drained pitted tart red cherries.

Light Cream Filling

1	egg
½	cup fat-free egg substitute
⅓	cup sugar
¼	cup cornstarch
2	cups 1% low-fat milk
1¼	teaspoons vanilla
½	teaspoon butter-flavored sprinkles

In a small bowl, whisk together the egg and egg substitute; set aside.

In a medium microwave-safe glass bowl, combine the sugar and cornstarch. Gradually whisk in the milk. Microwave on high power for 5 to 7 minutes, or until thickened and bubbly; stop and stir every 2 minutes.

Whisk some of the hot milk mixture into the egg mixture. Then whisk the egg-milk

mixture into the remaining hot milk mixture. Microwave on high power for 1½ to 2½ minutes, or until thickened; stop and stir every 45 seconds.

Whisk in the vanilla and butter-flavored sprinkles. Cover and refrigerate, stirring occasionally, for 30 minutes, or until the filling has cooled to lukewarm.

Makes about 2 cups. Per ¼ cup: 91 calories, 1.3 g. fat (13% of calories), 4.1 g. protein, 68.6 g. carbohydrates, 0 g. dietary fiber, 29 mg. cholesterol, 68 mg. sodium

NOTE
• This cream filling can be used in any pie or tart crust. Simply top with sliced fresh berries for a delicious dessert.

VARIATIONS
Strawberry-Kiwi Cream Tart: Spoon the cooled Light Cream Filling into a prebaked Basic Tart Crust (page 450). Cover and refrigerate for 30 minutes, or until the filling is set. In concentric circles over the filling, arrange 1 cup hulled and sliced fresh strawberries and 1 cup peeled and sliced kiwifruit (about 3 kiwi). Place 1 whole hulled strawberry, pointed end up, in the center. Drizzle with ¼ cup warmed apricot all-fruit spread. Refrigerate for 30 minutes before serving.
Blueberry Cream Tart: Follow the directions for Strawberry-Kiwi Cream Tart above. Replace the strawberries and kiwi with 2 cups fresh blueberries.

Apple Crisp

Filling

8	cups peeled, cored and thinly sliced Granny Smith apples
2	tablespoons water
3	tablespoons sugar
½	teaspoon ground cinnamon

Topping

¾	cup rolled oats
½	cup all-purpose flour

⅓ cup packed brown sugar
¾ teaspoon ground cinnamon
1 tablespoon dark corn syrup
1 tablespoon canola oil
2 teaspoons nondiet tub-style margarine or butter, softened

To make the filling: Place the apples and water in a 2-quart baking dish.

In a cup, stir together the sugar and cinnamon. Sprinkle over the apples and toss to coat well.

To make the topping: Preheat the oven to 375°.

In a medium bowl, stir together the oats, flour, brown sugar and cinnamon. Add the corn syrup, oil and margarine or butter. Using a fork or pastry blender, mix until crumbly. Sprinkle evenly over the apples.

Bake for 35 to 40 minutes, or until the apples are tender and the topping begins to brown.

Makes 6 servings. Per serving: 276 calories, 4.8 g. fat (15% of calories), 3 g. protein, 58.2 g. carbohydrates, 4.4 g. dietary fiber, 0 mg. cholesterol, 25 mg. sodium

NOTES

• For a richer oat flavor, toast the oats in a dry no-stick skillet over medium heat until fragrant. Then stir together with the flour, brown sugar and cinnamon.

• Top with a dollop of nonfat vanilla frozen yogurt for crisp à la mode.

• This crisp can be made ahead and served either cold or warm. To reheat a single serving, microwave on high power for 30 to 60 seconds.

VARIATIONS

Apple-Cranberry Crisp: Add ¼ cup dried cranberries along with the apples and water.

Pear or Peach Crisp: Replace the apples with 8 cups peeled, cored and thinly sliced pears or pitted and sliced peaches.

Berry Crisp: Replace the 2-quart baking dish with a 1½-quart baking dish. Replace the apple filling with 6 cups fresh or frozen mixed berries tossed with 3 tablespoons lemon juice and 3 tablespoons sugar. Sprinkle with the topping. Cover with foil

and bake for 30 minutes, or until the berries are bubbly. Remove the foil and bake for 5 to 10 minutes more, or until the topping is lightly browned.

Blueberry Cobbler

Blueberries
4 cups fresh or frozen blueberries
½ cup sugar
2 tablespoons cornstarch
1 tablespoon lemon juice
½ teaspoon cinnamon (optional)

Topping
1 cup unbleached flour
1½ tablespoons sugar
¼ teaspoon salt (optional)
1 teaspoon baking soda
½ teaspoon baking powder
2 tablespoons nondiet tub-style margarine or butter, softened
¾ cup low-fat buttermilk
½ teaspoon vanilla

To make the blueberries: Coat a 9″ no-stick pie pan with no-stick spray and set aside.

In a medium saucepan, combine the blueberries, sugar, cornstarch, lemon juice and cinnamon (if using). Bring to a boil over high heat. Reduce the heat to low. Cook and stir for 2 to 3 minutes, or until the mixture begins to thicken. Pour into the prepared pie pan.

To make the topping: Preheat the oven to 350°.

In a medium bowl, mix the flour, sugar, salt (if using), baking soda and baking powder. Using a pastry blender or table knives, cut in the margarine or butter until the mixture resembles coarse crumbs. Add the buttermilk and vanilla. Mix just until moistened.

Spoon heaping tablespoons of the batter evenly over the blueberries.

(continued)

Bake for 20 to 25 minutes, or until the blueberries are bubbly and the topping is golden brown.

Makes 6 servings. Per serving: 264 calories, 4.4 g. fat (15% of calories), 3.9 g. protein, 53.9 g. carbohydrates, 3.2 g. dietary fiber, 0.5 mg. cholesterol, 327 mg. sodium

VARIATIONS

Cherry Cobbler: Replace the blueberries with 2 cups pitted sweet cherries and 2 cups pitted sour cherries. Increase the sugar to ⅔ cup.

Peach Cobbler: Replace the blueberries with 4 cups fresh or frozen sliced peaches. Increase the sugar to ⅔ cup.

Strawberry-Rhubarb Slump

Filling

- ⅔ cup sugar
- 2½ tablespoons cornstarch
- ¼ teaspoon ground cinnamon
- 1 package (10 ounces) frozen strawberries (packed in syrup), thawed
- 1 package (16 ounces) frozen cut rhubarb, thawed

Dumplings

- 1¼ cups unbleached flour
- 2 tablespoons sugar
- 1 teaspoon baking powder
- ¼ teaspoon baking soda
- ⅛ teaspoon salt
- 1½ tablespoons canola oil
- 1½ tablespoons nondiet tub-style margarine or butter, cut into small pieces
- ½ cup low-fat buttermilk

To make the filling: In a Dutch oven or large ovenproof saucepan, combine the sugar, cornstarch and cinnamon.

Drain the juice from the strawberries into the pan; set the stawberries aside. Stir the sugar mixture until smooth.

Stir in the rhubarb. Bring the mixture to a boil over medium-high heat. Boil for 2 minutes, or until the mixture thickens and turns clear. Remove from the heat and stir in the strawberries. Set aside.

To make the dumplings: In a large bowl, combine the flour, sugar, baking powder, baking soda and salt. Add the oil and margarine or butter. Using a fork or pastry blender, mix until crumbly. Add the buttermilk and mix just until moistened.

Drop large spoonfuls of the dough over the fruit mixture, spacing them so that they don't touch each other. Cover with a lid or foil. Cook over medium heat for 10 minutes.

Preheat the oven to 375°.

Uncover and transfer the pan to the oven. Bake for 15 to 20 minutes, or until a toothpick inserted in a dumpling comes out clean. Cool for 10 minutes before serving.

Makes 6 servings. Per serving: 406 calories, 6.7 g. fat (14% of calories), 4 g. protein, 86.4 g. carbohydrates, 3.4 g. dietary fiber, 0.4 mg. cholesterol, 215 mg. sodium

Cherry Clafouti

Clafouti is a French dessert that could be described as a cross between a soufflé and a fruit-filled oven-baked pancake. No matter what you call it, it's delicious.

- 2½ cups pitted tart red cherries
- 2 eggs
- ½ cup fat-free egg substitute
- ⅔ cup skim milk
- ¼ cup honey
- ½ cup unbleached flour
- 1 tablespoon canola oil
- ½ teaspoon vanilla
- Pinch of salt

Preheat the oven to 400°. Coat a 9″ no-stick pie pan with no-stick spray. Add the cherries and set aside.

In a food processor or blender, process the eggs, egg substitute, milk, honey, flour, oil, vanilla and salt until smooth. Stop the machine occasionally to scrape down the sides of the container. Pour the egg mixture over the cherries.

Bake for 25 to 30 minutes, or until puffy and golden.

Makes 6 servings. Per serving: 178 calories, 4.3 g. fat (21% of calories), 6.4 g. protein, 29.1 g. carbohydrates, 1.1 g. dietary fiber, 71 mg. cholesterol, 72 mg. sodium

NOTE
• For an elegant finish, dust the baked clafouti with confectioners' sugar.

VARIATIONS
Blueberry Clafouti: Replace the cherries with 2½ cups fresh or frozen blueberries.
Apricot-Orange Clafouti: Replace the cherries with 2½ cups pitted and sliced apricots. Place the apricots in a large bowl with 1 tablespoon orange juice and 1 teaspoon grated orange rind. Allow to soak for 20 to 30 minutes, stirring occasionally. Drain. Place the drained apricots in the pie pan and proceed with the recipe.

pple Strudel

2 medium Granny Smith or Golden Delicious apples, peeled, cored and thinly sliced
2 tablespoons raisins
3 tablespoons brown sugar
½ teaspoon cinnamon
¼ teaspoon ground nutmeg
2 tablespoons fine unseasoned dry bread crumbs
2 tablespoons sugar
1 tablespoon melted butter
1 tablespoon canola oil

8 sheets frozen phyllo pastry, thawed
½ cup apricot all-fruit spread, warmed
1 tablespoon confectioners' sugar

Preheat the oven to 400°. Line a no-stick baking sheet with parchment paper.

In a large bowl, combine the apples, raisins, brown sugar, cinnamon and nutmeg.

In a small bowl, mix the bread crumbs and sugar.

In a cup, combine the butter and oil.

Remove one sheet of thawed phyllo from the package. Keep the remaining phyllo covered with a damp towel. Using a pastry brush, gently brush the phyllo with the oil mixture. Sprinkle with 2 teaspoons of the crumb mixture. Top with a second sheet of phyllo. Brush with the oil mixture and sprinkle with 2 teaspoons of the crumb mixture. Top with a third sheet of phyllo. Brush with the oil mixture and sprinkle with 2 teaspoons of the crumb mixture. Top with a fourth sheet of phyllo and brush with the oil mixture only.

Spread the top sheet of phyllo with half of the all-fruit spread to within 1″ of the edges. Spoon half of the apple mixture over the fruit spread to within 1″ of the edges. Fold 1″ of each long edge of the phyllo over the apple mixture. Starting with the short edge, roll up as tightly as possible. Gently place the strudel, seam side down, on the prepared baking sheet.

Repeat the filling and folding process to make a second strudel. Place next to the other strudel on the baking sheet. Brush both strudels with any remaining oil mixture and sprinkle with any remaining crumbs. Using a sharp knife, make several slashes in the top of each strudel. Bake for 15 to 20 minutes, or until crisp and golden brown. Sprinkle with the confectioners' sugar. Serve warm.

Makes 8 servings. Per serving: 153 calories, 3.4 g. fat (19% of calories), 0.6 g. protein, 31.7 g. carbohydrates, 0.7 g. dietary fiber, 4 mg. cholesterol, 40 mg. sodium

Chocolate

For millions of dessert lovers, chocolate is the ultimate finale to a special meal. It seems only natural that the tree that gives us chocolate and cocoa is called *Theobroma cacao*, or "food of the gods."

The problem with many chocolate desserts, of course, is that they're often very high in fat. Yet there are ways to enjoy your traditional favorites—like devil's food cake, chocolate brownies and chocolate mousse—without the traditional calories. By replacing chocolate with cocoa powder or by using very small amounts of the best chocolate that you can find, you can have wonderful desserts that won't break your diet or expand your waistline.

Later we'll discuss cocoa, which truly is the healthy cook's best friend. In the meantime, let's take a look at "real" chocolate. Yes, it's high in fat, and you'll never want to use a lot of it, yet it gives desserts a complex, richly satisfying taste that's hard to beat. In small amounts, it can play a valuable role in the healthy cook's repertoire.

TYPES OF CHOCOLATE

Chocolate begins its life as a bean. Long before it reaches your kitchen, it has been picked, roasted, shelled and ground. The resulting brown paste, called chocolate liquor, is combined with varying amounts of sugar and cocoa butter to create the different types of chocolate.

Every chocolate maker has its own formula. Once you find a brand that you like, it's often a good idea to stick with it, since you may not find exactly the same flavor elsewhere.

Different recipes call for different types of chocolate. Here are the main types.

☞ **Milk chocolate.** The stuff that candy bars are made of, milk chocolate does indeed contain milk solids. It's sweet, with a uniquely smooth, creamy texture.

☞ **Semisweet and bittersweet chocolates.** Used both for snacking and in cooking, these chocolates are essentially interchangeable. Bittersweet has a somewhat deeper chocolate taste, while semisweet has a more prominent sugar flavor.

☞ **Sweet chocolate.** Usually used in cakes, it has a very rich chocolate flavor and is very sweet.

☞ **Unsweetened chocolate.** Also known as baking chocolate, it contains no sugar at all and, eaten alone, is unpleasantly bitter. What it lacks in sweetness, however, it makes up for in richness; it's the richest of all chocolates and is usually used in baking. Sugar in the recipe offsets the chocolate's natural bitterness.

☞ **White chocolate.** Although it contains large amounts of cocoa butter, white chocolate isn't technically chocolate at all, because it doesn't contain chocolate liquor. It's often used in frostings and cheesecakes. White chocolate chunks can also be added to cookies or other desserts.

GREAT DECORATIONS

When you want a hint of chocolate in your low-fat desserts, try these decorative touches.

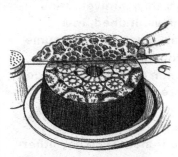

Dust cakes or baked goods with a 50–50 combination of cocoa and confectioners' sugar. To create an attractive pattern, place a doily, decorative stencil, small leaves or small cookie cutters on the dessert before dusting; remove carefully to avoid smudging the design.

Pour melted semisweet or bittersweet chocolate into a pastry bag or a small resealable plastic bag. If using the plastic bag, cut off a small piece of one corner. Pipe the chocolate on top of your dessert in a decorative pattern.

Dip fresh fruit, such as strawberries, orange sections, banana pieces or cherries, into melted semisweet, bittersweet, milk or white chocolate. Allow the chocolate to solidify and arrange the fruit on top of the dessert.

Use a small-hole grater to add a sprinkle of chocolate shavings to desserts. Make sure that the grater is cool and completely dry before using.

To make chocolate curls, quickly draw a vegetable peeler down a block of chocolate. Chocolate curls melt at the slightest touch, so use tweezers to place them on a cake or pie.

To make chocolate leaves, wash and dry unsprayed nonpoisonous leaves, such as ivy, lemon, rose or camellia. Paint the veiny side with melted chocolate. Chill for 1 hour, then carefully peel away the leaf.

Chocolate in its solid form is ideal for storage. Unless it's used in chunks or decorative pieces, however, it's generally melted before being added to recipes. Despite its robust appearance, chocolate is exceedingly delicate; it can scorch in an instant and readily gives up its delicate bouquet.

Always store it carefully. Chocolate should be stored in a cool, dry place, preferably between 60° and 75°F. At higher temperatures, a white "bloom" can appear on the surface. The discoloration is harmless and will not affect the taste, but it can make the chocolate unappealing to look at.

Never refrigerate or freeze chocolate, since the moisture that forms on the surface makes it troublesome to melt.

Cut it small. Putting a big block of chocolate in a pan causes one side to stay in constant contact with the heat, while the other sides stay maddeningly cool. Chocolate melts quickest and easiest when it's grated or chopped.

To best melt chocolate, place it on a cutting board. Using a large, sharp knife, shave off small pieces, then drop them all at once into the pan.

Stay alert. When melting chocolate, the difference between "just right" and "burned" is often measured in seconds.

☞ Chocolate doesn't look melted until you stir, so don't let your eyes deceive you.

☞ Unsweetened, sweet, semisweet and bittersweet chocolates should be stirred every minute or so; milk and white chocolate require nearly constant stirring.

☞ When working on the stove top, put the chopped chocolate in the top of a stainless-steel or glass double boiler over gently simmering water. As long as the water doesn't come to a boil, the temperature will stay in a safe range. For extra measure, remove the chocolate from the heat as soon as it's melted.

☞ To melt chocolate in the microwave, put it in a glass measuring cup or custard cup.

Chocolate
Is It Good for You?

It's no accident that chocolate tops the list of special gifts—on Valentine's Day, anniversaries and birthdays. Indeed, in a single year, Americans consume over 5 billion pounds of it.

For women particularly, chocolate is more than just a sweet food. Not only do women crave chocolate more than men do, they crave it more than any other food. Researchers speculate that chemical compounds in chocolate, like phenylethylamine, act on the brain to produce feel-good moods.

There's a bitter story behind all this sweetness. For one thing, chocolate is high in fat. An ounce of semisweet chocolate contains 10 grams of fat. An ounce of bittersweet chocolate is a bit worse, with more than 11 grams.

In addition, chocolate contains chemicals such as caffeine and tyramine, which in large amounts can cause changes in blood vessels that lead to headaches.

If you're like most people, of course, having small amounts of chocolate isn't likely to hurt either your head or your waistline. The bottom line is this: Eat chocolate as you would any other sweet—with enjoyment and moderation.

Microwave on high power, uncovered, stirring every 15 seconds.

Keep it dry. When water or even steam gets into chocolate, it can seize during melting; the melted chocolate turns into a gooey lump and refuses to return to a liquid state.

You can relax seized chocolate by stirring in ½ teaspoon solid vegetable shortening or butter for each ounce of chocolate. However, since this will increase the amount of fat, you may want to discard the chocolate and start over with fresh.

COCOA POWDER

To get the full-bodied taste of chocolate without the fat, healthy cooks often use cocoa instead. Like chocolate, cocoa is made from chocolate liquor refined from beans. Unlike chocolate, it contains far less cocoa butter. One ounce of cocoa has only about 3 grams of fat, compared with about 8 grams in semisweet chocolate and 16 grams in unsweetened. (Amounts vary by brand; read labels to see what you're getting.)

There are two main types of cocoa.

☞ **Unsweetened regular (nonalkalized) cocoa.** Recipes made with nonalkalized cocoa always require the addition of baking soda to help neutralize the mix and darken the color. Most American brands are nonalkalized. These have a slightly lighter, less intense flavor than Dutch-processed cocoa.

☞ **Unsweetened Dutch-processed cocoa.** Used in recipes that don't call for baking soda, this type of cocoa contains an alkali that neutralizes acids in the recipe. Most European and European-style cocoas, such as Droste and Van Houten's, are Dutch-processed. They have a richer color and more intense chocolate flavor.

To make cocoa work for you, here's what chefs advise.

Sift it well. You don't have to sift cocoa before measuring. However, sifting it before adding it to the recipe will help prevent lumps from forming.

☞ Refrigerating or freezing cocoa makes it difficult to sift. Chefs advise storing it at room temperature, preferably in an airtight container.

☞ Since cocoa readily absorbs flavors, be sure not to store it near onions, garlic or other strong-flavored ingredients.

Boost the flavor. Before adding cocoa to a recipe, dissolve it first in a little warm water. This enhances the cocoa flavor, making it more intense and flavorful.

Add the real thing. Although cocoa can impart a more intense flavor than bar chocolate, it may seem to lack a certain something in depth and richness. To boost the flavor of cocoa desserts, try adding a small amount—up to ½ ounce—of finely grated semisweet or bittersweet chocolate.

Michel Richard

One of America's finest chefs and restaurateurs, Michel Richard was trained early on in France as a pastry maker. His training paid off handsomely. Today, he owns restaurants nationwide, including Citrus in Los Angeles and Citronelle, with locations in Santa Barbara, Washington, D.C., and other cities.

"My favorite desserts are chocolate," he says. "All my life, I have eaten spice bread a few times a year, but by adding chocolate, I could eat it every day. It is the best."

Chocolate Spice Bread

1¾   cups unbleached flour
1½   teaspoons baking powder
 1   teaspoon baking soda
 1   teaspoon ground cinnamon
 ½   teaspoon ground ginger
 ½   teaspoon ground anise seeds
 ¼   teaspoon curry powder
     Pinch of salt
 ⅔   cup honey
 ⅔   cup cocoa powder
 ½   cup + 2 tablespoons orange juice
 2   eggs, lightly beaten

Preheat the oven to 325°. Coat an 8″ × 4″ no-stick loaf pan with no-stick spray and set aside.

Into a medium bowl, sift the flour, baking powder, baking soda, cinnamon, ginger, anise seeds, curry powder and salt.

In a large saucepan, combine the honey, cocoa powder and orange juice. Stir over low heat until well-mixed. Set aside to cool.

Mix the eggs into the chocolate mixture. Gradually incorporate the flour mixture into the chocolate mixture and mix well.

Pour the batter into the prepared pan and bake for 50 to 60 minutes, or until a toothpick inserted in the center comes out clean.

Unmold the bread onto a wire rack and allow to cool.

Makes 1 loaf; 16 slices. Per slice: 110 calories, 0.8 g. fat (6% of calories), 2.6 g. protein, 25.1 g. carbohydrates, 0.5 g. dietary fiber, 13 mg. cholesterol, 117 mg. sodium

Cherry Chocolate Cake

Here's a delightfully flavorful low-fat version of black forest cake. We used fat-free egg substitute instead of whole eggs and replaced the traditional fatty frosting with a decadent cherry topping.

Cherry Topping

1 package (12 ounces) frozen unsweetened pitted dark sweet cherries (about 1½ cups)
3 tablespoons sugar
2 teaspoons cornstarch
1½ tablespoons brandy or water

Cake

2 cups cake flour
2 teaspoons baking powder
½ teaspoon baking soda
¼ teaspoon salt
½ cup unsweetened cocoa
½ ounce semisweet chocolate, finely grated
1 teaspoon instant espresso coffee powder
1 cup packed light brown sugar
⅓ cup unsweetened applesauce
¼ cup canola oil
½ cup fat-free egg substitute
⅔ cup skim milk
½ cup warm water
2 teaspoons vanilla
⅓ cup cherry all-fruit spread
Nondairy reduced-calorie whipped topping or confectioners' sugar (optional)
Semisweet chocolate curls (optional)

To make the cherry topping: In a medium saucepan over low heat, combine the cherries (with any juice) and sugar. Cook and stir for 3 minutes, or until the sugar is dissolved and the cherries are heated through.

In a cup, dissolve the cornstarch in the brandy or water. Gently stir into the cherry mixture and bring to a boil. Boil for 1 minute, or until the sauce is thickened. Transfer the sauce to a bowl, scraping the sides of the pan with a rubber spatula to remove all the sauce. Cover and refrigerate for at least 20 minutes, or until completely cooled.

To make the cake: Preheat the oven to 350°. Coat two round 8" no-stick cake pans with no-stick spray and set aside.

In a large bowl, combine the flour, baking powder, baking soda, salt, cocoa, chocolate, coffee powder and brown sugar.

In a medium bowl, combine the applesauce, oil, egg substitute, milk, water and vanilla. Stir the applesauce mixture into the flour mixture and mix until the batter is smooth.

Spread the batter in the prepared cake pans. Bake on the center rack of the oven for 20 to 25 minutes, or until a toothpick inserted in the center comes out clean. Cool on a wire rack for 10 minutes; then invert and remove the pans. Cool the cake layers completely.

Place one cooled cake layer on a serving platter. Evenly spread with the all-fruit spread. Top with the second cake layer. Evenly spoon the brandied cherry topping over the top. Top with the whipped topping or dust with the confectioners' sugar (if using). Garnish with the chocolate curls (if using).

Makes 10 servings. Per serving: 310 calories, 6.7 fat (19% of calories), 4.7 g. protein, 59.6 g. carbohydrates, 1.3 g. dietary fiber, 0.3 mg. cholesterol, 225 mg. sodium

NOTES

• If cake flour is unavailable, use 1¾ cups all-purpose flour mixed with 2 tablespoons cornstarch.

• For a stunning presentation, spread the sides of the cake with nondairy reduced-calorie whipped topping. Then garnish with chocolate curls.

• For tips on making chocolate curls, see page 461.

Devil's Food Chocolate Layer Cake

1½ cups all-purpose flour
1 cup sugar
½ cup unsweetened cocoa
1 teaspoon baking soda
¼ teaspoon salt
1 cup low-fat buttermilk
¼ cup canola oil
⅓ cup unsweetened applesauce
2 teaspoons vanilla
⅓ cup apricot, raspberry or strawberry all-fruit spread
1¼ cups Chocolate Frosting (page 496)

Preheat the oven to 350°. Coat two round 8″ no-stick cake pans with no-stick spray and set aside.

In a medium bowl, combine the flour, sugar, cocoa, baking soda and salt.

In a small bowl, combine the buttermilk, oil, applesauce and vanilla. Stir the buttermilk mixture into the flour mixture and mix until the batter is smooth.

Spoon the batter evenly into the prepared pans. Bake for 25 minutes, or until a toothpick inserted in the center comes out clean. Cool on a wire rack for 10 minutes; then invert and remove the pans. Cool the cake layers completely.

Place one cooled cake layer on a serving platter. Evenly spread with the all-fruit spread. Top with the second cake layer. Spread the top and sides of the cake with the frosting.

Makes 10 servings. Per serving: 319 calories, 6.6 g. fat (18% of calories), 5.1 g. protein, 64.5 carbohydrates, 0.8 g. dietary fiber, 1 mg. cholesterol, 220 mg. sodium

NOTE

• For a beautiful presentation, use raspberry all-fruit spread and decorate with fresh raspberries.

Chocolate Ring Cake

Nonfat dairy products and a small amount of real chocolate make a healthy yet satisfying cake.

2⅓ cups all-purpose flour
⅔ cup unsweetened Dutch processed or European-style cocoa
2 ounces semisweet chocolate, finely grated
2 teaspoons baking powder
¾ teaspoon baking soda
1½ cups sugar
⅔ cup nonfat sour cream
¾ cup fat-free egg substitute
2 teaspoons vanilla
1 cup skim milk
Confectioners' sugar (optional)

Preheat the oven to 350°. Coat a 12-cup no-stick Bundt or tube pan with no-stick spray and lightly dust the inside with flour. Set aside.

In a small bowl, combine the flour, cocoa, chocolate, baking powder and baking soda; set aside.

In a medium bowl, beat together the sugar and sour cream for about 2 minutes, or until smooth. Beat in the egg substitute and vanilla. Alternately beat in ½ cup of the milk and half of the flour mixture, ending with the flour mixture. Beat until a smooth batter is formed.

Spoon the batter into the prepared pan. Bake for 40 to 45 minutes, or until a toothpick inserted in the center comes out clean.

Cool in the pan on a wire rack for 10 minutes; then invert and remove the pan. Cool completely. Dust with the confectioners' sugar (if using).

Makes 16 servings. Per serving: 181 calories, 1.7 g. fat (8% of calories), 5 g. protein, 39 g. carbohydrates, 0.7 g. dietary fiber, 1 mg. cholesterol, 137 mg. sodium

NOTE

• For a more decadent cake, microwave 2 ounces semisweet chocolate on high power, stirring every 15 seconds, until just melted. Stir in 1 to 2 teaspoons warmed 1% low-fat milk to make a pourable glaze. Drizzle the glaze evenly over the cooled cake.

Chocolate-Raspberry Roll

Raspberry Filling

1⅓	cups fat-free ricotta cheese
2	tablespoons unsweetened Dutch processed or European-style cocoa
3	tablespoons confectioners' sugar
2	tablespoons raspberry all-fruit spread

Chocolate Cake

½	cup cake flour
2	tablespoons unsweetened Dutch processed or European-style cocoa
½	teaspoon instant espresso coffee powder
2	egg yolks
⅔	cup sugar
1	teaspoon vanilla
¼	cup low-fat buttermilk
3	egg whites
½	teaspoon cream of tartar
	Confectioners' sugar (optional)
1	cup fresh raspberries (optional)

To make the raspberry filling: In a food processor or blender, combine the ricotta, cocoa, confectioners' sugar and all-fruit spread. Process until smooth. Set aside.

To make the chocolate cake: Preheat the oven to 375°. Coat a 15″ × 10″ no-stick jelly-roll pan with no-stick spray. Line the pan with parchment or wax paper. Coat the paper with no-stick spray and set aside.

In a small bowl, sift together the flour, cocoa and coffee powder.

In a medium bowl, using an electric mixer or a wire whisk, beat the egg yolks and ⅓ cup of the sugar until light and lemon-colored. Beat in the vanil-la and buttermilk. Beat the flour mixture into the egg mixture until well-blended; set aside.

In a large, clean bowl, combine the egg whites and cream of tartar. Using an electric mixer with clean, dry beaters, beat until soft peaks form. Gradually beat in the remaining ⅓ cup sugar.

Fold a third of the egg-white mixture into the batter. Add the remaining egg-white mixture all at once, folding quickly until the mixture is well-blended.

Spoon the batter evenly in the prepared pan. Bake for 12 to 15 minutes, or until the cake springs back when lightly touched.

Remove the cake from the oven and loosen from the sides of the pan with a knife. Invert the pan onto a clean nonterry dish towel. Remove the parchment or wax paper. Using a sharp knife, trim the edges of the cake if they are not even. Starting from the short end, roll up the towel and the cake together, jelly-roll style. Transfer the cake to a wire rack and cool completely.

Gently unroll the cooled cake. Spread the filling evenly over the cake to within ½″ of the edges. Then reroll the cake without the towel. Transfer the rolled cake to a serving plate. Refrigerate for at least 30 minutes and up to 1 hour before serving. Dust the cake roll with the confectioners' sugar (if using). Garnish with the raspberries (if using).

Makes 8 servings. Per serving: 173 calories, 1.7 g. fat (8% of calories), 8.8 g. protein, 33.4 g. carbohydrates, 0.2 g. dietary fiber, 53 mg. cholesterol, 53 mg. sodium

VARIATION

Chocolate-Strawberry Roll: Replace the raspberry all-fruit spread with strawberry all-fruit spread in the filling. Garnish with fresh strawberries.

Black-Bottom Chocolate Brownie Torte

This dense and rich dessert gets its low-fat profile from nonfat cream cheese and egg substitute.

Crust
- ½ cup chocolate wafer cookie crumbs
- 1 tablespoon sugar
- 1 tablespoon canola oil

Filling
- ½ cup all-purpose flour
- 1 tablespoon unsweetened cocoa
- 1 teaspoon instant espresso coffee powder
- ½ teaspoon cinnamon
- 2 ounces bittersweet or semisweet chocolate
- ½ cup nonfat cream cheese
- ½ cup packed dark brown sugar
- 1 tablespoon canola oil
- 1 teaspoon vanilla
- ½ cup fat-free egg substitute
- ⅓ cup toasted and chopped walnuts or pecans (optional); see note

  Confectioners' sugar (optional)

To make the crust: Preheat the oven to 350°. In a small bowl, combine the cookie crumbs, sugar and oil. Mix until moistened. Press the mixture into the bottom of an 8″ springform pan or loose-bottom tart pan. Bake for 10 minutes. Cool on a wire rack.

To make the filling: Lower the oven temperature to 325°.

In another small bowl, combine the flour, cocoa, coffee powder and cinnamon; set aside.

In the top of a double boiler, over gently simmering water, melt the chocolate. (Or microwave on high power, stirring every 15 seconds, until just melted.)

In a medium bowl, beat together the cream cheese and brown sugar. Beat in the oil and vanilla. Using a wooden spoon, stir in the egg substitute and chocolate until smooth. Add the flour mixture and stir until just blended. Quickly stir in the walnuts or pecans (if using).

Spread the batter evenly over the crumb crust. Bake for 30 minutes, or until a toothpick inserted in the center comes out almost clean. Do not overbake. Cool for 10 minutes on a wire rack.

Loosen the brownie torte by running a knife around the edge of the pan. Remove the sides of the pan. Cool slightly and dust with the confectioners' sugar (if using). Serve warm or at room temperature.

Makes 8 servings. Per serving: 202 calories, 8.2 g. fat (35% of calories), 5.4 g. protein, 28.9 g. carbohydrates, 1.3 g. dietary fiber, 0 mg. cholesterol, 154 mg. sodium

NOTE
• To toast the nuts, place them in a dry no-stick skillet over medium heat. Toast them, shaking the skillet often, for 3 to 5 minutes, or until fragrant.

Chocolate Cream Pie

- 1 cup sugar
- ¼ cup cornstarch
- ¼ cup cocoa
- ¼ teaspoon salt
- 3 cups skim milk
- 1 egg, lightly beaten
- 1 teaspoon unsalted butter, at room temperature
- 1 prebaked Basic Pie Crust (page 449)

In a large saucepan, whisk together the sugar, cornstarch, cocoa and salt until thoroughly blended. Slowly whisk in the milk. Then whisk in the egg. Cook over medium heat, whisking constantly until the mixture comes to a boil and thickens.

Cook and stir for 3 minutes. Remove from the heat. Whisk in the butter. Place a piece of plastic wrap directly on the surface of the filling. Let cool for 20 minutes. Remove the plastic wrap and pour the filling into the pre-baked pie crust. Refrigerate for 15 minutes before serving.

Makes 8 servings. Per serving: 319 calories, 9 g. fat (25% of calories), 7.6 g. protein, 53.2 g. carbohydrates, 0.7 g. dietary fiber, 32 mg. cholesterol, 231 mg. sodium

NOTE
• This pie is delicious with a light whipped topping.

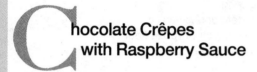

Chocolate Crêpes with Raspberry Sauce

Raspberry Sauce
1   package (10 ounces) frozen unsweetened raspberries (about 1½ cups)
6   tablespoons sugar or honey

Chocolate Crêpes
½   cup all-purpose flour
2   tablespoons unsweetened cocoa, sifted
1½   tablespoons sugar
1¼   cups skim milk
1½   teaspoons canola oil
1   egg
2   egg whites
1   pint nonfat chocolate or vanilla frozen yogurt
½   cup fresh raspberries (optional)

To make the raspberry sauce: Place the raspberries and sugar or honey in a medium saucepan. Cook over medium heat for 5 minutes, or until the berries release their juice and are no longer frozen.

Transfer to a food processor or blender and process until smooth. Press the mixture

through a strainer or fine sieve. Remove and discard the seeds. (This should yield about ¾ cup sauce.)

To make the chocolate crepes: In a medium bowl, combine the flour, cocoa and sugar.

In another medium bowl, whisk together the milk, oil, egg and egg whites. Whisk the milk mixture into the flour mixture, mixing until well-blended. Cover and refrigerate the batter for 1 hour.

Coat an 8″ no-stick, slope-sided no-stick skillet with no-stick spray. Warm the skillet over medium heat until hot. Pour in ¼ cup of the batter, quickly tilting the pan in all directions to evenly spread the batter into a circle. Cook the crêpe for about 1 minute, or until the bottom is lightly golden. Carefully flip the crêpe over and cook for 1 minute longer.

Transfer the cooked crêpe to a piece of wax paper. Repeat the process until all the batter is used, stacking each crêpe between pieces of wax paper.

To assemble, spoon ¼ cup of the frozen yogurt evenly down the center of each crêpe. Fold over one side, then the other. Place the crêpes, seam side down, on a freezer-safe plate. Freeze for 10 minutes. Serve with the raspberry sauce and raspberries (if using).

Makes 4 servings. Per serving (2 crêpes): 346 calories, 3.9 g. fat (10% of calories), 12.8 g. protein, 67.9 g. carbohydrates, 4.3 g. dietary fiber, 54 mg. cholesterol, 145 mg. sodium

NOTES
• To freeze any leftover crêpes, stack them between sheets of wax paper and tightly wrap in plastic.

• A crêpe pan works best for cooking crêpes. If you don't have one, a slope-sided skillet works fine (most no-stick skillets are slope-sided). Avoid using a skillet with straight sides, because it will make it difficult to flip the crêpes without damaging them.

VARIATION
Chocolate Crêpes with Strawberry or Cherry Sauce: Replace the raspberries with 1 package (12 ounces) frozen unsweetened strawberies or cherries.

Hot Chocolate Soufflé

1 tablespoon cornstarch
⅓ cup sugar
3 tablespoons unsweetened cocoa powder
¾ cup skim milk
2 tablespoons dark rum or ½ teaspoon rum extract + 2 tablespoons water
2 egg yolks
5 egg whites
½ teaspoon cream of tartar
1 tablespoon confectioners' sugar

Preheat the oven to 375°.

In a large saucepan, dissolve the cornstarch, sugar and cocoa powder in the milk. Cook over medium heat, stirring constantly, until the mixture comes to a boil and thickens.

In a small bowl, combine the rum or rum extract and water with the egg yolks. Stir about a quarter of the cornstarch mixture into the egg-yolk mixture. Stir back into the remaining cornstarch mixture. Cook and stir for 1 minute. Remove from the heat and set aside.

In a small bowl, using an electric mixer, beat the egg whites at high speed until foamy. Add the cream of tartar and beat until stiff peaks form.

Gradually stir a quarter of the egg-white mixture into the cornstarch mixture. Gently fold in the remaining egg-white mixture.

Spoon the mixture into a 1-quart soufflé dish. Bake for 30 to 35 minutes, or until the soufflé is puffed and lightly browned. Dust with the confectioners' sugar. Serve immediately.

Makes 4 servings. Per serving: 168 calories, 3.4 g. fat (19% of calories), 8.1 g. protein, 24 g. carbohydrates, 1.2 g. dietary fiber, 107 mg. cholesterol, 97 mg. sodium

VARIATIONS

Hot Chocolate-Orange Soufflé: Replace the rum with 2 tablespoons Grand Marnier or orange-flavored liqueur.

Orange Soufflé: Omit the cocoa. Add 1 teaspoon grated orange rind to the cooked mixture. Replace the rum with 2 tablespoons Grand Marnier or orange-flavored liqueur.

Easy Fudge Brownies

1½ cups sugar
⅓ cup nondiet tub-style margarine or butter
¼ cup low-fat buttermilk
¾ cup Dutch processed or European-style cocoa
2 eggs
2 teaspoons vanilla
1¼ cups all-purpose flour
¼ teaspoon baking soda

Preheat the oven to 350°. Coat a 9″ × 13″ no-stick baking dish with no-stick spray and set aside.

In a medium saucepan, combine the sugar, margarine or butter and buttermilk. Cook and stir over medium heat, bringing the mixture just to the boiling point. Remove from the heat. Stir in the cocoa until the mixture is smooth.

Stir in the eggs, one at a time. Stir in the vanilla. Add the flour and baking soda. Mix just until combined.

Spoon the batter into the prepared baking dish. Bake for 18 to 20 minutes, or until the brownies are set and still seem slightly sticky. Remove from the oven and cool in the pan before cutting.

Makes 24. Per brownie: 108 calories, 3.3 g. fat (26% of calories), 1.8 g. protein, 19.3 g. carbohydrates, 0.2 g. dietary fiber, 18 mg. cholesterol, 57 mg. sodium

VARIATIONS

Caramel-Glazed Brownies: In a small saucepan, combine ⅓ cup evaporated skim milk and 1 package (10 ounces) caramels. Gradually stir over low heat until melted. Remove from the heat and cool slightly. Drizzle the caramel glaze over the cooled brownies.

Easy Fudge-Nut Brownies: Add ½ cup finely chopped toasted walnuts or pecans to the batter.

Frosted Brownies: In a medium bowl, using an electric mixer, beat together 3 ounces low-fat cream cheese, 3 ounces nonfat cream cheese and 2 tablespoons low-fat milk. Spread evenly over the cooled brownies.

Peanut Butter or Chocolate Chip Brownies: Add ½ cup semisweet peanut butter or white chocolate chips to the batter.

Chocolate Bread Pudding

- 4 cups cubed day-old bread, such as white, raisin, sourdough or oatmeal
- 2 cups skim milk, scalded
- ¼ cup unsweetened Dutch processed or European-style cocoa, sifted
- ¾ cup fat-free egg substitute
- ¾ cup packed dark brown sugar
- 1 teaspoon vanilla
- 1 teaspoon brandy or rum (optional)
  Confectioners' sugar (optional)

Preheat the oven to 350°. Coat a 2-quart no-stick baking dish with no-stick spray.

Place the bread cubes in the prepared baking dish and set aside.

In a medium bowl, stir together the milk and cocoa until the cocoa is dissolved. Stir in the egg substitute, brown sugar, vanilla and brandy or rum (if using).

Pour the milk mixture over the bread. Bake for 35 to 40 minutes, or until set. Cool on a wire rack for 10 minutes. Lightly dust the top with confectioners' sugar (if using). Serve warm.

Makes 8 servings. Per serving: 156 calories, 1 g. fat (5% of calories), 5.8 g. protein, 32.4 g. carbohydrates, 0.4 g. dietary fiber, 1 mg. cholesterol, 157 mg. sodium

Old-Fashioned Chocolate Pudding

This dessert will bring out the kid in anyone. We lightened it up by replacing whole milk with skim milk and thickening the pudding with cornstarch instead of eggs.

- 2 cups skim milk
- ¾ teaspoon instant espresso coffee powder
- ½ cup sugar
- 2 ounces bittersweet or semisweet chocolate, finely chopped
- 3 tablespoons cornstarch, sifted

In a 2-quart saucepan, scald 1¾ cups of the milk. Stir in the coffee powder and sugar until dissolved.

In the top of a double boiler, over gently simmering water, melt the chocolate. Gradually add the milk mixture, stirring until smooth. Continue to cook in the double boiler, stirring often.

In a cup, dissolve the cornstarch in the remaining ¼ cup milk. Gradually whisk the cornstarch mixture into the chocolate mixture. Whisk constantly for 5 minutes, or until the pudding is thickened.

Transfer the pudding to a serving dish. Cover with plastic wrap and refrigerate for at least 45 minutes before serving.

Makes 4 servings. Per serving: 236 calories, 7.7 g. fat (27% of calories), 5.7 g. protein, 40.6 g. carbohydrates, 2.2 g. dietary fiber, 2 mg. cholesterol, 65 mg. sodium

VARIATION

Mocha Chocolate Pudding: Increase the instant espresso coffee powder to 2 teaspoons.

Glazed Chocolate Snack Bars

Bars

- ⅔ cup all-purpose flour
- ¼ cup unsweetened Dutch processed or non-alkalized cocoa
- ½ ounce semisweet chocolate, finely grated
- ¼ teaspoon baking powder
- ¼ teaspoon instant espresso coffee powder (optional)
- ⅔ cup packed dark brown sugar
- 2 tablespoons nondiet tub-style margarine or butter, softened
- ½ cup unsweetened applesauce
- 3 egg whites
- 1 teaspoon vanilla

Glaze

- 2 ounces semisweet chocolate

To make the bars: Preheat the oven to 350°. Coat an 8″ × 8″ no-stick baking dish with no-stick spray.

In a small bowl, combine the flour, cocoa, chocolate, baking powder and coffee powder (if using); set aside.

In a medium bowl, combine the brown sugar, margarine or butter and applesauce until smooth. Stir in the egg whites and vanilla. Stir the flour mixture into the brown-sugar mixture until just blended. Do not overmix.

Spread the batter evenly in the prepared dish. Bake for 20 to 25 minutes, or until a toothpick inserted in the center comes out almost clean. Do not overbake. Cool on a wire rack.

To make the glaze: Place the chocolate in a microwave-safe plastic bag (do not seal). Microwave on high, stirring every 15 seconds, until just melted. (Or melt the chocolate in a double boiler and spoon into a plastic bag.) Cut a small piece of plastic off the corner of the bag to make a tip. Gently pipe decorative lines of the chocolate over the top of the cooled and uncut bars. Cool slightly before cutting.

Makes 12. Per bar: 131 calories, 4.1 g. fat, (27% of calories), 2.3 g. protein, 23 g. carbohydrates, 0.7 g. dietary fiber, 0.5 mg. cholesterol, 53 mg. sodium

VARIATION

Chocolate-Nut or Raisin Snack Bars: Stir ½ cup chopped walnuts, raisins or a combination into the finished batter.

Chocolate Sauce

We reduced the fat in this chocolate sauce by using cocoa powder and espresso coffee for flavor and cornstarch for texture. It's irresistible on ice cream. Or try it as a dip for strawberries, bananas and dried apricots.

- ⅔ cup strong espresso coffee, cooled
- ¼ cup sugar
- 3 tablespoons unsweetened cocoa powder
- 2 teaspoons cornstarch
- 1 teaspoon vanilla
- ½ teaspoon butter, softened

In a medium saucepan, combine the coffee, sugar, cocoa powder and cornstarch. Whisk until smooth. Cook over medium heat, stirring constantly, until smooth and thickened. Stir in the vanilla and butter. Cool slightly before using.

Makes ¾ cup. Per tablespoon: 22 calories, 0.4 g. fat (15% of calories), 0.2 g. protein, 5.1 g. carbohydrates, 0.4 g. dietary fiber, 0.4 mg. cholesterol, 0.4 mg. sodium

NOTE

• The brewed espresso can be replaced with ⅔ cup hot water mixed with 2 teaspoons instant espresso coffee powder.

Cookies, Cakes and Bars

It's hard to imagine a birthday party, Christmas celebration or wedding anniversary at which cakes, cookies or bars don't play a leading role. The problem, of course, is that the amount of fat in these perennial favorites can be truly staggering.

Fats provide a velvety texture, aid in rising and help release flavors from other ingredients, such as vanilla or cinnamon. For the healthy cook, reducing the amount of fat in baked goods while maintaining the rich taste and distinctive mouthfeel can be a challenge.

Many cooks play it safe by making only recipes that are naturally low in fat, like angel food cake. But you don't have to limit yourself. Whether you're making a chocolate layer cake or whipping up a batch of sugar cookies, there are many ways to cut back on fat without giving up great taste or a pleasing texture.

STOCKING UP

You don't need a lot of fancy equipment to make cakes, cookies and bars. Indeed, many cooks use little more than a sturdy mixing bowl, measuring cups and spoons and a couple of baking sheets and cake pans. But since baking really is a science and since some batters require vigorous mixing, you may find yourself wanting precision equipment. Here's a look at some of the things you might need.

☞ **Free-standing mixer**. A good mixer is expensive but can save you considerable

amounts of arm strain. This is particularly true when making sponge cakes, which require long beating times.

☞ **Hand mixer**. Inexpensive and built to last, this is almost indispensable when it comes to creaming or mixing ingredients or for whipping up egg whites in a flash.

☞ **Food processor**. This powerful appliance can be used for an impressive variety of tasks, from pureeing fruit and mixing soft doughs to chopping nuts and making bread crumbs. This isn't really an essential appliance, but it's one that's very nice to have.

☞ **Mixing bowls**. These come in a variety of sizes, from tiny bowls used for holding egg whites to multiquart monsters that come out only when you're baking for crowds. Bowls made from stainless steel are the most practical and last forever. You may want a few ceramic microwave-safe bowls as well.

☞ **Narrow metal spatulas**. These are essential for spreading glazes and frostings on cakes and cookies.

☞ **Rubber spatulas**. These are designed to neatly scrape the sides of a bowl, making it possible to remove every last bit of batter or frosting.

☞ **Wire whisk**. This is used for blending batters and whipping egg whites.

☞ **Pastry bags**. Used for decorating cakes, these can be fitted with an almost limitless number of tips for creating exactly the shapes or designs that you need.

MAKING DROP COOKIES

The texture of the dough used for making drop cookies varies from recipe to recipe. Some doughs slip easily off the spoon, while others need to be pushed off. You can leave them in a mound or you can alter them as follows.

To slightly flatten drop cookies, press gently with the bottom of a small water glass. If the dough sticks, lightly flour the glass between pressings.

To make an attractive pattern, press down on each cookie with the back of a fork. Pressing down twice—the second time at right angles to the first—will make a cross-hatched pattern.

☞ **Cake-decorating turntable.** A small rotating metal disk, this makes filling and frosting cakes as easy as pie.

☞ **Baking sheets.** These come in a variety of styles. Black trays absorb heat and are used to put a nice crisp on the bottom of cookies. Shiny sheets reflect heat and are used when a more delicate crust is required. The most recent development is the air-cushioned sheet, which helps prevent burning or overbaking.

☞ **Jelly-roll pan.** Usually measuring approximately $10'' \times 15''$ with a $1''$ lip, a jelly-roll pan is used for cake rolls and some bar cookies.

☞ **Cake pans.** Chefs recommend straight-sided metal pans for layer cakes. The most useful sizes are $8''$ round and $9''$ round. For other cakes, $8'' \times 8''$ or $9'' \times 9''$ and $7'' \times 11''$ or $8'' \times 12''$ are handy. For making bar cookies, you'll also want a $9'' \times 13''$ pan.

☞ **Tube pan.** This is used for making chiffon and angel food cakes.

☞ **Pastry brush.** Made with soft bristles, this is used for brushing syrup onto cake layers and for spreading warm jam glazes over fruit-topped cakes.

☞ **Citrus zester.** An inexpensive little gadget, this is used to remove a thin layer of rind (the zest) from oranges, lemons and limes.

☞ **Wire racks.** These allow air to circulate under the pans, helping cakes and cookies cool quickly.

☞ **Parchment paper.** Essential for lining cake pans, jelly-roll pans and baking sheets, parchment keeps food from sticking—even without added fat.

COOKIES AND BARS

Cookies come in all shapes, sizes and textures, from thin and crispy to chunky and chewy. They can be cut into shapes or dropped onto baking sheets. For the ultimate in simplicity, they can even be poured into a pan and later cut into bars. Regardless of the style, cookies are very easy to make.

Start at room temperature. Allowing all the ingredients to warm slightly will make mixing easier and help ensure that each ingredient is thoroughly incorporated into the mix.

Slightly chilling cookie dough after mixing makes it easier to work with.

Use flour sparingly. You need some extra flour to prevent rolled cookies from sticking to the rolling pin or counter. Using too much, however, causes the cookies to toughen.

To prevent sticking without using a lot of flour, try rolling soft, slightly chilled cookie dough between sheets of wax paper.

Consistency counts. When making drop or rolled cookies, make sure that they're all approximately the same size. Otherwise, they'll bake at different rates, causing larger cookies to be underdone, while smaller ones will burn.

Put down protection. An easy way to prevent cookies from sticking is to line the pan with parchment paper or to give the pan a light misting with no-stick spray.

Keep an eye on the time. Since cookies bake so quickly, leaving them in the oven for even a minute or two longer than required will make them dry and tough. In addition, cookies continue cooking for a minute or two after they're out of the oven, so bakers advise removing them just before you think that they're done.

☞ Bar cookies are done when the edges appear dry and begin to pull away from the sides of the pan.

☞ Drop and rolled cookies are done when the edges are firm and the bottoms are slightly brown.

Melt the butter. You can reduce the amount of butter in a recipe by about half by melting it before adding it to the other ingredients. Essentially, this makes the butter go farther, which helps cookies bake up properly, despite the lower amount of fat.

Fight fat with fruit. Another way to reduce the amount of butter or other fats is to replace ½

Butter and Margarine
Is It GOOD for You?

They're two of the most common kitchen ingredients, used for everything from baking and sautéing to dressing up toast. Yet the health impact of butter and margarine remains controversial.

No one says that butter or margarine is good for you. Both are essentially pure fat, which isn't good for your waistline or your heart. The real debate is which slippery character is worse for you—the saturated fat found in butter (as well as cheese, whole milk, ice cream and meat) or the trans-fatty acids used in margarines and commercial baked goods.

According to the American Heart Association, research indicates that the worst offender by far is the saturated fat and cholesterol in butter. Yet scientists at the Harvard School of Public Health have tagged trans-fat (created when processors add hydrogen to vegetable oil) as the nastier of the two.

At present, there's no clear answer to which is worse. Both butter and margarine have the potential to clog arteries. Your best bet, experts say, is to cut way back on all fats.

cup of it with an equal amount of applesauce or another fruit puree.

Cut back on nuts. Walnuts, almonds and other nuts are very high in fat. Since a little goes a long way, you can often reduce the amount of nuts in a recipe by about half without really noticing the difference. Chopping the nuts also makes the flavor of a smaller amount go further.

☞ Many healthy cooks replace some or all of the nuts in a recipe with toasted rolled oats.

☞ Toasting nuts before adding them to a recipe gives them extra flavor, so that you can use less. To toast nuts, place them in a dry nostick skillet over medium heat. Toast the nuts, shaking the skillet often, for 3 to 5 minutes, or until fragrant and golden.

Go easy on the chips. Chocolate chips have a fair amount of fat. You can often cut back on them without adversely affecting the recipe.

☞ When making chocolate chip cookies, automatically reduce the amount of chocolate chips to about half the amount called for in the recipe.

☞ Substitute miniature chocolate chips for the full-size kind. You'll think that you're getting more chocolate than you are.

☞ Another way to cut back on chocolate chips is to replace some of them with dried apricots, raisins or chopped dates.

Add some oats. Substituting oat flour for about one-third of the all-purpose flour called for in the recipe will give the cookie or bar a moister, chewier texture.

To make your own oat flour, grind rolled oats in the food processor.

CAKES

We often think of cakes as being sinfully rich, and in fact, many are high in butter, margarine or other fats. Yet there are a number of strategies for reducing the fat in cakes without reducing taste. So before we get into the different kinds of cakes, here are some ways to make all your baking leaner.

Helpful Hint

To make an attractive fat-free topping, place a paper doily on top of a cake and sprinkle with confectioners' sugar. Then remove the doily and serve.

Whip the fat. The advantage of baking with butter or shortening is that air pockets are formed when these ingredients are creamed together with sugar. This is what makes the finished product light and tender. You can get similar effects by whipping sugar with egg whites. This will make the final product light and tender without the fat.

☞ An easy way to cut back on butter or shortening is to replace it with an equal amount of fruit puree. With most recipes, you can replace up to half the butter with puree without noticing the difference.

☞ When making chocolate desserts, prune puree is ideal. To make it, soften prunes briefly in hot water, drain and puree with a mixer or in a food processor until smooth. Or use baby-food prunes.

Shop for fat substitutes. Cakes contain a number of ingredients that can often be replaced with low-fat or even nonfat equivalents, with essentially no change in the resulting taste or texture.

☞ Replace whole milk with skim or low-fat milk.

☞ Substitute buttermilk, low-fat or nonfat plain yogurt or low-fat sour cream for regular sour cream.

☞ Replace full-fat cream cheese with low-fat cream cheese.

Cut back on chocolate. When you want the full, rich taste of chocolate without all the saturated fat, try using cocoa powder. Cocoa contains a small amount of fat yet still packs a big punch of chocolate flavor.

☞ For every ounce of melted unsweetened chocolate, substitute 3 tablespoons cocoa powder dissolved in 2 tablespoons water and mixed with 1 tablespoon prune puree.

☞ When using cocoa, dissolving it first in warm water helps the cocoa flavor bloom, making it more intense.

Get the freshest ingredients. To a certain extent, butter and shortening mask a cake's more subtle flavors; once you cut back on fat, the other flavors take on unexpected prominence. To make sure that you get the best taste, it's important to use only the best, freshest ingredients that you can find. Your taste buds will immediately tell the difference.

Add extra taste. Since cutting back on fat naturally makes recipes a little less robust, don't hesitate to use big flavors when making cakes.

☞ Flavored sugar pumps extra taste into any recipe without adding a lick of fat. To make flavored sugar, press a vanilla bean into a jar of sugar and let it stand for two weeks.

☞ Another way to add flavor is with citrus rind or by adding generous amounts of cinnamon, cloves, mace or other baking spices.

Baking Basics

Despite the mystique surrounding great cakes, they really aren't that hard to make. As long as you measure ingredients exactly and follow the recipe, you'll have delicious desserts every time.

Start hot. To ensure even baking and get the rising process started, always preheat the oven. An easy way to remember is to turn on the oven when you begin assembling ingredients. It will be at the right temperature by the time the batter is mixed.

Adjust for altitude. If you live at an altitude of more than 3,000 feet, increase the oven temperature by 25° and slightly decrease the baking time. (For more on high-altitude baking, see page 337.)

Helpful Hint

To remove a cake from its pan, run a thin knife around the edge to loosen the sides. Place a wire rack on top of the pan and quickly invert the pan onto the rack. Lift off the pan (if the cake sticks, hold on to the pan and rack and give a quick shake). Peel off any parchment or wax paper that's on the bottom of the cake. Place a wire rack on top of the cake and invert it so that the cake can finish cooling right side up.

Beat it slowly. When folding whipped egg whites into batter, a delicate hand is required to prevent deflating the whites and rendering the cake tough. First fold in one-third of the egg whites to lighten the batter and make mixing easier. Then gently fold in the rest.

Line the pans. To prevent sticking, line cake pans with parchment paper. Although parchment has a no-stick surface, you might want to lightly mist the paper with no-stick spray to guarantee that it will lift easily from the finished cake.

Bake in the middle. To ensure even heat circulation, it's best to bake cakes on the center rack in the oven. This helps the layers rise evenly and prevents burning.

CLASSIC CAKES

While the number of cake recipes is nearly infinite, most are variations on a few simple themes. Here are some of our favorite cakes, along with hints for having excellent results every time.

TROUBLESHOOTING CAKE PROBLEMS

Have you ever waited impatiently for a cake to rise, only to see it fall? Or watched in dismay as it crumbled into pieces instead of slipping smoothly from the pan? To see what went wrong—and learn how to prevent it in the future—see the chart below.

PROBLEM	POSSIBLE CAUSE	SOLUTION
Cake falls	Baking at too high a temperature	Reduce the temperature
	Overbeating egg whites	Beat egg whites until they're stiff, yet still glossy
Cake doesn't rise	Leavening is outdated	Test baking powder by placing a spoonful in cold water; it should bubble immediately
Cake breaks	Improper cooling	Let the cake cool on a wire rack for 15 minutes before removing from the pan
Cake has irregular holes	Overmixing batter	Mix for a shorter time, usually until the ingredients are just blended
Cake is lopsided	Uneven heating	Use an oven thermometer to check the temperature in different areas
	Oven is not level	Use a carpenter's level to make sure that the oven is level
Crumbly texture	Too much shortening	Check amount of shortening in recipe
	Undermixing batter	Mix until the ingredients are well-incorporated

Angel Food Cake

Pure white and a mile high, this fat-free masterpiece is a simple combination of cake flour, cream of tartar and sugar, plus stiffly beaten egg whites. It doesn't use baking powder or baking soda; the only rise comes from the egg whites.

☞ Angel food can be spiced up with the addition of ginger or cinnamon or with almond or orange extract.

☞ Adding a little cocoa to the batter quickly transforms a white cake into a chocolate one.

☞ To get the best lift from the egg whites, it's important that they be at room temperature before beating. They must also be neatly separated from the yolks, without a trace of fat

remaining; any yolk that gets into the whites will interfere with rising.

☞ The whites should be whipped until they form soft, billowy mounds. If you are adding sugar, this is the time to add it, a little bit at a time. The sugar will make the whites glossy and will cause soft peaks to form when the beaters are lifted.

☞ Chefs recommend using a copper bowl when beating egg whites; a reaction with the copper helps the whites achieve greater volume and stability.

☞ In the absence of a copper bowl, cream of tartar is usually added to egg whites to increase stability.

☞ Whites that are overbeaten begin to lose their glossy appearance and won't hold a peak, so beat them just to the point of stiffness.

☞ Use cake flour rather than all-purpose. Cake flour has a softer texture, which makes a more tender cake.

☞ Don't grease the pan, as the presence of oil will prevent the batter from rising. In fact, it's a good idea to wash the pan thoroughly before using to remove even a hint of oil.

☞ Put the batter in the oven as soon as the pan is filled. Egg whites that are left to stand can start to deflate, causing a denser cake.

Chiffon Cake

Chiffon cakes differ from angel food in that they include egg yolks and a little bit of oil. They're very light and moist and are usually fla-vored with coffee, chocolate, orange or lemon.

☞ The yolks benefit from vigorous beating, preferably with an electric mixer.

☞ As with angel food cakes, the whites should be whipped until peaks form. Use clean beaters, or the whites won't whip up.

☞ To make chiffon cupcakes, use paper liners or coat muffin cups with no-stick spray and fill about two-thirds full. The resulting cakes can be used as a base for strawberry short-cake.

☞ The crumb of chiffon cake is sufficiently dense that you can bake it in layers as well as in a tube pan.

Layer Cakes

In traditional recipes, layer cakes are high in butter, eggs and sometimes sour cream or heavy

ASSEMBLING A CAKE

Perhaps no other dessert is as elegant as an iced and nicely decorated layer cake. To get professional-looking results, follow these steps.

Chill the cake for easier handling. If de-sired, cut individual layers in half horizon-tally. (Before slicing, make a slight vertical cut, so that it will be easier to line up the pieces later on.)

Brush off any loose crumbs. Spread frosting between the layers and put them back together, lining up the parts of the ver-tical cut. Place on a serving plate and add other layers, applying frosting between them.

Apply a very thin layer of icing over the top and sides of the cake to seal in any crumbs. Then add a generous amount of frosting to the top and spread it to the outer edges and down the sides. Smooth or swirl the icing as desired.

Repeatedly pulling a fork at right angles across the top of the cake will add a graceful finishing touch.

cream. Here are a few ways to enjoy the richness of layer cakes without all the fat.

☞ Replace half the butter called for in the recipe with an equal amount of applesauce or pureed bananas, pumpkin or carrots.

☞ For chocolate cakes, chefs advising using raisin, prune or banana puree. Applesauce or pear sauce works well in yellow cakes, and carrots or pumpkin is recommended for spice cakes.

☞ One way to cut back on saturated fat is to replace the butter in a recipe with reduced-fat margarine. Just be sure to reduce the liquid in the recipe by 2 or 3 tablespoons to accommodate the water that's usually added to reduced-fat margarines.

☞ You can substitute nonfat yogurt for sour cream. For an extra taste twist, try using flavored yogurts, like coffee, vanilla or banana.

☞ Another ingredient that can fill in for sour cream is buttermilk. To keep the liquids in balance, use ¾ cup buttermilk for every cup of sour cream called for in the recipe.

Roll Cake

Roll cakes are made by baking a thin layer of batter in a parchment-lined jelly-roll pan. The resulting cake is then rolled around a filling, like fresh fruit or preserves. The cake can be eaten plain or frosted with icing or confectioners' sugar.

Flourless Cakes and Tortes

As the name suggests, these are made with no flour. Instead, they use egg yolks, ground nuts or bread crumbs. The resulting cake is light, rich and very moist.

☞ The yolks are beaten with sugar until they fall from the beaters in a thick ribbon. The thorough mixing assists in aerating the cake and dissolving the sugar crystals.

☞ To get the best rise, put the pan into the oven as soon as it's filled with batter. Flourless cakes don't rise much in any event, so don't expect the final product to be particularly puffy.

☞ Flourless cakes and tortes are often dusted with confectioners' sugar, covered with a flavored glaze or served with fresh fruit.

Fruitcake

Made by combining grated or pureed fruits or vegetables—like carrots, bananas, apples, pumpkin and dates—with a little oil and eggs, fruitcakes are both incredibly moist and easy to make.

☞ Store-bought fruitcakes often use candied fruits, which may be why they often sit around for months without being eaten. When making your own, use dried fruit, such as raisins, prunes, peaches or currants.

☞ Let your imagination flourish. Fruitcakes typically contain half a dozen or more varieties of fruit; the more, the merrier.

☞ To reduce the amount of fat, replace the traditional nuts with an equal amount of chopped fruit.

☞ Another way to reduce the amount of fat is to replace it with an equal amount of pureed fruit. To complement the spicy flavor of fruitcakes, pumpkin puree is always a good choice.

ICING ON THE CAKE

Having cake is always a special event, but to make it even more special, you'll want to add something extra to top it off.

Traditional frostings are sugar-based mixtures that often contain extraordinary amounts of fat. It's possible, however, to enjoy the taste and elegant finish of a great topping without all the fat. Here are some tips that you may want to try.

Put on a light glaze. Made by combining a warm liquid with confectioners' sugar until the mixture is the consistency of warm honey, a glaze is an easy way to dress up any cake.

☞ To use a glaze, simply spread it on top of the cake and allow it to dribble down the sides.

☞ The flavor of the glaze depends on the liquid that you use; many cooks use preserves

MAKING CAKE ROLL

Delicious and a delight to the eye, a cake roll only looks complicated. In fact, it's very easy to make. Here's how. Cooks typically use parchment paper to make the roll, although a clean dish towel will also work. Here's what you need to do.

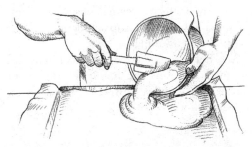

Coat a 10″ × 15″ no-stick jelly-roll pan with no-stick spray, then line it with parchment or wax paper, pressing the paper into the corners and along the sides. The paper should extend over the short ends of the pan by a few inches. Coat it with no-stick spray. Pour in the batter and bake as directed (usually 375° for about 10 to 12 minutes, or until puffed and lightly golden).

Remove the pan from the oven and cover with another piece of parchment paper and a flat baking sheet. Using pot holders, invert the pan onto the sheet. Remove the pan and immediately peel off the paper that the cake was baked on.

Lightly sprinkle the cake with confectioners' sugar and immediately roll it up. (You may start at either a long end or a short end. Roll up the paper along with the cake for easier handling.) Set on a wire rack and cool completely.

Unroll the cooled cake and spread the filling evenly over the entire surface.

Leaving the paper behind, reroll the cake as tightly as you can without crushing it or squeezing out the filling. You can decorate the cake with a sprinkling of confectioners' sugar, a layer of frosting or a flavored glaze. Chill slightly, then slice and serve.

thinned with lemon juice or with warm milk flavored with vanilla extract.

☞ You can make a flavorful citrus glaze by grating the rind from a lemon, orange or lime and beating it with freshly squeezed juice from the same fruit. Combine the mixture with confectioners' sugar until it's the consistency of honey, then spread it on the cake.

☞ For a low-fat chocolate glaze, sift Dutch-processed cocoa powder with confectioners' sugar and thin with hot water. To give it a mocha twist, use coffee instead of water.

☞ For a fresh-fruit glaze, combine ½ cup preserves with about 1 teaspoon unflavored gelatin. Cook over medium heat until the glaze

is slightly thickened. Let cool slightly, then apply to the cake.

Put on a cream-cheese frosting.
Traditional cream-cheese frosting, the classic accompaniment to carrot cakes, is very high in fat. To enjoy the flavor and texture of cream cheese without so much fat, try combining low-fat or nonfat cream cheese with some marshmallow creme. For 8 ounces cream cheese, use 1 cup marshmallow creme, 1 cup confectioners' sugar and 1 teaspoon vanilla.

Another way to make over a cream-cheese topping is to reduce the amount of full-fat cream cheese by half and substitute an equal amount of yogurt cheese.

USING A PASTRY BAG

Whether you're making graceful rosettes on a bar cookie or spelling "Happy Birthday" on a cake, you're going to need a pastry bag. Inexpensive and easy to use, pastry bags can be fitted with an enormous variety of tips, from round and flat to fluted and star-shaped.

If you'll need to switch tips midway through decorating, get a coupling device, which allows a change without emptying the bag.

To get the most from your pastry bag, here's what chefs advise.

Position the tip (or the inner part of the coupling device) inside the empty pastry bag. If using the coupling device, add the tip and outer ring outside the bag.

Fold down the top of the bag to make a cuff all around, so that you can easily insert the filling. Place the bag inside a 2-cup (or larger) measuring cup to hold it upright. Carefully spoon in the filling, using a rubber spatula.

Fold up the cuff and press the filling tightly into the bottom of the bag, just as you would squeeze a tube of toothpaste. Twist the top of the bag to hold in the filling. Use steady pressure as you make your designs.

Flo Braker

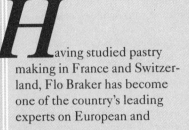

*H*aving studied pastry making in France and Switzerland, Flo Braker has become one of the country's leading experts on European and American baking. From her home in Palo Alto, California, she develops dishes that look as wonderful as they taste.

"When I modify a recipe, I try not to change it too drastically," she says. "By keeping some fat, you don't remove the flavor or adversely affect the texture."

Sponge Cake with Strawberry Filling

Sponge Cake
1½ cups sifted cake flour
1 teaspoon baking powder
¼ teaspoon salt
1 cup sugar
3 egg yolks
¼ cup orange juice
6 egg whites
1 teaspoon cream of tartar
1 teaspoon vanilla
1 teaspoon finely grated orange rind

Strawberry Filling
2½ cups strawberries, hulled and sliced
¼ cup granulated sugar
¼ cup confectioners' sugar (optional)

To make the sponge cake: Position the oven rack so that it's in the lower third of the oven. Preheat the oven to 325°.

Sift the flour, baking powder, salt and 2 tablespoons of the sugar onto wax paper.

Place the egg yolks in a small bowl. Using an electric mixer, beat in 6 tablespoons of the remaining sugar until the mixture is thick and pale in color. Add the orange juice and beat for 4 minutes, or until thickened.

Place the egg whites in a large bowl. Using clean beaters, whip the egg whites until frothy. Add the cream of tartar and whip until soft peaks form. Add the remaining ½ cup sugar and whip for 2 to 3 minutes, or until stiff peaks form. Beat in the vanilla.

Pour the egg-yolk mixture over the egg-white meringue. Sprinkle with the orange rind. Gently fold the two mixtures together.

Sprinkle one-third of the flour mixture over the egg mixture and fold in. Repeat two more times, folding just until incorporated.

Pour the mixture into an ungreased 10″ no-stick tube pan with a removable bottom. Level the surface.

Bake for 35 to 40 minutes, or until the top springs back slightly when lightly touched.

Remove from the oven and invert over a heavy long-necked bottle. Allow to cool for 45 minutes. Remove the cake from the pan.

To make the strawberry filling: In a large bowl, toss the strawberries with the granulated sugar. Set aside for 2 hours. Mash the berries, toss gently and let stand for 1 hour.

When the cake is cool, split it into three layers and fill with the strawberries and some of their juices. Sprinkle the confectioners' sugar (if using) over the top of the cake.

Makes 10 servings. Per serving: 200 calories, 1.8 g. fat (8% of calories), 4.6 g. protein, 41.8 g. carbohydrates, 1.1 g. dietary fiber, 64 mg. cholesterol, 123 mg. sodium

Glazed Golden Bundt Cake

Cake

- 3 cups all-purpose flour
- 2 cups sugar
- 2 teaspoons baking powder
- ½ teaspoon baking soda
- ½ teaspoon salt
- ¾ cup butter (1½ sticks), softened
- 1 tablespoon vanilla
- 3 large eggs
- 1 cup nonfat sour cream
- 1 cup skim milk

Glaze

- ¾ cup confectioners' sugar
- 1 teaspoon vanilla
- 1–2 tablespoons warm water (105° to 115°F)

To make the cake: Preheat the oven to 350°. Generously coat a 12-cup no-stick Bundt or ring pan with no-stick spray and dust with flour.

In a large bowl, combine the flour, sugar, baking powder, baking soda and salt. Add the butter. Using an electric mixer, mix until the butter is thoroughly incorporated into the flour mixture.

Add the vanilla, eggs, sour cream and milk. Beat for 1 minute at low speed, scraping the bowl often. Beat at high speed for 2 minutes, or until the batter is light and fluffy.

Spoon the batter into the prepared pan and smooth it evenly. Bake for 60 to 70 minutes, or until a toothpick inserted in the center comes out clean. Cool in the pan for 45 minutes. Turn out onto a serving plate and cool completely.

To make the glaze: In a small bowl, whisk together the confectioners' sugar, vanilla and water until smooth. Evenly drizzle over the cooled cake.

Makes 16 servings. Per serving: 304 calories, 9.8 g. fat (29% of calories), 5.0 g. protein, 49.5 g. carbohydrates, 0.6 g. dietary fiber, 63.5 mg. cholesterol, 226 mg. sodium

VARIATION

Chocolate-Glazed Marble Cake: Using separate bowls, divide the prepared batter into 2 portions. Into half of the batter, stir ¼ cup unsweetened dark cocoa powder and ⅛ teaspoon baking soda. Scoop the chocolate batter and yellow batter alternately into the pan. Bake as directed. To make the glaze, add 2 tablespoons unsweetened cocoa powder along with the confectioners' sugar. Increase the water to 2 to 3 tablespoons, as necessary. Whisk until smooth and drizzle over the cooled cake.

Raspberry Jelly Roll

- 1 cup all-purpose flour
- 1 teaspoon baking powder
- ¼ teaspoon salt
- 4 eggs
- ¾ cup sugar
- ¼ cup cold water
- 1 teaspoon vanilla
- 2 teaspoons confectioners' sugar
- ¾ cup seedless raspberry all-fruit spread

Preheat the oven to 375°. Generously coat a 15″ × 10″ no-stick jelly-roll pan with no-stick spray and dust with flour.

In a small bowl, combine the flour, baking powder and salt.

In a large bowl, beat the eggs with an electric mixer at the highest speed for 5 minutes, or until thick and lemon-colored. Add the sugar, 1 tablespoon at a time, beating constantly until light and fluffy. Stir in the water and vanilla. Add the flour mixture and blend at low speed just until the dry ingredients are incorporated.

Spoon the batter into the prepared pan and smooth it evenly. Bake for 8 to 12 minutes, or just until the top springs back when lightly touched in the center.

While the cake bakes, cut a length of paper towel about 20″ long. Sprinkle evenly with 1 teaspoon of the confectioners' sugar.

Loosen the edges of the baked cake and immediately invert onto the toweling. Roll up starting from a short end, rolling the towel into the cake. Cool on a wire rack. Carefully unroll the cake and remove the towel. Spread the inside of the cake with the all-fruit spread; reroll the cake. Wrap in plastic wrap or foil and refrigerate. Dust with the remaining 1 teaspoon confectioners' sugar before serving.

Makes 12 servings. Per serving: 165 calories, 1.8 g. fat (10% of calories), 3.4 g. protein, 34.5 g. carbohydrates, 0.4 g. dietary fiber, 71 mg. cholesterol, 97 mg. sodium

VARIATION

Pineapple-Filled Roll Cake: Omit the all-fruit spread. Instead, while the cake bakes, prepare a pineapple filling. Drain 1 can (8 ounces) crushed pineapple, reserving the juice. Add water to yield ½ cup liquid. Sprinkle 1½ teaspoons unflavored gelatin over the liquid and let stand until softened. Place over hot water and stir until dissolved. Chill until the mixture is partially set. Add ½ cup nonfat lemon-flavored yogurt and beat with an electric mixer until the mixture is light and fluffy. Fold in the pineapple. Spread onto the cooled cake and roll up loosely to incorporate the filling into the roll.

Lemon Pound Cake

2¼ cups cake flour
1¼ cups sugar
  2 teaspoons baking powder
¼ teaspoon baking soda
¼ teaspoon salt
½ cup butter, at room temperature
  1 cup nonfat sour cream
¼ cup skim milk
  2 egg whites
  1 teaspoon grated lemon rind
  1 teaspoon lemon extract
  1 teaspoon vanilla

Preheat the oven to 350°. Coat a 9″ × 5″ no-stick loaf pan with no-stick spray and dust lightly with flour.

In a large bowl, combine the flour, sugar, baking powder, baking soda, salt, butter, sour cream, milk, egg whites, lemon rind, lemon extract and vanilla. Using an electric mixer, mix at low speed for 1 minute, scraping the sides of the bowl often. Mix at medium speed for 2 minutes longer, or until the batter is light and fluffy.

Spoon the batter into the prepared pan and smooth it evenly. Bake for 55 to 65 minutes, or until a toothpick inserted in the center comes out clean. Cool in the pan for 10 minutes. Turn out onto a wire rack and cool completely.

Makes 16 servings. Per serving: 186 calories, 5.9 g. fat (28% of calories), 2.9 g. protein, 30.4 g. carbohydrates, 0.4 g. dietary fiber, 16 mg. cholesterol, 98 mg. sodium

VARIATIONS

Cocoa-Spice Pound Cake: Replace ¼ cup of the cake flour with ¼ cup unsweetened cocoa powder. Add 1 teaspoon ground cinnamon, ¼ teaspoon ground nutmeg and ¼ teaspoon ground cloves. Omit the lemon rind and lemon extract.

Rum Baba Pound Cake: Add 1 tablespoon light rum to the batter along with the vanilla. While the cake bakes, bring ¼ cup sugar and ⅓ cup water to a boil. Simmer for 5 minutes. Remove from the heat and cool slightly. Stir in ¼ cup light rum. Pierce the warm cake with a toothpick or skewer in several places. Drizzle evenly with the rum syrup.

Luscious Lemon Cheesecake

20 reduced-fat vanilla wafers, finely crumbled
 2 packages (8 ounces each) nonfat cream cheese
 1 package (8 ounces) Neufchâtel cheese
 1 cup fat-free ricotta cheese
 3 large eggs
 1 cup sugar
 1 tablespoon cornstarch
 ¼ cup fresh lemon juice
 1 teaspoon grated lemon rind

Preheat the oven to 350°. Coat a 9″ or 10″ no-stick springform pan with no-stick spray. Spread the vanilla wafer crumbs evenly over the bottom of the pan.

In a large bowl, combine the cream cheese, Neufchâtel, ricotta, eggs, sugar, cornstarch, lemon juice and lemon rind. Using an electric mixer, beat until smooth.

Spoon the mixture into the prepared pan and smooth it evenly. Place the pan on a baking sheet. Bake for 45 to 50 minutes, or until the center is almost set. Cool in the pan. Refrigerate for 3 hours or overnight before serving.

Makes 12 servings. Per serving: 202 calories, 6.3 g. fat (29% of calories), 11.8 g. protein, 24.6 g. carbohydrates, 0.2 g. dietary fiber, 77 mg. cholesterol, 353 mg. sodium

VARIATION

Raspberry-Swirl Cheesecake: Thaw 1 package (10 ounces) frozen raspberries in light syrup. Press the berries through a sieve to remove the seeds. Remove 2 cups of the cheesecake mixture to a medium bowl. Add the pureed raspberries and 2 teaspoons cornstarch; mix well. Pour half the plain filling over the crust. Over the plain filling, spoon the raspberry mixture alternately with the remaining plain filling. Using a table knife, swirl the raspberry filling through the plain filling.

Sour Cream Layer Cake

 6 egg whites
 1 teaspoon cream of tartar
 2 cups sifted cake flour
 1 cup sugar
 2 teaspoons baking powder
 2 teaspoons vanilla
 1 cup reduced-fat or nonfat sour cream
 ¼ cup canola oil
 ¼ cup water
 ½ cup strawberry, raspberry or apricot all-fruit spread
 1 cup confectioners' sugar
2–3 teaspoons lemon juice

Preheat the oven to 350°. Coat two 8″ or 9″ no-stick round cake pans with no-stick spray.

In a clean and dry large bowl, using an electric mixer, whip the egg whites until frothy. Add the cream of tartar and beat until the whites are stiff.

In another large bowl, combine the flour, sugar, baking powder, vanilla, ¾ cup of the sour cream, oil and water. Stir until well-blended and the mixture is smooth. Fold in the egg whites.

Divide the batter between the cake pans and smooth it evenly. Bake for 25 to 30 minutes, or until the cakes spring back when lightly touched in the center. Cool for 10 minutes in the pans. Carefully turn out onto a wire rack and cool completely.

Place one cake layer on a serving plate. Spread the all-fruit spread evenly over the surface. Top with the second cake layer. Spread the center of the top layer with the remaining ¼ cup sour cream to make a 3″ circle. In a 2-cup measuring cup, mix the confectioners' sugar and lemon juice until smooth. Spread the mixture around the edge of the cake up to the sour cream, allowing the mixture to drizzle down the sides of the cake.

Makes 12 servings. Per serving: 263 calories, 7.7 g. fat (24% of calories), 4.5 g. protein, 50.8 g. carbohydrates, 0.8 g. dietary fiber, 3 mg. cholesterol, 85 mg. sodium

VARIATIONS

Fresh Strawberry Layer Cake: Omit the all-fruit spread. Increase the remaining sour cream to ½ cup and spread over the bottom cake layer. Arrange 1 cup sliced fresh strawberries over the sour cream and sprinkle with 2 tablespoons confectioners' sugar. Place the second cake layer on top. Drizzle with the confectioners'-sugar mixture.

Poppy Seed Layer Cake: Soak ¼ cup poppy seeds in 2 tablespoons 1% low-fat milk for 30 minutes. Add to the batter along with the egg whites. Fill and frost as directed.

Light Lemon Cupcakes

Cupcakes

- 1 cup all-purpose flour
- ½ cup sugar
- ¼ cup instant dry milk powder
- 1 teaspoon baking powder
- ¼ teaspoon baking soda
- ¼ teaspoon salt
- 5 tablespoons softened butter
- ½ cup nonfat lemon-flavored yogurt
- 1 large egg
- ¼ cup water
- ¼ teaspoon lemon extract

Icing

- 1 cup confectioners' sugar
- 2 teaspoons lemon juice
- 1 tablespoon water

To make the cupcakes: Preheat the oven to 350°. Line a 12-cup no-stick muffin pan with paper liners.

In a large bowl, combine the flour, sugar, milk powder, baking powder, baking soda, salt, butter and yogurt. Using an electric mixer, blend until the butter is thoroughly incorporated into the dry ingredients.

In a cup, mix the egg with the water and lemon extract. Add to the flour mixture and beat until smooth.

Spoon the batter into the paper-lined cups. Bake for 25 minutes, or until the cupcakes are lightly browned and spring back when lightly touched in the center. Remove from the pans and cool completely on wire racks.

To make the icing: In a 2-cup measuring cup or small bowl, mix together the confectioners' sugar, lemon juice and water. Evenly drizzle over the cupcakes.

Makes 12. Per cupcake: 170 calories, 5.3 g. fat (28% of calories), 3 g. protein, 27.9 g. carbohydrates, 0.3 g. dietary fiber, 31 mg. cholesterol, 59 mg. sodium

VARIATION

Pineapple Upside-Down Cupcakes: Coat the 12-cup muffin pan with no-stick spray; omit the paper liners. Spoon 2 teaspoons brown sugar into each cup. Top with ½ teaspoon butter and ¼ of one ring of pineapple. Spoon the cupcake batter into the cups on top of the pineapple. Bake as directed. Invert onto a serving tray while the cupcakes are hot. Omit the icing.

Angel Food Cake

- 1 cup + 2 tablespoons sifted cake flour
- 1¼ cups + 2 tablespoons sugar
- 12 egg whites, at room temperature
- 1¼ teaspoons cream of tartar
- ¼ teaspoon salt
- 1½ teaspoons vanilla
- ½ teaspoon almond extract

Preheat the oven to 350°.

Sift the flour with ½ cup of the sugar three times. Set aside.

In a clean and dry large bowl, combine the egg whites, cream of tartar and salt. Using an electric mixer, beat until the egg whites form soft peaks. Gradually beat in the remaining sugar, ¼ cup at a time. Add the vanilla and almond extract. Beat until glossy.

Gently fold the flour mixture into the egg-white mixture in 3 stages, folding just enough to mix each time. Gently pour the batter into an ungreased 9″ or 10″ straight-sided no-stick tube pan and smooth the surface of the batter evenly.

Bake for 40 to 45 minutes, or until the cake is golden brown. Invert the pan over the top of a heavy long-necked bottle or funnel and let cool for 1½ to 2 hours. Gently remove to a serving platter.

Makes 12 servings. Per serving: 146 calories, 0.1 g. fat (1% of calories), 4.4 g. protein, 31.7 g. carbohydrates, 0.2 g. dietary fiber, 0 mg. cholesterol, 100 mg. sodium

NOTES

- For a colorful angel food cake, fold 3 to 4 tablespoons colored crystal sprinkles into the batter with the last addition of flour.
- Top the cake with fresh berries, frozen yogurt, Chocolate Glaze (page 497), or one of the sauces in Baked Fruit, Compotes, Sauces and Soufflés.
- To stabilize an empty bottle, fill it with water before inverting the cake pan over it.

Pineapple Upside-Down Cake

We updated this classic upside-down cake by using fat-free egg substitute and reduced amounts of margarine and sugar. We also added ground ginger and cinnamon to give it a spicy boost of flavor.

Topping

- 1 can (20 ounces) pineapple rings (packed in juice)
- 6 tablespoons packed brown sugar
- 2 teaspoons nondiet tub-style margarine or butter

Cake

- 1½ cups all-purpose flour
- 1¼ teaspoons baking powder
- ½ teaspoon baking soda
- ¼ teaspoon salt
- ¼ teaspoon ground ginger
- ¼ teaspoon ground cinnamon
- 6 tablespoons sugar
- 1½ tablespoons nondiet tub-style margarine or butter, softened
- 1½ tablespoons canola oil
- ¼ cup fat-free egg substitute
- ¾ teaspoon grated orange rind
- 2 teaspoons vanilla
- ⅔ cup nonfat plain yogurt
- 2 tablespoons dark rum or ½ teaspoon rum extract + 1½ tablespoons orange juice

To make the topping: Drain the pineapple, reserving ¾ cup of the juice.

In a large cast-iron or ovenproof skillet, combine the brown sugar, margarine or butter and the reserved pineapple juice. Bring the mixture to a boil over medium heat. Cook, stirring frequently, for 3 to 4 minutes, or until reduced by half. Add the pineapple rings. Bring to a boil again and cook for 3 to 4 minutes, turning the pineapple occasionally, until the syrup is slightly thickened and the pineapple is slightly browned. Remove from the heat.

To make the cake: Preheat the oven to 375°.

In a medium bowl, combine the flour, baking powder, baking soda, salt, ginger and cinnamon. Set aside.

In a large bowl, combine the sugar, margarine or butter and oil. Using an electric mixer, beat until smooth. Add the egg substitute, orange rind and vanilla. Beat until well-blended. Stir in the yogurt.

Add the flour mixture and stir just until blended. Do not overmix.

Immediately spoon the batter evenly over the pineapple. Bake for 20 to 25 minutes, or until a toothpick inserted in the center comes out clean. Remove from the oven and let stand for 5 minutes.

Run a metal spatula around the sides to loosen the cake. Place a serving platter on top of the skillet and carefully flip the skillet over onto the platter. Let sit, with the pan on top, for 2 minutes. Then carefully remove the skillet. If any pineapple rings stick to the skillet, remove them with a knife and put them in their places. Drizzle with the rum or rum extract and orange juice. Let cool slightly before serving.

Makes 8 servings. Per serving: 293 calories, 6 g. fat (18% of calories), 4.6 g. protein, 53.9 g. carbohydrates, 1.2 g. dietary fiber, 0.3 mg. cholesterol, 271 mg. sodium

VARIATION

Peach Upside-Down Cake: Replace the pineapple with 1 can (20 ounces) sliced peaches in light syrup. Reduce the brown sugar to 4 tablespoons.

Chocolate Chip Blondies

1	cup flour
½	teaspoon baking soda
⅓	cup nondiet tub-style margarine or butter, softened
⅓	cup sugar
⅓	cup packed brown sugar
1½	teaspoons vanilla
1	egg
½	cup semisweet miniature chocolate chips

Preheat the oven to 375°. Coat an 8″ × 8″ no-stick baking dish with no-stick spray and set aside.

In a small bowl, combine the flour and baking soda; set aside.

In a large bowl, cream together the margarine or butter, sugar, brown sugar and vanilla. Stir in the egg. Add the flour mixture and stir until well-blended.

Spoon the batter into the prepared dish and smooth it evenly. Sprinkle the chocolate chips over the surface.

Bake for 2 minutes to melt the chips. Remove from the oven and run a knife through the batter to create a marbleized effect.

Return to the oven and bake for 14 to 16 minutes, or until the mixture is set and a toothpick inserted into the center comes out almost clean. Cool in the dish. When completely cool, cut into bars.

Makes 24. Per bar: 84 calories, 3.8 g. fat (39% of calories), 0.9 g. protein, 12.2 g. carbohydrates, 0.2 g. dietary fiber, 9 mg. cholesterol, 64 mg. sodium

VARIATION

Butterscotch Blondies: Replace the chocolate chips with ¾ cup miniature butterscotch chips.

Carrot Cake

Cake

1¼	cups all-purpose flour
1½	teaspoons baking powder
½	teaspoon baking soda
1	teaspoon ground cinnamon
¼	teaspoon ground nutmeg
⅛	teaspoon ground cloves
⅛	teaspoon salt
⅔	cup sugar
2	tablespoons nondiet tub-style margarine or butter, softened
3	egg whites
⅓	cup applesauce
1⅔	cups grated carrots
¼	cup raisins

Frosting

¾	cup confectioners' sugar
3	tablespoons tub-style nonfat cream cheese
½	teaspoon skim milk
½	teaspoon vanilla

To make the cake: Preheat the oven to 350°. Coat an 8″ × 8″ no-stick baking dish with no-stick spray and set aside.

In a medium bowl, combine the flour, baking powder, baking soda, cinnamon, nutmeg, cloves and salt.

In a large bowl, cream together the sugar and margarine or butter. Using an electric mixer, beat in the egg whites and applesauce until well-blended. Add the flour mixture and beat, stopping once to scrape down the bowl, until just combined. Stir in the carrots and raisins.

Pour the batter into the prepared dish and smooth it evenly. Bake for 30 to 35 minutes, or until the top is lightly browned and a toothpick inserted in the center comes out clean. Cool completely in the dish.

To make the frosting: Sift the confectioners' sugar into a medium bowl. Add the cream cheese, milk and vanilla. Blend until smooth. Spread the frosting evenly over the cooled cake.

Makes 8 servings. Per serving: 247 calories, 3.2 g. fat (11% of calories), 4.5 g. protein, 50.7 g. carbohydrates, 1.6 g. dietary fiber, 0 mg. cholesterol, 274 mg. sodium

NOTE

• Some brands of nonfat cream cheese taste better than others. Experiment to find your favorite.

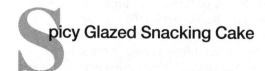

Spicy Glazed Snacking Cake

Cake

1¾	cups all-purpose flour
1	teaspoon baking powder
½	teaspoon baking soda
1	teaspoon ground cinnamon
1	teaspoon ground ginger
¼	teaspoon ground cloves
⅛	teaspoon ground nutmeg
¾	cup low-fat buttermilk
⅔	cup packed brown sugar
¼	cup applesauce
1	egg white
3	tablespoons canola oil
1	teaspoon vanilla

Glaze

¾	cup confectioners' sugar
½	teaspoon ground ginger
¼	teaspoon ground cinnamon
1	tablespoon honey
4	teaspoons apple juice or water
½	teaspoon vanilla

To make the cake: Preheat the oven to 350°. Coat an 8″ × 8″ no-stick baking dish with no-stick spray and set aside.

In a medium bowl, combine the flour, baking powder, baking soda, cinnamon, ginger, cloves and nutmeg.

In a large bowl, combine the buttermilk, brown sugar, applesauce, egg white, oil and vanilla. Add the flour mixture and stir until just combined.

Spoon the batter into the prepared dish and smooth it evenly. Bake for 30 to 35 minutes, or until a toothpick inserted in the center comes out clean. Cool on a wire rack for 10 to 15 minutes.

To make the glaze: Sift the confectioners' sugar into a medium bowl. Stir in the ginger and cinnamon. Add the honey, apple juice or water and vanilla. Stir until smooth. Drizzle the glaze over the top of the cooled cake and spread it evenly over the surface.

Makes 8 servings. Per serving: 287 calories, 5.6 g. fat (18% of calories), 4.1 g. protein, 55.3 g. carbohydrates, 0.9 g. dietary fiber, 1 mg. cholesterol, 159 mg. sodium

NOTE

• Wrap any leftover cake in plastic wrap. It will keep for 2 to 3 days at room temperature.

Raisin-Fig Bars

18	dried figs (about 12 ounces), stems removed
¾	cup raisins
1½	cups water
¼	cup honey
⅛	teaspoon ground cinnamon
1¼	cups all-purpose flour
1	cup oat bran
¼	cup packed brown sugar
⅛	teaspoon salt
2	tablespoons canola oil
3	tablespoons nondiet tub-style margarine or butter, cut into small pieces

Preheat the oven to 400°. Coat a 9″ × 13″ no-stick baking dish with no-stick spray and set aside.

Coarsely chop the figs and place in a food processor. Add the raisins and process, using on/off turns, until fairly smooth. Transfer to a medium saucepan. Add the water, honey and cinnamon. Bring to a boil over medium-high heat. Reduce the heat to medium and cook, stirring occasionally, for 8 minutes, or until the mixture thickens. Remove from the heat and set aside.

In a food processor, combine the flour, oat bran, brown sugar and salt. Process using on/off turns. Add the oil and margarine or butter. Process well using on/off turns.

Press half the mixture into the prepared dish. Spoon dollops of the fig mixture over the crust. Spread it out evenly with the back of a spoon. Sprinkle the remaining crust mixture over the top and spread it out evenly with the back of a spoon. Gently press it into place.

Bake for 20 to 25 minutes, or until lightly browned. Cut into bars while warm. Serve warm or at room temperature.

Makes 24. Per bar: 125 calories, 3.1 g. fat (20% of calories), 1.9 g. protein, 25.5 g. carbohydrates, 2.2 g. dietary fiber, 0 mg. cholesterol, 34 mg. sodium

NOTE

• Wrap leftover bars in plastic wrap. They will keep for 4 to 5 days at room temperature.

Crunchy Peanut Butter Cookies

Low-fat peanut butter cookies? You bet. We slimmed down this favorite by using a reduced amount of peanut butter and an egg white in place of eggs.

¾ cup packed brown sugar
¼ cup sugar
5 tablespoons vegetable shortening or butter
¼ cup crunchy peanut butter (see note)
1 teaspoon vanilla
1 egg white
3 tablespoons water
1¾ cups all-purpose flour
¾ teaspoon baking soda
¼ teaspoon salt

Preheat the oven to 350°. Coat no-stick baking sheets with no-stick spray or line with parchment paper.

In a medium bowl, cream together the brown sugar, sugar, shortening or butter and peanut butter until smooth. Add the vanilla, egg white and water. Beat until light.

In another medium bowl, combine the flour, baking soda and salt. Stir the flour mixture into the peanut-butter mixture.

Shape the batter into 1″ balls and place on the prepared baking sheets, leaving 2″ between cookies. Using a fork that has been dipped in water, flatten the cookies. Bake for 10 to 12 minutes, or just until the cookies are set. Cool on the sheets for 2 minutes. Remove the cookies to a wire rack and cool completely.

Makes 30. Per cookie: 45 calories, 1.8 g. fat (35% of calories), 0.7 g. protein, 6.8 g. carbohydrates, 0.7 g. dietary fiber, 0 mg. cholesterol, 23 mg. sodium

NOTE
• Unsalted peanut butter works best for these cookies. Look for "natural" or "no-salt-added" peanut butter in your supermarket.

Chocolate Chip and Raisin Cookies

¾ cup packed brown sugar
¼ cup sugar
6 tablespoons butter, softened
½ teaspoon vanilla
1 egg white
3 tablespoons water
1½ cups all-purpose flour
¾ teaspoon baking soda
¼ teaspoon salt
½ cup miniature semisweet chocolate chips
½ cup raisins

Preheat the oven to 350°. Coat no-stick baking sheets with no-stick spray or line with parchment paper.

In a medium bowl, cream together the brown sugar, sugar and butter until smooth. Add the vanilla, egg white and water. Beat until light.

In another bowl, combine the flour, baking soda and salt. Stir the flour mixture into the brown-sugar mixture. Fold in the chocolate chips and raisins.

Drop by rounded teaspoonfuls onto the prepared baking sheets, leaving 2″ between cookies. Bake for 8 to 10 minutes, or just until the cookies are set. Cool on the sheets for 2 minutes. Remove to a wire rack and cool completely.

Makes 45. Per cookie: 61 calories, 2.3 g. fat (32% of calories), 0.6 g. protein, 10.1 g. carbohydrates, 0.3 g. dietary fiber, 4 mg. cholesterol, 29 mg. sodium

White Chocolate Chip and Dried Cranberry Cookies: Replace the semisweet chocolate chips with miniature white chocolate chips. Replace the raisins with dried cranberries.

Spicy Gingerbread Cookies

6	tablespoons vegetable shortening or butter
¾	cup packed brown sugar
2½	cups all-purpose flour
1	tablespoon ground cinnamon
2	teaspoons ground ginger
1½	teaspoons ground cloves
1	teaspoon baking soda
2	tablespoons molasses
¼–⅓	cup water

Preheat the oven to 375°. Coat no-stick baking sheets with no-stick spray or line with parchment paper.

In a large bowl, cream together the shortening or butter and brown sugar.

In another large bowl, combine the flour, cinnamon, ginger, cloves and baking soda. Add to the flour mixture and stir until well-blended.

In a cup, stir the molasses into 2 tablespoons of the water. Add to the dough and mix well. Add more water, as necessary, to form a stiff dough.

Divide the dough into four equal-size pieces. Roll each piece out to ⅛″ thickness. Using cookie cutters or a sharp knife, cut out cookies and place them on the prepared baking sheets, leaving 1″ between cookies.

Bake for 7 to 10 minutes, or until the cookies are lightly browned.

Makes 60. Per cookie: 60 calories, 1.3 g. fat (20% of calories), 0.5 g. protein, 11.6 g. carbohydrates, 0.1 g. dietary fiber, 0 mg. cholesterol, 16 mg. sodium

NOTE

• To decorate the cookies with Royal Icing, beat 1 egg white and gradually add 3 cups confectioners' sugar and 1 teaspoon vanilla. Add more water as necessary to make a smooth icing. Drizzle or pipe the icing over the cookies.

Chocolate Oatmeal Cookies

½	cup whole-wheat flour
½	cup all-purpose flour
3	tablespoons unsweetened cocoa powder
1	teaspoon baking powder
½	teaspoon baking soda
½	teaspoon salt
½	teaspoon ground cinnamon
¼	cup unsweetened applesauce
¼	cup canola oil
½	cup packed brown sugar
¾	cup confectioners' sugar
1	large egg
1	teaspoon vanilla
1¼	cups rolled oats
½	cup raisins or chopped dates

Preheat the oven to 350°. Coat no-stick baking sheets with no-stick spray or line with parchment paper.

In a small bowl, combine the whole-wheat flour, all-purpose flour, cocoa powder, baking powder, baking soda, salt and cinnamon.

In a large bowl, combine the applesauce, oil, brown sugar, confectioners' sugar, egg and vanilla. Mix until well-blended. Add the flour mixture and mix well. Stir in the oats and raisins or dates. Drop by rounded teaspoonfuls onto the prepared baking sheets, leaving 2″ between cookies. Bake for 10 to 12 minutes, or until very lightly browned. Do not overbake. Remove the cookies to a wire rack to cool. Or, if using parchment paper, slide the cookies and parchment paper onto a countertop to cool.

Makes 40. Per cookie: 57 calories, 1.6 g. fat (24% of calories), 0.9 g. protein, 10.4 g. carbohydrates, 0.8 g. dietary fiber, 0 mg. cholesterol, 47 mg. sodium

Raspberry Thumbprint Cookies

These classic homestyle cookies get a healthy makeover with an innovative puree of dried apples, hot water and a reduced amount of butter. Fill them with your favorite jam to vary the flavor.

- ½ cup dried apples, packed
- 3 tablespoons hot water
- 6 tablespoons butter, cut up
- 1 egg white
- 1 tablespoon vanilla
- 1 cup sugar
- 3 cups whole-wheat pastry flour or cake flour
- 1 teaspoon baking soda
- ½ teaspoon salt
- ½ cup raspberry all-fruit spread

Preheat the oven to 350°. Coat no-stick baking sheets with no-stick spray or line with parchment paper.

In a food processor or blender, process the apples and water until smooth. Add the butter, egg white and vanilla. Process until well-blended.

Add the sugar, flour, baking soda and salt. Process until well-blended.

Using a wet spoon, shape the mixture into 1″ balls and place on the prepared baking sheets, leaving 2″ between cookies. Dip your thumb in water and make an indentation in the center of each cookie. Spoon a scant ½ teaspoon of the all-fruit spread into the center of each cookie.

Bake for 12 to 15 minutes, or until the cookies are lightly browned and feel firm to the touch.

Remove the cookies to a wire rack to cool. Or, if using parchment paper, slide the cookies and parchment paper onto a countertop to cool.

Makes 50. Per cookie: 66 calories, 1.4 g. fat (19% of calories), 0.6 g. protein, 12.8 g. carbohydrates, 0.5 g. dietary fiber, 4 mg. cholesterol, 42 mg. sodium.

VARIATIONS

Chocolate-Filled Thumbprint Cookies: Omit the raspberry all-fruit spread. Bake the cookies as directed. While the cookies bake, stir together ¾ cup confectioners' sugar, 1 tablespoon cocoa powder, 1 teaspoon vanilla and 1 to 2 teaspoons hot coffee. Fill each baked cookie with ½ teaspoon of this mixture.

Lemon Curd Thumbprint Cookies: Omit the raspberry all-fruit spread. Instead, fill each cookie with ½ teaspoon lemon curd before baking. Lemon curd is most often found in lemon meringue pie. You can buy prepared lemon curd in specialty stores and large supermarkets near the jams and jellies.

Orange Thumbprint Cookies: Omit the raspberry all-fruit spread. Instead, fill each cookie with ½ teaspoon orange marmalade before baking.

Oatmeal-Raisin Cookies

1 cup unbleached flour
½ teaspoon baking soda
1½ cups rolled oats
½ teaspoon ground cinnamon
⅔ cup packed brown sugar
6 tablespoons nondiet tub-style margarine or butter, softened
2 egg whites, lightly beaten
½ cup skim milk
1 teaspoon vanilla
1 cup raisins

Preheat the oven to 375°. Coat no-stick baking sheets with no-stick spray or line with parchment paper and set aside.

Over a medium bowl, sift together the flour and baking soda. Stir in the oats and cinnamon; set aside.

In a large bowl, cream together the brown sugar and margarine or butter. Stir in the egg whites, milk and vanilla. Gradually add the flour mixture, stirring well after each addition. Fold in the raisins.

Drop by teaspoonfuls onto the prepared baking sheets, leaving 2″ between cookies.

Bake for 10 to 12 minutes. Cool on the sheets for 2 minutes. Remove to wire racks to cool completely.

Makes 40. Per cookie: 65 calories, 2 g. fat (26% of calories), 1.2 g. protein, 11.1 g. carbohydrates, 0.5 g. dietary fiber, 0.1 mg. cholesterol, 45 mg. sodium

NOTE
• For a more hearty-tasting cookie, add ¼ cup toasted wheat germ.

Dried Fruit Truffles

½ cup dried pitted prunes
½ cup pitted dates
½ cup dried apricots
1 tablespoon dried lemon rind
2 tablespoons butter
½ cup sugar
1 tablespoon honey
2 tablespoons frozen orange juice concentrate, thawed
1 teaspoon cinnamon
1½ cups crispy rice cereal
2 tablespoons confectioners' sugar

In a food processor, combine the prunes, dates, apricots and lemon rind. Process until finely chopped.

In a heavy saucepan over medium-low heat, combine the butter, sugar, honey, frozen juice concentrate and cinnamon. Cook, stirring occasionally, until the sugar is dissolved. Add the fruit mixture and cereal. Stir to coat. Remove from the heat and set aside to cool.

When cooled, pinch off small pieces of the mixture and roll into 1″ balls. Place the confectioners' sugar in a shallow bowl or pie pan. Roll the balls in the sugar and set on wax paper to dry.

Makes 36. Per truffle: 46 calories, 0.7 g. fat (13% of calories), 0.3 g. protein, 10.1 g. carbohydrates, 0.8 g. dietary fiber, 2 mg. cholesterol, 15 mg. sodium

VARIATION
Dried Berry Truffles: Replace the prunes, dates and apricots with ½ cup dried strawberries, ½ cup dried blueberries and ½ cup dried cranberries or cherries. Replace the sugar with brown sugar. Replace the rice cereal with 1 cup reduced-fat vanilla wafer crumbs.

Almond-and-Anise Biscotti

½ cup sugar
2 tablespoons unsalted butter, softened
¼ cup honey, warmed
2 egg whites
1 teaspoon vanilla
1½ cups all-purpose flour
1 teaspoon anise seeds
½ cup coarsely ground almonds
¼ teaspoon salt
1 teaspoon baking powder

Preheat the oven to 350°. Coat a no-stick baking sheet with no-stick spray or line with parchment paper.

In a large bowl, cream together the sugar, butter, honey, egg whites and vanilla until smooth. Add the flour, anise seeds, almonds, salt and baking powder. Mix until the dough is smooth and thick. Divide the dough into two equal-size pieces. Refrigerate for 30 minutes, or until firm.

Shape each piece into a 12″-long log and place both on the prepared baking sheet. Bake for 20 to 25 minutes, or until golden. Remove the logs to wire racks to cool.

Slice the cooled logs on a slight diagonal into ¼″ to ⅓″ slices. Place on the baking sheet. Reduce the oven temperature to 300° and bake for 15 minutes. Turn the biscotti over and bake for 10 to 15 minutes longer, or until dry. Cool on wire racks.

Makes 48. Per biscotto: 40 calories, 1.2 g. fat (28% of calories), 0.8 g. protein, 6.6 g. carbohydrates, 0.3 g. dietary fiber, 1 mg. cholesterol, 21 mg. sodium

VARIATIONS
Chocolate Biscotti: Replace the sugar with ½ cup packed brown sugar. Replace ¼ cup of the flour with ¼ cup unsweetened cocoa powder. Stir 1 tablespoon instant espresso or coffee powder into the dough.
Orange-and-Walnut Biscotti: Replace the anise seeds with 1 teaspoon grated orange rind. Replace the almonds with ½ cup coarsely ground walnuts.

Chocolate Frosting

We updated this classic frosting to make it healthy. Nonfat sour cream and skim milk did the trick.

6 tablespoons unsweetened cocoa powder
1¼ cups confectioners' sugar
½ cup nonfat sour cream
1 tablespoon skim milk

Into a medium bowl, sift together the cocoa powder and confectioners' sugar. Add the sour cream and milk. Stir until smooth. Cover with plastic wrap and refrigerate for at least 1 hour before using.

Makes 1¼ cups; 20 tablespoons. Per 2 tablespoons: 72 calories, 0.3 g. fat (4% of calories), 1.4 g. protein, 17.9 g. carbohydrates, 0 g. dietary fiber, 0 mg. cholesterol, 11 mg. sodium

NOTES
• If the frosting is too thick, stir in more skim milk, 1 teaspoon at at time.
• After frosting cakes, refrigerate them for 10 minutes before serving.
• Refrigerate leftover cakes iced with this frosting.

VARIATION
Mocha Chocolate Frosting: Add 2 teaspoons instant espresso coffee powder to the cocoa.

Seven-Minute Frosting

2 egg whites
1 cup sugar
⅛ teaspoon cream of tartar
¼ cup water
1 teaspoon vanilla

In the bottom of a double boiler or a large saucepan, bring a small amount of water to a simmer. In the top of the double boiler or in a large metal bowl, combine the egg whites, sugar, cream of tartar and water. Place over the simmering water. Using an electric mixer, beat for 7 minutes, or until the mixture holds its shape.

Remove from the heat and beat in the vanilla, then beat until the frosting is cool. Spread over your favorite two-layer cake.

Makes 3 cups. Per ¼ cup: 67 calories, 0 g. fat (0% of calories), 0.6 g. protein, 17 g. carbohydrates, 0 g. dietary fiber, 0 mg. cholesterol, 10 mg. sodium

VARIATION
Sea-Foam Frosting: Replace the sugar with 1 cup packed brown sugar.

Chocolate Glaze

This rich-tasting glaze is almost fat-free. Try it on ring cakes or brownies.

1 cup confectioners' sugar
1 teaspoon instant espresso coffee powder
2 tablespoons unsweetened dark cocoa powder
1 teaspoon vanilla
  Pinch of salt
1½ tablespoons hot water

In a small bowl, combine the confectioners' sugar, coffee powder, cocoa powder, vanilla, salt and water. Stir until the frosting is well-blended and of spreading consistency.

Makes ½ cup; 8 tablespoons. Per tablespoon: 52 calories, 0.2 g. fat (4% of calories), 0.2 g. protein, 13 g. carbohydrates, 0.4 g. dietary fiber, 0 mg. cholesterol, 0.5 mg. sodium

VARIATION
Chocolate-Orange Glaze: Replace the hot water with 1½ tablespoons orange-flavored liqueur or frozen orange juice concentrate, thawed. Add 1 teaspoon grated orange rind.

Great *Additions*

Sauces and Salsas

Whether served on the side, swirled underneath or drizzled on top, sauces and salsas embellish, adorn and enhance a huge variety of foods. They can be used to enliven a plate of plain pasta, spruce up a baked potato or invigorate a medley of simple vegetables. Whatever the recipe, sauces and salsas add big flavor while requiring relatively little effort.

For the cook in search of healthy recipes, traditional sauce cookery poses certain challenges. Many classically prepared sauces are oozing with full-fat ingredients—heavy cream, butter, egg yolks and cheese. Hollandaise, a traditional symbol of culinary elegance, is really nothing more than a fat-drenched emulsion of melted butter and egg yolks.

Things are beginning to change as a new generation of healthful sauces captures the fancy of cooks nationwide. Sauce cookery is no longer the sole province of French cuisine. Relying on healthful staples such as tomatoes, herbs, skim milk, yogurt, beans and low-fat thickeners, today's sauces encompass a cornucopia of adventurous tastes and textures—a bounty of flavors with a lot less fat.

SAVORY SAUCES

Perhaps because of their French pedigree, sauces have a reputation for being difficult to make. While it's true that sauces can separate, curdle or otherwise give up their wonderful textures—usually at the worst possible time, such as when company is waiting for dinner—careful handling and attention to detail can usually prevent this. Many sauces are delicate, but they're not particularly temperamental.

Here are a few general principles of sauce cookery, plus some ways to keep sauces lean and flavorful.

Temper the ingredients. Rather than adding cold ingredients to a simmering sauce, which can impede thickening, chefs advise mixing add-ins in a small bowl with some of the hot liquid before putting them in the pot.

Cook flour first. When using flour to thicken a sauce, browning it first will help eliminate the floury taste. If the sauce is to remain light colored, stir the flour in a dry saucepan for 2 minutes without letting it brown.

Keep the lid off. Cooking sauces in a covered pan causes steam to condense, thinning the sauce and making a watery texture.

Stir it well. To thoroughly incorporate ingredients and make an evenly textured sauce, it's important to stir frequently.

For fragile sauces, chefs advise using a wooden spoon. When using a metal spoon to stir sauces, be sure that it's made from stainless steel; other metals may discolor the sauce.

Make them lean. Since traditional sauces can be very high in butter, cream and other fatty items, you may want to make over some of your favorites. For example:

☞ **Alfredo.** Replace the cream with 1% low-fat milk and replace the egg yolks with fat-free egg substitute. Use low-fat cheese. You may also want to thicken the sauce with cornstarch.

☞ **Béarnaise.** Forget it. There's no healthy way to make béarnaise. Consider using a low-fat tomato salsa or yogurt sauce for a different slant to the dish.

☞ **Gravy.** Defat the pan drippings. Replace the flour-and-butter roux (a cooked combination of flour and fat used as a thickening agent) with cornstarch. Use 1% low-fat milk in place of cream.

☞ **Hollandaise.** Choose another sauce, such as salsa or a yogurt sauce, since Hollandaise is impossible to make low-fat.

☞ **Hummus.** Replace half of the tahini with low-fat plain yogurt and eliminate the oil. Double up on the parsley.

☞ **Pesto.** Replace half of the oil with an equal amount of diced plum tomatoes. Reduce the cheese by half and increase the amount of basil. If desired, add some chopped spinach leaves for extra color.

White Sauces

Traditional white sauces, also known as béchamel sauces, should almost always be approached with caution. Most contain a bevy of high-fat ingredients, such heavy cream, cheese, eggs and a flour-and-butter roux. Cheese sauces for vegetables may sound healthy, but they're really cream sauces in disguise.

Here are a few ways to lighten dairy-based sauces, while still maintaining the silky textures and smooth flavors.

☞ Replace heavy cream with a mixture of 1% low-fat milk and cornstarch. The mix mimics the appearance of heavy cream while dramatically reducing the amount of fat.

☞ Replace high-fat sour cream with low-fat plain yogurt.

☞ Add fresh herbs and spices for an assertive presence that makes up for missing fat.

White sauces are recommended for such dishes as pasta primavera, cooked vegetables (especially broccoli), grilled or broiled fish, chicken entrées (like chicken and biscuits) and potatoes au gratin.

Start with a sauté. In a medium saucepan, sauté 1 small onion and 1 or 2 cloves garlic until tender. Stir in about 2 cups 1% low-fat milk, 2 tablespoons chopped fresh parsley and a little salt and pepper. Bring to a gentle simmer.

If you're trying to reduce your intake of sodium, you can replace the salt with a splash of dry white wine.

Make your thickener. In a small bowl, mix 2 tablespoons cornstarch and 2 tablespoons cold water until smooth. Stir into the simmering sauce and cook for about 2 minutes, stirring frequently.

☞ For extra thickening and rich taste, blend in 2 to 3 tablespoons Parmesan cheese or shredded reduced-fat Swiss cheese.

☞ To add a bit of zest, squeeze some lemon juice into the sauce just before serving.

☞ To transform a simple white sauce into an herb sauce, add the chopped fresh herbs of your choice.

☞ For a mushroom sauce, sauté mushrooms along with the onions and garlic.

☞ If you want the sauce to have a little bite, add a bit of horseradish, parsley and mustard.

Brown Sauces

Old-fashioned gravy may be as American as turkey with all the fixings, but it can present a real problem for the healthy cook. Made with the pan drippings and juice of oven-roasted chicken, turkey or beef, brown sauces are literally swimming in calories and saturated fat.

To make gravy that's fresh-tasting and surprisingly light, here's what chefs advise.

Defat the drippings. When the meat is finished cooking, remove it from the pan and set aside.

☞ Pour the drippings into a fat-separating measuring cup, sold in kitchen supply stores. Fat rises to the top, so the spout on this type of cup originates at the bottom, making it easy to pour off the fat-free liquid.

☞ Add some water, wine or other liquid to the roasting pan. Place over heat and scrape with a wooden spoon to loosen the browned bit on the bottom. They contain a good deal of flavor. Add to the measuring cup and defat as above.

☞ Another way to remove fat is to refrigerate the drippings for at least 4 hours in a small container. When the liquid has chilled, skim off the layer of fat that forms on the surface. The remaining jellylike liquid will be your gravy base.

Cook it slowly. In a saucepan, bring the defatted base to a gentle simmer. Cook over medium heat for about 5 minutes, stirring frequently.

☞ Whisk in 1% low-fat milk to get the proper consistency. Chefs recommend using about ½ cup milk for every 1 cup defatted base. Reduce the heat to low after pouring in the milk.

☞ In a small bowl, combine equal amounts of cornstarch and cold water. (About 2 table-spoons of cornstarch will thicken 2 cups of gravy). Whisk the cornstarch mixture into the simmering liquid and cook for 2 minutes longer. Continue to whisk until there are no lumps and the liquid has thickened.

☞ Lightly season the gravy with chopped fresh parsley, minced garlic, ground sage, dried thyme, salt and pepper. Pour into a gravy boat and serve.

Basic Tomato Sauce

When it comes to hearty and healthful sauces, tomatoes are a cook's best friend. Tomatoes form the basis of a variety of robustly flavored low-fat sauces. The many forms of tomatoes—fresh, canned whole, stewed, paste and so forth—inspire a variety of versatile sauces, all with different personalities and flavors. Some chefs like to grill tomatoes before using them in a sauce to add a distinctive smoky taste.

To make a delicious basic tomato sauce:

☞ In a medium saucepan, sauté some diced onions and some minced garlic until tender.

☞ Stir in a combination of stewed tomatoes and tomato puree. Sprinkle in dried basil and oregano plus red-pepper flakes and salt.

☞ Simmer over low heat, stirring often, for 20 minutes or longer.

☞ Near the finish, stir in a few tablespoons chopped fresh herbs, such as parsley, basil and oregano.

While tomatoes provide the body of a sauce, aromatic ingredients like garlic, shallots and onions lend delicious accents. Mushrooms, egg-plant, sweet peppers and other vegetables can also be included, as can herbs like oregano, basil, parsley and sage.

☞ When adding meat to the sauce, choose lean cuts and do your best to remove as much fat as possible before cooking. Or brown the meat separately and drain it well on paper towels before adding to the sauce.

☞ You can leave out the meat altogether and replace it with seasonal vegetables like eggplant, zucchini, yellow summer squash or spinach.

Creole Sauce

This is a classic Louisiana red sauce made with the "holy trinity" of Cajun and Creole cooking: onions, sweet peppers and garlic. Creole sauce is further flavored with a plethora of spices, including red pepper, black pepper, thyme, oregano and parsley. The sauce makes a spicy embellishment for shrimp, scallops, chicken and vegetable medleys.

Creole sauce is prepared just like a basic red tomato sauce, except it uses crushed tomatoes instead of tomato puree.

Creole sauce can be simmered with sautéed shrimp or other shellfish, folded into rice (for a Spanish rice–type dish) or spooned over grilled chicken or fish steaks.

Sofrito

This is a simple sauce popular in Spanish-speaking countries. It is very easy to make: Sauté onions, peppers, tomatoes, garlic, cilantro and parsley in a little oil until the vegetables are tender but still have crunch. Serve over rice, grains, beans, potatoes or roasts as a high-flavor replacement for such fatty fare as butter and sour cream.

To transform this simple sauce into a more filling condiment, add cooked black beans, red kidney beans or chick-peas to the mix.

Bean Sauces

When you want a low-fat topping that won't overwhelm a delicate dish, try a bean sauce. Bean sauces are a wonderful accompaniment for chicken and other meats. They can also be served with grilled foods, such as firm-textured fish or vegetables. Here's how to make a super bean sauce.

☞ Begin by sautéing diced onions, red peppers and garlic in a little oil. For extra bite, add a small chili pepper to the mix.

☞ Add about 2 cups cooked or canned beans and 14 ounces stewed tomatoes. Season with dried oregano, ground cumin, salt and pepper. Cook, stirring occasionally, for about 20 minutes. If desired, mash or puree the beans.

☞ For the best flavor, season bean sauces with fresh herbs toward the end of the cooking time to prevent the flavors from dissipating.

Curry Sauce

To get an intense flavor with little or no added fat, try a curry sauce. The core flavor, of course, is curry powder, a potent blend of aromatic seasonings. Most curry sauces also contain a fragrant base of sautéed onions, tomatoes, garlic, ginger and chili peppers. To thicken the

THE THICKENING

To give a sauce the necessary body and rich texture, you need to use a thickener. Traditional recipes call for high-fat ingredients like egg yolks, heavy cream and butter-based roux (a cooked combination of flour and fat used as a thickening agent). Yet there are healthy alternatives. A small amount of cornstarch or arrowroot will transform a thin, soupy sauce into one with a silken texture and pleasingly thick body.

Arrowroot thickens at lower temperatures than cornstarch, so it's good for delicate sauces that should not boil. Cornstarch needs to come to a boil for best results; cook for an additional 1 or 2 minutes to take away the raw taste.

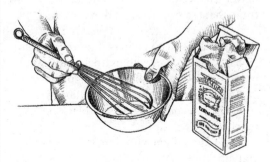

Whisk together equal amounts of cornstarch or arrowroot and cold water in a small mixing bowl. As a general rule, about 1½ to 2 tablespoons starch will thicken 2 cups sauce.

While the sauce is simmering, gradually whisk in the mixture. Gently simmer, continuing to whisk, until the sauce has thickened.

sauce, chefs often add a medley of potatoes, carrots and legumes. In addition, chick-peas and lentils are often added to curry dishes.

☞ Sauté diced onions, minced garlic and minced ginger in a small amount of oil until tender.

☞ Stir in diced tomatoes, curry powder, ground cumin, salt and pepper. Sauté for 2 minutes more.

☞ Stir in diced white potatoes, diced carrots and enough water or defatted chicken broth to cover. Simmer over medium-low heat, stirring occasionally, for 20 to 30 minutes, or until the vegetables are tender.

☞ If using cooked beans or lentils, add them 5 to 10 minutes before the sauce is done.

☞ Near the finish, stir in a few tablespoons chopped fresh herbs, such as parsley or cilantro.

☞ To thicken, mash the potatoes against the side of the pan with the back of a spoon.

Yogurt Sauce

Sauces made with yogurt add a refreshing tang to meals. One common and easy-to-prepare yogurt sauce is called raita. It's a blend of yogurt, cucumbers, herbs and spices. It doesn't require cooking, and it makes a soothing companion to grilled and broiled fish and vegetables, spicy dishes, curries and baked potatoes.

☞ In a medium bowl, combine 2 cups nonfat plain yogurt with 1 chopped cucumber (peeled, if waxed), minced garlic and a few tablespoons chopped fresh herbs, such as mint, parsley, basil or cilantro.

☞ For a slightly spicy variation, add minced ginger, minced chili peppers and ground cumin.

Other sauces mix nonfat plain yogurt with low-fat or nonfat sour cream, reduced-fat or fat-free mayonnaise, chutney, chopped scallions or fresh herbs, hot sauce, horseradish, chili sauce, salsa or ketchup. The blends are nearly limitless.

SALSAS

Once seen only on the chip-and-dip circuit, salsas have steadily grown in popularity—not just as condiments but as sauces, too. In fact, the word *salsa* means "sauce" in Spanish.

While there are many varieties of salsa, most contain three key flavors: cilantro, lime and chili peppers. Cilantro contributes a pungent earthiness; fresh lime weighs in with tartness; and chili peppers provide the spice kicker. Garlic is often added, as are basil, parsley and cumin.

Most salsas are made with tomatoes. Like other tomato-based sauces, the form of tomatoes varies according to taste and season. In midsummer, a salsa prepared with vine-ripened tomatoes is a wonderful thing. In the heart of winter, salsas may be made by blending stewed tomatoes with crushed fresh tomatoes.

To make a basic salsa, dice 2 large tomatoes, 1 small red onion, 1 clove garlic and 1 small jalapeño pepper (wear plastic gloves when handling). Stir in the juice of 1 lime, 2 or 3 tablespoons chopped fresh cilantro and a sprinkling of ground cumin, dried oregano, salt and red pepper. Let the mixture marinate for 1 hour at room temperature. Then refrigerate or serve.

Salsas can also be made by combining chopped fresh fruit, such as pineapple, kiwifruit, peaches, papayas and mangoes. When making a fruit salsa, it is best to use a combination of fruits, such as diced pineapple with kiwifruit or mangoes with papaya, since fruit blends offer a better balance of sweet and tart flavors. Choose fruits that are ripe, fresh and in season.

There's a huge variety of possible salsa combinations. Salsas that you may want to try include:

☞ Roasted vegetables, including sweet peppers, onions, zucchini and eggplant

☞ Cherry tomatoes and scallions

☞ Corn and avocado with black beans, tomatoes and garlic

☞ Cucumbers with pimentos, red onions and dill

☞ Pineapple and kiwifruit with red peppers, onions and ginger

☞ Peaches and pineapple with peppers, mint and shallots

☞ Raspberries with peppers and mint

Jan Birnbaum

Jan first learned about sauces and salsas during his culinary apprenticeship at New Orleans' renowned K-Paul's restaurant. Since then, he has continued to create bold and exciting flavors—as executive chef and owner of Catahoula Restaurant and Saloon in Calistoga, California.

"Ounce for ounce, Beluga caviar is second to salsa for the most excitement you can get in one tablespoon," he explains. "Food doesn't have to be hot, but it has to be exciting in your mouth. It has to make you want to take the next bite."

This recipe is a spicy salsa. If you want it on the milder side, cut back on the amount of peppers, especially the habanero. Serve the salsa with chips or as an accompaniment to grilled fish or meat (this will reduce the total calories from fat).

Very Spicy Tomato Salsa

½ cup lime juice
¼ cup olive oil
1 teaspoon cumin seeds, toasted and ground (see note)
2 cloves garlic, minced
Pinch of salt
Pinch of ground black pepper
6 ripe tomatoes, seeded and diced
1 large red onion, diced
4 poblano peppers, charred, peeled, seeded and diced
2 jalapeño peppers, minced (wear plastic gloves when handling)
1 habanero pepper, minced (wear plastic gloves when handling)
3 tablespoons chopped fresh cilantro

In a large bowl, whisk together the lime juice, oil, cumin, garlic, salt and black pepper. Stir in the tomatoes, onions, poblano peppers, jalapeño peppers, habanero peppers and cilantro. Mix well. Chill.

Makes 6 cups. Per ¼ cup: 35 calories, 2.4 g. fat (62% of calories), 0.5 g. protein, 3.4 g. carbohydrates, 0.8 g. dietary fiber, 0 mg. cholesterol, 9 mg. sodium

NOTE

• To toast cumin seeds, place them in a dry nostick skillet over medium heat. Toast the seeds, shaking the skillet often, for 3 to 5 minutes, or until fragrant. Then grind the seeds with a mortar and pestle or in a spice grinder.

Basic Tomato Sauce

Makes 3 cups. Per ¼ cup: 37 calories, 1.4 g. fat (34% of calories), 1.3 g. protein, 6 g. carbohydrates, 1.4 g. dietary fiber, 0 mg. cholesterol, 161 mg. sodium

Perk up pasta or meat loaf with this simple, delicious red sauce. Or use it in any recipe that calls for prepared sauce. This makes enough for 1½ pounds of pasta.

4	medium tomatoes, cored
1	tablespoons olive oil
3–4	cloves garlic, minced
¼	cup + 2 tablespoons tomato paste
1	cup reduced-sodium tomato puree
1	cup water or reduced-sodium vegetable broth
1	tablespoon chopped fresh basil
1	teaspoon chopped fresh oregano
1	teaspoon chopped fresh thyme
2	tablespoons reduced-sodium soy sauce
⅛	teaspoon ground black pepper

Place the tomatoes in a pot of gently boiling water. Blanch for 30 seconds, or until the skins begin to crack. Remove the tomatoes with a slotted spoon and transfer to a bowl of ice water to stop the cooking process. When cool enough to handle, slip off and discard the tomato skins. In a food processor or blender, blend the tomatoes until smooth. Or pass them through a food mill and discard the seed residue. Set aside.

In a medium saucepan over medium-low heat, warm the oil. Add the garlic. Sauté for 4 minutes, or until lightly browned. Add the tomatoes, tomato paste and tomato puree. Gradually stir in the water or broth. Cook over medium heat for about 45 minutes, stirring occasionally. Add the basil, oregano, thyme and soy sauce. Simmer for 15 to 20 minutes.

Refrigerate any remaining sauce for up to 10 days. Or freeze for up to 6 months.

VARIATIONS

Chunky Tomato Sauce: After peeling the tomatoes, remove the seeds. Coarsely chop the tomatoes and add them directly to the saucepan without pureeing them. Adjust the degree of chunkiness by mashing tomatoes with the back of a spoon.

Quick Marinara Sauce: Add 1 chopped onion along with the garlic. Sauté until soft. Use 1 can (28 ounces) reduced-sodium peeled plum tomatoes in place of the fresh tomatoes. Chop the tomatoes in the can. Add the tomatoes (with juice) to the onions and garlic. Omit the tomato puree and water. Reduce the tomato paste to 2 tablespoons and stir into the tomato mixture. Add the basil, oregano and thyme. Replace the soy sauce with 1 tablespoon red-wine vinegar. Simmer over medium heat for 15 to 20 minutes.

Quick Tomato Sauce: Puree all of the ingredients in a food processor or blender. Pour the sauce into a medium saucepan. Bring to a boil over medium heat. Reduce the heat to medium-low, cover and simmer for 30 minutes. Stir occasionally.

Tomato-Chicken Sauce: Add 2 cups diced cooked chicken along with the herbs.

Tomato-Meat Sauce: Coat a no-stick skillet with no-stick spray and warm over medium heat. Brown ⅓ pound extra-lean ground beef. Drain off all of the visible fat. Add the browned beef to the tomato mixture along with the herbs.

Tomato-Vegetable Sauce: Add 1 chopped onion and 1 cup chopped vegetables to the garlic. Sauté until soft. Use any combination of vegetables, such as peppers, mushrooms, carrots, celery or zucchini.

Pesto

Toss this delicious Italian paste with hot pasta or spread on toasted slices of Italian bread, use as a baked-potato topping or stir it into soups at the last minute.

2¼	cups fresh basil leaves
¼	cup toasted walnuts
¼	cup scallions, cut into 1" pieces
2	tablespoons lemon juice
2	cloves garlic
¼	teaspoon freshly ground black pepper
¾	cup defatted chicken broth or vegetable broth
3	tablespoons grated reduced-fat Parmesan cheese

Place the basil in a food processor or blender. Process until finely chopped. Add the walnuts, scallions, lemon juice, garlic and pepper. Process with on/off pulses until the walnuts are finely chopped.

With the motor running, gradually add the broth and Parmesan, blending until well-mixed.

Makes ⅔ cup. Per 2 tablespoons: 58 calories, 4 g. fat (62% of calories), 4.1 g. protein. 3.2 g. carbohydrates, 0.5 g. dietary fiber, 0 mg. cholesterol, 106 mg. sodium

NOTE
• Pesto can be frozen in airtight containers for up to 3 months.

VARIATION
Mixed Herb Pesto: Replace the 2¼ cups fresh basil leaves with ¾ cup fresh Italian parsley, ¾ cup fresh dill and ¾ cup fresh basil leaves. Or, substitute any available fresh herbs. Just make sure that amounts stay the same.

Creamy Peanut Sauce

Cooked soba noodles make a great match for this sauce. Add shredded cooked chicken or pork for variety. Or use the sauce as a dip for crudités (fresh cut vegetables), as a topping for freshly steamed vegetables or spooned over grilled poultry.

4	tablespoons warm water
4	tablespoons reduced-fat smooth peanut butter
¼	cup nonfat sour cream
3	tablespoons rice vinegar
1	tablespoon reduced-sodium soy sauce
1	tablespoon grated fresh ginger
2	cloves garlic, minced
½	teaspoon sesame oil
¼	cup coarsely chopped cilantro
¼	teaspoon red-pepper flakes (optional)

In a food processor or blender, combine the water and peanut butter. Blend until smooth. Add the sour cream, vinegar, soy sauce, ginger, garlic, sesame oil and cilantro. Blend until the ginger and garlic are finely chopped.

Spoon the sauce into a medium bowl. Stir in the pepper flakes (if using).

Makes ¾ cup. Per 2 tablespoons: 78 calories, 4.4 g. fat (49% of calories), 4 g. protein, 6.3 g. carbohydrates, 0.4 g. dietary fiber, 0 mg. cholesterol, 102 mg. sodium

VARIATION
Spicy Peanut Sauce: Replace the nonfat sour cream with nonfat plain yogurt. Add ⅛ to ¼ teaspoon hot-pepper sauce.

Green Chili Sauce

Serve this tangy chili sauce with almost any Southwestern main dish. Or try it spooned over burgers. Any of these serving suggestions will lower the total percent of calories from fat.

2	tablespoons canola oil
½	onion, chopped
1	large clove garlic, minced
2	tablespoons all-purpose flour
¼	teaspoon ground cumin
¼	teaspoon ground black pepper
1½	cups defatted chicken broth or vegetable broth
2	cans (4 ounces each) chopped mild green chili peppers
¼	teaspoon dried oregano
⅛	teaspoon salt
1–2	teaspoons canned jalapeño peppers, diced (optional); wear plastic gloves when handling

In a heavy medium no-stick skillet over medium heat, warm the oil. Add the onions and garlic. Sauté for 3 minutes, or until soft. Stir in the flour, cumin and black pepper. Cook and stir for 2 minutes.

Whisk in the broth. Cook, whisking, until the mixture is smooth. Add the chili peppers, oregano and salt. Reduce the heat to medium-low and simmer for 10 minutes.

Remove from the heat. Stir in the jalapeño peppers (if using). If the sauce is too thick, whisk in additional broth until the desired consistency is reached.

Makes 2½ cups. Per ¼ cup: 40 calories, 2.8 g. fat (61% of calories), 1.1 g. protein, 2.9 g. carbohydrates, 0.4 g. dietary fiber, 0 mg. cholesterol, 343 mg. sodium

Fresh Tomato Salsa

1	cup seeded and diced tomatoes
⅔	cup diced seedless small cucumbers
2	tablespoons thinly sliced scallions
½	teaspoon minced garlic
½	teaspoon sugar
¼	teaspoon dried oregano, crumbled
¼	teaspoon salt
⅛	teaspoon ground red pepper
2	tablespoons coarsely chopped fresh cilantro

In a medium bowl, combine the tomatoes, cucumbers, scallions, garlic, sugar, oregano, salt, pepper and cilantro. Mix well.

Let stand for 30 minutes before serving. Serve at room temperature.

Makes 2 cups. Per ¼ cup: 10 calories, 0.1 g. fat (10% of calories), 0.4 g. protein, 2.1 g. carbohydrates, 0.4 g. dietary fiber, 0 mg. cholesterol, 70 mg. sodium

VARIATIONS

Black Bean–Tomato Salsa: Follow the directions for Salsa Cruda below. Add 1 cup cooked or canned black beans.

Salsa Cruda: Omit the cucumbers. Replace the scallions with 2 tablespoons diced onions or red onions. Omit the oregano. Replace the ground red pepper with 1 seeded and minced jalapeño or serrano pepper (wear plastic gloves when handling).

Smoky Chipotle Salsa: Replace 3 tablespoons of the cucumbers with 2 seeded and chopped chipotle chili peppers in adobo sauce. Omit the oregano and ground red pepper. Add ½ teaspoon lime juice.

Tropical Black Bean Salsa

2 cups finely chopped fresh pineapple
1 cup peeled and finely chopped kiwifruit
1 cup canned black beans, rinsed and drained
½ cup finely chopped red onions
1 jalapeño pepper, seeded and minced (wear plastic gloves when handling)
2 tablespoons fresh lime juice
½ teaspoon salt
¼ cup minced fresh cilantro

In a medium bowl, combine the pineapple, kiwi, beans, onions, peppers, lime juice, salt and cilantro. Mix well. Cover and refrigerate for at least 1 hour to allow the flavors to blend. Allow the salsa to come to room temperature before serving.

Makes 4 cups. Per ¼ cup: 28 calories, 0.2 g. fat (7% of calories), 1.2 g. protein, 6.5 g. carbohydrates, 1.4 g. dietary fiber, 0 mg. cholesterol, 111 mg. sodium

NOTE
• The fresh pineapple can be replaced with 2 cups canned pineapple chunks (packed in juice).

VARIATIONS
Mango and Black Bean Salsa: Reduce the pineapple to 1 cup. Replace the kiwifruit with 2 cups peeled and chopped fresh mango.
Smoky Tropical Black Bean Salsa: Grill, broil or pan-sear the pineapple until lightly browned before adding to the salsa mixture. Replace the jalapeño pepper with 1 seeded and chopped chipotle pepper in adobo sauce (or add 2 to 3 drops liquid smoke seasoning along with the jalapeño pepper).

Salsa Verde

8 ounces tomatillos (about 5–6 medium), husked
1 jalapeño pepper, seeded and minced (wear plastic gloves when handling)
½ cup chopped onions
5–6 sprigs fresh cilantro, coarsely chopped
¼ cup water
½ teaspoon salt

Preheat the oven to 400°. Coat a no-stick jelly-roll pan with no-stick spray. Place the tomatillos in the pan. Roast, turning every 5 minutes, until the tomatillos are browned and almost cooked through.

Place the tomatillos in a food processor or blender. Add the peppers, onions and cilantro. Process until coarsely pureed.

Pour the puree into a small bowl. Stir in the water, 1 tablespoon at a time, until the sauce achieves the desired consistency. Stir in the salt. Let stand for 30 minutes before serving.

Makes 1½ cups. Per ¼ cup: 18 calories, 0.4 g. fat (19% of calories), 0.6 g. protein, 3.4 g. carbohydrates, 0.3 g. dietary fiber, 0 mg. cholesterol, 190 mg. sodium

White Sauce

1 cup 1% low-fat milk
1 tablespoon cornstarch
¼ teaspoon salt
Ground black pepper

In a small saucepan over medium heat, bring ¾ cup of the milk to a boil. In a small bowl, combine the remaining ¼ cup milk and cornstarch. Stir until the cornstarch is dissolved.

Pour half of the hot milk into the cornstarch mixture to warm it gradually. Pour the cornstarch mixture back into the saucepan. Cook and stir until the sauce returns to a boil and begins to thicken.

Cook over medium-low heat for 2 minutes. Remove from the heat and season with the salt and pepper.

Makes 1 cup. Per ¼ cup: 38 calories, 1.2 g. fat (28% of calories), 2 g. protein, 4.7 g. carbohydrates, 0 g. dietary fiber, 4 mg. cholesterol, 164 mg. sodium

VARIATIONS

Cheddar Cheese Sauce: Add ½ cup finely shredded reduced-fat Cheddar cheese toward the end of cooking time. Stir until the cheese is melted. Remove from the heat and add the salt and pepper.

Deviled Cheese Sauce: Follow the directions for Cheddar Cheese Sauce above. In a small bowl, whisk together 1½ teaspoons dry mustard and 1 tablespoon cold water. Stir the mustard mixture into the completed sauce, 1 teaspoon at a time, until the desired intensity is reached.

Easy Gravy: Replace the milk with defatted chicken or beef broth. Add an additional teaspoon of cornstarch. If desired, add ½ teaspoon minced fresh herbs such as parsley, thyme or rosemary.

Herbed Cheese Sauce: Follow the directions for Cheddar Cheese Sauce above. Stir 2 tablespoons minced fresh herbs, such as parsley, chives, tarragon, dill or a combination, into the completed sauce.

Mushroom Gravy: Follow the directions for Easy Gravy above. In a separate no-stick skillet coated with no-stick spray, sauté 4 ounces sliced mushrooms (about 1⅓ cups) for 2 minutes. Gradually stir in the Easy Gravy and strained or defatted pan juices from cooked beef, chicken or turkey. Bring to a simmer and add 1 teaspoon lemon juice. Add salt and ground black pepper to taste.

Savory White Sauce: Coat the saucepan with no-stick spray and warm over medium heat. Add 2 tablespoons each of finely chopped onions, carrots and celery. Sauté for 2 minutes, or until soft. Add a bay leaf along with the milk. Cook as directed. Remove and discard the bay leaf before using the sauce. For a smoother sauce, pass the vegetables through a food mill.

Wild Mushroom Gravy: Soak ½ ounce dried wild mushrooms in ½ cup hot water for 20 minutes, or until softened. Meanwhile, follow the directions for Mushroom Gravy above. Drain the wild mushrooms, reserving the soaking liquid. Mince the mushrooms and add to the skillet along with the sautéed fresh mushrooms. Cook for 30 seconds. Add the reserved soaking liquid and cook until reduced by half. Finish the sauce as directed above.

Tartar Sauce

QUICK!

1 cup fat-free mayonnaise
1 dill pickle spear, finely chopped
2 tablespoons minced fresh parsley
1 tablespoon lemon juice
2 teaspoons capers, chopped

In a small bowl, combine the mayonnaise, pickles, parsley, lemon juice and capers. Mix well. Cover and refrigerate for 15 minutes to allow the flavors to blend.

Makes 1 cup. Per 2 tablespoons: 26 calories, 0 g. fat (0% of calories), 0.1 g. protein, 6.6 g. carbohydrates, 0 g. dietary fiber, 0 mg. cholesterol, 511 mg. sodium

Creamy Tarragon-and-Dill Sauce

QUICK!

½ cup dry-curd cottage cheese
¼ cup fat-free mayonnaise
¼ cup skim milk
1 tablespoon lemon juice
1 clove garlic, minced
1½ teaspoons chopped fresh tarragon
1½ teaspoons chopped fresh dill

Place the cottage cheese in a food processor or blender and process until smooth, stopping to scrape down the sides of the container as necessary. Add the mayonnaise, milk, lemon juice, garlic, tarragon and dill. Process with on/off turns until well-blended.

Makes 1 cup. Per 2 tablespoons: 17 calories, 0.1 g. fat (3% of calories), 1.9 g. protein, 2.3 g. carbohydrates, 0 g. dietary fiber, 1 mg. cholesterol, 100 mg. sodium

Horseradish Sauce

QUICK!

1 cup nonfat sour cream
2 tablespoons minced fresh parsley
1 tablespoon prepared horseradish
1 tablespoon lemon juice
1 teaspoon Dijon mustard
2–3 drops hot-pepper sauce

In a small bowl, combine the sour cream, parsley, horseradish, lemon juice, mustard and hot-pepper sauce. Mix well. Refrigerate for 15 minutes to allow the flavors to blend.

Makes 1 cup. Per 2 tablespoons: 19 calories, 0.1 g. fat (5% of calories), 2 g. protein, 3.3 g. carbohydrates, 0.1 g. dietary fiber, 0 mg. cholesterol, 48 mg. sodium

Tarragon-Mustard Sauce

QUICK!

¾ cup nonfat plain yogurt
¼ cup fat-free mayonnaise
2 tablespoons chopped fresh chives
1 tablespoon minced fresh tarragon
1 teaspoon Dijon mustard
1 teaspoon brown mustard
½ teaspoon ground black pepper

In a small bowl, combine the yogurt, mayonnaise, chives, tarragon, Dijon mustard, brown mustard and pepper. Mix well. Refrigerate for 15 minutes to allow the flavors to blend.

Makes 1 cup. Per 2 tablespoons: 20 calories, 0.1 g. fat (6% of calories), 1.3 g. protein, 3.3 g. carbohydrates, 0 g. dietary fiber, 0.4 mg. cholesterol, 128 mg. sodium

Rémoulade Sauce

⅓ cup nonfat plain yogurt
⅓ cup fat-free mayonnaise
¼ cup minced sweet red peppers
2 tablespoons white-wine vinegar
4 teaspoons chili sauce
4 teaspoons prepared horseradish
1½ teaspoons chopped fresh parsley
1 teaspoon chopped fresh tarragon
1 teaspoon chopped fresh chervil
1 teaspoon paprika

In a small bowl, combine the yogurt, mayonnaise, peppers, vinegar, chili sauce, horseradish, parsley, tarragon, chervil and paprika. Cover and refrigerate overnight. Serve chilled.

Makes about 1 cup. Per 2 tablespoons: 21 calories, 0.1 g. fat (3% of calories), 0.8 g. protein, 4.5 g. carbohydrates, 0.2 g. dietary fiber, 0.2 mg. cholesterol, 195 mg. sodium

Sweet Red-Pepper Sauce

Serve this simple creamy sauce over fish, chicken, omelets or polenta.

- 1 tablespoon olive oil
- 1 medium onion, chopped
- 4 medium red peppers, diced
- 2 cloves garlic, minced
- 1 bay leaf
- ½ cup defatted chicken broth or water
- 1½ tablespoons minced fresh basil or 1½ teaspoons dried
- 1½ tablespoons minced fresh parsley

In a no-stick skillet over medium heat, warm the oil. Add the onions and peppers. Sauté for 12 minutes. Add the garlic and sauté for 3 minutes. Add the bay leaf and broth or water. Reduce the heat to low, cover and simmer for 20 minutes.

Transfer the mixture to a food processor or blender. Remove and discard the bay leaf. Add the basil and parsley. Process until smooth.

Pour the sauce into a medium saucepan and bring to a boil. Reduce the heat slightly and cook, stirring frequently, for 5 minutes, or until slightly thickened.

Makes about 1½ cups. Per ¼ cup: 83 calories, 2.8 g. fat (27% of calories), 3.1 g. protein, 14.1 g. carbohydrates, 3.1 g. dietary fiber, 0 mg. cholesterol, 29 mg. sodium

VARIATION

Roasted Red-Pepper Sauce: Roast the peppers before adding them to the skillet. Preheat the broiler. Place the whole peppers on a foil-lined baking sheet. Broil 3″ from the heat, turning often, until the skin begins to bubble and blacken. Transfer to a paper bag. Seal and let sweat for 15 minutes. When cool, peel and discard the skin from the peppers. Remove and discard the cores and seeds. Chop the flesh and add to the skillet along with the garlic.

Creamy Curry Sauce

QUICK!

This sauce tastes great on steamed vegetables or baked potatoes.

- 2 cups nonfat plain yogurt
- 1 tablespoon cornstarch
- 1 tablespoon water
- 2 teaspoons curry powder
- ½ teaspoon ground coriander
- 3 teaspoons honey
- 1 teaspoon lemon juice
- ½ teaspoon ground ginger
  Ground black pepper

Place the yogurt in a medium saucepan over medium-low heat. In a cup, dissolve the cornstarch in the water. Stir into the yogurt and mix well.

Stir in the curry powder, coriander, honey, lemon juice, ginger and pepper to taste. Cook and stir over medium heat just until the sauce comes to a boil. Remove from the heat and serve immediately.

Makes about 2 cups. Per ¼ cup: 46 calories, 0.2 g. fat (4% of calories), 3.3 g. protein, 7.8 g. carbohydrates, 0.2 g. dietary fiber, 1 mg. cholesterol, 44 mg. sodium

Basic Barbecue Dry Rub

QUICK!

Rub this mixture into the entire exposed surface of meat, poultry or fish before grilling to create a zesty-flavored crust.

- 2 tablespoons paprika
- 2 tablespoons brown sugar
- 1 tablespoon garlic powder

1 tablespoon chili powder
1 tablespoon ground cumin
1 tablespoon freshly ground black pepper-corns
1 teaspoon ground red pepper
1 teaspoon dry mustard

In a small bowl, combine the paprika, brown sugar, garlic powder, chili powder, cumin, black pepper, red pepper and mustard. Mix well. Store in an airtight container in a cool, dark place.

Makes about ½ cup. Per tablespoon: 31 calories, 0.7 g. fat (18% of calories), 0.9 g. protein, 6.5 g. carbohydrates, 0.6 g. dietary fiber, 0 mg. cholesterol, 14 mg. sodium

QUICK!
Basic Barbecue Baste

Brush or spoon this mixture over meat, poultry or fish while grilling to keep the food moist.

1 cup defatted chicken broth
½ cup white vinegar
2 tablespoons reduced-sodium Worcester-shire sauce
¼ cup minced onions
1 tablespoon Basic Barbecue Dry Rub (opposite page)

In a small saucepan over medium heat, combine the broth, vinegar, Worcestershire sauce, onions and Basic Barbecue Dry Rub. Mix well. Cook for 5 minutes. Remove from the heat.

Makes about 1½ cups. Per tablespoon: 4.4 calories, 0 g. fat (0% of calories), 0.3 g. protein, 0.9 g. carbohydrates, 0.1 g. dietary fiber, 0 mg. cholesterol, 23 mg. sodium

QUICK!
Basic Barbecue Sauce

1 tablespoon butter or margarine
¼ cup minced onions
1 small clove garlic, minced
1 cup tomato sauce
1 tablespoon brown sugar
1 tablespoon soy sauce
1 teaspoon apple cider vinegar
1 teaspoon Worcestershire sauce
½ teaspoon dry mustard
⅛ teaspoon ground black pepper

In a medium no-stick skillet over medium heat, melt the butter or margarine. Add the onions and garlic. Sauté for 4 minutes. Stir in the tomato sauce, brown sugar, soy sauce, vinegar, Worcestershire sauce, mustard and pepper. Cook for 5 minutes, or until heated through. Cool slightly before using.

Makes about 1 cup. Per tablespoon: 16 calories, 0.7 g. fat (38% of calories), 0.3 g. protein, 2.4 g. carbohydrates, 0.3 g. dietary fiber, 2 mg. cholesterol, 168 mg. sodium

NOTE
• This sauce makes enough for 2 boneless, skinless chicken breasts or 16 ounces flank steak. Before cooking, coat the meat with ¾ cup of the sauce, cover and refrigerate for at least 30 minutes. Use the remaining ¼ cup sauce to baste the meat. Or warm the remaining sauce and serve it with the cooked meat.

VARIATIONS
Herbed Barbecue Sauce: Toward the end of cooking time, add 1 tablespoon chopped fresh parsley and 1 teaspoon chopped fresh thyme or rosemary to the sauce.
Spicy Barbecue Sauce: Add 2 to 3 drops hot-pepper sauce, a pinch of ground cloves and a pinch of ground ginger along with the black pepper.

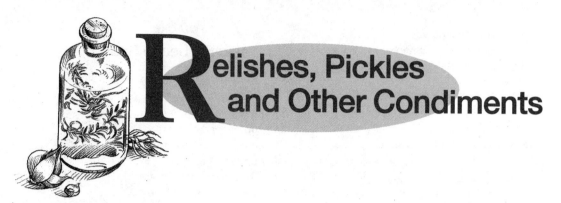

Relishes, Pickles and Other Condiments

The days are past, thank goodness, when "good for you" meant food that was basic, brown and bland. Today's healthy cooks want big flavors, which is why they're stocking up on relishes, pickles, chutneys, vinegars and other highly flavored condiments.

Depending on your tastes, condiments can be spooned over grilled chicken, drizzled on salads, served over rice or swirled into soup. They heighten and brighten the menu with good-for-you flavors and textures. Best of all, they embellish a meal while adding virtually no fat or cholesterol.

PICKLES AND RELISHES

It's hard to imagine a world without relishes and pickles. No more cranberry relish at Thanksgiving. Good-bye to corn relish on the barbecue platter. No more pickles on hamburgers and hot dogs. Why, it would almost be like omitting the bun.

Relishes and pickles provide more than just great tastes. Since they contain mostly fruits or vegetables and vinegar and spices, they're very low in fat and calories. What's more, they provide flavorful alternatives to fat-laden condiments like mayonnaise, sour cream, buttery spreads and salty chips.

There's an enormous variety of relishes and pickles to choose from. When you get bored with one kind, buy another. Better yet, make your own. It's that easy!

Follow your tastes. No matter how much you enjoy hot dog relish and sweet pickles, sooner or later you're going to want to try something new. You can make fantastic condiments from virtually any fruit or vegetable, including beets, tomatoes, corn, peaches, apples, pears and nectarines. Some cooks even add dried fruits like dates and raisins to the jar.

Combine the flavors. Are you tired of Aunt Ethel's delicious but ancient recipe for corn relish? Shake up your taste buds by combining new flavors and ingredients. For example:

☞ **Beet-apple relish.** Combine diced beets, apples, onions, cider vinegar, allspice, cinnamon and sugar.

☞ **Green-tomato relish.** Combine diced green tomatoes, onions, pears or apples, wine vinegar, minced garlic and sugar.

☞ **Peach-apricot relish.** Combine diced peaches, dried apricots, onions, minced ginger, white vinegar, dry mustard and sugar.

☞ **Corn-and-pepper relish.** Combine corn, red and green peppers, diced onions, ground red pepper, white vinegar and sugar.

Homemade Tastes

Pickling—whether it involves whole cucumbers or finely chopped vegetables—is one of the oldest methods for preserving food. In the days before refrigeration, it enabled cooks to enjoy summer's bounty all year long. The combination of sugar, salt and vinegar virtually guarantees that bacteria can't survive. When properly

SAFETY FIRST

Although pickles and relishes can be stored in the refrigerator without special handling, long-term storage requires that the jars be sterilized and sealed to prevent spoilage. Cooks who do a lot of canning may choose to invest in a special water-bath canner. It's less expensive but equally safe to use equipment that you already have.

Fill canning jars three-quarters full with water and place them in a pot partly filled with water. Place the lids loosely on top of the jars and simmer on the stove top for 15 to 20 minutes. Keep the jars hot and filled with water right up to the time when you're ready to fill them.

Empty the water and dry the jars. Immediately ladle the relish or pickles into the jars (a wide-mouth canning funnel makes this easy and neat). Leave ½" to 1" headspace at the top of each jar to allow for expansion. Wipe the rims clean of any spills, then screw the lids all the way down.

Completely submerge the jars in a pot of water and simmer for about 10 minutes. Use canning tongs to remove the jars from the water. Place on kitchen towels to drain and cool. Listen for popping or sucking sounds as the jars cool, which means that the seals are taking hold.

To test the seal, press down on the center of each lid. If it presses down and then pops up, the seal didn't hold and should be redone. If the lid won't push down, the jar is properly sealed.

canned, pickled foods last indefinitely if stored unopened in a cool, dark place.

There are two common techniques for making pickles. Pickles that you buy at the deli are often brined—steeped and fermented in a saltwater solution (brine) for several weeks. For home cooks, the preferred method for preparing relishes and pickles is simply to cover the vegetables with a simmering broth of vinegar, spices, salt, sugar and assorted garnish vegetables and let stand for 5 to 10 minutes. You then transfer the mixture to canning jars or refrigerate it for immediate use.

Buy them bright. When making relishes and pickles, it's important to start with the brightest, crispest items that you can find. Bruised, wilted or overripe vegetables and fruits deteriorate during the cooking, or curing, process. Further, the texture of a condiment is almost as important as the flavor, so a firm pickle with a loud snap is much more desirable than a limp, tepid specimen.

MAKING RELISH

Even if you eat relish only when there's a hot dog to go with it, you'll appreciate the fresh flavors of homemade.

Slice or coarsely chop the vegetables or fruits. With the exception of beets and mangoes, you don't have to peel them first.

Mince strongly flavored aromatic ingredients, like garlic, ginger or chili peppers.

Combine the ingredients, along with spices, vinegar and sugar, in a heavy nonreactive saucepan. Make sure that the liquid barely covers the ingredients. Bring the mixture to a gentle simmer. Cook over medium-low heat, uncovered, until the ingredients are tender.

Let cool slightly, then ladle the relish into jars for storage.

When making pickles, use pickling cucumbers rather than the slicing kind that you use on salads. Pickling cukes are small and wide with a firm texture, stubbly skin and a slightly bitter taste. Slicing cucumbers aren't as firm and crisp, so they become quite limp.

Use the right gear. The high acid content of relishes and pickles may react with aluminum, copper or cast-iron cookware, causing unsightly colors or an unpleasantly off flavor. It's best to use pots and other utensils made from stainless steel, enamelware or food-grade plastic.

Use simple vinegar. Although you can use apple cider vinegar or red-wine vinegar for making relishes and pickles, they tend to darken the ingredients. They can also be somewhat expensive. If you want to preserve the original colors of light-colored ingredients and keep your costs down, distilled white vinegar is your best bet.

Try a spice combo. Many pickle and relish recipes call for a dozen or more spices. Rather than loading your pantry with ingredients that you'll rarely use, you may want to buy a commercial blend. These typically include such spices as whole cloves, allspice berries, celery seeds, mustard seeds, bay leaves, coriander seeds, black peppercorns, dill seeds, mace, dried chilies and cinnamon sticks.

Choose your texture. Cooks who desire a rustic pickle usually sprinkle spices directly into the pan. Those who favor a clearer broth wrap the flavorings in cheesecloth before adding them to the pot. Both methods work well and are a matter of personal choice.

Choose your sweetener. Most pickles and relishes are made with granulated sugar, although honey can be used instead. You can replace 1 cup sugar with ¾ cup honey. Replacing white sugar with an equal amount of brown sugar creates a darker hue.

Keep the crispness. To help vegetables maintain maximum crispness, some recipes call for adding ⅛ teaspoon alum per quart of liquid. If your ingredients are fresh, however, and you don't overcook them, added alum really isn't necessary.

Preserve them well. If you're planning to eat the relishes or pickles within a few weeks, you can store them in the refrigerator. Otherwise, it's important to pack them well to prevent spoilage.

An unopened jar of pickles that has been properly sterilized and sealed will last for at least a year when it's stored in a cool, dark place. Once the jar has been opened, however, it should be refrigerated and used within several weeks.

CHUTNEY

A sweet-and-tart blending of fruit, onion, vinegar and spices, chutney is a vibrant Indian condiment (*chutna* means "relish") that jazzes up almost any food.

Chutney differs from relish in that the flavors are more complex. Spicy seasonings like fresh ginger, garlic and chili peppers add sharp nuances, while aromatic spices like cloves, cinnamon, coriander and cumin add their own pronounced flavors. Also, while the spices in relishes and pickles are often used whole, they're usually ground finely for chutneys, which causes them to penetrate more deeply.

Fear no fruits. While relishes and pickles draw mainly from the vegetable kingdom, chutneys are made from fresh fruits, like mangoes, apples, peaches, rhubarb or tomatoes. The sweetness of the fruit provides a pleasing counterpart to the spicy or sour sensations.

When buying fruits, make sure that they're ripe but firm. Fruits that are past their peak will be soft and won't hold up well during cooking.

Bring out the vinegars. Since chutneys are naturally darker than pickles, it's perfectly acceptable to use darker vinegars, like red-wine or cider vinegar.

Cook them well. Chutneys require a fairly long cooking time to allow the flavors to mingle.

After chopping the ingredients and adding the vinegar and spices, let the mixture simmer for 30 to 60 minutes over low heat, stirring occasionally. It's done when it begins to thicken and resemble jam.

Experiment. Since chutney is so easy to make, the flavors are limited only by your imagination. Here are some classic combinations for you to try.

☞ **Cranberry chutney.** Combine cranberries, apples or pears, onions, raisins, orange rind, ginger, garlic, cumin, cloves, black pepper, wine vinegar and sugar.

☞ **Mango chutney.** Combine mango, apples, onions, raisins, ginger, garlic, chili peppers, cloves, black pepper, wine vinegar and sugar.

☞ **Peach-apricot chutney.** Combine peaches, apples, dried apricots, onions, nutmeg, ginger, dry mustard, black pepper, wine vinegar and sugar.

☞ **Pineapple chutney.** Combine diced fresh pineapple, apples, onions, ginger, chili peppers, garlic, curry powder, turmeric, cumin, black pepper, wine vinegar and sugar.

☞ **Rhubarb-plum chutney.** Combine rhubarb, plums, onions, ginger, cloves, black pepper, wine vinegar and sugar.

☞ **Tomato-fruit chutney.** Combine tomatoes, apples, pears, onions, cider vinegar, garlic, chili peppers, cinnamon, cumin, black pepper and sugar.

VINEGAR

A centerpiece of the healthy pantry, vinegar brings a sharp, clean flavor to vinaigrettes, marinades, salads and soups. It also acts as a preservative in pickles, relishes and chutneys.

There is a growing array of vinegars on the market, from basic red wine and apple cider to premium balsamic. You can even buy trendy and expensive vinegars made from wine grapes like Cabernet and Chardonnay. Here are some of the best.

☞ **Balsamic vinegar.** A smooth, well-aged vinegar imported from Italy, it has a deep, reddish-brown hue and a mellow flavor. Balsamic vinegar lends a sophisticated touch to dressings, marinades and sauces.

☞ **Champagne vinegar.** A smooth, mildly flavored vinegar with a hint of champagne flavor, it's often used in vinaigrettes or is lightly drizzled on salads.

☞ **Chili pepper vinegar.** This adds a piquant jolt to any recipe. You can buy it ready-made, or you can create your own by dropping two or three hot red chili peppers of different varieties into vinegar and steeping them for two to three weeks.

☞ **Cider vinegar.** This fruity, mildly tart vinegar has a caramel color and an undercurrent flavor of apples. A versatile vinegar, it's often added to salad dressings, relishes, chutneys and marinades.

☞ **Distilled vinegar.** Also called white vinegar, this strong, clear liquid is made from grains such as barley, rye and corn. It's the favored vinegar for pickling.

☞ **Fruit vinegars.** Often made with raspberries, blackberries and blueberries, these make excellent salad vinegars.

☞ **Herb vinegars.** Made by infusing vinegar with herbs like tarragon, basil, oregano, garlic and mint, these can be used on salads, rice or steamed vegetables.

☞ **Malt vinegar.** An English vinegar often made from potatoes, it has a yeasty, heavy flavor. Malt vinegar is often used as a table condiment for fish and chips. Cider vinegar is a close substitute.

☞ **Red-wine vinegar.** The workhorse of the healthy kitchen, this mellow-tart vinegar is a favorite for chutneys, marinades, salads and vinaigrettes as well as for adding a splash of zest to soups and sauces.

☞ **Rice vinegar.** Made from Japanese rice wine (sake), this clear vinegar has a smooth, mild, almost sweet flavor. It is a popular flavoring in Asian salads, soups, sauces and lightly flavored dressings.

☞ **White-wine vinegar.** Not to be confused with white distilled vinegar, white-wine vinegar is mildly flavored and similar in character to champagne vinegar. Use in salad dressings and bland soups.

While specialty stores and supermarkets stock a wide variety of flavored vinegars, it's easy to make your own at home.

☞ Combine a plain vinegar with your favorite seasonings, like raspberries, tarragon or garlic, and briefly simmer in a saucepan.

☞ Pour the mixture into sterile jars, cover and allow to steep for two to four weeks, or until the mixture tastes right to you.

☞ Strain the infused liquid and pour into bottles for storage.

Vinegar is a good keeper, but once the bottle is opened, it won't last forever. Herb vinegars usually keep for several months when stored in a cool, dark place. Fruit vinegars spoil more quickly, however, and should be kept in the refrigerator.

Once you discover the flavors of various vinegars, you'll find yourself using them more and more generously—not just as a condiment but also to replace some of the fat that you depended on for flavor. When sautéing chicken, seafood or vegetables, for example, reduce the oil by half and replace it with an equal amount of rice or wine vinegar.

☞ Drizzle balsamic or wine vinegar over a salad of fresh tomatoes, chopped basil and garlic.

Helpful Hint

To enjoy the rich taste of balsamic vinegar without the high cost, mix it half-and-half with red-wine vinegar.

☞ Swirl a touch of wine or rice vinegar into low-sodium chowders or bisques as a last-minute flavor enhancer.

☞ Drizzle a few drops of vinegar over a side dish of braised spinach, escarole, kale or broccoli rabe.

☞ Add a hint of balsamic vinegar to roasted new potatoes.

☞ Zip up the flavor of prepared salad dressings by mixing in raspberry or other flavored vinegars.

FIERY LIQUIDS

Once used only in ethnic and regional cuisines, bottled hot sauces have become nearly as common on tables as salt and pepper shakers. These piquant liquids add intensive flavors to food without contributing fat or cholesterol. And although some of them do contain salt, their big flavors lessen the need for additional salt in many recipes.

Tabasco sauce from Louisiana is the most renowned of the peppery libations, but it's hardly the only one. Virtually every region in the country has its own favorites. You'll find hot sauces made from fiery habaneros, Scotch bonnet peppers, green jalapeño peppers and many more. Let your taste buds be your guide—but don't overdo it. A few drops is usually all that you need.

CITRUS JUICES

You don't have to look far to find a healthful, inexpensive ingredient that adds zip to any meal. A squeeze of lemon, lime or orange juice enlivens most anything, from soups, salads and marinades to grains, legumes and vegetable side dishes.

While cooking with citrus juices has only recently come into vogue in this country, it has long been a favored flavoring tool in other parts of the world. In Southeast Asia, for example,

Helpful Hint

When making muffins, cakes or other baked goods, try replacing half of the oil with an equal amount of orange juice.

lime juice and lime leaves are often used to enhance soups, sauces and salads. Many Mexican and Latin American dishes—like fajitas, salsa and guacamole—call for a squeeze of lime. And in Middle Eastern and Greek cooking, lemon juice is used to flavor everything from lentil stews and bean soups to hummus and grain salads.

☞ Fresh-squeezed juice is best, but bottled or chilled juice also works well.

☞ One lemon or lime can flavor about 4 cups of a grain or bean salad.

☞ When making a vinaigrette, start by adding one part citrus juice to two parts oil. You can gradually alter the mix in favor of the juice until you find the taste that's right for you.

☞ A squeeze of fresh lemon is a delicious addition to braised kale, spinach or other greens. One lemon can season about 1 pound leafy greens.

☞ Grilled vegetables are delicious when tossed with lemon juice, chopped garlic, a touch of oil and fresh herbs.

☞ Sauté strips of boneless, skinless chicken breasts in a lemon–olive oil mixture. Plan to use at least one lemon for every 8 ounces of chicken breast.

☞ Baste swordfish or tuna steaks on the grill with fresh lime juice. Plan to use at least one lime for every 8 ounces of fish.

THE INTERNATIONAL PANTRY

If your experience with flavored condiments hasn't gone beyond relish, there's a whole world of flavors waiting for you. Virtually every country and culture has its own special ingredients and combinations. Some of these you'll find in ethnic markets. Others you may discover accidentally when going out to eat. Don't hesitate to try them. They add exhilarating flavors to the menu, and they may change your mind about needing salt and butter.

☞ **Chow-chow.** A staple of Pennsylvania Dutch kitchens, this is a sour, vinegary combination of cabbage, corn and other vegetables.

☞ **Ketjap manis.** This is a sweetened version of soy sauce that's often used in Indonesian and Far Eastern cuisine. The syrupy brown liquid can be poured over rice, stir-fries, soups and salads. Interestingly enough, the American word *ketchup* is thought to be derived from *ketjap manis*.

☞ **Miso.** A thick paste made from fermented soybeans, salt and grains, miso imparts a mild soy-like flavor to Japanese soups and sauces.

☞ **Pickapeppa sauce.** This dark spicy-sweet sauce comes from Jamaica. With a syrupy texture and Worcestershire-like taste, it can be poured over rice or potatoes, brushed on roasted chicken or used as a sandwich spread.

☞ **Sambal.** A sweet-and-spicy chili paste, it can be served with everything from stir-fries and barbecued chicken to rice casseroles.

☞ **Tamari.** A rich Japanese soy sauce, it's slightly more concentrated than the Chinese kind.

☞ **Wine mustard.** A smooth paste with an occasional sharp bite, this mustard is prepared from pungent mustard seeds, vinegar or wine and spices. Dijon mustard—named for the Dijon region in France—is the best known.

Cindy Pawlcyn

Despite being busy with six restaurants in the San Francisco area—including Mustards Grill, Fog City Diner and Buckeye Road-house—Cindy Pawlcyn continues to develop trademark side dishes and condiments to enhance her upbeat cuisine. One of her favorites is this mango chutney.

"I like this over grilled poultry or any meat, because it is so simple and adds no fat—just a wallop of flavor," she says.

If you can't get mango, ex-periment with different fruits or fruit combinations, she ad-vises. The combination of sweet mango, spicy jalapeño pepper and aromatic ginger gives this a very special flavor. If you like less heat in your foods, decrease the amount of jalapeño pepper.

Pickled Mango-Ginger Chutney

- 1 cup water
- 1 cup rice-wine vinegar
- 1 cup sugar
- 6 ounces fresh ginger, thinly sliced
- ½ jalapeño pepper, finely cut into strips (wear plastic gloves when handling)
- 2 tablespoons red-pepper flakes
- 2 shallots, very thinly sliced
- 3 ripe mangoes

In a medium saucepan, combine the water, vinegar, sugar, ginger, jalapeño peppers, red-pepper flakes and shallots. Bring to a full boil over medium-high heat. Remove from the heat and allow to cool.

Peel the mangoes and slice the flesh off the pits. Thinly slice the flesh and place in a large bowl. Pour the ginger mixture over the mangoes. Mix well. Store in the refrigerator.

Makes about 5 cups. Per ¼ cup: 57 calories, 0.2 g. fat (3% of calories), 0.3 g. protein, 14.7 g. carbohydrates, 0.7 g. dietary fiber, 0 mg. cholesterol, 3 mg. sodium

Quick!
Cranberry-Apple Chutney

2 cups whole fresh cranberries, rinsed and drained
1 Granny Smith apple, unpeeled, cored and chopped
1 cup finely chopped red onions
1 cup brown sugar
½ cup dried cranberries
2 tablespoons strong coffee
2 tablespoons red-wine vinegar
  Grated rind of 1 lemon
½ teaspoon red-pepper flakes
3 tablespoons cranberry juice concentrate (see note)
2 tablespoons chopped fresh mint

In a large stainless steel saucepan, combine the fresh cranberries, apples, onions, brown sugar, dried cranberries, coffee, vinegar, lemon rind and red-pepper flakes. Bring to a simmer over medium heat. Reduce the heat to medium-low and simmer gently for 15 to 20 minutes, or until almost all of the liquid has evaporated.

Remove from the heat and stir in the juice concentrate and mint.

Pour the chutney into hot, scalded preserving jars, leaving ⅛″ headspace. Wipe the rims clean, attach the lids and tightly screw on the caps. Invert the jars for 10 seconds.

Cool on a wire rack. Store in the refrigerator.

Makes 3 cups. Per tablespoon: 26 calories, 0.03 g. fat (1% of calories), 0.1 g. protein, 6.9 g. carbohydrates, 0.4 g. dietary fiber, 0 mg. cholesterol, 2 mg. sodium

NOTE

• Cranberry juice concentrate is sold in aseptic packages in most supermarkets. It is different from frozen cranberry juice concentrate. Look for it on supermarket shelves rather than in the freezer case.

VARIATION

Cherry-Apple Chutney: Replace the fresh cranberries with pitted tart cherries. Replace the dried cranberries with dried cherries. Add 3 tablespoons frozen apple juice concentrate.

Mango Chutney

2 cups chopped fresh mangoes
1 cup finely chopped red onions
1 cup brown sugar
⅓ cup currants
1 small jalapeño pepper, seeded and minced (wear plastic gloves when handling)
  Grated rind of 1 lime
  Juice of 2 limes
2 tablespoons minced fresh ginger
1 cinnamon stick

In a large stainless steel saucepan, combine the mangoes, onions, brown sugar, currants, peppers, lime rind, lime juice, ginger and cinnamon. Bring to a simmer over medium heat. Reduce the heat to medium-low and simmer gently for 30 to 40 minutes, or until almost all of the liquid has evaporated.

Remove and discard the cinnamon stick.

Pour the chutney into hot, scalded preserving jars, leaving ⅛″ headspace. Wipe the rims clean, attach the lids and tightly screw on the caps. Invert the jars for 10 seconds.

Cool on a wire rack. Store in the refrigerator.

Makes 2 cups. Per tablespoon: 42 calories, 0.1 g. fat (1% of calories), 0.2 g. protein, 10.9 g. carbohydrates, 0.6 g. dietary fiber, 0 mg. cholesterol, 5 mg. sodium

Sweet-and-Sour Refrigerator Pickles

- 2 pounds cucumbers (8 to 10 small), peeled and sliced crosswise
- Kosher salt
- 1½ cups white-wine vinegar or apple cider vinegar
- 1 cup sugar

Place the cucumbers in a nonreactive bowl. Sprinkle lightly with the salt and toss to coat. Cover and refrigerate for 24 hours.

Rinse the cucumbers and set in a colander to drain for 15 minutes.

Meanwhile, in a large stainless steel saucepan, combine the vinegar and sugar. Cook and stir over medium-low heat until the sugar dissolves.

Pack the cucumbers into hot, scalded preserving jars, leaving ⅛″ headspace. Pour in the hot vinegar mixture to cover. Wipe the rims clean, attach the lids and tightly screw on the caps.

Cool on a wire rack. Refrigerate the pickles for 2 weeks before opening. Store in the refrigerator.

Makes about 8 cups. Per 2 tablespoons: 14 calories, 0 g. fat (0% of calories), 0.1 g. protein, 3.8 g. carbohydrates, 0 g. dietary fiber, 0 mg. cholesterol, 0.4 mg. sodium

VARIATIONS

Herb-Scented Refrigerator Pickles: While packing the vegetables into the jars, sprinkle them with crumbled bay leaves, fresh parsley sprigs, fresh dill sprigs, halved cloves of garlic and whole mustard seeds.

Mixed Vegetable Pickles: Replace the cucumbers with a mixture of 1½ cups carrots (peeled and cut diagonally into 1″ lengths), 1½ cups red pepper pieces, 1 cup cauliflower florets, 1 cup broccoli florets and 1 cup zucchini slices.

Herb Vinegar

- 4 sprigs fresh tarragon, thyme, rosemary, savory, basil, oregano, marjoram or dill
- 1 cup apple cider vinegar
- 1 cup distilled white vinegar

Rinse and pat dry the herbs. Place in a scalded jar big enough to hold 2 cups liquid.

In a small stainless steel saucepan over medium heat, warm the apple cider vinegar and white vinegar until hot. Using a canning funnel, pour the vinegar into the jar. Cool slightly. Wipe the rim clean and tightly screw on the cap.

Let stand for at least 2 weeks before using. Store in a cool, dark place.

Makes 2 cups. Per tablespoon: 1 calorie, 0 g. fat (0% of calories), 0 g. protein, 0.9 g. carbohydrates, 0 g. dietary fiber, 0 mg. cholesterol, 0.2 mg. sodium

NOTES

• If you prefer not to have them in the jar, strain the liquid after 2 weeks, discarding the herbs. Return the strained liquid to the jar.

• Use this vinegar and all its variations to perk up steamed vegetables or pasta dishes.

VARIATIONS

Berry Vinegar: Omit the herbs. Omit the white vinegar; instead, use 2 cups cider vinegar. To the saucepan of warm vinegar, add ½ cup raspberries, strawberries or blueberries, 1 tablespoon sugar, 1 slice orange or lemon and a sprig of mint. Crush the berries with the back of a spoon. Remove from the heat to cool. Cover and let steep in a cool place for 2 to 3 days. Place the pan over medium heat and bring to simmer. Remove from the heat and strain the liquid into the jar. Discard the solids.

Garlic-Herb Vinegar: Add 2 peeled and halved cloves garlic to the jar. After 2 weeks, use a skewer to remove and discard the garlic.

Hot-Pepper Vinegar: Replace the herbs with 2 small chili peppers, halved (wear plastic gloves when handling).

Fresh Cranberry Relish

- 2 cups fresh cranberries
- 1 Granny Smith apple, chopped
- 1 navel orange, unpeeled and chopped
- ½ cup sugar

In a food processor, combine the cranberries, apples, oranges and sugar. Process with on/off turns just until chunky.

Transfer to a bowl, cover and refrigerate for at least 2 hours before serving.

Makes 4 cups. Per 2 tablespoons: 10 calories, 0 g. fat (0% of calories), 0 g. protein, 2.8 g. carbohydrates, 0.2 g. dietary fiber, 0 mg. cholesterol, 0.1 mg. sodium

Zesty Pepper-Onion Relish

- 6 medium sweet red peppers, stems and seeds removed
- 1 cup chopped onions
- 1 cup white vinegar
- 1½ cups sugar
- 1 teaspoon salt
- ½ lemon, sliced
- 2 teaspoons whole allspice
- 1 slice fresh ginger (¼" thick) or ¼ teaspoon ground

Place the peppers in a large bowl. Cover with boiling water and let stand for 5 minutes; drain. Repeat and drain well.

Transfer the peppers to a food processor. Coarsely chop using on/off turns.

In a large stainless steel saucepan, combine the onions, vinegar, sugar, salt and chopped peppers. In a cheesecloth, tie the lemon slices, allspice and ginger. Add to the pan. Bring the mixture to a boil over medium heat. Simmer for 30 minutes, stirring occasionally. Remove from the heat, cover and let stand overnight.

The next day, bring the mixture to a boil and simmer for 10 minutes.

Pour the relish into hot, scalded preserving jars, leaving ⅛" headspace. Wipe the rims clean, attach the lids and tightly screw on the caps. Invert the jars for 10 seconds.

Cool on a wire rack. Store in the refrigerator.

Makes 3 cups. Per 2 tablespoons: 71 calories, 0.2 g. fat (2% of calories), 1 g. protein, 18 g. carbohydrates, 1.2 g. dietary fiber, 0 mg. cholesterol, 89 mg. sodium

Sweet-and-Spicy Ketchup

- 1 tablespoon canola oil
- 1 large onion, chopped
- 1 can (16 ounces) plum tomatoes
- ½ cup apple cider vinegar
- ½ cup frozen white grape juice concentrate
- 3 tablespoons tomato paste
- 1 teaspoon chili powder
- 1 tablespoon chopped fresh parsley
  Salt and ground black pepper

In a large no-stick skillet over medium heat, warm the oil. Add the onions and sauté for 4 minutes, or until soft.

Add the tomatoes and vinegar. Bring to a boil. Stir in the frozen juice concentrate. Reduce the heat to low and simmer, stirring occasionally, for 30 minutes.

Stir in the tomato paste, chili powder and parsley. Simmer until heated through.

Transfer the mixture to a food processor or blender. Process until smooth. Season with the salt and pepper.

Makes about 3 cups. Per tablespoon: 12 calories, 0.3 g. fat (23% of calories), 0.2 g. protein, 2.4 g. carbohydrates, 0 mg. cholesterol, 24 mg. sodium

Yellow Mustard

QUICK!

½ cup dry mustard powder
⅓ cup cold water
¾ cup all-purpose flour
⅓ cup white-wine vinegar
2 tablespoons honey
1½ teaspoons salt
¾ teaspoon coarsely ground black pepper

In a medium bowl, whisk together the mustard and water. Let soak for 10 minutes.

Add the flour, vinegar, honey, salt and pepper. Stir until smooth.

Let stand for 15 minutes. Refrigerate in a glass jar or airtight container for up to 6 months.

Makes 1 cup. Per tablespoon: 46 calories, 1.2 g. fat (23% of calories), 1.5 g. protein, 7.3 g. carbohydrates, 1.6 g. dietary fiber, 0 mg. cholesterol, 200 mg. sodium

Spicy Grainy Mustard

⅓ cup yellow mustard seeds
1 tablespoon brown mustard seeds
¼ cup dry mustard powder
½ cup cold water
1 cup apple cider vinegar
2 tablespoons brown sugar
1 small clove garlic, pressed or finely minced
¼ teaspoon ground cinnamon
¼ teaspoon ground allspice
¼ teaspoon dill seed
¼ teaspoon dried tarragon, crumbled
⅛ teaspoon ground cloves

In a medium bowl, stir together the yellow mustard seeds, brown mustard seeds, mustard powder and water. Let soak for 3 hours.

In a small stainless steel pan, combine the vinegar, brown sugar, garlic, cinnamon, allspice, dill seed, tarragon and cloves. Bring to a boil over medium heat. Simmer for 10 to 15 minutes or until the mixture is reduced by half. Pour through a strainer onto the mustard mixture.

Transfer the mixture to the top of a double boiler. Cook for 10 minutes, or until thickened. Remove from the heat and allow to cool.

Pour the cooled mixture into a glass jar or airtight container. Refrigerate for 3 days before serving.

Makes about ¾ cup. Per tablespoon: 41 calories, 2.1 g. fat (46% of calories), 1.8 g. protein, 5.6 g. carbohydrates, 1 g. dietary fiber, 0 mg. cholesterol, 18 mg. sodium

Corn Relish

QUICK!

1½ cups fresh or frozen corn
1 tablespoon water
⅛ teaspoon salt
1 small sweet red pepper, chopped
¼ cup thinly sliced scallions
1 jalapeño pepper, seeded and minced (wear plastic gloves when handling)
1 teaspoon extra-virgin olive oil
1 teaspoon lime juice
¼ teaspoon ground black pepper

In a small saucepan, combine the corn, water and salt. Cook over low heat for 2 to 4 minutes, or until the corn is heated through and tender. Remove from the heat and drain.

Stir in the red peppers, scallions, jalapeño peppers, oil, lime juice and black pepper. Let sit for at least 15 minutes before serving.

Makes about 2 cups. Per 2 tablespoons: 18 calories, 0.3 g. fat (14% of calories), 0.6 g. protein, 3.8 g. carbohydrates, 0.5 g. dietary fiber, 0 mg. cholesterol, 22 mg. sodium

Celebrate!

HORS D'OEUVRES, DIPS AND SNACKS, PAGE 528

HOLIDAY DINNERS, PAGE 554

Hors d'Oeuvres, Dips and Snacks

Holidays, family get-togethers and spontaneous celebrations with friends create some of our most vivid memories. At the heart of any good party is food. Food brings people together and turns ordinary gatherings into special occasions.

Party menus of the past usually featured deep-fried appetizers and the fattiest desserts imaginable. Today's party fare leans more toward the light and festive, with an abundance of fresh fruits, vegetables, whole-grain breads and slimmed yet satisfying desserts.

Of course, having a successful party is a bit more complicated than just throwing together a few snacks. You have to plan a menu. You need to estimate how much people will eat and drink. You have to prepare the food, arrange it so that it looks pretty and place it so that it's easy to reach. And in the midst of all this, you have to play host and make sure that everyone has a good time. A lot to think about, for sure.

Having a party, whether the guest list includes 5 people or 50, needn't be a huge chore. With a little creativity, you and your guests will enjoy yourselves immensely.

LAYING THE FOUNDATION

Careful planning is the key to successful parties, caterers say. Obviously, you can't anticipate every possible problem, but there are ways to bring your party into focus right from the start. Here's what experts advise.

Start with a list. When you're busy making arrangements, it's extremely easy to overlook small but essential details, like getting those extra chairs or buying scallions for the dip. To prevent this, caterers always prepare a master to-do list. Your own list might include reminders such as "mow the lawn," "pick up ice" or "borrow an extra platter." By checking off each item as soon as it's completed, you'll know at any given moment how far you've come and how much remains to be done.

Create extra space. Even a small party can use up a lot of refrigerator and freezer space. To make room for such things as ice cubes, cold drinks or crudité platters, it's a good idea to clean out your refrigerator and freezer ahead of time.

Get help. We're often reluctant to impose on friends, but once a party reaches a certain size—say, more than ten guests—it's really too much for one person to handle alone. Don't hesitate to ask friends or family members to pitch in. Or check with your neighbors to see if their teenagers would like to earn a little money. Dividing the work among several people makes it easier for everyone—and will help ensure that you have as good a time as your guests.

PLANNING MENUS

The big question is usually, "What should I make?" To help you decide, here are some points to consider.

Think in season. The key to freshness and

To give your party a special "something's cooking" aroma, sprinkle a little cinnamon and sugar in a skillet and cook slowly over medium-low heat. Continue cooking until fragrant, usually about 5 minutes.

quality as well as low price is to always plan your menu around foods that are currently in season.

☞ In spring, rely on fresh vegetables for dishes like new-potato salad with chives or fresh steamed asparagus with low-fat mustard dipping sauce.

☞ In summer, try cool seafoods, like shrimp cocktail, or a refreshing fruit platter.

☞ For fall and winter, choose hearty dishes, like creamy squash soup or stuffed potatoes.

Balance the flavors. Even exotic foods quickly lose excitement when that's all there is on the table. That's why chefs like to combine foods with complementary flavors—a chilled soup, for example, balances bold-flavored kebabs.

Consider convenience. More is involved in planning a menu than just what tastes good. You'll also have to ask yourself where and how people will be eating. At a sit-down dinner, for example, light dipping sauces work well. But for a cocktail party in which people are milling around, you're going to want food that's easier to eat—solid food like stuffed mushrooms, small spring rolls and mini-pizzas.

Keep it simple. Unless you're inviting fewer than ten people (or you're already an expert caterer), you aren't going to have time to put together a fancy presentation. For larger gatherings, chefs say, the simplest menu is the best. Finger foods are always a good choice: whole pizzas cut into bite-size pieces, for example, or platters of crisp raw vegetables.

Take a culinary tour. An easy and exciting way to plan a menu is to group it around an ethnic theme. Ethnic theme parties can be as simple as serving related foods, such as tortillas and beans. Or they can be as elaborate as to include the appropriate music and decorations. Menus that you may want to try include:

☞ **Asian.** Wonton soup, California sushi, steamed dumplings, cold sesame noodles and almond cookies

☞ **Southwestern.** Gazpacho soup, quesadil-las with low-fat cheese, burritos, Spanish rice, refried beans and sautéed bananas

☞ **Middle Eastern.** Pita triangles and hummus, tabbouleh, stuffed grape leaves, baba ghanoush (roasted eggplant) and cucumbers with yogurt and dill

WORKING AHEAD

By the time guests arrive, the tables should be set and the food ready to serve—or at least ready for last-minute preparations. To get organized and make the most of your time:

Prepare foods early. Even when the menu calls for foods to be cooked just before the party, there are usually many ingredients that you can prepare ahead of time and store in the refrigerator until they're needed. For example:

☞ Salad greens, washed and dried

☞ Cut-up raw vegetables (Carrots, celery and radishes should be stored in a bowl of cold water in the refrigerator.)

☞ Blanched or steamed vegetables

☞ Peeled garlic cloves

☞ Cubed or shredded cheese

☞ Bunches of fresh herbs (Trim the stems about ¼" from the end, then wrap the stems in dampened paper towels and seal in a plastic bag.)

When preparing vegetables ahead of time, be sure to store assertive items like onions and garlic separately to prevent their flavors from mingling with milder foods.

Buy them precut. Perhaps the ultimate time-saver is to buy salad mixes and precut,

ESTIMATING AMOUNTS

The worst thing that can happen to a party is running out of food early. Almost as bad is eating leftovers for two weeks because you made too much. These guidelines from caterers will help you prepare just the right amount. The amounts are calculated for a buffet party with 12 guests, allowing 2 servings per guest.

FOOD	AMOUNT PER SERVING	TOTAL AMOUNT NEEDED
BEVERAGES		
Coffee	¾ cup	8–12 ounces, ground
Ice	—	15 pounds
Soft drinks	1 cup	Three 2-liter bottles
Tea, hot	¾ cup	5 quarts (20–25 tea bags)
Tea, iced	1 cup	6 quarts (25–30 tea bags)
SNACKS AND CRUDITÉS		
Chips or pretzels	¾ ounce	1¼ pounds
Broccoli or cauliflower florets	½ cup	Four 1-pound heads
Carrot sticks	Two to three 2″ sticks	1¼ pounds
Celery sticks	Two to three 2″ sticks	2–3 bunches
Olives	3–4	5 cups
Pickles, sliced	3–4 slices	1 quart
MAIN DISHES		
Pizza	⅓ pizza	Eight 12″ pizzas
Rice	¾ cup, cooked	6 cups, uncooked
Salad (green)	1 cup	6 quarts
Salad (pasta or potato)	½ cup	3 quarts
Soup	1½ cups	2½ gallons
DESSERTS		
Cake	1/12 cake	Two 13″ × 9″ cakes
Ice cream or frozen yogurt	½ cup	3 quarts
Pie	⅛ pie	Three 9″ pies

bagged vegetables, such as broccoli, cauliflower and baby carrots. Supermarkets even stock cut celery and carrot sticks for use in crudités.

Put the freezer to work. Rather than doing all your cooking the day of the party, cook some foods ahead and freeze them. Soups, sauces, stews, cookies, cakes and pizza dough all can be made days or even weeks in advance.

Consolidate your efforts. When preparing food ahead of time, save time by specializing. For example, if you're chopping one onion for use in a dip, go ahead and chop all the onions that you're going to use for the whole party. Then move on to the next ingredient.

Make a tent. When storing foods with soft or decorative toppings, like stuffed vegetables, it's important to raise the plastic wrap above the food to prevent it from smearing. An easy way to do that is to stand corks on the platters so that they are slightly higher than the surface of the food. Cover with plastic wrap and refrigerate.

BUFFET BASICS

You can't beat the simple beauty of a buffet. Whether indoors or out, formal or informal, large or small, a buffet provides atmosphere and variety for your guests, while leaving less cleanup for you. Plus, this type of entertaining is perfect for the healthy cook. In addition to heart-healthy seafoods and lean meats, you can easily serve nutrition-packed items like fresh crudités, stuffed vegetables and colorful fruit platters.

When planning a buffet, heed these tips from caterers.

Keep the sides open. Rather than placing the buffet table against a wall, put it in an area where guests can line up along both sides. This effectively doubles the number of people who can serve themselves at one time, keeping the line moving smoothly.

Split the crowd. When using more than one buffet table, place them on opposite sides of the room. Since guests naturally huddle around the

food, this will encourage them to move about, resulting in a livelier party.

You can make additional buffet stations by using end tables, card tables or extra counter space.

Get the right plates. For hungry guests, nothing is more frustrating than approaching an extravagant buffet with a plate just large enough to hold a carrot stick and perhaps a little dip. As a rule, any buffet with more than five items should be equipped with dinner plates. For buffets with less than five items, salad plates will suffice.

Provide two paper plates for every guest. When using china dinnerware, provide one plate per guest.

Make food easy to reach. For easy self-service, "whole" dishes like lasagna or soup should be placed about 6″ from the edge of the table. Easy-to-serve finger foods can be placed further toward the middle.

Always leave a little extra room on buffet tables so that guests can set down their plates or glasses.

Prepare the portions. Buffet lines move fastest when individual portions have already been prepared. So rather than just placing a pan of lasagna or a whole chicken on the table, cut the appropriate serving sizes ahead of time.

Keep drinks separate. To prevent beverages from sloshing into food bowls or platters, set aside a table just for drinks. Items to set out on the beverage table usually include:

- ☞ Hot cups
- ☞ Cold cups
- ☞ Ice
- ☞ Tongs or spoon for ice
- ☞ Sugar
- ☞ Milk
- ☞ Stirring spoons
- ☞ Napkins
- ☞ Bottle opener
- ☞ Corkscrew

Provide plenty of water. Since many people these days are drinking more water and less soda or alcohol, it's always a good idea to put

SETTING UP THE BUFFET

To keep buffet lines moving swiftly, it's helpful to arrange items in the order in which they'll be needed. Beginning at the right side of the table and moving left, here's how to set things up.

Plates and bowls. Your guests can't load up without them, so they should go at the beginning.

Foods. Set them back 6" from the edge of the table so that your guests will have room to set down their plates.

Dressings, dips and condiments. These go toward the end, since they're used to embellish items that have gone before.

Napkins and silverware. At the very end, put individual sets of silverware rolled up in napkins. Rolling them makes them easier to pick up and carry.

Desserts. These usually go on a separate table, since guests will want to eat their main dishes first. It's traditional to put the coffee pot or urn on the same table as the desserts.

---

a pitcher of water on the beverage table. To add elegance and a delicate citrus taste, toss a few slices of fresh lemon or lime into the pitcher.

Set up collection stations. To keep the buffet tables clear, put out several trash bins at the beginning of the party. They should be out of the way of traffic but not out of reach. This way people can toss their own trash, saving you hours of cleanup time later.

Beautiful Buffets

When guests arrive, the alluring sights and smells of a well-planned buffet will set the stage for a great party. To dress your buffet for maximum success, try these caterers' tips.

Cover it well. An attractive tablecloth not only protects the table but also brings out the wonderful colors of the food itself. White is usually the color of choice, since it doesn't compete with food. But don't feel restricted to a bland color. Gather your serving dishes ahead of time and see how they look against your chosen background.

Create colorful cuisine. Rather than making single-ingredient platters, go for eye appeal by mixing and matching a variety of shapes and colors.

☞ Combine golden pineapple, red watermelon and green grapes for a dazzling fruit platter.

☞ Make the traditional crudité platter a visual treat by complementing carrot and celery sticks with strips of sweet yellow and red peppers.

☞ Combine red radishes with lightly blanched broccoli florets.

☞ Cut quiche into diamond shapes.

☞ Make small pizza triangles.

☞ Balance round scones with square bar cookies.

☞ Vary long and short vegetables in a decorative pattern.

☞ Cut carrots on the diagonal to make "chips."

☞ Combine long vegetables like asparagus or celery with small, round vegetables like halved brussels sprouts and radishes.

Bring out the platters. Parties are perfect for those large, colorful platters that you don't normally use. They lend a festive touch to the gathering, while doing the work of many smaller plates.

Decorate with savvy. Candles and flowers lend an exuberant air to any gathering. When putting them on the buffet, however, make sure that they're in the middle of the table so that they don't get in the way of the food.

☞ Spring calls for fresh flower bouquets. Or try floating single gardenias, roses or other large blossoms in bowls of cold water.

☞ In autumn, Indian corn, gourds and dried leaves make beautiful decorations.

☞ For winter, decorate with holly, pine cones or decorative twigs.

☞ For summer, use halved coconuts, whole melons or squash blossoms floated in a bowl of water.

Go wild with garnishes. Why serve food plain when you can dress it up? Sometimes just adding some sprigs of parsley or a sprinkling of

ARTFUL ARRANGEMENTS

Raw vegetables don't have to be boring. With crudité platters, you can alternate colors and shapes to your heart's—and eye's—content. Put long next to short, round next to rectangular, red next to green. It's entirely up to you. Here are some arrangement possibilities.

Circles. Place a bowl of dip in the center of a round platter. Cut vegetables into even lengths and arrange around the dip in concentric circles.

Fan. Place 3 bowls of dip at the top of a round platter. Cut vegetables into even lengths and arrange in front of the dip in the shape of a fan.

Zigzag. Place bowls of dip along each of the short sides of a rectangular platter. Cut vegetables into even lengths. Arrange lengthwise in alternating diagonal rows between the dips.

chopped herbs gives a buffet dish that professional finish. To be more creative:

☞ Place small whole vegetables like cherry tomatoes or colorful chili peppers around the edge of the plate.

☞ Line platters of seafood with ornamental kale and halved slices of lemon.

☞ Place stuffed vegetables on beds of decorative lettuces, such as radicchio or red oak leaf.

☞ Garnish platters of fruit or fruit salads with sprigs of fresh mint. Variegated pineapple mint is an especially decorative variety.

☞ Embellish savory dishes like lasagna with whole sprigs of fresh herbs. Good choices include parsley, rosemary, green or purple basil, sage, dill and thyme.

☞ Add colorful edible flowers to casseroles, platters or punch bowls. Squash blossoms and nasturtiums are good choices.

Make edible containers. To add an exciting touch to the buffet, replace your regular bowl with edible containers.

☞ **Sweet pepper cups.** Choose peppers that can stand upright without toppling. Cut a wide hole around the stems and remove the tops. (Or leave the stem intact and cut the pepper in half lengthwise.) Remove the cores and seeds. Fill with savory dips, spreads or sauces.

☞ **Bread bowls.** Preheat the oven to 350°. Cut a large hole in the top of a crusty round loaf or a long French or Italian bread. Pull out the soft bread inside, leaving ½″ shell. Place the shell on a no-stick baking sheet and bake until crisp, about 20 minutes. Remove from the oven and let cool. Fill with hot or cold dips or spreads. If desired, cut the bread from the interior into squares and serve with toothpicks alongside the filled bread bowl.

☞ **Cabbage bowls.** Remove the loose outer layers of a head of red or green cabbage. Cut off the stem end to make the cabbage sit flat. Cut off the top third and scoop out the insides with a grapefruit knife, leaving ½″ of shell intact. Fill with savory dips or sauces.

☞ **Pineapple boats.** Cut a pineapple in half lengthwise. Remove the fruit with a grapefruit knife, leaving a ½″ shell. Fill with fruit salad, sweet dips or sauces.

☞ **Squash tureen.** Preheat the oven to 350°. Cut off the top third of a large acorn squash or pumpkin. Carefully scoop out the seeds, leaving a ½″ shell. Place on a no-stick baking sheet and bake for 20 minutes. Remove from the oven, cool and fill with soup; squash and pumpkin soup are good choices.

☞ **Zucchini boats.** Cut a large zucchini in half lengthwise. Remove the seeds, leaving ½″ shell. Fill with savory dips or spreads.

Buffet Safety

Since party food is usually kept at room temperature for the duration of the festivities, it's extremely important to keep it sufficiently hot or cold to prevent contamination. Obviously, most home cooks don't have sophisticated steam tables or cooling stations. But there are other ways to keep the food safe.

Put like with like. Grouping all the hot foods in one place and all the cold ones in another will help keep the temperatures constant, so that bacteria are less likely to move in.

Serve in stages. Rather than putting all the food out at once, surprise your guests by bring-ing out two or three dishes at a time. They'll appreciate the variety, and you'll be better able to keep the various courses at safe

GREAT GARNISHES

Any dish becomes more attractive and appetizing with the addition of a garnish. Give your buffet a professional finish with these simple eye-catching decorations. (Putting the garnishes in ice water will keep them crisp and bright until you're ready to use them.)

TOMATO ROSES

Using a sharp paring knife, peel the skin from a tomato in one continuous strip.

Roll into a spiral to create a rosebud. Finish the flower with a sprig of fresh basil.

SCALLION FLOWERS

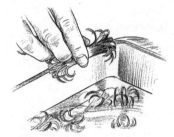

Cut off the root end of a scallion. Cut off excess greens, leaving a scallion about 4" long. Make slits through the bottom that reach about 1½" up through the white part.

Shred the green top in a similar manner, leaving about ½" in the middle uncut.

Place in a bowl of ice water until the petals curl, usually about 2 hours.

CHILI FLOWERS

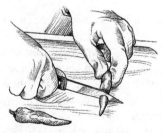

Cut the tip off an elongated jala-peño, serrano or Tabasco pepper and discard the pointed end. (Wear plastic gloves when handling.)

Using scissors or a paring knife, cut long petals that widen toward the stem end, stopping about ½" from the base.

Rinse the pepper under running water and remove the seeds. Place in a bowl of ice water until the petals curl.

EDIBLE FLOWERS

Flowers make beautiful garnishes that add unique flavors to the buffet table. Just be sure to use flowers that are grown for eating; those used for floral arrangements have generally been treated with pesticides.

FLOWER	FLAVOR	USES
Begonia	Lemony-sweet	Fruit salads, desserts
Borage	Similar to cucumber	Salads
Calendula	Mildly tangy	Salads, soups, dips, spreads and egg dishes
Chive blossoms	Onion-like	Salads, soups
Daisy	Mild	Salads
Dandelion	Mild	Soups
Daylily	From sweet to tart	Salads
Dianthus	Similar to clove or nutmeg	Salads
Hollyhock	Mild	Salads, savories
Lavender	Sweet	Fruit salads, desserts
Marigold	Citrusy	Salads, soups, savories
Nasturtium (flowers and leaves)	Tangy, a bit like watercress	Salads, egg dishes or stuffed as an appetizer
Pansy	Mild, a bit like lettuce	Salads, savories
Rose	Strong and fragrant	Beverages, desserts
Squash blossoms	Mildly sweet	Salads, egg dishes or stuffed as an appetizer
Viola (Johnny-jump-up)	Mild	Salads, desserts
Violet	Sweet	Fruit salads, desserts

temperatures in the kitchen until they're needed.

☞ Store dips, spreads, chilled seafood and other cold recipes on the bottom shelf of the refrigerator (the coldest spot) until they're needed.

☞ Whenever possible, divide recipes into two or more batches. While one batch is being eaten, keep another at a safe temperature in the kitchen. Then you can bring it out as soon as the first plate is emptied.

Use the right cookware. Serving food in heavy baking dishes keeps it at a more constant temperature than using glass or thin metal containers.

Heat at the table. An electric warming tray is an easy, inexpensive way to keep foods warm for the duration of the party. Or use a chafing dish, which is simply a large double boiler with a heating unit beneath.

Don't forget the slow-cooker. Traditionally used for long-cooking items like stews or beans, slow cookers are perfect for keeping chili, soups, dips or pilafs warm without overheating.

Warm the plates. Putting hot food on a

MAKING EDIBLE BOWLS

It's possible to have a pretty melon and eat it too. The secret is making it into an edible food bowl. Hollowed-out edibles create a festive look for any occasion. Here's how it's done. (The technique works with winter squash, cabbages and other large items that can have their centers scooped out.)

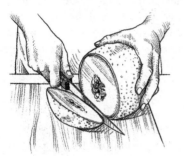

Cut a thin slice from the bottom of a large cantaloupe or honeydew melon so that it will sit steady. Then cut off the top.

Scoop out the seeds and some of the flesh, leaving ½" of shell intact.

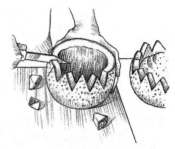

For added effect, make 1" diagonal cuts around the top of the bowl to create a decorative crown. Fill with fruit salad, sweet dips or sauces.

Helpful Hint

To make an instant warming tray, open a waffle iron until it lies flat. Cover it with heavy-duty foil and set it at the lowest temperature setting. If it has flat plates in addition to the waffled ones, use them.

cold plate causes it to instantly drop a few degrees. When using china, chefs advise first warming the plates to a comfortable holding temperature of about 100° in an oven set on very low heat.

Keep them cool. When serving cold foods, chill the plates in the refrigerator for one hour before using. Or put them in the freezer for 20 minutes.

Put them on ice. To keep a bowl or small platter chilled at the table, rest it on a nest of crushed ice in a larger bowl or platter.

Before the party, place an inverted bowl in the freezer with a pliable freezer gel pack on top. The gel pack will freeze in the shape of the bottom of the bowl. The pack can later be used as a cold base when you're ready to serve.

LOW-FAT PARTY FARE

Party food has traditionally consisted of deep-fried appetizers and high-fat dipping sauces. Today, however, hosts and guests are looking for lighter fare—fresh foods that won't fill them up or stay with them long after the party is over. Here are some festive, healthy foods that you may want to try.

Party Soups

Soup is inexpensive, easy to make and a delight to the senses. You can serve it in mugs, which allows guests to eat and mill around without fiddling with bowls and spoons.

Make it smooth. For guests with a beverage in one hand and a mug of soup in the other, holding a spoon is almost impossible. So avoid chunky soups. "Sipping" soups are a better choice, like smooth tomato or cream of vegetable.

Use sturdy mugs. To prevent hot hands and messy spills, serve the soup in coffee mugs. If you're using disposable china, be sure to pick cups or mugs with a sturdy design and strong handles.

Make the service easy. Put the empty mugs near the soup tureen or slow cooker. Include a ladle and, of course, plenty of napkins.

Canapés

Like little open-faced sandwiches, canapés are simply crackers or pieces of bread or toast that have been topped with a savory spread and perhaps embellished with chopped vegetables or herbs.

The great thing about canapés is that they lend an elegant touch to a party. Despite this, they are very easy to make. All the ingredients can be prepared in advance so that the canapés can be assembled just before it is time to serve them.

☞ Slice crusty French bread into ½" slices. Lightly brush one side of the slices with olive oil. Broil for 1 minute per side, then rub all over with the cut side of a garlic clove. Top with diced fresh tomatoes, chopped fresh basil and grated Parmesan cheese.

ROASTING GARLIC

When roasted, garlic gives up its wild character and takes on a milder flavor. It also becomes soft enough to spread on toasted slices of bread, making a perfect party snack. It can be eaten alone or combined with such ingredients as fresh basil, roasted peppers, sun-dried tomatoes or low-fat cream cheese.

Put unpeeled garlic cloves in an 8" × 8" no-stick baking dish and drizzle with a little olive oil. Roast in a 350° oven for 30 minutes, or until soft. Remove from the oven and allow to cool.

To remove the garlic from its peel, squeeze one end. Mash the garlic, then spread it on crackers or bread.

☞ Top toasted slices of French bread with a layer of low-fat pesto and slivered sun-dried tomatoes. Or top the bread and pesto with reduced-fat mozzarella cheese and run under the broiler before serving.

☞ Top slices of pumpernickel or rye bread with thin strips of smoked salmon. Season with a squeeze of lemon juice and freshly ground black pepper.

☞ Combine low-fat cream cheese with minced parsley, dill, garlic and scallions. Spread on whole-grain crackers or rye bread and top with thin slices of cucumber and black pepper. Finish with a small sprig of fresh dill.

☞ Combine low-fat cream cheese with flaked lump crabmeat and Old Bay seasoning. Spread on water crackers and spritz with lemon juice.

☞ Combine low-fat cream cheese with smoked bluefish and horseradish. Spread on whole-grain crackers and top with thin slices of cucumber.

☞ Combine low-fat cream cheese with Dijon and dill, basil, thyme or sage. Spread on toasted rye bread and top with steamed asparagus tips. Spritz with fresh lemon juice.

☞ Combine low-fat cream cheese with capers and snipped fresh chives. Spread on thin slices of toasted black bread and top with nasturtium petals.

Crudités

Platters of raw and blanched vegetables are the backbone of any buffet. They're healthy and easy to prepare ahead of time. When decoratively arranged and accompanied by tasty dips, crudités often become the most popular item on the party table.

Begin by blanching. To slightly tenderize certain vegetables and help set their color, it's helpful to blanch them for 30 seconds in boiling water, then transfer them to a bowl of ice water to stop the cooking. Items that should be blanched include brussels sprouts, broccoli, cau-

LOW-FAT DIPS

It's easy to gain weight snacking your way through a party, but with low-fat dips, you can enjoy delicious snacks without worrying about your waistline. After mixing the ingredients, refrigerate for at least 2 hours to blend the flavors. Serve the dips with fresh crudités or whole-grain crackers. Nonfat versions of sour cream and yogurt cheese are the base of these dips. You can buy yogurt cheese in some supermarkets or make your own (see page 279).

☞ **Curried yogurt dip.** Combine 2 cups nonfat yogurt cheese, ¼ cup minced fresh parsley, ¼ cup chopped fresh chives, 2 tablespoons minced shallots, 1½ tablespoons curry powder and ½ teaspoon salt. Makes about 2¼ cups.

☞ **Spinach dip.** Thaw 1 package (10 ounces) frozen chopped spinach and squeeze out excess liquid. Mix with ¾ cup nonfat yogurt cheese, ⅓ cup reduced-fat mayonnaise, ½ envelope vegetable soup mix and 1 tablespoon chopped scallions. Makes about 2½ cups.

☞ **Sour cream and chive dip.** Combine 2 cups nonfat sour cream, 2 tablespoons minced fresh parsley, 2 tablespoons chopped fresh chives, ½ teaspoon paprika, ¼ teaspoon curry powder and ¼ teaspoon salt. Makes about 2 cups.

☞ **Creamy horseradish dip.** Combine 2 cups nonfat sour cream, 2 tablespoons prepared horseradish, ½ teaspoon paprika and ¼ teaspoon salt. Makes about 2 cups.

liflower, green beans, asparagus, baby yellow squash and zucchini.

Make them pretty. While carrots, celery and peppers are generally cut into slender lengths, other vegetables may be cut, trimmed or arranged to suit your tastes. Strive for a variety of shapes and a good mix of textures and colors.

Stuffed Vegetables

Many small vegetables make colorful and delicious appetizers when hollowed out and stuffed. Guests love to graze their way through an array of these tasty little morsels. In addition, they're easy to make ahead and keep in the refrigerator until party time. Here are some easy edible containers.

☞ **Cherry tomato cups.** Remove the stems and cut a thin slice from the tops. Carefully scoop out the seeds and flesh, leaving the shell intact. Lightly salt the insides of the tomatoes to draw out excess liquid. Invert on a wire rack to drain for 10 minutes. Rinse and stuff.

☞ **Cucumber cups.** Using a fork, score the skin of a cucumber lengthwise. Cut crosswise into ¾″ slices. Using a melon baller or teaspoon, scoop out flesh from each slice, leaving a ¼″ shell. Lightly salt the cups and invert them onto a wire rack to drain for 10 minutes. Rinse and stuff.

☞ **Lettuce-leaf saucers.** Rinse the small inner leaves of a leaf lettuce, like Boston, romaine, radicchio or even Belgian endive. Dry well and stuff.

☞ **Mushroom caps (for cold stuffing).** Rinse mushrooms, remove stems and place, rounded side down, on a no-stick baking sheet. Bake at 425° for 10 minutes. Remove, cool and stuff.

☞ **Mushroom caps (for hot stuffing).** Rinse mushrooms, remove stems and add stuffing. Place on a no-stick baking sheet. Bake at 375° for 10 minutes, or until heated through.

☞ **Snow pea purses.** Blanch snow peas in boiling water for 30 seconds. Plunge into cold water. Carefully slit open the curved side of each pod and stuff.

☞ **Squash boats.** Cut very small yellow squash or zucchini in half lengthwise and blanch in boiling water for 30 seconds. Plunge into cold water to stop the cooking process. Carefully scoop out the flesh and set aside, leaving a ½″ shell. Chop the flesh and mix with stuffing, if desired.

Fruit Platters

Few things liven up the buffet table like fresh fruit. Fruit is sweet and juicy and provides a refreshing change from savory items on the menu. Preparation time is minimal, and dips can be as simple as nonfat vanilla yogurt.

☞ **Berries.** Use fresh strawberries, raspberries and blueberries. (Large strawberries can be left whole—especially if they still contain their stems—or cut in half.) Arrange on a platter and serve.

☞ **Cherries.** Serve whole. Leave on the stems for a nice presentation.

☞ **Grapes.** Combine seedless green and red grapes on a platter. Cut large bunches into small ones. If tiny champagne grapes are available, use them.

☞ **Mangoes.** Peel and pit, then cut into chunks. Serve with toothpicks.

☞ **Melons.** Cut cantaloupe, watermelon and honeydew into small wedges with the rind included. Or use a melon scoop to make small balls. Serve with toothpicks.

☞ **Oranges and tangerines.** Remove the rind and separate into sections.

☞ **Pineapple.** Cut lengthwise into quarters and slice into small wedges with the rind included. Or cut into chunks and serve with toothpicks. Can be served in a hollowed-out pineapple boat, if desired.

Finger Foods

The deep-fried appetizers of yesteryear have given way to a variety of healthy new finger foods, such as spring rolls and baked potato skins. You'll find an abundance of low-fat appetizer recipes beginning on page 546. For something quick, here are a few delicious morsels to try.

☞ **Shrimp cocktail.** Line a large platter with lettuce leaves and lemon wedges. Fill with chilled cooked shrimp.

To make 2 cups cocktail sauce, combine 1½ cups ketchup, ½ cup lemon juice, ¼ cup prepared horseradish, 2 tablespoons Worcestershire sauce, 2 teaspoons minced onions and 4 teaspoons maple syrup. Chill and serve with the shrimp.

☞ **Lean potato skins.** Prick the skins of small potatoes with a fork. Bake at 350° until tender. Cut the potatoes in half lengthwise and scoop out the flesh, leaving ½" shells (may be done ahead to this point). Return to the oven for 10 minutes.

In a small bowl, combine equal parts softened reduced-fat margarine, chopped fresh chives and grated Parmesan cheese. Add black pepper to taste. Spread the potato skins with the margarine mixture and bake for 10 minutes, or until the skins are brown and crisp. Serve hot.

☞ **Quick low-fat quesadillas.** Coat a no-stick skillet with no-stick spray. Place over medium heat and add 1 large flour tortilla. Top the tortilla with a thin layer of shredded reduced-fat Monterey Jack cheese. Add your favorite Mexican toppings such as cooked black beans, cut corn, sliced jalapeño peppers, refried beans, chopped sweet peppers or thick salsa. Sprinkle with chopped fresh cilantro and another thin layer of shredded reduced-fat Monterey Jack cheese. Place another tortilla on top. Cook about 4 minutes per side, or until browned on both sides and the cheese is melted.

☞ **Tasty tofu bites.** Cut a 1-pound block of pressed firm tofu into bite-size cubes. Coat a no-stick skillet with no-stick spray and place over medium-high heat. Sauté the tofu until browned on all sides. Toss with minced garlic and 2 tablespoons reduced-sodium soy sauce. Serve hot or cold with toothpicks.

PIZZA

Pizza has long been appreciated as the ultimate in convenience foods. But you don't have to order out to get great taste.

This traditional party favorite will accommodate just about any ingredient that you want to put on it, from reduced-fat cheese and lightly sautéed vegetables to broiled seafood and roasted lean meats.

Briefly sautéing vegetables such as onions, mushrooms, peppers, zucchini and eggplant before adding them to the crust will reduce the amount of liquid that's released during baking. This in turn helps keep the crust from getting soggy. In addition, briefly steaming or blanching vegetables first helps ensure that they cook all the way through.

Here are a few easy topping ideas for you to try out.

☞ **Fresh tomato-and-roasted-pepper pizza.** Sprinkle 1 tablespoon minced garlic over the crust. Top with thinly sliced plum tomatoes, chopped fresh oregano and shredded part-skim mozzarella cheese. Finish with strips of roasted red peppers and sliced black olives.

☞ **Greek pizza.** Top the crust with tomatoes, sweet and hot peppers, wilted spinach, feta cheese, kalamata olives and oregano.

☞ **Mexican pizza.** Spread the crust with well-drained salsa and top with shredded reduced-fat Monterey Jack cheese.

☞ **Neapolitan pizza.** Add sliced tomatoes, garlic and oregano or basil to a plain crust.

☞ **Pizza Provençal.** Top the crust with tomatoes, onions, anchovies, olives, fennel and chopped fresh herbs.

☞ **Sour-cream-and-broccoli pizza.** Sauté chopped onions until soft, then remove from the heat and stir in nonfat sour cream and fresh dill. Spread over the pizza crust and top with steamed broccoli florets and shredded reduced-fat Cheddar cheese.

PIZZA PIZZAZZ

It's inexpensive, guests love it and it's easy to prepare. No wonder pizza is one of the most popular party foods. But the typical restaurant pizza contains up to 18 grams of fat per slice—and that's without fancy toppings. Add pepperoni and your two-slice snack could deliver up to 40 grams of fat and more than 1,000 milligrams of sodium.

Here are great recipes for crusts and sauces. Remember that you can save time by preparing the ingredients in advance, then freezing the crust and refrigerating the sauce. When you're ready to eat, simply put the toppings together.

THE CRUST

Restaurants generally use extra oil to make a crisp crust, but there's a low-fat way that works just as well. This basic dough recipe will make four 6″ pizzas, which can be quartered to make party-size slices.

Since the consistency of pizza dough can be affected by subtle factors such as room temperature, you may need to add a little extra water or flour (1 tablespoon at a time) to create a smooth and elastic dough as you knead.

Basic Pizza Dough

1⅓ cups warm water (105°–115°F)
1 package (¼ ounce) quick-rising yeast
1 tablespoon olive oil
1 teaspoon salt
3 cups all-purpose flour
1 tablespoon cornmeal
   Sauce and toppings

Place the water in a large bowl and sprinkle with the yeast. Set aside for 5 minutes, or until the yeast gets foamy. Then stir in the oil, salt and 2½ cups of the flour. Gradually mix in the remaining ½ cup flour to form a kneadable dough.

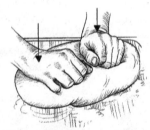

Place the dough on a lightly floured surface and knead for about 8 minutes, or until smooth and elastic. Add flour as needed to keep the dough from sticking.

Coat another large bowl with no-stick spray. Shape the dough into a ball and put it in the bowl, rolling it around to coat it with spray. Cover the bowl with a kitchen towel and set in a warm, draft-free place. Allow to rise for about 30 minutes, or until the dough doubles in bulk.

Punch down the dough and divide it into 4 equal pieces. On a lightly floured surface, roll each piece into a round no thicker than ¼". Keep the other pieces covered with a dish towel as you work.

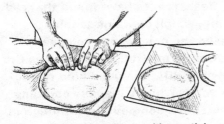

Coat 2 no-stick baking sheets with no-stick spray. Sprinkle lightly with the cornmeal and place 2 crusts on each sheet. Roll the edge of each crust slightly inward and pinch to form a rim. Top with the sauce and toppings of your choice. Bake in a preheated 475° oven for 15 minutes, or until the crust is brown and crisp.

NOTES

• Rather than a baking sheet, use a pizza stone or unglazed quarry tiles. These porous baking stones create crispy crusts, because they absorb excess moisture from the dough.

• If you don't have a pizza stone, try this: Bake the pizza on a no-stick baking sheet for half the required time to firm up the crust. Then slide it directly onto the oven rack to finish cooking.

• To make a whole-wheat crust, replace 1 cup all-purpose flour with 1 cup whole-wheat flour.

• To prevent the crust from getting soggy, lightly brush it with olive oil and partially bake the crust for 10 minutes in a 475° oven. Remove from the oven and let cool before adding toppings.

The key to a good pizza sauce is cooking off enough liquid to make a thick sauce that isn't too watery. Watery sauce will make a soggy pizza. The no-fuss combination of canned tomato sauce and tomato paste below works great every time. This recipe makes about 2¼ cups, enough for the Basic Pizza Dough.

Basic Pizza Sauce

1 small onion, diced
1 clove garlic, minced
1 tablespoon dried oregano
1 tablespoon olive oil
1 can (15 ounces) tomato sauce
1 can (6 ounces) tomato paste

In a medium no-stick skillet over medium heat, sauté the onions, garlic and oregano in the oil for 5 minutes, or until the onions are softened.

Stir in the tomato sauce and tomato paste. Simmer for 10 minutes. Remove from the heat and allow to cool before using.

NOTES

• For a richer flavor, stir in 2 teaspoons balsamic vinegar along with the tomato sauce.

• For a robust tomato flavor, pour ¼ cup boiling water over 4 to 5 sun-dried tomato halves. Set aside for 10 minutes, or until soft. Finely chop the softened tomatoes. Add the tomatoes and their soaking liquid along with the tomato sauce. Increase the simmering time to 15 minutes, or until the sauce is thick.

VARIATION

Chunky Tomato Sauce: Omit the oregano, reduce the amount of tomato paste to 2 tablespoons and replace the tomato sauce with 1 can (15 ounces) Italian-style stewed tomatoes with herbs.

Eating and making merry are only two-thirds of the party equation. The final ingredient is drinking. Whether it's iced tea on the Fourth of July or hot mulled cider for the Christmas holidays, the beverages that you serve put your personal stamp on the occasion. Great drinks are easy to make.

Warm Beverages

During the cold months, handing guests a warm drink is sure to get things off to a hospitable start. Most warm beverages have just a few ingredients and are ready in minutes.

☞ **Hot mulled cider.** In a saucepan, combine 2 quarts apple cider, 4 cinnamon sticks, 3 whole cloves, 6 whole allspice berries and a ¼"-thick slice fresh ginger. Heat over medium heat for 15 minutes, or until steaming. Discard the spices and pour into mugs or a punch bowl. Makes eight 1-cup servings.

☞ **Make-ahead hot cocoa.** In a large microwave-safe bowl, combine 2¾ cups instant nonfat dry milk powder, ½ cup sugar and 6 tablespoons unsweetened cocoa powder. Mix with 8 cups water and 2½ teaspoons vanilla extract. Microwave on high power for 6 minutes, or until very hot. Ladle into mugs. Makes eight 1-cup servings.

☞ **Hot berry wassail.** Wassail is a traditional English holiday drink containing alcohol. Here's a festive alcohol-free version that can be served warm or cold. In a saucepan, combine 3 cups cranberry-apple juice, 2 cups cranberry-raspberry juice, 1 cup orange juice, 4 strips orange rind, 8 whole cloves and 2 cinnamon sticks. Bring to a boil over medium heat. Reduce the heat to low and simmer for 15 minutes. Strain into mugs or a punch bowl. Makes six 1-cup servings.

☞ **Spicy tomato warm-up.** Finally, an alcohol-free Bloody Mary. In a large glass bowl, combine 1 can (46 ounces) reduced-sodium tomato

Wine
Is It GOOD for You?

An old Russian proverb advises, "Drink a glass of wine after your soup, and you will steal a ruble from the doctor."

In recent years, a number of large studies have confirmed that drinking moderate amounts of wine can substantially lower the risk for heart disease.

Researchers have found that red wine, which contains tannins (flavoring compounds released during fermentation), increases the level of HDL, the good kind of cholesterol. White wine also contains protective compounds, although in lower concentrations than the reds.

While some wine is good, however, experts are reluctant to recommend imbibing as part of a healthy lifestyle. Sipping a little wine may be healthy, but drinking too much can have dangerous, sometimes catastrophic effects. In addition, the protective effect found in a glass or two quickly tapers off when people drink more. There's also the issue of sulfites, preservatives added to wine that may cause allergic symptoms in some people.

What's the bottom line? If you don't drink, there's no reason to start. If you do enjoy an occasional glass of wine, go ahead and toast your good health—you may be giving it a little boost.

juice, ¼ cup lemon juice, 1½ teaspoons Worcestershire sauce, 1 teaspoon sugar, ½ tea-spoon hot-pepper sauce and ¼ teaspoon garlic powder. Microwave on high power, stirring occasionally, for 8 minutes, or until hot. Pour into mugs or a punch bowl and top with freshly ground black pepper. Makes eight 1-cup servings.

Heat them up. To keep drinks from cooling too quickly, it's important to prewarm the mugs and punch bowl. The easiest way to do this is to fill them with hot tap water and let them sit for 10 minutes. Empty and dry before using.

Leave room at the top. Since guests are typically moving about with their party drinks, don't fill the mugs more than three-quarters full.

Cold Beverages

When the party is hot and the weather is warm, the first thing that guests want is something cold to drink. Why do the same-old with cans of beer or sugary sodas? Here are some different refreshing thirst quenchers.

☞ **Fruit punch.** In a punch bowl, combine the juice from 2 limes and 2 oranges with 3 quarts cranberry juice, 1 quart sparkling water and 3 tablespoons sugar. Stir to dissolve the sugar and add lime and orange slices to the bowl. Serve over ice.

☞ **Fruit spritzers.** In a punch bowl, combine thawed frozen juice concentrate with

---

KEEPING ICE COLD

In the heat of a party, it can be tough to keep the ice frozen and the beverages cold. To prevent ice from running out (and over), try these tips.

☞ Keep the ice bucket away from the stove and out of the kitchen during the party.

☞ Put the empty ice bucket in the refrigerator or freezer two hours before the party. When it's thoroughly cold, add ice.

☞ Put a freezer gel pack beneath the ice bucket.

☞ For use in punch bowls, make large blocks of ice in milk or juice cartons. Large blocks melt more slowly than smaller cubes.

---

seltzer water. For variety, mix two or more concentrates, like orange and cranberry juice.

☞ **Sun tea.** In a 2-quart glass pitcher, combine 4 tea bags and 1½ quarts cold water. You also may want to add several sprigs fresh lemon balm or mint. Place the pitcher in a sunny spot for at least 3 hours. Remove the tea bags and sweeten to taste. Chill and serve over ice.

☞ **Mock mimosas.** Mimosas are traditionally made with champagne. You can make a non-alcoholic version by combining equal parts orange juice and sparkling water. Serve in champagne glasses.

Helpful Hint

Punch that's delicious at the beginning of the night can gradually turn dull and watery from all the melting ice. To help maintain the full flavor, don't use ice cubes made from water; make them from punch, instead.

Mark Militello

With recipes fusing Caribbean ingredients and Californian and Mediterranean techniques, Mark Militello's cuisine—at Mark's Place in North Miami and Mark's Las Olas in Fort Lauderdale—can be deliciously complex. When cooking for guests at home, however, he takes a simpler approach.

"I want to enjoy my guests rather than spend all my time in the kitchen, so I keep things simple," he says. "I prepare as many things as possible ahead of time. I serve room-temperature hors d'oeuvres and use interesting platters and colorful presentations for a casual feeling."

This recipe can be made early in the day and then reheated when you are ready to serve. The percentage of calories from fat is on the high side only because there are so few calories—and so little fat—in the dish.

Grilled Skewered Portobello Mushrooms

- 4 medium portobello mushrooms (each about 4″ across)
- 2 cloves garlic
- 1 tablespoon extra-virgin olive oil
- 1 tablespoon lemon juice
- 1 tablespoon balsamic vinegar
- 1½ teaspoons chili oil
- 3 tablespoons minced fresh basil
- 1 tablespoon finely chopped garlic
  Pinch of salt
  Pinch of ground black pepper

Remove and discard the stems from the mushrooms. Cut the garlic cloves into thin lengthwise slivers. Make a series of tiny incisions in the tops of the mushrooms, using the tip of a paring knife. Insert the garlic slivers.

Place the mushrooms in a single layer in a 9″ × 13″ no-stick baking dish.

In a small bowl, whisk together the olive oil, lemon juice, vinegar and chili oil. Stir in the basil, chopped garlic, salt and pepper. Pour over the mushrooms. Let marinate at room temperature for 2 hours, turning the caps once or twice.

Coat an unheated grill rack with no-stick spray. Light the grill according to the manufacturer's directions. Place the rack on the grill. Just before serving, grill the mushrooms for 2 to 3 minutes per side over medium-hot coals, basting with any leftover marinade. Transfer the mushrooms to a cutting board and cut into quarters. Thread each quarter onto a tiny wooden skewer. Arrange on a platter and serve at once.

Makes 16 servings. Per serving: 15 calories, 1.3 g. fat (74% of calories), 0.1 g. protein, 0.9 g. carbohydrates, 0 g. dietary fiber, 0 mg. cholesterol, 0.4 mg. sodium

Pierogi

Wonton wrappers and reduced-fat ricotta cheese make a quicker and healthier version of Polish pierogi.

1	cup finely chopped cremini or button mushrooms
2	tablespoons chopped scallions
1	large clove garlic, minced
1	cup fat-free or reduced-fat ricotta cheese
1	teaspoon lemon juice
2	teaspoons minced parsley
¾	teaspoon dried dill
¼	teaspoon salt
¼	teaspoon ground black pepper
1	large egg white
42–46	wonton wrappers

Coat a small no-stick skillet with no-stick spray. Warm over medium heat until hot. Add the mushrooms, scallions and garlic. Cover and cook for 3 to 5 minutes, or until the mushrooms release their liquid. Uncover, reduce the heat to medium-low and cook for 3 to 4 minutes, or until the liquid has evaporated.

In a small bowl, combine the ricotta, lemon juice, parsley and dill. Stir in the mushroom mixture, salt and pepper. Add the egg white and mix well.

Using a 3″ cookie cutter, cut rounds from the wonton wrappers. Place rounded teaspoonfuls of the cheese mixture in the center of each wonton round. Brush the edges of the wonton with water and fold in half over the filling. Crimp the edges with a fork to seal. Repeat with the remaining wrappers and cheese mixture.

In a large saucepan, bring 6″ to 8″ of water to a boil over high heat. Reduce the heat to medium, maintaining a rapid simmer. Add the pierogi in batches, cooking until they rise to the top of the water. Remove with a slotted spoon and transfer to paper towels. Serve hot.

Makes 8 servings. Per serving (about 5 pierogi): 145 calories, 0.9 g. fat (5% of calories), 9.3 g. protein, 26 g. carbohydrates, 0.1 g. dietary fiber, 5 mg. cholesterol, 320 mg. sodium

NOTES

• Traditional pierogi are round, but you can save time by making rectangular pierogi instead of cutting the wonton wrappers into rounds. Use a bit more filling in each pierogi.

• For a tasty topping, sauté thinly sliced onions in a small amount of olive oil over medium heat until browned.

• When serving pierogi on a platter, lightly coat them with no-stick spray to prevent sticking.

VARIATIONS

Mushroom Pierogi: Omit the filling above. Instead, in a large no-stick skillet coated with no-stick spray, sauté 3½ cups finely chopped mushrooms and ¼ cup chopped scallions until tender. Remove from the heat. Stir in 2 to 4 tablespoons nonfat or low-fat sour cream and ¼ to ½ teaspoon dried thyme or dill. Season to taste with salt and black pepper.

Potato Pierogi: Omit the filling above. Instead, in a small bowl, combine 1¼ cups mashed potatoes with ¼ cup sautéed sliced scallions. Season to taste with salt and black pepper.

Sauerkraut Pierogi: Omit the filling above. Instead, in a small bowl, combine 1¼ cups drained chopped sauerkraut, ¼ cup sautéed chopped onion and 2 to 3 tablespoons nonfat or low-fat sour cream. Season to taste with black pepper.

Spring Rolls with Dipping Sauce

Spring Rolls

3	cups bean thread noodles
2¼	cups thinly sliced Napa cabbage
1	cup grated carrots
½	cup roasted, unsalted peanuts, finely chopped
⅔	cup thinly sliced scallion greens
2	teaspoons toasted sesame oil
16	rice papers (8″ diameter)

Dipping Sauce

2	teaspoons cornstarch or arrowroot
1	cup water
½	cup unseasoned rice vinegar
2	tablespoons reduced-sodium soy sauce
¼	cup sugar
4	cloves garlic, minced
4	teaspoons minced fresh ginger
¼	teaspoon crushed red-pepper flakes

To make the spring rolls: Cook the noodles according to the package directions. Drain and coarsley chop.

In a large bowl, combine the noodles, cabbage, carrots, peanuts, scallions and sesame oil. Set aside.

Fill a 10″ pie plate with warm water. Place one of the rice papers in the water and soak for 30 to 60 seconds, or until the paper is pliable. Transfer to a clean kitchen towel and blot gently to dry.

Place ⅓ cup of the noodle mixture on the bottom third of the rice paper. Lift the bottom edge of the paper over the filling and fold the sides toward the center. Roll up as tightly as possible.

Repeat with the remaining papers and filling. Serve at room temperature within 1 to 2 hours.

To make the dipping sauce: In a small saucepan, combine the cornstarch or arrowroot and water. Stir until dissolved. Add the rice vinegar, soy sauce, sugar, garlic, ginger and red-pepper flakes.

Bring to a boil over medium-high heat, stirring constantly, or just until thickened (this will happen very quickly). Remove from the heat and cool to room temperature. Transfer to a small serving bowl and serve with the spring rolls.

Makes 8 servings. Per serving (2 spring rolls): 195 calories, 5.9 g. fat (27% of calories), 5.6 g. protein, 31.6 g. carbohydrates, 1.9 g. dietary fiber, 0 mg. cholesterol, 240 mg. sodium

NOTES

• Rice papers are like thin, white tortillas with a delicate texture when soaked in water. They are available in large supermarkets and Asian grocery stores.

• For a decorative presentation, roll one leaf Thai lemon basil into each spring roll. After placing the filling on the rice paper, place the leaf upside down in the center third of the paper. Roll up so that the leaf is visible through the top of the completed spring roll.

QUICK!
Sesame Chicken Skewers

½	cup defatted reduced-sodium chicken broth
¼	cup minced fresh parsley
¼	cup finely chopped scallions
2	tablespoons reduced-sodium soy sauce
4	teaspoons toasted sesame oil
2	cloves garlic, minced
2	teaspoons grated fresh ginger
½	teaspoon ground coriander
2–3	drops hot-pepper sauce

24 ounces boneless, skinless chicken breasts (about 6 breast halves), cut into ½"-wide strips

2 tablespoons sesame seeds

In a medium bowl, combine the broth, parsley, scallions, soy sauce, oil, garlic, ginger, coriander and hot-pepper sauce. Add the chicken and toss to coat. Cover and refrigerate for at least 15 minutes.

Preheat the broiler.

Drain the chicken. Discard the marinade. Thread the chicken strips on separate 6" metal skewers in loose S shapes. (See note if using wooden skewers.) Sprinkle with the sesame seeds.

Place the skewers on the rack of a broiling pan. Broil 4" from the heat for 3 minutes. Turn the skewers over and broil for 3 to 5 minutes more, or until the chicken is no longer pink.

Makes 8 servings. Per serving (3 skewers): 139 calories, 5.6 g. fat (37% of calories), 20.3 g. protein, 1.1 g. carbohydrates, 0.3 g. dietary fiber, 52 mg. cholesterol, 200 mg. sodium

NOTES

• For more intense flavor, marinate the chicken for up to 8 hours.

• If using wooden skewers, place them in a shallow pan and cover with water. Set aside to soak. This will keep the skewers from burning.

Meatballs in Sweet-and-Hot Sauce

Meatballs
10 ounces lean ground turkey breast
6 ounces extra-lean ground beef
¼ cup fat-free egg substitute
1 can (8½ ounces) water chestnuts, drained and chopped
¼ cup thinly sliced scallions

¼ cup unseasoned dry bread crumbs
¼ teaspoon ground black pepper

Sweet-and-Hot Sauce
¾ cup defatted reduced-sodium chicken broth
⅓ cup tomato ketchup
2 tablespoons brown sugar
½ teaspoon ground ginger
2–3 drops hot-pepper sauce
2 teaspoons cornstarch
3 tablespoons seasoned rice vinegar

To make the meatballs: Preheat the oven to 400°. Coat a no-stick baking sheet with no-stick spray and set aside.

In a large bowl, combine the turkey, beef, egg substitute, water chestnuts, scallions, bread crumbs and pepper. Mix well. Form the mixture into thirty 1" balls.

Place the meatballs on the prepared baking sheet. Bake for 15 minutes, or until no longer pink in the center when tested with a sharp knife. Keep warm in a serving bowl until ready to serve.

To make the sweet-and-hot sauce: In a small saucepan, whisk together the broth, ketchup, brown sugar, ginger and hot-pepper sauce. Dissolve the cornstarch in the vinegar and stir into the sauce. Cook over medium heat until the mixture comes to boil. Reduce the heat to low. Cook and stir for 1 minute, or until slightly thickened. Pour over the meatballs and gently toss to coat. Serve with toothpicks.

Makes 30. Per meatball: 38 calories, 0.8 g. fat (20% of calories), 3.8 g. protein, 3.8 g. carbohydrates, 0.3 g. dietary fiber, 10 mg. cholesterol, 57 mg. sodium

Stuffed Mushrooms

16 large mushrooms, cleaned
1 tablespoon olive oil
3 tablespoons dry sherry or nonalcoholic white wine
¼ cup chopped fresh parsley
1 tablespoon grated Parmesan cheese
1 tablespoon unseasoned dry bread crumbs
1 clove garlic, minced
¼ teaspoon dried thyme
¼ teaspoon dried oregano
Salt and ground black pepper

Preheat the oven to 375°. Coat a 9″ × 13″ no-stick baking dish with no-stick spray and set aside.

Remove and finely chop the mushroom stems; set aside.

In a cup, combine the oil and sherry or wine. Pour 2 tablespoons of the mixture into a medium no-stick skillet, reserving 2 table-spoons. Warm the skillet over medium-low heat. Add the chopped stems and sauté for 6 minutes, or until the mixture is dry.

Add the parsley, Parmesan, bread crumbs, garlic, thyme, oregano, salt and pepper. Remove from the heat and stir in 1 tablespoon of the remaining sherry mixture until moistened.

Spoon the mushroom mixture into the caps. Place in a single layer in the prepared dish. Bake for 15 to 20 minutes, or until the caps are tender and heated through. Halfway through the cooking time, brush the caps with the remaining 1 tablespoon sherry mixture. Serve hot.

Makes 16. Per cap: 19 calories, 1 g. fat (48% of calories), 0.5 g. protein, 1.3 g. carbohydrates, 0.3 g. dietary fiber, 0.3 mg. cholesterol, 12 mg. sodium

Greek Dolmades

These rice-stuffed grape leaves are best made a day ahead so the flavors have time to blend.

1 jar (16 ounces) grape leaves, rinsed
1¼ cups uncooked short-grain white rice
3½ cups defatted reduced-sodium chicken broth
5 tablespoons extra-virgin olive oil
1 onion, finely chopped
1 clove garlic, minced
2 tablespoons minced fresh dill
½ cup minced fresh parsley
½ cup lemon juice
Salt and ground black pepper

Using a knife, remove and discard the stems from the grape leaves. Set aside.

In a medium saucepan, combine the rice and broth. Bring to a boil. Reduce the heat to low, cover and simmer for 20 to 25 minutes, or until the liquid is absorbed. Set aside.

In a medium no-skillet over medium heat, warm 1 tablespoon of the oil. Add the onions and sauté for 5 to 8 minutes, or until softened but not browned. Stir in the garlic, dill, parsley and ¼ cup of the lemon juice. Remove from the heat.

Stir the onion mixture into the rice. Season with salt and pepper to taste. Set aside.

Preheat the oven to 350°.

On a flat surface, place one grape leaf, smooth side down, with the stem end toward you. Using a spoon, place about 1½ teaspoons of the rice mixture on the leaf 1″ from the stem end. Shape the mixture into a cylinder. Fold the stem end over the filling. Roll over once, then fold in the sides and roll up to en-close the filling. Place in a 9″ × 13″ glass or ceramic baking dish. Repeat with the remaining grape leaves and rice mixture.

Drizzle the bundles with the remaining 4 tablespoons oil and ¼ cup lemon juice. Cover with foil and bake for 30 minutes.

Remove from the oven and allow to cool for 10 minutes. Refrigerate for at least 4 hours, basting occasionally with the liquid. Serve chilled.

Makes 30. Per dolmade: 63 calories, 2.4 g. fat (34% of calories), 2.1 g. protein, 8.3 g. carbohydrates, 0.1 g. dietary fiber, 0 mg. cholesterol, 87 mg. sodium

QUICK!

Spinach-Cheese Quesadillas

1 small onion, finely chopped
1 cup washed and finely chopped fresh spinach
   Pinch of nutmeg
3 tablespoons shredded reduced-fat Cheddar cheese
3 tablespoons shredded reduced-fat Monterey Jack cheese
½ teaspoon chili powder
   Pinch of ground red pepper (optional)
2 large flour tortillas (12" diameter)

Generously coat a large no-stick skillet with no-stick spray and warm over medium heat. Add the onions and sauté for 6 minutes, or until lightly browned. Add the spinach and nutmeg. Cook for 1 to 2 minutes, or until the spinach is just wilted and heated through. Transfer to a medium bowl and set aside.

Meanwhile, in a small bowl, stir together the Cheddar, Monterey Jack, chili powder and pepper (if using). Set aside.

Return the skillet to medium-low heat and place 1 tortilla in the skillet. Quickly spread half of the cheese mixture over the surface of the tortilla. Spread the spinach mixture evenly over the cheese. Sprinkle with the remaining half of the cheese mixture and top with the second tortilla. Using a spatula, gently press the quesadilla to combine the layers.

Cook for 4 minutes per side, or until lightly browned and the cheese is melted. Cool slightly and cut into wedges. Serve warm.

Makes 8 wedges. Per wedge: 49 calories, 1.5 g. fat (28% of calories), 2.5 g. protein, 6.3 g. carbohydrates, 0.4 g. dietary fiber, 3 mg. cholesterol, 106 mg. sodium

NOTE
• Serve with your favorite salsa for dipping.

Spicy Roasted Chick-Peas

2 cups canned chick-peas, rinsed and drained
1½ teaspoons extra-virgin olive oil
½ teaspoon ground cumin
½ teaspoon ground coriander
¼ teaspoon ground red pepper
¼ teaspoon ground black pepper

Preheat the oven to 400°. Coat a no-stick baking sheet with no-stick spray and set aside.

In a small bowl, toss the chick-peas with the oil, cumin, coriander, red pepper and black pepper.

Place the chick-peas in a single layer on the prepared baking sheet. Bake for 30 to 40 minutes, or until crisp and golden.

Makes about 2 cups; 8 servings. Per serving: 50 calories, 1.6 g. fat (29% of calories), 2.0 g. protein, 7.1 g. carbohydrates, 2.1 g. dietary fiber, 0 mg. cholesterol, 170 mg. sodium

VARIATIONS
Southwestern Roasted Chick-Peas: Replace the coriander with chili powder.
Cajun Roasted Chick-Peas: Replace the cumin, coriander, red pepper and black pepper with 1 teaspoon Cajun Spice (page 33).

Herbed Ricotta Cherry Tomatoes

QUICK!

32 cherry tomatoes, stems removed
   Salt
10 dry-pack sun-dried tomato halves
¾ cup part-skim ricotta cheese
1 tablespoon grated Parmesan cheese
1 tablespoon snipped fresh chives
2 cloves garlic, minced
   Pinch of ground black pepper
2 tablespoons minced fresh basil

Cut a thin slice from the top of each cherry tomato. Carefully scoop out the seeds and flesh, leaving the shell intact. Lightly salt the insides of the tomatoes to draw out excess liquid. Invert on a rack to drain for 10 minutes. Rinse the tomatoes and set aside.

Meanwhile, place the sun-dried tomatoes in a small bowl. Cover with boiling water and set aside for 15 minutes, or until softened. Remove the tomatoes from the water. Finely chop the tomatoes and transfer to a medium bowl. Stir in the ricotta, Parmesan, chives, garlic and pepper. Mix well.

Spoon the cheese mixture into a pastry bag fitted with a small star tip. Pipe the mixture into each cherry tomato. Sprinkle each with a small amount of the basil. Serve chilled or at room temperature.

Makes 8 servings. Per serving (4 tomatoes): 86 calories, 2.5 g. fat (24% of calories), 5.1 g. protein, 13.1 g. carbohydrates, 2.1 g. dietary fiber, 8 mg. cholesterol, 65 mg. sodium

NOTE

• The sun-dried tomato soaking liquid may be reserved to use in sauces, soups or other dishes where a rich tomato flavor is desired. Freeze the liquid in an airtight container until ready to use.

VARIATION

Herbed Ricotta Snow Peas: Replace the cherry tomatoes with 32 snow peas. Remove the strings and ends from the snow peas. In a medium saucepan, bring a small amount of water to a boil. Add the snow peas and cook for 2 minutes. Drain and rinse with cold water.

Chili Bean Dip

QUICK!

1 can (15 ounces) red kidney or pinto beans, rinsed and drained
1½ teaspoons extra-virgin olive oil
1 teaspoon chili powder
1 teaspoon dried oregano
1 scallion, thinly sliced
1 clove garlic, minced
2 teaspoons chopped canned green chili peppers
¼ teaspoon ground red pepper

In a food processor or blender, combine the beans and oil. Process until smooth.

Add the chili powder, oregano, scallions, garlic, chili peppers and red pepper. Process using on/off turns, just until blended.

Makes about 1½ cups. Per 2 tablespoons: 38 calories, 0.9 g. fat (21% of calories), 2.9 g. protein, 7 g. carbohydrates, 2.3 g. dietary fiber, 0 mg. cholesterol, 69 mg. sodium

Hummus
QUICK!

Hummus is a popular Middle Eastern dip made from pureed chick-peas. Serve it with warm wedges of pita bread, whole-grain crackers or crudités (fresh cut vegetables).

- 1 can (16 ounces) chick-peas, rinsed and drained
- ⅓ cup nonfat plain yogurt
- ¼ cup minced scallions
- ¼ cup packed finely minced fresh parsley
  Juice of 2 lemons
- 5 teaspoons tahini (see note)
- 1 tablespoon extra-virgin olive oil
- 3 cloves garlic, minced
- ⅛ teaspoon ground black pepper
  Dash of reduced-sodium soy sauce
  Pinch of ground red pepper

In a food processor or blender, process the chick-peas until smooth. Occasionally stop to scrape down the sides of the bowl if necessary.

Add the yogurt, scallions, parsley, lemon juice, tahini, oil, garlic, black pepper and soy sauce. Process until smooth and creamy. (If necessary, add a small amount of water or canned bean liquid to achieve the desired consistency.)

Transfer to a serving bowl. Sprinkle with the red pepper. Serve at room temperature.

Makes about 1¾ cups. Per 2 tablespoons: 54 calories, 2.4 g. fat (39% of calories), 2.1 g. protein, 6.5 g. carbohydrates, 0 g. dietary fiber, 0.1 mg. cholesterol, 126 mg. sodium

NOTE
• Tahini, or sesame butter, is available in most supermarkets or Middle Eastern grocery stores.

Zucchini Bites

- 2 eggs
- 5 egg whites
- 4 cups shredded zucchini
- 1½ cups shredded fat-free mozzarella cheese
- 1 cup chopped onions
- ½ cup grated Parmesan cheese
- ½ cup all-purpose flour
- 1 tablespoon chopped fresh dill
- ¼ teaspoon baking powder

Preheat the oven to 350°. Coat a 9″ × 13″ no-stick baking dish with no-stick spray and set aside.

In a large bowl, beat together the eggs and egg whites. Stir in the zucchini, mozzarella, onions, Parmesan, flour, dill and baking powder.

Spoon the mixture into the prepared dish. Bake for 30 to 35 minutes, or until a toothpick inserted into the center comes out clean. Cool in the pan for 5 minutes. Cut into 24 squares. Serve warm or cold.

Makes 8 servings. Per serving (3 squares): 137 calories, 3.3 g. fat (22% of calories), 15.6 g. protein, 10.9 g. carbohydrates, 1.1 g. dietary fiber, 58 mg. cholesterol, 329 mg. sodium

VARIATION
Sun-Dried Tomato Zucchini Bites: Replace the dill with 1 tablespoon chopped fresh basil. Place 8 dry-pack sun-dried tomatoes in a cup or small bowl. Cover with boiling water and let soak for 15 minutes, or until softened. Finely chop and stir into the zucchini mixture.

Holiday Dinners

True, holidays are meant for a little indulgence. But too much festive food invariably results in unwanted pounds later on. The question becomes, "How can I enjoy the holidays without paying for them later?"

It's really quite simple. With a few tips from the experts, you can serve all the traditional holiday trimmings—without all the fat.

TALKING TURKEY

Typically the centerpiece of the Thanksgiving and Christmas feasts, turkey is perhaps the most popular holiday food. To enjoy your holiday bird without all the fat, here's what chefs advise.

Buy it lean. Look for the leanest varieties. These will be the ones that haven't been pumped up with butter or other fattening additives. Check the label: If it says "self-basting," it's high in fat—and you should pick another bird.

Spice up the flavor. To get the full-fledged flavor of your holiday bird without the fat, slip spices and herbs underneath the skin right against the meat. That way, you'll get their full flavor even after the skin has been removed.

Use a fat-free baste. Basting is essential to get that tender white meat that people love. Instead of drenching the bird in high-fat pan drippings, baste it with fat-free broth. You can even baste with fruit juice for a more zesty flavor.

STUFFINGS AND GRAVIES

A holiday dinner wouldn't be complete without stuffing and gravy. Here's how to include these favorites without tipping the scale.

Skip the giblets. Although organ meats have traditionally been added to holiday stuffings, they're high in fat and cholesterol. What's more, they really don't add very much to the overall flavor. Chances are, you'll never even notice that they're missing.

Trust broth. To moisten the stuffing, replace fatty butter, oil or pan drippings with defatted chicken broth. To boost the flavor, add fruit juices or dried herbs.

Bake it separately. Rather than cooking stuffing inside the bird, where it absorbs fat like a sponge, bake it in a separate dish. It will stay just as moist without picking up the extra calories.

Defat the pan juices. When making gravy using pan juices, pour off as much accumulated fat as possible. Then add some broth or water to the pan and scrape up the browned bits from the bottom. Transfer the liquid to a fat separator and pour off the fat-free liquid on the bottom.

Thicken with cornstarch. Rather than making gravy using the traditional butter-and-flour roux (a cooked combination of flour and fat used as a thickening agent), chefs advise thickening the gravy with cornstarch. Replace heavy cream with 1% low-fat milk to help keep the fat to a minimum.

LEAN DESSERTS

Cookies, cakes and pies are virtually synonymous with the holidays. The healthy cook can serve these desserts and still keep fat and calories to a minimum. Here's how.

Mix and match. An easy way to reduce fat in baked goods is to replace whole milk with 1% low-fat milk or skim milk. Of course, fat-free versions of dairy products by themselves don't always produce completely satisfying results. But you can often use a combination of fat-free and low-fat, or even fat-free and regular, for a healthier version of the original.

Cut fat with fruit. You can reduce fat in traditional cookies and cakes by up to 50 percent by replacing some of the butter or shortening with an equal amount of applesauce or another fruit puree.

Give pumpkin a try. Pecan pie is a holiday favorite. Unfortunately, the large amount of nuts used makes it high in fat. Instead of eliminating pie altogether, try celebrating with pumpkin. Everyone loves pumpkin pie, and it has about half the fat of traditional pecan pie.

Use skim milk. When making pumpkin pie, evaporated skim milk is a good low-fat substitute for heavy cream or half-and-half.

Serve pie à la yogurt. You can trim lots of fat from your holiday table by serving pie with low-fat frozen yogurt instead of ice cream.

Toast the nuts. All nuts (except chestnuts) are a high-fat ingredient. To reduce the fat, simply reduce the amount of nuts. To get more flavor from smaller amounts, toast them first in a dry no-stick skillet until fragrant. You can also replace some of the nuts with raisins, chopped dates or other dried fruit or even skillet-toasted rolled oats.

Add flavor without fat. When using reduced amounts of fat in desserts, enhance the flavor with grated citrus rind or baking spices like cinnamon, cloves or mace.

HEALTHY HOLIDAY EATING

If the holidays are a challenge for the healthy cook, they're even tougher on the guest. Temptations abound, from buttery cookies at Christmas to hot dogs and macaroni salad on the Fourth of July. Navigating the buffet table is like finding your way through a minefield. But it is possible to enjoy all the holidays without guilt. Here's how.

Don't starve yourself. Around the holidays, you may be tempted to skip a few meals to leave room for the big buffet looming in the near future. That's about the worst thing that you can do. You'll be so hungry that you'll end up hovering by the food, wolfing down everything in sight. It's better to eat regular meals and then snack lightly before heading to the party, preferably filling up on complex carbohydrates like potatoes, rice and pasta. These foods will help you feel satisfied, enabling you to make smart decisions about what to eat at the party.

Drink lots of water. If you really want to control your hunger, drink plenty of water. In generous amounts, water satisfies the appetite and curbs your food cravings.

Look lean. When you're scanning the buffet choices, look for the leanest foods. Good appetizer and snack choices include shrimp with cocktail sauce (not tartar sauce), pizza (if not too heavy on the cheese), fruit salad, fresh vegetable crudités, pretzels, crackers and unbuttered popcorn.

Choose turkey. Roast duck and goose are Christmas staples on some menus. But even without the skin, these birds contain twice as much fat as white-meat turkey.

Skip the skin. The skin is virtually the fattiest part of any bird. Baste it with butter or pan drippings, and you worsen the situation. Do yourself a favor by leaving it on your plate.

Trim the fat. If you're dining on roast beef or ham, trim away any visible fat, including the crispy bits. These are pure fat.

HOLIDAY TRIMMINGS WITHOUT THE FAT

You're heading off to a holiday party. You know that there will be lots of tempting food, and you want to make the best choices. Here are some traditionally fatty foods and some leaner alternatives for them.

TRADITIONAL FOOD	FAT (G.)	HEALTHIER CHOICE	FAT (G.)
½ cup eggnog	9	1 cup mulled cider	0
1 ounce cheese with crackers	17	¼ cup herbed yogurt dip with vegetable crudités	0
1 oz. roasted mixed nuts	15	1 oz. pretzels	1
1 oz. tortilla chips	8	1 cup unbuttered popcorn	0
3½ oz. fried chicken nuggets	18	3 oz. shrimp cocktail	1
½ cup potato salad	10	½ cup three-bean salad	0
4 oz. dark-meat turkey without skin	13	4 oz. white-meat turkey without skin	4
½ cup sweet potato casserole	7	1 baked sweet potato	0
½ cup green bean casserole	12	½ cup steamed green beans	0
1 crescent roll	4	1 brown-and-serve roll	1
½ cup sausage stuffing	16	½ cup cornbread stuffing	6
1 nut brownie	6	1 cup fruit salad	1
1 slice cheesecake	16	1 slice angel food cake with fruit	0
1 slice pecan pie with ice cream	31	1 slice pumpkin pie with frozen yogurt	15

Fresh is best. When it comes to the Thanksgiving cranberry sauce, choose fresh cranberry relish. It often contains a lot less sugar than regular canned cranberry sauce.

Pick a pilaf. If you have a choice between stuffing and rice pilaf, choose the pilaf—especially if the stuffing was cooked in the bird, where it soaks up extra fat during baking. Rice pilaf has far less fat than most stuffings.

Gobble up the greens. Vegetables are always a big part of holiday buffets. By filling up on salads and other vegetables, you'll get the best of the buffet table and still have room for a few sweets.

Feed on fruit. Fresh fruit is a holiday buffet staple. It's sweet, delicious and good for you, too. To satisfy your sweet tooth, seek out the grapes, apples, oranges, pineapple and other fresh fruits on the table.

Take a sample. Some of the more sinful buffet offerings may be too tempting to pass up. Rather than deny yourself, take a small sampling of these decadent foods. This way, you can enjoy them, not feel deprived and still not do yourself any real damage.

Christian Chavanne

All too often, the excitement and abundant good feelings of the holidays are accompanied by a similar abundance of delicious but calorie-laden fare. For Christian Chavanne of Marabella Restaurant in Corpus Christi, Texas, the trick is taking traditional (and overly rich) dishes and transforming them into something new and lean.

"I simply break them into components and analyze their texture, mouthfeel and flavor," he says. "Then I recreate the dish with the same eye appeal and overall good flavor."

The traditional version of this harvest salad contains diced cheese, crispy fried bacon and a dressing containing ¾ cup oil. Christian cut way back on the oil and cheese (he uses shredded cheese to make the smaller amount go further). He replaces the crunchiness of bacon with croutons and gets bacon's flavor from a little liquid smoke.

He uses a mix of mesclun greens as the base of the salad. If you like, you can use a mixture of Bibb lettuce, radicchio, red-leaf lettuce, spinach and watercress.

Harvest Salad

Dressing
- 2 beets, cooked, peeled and diced
- 1 cup cranberry juice
- 3 tablespoons red-wine vinegar
- 2 tablespoons Dijon mustard
- 2 tablespoons extra-virgin olive oil
- 1 shallot, minced
- 1 clove garlic, minced
- 4 drops liquid smoke
  Salt and ground black pepper

Salad
- 2 quarts torn mixed greens
- 4 thick slices crusty French bread, diced and oven-toasted
- 1 large firm pear, cut into 16 wedges
- 1 Fuyu persimmon, diced
- 2 cups pomegranate seeds
- ¼ cup shredded Parmesan or Romano cheese
- 2 tablespoons chopped toasted walnuts (see note)

To make the dressing: In a blender, combine the beets, cranberry juice, vinegar, mustard, oil, shallots, garlic and liquid smoke. Blend for 1 to 2 minutes, or until smooth. Season with the salt and pepper.

To make the salad: In a large bowl, toss the greens with the croutons and one-quarter of the dressing. Divide among salad plates. Top with the pears and persimmons. Drizzle with the remaining dressing. Sprinkle with the pomegranate seeds, Parmesan or Romano and walnuts.

Makes 6 servings. Per serving: 281 calories, 8.8 g. fat (27% of calories), 7.6 g. protein, 46.8 g. carbohydrates, 4.9 g. dietary fiber, 3 mg. cholesterol, 342 mg. sodium

NOTE
• To toast the walnuts, place them in a dry no-stick skillet over medium heat. Toast the nuts, shaking the skillet often, for 3 to 5 minutes, or until fragrant.

THANKSGIVING

Having a healthy holiday doesn't mean depriving yourself of great food. To prove it, we've put together a Thanksgiving feast that you and your family will love. Indulge in pumpkin soup and chive biscuits, roast turkey, cranberry sauce, green beans, candied sweet potatoes and delicious poached pears for dessert. All that, and the whole meal has just 12 grams of fat per serving. This Thanksgiving dinner is so lean, there's even room for a slice of Pumpkin Pie (page 454).

Thanksgiving Dinner Menu

Serves 8

Pumpkin Soup, **120**
Rolled Biscuits, **353**
*Roasted Turkey Breast with Cranberry
 Sauce,* **558**
Ginger Green Beans, **559**
Candied Sweet Potatoes, **559**
Spiced Poached Pears with Cranberries, **429**

Roasted Turkey Breast with Cranberry Sauce

Here's a clever way to reduce the fat in your holiday bird. Use only the lean, tasty breast and marinate it overnight in a flavorful mixture of crushed spices and yogurt. The sweet-tart cranberry sauce makes this dish a winner that the whole family will love.

Turkey
1 boneless, skinless turkey breast half (about 2¼ pounds)
¾ cup nonfat plain yogurt
2 cloves garlic, minced
1 tablespoon apple cider vinegar
1 teaspoon black peppercorns, crushed
1 teaspoon cumin seed, crushed
1 teaspoon dried rosemary, crushed
1 teaspoon minced fresh ginger
½ teaspoon ground cinnamon

Cranberry Sauce
2 cups fresh cranberries
½ cup dried apple slices
  Grated rind of 1 orange
1 cup orange juice
½ cup all-fruit apple butter
3 tablespoons maple syrup

To make the turkey: Rinse the turkey with cold water and pat dry with paper towels. Set aside.

In a large nonreactive bowl, combine the yogurt, garlic, vinegar, pepper, cumin, rosemary, ginger and cinnamon. Add the turkey and turn to coat evenly. Cover and refrigerate overnight, turning the meat occasionally.

To make the cranberry sauce: While the turkey is marinating, in a food processor or blender, combine the cranberries, apples, orange rind and orange juice. Process using on/off turns until finely chopped but not pureed. Transfer the mixture to a medium saucepan. Add the apple butter and maple syrup. Bring to a boil over high heat. Reduce the heat to low and simmer, uncovered, for about 10 minutes. Transfer to a serving bowl and allow to cool.

Cover and refrigerate until serving time.

To roast the turkey, remove it from the marinade and place it in an oven cooking bag. Discard the marinade. Roast the turkey according to the manufacturer's directions, or until the internal temperature of the turkey reaches 170°. Start checking the internal temperature after 1 hour.

Remove the turkey from the cooking bag and let stand for 10 minutes before slicing and serving. Serve with the cranberry sauce.

Makes 8 servings. Per serving: 252 calories, 1.2 g. fat (4% of calories), 32.6 g. protein, 27.5 g. carbohydrates, 1.9 g. dietary fiber, 85 mg. cholesterol, 76 mg. sodium

NOTE
• This recipe works well in a clay cooker. Simply place the marinated turkey breast in the clay cooker, cover and bake at 350° for 1 to 1½ hours, or until cooked through. The turkey is cooked through when the internal temperature reaches 170°.

QUICK!
Ginger Green Beans

Need a quick dish? These fragrant green beans are ready in less than 15 minutes. And they taste great.

1	package (16 ounces) frozen whole green beans
1	tablespoon nondiet tub-style margarine or butter
½	cup chopped shallots
1	tablespoon crystallized ginger
½	teaspoon grated lemon rind
⅛	teaspoon ground black pepper

In a medium saucepan, bring 1″ of water to a boil. Place the green beans on a steaming rack and set the rack in the pan. Cover and steam for 7 to 9 minutes, or until the beans are tender. Remove the steaming rack and set aside. Drain the pan.

In the same pan over low heat, melt the margarine or butter. Add the shallots and ginger. Sauté for 4 minutes, or until the shallots are tender. Add the green beans, lemon rind and pepper. Cook for 1 minute, or until heated through.

Makes 8 servings. Per serving: 39 calories, 1.5 g. fat (32% of calories), 1 g. protein, 6.4 g. carbohydrates, 0 g. dietary fiber, 0 mg. cholesterol, 28 mg. sodium

QUICK!
Candied Sweet Potatoes

Yes! This holiday favorite can be included in a healthy menu. We kept in just enough of the "candy" so it tastes delicious but isn't overloaded with excess fat and sugar.

1¼	pounds sweet potatoes, peeled and cut into 2″ pieces
½	cup chopped onions
1	Granny Smith apple, cut into 1″ pieces
¼	cup raisins
¼	cup orange juice
2	tablespoons brown sugar
2	tablespoons nondiet tub-style margarine or butter
½	teaspoon grated orange rind

In a large saucepan, combine the potatoes and onions. Add 1″ of water to the pan. Cover and simmer over medium heat for 8 minutes, or until the potatoes are tender. Drain, returning the vegetables to the pan.

Add the apples, raisins, orange juice, brown sugar, margarine or butter and orange rind. Cook over low heat, stirring frequently, until the liquid reduces slightly and glazes the potatoes and apples.

Makes 8 servings. Per serving: 127 calories, 3.1 g. fat (21% of calories), 1.3 g. protein, 24.7 g. carbohydrates, 0.8 g. dietary fiber, 0 mg. cholesterol, 48 mg. sodium

CHRISTMAS

Every year at Christmas, many of us serve the same old fatty roast beef, turkey or ham, with sugary cakes and pies for dessert. This year, make something special. Give your family a Christmas dinner that has all the holiday trimmings with just a fraction of the fat. The centerpiece of this meal is a savory roast pork tenderloin. For dessert, indulge in a beautiful holiday stollen jeweled with fruit and drizzled with a snow-white glaze. If you like more than one dessert on your Christmas table, round out the meal with moist and tender Apple Crumb Pie (page 452).

Christmas Dinner Menu

Serves 8

Hot Mulled Apple-Cranberry Punch, **560**
Glazed Roast Pork Tenderloin, **561**
Mashed Potatoes with Root Vegetables, **387**
Herbed Peas and Onions, **561**
Glazed Acorn Squash Rings, **390**
Fruit-Stuffed Stollen with Almond Glaze, **334**

QUICK!
Hot Mulled Apple-Cranberry Punch

Looking for a little Christmas spirit? This warm beverage is spiced just right to put you and your guests in the holiday mood.

    4 cups water
    3 cups fresh or frozen cranberries
    3 cups apple cider
    ½ cup sugar
    1 cinnamon stick, broken into pieces
    1 teaspoon whole cloves
    ⅛ teaspoon ground nutmeg
       Rind of 1 orange, cut in 1 continuous strip
       Cinnamon sticks
       Orange slices

In a large saucepan over medium-high heat, combine the water, cranberries, apple cider, sugar, cinnamon stick, cloves, nutmeg and orange rind. Bring to a boil. When the cranberries begin to pop, reduce the heat to low. Cover and simmer for 10 to 15 minutes, or until the berries are tender. Remove from the heat.

Strain the mixture, discarding the solids. Pour into mugs and serve warm garnished with the cinnamon sticks and orange slices.

Makes 6 cups. Per ¾ cup: 118 calories, 0.2 g. fat (1% of calories), 0.3 g. protein, 31.4 g. carbohydrates, 1.9 g. dietary fiber, 0 mg. cholesterol, 3 mg. sodium

NOTE
• If cranberries are unavailable, you can replace the cranberries, water and sugar with 3 cups cranberry juice cocktail.

VARIATIONS
Hot Mulled Cranberry-Apricot Punch: Replace the apple cider with apricot nectar.
Hot Mulled Cranberry-Pear Punch: Replace the apple cider with pear nectar.

Glazed Roast Pork Tenderloin

Here's a surefire hit for the holidays. Juicy roast pork tenderloin is glazed with an irresistible mixture of honey, mustard, orange and cinnamon. And it only takes 30 minutes to cook.

¼ cup Dijon mustard
2 tablespoons orange juice
2 tablespoons honey
1 teaspoon grated orange rind
¼ teaspoon ground cinnamon
⅛ teaspoon ground allspice
2 pounds pork tenderloin, trimmed of all visible fat

Preheat the oven to 325°.

In a small bowl, whisk together the mustard, orange juice, honey, orange rind, cinnamon and allspice. Set aside.

Place the pork on a rack in a shallow roasting pan. Insert a meat thermometer into the center of the pork. Roast for 30 minutes, or until the thermometer registers 160°. During the last 10 minutes of roasting, brush the pork occasionally with the mustard mixture.

Remove from the oven and let stand for 5 minutes before slicing and serving.

Makes 8 servings. Per serving: 162 calories, 4.5 g. fat (26% of calories), 23.9 g. protein, 5.2 g. carbohydrates, 0.1 g. dietary fiber, 65 mg. cholesterol, 147 mg. sodium

Herbed Peas and Onions

QUICK!

Thyme, dill and sautéed onions give sweet peas a savory flavor that pairs well with almost any main dish.

1 tablespoon extra-virgin olive oil
2 onions, thinly sliced and separated into rings
1 cup reduced-sodium chicken broth
2 teaspoons dried thyme
1 teaspoon salt-free lemon-herb seasoning
2 packages (10 ounces each) frozen peas, thawed
2 tablespoons chopped fresh dill

In a large no-stick skillet over medium heat, warm the oil. Add the onions and cook, stirring frequently, for 6 to 8 minutes, or until the onions are lightly browned.

Stir in the broth, thyme and lemon-herb seasoning. Bring to a boil over high heat. Reduce the heat to low and stir in the peas. Cover and cook for 6 to 8 minutes more, or until the peas are heated through and tender. Uncover and cook 1 minute longer, or until most of the liquid evaporates. Sprinkle with the dill before serving.

Makes 8 servings. Per serving: 89 calories, 2.1 g. fat (20% of calories), 4.4 g. protein, 14 g. carbohydrates, 3.4 g. dietary fiber, 0 mg. cholesterol, 71 mg. sodium

EASTER

Easter supper provides the perfect opportunity to showcase the bounty of spring in one special meal. This menu includes asparagus, dill, potatoes, watercress, arugula and an extraordinary roast lamb loin. Dessert is a deliciously simple peach sherbet parfait. If you prefer a more traditional holiday ham in place of the lamb, this menu works wonderfully with the Orange-Braised Pork Tenderloins (page 273).

QUICK!

Spring Greens and Strawberries with Poppy Seed Dressing

Here's a lively salad. Tangy watercress and arugula get a touch of sweetness from orange juice, poppy seeds and strawberries.

3   cups watercress leaves
3   cups torn arugula leaves
3   cups sliced strawberries
¼   cup orange juice
2   teaspoons olive oil
2   teaspoons poppy seeds
½   teaspoon grated orange rind

In a large bowl, combine the watercress, arugula and strawberries.

In a small bowl, whisk together the orange juice, oil, poppy seeds and orange rind. Pour the dressing over the salad and toss gently to combine.

Makes 8 servings. Per serving: 37 calories, 1.7 g. fat (38% of calories), 1 g. protein, 5.4 g. carbohydrates, 1.2 g. dietary fiber, 0 mg. cholesterol, 8 mg. sodium

NOTE
• For a delicious twist on this salad, add 1 cup fiddlehead ferns. Fiddlehead ferns taste like a cross between green beans and asparagus. You can use blanched green beans or asparagus as a substitute for fiddlehead ferns.

VARIATION
Spinach Salad with Strawberries: Replace the watercress and arugula with 6 cups torn tender spinach leaves. For a nutty crunch, add ⅓ cup sliced toasted almonds.

Spicy Lamb Loin

If only every entrée could be this good. Tender lamb loin is rubbed with spices, pan-seared then oven-roasted. It's then served over orzo pasta and topped with a simple sauce featuring thyme, shallots and balsamic vinegar. The whole dish comes together in less than 45 minutes.

- 2 pounds boneless lamb loin, trimmed of all visible fat
- 2 tablespoons freshly cracked peppercorns
- 2 tablespoons freshly cracked coriander seeds
- ½ cup balsamic vinegar
- 2 tablespoons minced shallots or onions
- 1 teaspoon dried thyme
- 2 bay leaves
- 2 cups defatted reduced-sodium beef broth
- 4 teaspoons butter or margarine
- ¼ cup minced fresh parsley
- 6 cups cooked orzo pasta

Preheat the oven to 400°.

Cut the lamb loin into 4 fillets. Firmly press the peppercorns and coriander into both sides of each fillet.

Coat a large no-stick skillet with no-stick spray and warm over medium-high heat. Sear the fillets on both sides, then transfer to an ovenproof pan.

Roast the fillets in the oven for 10 to 15 minutes. Remove from the oven and set aside for 5 minutes.

Meanwhile, return the skillet to medium heat. Add the vinegar, shallots or onions, thyme and bay leaves. Cook for 3 to 4 minutes, scraping any browned bits from the bottom of the skillet. Stir in the broth and bring to a boil. Boil for 2 to 3 minutes, or until the liquid is slightly reduced.

Reduce the heat to low and whisk in the butter or margarine. Stir in the parsley. Remove and discard the bay leaves. Keep the mixture warm.

To serve, cut the lamb into very thin slices. Serve with the orzo and drizzle the sauce over the lamb.

Makes 8 servings. Per serving: 380 calories, 11.2 g. fat (27% of calories), 29.6 g. protein, 38.9 g. carbohydrates, 0.4 g. dietary fiber, 79 mg. cholesterol, 97 mg. sodium

Candied Carrot Coins

The sweet flavor of candied carrots is welcome in any menu. Plus, they're packed with health-boosting beta-carotene.

- 2 pounds carrots, sliced ¼" thick
- 1 cup brown sugar
- 1 tablespoon nondiet tub-style margarine

In a medium saucepan, bring 2" water to a boil. Place the carrots on a steaming rack and set the rack in the pan. Cover and steam for 15 to 20 minutes, or until the carrots are tender. Remove the steaming rack and set aside.

Measure 1 cup cooking liquid and discard the remainder. Return the liquid to the pan and add the sugar and margarine. Bring to a boil over high heat. Stir until the brown sugar dissolves. Reduce the heat to low and simmer for 10 minutes, or until the liquid reduces slightly. Add the carrots and cook for 10 minutes, or until the liquid is reduced and the carrots are glazed.

Makes 6 servings. Per serving: 221 calories, 2.2 g. fat (9% of calories), 1.5 g. protein, 51.2 g. carbohydrates, 0 g. dietary fiber, 0 mg. cholesterol, 138 mg. sodium

PASSOVER

The Passover seder meal commemorates Jewish heritage with a variety of symbolic foods. We've updated these dishes to cut fat, calories and cholesterol without sacrificing flavor. Egg whites replace whole eggs in a delicious version of matzo ball soup. And the main-dish turkey cutlets have less than 1 gram of fat per serving. In keeping with Kosher dietary laws, dishes made without meat or dairy products are labeled "pareve."

Passover Dinner Menu

Serves 6

Charoset, **564**
Matzo Ball Soup, **565**
Passover Spinach Squares, **565**
Baked Turkey Cutlets with Vegetables, **566**
Passover Sponge Cake with Strawberries, **566**

Charoset (pareve)

Charoset is a simple fruit-and-nut mixture that represents the mortar and bricks that the captive Israelites used to build the cities of Egypt. This version has less fat and sugar than traditional recipes and still tastes delicious.

1	Red Delicious apple, finely chopped
¼	cup finely chopped toasted walnuts (see note)

¼	cup chopped dates
¼	cup dark raisins
1	tablespoon sugar
2	tablespoons sweet red wine or grape juice
¼	teaspoon ground cinnamon

In a medium bowl, stir together the apples, walnuts, dates, raisins, sugar, wine or grape juice and cinnamon. Refrigerate for 10 minutes before serving.

Makes about 2 cups. Per ¼ cup: 72 calories, 2.3 g. fat (27% of calories), 1.2 g. protein, 12.5 g. carbohydrates, 1.2 g. dietary fiber, 0 mg. cholesterol, 3 mg. sodium

NOTE
• To toast the walnuts, place them in a dry no-stick skillet over medium heat. Toast the nuts, shaking the skillet often, for 3 to 5 minutes, or until fragrant.

Matzo Ball Soup

We updated these matzo balls by using egg whites and a reduced amount of oil. The soup is simple and flavorful, and the matzo balls are as tender as can be.

4	egg whites
1	tablespoon canola oil
⅓	cup matzo meal
3	carrots, sliced
6	cups defatted chicken broth
2	tablespoons chopped fresh parsley
	Pinch of ground black pepper

In a large clean bowl, using an electric mixer, beat the egg whites until foamy. Stir in the oil. Add the matzo meal and blend well. Cover and refrigerate for 20 minutes. Shape the mixture into 6 balls and set aside.

Bring a large pot of water to a boil over high heat. Carefully drop the matzo balls into the water. Add the carrots. Reduce the heat to medium-low, cover and simmer for 30 minutes.

Drain the mixture, returning the carrots and matzo balls to the pot. Add the broth and cook over medium heat until heated through. Divide the soup among 6 soup bowls. Garnish each serving with equal amounts of the parsley and pepper.

Makes 6 servings. Per serving: 98 calories, 3.2 g. fat (29% of calories), 5.7 g. protein, 11.4 g. carbohydrates, 1.1 g. dietary fiber, 0 mg. cholesterol, 114 mg. sodium

Passover Spinach Squares (pareve)

Serve these nibbles as an appetizer with the main course. You can replace the fresh spinach with 3 packages (10 ounces each) frozen and thawed chopped spinach.

1½	pounds fresh spinach, stemmed and washed
1½	teaspoons canola oil
1	leek, thinly sliced (white part only)
2	cloves garlic, minced
2	teaspoons lemon juice
¾	teaspoon dried oregano
⅛	teaspoon ground black pepper
3	egg whites

Preheat the oven to 350°. Coat an 8″ × 8″ no-stick baking dish with pareve no-stick spray and set aside.

In a large pot, bring a small amount of water to a boil. Add the spinach, cover and cook over medium heat for 5 minutes, or until the spinach is wilted. Squeeze the spinach dry, chop and place in a large bowl.

In a small no-stick skillet over low heat, warm the oil. Add the leeks and garlic. Sauté for 10 minutes, or until tender but not browned. Add the leek mixture to the bowl with the spinach. Stir in the lemon juice, oregano and pepper.

In another clean large bowl, using an electric mixer, beat the egg whites until foamy. Fold into the spinach mixture.

Pour the mixture into the prepared pan and bake for 35 minutes, or until set. Remove from the oven and set aside to cool slightly. Cut into 16 squares and serve warm.

Makes 16. Per square: 22 calories, 0.6 g. fat (22% of calories), 2 g. protein, 2.9 g. carbohydrates, 1.3 g. dietary fiber, 0 mg. cholesterol, 45 mg. sodium

Baked Turkey Cutlets with Vegetables

You couldn't ask for an easier holiday main dish. Just combine lean turkey cutlets with vegetables and herbs and bake for 30 minutes. It's perfect for Passover.

1¼ pounds turkey breast cutlets
1 onion, thinly sliced
1 sweet red pepper, thinly sliced
1 green pepper, thinly sliced
8 ounces mushrooms, thinly sliced
½ teaspoon dried thyme
½ teaspoon dried sage
⅛ teaspoon salt (optional)
⅛ teaspoon ground black pepper

Preheat the oven to 350°.

Cut the turkey cutlets into 6 equal-size pieces and place them in a nonreactive 8″ × 8″ no-stick baking dish. Top with the onions, red peppers, green peppers and mushrooms. Sprinkle with the thyme, sage, salt (if using) and black pepper.

Cover with foil and bake for 30 minutes, or until the vegetables are tender and the turkey is cooked through and no longer pink.

Makes 6 servings. Per serving: 138 calories, 0.9 g. fat (6% of calories), 24.5 g. protein, 8.1 g. carbohydrates, 1.9 g. dietary fiber, 63 mg. cholesterol, 42 mg. sodium

NOTE

• This dish can be prepared ahead up to the point of baking. After covering the dish with foil, refrigerate for up to 24 hours. Before serving, remove the dish from the refrigerator and bake as directed.

Passover Sponge Cake with Strawberries (pareve)

This tender sponge cake makes a wonderful finale for a spring Passover meal. The crowning touch is a delicious strawberry topping. You'd never guess the whole cake has less than 3 grams of fat per serving.

1 quart strawberries, hulled and sliced
1 cup sugar
⅓ cup matzo cake meal
2 tablespoons potato starch
4 eggs, separated
2 tablespoons lemon juice
1 teaspoon grated lemon rind

Preheat the oven to 325°. Coat a 9″ no-stick pie pan with no-stick spray and set aside.

In a medium bowl, toss the strawberries with ¼ cup of the sugar. Set aside for about 1 hour, stirring occasionally.

Meanwhile, in a cup or small bowl, whisk together the cake meal and potato starch; set aside.

In a large clean bowl, using an electric mixer, beat the egg whites until soft peaks form. Set aside.

In another large bowl, beat the egg yolks until light and lemon colored. Add the remaining ¾ cup sugar and beat well. At low speed, blend in the cake-meal mixture, lemon juice and lemon rind. Fold in the egg whites.

Pour the batter into the prepared pan. Bake until the top is golden brown and springs back when lightly touched. Remove from the pan and cool completely on a wire rack.

When completely cool, cut the cake into 8 wedges. Serve with the strawberries.

Makes 8 servings. Per serving: 193 calories, 2.8 g. fat (13% of calories), 4.1 g. protein, 39.1 g. carbohydrates, 1.5 g. dietary fiber, 106 mg. cholesterol, 33 mg. sodium

MENUS FOR SPECIAL OCCASIONS

Whether it's a holiday, birthday party or just time to celebrate, some meals should be more special than others. Planning these feasts is half the work, so we've done it for you. The menus below coordinate this book's best dishes into complete and healthy meals. Here's to a special occasion that celebrates good taste and good health.

Valentine's Day Dinner Menu

Spinach and Mandarin Orange Salad, **98**
Sun-Dried Tomato and Goat Cheese Risotto, **172**
Roast Swordfish with Herbed Crust, **247**
Hot Chocolate Soufflé, **470**

Outdoor Picnic

Zucchini Bites, **553**
Chicken Salad, **97**
Three-Bean Picnic Salad, **101**
Marinated Summer Berries, **427**
Glazed Golden Bundt Cake, **484**

Mother's Day Dinner Menu

Tomato-and-Cucumber Salad, **98**
Asparagus and Couscous, **373**
Poached Salmon with Horseradish-Dill Sauce, **248**
Sponge Cake with Strawberry Filling, **483**

Child's Birthday Party

Devil's Food Chocolate Layer Cake, **466**
Banana Ice Cream, **433**
Chocolate Sauce, **472**
Easy Fudge Brownies, **470**
Crunchy Peanut Butter Cookies, **492**

Sunday Brunch

Strawberry Waffles, **351**
Spinach-and-Mushroom Frittata, **305**
White Bean Soufflé, **193**
Cranberry-Orange Muffins, **345**

Wedding Anniversary

Warm Peach Soup with Fruit Sorbets, **411**
Lemon Chicken, **209**
Italian Wild Rice Pilaf, **164**
Apple Strudel, **459**

Summer Barbecue

Grilled Skewered Portobello Mushrooms, **546**
Zesty Barbecued Chicken Breasts, **76**
Potato Salad, **100**
Apricot-Blackberry Pie, **452**

Father's Day Dinner Menu

French Onion Soup, **115**
Herb Dinner Rolls, **325**
Savory Beef Tenderloin, **265**
Cherry Pie, **451**

Index

Note: <u>Underscored</u> page references indicate boxed text. **Boldfaced** references indicate illustrations.

Croutons, homemade, 90–91
Crudités, 539–40
   arranging platters of, <u>533</u>, **533**
Crumb crusts, 438
   Chocolate Crumb Crust, 450
   Gingersnap Crumb Crust, 450
   Graham Cracker Crust, 449–50
   Vanilla-Nut Crumb Crust, 450
Crumble, <u>439</u>
Crusts
   crumb, 438
     recipes
      Chocolate Crumb Crust, 450
      Gingersnap Crumb Crust, 450
      Graham Cracker Crust, 449–50
      Vanilla-Nut Crumb Crust, 450
   herb, 253–54, <u>255</u>
   meringue
     Meringue Pie Shell, 451
   pastry, 438–46
     decorative finishes for, <u>444–45</u>, **444–45**
     dough consistency for, <u>440</u>
     filled vs. unfilled, 445–46
     glazing, 446
     moving, <u>446</u>
     problems with, 440
     recipes
      Basic Pie Crust, 449
      Basic Tart Crust, 450
      Basic Whole-Wheat Tart Crust, 450
      Whole-Wheat Pie Crust, 449
Cuban-style dishes
   Cuban Beans, 190–91
Cubing foods, <u>17</u>, 17
Cucumbers, 362, <u>362</u>, 362
   Herb-Scented Refrigerator Pickles, 523
   Mustard-Glazed Salmon with Cucumber Relish, 248
   Sweet-and-Sour Refrigerator Pickles, 523
   Tomato-and-Cucumber Salad, 98
Cupcakes
   Light Lemon Cupcakes, 487
   Pineapple Upside-Down Cupcakes, 487
Currants
   Currant Scones, 347
Curry
   recipes (*see* Curry recipes)
   sauce, 503–4

Curry recipes
   Chick-Pea and Potato Curry, 194
   Creamy Curry Sauce, 512
   Curried Brown Rice with Mushrooms and Peas, 166
   Curried Chicken Salad, 97
   Curried Potatoes and Peas, 297
   Curried Red Lentils, 189
   Curried Tofu with Squash and Lima Beans, 291
   Curry Powder, <u>33</u>
Custard
   Blueberry Compote with Vanilla Custard, 430
   Blueberry Custard Tart, 455–56
   Cherry Compote with Vanilla Custard, 430
   Cherry Custard Tart, 456
Cutlery. *See* Knives
Cutting
   foods by hand, <u>16–17</u>, **16–17**
   mangoes, <u>406</u>, **406**
   onions, <u>42</u>, **42**

D

Daily Value, on food label, <u>3</u>
Dairy products, calcium in, 8
Dates
   Charoset, 564
   Dried Fruit Truffles, 495
Defrosting
   meat, 22
   poultry, 201–2
Desserts
   chocolate, 460–72
   cookies, cakes and bars, 473–97
   fruit, 419–35
   low-fat, 555
   pies, crisps and other sweets, 438–59
Dicing foods, <u>16</u>, 16
Dill, 90, <u>103</u>
   Creamy Tarragon-and-Dill Sauce, 511
   Grilled Tuna Steaks with Chive and Dill Sauce, <u>77</u>, **77**
   Mixed Herb Pesto, 507
   Poached Salmon with Horseradish-Dill Sauce, 248
   Steamed Sole with Creamy Dill Sauce, <u>237</u>, **237**
Dips, 552–53
   beans in, <u>183</u>
   low-fat, <u>539</u>

Dolmades
   Greek Dolmades, 550–51
Dough
   bread
     kneading, 315–16, <u>316</u>, **316**
     making, <u>315</u>, 315–17
     microwaving, <u>317</u>
     shaping, <u>318–19</u>, **318–19**
     stickiness of, <u>317</u>
   pasta, recipes
     Basic Pasta Dough, <u>132–33</u>, **132**
     Beet Pasta Dough, <u>133</u>
     Herbed Pasta Dough, <u>133</u>
     Lemon-Pepper Pasta Dough, <u>133</u>
     Spinach Pasta Dough, <u>133</u>
     Tomato Pasta Dough, <u>133</u>
     Whole-Wheat Pasta Dough, <u>133</u>
   pastry (*see also* Crusts, pastry)
     consistency of, <u>440</u>
     freezing, <u>442</u>
     mixing, 442–43
     moving, <u>446</u>
     rolling, 443–44
   phyllo, <u>441</u>
   pizza
     Basic Pizza Dough, <u>542–43</u>, **542, 543**
Dough scraper, 310
Dressings
   poultry (*see* Stuffings)
   salad (*see* Salad dressings)
Dried fruit. *See* Fruit(s), dried
Duck, 207
   Grilled Herbed Duck Breasts, 219–20
Dumplings
   Turkey Stew with Herb Dumplings, 127
Dutch oven, heavy-gauge, 13
DV, on food label, <u>3</u>

E

Easter menu, 562–63
   Egg noodles, cholesterol in, <u>131</u>
Eggplant, 361–62
   Balsamic Barbecue Kebabs, 300
   Chick-Pea, Eggplant and Tomato Casserole, 194
   Eggplant Caponata, 374
   Eggplant Chili, 197, 304
   Eggplant Parmesan, 307
   Garden Vegetable Kebabs, 300

legumes and, 179
for salads, 89–90
for seasoning vegetables, 281
in soups, 110
storing, 30
Holiday dinners, 554–67
Hominy, 160, 161
Honey, 342
Honey-Oatmeal Bread, 330–31
Pork Tenderloin with Honey-Mint Sauce, 275
Honeydew melon
Cold Melon Soup, 435
Melon Sorbet, 432
Sparkling Fruit Salad with Mint, 412
Honey mustard
Honey-Mustard Catfish, 272
Honey-Mustard Pork Tenderloins, 272
Hors d'oeuvres, 538–41, 546–53
Horseradish, 8, 8
Horseradish Sauce, 511
Mashed Potatoes with Horseradish, 387
Poached Salmon with Horseradish-Dill Sauce, 248
Hot-air corn popper, 20
Hot sauces, bottled, 519
Hummus, 553

I

Ice, for entertaining, 545
Ice cream
Banana Ice Cream, 433
Berry-Banana Ice Cream, 433
Icings. *See* Frostings; Glazes
Immersion blender, 14
Indian-style dishes. *See also* Curry
Indian Burger, 302
Indian-Style Pork, 270
Indoor countertop grills, 69, 69
Instant-read thermometer, 21, 21
Italian green beans, 184
Italian-style dishes. *See also* Pasta; Pizza
Chicken Cacciatore, 211
Creamy Italian Dressing, 103
Italian Herb Crust, 255
Italian Herb Seasoning, 32
Italian Minestrone, 119
Italian-Style Pork over Linguine, 273

Italian-Style Vegetable Stew, 304
Italian Wild Rice Pilaf, 164
Meatballs Cacciatore, 211
Poached Flounder Italian-Style, 51, 51
Sausage Sandwiches, 211

J

Jacob's cattle beans, 183
Jalapeño pepper jelly
Lamb with Jalapeño Mint Sauce, 275
Jalapeño peppers
Jalapeño Corn Muffins, 345
Jambalaya
Chicken-and-Ham Jambalaya, 225
Turkey-and-Sausage Jambalaya, 225
Vegetarian Jambalaya, 305
Jam recipes
Blueberry Jam with Mint, 414
Blueberry-Rhubarb Jam, 414
No-Sugar Apple-Blackberry Jam, 416
No-Sugar Apple-Grape Jam, 416
No-Sugar Pear-Grape Jam, 416
Raspberry-Cherry Jam, 415
Strawberry Jam, 414
Strawberry Jam with Chamomile, 414
Jams, 408
freezer, 410
light, 416
making, 409
storing, 410
Jelly, 408
making, 408–9
storing, 410
Jelly bag, 409, 409
Jelly roll
Raspberry Jelly Roll, 484–85
Juicer, electric, 20
Juices
citrus, uses for, 519–20
in yeast breads, 314
Julienning foods, 17, 17

K

Kalamata olives
Focaccia with Mediterranean Vegetables, 333

Kamut, 162
Kasha, 160
Kebabs, 72, 72
Balsamic Barbecue Kebabs, 300
Chinese Turkey Kebabs, 221
Garden Vegetable Kebabs, 300
Greek-Style Lamb-and-Vegetable Kebabs, 275–76
Grilled Sea-Scallop Kebabs, 250
Grilled Shrimp Kebabs, 250
Southwestern-Style Kebabs, 300
Spicy Sesame Kebabs, 300
Kelp, for cooking beans, 182
Ketchup
Sweet-and-Spicy Ketchup, 524
Ketjap manis, 520
Key limes, 401
Kidney beans
Chicken-and-Bean Enchilada Casserole, 214
Chili Bean Dip, 552
Chili con Carne, 197
Eggplant Chili, 197
Mexican Rice and Beans, 169
Red Beans and Rice, 191
Three-Bean Picnic Salad, 101
Turkey-and-Bean Burritos, 222–23
Vegetarian Chili, 303
Vegetarian Jambalaya, 305
Kitchen equipment. *See* Equipment, kitchen
Kiwifruit, 405
Fresh Fig Salad with Kiwi-Lime Dressing, 412
Smoky Tropical Black Bean Salsa, 509
Strawberry-Kiwi Cream Tart, 456
Tropical Black Bean Salsa, 509
Knives
care of, 14, 16–17
sharpening, 15, 15
steeling, 18, 18
for stir-fry preparation, 41–42
types of, 14
Kumquats, 401

L

Labels, food
fat listed on, 6
reading, 3
on whole-grain products, 5
Lamb, 260
recipes (*see* Lamb recipes)
seasoning for, 33

Sauces
bottled hot, 519
cooking, 500–501
fruit, 424–25, _425_
instant tomato, _358_
for poached food, _50_
recipes (_see_ Sauce recipes)
reducing fat in, 500–501
thickening, _503_, **503**
types of, 501–4
Sauerkraut
Sauerkraut Pierogi, 547
Sausage
Cheese-and-Meat Filling for
Pasta, 142
Paella, 173
Sausage Sandwiches, 211
Spaghetti and Meatballs, 146–47
Turkey-and-Sausage Jambalaya,
225
Turkey Sausage–Stuffed
Peppers, 375
Sautéing
chicken and vegetables, _48–49_,
48–49
as cooking technique, 47–50
fish, 235–36
meats, 254
poultry, 204
vegetables, for soups, 109
Sauté pans, 47, 48
Scaling fish, _234_, 234
Scallions
Chicken Sauté with Vegetables
and Herbs, _48–49_, **48–49**
Creamy Primavera Sauce, _175_
Scallop-and-Vegetable Stir-Fry,
244
Shrimp-and-Vegetable Stir-Fry,
244
Stir-Fry with Tofu and
Vegetables, 297
Scallops
All-American Bouillabaisse, 247
Couscous with Tomato, Fennel
and Scallops, 177
Grilled Sea-Scallop Kebabs, 250
Mediterranean Pasta with Scal-
lops, 151
Scallop-and-Vegetable Stir-Fry,
244
Sea-Scallop Scampi, 243
Scampi
Sea-Scallop Scampi, 243
Skinny Shrimp Scampi, 243
Scones
Apricot Scones, 347
Basic Scones, 346–47

Currant Scones, 347
Lemon-Thyme Scones, 347
Raisin Scones, 347
Seafood. _See also_ Fish; Shellfish
as low-fat food, 6
Seasoning recipes
Beef Seasoning, _32_
Italian Herb Seasoning, _32_
Lamb Seasoning, _33_
Poultry Seasoning, _32_
Vegetable Seasoning, _32_
Seasonings. _See also_ Herbs;
Spices
for beans, 182
chili peppers, 34
citrus rind, 36
garlic, 34–36
ginger, 36
for quick breads, _340_
recipes (_see_ Seasoning recipes)
for vegetables, 281
in yeast breads, 314
Seeds
as bread topping, 322
as salad garnish, 86, 88
toasting, 282
Serving size, on food label, _3_
Sesame oil
Spicy Sesame Kebabs, 300
Sesame seeds
Sesame Beef-and-Cauliflower
Stir-Fry, 269
Sesame Chicken-and-
Broccoflower Stir-Fry,
269
Sesame Chicken Skewers,
548–49
Sesame Pork-and-Broccoli Stir-
Fry, 269
Sesame Turkey Cutlets, 221
Shakes
Banana-Mango Shake, 435
Blueberry-Banana Shake, 435
Blueberry-Peach Shake, 435
Strawberry-Apricot Shake, 435
Strawberry-Banana Shake, 435
Shallots, _380_, 380
Ratatouille Strudel, 290
Salmon in Vegetable Broth with
Potato Slices, _53_
Summer Vegetable Strudel, 290
Vegetable and Wild Rice Strudel,
290
Vegetable Strudel, 289–90
Shellfish. _See also_ Fish
in chowders, 236, 238
cooking times for, _232_, 241
grilling, 75, 78

health benefits of, _239_
in main-dish salads, 91
preparing, 241
recipes (_see_ Shellfish recipes)
selecting, 239, 241
serving sizes of, 230
in soups, 111
in stews, 236, 238
Shellfish recipes. _See also_ Fish
recipes
All-American Bouillabaisse, 247
Baked Rockfish with Mussels,
_242_
Couscous with Tomato, Fennel
and Scallops, 177
Couscous with Tomato, Fennel
and Shrimp, 177
Crab Cakes, 245
Grilled Sea-Scallop Kebabs, 250
Grilled Shrimp Kebabs, 250
Linguine with White Clam
Sauce, 149
Manhattan Clam Chowder,
122–23
Mediterranean Pasta with Scal-
lops, 151
Mediterranean Pasta with
Shrimp, 150–51
Mussels Marinara, 250
New England Clam Chowder,
122
Paella, 173
Scallop-and-Vegetable Stir-Fry,
244
Seafood Salad, 98
Sea-Scallop Scampi, 243
Shrimp-and-Vegetable Stir-Fry,
244
Skillet Shrimp with Cilantro
Pesto, 244–45
Skinny Shrimp Scampi, 243
Spaghetti with Red Clam Sauce,
149
Shell pasta
Lentil-and-Pasta Soup, 124
Red Lentil and Pasta Soup, 124
Shells and Beans with Basil, _141_
Stuffed Shells Florentine,
142–43
Tomato Soup with Pasta, 116
Shepherd's pie
Ratatouille Shepherd's Pie, _286_
Sherbet, 425–26
Orange Sherbet Parfaits with
Walnuts, 434
Peach Sherbet Parfaits, 434
Raspberry Sherbet Parfaits with
Pecans, 434

U

V

Vanilla
   Fruit-Stuffed Stollen with Vanilla Glaze, 335
Veal
   Meat Ravioli, 146
Vegetable broth, 108
Vegetable oil, for pastry crusts, 442
Vegetable recipes
   Baked Turkey Cutlets with Vegetables, 566
   Black-Eyed Pea and Vegetable Stew, 126
   Cheese-and-Vegetable Filling for Pasta, 142
   Chicken Sauté with Vegetables and Herbs, 48–49, **48–49**
   Chinese Vegetable Stir-Fry, <u>46</u>
   Chunky Chicken-Vegetable Soup, 116
   Focaccia with Mediterranean Vegetables, 333
   Garden Vegetable Kebabs, 300
   Greek-Style Lamb-and-Vegetable Kebabs, 275–76
   Greek-Style Vegetable Stew, 304
   Herbed Summer Vegetables, <u>175</u>
   Italian-Style Vegetable Stew, 304
   Mixed Vegetable Pickles, 523
   Mixed Vegetable Stir-Fry, 296
   Moroccan Vegetable Stew, 304
   Roast Chicken with Winter Vegetables, 218–19
   Salmon in Vegetable Broth with Potato Slices, <u>53</u>
   Scallop-and-Vegetable Stir-Fry, 244
   Shrimp-and-Vegetable Stir-Fry, 244
   Stir-Fry with Tofu and Vegetables, 297
   Summer Vegetable Frittata, 306
   Summer Vegetable Strudel, 290
   Tomato-Vegetable Sauce, 506
   Vegetable and Wild Rice Strudel, 290
   Vegetable Casserole and Biscuits, 287
   Vegetable Potpie, 287
   Vegetable Sloppy Joes, 303
   Vegetable Strudel, 289–90
Vegetables. *See also specific vegetables*

blanching, <u>86</u>
cooking techniques for, 279–81, 368, 384–85
for crudités, <u>533</u>, **533**, 539–40
daily servings of, 4
fast-cooking, for stir-fries, <u>43</u>
frozen vs. canned, 4–5
grilling, 78
microwaving, <u>56</u>, 57
pureed, as thickener, <u>279</u>
as salad garnishes, 86, <u>87</u>, **87**, 88
sautéing, <u>48–49</u>, **48–49**
seasonings for, <u>32</u>, 281
slow-cooking, for stir-fries, <u>43</u>
for soups, 112, 113
spring and summer
   buying, 356
   storage and preparation of, 357
stir-frying, <u>46</u>, **46**
stuffed, 540
in vegetarian diet, 281–82
winter, 376
   care of, 376–77
   preparing, 377, 381–84
   storage and preparation of, 378–79
Vegetable shortening, for pastry crusts, 441
Vegetarianism
   benefits of, 277, <u>278</u>
   cooking strategies for, 281–82
   cooking techniques for, 279–81
   health effects of, <u>278</u>
   proteins and, <u>278</u>
   reducing fat intake with, 277–79
Vegetarian main dishes, 46, 142, 286, 287–307
Vichyssoise, 105
Viennese-style dishes
   Vienna Bread, 330
Vinaigrette, 88
   Balsamic Vinaigrette, 102
   Tomato-Basil Vinaigrette, 102
Vinegar recipes
   Berry Vinegar, 523
   Garlic-Herb Vinegar, 523
   Herb Vinegar, 523
   Hot-Pepper Vinegar, 523
Vinegars, 518–19
   for chutneys, 517
   for pickles and relishes, 517
   recipes (*see* Vinegar recipes)
   types of, for salad dressings, <u>90</u>, <u>103</u>
Vitamin B$_{12}$, vegetarianism and, <u>278</u>

W

Waffle iron, as warming tray, <u>537</u>
Waffle recipes
   Basic Waffles, 350–51
   Strawberry Waffles, 351
   Whole-Wheat Waffles, 351
Waffles, 342–43
   recipes (*see* Waffle recipes)
   toppings for, <u>350</u>
Walnuts
   Banana-Nut Muffins, 345
   Charoset, 564
   Chocolate-Nut Snack Bars, 472
   Easy Fudge-Nut Brownies, 471
   Fruit-and-Nut Stuffed Squash, 392–93
   Nut Streusel, <u>349</u>
   Nutty Granola, 177
   Orange-and-Walnut Biscotti, 496
   Orange Sherbet Parfaits with Walnuts, 434
   Spice-Nut Muffins, 346
   Walnut Ravioli, <u>135</u>
Water, in yeast breads, 314
Water chestnuts
   Chinese Vegetable Stir-Fry, <u>46</u>
   Mixed Vegetable Stir-Fry, 296
   Scallop-and-Vegetable Stir-Fry, 244
   Shrimp-and-Vegetable Stir-Fry, 244
Watercress
   Spring Greens and Strawberries with Poppy Seed Dressing, 562
Watermelon
   Melon Sorbet, 432
Wheat, 162
Wheat germ
   Basic Granola, 177
   Fruited Granola, 177
   Nutty Granola, 177
White beans
   Cannellini Beans with Rosemary, 190
   Cassoulet, 196–97
   Cassoulet with Spinach, 197
   Frittata Florentine with White Beans, 193
   Risotto with Greens and Beans, 171
   Simmered White Beans and Sweet Potatoes, 190
   White Bean Soufflé, 193
White pepper, 31

COMMON MEASURES

Dash or pinch = less than ⅛ teaspoon

1 tablespoon = 3 teaspoons

1 fluid ounce = 2 tablespoons

¼ cup = 4 tablespoons or 2 fluid ounces

⅓ cup = 5 tablespoons + 1 teaspoon

½ cup = 8 tablespoons or 4 fluid ounces

1 cup = 16 tablespoons or 8 fluid ounces

1 pint = 2 cups or 16 fluid ounces

1 quart = 2 pints or 32 fluid ounces

1 gallon = 4 quarts or 128 fluid ounces

1 pound = 16 ounces

PASTA EQUIVALENTS

Type	Dry Measure (4 servings)
Long, skinny pastas, like spaghetti	a 1½″-diameter bunch
Broad noodles	4 cups
Fine or medium noodles	4½ cups
Macaroni	2 cups
Rigatoni	4 cups
Ziti, rotini or fusilli	3 cups
Bow ties	4 cups
Orzo, ditalini, stelline or acini di pepe	1⅓ cups

MEAT: IS IT DONE?

To gauge the doneness of beef, veal or lamb, you should use a meat thermometer inserted into the thickest part of the meat, but not touching bone.

You can look for these signs as well.

☞ **Rare.** The meat should be pink at the edges and quite red in the center.

☞ **Medium-rare.** The meat should be pink at the edges and dark pink in the center.

☞ **Medium-well.** Beef and lamb should be brown at the edges; pork should be white. All three types of meat should be slightly pink in the center.

☞ **Well-done.** No pink should be visible.

COOKING TEMPERATURES

Food	Cook Until . . .
GROUND MEAT	
Turkey or chicken	165°
Veal, beef, lamb or pork	160°
MEAT CUTS	
Veal, beef or lamb	145° (medium-rare) 160° (medium) 170° (well-done)
Pork	160° (medium) 170° (well-done)
POULTRY	
Chicken, whole	180°
Turkey, whole	180°
Poultry breasts	170°
Poultry thighs, wings	cook until juices run clear

SEAFOOD AND POULTRY COOKING TIMES

SEAFOOD	MICROWAVE TIME (MIN.)	STEAMING TIME (MIN.)
Fish fillet, ¾"–1" thick	4–6	4–5
Fish fillet, 1" thick	4–7	7–8
Fish steak	4–7	7–9
Whole fish	4–5 per inch of thickness	10 per inch of thickness
Shrimp, medium, shelled	3–5	2
Clams, 1 pound, in the shell	3–5, or until shells open	5–7, or until shells open
Mussels, 1 pound, in the shell	2–4, or until shells open	3–4, or until shells open
Scallops, 1 pound	5–8 on medium-high power	4–6
Lobster tails, 2, in the shell	7–11 on medium power, until bright red	10–12, wrapped in parchment paper

FISH	POACHING TIME (MIN.)	CHICKEN	POACHING TIME (MIN.)
Chunks, 1 pound	6–8	Split breasts, 1½ pounds	20–25
Whole fish	6–8 per pound	Boneless breasts, 1 pound	12–15
Steaks, 8–10 ounces	5–10	Boneless thighs, 1½ pounds	18–22
Fillet (delicate), 4–6 ounces	5–7		
Fillet (rolled and stuffed), 6–8 ounces	8–10		
Fillet (firm), 6–8 ounces	10–12		

CHICKEN SIZE, STUFFED	ROAST AT 400° FOR . . .	THEN ROAST AT 325° FOR . . .
4 pounds	30 minutes	1 hour
5 pounds	30 minutes	1–1¼ hours
6 pounds	30 minutes	1¼–1½ hours
7 pounds	30 minutes	1½–2 hours

TURKEY SIZE, STUFFED	ROAST AT 325° FOR . . .
6–8 pounds	3–3½ hours
8–12 pounds	3½–4¼ hours
12–16 pounds	4–5 hours
16–20 pounds	4½–5½ hours

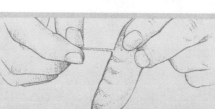